ENCYCLOPEDIA OF AMERICAN WAR LITERATURE

ENCYCLOPEDIA OF AMERICAN WAR LITERATURE

Edited by
Philip K. Jason and Mark A. Graves

Associate Editors
Robert D. Madison and Michael W. Schaefer

Greenwood Press
Westport, Connecticut • London

Library of Congress Cataloging-in-Publication Data

Encyclopedia of American war literature / edited by Philip K. Jason and Mark A. Graves.
    p. cm.
  Includes bibliographical references (p.) and index.
  ISBN 0–313–30648–6 (alk. paper)
    1. American literature—Encyclopedias. 2. War in literature—Encyclopedias. I. Jason,
  Philip K., 1941– II. Graves, Mark A., 1963–
  PS169.W27E53   2001
  810.9'358—dc21   00–042225

British Library Cataloguing in Publication Data is available.

Library of Congress Catalog Card Number: 00–042225
ISBN: 0–313–30648–6

First published in 2001

Greenwood Press, 88 Post Road West, Westport, CT 06881
An imprint of Greenwood Publishing Group, Inc.
www.greenwood.com

Printed in the United States of America

The paper used in this book complies with the
Permanent Paper Standard issued by the National
Information Standards Organization (Z39.48–1984).

10 9 8 7 6 5 4 3 2 1

CONTENTS

INTRODUCTION

People read war literature for many reasons. For some, it provides a high level of excitement. These readers enjoy the details of combat: the emotions of anger and fear, the physical challenges, the employment of soldierly skills. Others read war literature for the historical knowledge it may impart. Few forms of historical fiction have a greater following than fiction about war. Still others are intrigued by the moral issues raised by such texts and by the implicit discussion of leadership that is hinged to characterizations of unit commanders. All of these interests are satisfied by the central type of war literature that may be termed *combat literature*. But the literature of war has a wider arc that takes in representations of causes and consequences of the battlefield action. It has political, cultural, and psychological dimensions. And these dimensions, too, find an avid readership. For all its popularity, and even though many of the major literary texts in Euro-American culture deal with war, there is no critical consensus on just how or why it is important or how it should be approached. Indeed, there is little critical discussion of the literature of war. It has not been systematically classified or theoretically addressed in a comprehensive way.

And yet it is clearly an important body of representation. The essential story line places individuals in extreme situations, often at the margins of their capacities for survival and effective behavior. The laboratory of the writer's imagination, entered by the reader, tests understandings of the human condition, of the limits of human or humane nature. This aspect of much war writing brings it under the umbrella of literature that explores related extremes of traumatic victimhood. Essential to the discussion of such works is Kali Tal's *Worlds of Hurt: Reading the Literatures of Trauma* (1996), a study that examines the interface between the personal and the political in the stories of survivors.

In the short history of that American nation known as the United States, war has marked the journey, and imaginative literature has reflected and shaped an understanding of that journey. Whatever is universal about war stories—assuming that there are universal attributes—takes on the local cultural color of creative transformers. To study the war literature of the United States, then, is to study the representation not only of individuals at war but also of the American experience, variously understood. Sometimes this rendering is self-conscious, sometimes unconscious. Sometimes it is the veneer, and other times it is the core.

The existing critical forays seem to us to be limited in ways that leave much room for further examinations. Wayne Charles Miller's *An Armed America: Its Face in Fiction* (1970) is both too broad and too narrow. Its subtitle—"A History of the American Military Novel"—sets its limits at a single genre but expands its subject reference beyond war to portrayals of the military establishment and military life. Thus, his chapter on Melville has little to do with war representation, except for the brief mention of Melville's Civil War poems that cannot get more than fleeting attention in a book about novels. At the same time, Miller's concern with handling many noncombat "military novels" leads him to exclude or merely refer to scores of key works that treat men at war. Miller's is a useful book in many ways, but it just does not get to an ideational level. Other critical efforts, like Peter Aichinger's 1975 study *The American Soldier in Fiction, 1880–1963*, Peter G. Jones's *War and the Novelist: Appraising the American War Novel* (1976), and Jeffrey Walsh's *American War Literature, 1914 to Vietnam* (1982), make no attempt to be comprehensive. Indeed, the very titles of these useful volumes announce their limitations of genre or temporal scope.

Before there can be meaningful assessments of the American literature of war, there needs to be a gathering of basic information—an overview. The aim of the present project is to indicate the abundance and richness of the material, an abundance that can only be hinted at in the space at our disposal. Still, an encyclopedic reference can at least point out the high and some of the middle ground of this enormous body of work.

The remarks that follow are intended to suggest some of the possible directions for critical projects on American war literature.

War literature, particularly fiction, lends itself to classification by duration and focus of conflict. That is, plots are derived from such frames as the tour of duty (James Webb's *Fields of Fire*), campaigns (John Del Vecchio's *The 13th Valley*), particular battles or skirmishes (Humphrey Cobb's *Paths of Glory*), and sometimes the contours of a single day (Harry Brown's *A Walk in the Sun* and David Halberstam's *One Very Hot Day*). Another mark of differentiation is the command or unit level, a focusing decision of crucial importance that is often related to point of view. Most American war fiction is pitched at the company level, notably William March's *Company K* and James Jones's *The Thin Red Line*. However, the narrower platoon or squad narratives are abundant, and the broader battalion-level narrative (which is likely to become a "headquarters" tale) is available. Works focused on air or sea combat have similar ranges of reference and focus. Many successful works, like James Michener's *The Bridges at Toko-ri*, gain their organizing strength from the combination of parameters: the military objective and the military unit.

As a subject for literary treatment, then, war—as combat action—has convenient handles and shapes. It is, therefore, a storyteller's delight.

In the American war narratives of the twentieth century, the command level of the company or subunit allows for the panorama of types—the "American boys" from varied backgrounds—that constitute a special version of the melting pot myth. In his essay "The War on the Home Front" (collected in *Americans at War*, 1997), Stephen E. Ambrose comments on the development of the melting pot motif:

Unlike the Civil War, when army units were recruited from a single state, in World War II men in most cases were thrown together willy-nilly—so much so that a war-spawned cliché of film and fiction is the squad made up of the hillbilly from Arkansas, the Jew from Brooklyn, the coal miner from Pennsylvania, the farmer from Ohio, the lumberman from Oregon, the Italian from Chicago, the Pole from Milwaukee, the Cajun from Louisiana. At first they hate each other; training draws them together; combat welds them into a band of brothers; they emerge by the final scene as just plain Americans with a strong sense of nationalism. And the truth is that this happened in life before it happened in art. (177–178)

The melting pot cliché informs popular and influential works like Leon Uris's *Battle Cry* and Norman Mailer's *The Naked and the Dead*. It is implicit in such World War I works as *Company K* and Dos Passos's *Three Soldiers*. However, it undergoes uneasy modification and expansion in the later Asian wars by the introduction of African Americans into the mix, as well as Hispanics and Native Americans. Webb's *Fields of Fire* is a case in point. The bonding step of training together vanishes in Vietnam fact and fiction, as men came to Vietnam individually as replacements rather than as part of replacement units that had trained together. And while combat often brings fighting men together as a band of brothers, in the case of Vietnam representation, and to some extent that of the Korean War, the strong sense of nationalism that characterizes the trailing action of World War II writing is rarely present. Often enough, veterans return as isolated, alienated individuals out of phase with anything like a national identity. Their loyalty, if to anything, is to one another.

On the other hand, much of the experience of war remains an individual business, a personal testing and act of becoming. Stephen Crane's *The Red Badge of Courage* acknowledges the power of the group and fashions metaphors that underscore the merging of individual identities into larger marching and fighting organisms, but his novel is nonetheless primarily about one man's initiation (to borrow a Dos Passos title). Similarly, for all the color and delight in the supporting cast, Tim O'Brien's *Going After Cacciato* is first and foremost Paul Berlin's story.

In fact, the great bulk of war narratives that focus on young men (as they so often and so unfortunately must) are essentially initiation or coming of age stories, and the complex of ways in which a tour of duty turns into a trial of selfhood needs detailed examination, as does the corollary motif of bonding and brotherhood.

Both of these motifs find particularly vivid expression in a major subset of war literature—the prisoner of war story. This kind of tale, which overlaps with nonmilitary narratives of incarceration, provides both a horrific range of particulars and a fascinating microcosm—a laboratory experiment, almost—for the creative imagination. Works like MacKinlay Kantor's *Andersonville*, e. e. cummings's *The Enormous Room*, and Francis Pollini's *Night* demand comparative exploration, in part for what they tell us about the human condition and in part for what we can discover about literary construction and the power latent in the confinement premise.

One version of the prisoner of war story is the narrative, largely interior, of solitary confinement. The circumstance, for all its literal reality, clearly has a dimension of metaphor and reminds readers of how psychological circumstances can (and do) create something like a solitary confinement of the mind. The mood or atmosphere of exile, alienation, or aloneness runs through much war literature. The state of mind is projected into and contained within plots that deal with the lost soldier—the individual who is cut off from or isolated from his unit by the chances of war and by his sole survivorship. Through much of his ordeal, Stephen Crane's Henry Fleming is alone, literally and figuratively lost. Because of its lack of extended action and character interchange, this kind of experience or sensation is more often rendered in short stories and poems than in novels.

The consequences of war—on the individual, on the war-torn country, and even on the culture of the participating nation whose borders remain secure— have generated a body of work that rivals the literary response to combat itself. Aftermath and homecoming stories have their own dimensions and motifs. Stephen Becker's *When the War Is Over*, Ernest Hemingway's *A Farewell to Arms* and "Soldier's Home," and Philip Caputo's *Indian Country* are only a few representative titles in this provocative category, a category of works that need to be sifted against one another for their lessons and their merits of craft and vision. How do Americans put war behind them? Literary artists can help us find out.

Any critique rooted in significant grouping or classification may overlook questions about changing responses through time. Certainly questions about how cultural change affects various genre need further exploration, though several critical studies have made inroads here. We can offer some statements about the poets' responses to war that invite elaboration and correction.

American war poetry has gone through several shifts, reflecting to some extent broad cultural shifts in sensibility. The poetry of the Revolutionary War tends to be anthemic and sentimental. Sometimes narrative, often focused on heroes and events, it is part of the process of national identification. Civil War poetry is more varied in tone. While a good portion of it is mawkish lament or ideologically driven, there are as well image-centered lyrics, like those of Whitman, capable of celebrating the innocent soldier while questioning the necessity of war. Some pieces aspire to popular mythmaking, as does the poetry (and other writings) of the Indian Wars. The little verse that we have from the Spanish-American War is journalistic and jingoistic.

The paradox of war's horror and grandeur begins with Stephen Crane and is a focal point of much World War I poetry. Irony is the grand device of much twentieth-century American War poetry, along with a grim—sometimes gruesome—realism. In part, these traits derive from the fact that we have more participant poetry. Many critics see modernist free verse as largely a response to war—its experiential chaos and the chaos of values that "world war" connotes. The poetry of the Korean and Vietnam Wars is largely an outcry of perceived betrayals, shame, loss, and cynicism. Its techniques are often in the service of undermining complacency and heroic clichés.

In all periods, the poetry that is not primarily narrative tends to fix frozen moments, presenting image snapshots of vivid sensory and emotional material, with or without editorial comment. Sometimes, as in Whitman's "Cavalry Crossing a Ford," the camera is stopped and a few consecutive frames explored. Often, as in Bruce Weigl's "Song of Napalm," it is the hideous image lodged in memory that is the fulcrum of the war poem.

Dramatists have had far less to do with the material of war, certainly of combat interludes, than have fiction writers and poets. This fact may have to do with the difficulty of such stage representation. (These very difficulties, of course, have been solved by the conventions and techniques of filmmaking.) Nonetheless, there is a significant body of dramatic literature that attempts to come to terms with the experience of war, thought it often relies on departures, homecomings, and lulls in the action. The problems of dramatizing war—revealed long ago in the selective scene building of the Greek masters and of Shakespeare, the stage convention of single combat, the reports of offstage bloodshed—on occasion bring forth an inspired impressionistic invention. David Rabe's *The Basic Training of Pavlo Hummel* is a case in point.

Having said this much, we will say little more by way of preamble to the main business of this volume. We must emphasize, for those who might be looking for a more inclusive selection of historical, biographical, and autobiographical texts, that our dominant concern is with imaginative responses (fiction, poetry, and drama) by American authors to wars in which Americans have participated. By "American authors" we mean here men and women writing in the regions of North America that became known as the United States. We have opened the door to significant literary nonfiction of various kinds, but we have made no attempt to provide a comprehensive overview of historical or theoretical writings. A few are included as they bear in some way on the imaginative literature itself.

The plan of this volume is simple and predictable: We have arranged the entries in a single alphabet by author, interspersing in the same alphabet several topic entries giving overviews on the literature of individual wars, special types of works, and categories of authorship. These topic entries are as follows: African American War Literature, Civil War, Civil War—Women's Diaries, *Corridos*, First World War, Ghost Dance Songs, Indian Captivity Narratives, King

Philip's War, Korean War, Revolutionary War, Revolutionary War—Women's Diaries, Second World War, Spanish-American War, Spanish Civil War, Vietnam War, and Vigilantes. Author entries provide short biographies focused on the subject's involvement in the issues or experience of war, a short critical discussion of the subject's important contributions to war literature, and a brief reference section. If an author or topic entry refers to a writer for whom there is a separate entry, that name appears in boldface to indicate that it is a cross-reference. Following the entries, we have provided a selected bibliography and an index of titles and topics.

A

ADAMS, JOHN TURVILL (1805–1882). Born in British Guiana in 1805, Adams migrated to Norwich, Connecticut, where he set up a law practice and began his literary career. Although he later became a state senator, Adams considered his two novels, his brief career as an editor, and his collection of poems to be his primary accomplishments. In particular, his novels are noteworthy for their insightful depiction of colonial New England. The second of these, *The Knight of the Golden Melice*, republished as *The White Chief among the Red Men* (1859), is one of many historical romances dealing with intrigues of the real-life figure Sir Christopher Gardiner in the early settlement of Boston, Massachusetts.

In Adams's depiction, Gardiner, or "Soog-u-Gest," is the spiritual brother of Sassacus, the Pequot Grand Sachem, and a spy for Father Le Vieux, a French Jesuit missionary. Although Gardiner, a British nationalist, believes himself to be working toward the supplanting of fanatical Puritanism by the milder religion of the church of Rome, Le Vieux is actually using him to further the territorial interests of France. Unknown to Gardiner, Le Vieux plans to aggravate relations between the Pequots and their surrounding tribes, thus thwarting the tribal unification that would make trade easier between British colonists and their Indian neighbors. Le Vieux's eventual goal is to eliminate the colonists and open British territory for the use of migrating French Catholics. At the novel's conclusion, Gardiner is exiled from the colony, but the expulsion occurs too late. Chaos has erupted in Governor John Winthrop's Boston, chaos among local tribes, between the British and the French, and among the colonists themselves.

As the novel *The Knight of the Golden Melice* details the adventures of the wily and charismatic Gardiner in a colony ruled by fanatical Puritans and malign magistrates, it also presents the growing conflict between English and French interests in the colonies and the tensions that resulted in the Pequot War.

REFERENCE

Adams, John Turvill. *The Knight of the Golden Melice*. New York: Derby & Jackson, 1859.

Priscilla Glanville

ADAMS, SAMUEL HOPKINS (1871–1958). Born in Dunkirk, New York, Adams began writing in the early 1900s. By the time he died at age eighty-seven, this prolific muckraker, biographer, and historian had written more than 500 articles, short stories, and novels. Adams is perhaps best known for a series of muckraker articles he published in *Collier's Magazine* to expose patent medicine quackery. This series is credited with furthering the passage of the Pure Food and Drug Act. Adams's novels also reflect muckraking concerns. One of Adams's early novels, *Common Cause: A Novel of the War in America* (1919), depicts the struggle of Jeremy Robson, a patriotic muckraker, at the onset of the First World War.

Robson is a reporter in Fenchester, Centralia, an American town whose elite constituents are German expatriates. Overrun with German sympathizers, corrupt politicians, and pandering newspapermen, Fenchester is thrown into chaos at the onset of the First World War. Robson and his newspaper, *The Guardian*, outrage the community with nationalistic editorials and muckraking exposés on German sympathizers who hide behind pacifist propaganda.

The more successful Robson becomes at exposing the fraudulent politics of the self-proclaimed pacifists, the more the community conspires against him. At one point, a member of Fenchester's pro-German "Deutscher Club" accuses Robson of avoiding military duty. When Robson, whose poor heart kept him from active duty, refuses to stop publishing nationalistic editorials and scathing exposés, he earns for himself the title "mud-slinger," which we know as "muck-raker."

Robson's patriotic zeal and unapologetic muckraking eventually earn the respect of the citizens of Fenchester. As Adams notes, "Men of all types of political belief, of all classes, of all economic and social creeds, abandoned their private feuds and bitterness in a fervor against the common enemy." Through the novel *Common Cause*, Adams demands that politicians and newspapermen who profit from the mechanisms of war not be allowed to create derision among nationalistic American citizens.

REFERENCES

Downs, Robert, and Jane Downs. *Journalists of the United States.* Jefferson, NC: McFarland, 1991.
Kennedy, Samuel V. *Samuel Hopkins Adams and the Business of Writing.* Syracuse: Syracuse University Press, 1999.

Priscilla Glanville

ADLER, MORTIMER JEROME (1902–). Adler was born in New York City. He received his Ph.D. in psychology from Columbia University in 1929. He taught philosophy of law at the University of Chicago from 1930 until 1952, with stints outside academe including serving as an Indoctrination Lecturer for the U.S. Air Transport Command. Known primarily as a popularizer of philosophy and a promulgator of the Great Books Reading Program, Adler is also a prolific writer, having authored or edited over sixty books and hundreds of articles, the most prominent being *How to Read a Book* (1940). Adler also served as chief editor and organizer of the *Encyclopaedia Britannica*, 15th edition.

Adler's direct involvement with war literature stems from three pieces of writing. In October 1940, he published in *Harper's Magazine* "This Pre-War Generation," which takes to task the moral relativism and subjectivism Adler sees all around him, as well as beginning to make a case against the isolationist stance espoused by (among others) the influential president of the University of Chicago, Robert Hutchins (also Adler's friend). In 1944, a short article, "Thinking Straight on War and Peace," appeared in *Vogue* (January 15). This is a redaction of a book Adler published later in the year, entitled *How to Think about War and Peace*. In this book, Adler favors U.S. involvement in the war, while he deplores the destruction that all wars bring. The work is a detailed philosophical disquisition on what might lead to a permanent and universal peace once this war is concluded (Adler never doubts that the powers of right and good will prevail). Adler contends that through rigorous thinking on what we mean by the words *war* and *peace*, we will be able to achieve perpetual peace, but only through the establishment of a world government. Truly reasonable and logical human beings should recognize that "membership in the human race should be enough to bring [our] virtues into play and to overcome [our] indifference in the long run" to the establishment of a federated conglomeration of nations, the only means whereby increasingly destructive wars can be avoided.

REFERENCES

Adler, Mortimer J. *Philosopher at Large: An Intellectual Autobiography*. New York: Macmillan, 1977.
Bowen, Ezra. "The Last Great Aristotelian." *Time* 4 May 1987: 84–85.

Brian Adler

AFRICAN AMERICAN WAR LITERATURE. In 1770, fugitive slave Crispus Attucks took two bullets in the chest during the Boston Massacre, the first of a series of volatile, often bloody conflicts leading to the American Revolution. While Attucks's active resistance against the British prompted white colonists to roundly hail him as both patriot and hero, blacks found something more in Attucks's display of loyalty to the fledging American republic—an argument for black citizenship rights. That argument, as compelling as it was, failed; legal enfranchisement would continue to be deferred for nearly a century. Indeed, Paul Revere's famous engraving of the massacre symbolized the long fight that lay ahead for African Americans: Revere depicted the five men slain as white, effectively erasing any sign of Attucks's involvement. Black historian William Nell (1816–1874) would later conclude in *Colored Patriots of the American Revolution* (1855), the first book-length treatment of black participation in

American warfare: "A combination of circumstances have veiled from the public eye a narration of those military services which are generally conceded as passports to the honorable and lasting notice of Americans."

Nell's work is, in one sense, a correction of Revere's engraving: The historian "unveils" an altogether different rendition of the American Revolution for the "public eye"—one decidedly inclusive of blacks. However, *Colored Patriots* stands as more than counternarrative. Nell hoped his book—replete with acts of valor, bravery, and heroism equal to those of whites—would serve as a "passport" allowing black Americans entry into the very nation they had faithfully served, undeterred by its continuing refusals. Although a fictionalized treatment of war by an African American would not appear until after the Civil War, thirteen years after Nell's publication, African American war literature as a whole finds its genesis in Nell's endeavor. With few exceptions, war becomes a site upon which black writers contest exclusionary historical narratives, battle notions of racial inferiority, and fight for their rights as American citizens. War, at home or abroad, serves as a trope for the "wars" for equality blacks continued to wage within the borders of their own nation.

In 1868, Frances Harper's first Civil War novel, *Minnie's Sacrifice*, appeared in serialized form in *The Christian Recorder*. A prominent nineteenth-century poet, activist, and feminist, Harper (1825–1911) turned to the novel to create idealized portraits of "live" black men and "earnest, lovely" women who could serve as models for African Americans struggling with their newly found status as freed people. Heavily influenced by conventions of sentimental women's fiction, *Minnie's Sacrifice* is essentially a melodramatic romance of passing: the tale of Minnie, a mulatta heroine, and Louis, a mulatto hero, whose black ancestral roots have been hidden from them by friends and relatives who wish to spare the two from slavery. Upon discovering the truth of their identities, they decide to "suffer" with their "own branch of the human race," marry, and join the war efforts as "pioneers of a new civilization." Harper's second war novel, *Iola Leroy* (1892), revises and expands upon the plot of the earlier work. The heroine, Iola, becomes reduced to slavery when her blackness is revealed; she, too, joins the war—as a nurse—and marries a "black" man as white as she. Despite these points of convergence, Harper's shifting attitudes toward the Civil War make these two works decidedly distinct from one another, a distinction due, no doubt, to the era in which *Iola Leroy* was published. Historians have dubbed the 1890s the "Black Nadir," a decade marked by lynch law, Jim Crow, poll taxes, and numerous other tactics threatening advances blacks had gained since Emancipation. Thus, while both novels flout their protagonists' patriotism, noble characteristics, and "whiteness" as evidence of blacks' readiness for citizenship, the increasingly urgent tone Harper adopts in *Leroy* attests to the author's growing doubt that the nation would make good on the promises made during wartime.

The Fanatics (1902), by **Paul Laurence Dunbar**, has little in common with Harper's works. Aside from "Nigger Ed," the town bell-ringer, the main characters in Dunbar's fictional community of Dorbury are white, and to Dunbar, this means they view blacks as merely pawns in an elaborate, destructive game of war. Dunbar drives this point home by emphasizing the negligible change in "Nigger Ed's" status after the war.

Though blacks undoubtedly produced many first-person Civil War narratives, only two major works have been recovered: Elizabeth Keckley's *Behind the Scenes, or Thirty Years a Slave and Four Years in the White House* (1868) and Susie King Taylor's *A Black Woman's Civil War Memoirs* (1902). Keckley (1818–1907) devotes less than one third of her fascinating postbellum autobiography to her life in bondage and instead focuses on the four years she spent serving the White House as Mary Todd Lincoln's modiste, the years of the Civil War. Writing out of dire financial necessity (aiding Mrs. Lincoln after the assassination rendered her penniless), Keckley fully exploits the most private details of the Lincolns' lives, in those details, however, lie invaluable insights into the president's frame of mind during the war. Regrettably, Keckley's own thoughts about the events engulfing the nation are far too brief—her only son's enlistment in the Union army and death in battle are mentioned in two short sentences, buried in pages describing the Lincolns' loss of their son Will.

Susie King Taylor's *Memoirs* might help elucidate what army life held for men like Keckley's son. Taylor (1848–1912), a laundress and soldier–teacher with the 1st South Carolina Volunteers, begins her slim volume with a preface written by **Thomas Wentworth Higginson** (*Army Life in a Black Regiment*), who lauds her contributions to the troops he commanded and welcomes her unique point of view. "Actual military life is rarely described by a woman," he writes, adding that her perspective is "wholly different" from his. In *Memoirs*, Taylor strives to minimize that difference, portraying herself as a woman fit to be a soldier. She boasts, for instance, of her ability to clean and shoot a rifle: hardly "feminine" behavior. Though the book is primarily autobiographical, Taylor offers frank analysis of the difficulties black men and their white commanders faced in an army still questioning the decision to engage African American troops.

Toward the end of *Memoirs*, Taylor also remarks on America's negative depictions of black Cubans during the Spanish-American Wars. Indeed, at the turn of the century, black newspapers and periodicals rippled with debates over the issue of imperialism. The wars divided blacks into two major camps: those who believed that the United States should be supported in their efforts to "democratize" and "civilize" Cuba and the Philippines, and those who felt that American imperialism amounted to little more than a disguised form of racial subjugation. **Theodore Roosevelt**'s conflicting accounts of the role black troops played in the famed battle of San Juan Hill complicated matters even further, first praising their performance immediately after the war, then later condemning them as "peculiarly dependent."

F. Grant Gilmore's Spanish-American War novel *The Problem: A Military Novel* (1915) seeks to restore full glory to the troops' tarnished image. To accomplish this task, Gilmore includes vivid descriptions of the battlefront—an aspect of war untouched by black novelists before him. The story of Sergeant William Henderson, who leads the Ninth Cavalry to victory in Cuba and the Philippines, *The Problem* abounds with acts of heroics performed under the most dangerous of circumstances. Lest Henderson's patriotism be dismissed as an anomaly, Gilmore halts his novel midway to insert a chapter outlining the history of black military service.

It is likely that Gilmore's research drew significantly from Herschel Cashin's invaluable collection of first-person narratives, letters, poems, and military documents, *Under Fire with the Tenth U.S. Cavalry* (1899). Cashin, a recorder with the U.S. Land Office, coedited *Under Fire* with the help of army chaplain Charles Alexander and other African Americans who served directly in the Tenth Cavalry. Their assemblage of primary material shares a purpose similar to Gilmore's: to demonstrate the national loyalty of those soldiers, who, in the editors' words, have been unfairly labeled "a so-called alien race."

Despite the significant role blacks played in Cuba and the Philippines, the fruits of their labor were few: The armed forces and the nation remained segregated. Upon America's entry into World War I, an increasing number of blacks discouraged military service and civilian displays of patriotism as a means of securing equality. While the majority of blacks received menial assignments, some fought—brilliantly, by many accounts—but no matter what their duties abroad, all faced notoriously poor treatment upon returning stateside, further infuriating blacks. As the African American population adopted a more radical political consciousness, so did black writers. As a whole, World War I novelists reject the optimism inherent in their predecessors' sentimentalism, examining war—both national and racial—through the sobering lens of realism. The idealized men and women of romantic war fiction are thus banned from these texts, supplanted by more complex protagonists whose patriotism strains under the weight of racial antagonism.

Claude McKay's *Home to Harlem* (1928), a novel so raw that W.E.B. Du Bois claimed it made him feel "unclean," introduces African American war literature to its first working-class hero. Jake Brown, a longshoreman, enlists in the navy, itching to "get a crack at the Germans." Instead, he finds himself armed with lumber, toting planks back and forth to build officers' housing in Brest. Disillusioned by the navy's refusal to recognize him as a man, he deserts his "happy chocolate company" to return to Harlem. Far from being the refuge he had imagined, he discovers a congested, bar-brawling Harlem overflowing with black men caught in the violent ethos of the nation. McKay (1889–1948) follows Brown's psychological awakening as he realized that his manhood must be defined on his own terms—neither the military nor the streets of Harlem can do that for him.

Sinclair Lewis praised Walter White's *The Fire in the Flint* as one of the two best novels produced in 1924. Another exploration of a veteran's bitter homecoming, it centers on Kenneth Harper, a doctor who returns to Georgia after serving in the army, believing his status as a physician and ex-soldier will insulate him from Southern small-town racism. His notions are quickly disabused when he attempts to help black farmers financially exploited by white landowners. Harper's emergent activism, sharpened when a cadre of white men rape his younger sister, brings him in direct confrontation with the Ku Klux Klan. Although black uproar over the numerous assaults against African American World War I veterans sparked the early civil rights movement, White (1893–1955) offers a bleak forecast: His novel ends with a newspaper report of Harper's lynching.

Victor Daly's short novel *Not Only War* (1932) returns black war literature to the battlefront. Montgomery Jason, a black college student, and Robert Casper, a young white Southern patrician, engage in a rivalry over an African American schoolteacher whom Casper has taken as a lover. Both men join the army, where they meet again in France, Casper serving, naturally, as Jason's superior officer. When Casper finds Jason residing in the home of a white French woman and her mother rather than in the assigned haylofts, he becomes incensed by the possibility that Jason is having an affair with a white woman. Casper accuses Jason of violating military housing law and orders the soldier court-martialed. Shortly thereafter, Casper is wounded on the front, forcing Jason to make an agonizing decision: exacting retribution—an eye for an eye—or getting his compatriot help. War, writes Daly (1895–1986), is not the only "hell": The battles for the "souls of men" are equally hellish and equally worth struggling for.

World War II renewed many of the debates surrounding other American wars. Letters from black soldiers describing the unfair conditions under which they served flooded African American newspapers. The irony of a war against fascism fought by a segregated military, heightened by the hypocrisy of a country touting democratic ideals globally but not fully practicing them locally, was hardly lost on African Americans. Black communities issued a galvanizing call: victory abroad and victory at home—the "Double V."

Poet Gwendolyn Brooks (1917–   ) models her series of war sonnets, "Gay Chaps at the Bar," from *A Street in Bronzeville* (1945), on "V" letters she received from black soldiers, including her brother, a sergeant in the army. Brooks uses the voices of these men to create moving first-person testimonies chronicling their experiences: the trepidation they felt before leaving for battle, the terror and glory of warfare during their tenure, and afterward, the haunting memories of war, exacerbated by an uncertainty over how they, as black men, would be received once stateside. Brooks notes this absurd state of American racial relations in "Negro Hero," a sonnet–ballad from the same book of poems: "(In a southern city a white man said / Indeed, I'd rather be dead; / Indeed, I'd rather be shot in the head / Or ridden to waste on the back of a flood / Than saved by a drop of a black man's blood.)"

Hayes Dawkins, the hero of William Gardner Smith's *Last of the Conquerors* (1948), shares the uncertainty of Brooks's narrators. Set in postwar Berlin and Bremberg, Smith's novel exposes the indignities black soldiers suffered at the

hands of racist military police (MPs) and commanding officers: beatings, indiscriminate VD (venereal disease) checks, and unjustified court-martials. Smith
(1927–1977) juxtaposes this treatment against the relatively prejudice-free
attitudes of German civilians toward African Americans. While Dawkins and
his fellow soldiers understand the contradiction—these were people complicit
in the Holocaust, after all—Germany offers the men a taste of what life might
hold in country that viewed them as human first and black second. When the
army institutes a series of expulsory regulations—designed, in their minds, to
rid the army of African Americans—they are forced to confront their mixed
feelings about returning to America. Two flee to Berlin's Russian Zone, but
Dawkins chooses to go back to the United States, which, for all of its injustices,
remains his home.

Chester Himes's *If He Hollers, Let Him Go* (1946) is a brilliant reversal of
the homecoming story, following the events that lead to a defense worker's
forced enlistment in the military. In the span of two days, Robert Jones, a tough,
defiant leaderman at a California war plant, is demoted for verbally insulting
Madge, a white woman with whom he works. Alternately drawn to and repulsed
by Madge, Jones ultimately rejects her. She subsequently accuses him of rape.
Although the judicial system recognizes the meritlessness of her claims, Jones
is given two alternatives—jail or the army.

And Then We Heard the Thunder (1963), by John Oliver Killens (1916–1987),
is a sprawling World War II narrative that is perhaps the most stunning—and
hopeful—of all African American World War II novels written before the Korean War. Killens's hero, Solomon Saunders, is drafted into the army shortly
after becoming married. While his wife views his recruitment as an opportunity
to succeed in the "white world," Saunders adamantly denies needing its acceptance. Nonetheless, he vows to ascend through the ranks of the military by being
"the best damn soldier in the Army of the United States," also vowing to remember who he is—a black man from the slums of Harlem. This dual allegiance, however, comes to haunt him. As the army rewards Saunders for his
strict abidance of military regulations, his junior officers—his friends—taunt
him for being an "Uncle Tom." He finds himself in a constant tug of war
between his professional aspirations as an officer and his personal repugnance
toward the relentless humiliation he and his soldiers are subjected to as black
Americans. Saunders can no longer avoid reconciling this conflict when his
efforts to rescue his unjustly imprisoned friend, "Quiet Man," from white MPs
sparks an armed racial war between black and white soldiers stationed in Australia. He fights—unleashing years of pent-up anger—and wins back his racial
pride. He also loses: His best buddies are killed in the violence. In the end,
however, when the fury has died down, he finds himself surrounded by dis-
traught soldiers, black and white, who wanted nothing to do with this particular
war, between countrymen, between races. "The world is waking up again,"
Saunders laments. "And we poor bastards sit here crying."

In 1948, President Harry Truman issued Executive Order 9981, effectively ending segregation in the military once and for all. The African American literature of the wars in which Americans fought separately for the same essential ideals—freedom, democracy, equality—stands as an uncomfortable record of a nation that too long kept these rights from the very people who risked their lives for them. The early and uneasy result of Truman's policy is reflected in *Stalemate at Panmunjon* (1980), Wilbert L. Walker's novel of the Korean War. Although the novel's hero, platoon leader Charlie Brooks, seems to prove Truman's policy a success by distinguishing himself in combat, Walker also emphasizes that lingering racial bigotry cannot be eradicated simply through legislation.

The complexities of African American experiences during the Vietnam War are captured in several significant novels, among them A. R. Flowers's *De Mojo Blues* (1985), George Davis's *Coming Home* (1971), and **John A. Williams**'s *Captain Blackman* (1972). In Flowers's novel, three veterans receive dishonorable discharges after fragging their white platoon leader. Focusing on their return from the war, *De Mojo Blues* explores the process of recovering from the psychological trauma they endured as both soldiers and as black men. *Coming Home* confronts war frankly with its horrifying scenes of daily bombing runs over Vietnam. The novel also suggests that the racism destroying American society was also a primary cause of the imperial warfare against the Vietnamese. Williams's classic subsumes the Vietnam experience into the larger vision of a dying African American soldier who dreams he is fighting in America's wars, beginning with the American Revolution.

David Parks's *GI Diary* (1968) is a powerful record of one individual's experience, while **Wallace Terry**'s *Bloods: An Oral History of the Vietnam War by Black Veterans* (1984) remains the most remarkable record of collective memory. Among the notable volumes of African American poetry of the war are *Dien Cai Dau* (1990) by **Yusef Komunyakaa**, *Mad Minute* (1990) by Lamont B. Steptoe, and *In the Grass* (1995) by Horace Coleman. Adrienne Kennedy's confrontational *An Evening with Dead Essex* (1983), an experimental drama, concerns itself with Vietnam on a symbolic level. It posits racism and societal capacity for betrayal and brutality as the link between violence at home and violence abroad.

REFERENCES

Daly, Victor. *Not Only War: A Story of Two Great Conflicts*. 1932. College Park, MD: McGrath, 1969.

Greene, J. Lee. "The Wars for Eden." *Blacks in Eden: The African American Novel's First Century*. Charlottesville: University Press of Virginia, 1996.

Keckley, Elizabeth. *Behind the Scenes, or Thirty Years a Slave and Four Years in the White House*. 1868. New York: Oxford University Press, 1988.

Lanning, Michael Lee. *The African American Soldier from Crispus Attucks to Colin Powell*. Seacaucus, NJ: Birch Lane Press, 1997.

McKay, Claude. *Home to Harlem*. 1928. Boston: Northeastern University Press, 1987.

Moebs, Thomas Truxtun, ed. *Black Soldiers—Black Sailors—Black Ink: Research Guide on African Americans in U.S. Military History, 1526–1900*. Chesapeake Bay, VA: Moebs Publishing Company, 1994.

Taylor, Susie King. *A Black Woman's Civil War Memoirs*. 1902. Princeton, NJ: Markus Weiner Publishers, 1988.

White, Walter. *The Fire in the Flint*. 1924. Athens: University of Georgia Press, 1996.

Jennifer C. James

AIKEN, CONRAD (1889–1979). Born in Savannah, Georgia, Conrad Aiken was sent to live in Cambridge, Massachusetts, with his relatives after the murder-suicide of his parents. In 1912, he graduated from Harvard, married Jessie McDonald, and traveled to London, where he befriended Rupert Brooke. In 1914, Aiken returned to the States to publish his first book of poetry, *Earth Triumphant and Other Verses*, but during World War I, he made several trips to England to work on various writing projects.

Although Aiken associated with many of the "war" poets, he did not want to go to war. Aiken's American citizenship spared him from conscription, and in 1917 when faced with the prospect of having to serve in the army, he argued that his profession as a poet was "essential." As a result, Aiken became the first American to be deferred from active duty because he was a poet. Despite the fact that Aiken's inexperience with the reality of war limited his interpretations of war, he did attempt to write poetry that reflected the sentiment of his generation. In "1915: The Trenches," first collected in *Nocturne of Remembered Spring and Other Poems* (1917), Aiken describes war as a "vast symphonic dance of death" and offers a critical view of war's destructive nature (7). In *Skepticisms: Notes on Contemporary Poetry* (1919), Aiken criticized writers who relied on common imagery to recreate the horrors of war: "What immediately suggests itself is that as war is hideously and predominantly real, an affair of overwhelmingly sinister and ugly forces, it can only be embodied successfully in an art which is realistic, or psycho-realistic" (222).

Following World War I, Aiken published several volumes of poetry in the 1920s and established himself as a critic of poetry. In 1930, he was awarded the Pulitzer Prize for his *Selected Poems* (1929) and received a Guggenheim Fellowship. Despite Aiken's literary success, his personal life was deeply troubled. In 1930, he divorced, and two years later, he attempted suicide. Following this turmoil, Aiken focused mainly on writing critical reviews, but he did continue to publish poetry. In 1944, he published *The Soldier*, a long narrative poem that presents the journey of a consciousness exposed to war. Although Aiken does not describe war, he attempts to recreate the psychological impact war has on one's perceptions of reality. Early in the poem, war's brutalities are rationalized, and "the business of bloodletting" is seen as an "ancient profession" (7). Yet near the end of the poem, the voice of the poem attempts to come to terms with the war: "Look home from the desert, soldier: / to the regenerate desert of the heart come home: / and know that this too needs heroes and endurance, and ardor" (31).

Toward the end of his life, Aiken wrote poetry for children and published several novels. In 1969, he received the National Medal for Literature, and in 1973 he was named the Poet Laureate of Georgia. He spent the end of his life near his boyhood home and died in Savannah at the age of eighty-four.

REFERENCES

Aiken, Conrad. *Collected Poems*. New York: Oxford University Press, 1970.

———. *Selected Letters of Conrad Aiken*. Ed. Joseph Killorin. New Haven: Yale University Press, 1978.

Butscher, Edward. *Conrad Aiken, Poet of White Horse Vale*. Athens: University of Georgia Press, 1988.

Hoffman, Frederick. *Conrad Aiken*. New York: Twayne, 1962.

Mary Hricko

ALCOTT, LOUISA MAY (1832–1888). Pennsylvania-born but reared in Boston and Concord, Alcott is best known today for *Little Women* (1868), her novel about a New England family's life on the Civil War home front. However, her long bibliography includes other abolitionist and Civil War literature in the genres of domestic melodrama, thriller, journalism, poetry, and fictionalized autobiography. Alcott's abolitionist position in her writings reflected her family background and her own beliefs and actions. Her father, [Amos] Bronson Alcott, an extremist among Transcendentalists and an innovator in education, was her principal instructor.

Hospital Sketches (1863) is Alcott's fictionalized version of her experiences as a volunteer nurse in a military hospital in wartime Washington, a service that lasted only six weeks before she contracted typhoid fever. By turns satiric and sentimental, Alcott's sketches also provide a realistic portrait, rare for the war literature of the time, of wounded soldiers and the hospitals in which they were tended. For example, Alcott tells of a soldier suffering from what would now be called posttraumatic stress disorder: "He had been reliving, in imagination, the scenes he could not forget, till his distress broke out in incoherent ravings, pitiful to hear." In another passage she responds frankly to a question about church services for dying men and critiques the chaplains, saying, "In most hospitals I hope there are [such services]; in ours, the men died, and were carried away with as little ceremony as on a battlefield." Also, as Elaine Showalter notes, Alcott's narrator, Nurse Tribulation Periwinkle, honestly criticizes doctors and acknowledges her own reluctance to treat Confederate soldiers because of their enemy status.

Alcott's abolitionism and propensity for strong female protagonists are clear in *Hospital Sketches*, but they are more fully developed in the short story "My Contraband" (1863, originally titled "The Brothers"). This tale focuses on a Civil War hospital nurse named Dane; a mulatto ex-slave named Robert, the "contraband" of the title; and Captain Fairfax, a wounded Confederate officer who is Robert's half brother and former master. Dane is outraged when Robert tells her that Fairfax raped Robert's wife, but remaining true to her Christian principles, she persuades Robert not to murder Fairfax, and she herself nurses the Confederate back to health. When Dane meets Robert again, it is he who is her patient, for he has enlisted in the Fifty-fourth Massachusetts regiment and been mortally wounded by Fairfax, who was then himself killed by one of Robert's comrades during the regiment's assault on Fort Wagner, South Carolina. Before Robert dies, he learns that his wife had committed suicide after the rape, but he is happy in the belief that, thanks to Dane's having talked him out of the sin of murder, he will be reunited with her in the afterlife. Dane also learns that as a mark of gratitude (and seemingly as a mark of Alcott's linking of race- and gender-based oppression) Robert has taken her last name for his own.

Alcott's other significant Civil War works include *Colored Soldiers' Letters* (1864), a collection of correspondence by African American troops; the short story "M. L." (1863), about an interracial romance; the short story "An Hour" (1864), which considers the issues of slave rebellion and emancipation; and the poem "With a Rose, That Bloomed on the Day of John Brown's Martyrdom," a tribute to the militant abolitionist whose cause Alcott and her family had actively supported.

REFERENCES

Alcott, Louisa May. *The Poems of Louisa May Alcott*. New York: Ironweed Press, 2000.

Elbert, Sarah, ed. *Louisa May Alcott on Race, Sex, and Slavery*. Boston: Northeastern University Press, 1997.

Sexton, Martha. *Louisa May: A Modern Biography of Louisa May Alcott*. Boston: Houghton Mifflin, 1977.

Showalter, Elaine, ed. *Alternative Alcott*. New Brunswick, NJ: Rutgers University Press, 1986.

Debra A. Benko

ALLEN, ETHAN (1738–1789). Born in Litchfield, Connecticut, Allen's formal education stopped with his father's death in 1755, but this loss did not prevent him from reading widely or from publishing a number of thoughtful works, including *The Narrative of Colonel Ethan Allen's Captivity* (1779) and *Reason, the Only Oracle of Man* (1784). Allen briefly served as a militiaman (1757) at Fort William Henry, New York, during the French and Indian War (1754–1763).

By 1770, Allen had moved his extended family to the Green Mountains and readily stepped forward as a political leader in the struggle to establish an autonomous Vermont, independent of New York. That same year he participated in the formation of the Green Mountain Boys and was elected colonel-commandant of the company. In May 1775, Allen scored an early and easy victory in the War of Independence in the seizure of Fort Ticonderoga, New

York. Later that year. Allen participated in and was captured during the disastrous campaign for Canada.

Allen's *Narrative* (an important source for **Herman Melville**'s *Israel Potter*) recounts his experiences as one of the first American prisoners of war in the Revolution, and in this work, he can be understood on two levels. First, *The Narrative* is a skillful piece of propaganda intended to bolster waning American morale. Allen elevated American captives to the stature of secular martyrs who suffered for liberty's sake at the hands of cruel Britons. On its second and more subtle level, *The Narrative* is an act of personal redemption. Taken prisoner at Montreal (1775), Allen was imprisoned by the British for over two years. During this time, Vermont attained statehood, was writing a constitution, and was developing an independent political identity. Allen feared that he had been forgotten and was no longer a hero or leader; thus, *The Narrative* served as a device to reassert his former identity. Vermont's struggle for independence is explicitly linked to the larger contest between the revolutionary states and Britain. Through this device, Allen helped to elevate himself from the status of local hero to a figure of national prominence.

REFERENCES

Allen, Ethan. *The Narrative of Colonel Ethan Allen's Captivity.* 1779. Reprinted, with Introductory Notes by John Pell. New York: Fort Ticonderoga Museum, 1930.
Belleisles, Michael A. *Revolutionary Outlaws: Ethan Allen and the Struggle for Independence on the Early American Frontier.* Charlottesville: University Press of Virginia, 1993.

Ricardo A. Herrera

ALLEN, HENRY WILSON (1912–1991). Allen was born in Kansas City, Missouri. His father was a dental surgeon, descended from American Revolutionary War hero **Ethan Allen** and numbering Confederate army veterans among his patients. After high school and brief study at the Kansas City Polytechnic Institute, Allen in 1932 headed west, where he worked as miner, cowboy, horse wrangler, blacksmith, and Hollywood polo-pony exerciser. He wrote Metro-Goldwyn-Mayer scripts until he was discharged in 1949 for writing fiction on company time. His first novel, *No Survivors* (1950), is a retelling of the **Custer** legend narrated by an army officer rescued by Crazy Horse and preferring the Indian way of life and an Indian maiden's love. Allen wrote four more novels featuring Custer—regarded as brave but foolhardy.

Allen wrote so rapidly that he adopted two pen names—"Will Henry" and "Clay Fisher." Of his fifty-four novels and short story collections, fully twenty concern American military action, mostly against Native Americans but also during the Civil War and the Spanish-American War.

Allen's finest novels are historical reconstructions featuring brave, oppressed Native Americans and almost always presented from an antiwhite perspective.

His masterpiece, *From Where the Sun Now Stands* (1960), narrated by a pony-herding Indian lad, details Nez Percé Chief Joseph's retreat from Idaho into Montana and his honorable October 1877 surrender to scathingly criticized U.S. Army generals. *Chiricahua* (1972), the best of Allen's four Apache novels, concerns justifiably violent raids in 1883 by Chato and other Chiricahuas frustrated by army mistreatment in Arizona. Allen also sympathizes with Native Americans when, for example, they were involved in such events as the December 1866 Fetterman Massacre (*Red Blizzard*, 1951), the May 1858 campaign against Yakima chief Kamiakin (*To Follow a Flag*, 1953, retitled *Pillars of the Sky*, 1956), and the November 1864 Sand Creek Massacre (*Maheo's Children*, 1968, retitled *The Squaw Killers*, 1971). Allen also bases brilliant fiction on Lewis and Clark's 1804–1806 expedition, quasi-military in nature, in *The Gates of the Mountains* (1963), making a savior–heroine of Sacajawea.

Journey to Shiloh (1960), Allen's bitter Civil War novel, narrates seven youthful Confederate soldiers' ruinous disillusionment. *San Juan Hill* (1962) presents an Arizona cowboy turned soldier who fights well, concludes that war is a pointless folly, but relishes camaraderie partly generated by real-life **Theodore Roosevelt** and Buckey O'Neill.

Many of Allen's roughly fifty short stories treat the same war themes his novels develop. Representative is "River of Decision," from *Red Brother and White* (1966); in it a young soldier deserts General Henry Sibley's Confederate army unit after his failure to wrest New Mexico and Arizona territories from Union control (ending May 1862), crosses the Rio Grande to share his life with an Apache bandit's daughter, and agrees with a friend that "no war is ever won."

REFERENCES

[Allen, Henry Wilson]. *Will Henry's West*. Ed. Dale L. Walker. El Paso: Texas Western Press, 1984.

Gale, Robert L. *Will Henry/Clay Fisher*. Boston: Twayne Publishers, 1984.

Kroll, Keith. "Henry W. Allen (Will Henry/Clay Fisher): A Bibliography of Primary and Secondary Sources." *Bulletin of Bibliography* 44.4 (December 1987): 219–231.

Robert L. Gale

ALLEN, HERVEY (1889–1949). Although Hervey Allen is remembered primarily for *Anthony Adverse* (1933), one of the most popular historical novels of the century, his memoir *Toward the Flame* (1926) stands among the finest combat narratives of World War I. Born in Pittsburgh, Allen completed a B.S. in economics at the University of Pittsburgh in 1915 and, several months later, joined the Pennsylvania National Guard. He served on the Mexican border, then in France, participating in the Second Battle of the Marne and—after recuperating from wounds received at Fismette—the Meuse-Argonne Offensive. After the war, Allen studied at Harvard before teaching at a variety of institutions. In 1927, he married, moved to Bermuda, and began work on the wildly successful

Anthony Adverse. The royalties from this novel enabled Allen to purchase a large estate in Maryland, where he died of a heart attack in 1949.

Perhaps more than any other American war memoir, *Toward the Flame* invites comparison with British works such as Robert Graves's *Good-bye to All That* (1929) or Edmund Blunden's *Undertones of War* (1928). Like these accounts by former subalterns, Allen's book presents warfare from the perspective of an extremely literate junior officer, one who composes poems by candlelight in his pup tent and, in one scene, takes turns reciting *The Rubaiyat of Omar Khayyam* with a similarly cultured New England officer. Yet such reminders of Allen's literary proclivities appear infrequently, and his narrative is, in fact, remarkably self-effacing: Focused on a period of only two months during the summer of 1918, it describes just enough of the author's personal suffering to convey the enormous stress inherent in a combat officer's duties and ends shortly before Allen's wounding at Fismette. Indeed, *Toward the Flame* concentrates primarily, and brilliantly, on what Allen saw around him—the infinite variety of outrages committed against flesh by high explosives, the eerie appearance of abandoned enemy positions, the columns of exhausted men marching by night.

The book also eludes categorization, resembling neither patriotic propaganda nor pacifistic literature. Of the Germans, Allen writes, "I disliked them because I feared them, knowing full well their dangerous capability" (140). Here, the enemy is neither vilified nor embraced. And while contemptuous of the antiquated "science" of "musketry" ("murder in print," Allen calls it [139]) and understandably indignant over command blunders (especially in regard to the fighting around Fismette, the climax of the narrative), Allen eschews heavy-handed irony or overly insistent rhetoric. He is content simply to describe his experiences, leaving the reader to judge.

Allen's subsequent writings include the Civil War novel *Action at Aquila* (1938) and *It Was Like This* (1940), a book of two short stories dealing with World War I. The latter work is uneven and, at times, preposterous—as when Allen, succumbing to folklore, shows a German machine gunner chained to his weapon. Nevertheless, the second story in the volume, entitled "Blood Lust," is an unforgettable portrait of brutalization, as the quintessential American innocent, Corporal Virgin, becomes a man capable of bayoneting a German prisoner and, after becoming a prisoner himself, decapitating his guard. Here, the anger and disgust so artfully suppressed in *Toward the Flame* find powerful expression.

REFERENCES

Cooperman, Stanley. *World War I and the American Novel*. Baltimore: Johns Hopkins University Press, 1967.
Davison, Edward. "Hervey Allen." *Carrell* (June 1960): 16–22.

Steven Trout

AMERICAN REVOLUTION. *See* **Revolutionary War.**

ANDERSON, MAXWELL (1888–1959). Although largely overshadowed by his contemporary **Eugene O'Neill**, Maxwell Anderson was a highly successful dramatist and screenwriter best remembered for his plays of social criticism and his attempts to revive verse drama. His paradoxical contribution to American war literature is *What Price Glory?* (1924), an antiwar play coauthored with **Laurence Stallings**, and his patriotic World War II dramas: *Key Largo* (1939), *Candle in the Wind* (1941), *The Eve of St. Mark* (1942), *Storm Operation* (1944), and *Truckline Café* (1946).

Anderson was born in Pennsylvania but raised in the Midwest, moving frequently as his father, a Baptist minister, was reassigned. After completing an undergraduate degree at the University of North Dakota in 1911 and an M.A. in English at Stanford University in 1914, he taught high school English in San Francisco for three years before becoming head of the English Department at Whittier College in 1917. He was fired a year later for his outspoken opposition to American involvement in World War I and for his defense of a student who wrote antiwar articles for the campus newspaper that were censored by the college administration. Thus, Anderson was dismissed from his job at a Quaker school for his antiwar beliefs, an irony that has not been lost on subsequent biographers and critics.

After several years of writing editorials for major New York newspapers by day and poetry and plays by night, Anderson had his first Broadway hit in 1924 with *What Price Glory?*, a play he coauthored with Laurence Stallings, a World War I combat veteran who lost both legs as a result of a wound received as a Marine at Belleau Wood. *What Price Glory?* is the first American antiwar play of any consequence, and it shocked audiences with its realistic language and irreverent debunking of jingoistic patriotism. The play follows a U.S. Marine infantry unit before, during, and after a brief but fierce battle for a small French town. Comic overtones at the beginning as a captain and sergeant vie for the favors of a French girl quickly give way to a darker and bleaker rendering of the impact of impersonal modern warfare on individual soldiers. The final irony is that after fighting the Germans to a draw the Marines wind up bypassing the town, which they could have done earlier and avoided casualties. *What Price Glory?* is best grouped with the war literature of the Lost Generation that began to appear at that time because it displays the same disillusionment with a spiritually empty modern world whose advanced technology has only made it possible for humanity to inflict more suffering and death on itself.

Not surprisingly, Hollywood chose Anderson to adapt Erich Maria Remarque's classic antiwar novel *All Quiet on the Western Front* for the screen, and when the film appeared in 1930, it was received as a Hollywood equivalent of Broadway's *What Price Glory?* With the marginal exception of *Valley Forge* (1934), a play more about the inner conflicts of a future president than about the Revolution, Anderson did not return to war as a theme in his work until *Key Largo* (1939), in which a veteran of the American Lincoln Brigade in the Spanish Civil War, believing the Loyalist cause to be lost, abandons his comrades to save himself. Once back in his own country he finds that he cannot live with his guilt and that the only way he can achieve peace is by finding a cause for which he is willing to die.

In its sanctioning of armed resistance to fascism, *Key Largo* represents a sea change in Anderson's hitherto antiwar stance. This profound shift in convictions is confirmed in the plays Anderson wrote during World War II. Set in occupied France, *Candle in the Wind* (1941) is propagandistic in its vilification of the Nazis and its shrill call to arms. Following the U.S. entry into the war, Anderson embarked on extended tours of army bases in North Carolina and Virginia and later visited American installations in England and North Africa. This firsthand observation of military life during wartime gave him the material for *The Eve of St. Mark* (1942), the story of the repercussions of the death of an American farm boy in World War II, and *Storm Operation* (1944), an account of a minor military operation during the invasion of North Africa. The last of his World War II plays, *Truckline Café* (1946), focuses on a veteran's homecoming and attempts to explore the emotional and psychological impact of war on the individual soldier. After the war, Anderson returned to writing historical verse tragedies until his death.

REFERENCES

Bailey, Mabel Driscoll. *Maxwell Anderson, the Playwright as Prophet*. New York: Abelard-Schuman, 1957.
Clark, Barrett H. *Maxwell Anderson, the Man and His Plays*. New York: Samuel French, 1933.
Shivers, Alfred S. *Maxwell Anderson*. Boston: Twayne, 1983.

Lucas Carpenter

ANDERSON, THOMAS (1929–   ). Born in Passaic, New Jersey, Thomas Anderson moved with his family to Denmark at age three and spent his childhood there. Papers fabricated by the Danish Underground obscured his family's identity as American citizens during the war years, and Anderson was educated in Danish schools. He served a tour of duty in the U.S. Army during the late 1940s; then after a trip to France as a deck hand on a Danish freighter and a hitchhiking sojourn in Europe, he was back in the army and headed for Korea at the end of 1950. A few weeks after Christmas that year, the reconnaissance company in which he served found itself trapped behind enemy lines and fought its way to a Dutch-held place called Hoengsung. To a large extent this action informed the story of Anderson's Korean War novel, *Your Own Beloved Sons* (1956), one of the most widely acclaimed novels of that war.

Perhaps because Anderson drew upon his own experience, this seems an unusually good first novel. Employing the familiar organizing principle of a combat patrol's movement over hostile terrain, the story deals especially with two American soldiers: the veteran Sergeant Stanley, who is nearing the end of his tour of duty in Korea; and the callow but eager Richard Avery, new to the war and all that it involves. Anderson excels at depicting the sights, sounds, and myriad small details of the soldier's life in the field, particularly under combat conditions. His battle scenes are nicely written, and his characters vary believably in temperament and personality without being stereotypes. *Your Own Beloved Sons* is valuable for its comment on the personnel rotation system and its effects on the attitude and behavior of what a later war would call "short-timers." Also noteworthy is the book's depiction of leadership in the person of Sergeant Stanley. His death, one of several among the patrol's members, prompts the reader to think about Stanley's obvious connection to the book's epigraph and title, drawn from Sun Tzu's prescription for effective leadership.

Anderson's other published novel is *Here Comes Pete Now* (1961), a book set in an urban hiring hall and remarkable only for its rather obscure thematic import.

REFERENCES

Crane, Milton. Rev. of *Your Own Beloved Sons*, by Thomas Anderson. *Saturday Review* 24 March 1956: 21.
Rev. of *Your Own Beloved Sons*, by Thomas Anderson. *Time* 26 March 1956: 112.
Rugoff, Milton. Rev. of *Your Own Beloved Sons*, by Thomas Anderson. *New York Herald Tribune Book Review* 25 March 1956: 5.

James R. Kerin, Jr.

ANDREWS, MARY RAYMOND SHIPMAN (1860–1936). Raised in Lexington, Kentucky, as the oldest child of an Episcopalian minister, Andrews spent most of her adult life in Syracuse, New York, the wife of a judge. A popular writer of fiction and poetry, Andrews published most of her work between 1902 and 1929 in *Scribner's Magazine* and other leading magazines of the age. Several of the stories and poems were later published in book form or anthologized. Fervent patriotism, didacticism, sentimentalism, and historical embellishment characterize Andrews's fiction and poetry.

Andrews's most famous story, *The Perfect Tribute* (1906), first published in *Scribner's* and then as a separate book, is one of her many works about Abraham Lincoln. Ignoring factual evidence, Andrews mythologizes the writing and reception of the Gettysburg Address. Built on a pattern of contrasts, the story depicts Lincoln as a humble man, all too aware of his faults, who feels incapable of adequately addressing the solemnity of Gettysburg. When, according to the story, no one applauds the speech, Lincoln feels he has failed. Later, back in Washington, he writes a will for a dying Confederate soldier held in prison. Not knowing he is speaking to the president, the soldier speaks of the country's admiration of the Gettysburg speech. Through the Confederate soldier, Andrews's suggests the healing power of the speech for the entire country: "Other people have spoken stirring words, for the North and for the South, but never before . . . with the love of both. . . . It is only the greatest who can be partisan without bitterness, and only such to-day may call himself not Northern or Southern, but American." The soldier's family, divided by the war, believes family union is more important than politics and serves as a metaphor for the national philosophy that must be adopted.

Other works include *Marshall* (1912), a historical novel about the Napoleonic wars, and *A Lost Commander* (1933), a biography of Florence Nightingale. The spirit that marks Andrews's writing is perhaps best illustrated in "Her Country" (1918), in which a destitute young woman with a beautiful voice reluctantly agrees to donate her talent by singing about the flag for factory workers. At the moment she sees the flag, "A thrill caught her. There it was, the flag that had guarded her working and sleeping all her life. . . . Suddenly, her whole vigorous fresh being rose to it in warmth and loyalty." Transformed, she dedicates her talents to the support of the war effort. The story was meant to encourage Americans to purchase war bonds and to be ready to make sacrifices for the good of the country.

The nine poems that make up Andrews's *Crosses of War* (1918) are unabashedly sentimental. Often picturing young friends or simply American youths on the battlefields of France, these pieces, in varied stanzaic forms, praise the young men, anticipate the potential loss of lives, and hope for divinely inspired victory. Titles like "The Vigil," "Flower of the Land," and "America Victorious" set the tone.

Several of her patriotic stories have been made into movies produced in cooperation with the U.S. Marine Corps. *The Perfect Tribute* was reissued in 1987 as a children's book.

REFERENCES

Baright, Irene Benthan. *An Appreciation of the Life and Writing of Mary Raymond Shipman Andrews*. Manchester, MA: North Shore Press, 1937.

Hopkins, J.G.E. "Introduction." *The Scribner Treasury: Twenty-two Classic Tales by Mary Raymond Shipman Andrews and Others*. New York: Charles Scribner's Sons, 1953.

Pamela Monaco

APESS, WILLIAM (1798–1839?). William Apess was born in Colrain, Massachusetts, among the impoverished Pequot Indians who were defeated by English colonists in the Pequot War of 1637. The Pequots were declared extinct in the Treaty of Hartford in 1638, and many survivors were either sold into slavery or absorbed into neighboring tribes, forbidden to ever use their name "Pequot" again. It is against this heritage of racial genocide that Apess's parents struggled, finally separating and leaving him with alcoholic grandparents who beat him. White Christian families took him in as an indentured servant, and he became drawn to the Methodists who professed equality among all races. After running away and briefly serving in the War of 1812, he returned to Colrain and was ordained a Methodist minister in 1829. He began preaching among the

Pequot Indians, using the God-given rights that white Christians espoused to demand the same for Native Americans.

Apess's autobiographical writing is a testament of his conviction that Native Americans could attain freedom through salvation, yet he also blamed white Christians for the poverty and prejudice Native Americans were suffering at their hands. In *A Son of the Forest* (1839), Apess struggled to understand the concept of sin. He deplored the hypocrisy of white Christians and denounced them for denying Native Americans their rightful place within the Christian community. He spoke out against the practice of paying Native Americans for their work with alcohol instead of money, calling the practice deliberate genocide. He pointed out that the very name "Indian" was a slur to his people and argued that they were the only ones who could rightly be called "Natives."

Apess was arrested as an agitator during the Marshpee Revolt from which he wrote *Indian Nullification of the Unconstitutional Laws of Massachusetts Relative to the Marshpee Tribe; or, The Pretended Riot Explained* (1835). Although *Indian Nullification* is a series of accounts from participants of the revolt, Apess is credited for giving perspective to the collection. The revolt called attention to the deplorable practices under which Native Americans lived, blaming white Christians who "instructed" and "converted" the Marshpee Indians by giving them liquor and stealing their land. Although the white community expected the Native Americans to quietly await their extinction, *Indian Nullification* affirmed that they were in fact not a dying people.

In the self-published *Eulogy on King Philip* (1836), Apess honored Wampanoag leader Metacomet, known to the English colonists as King Philip, who was killed during King Philip's War (1675–1676). Apess challenged **Increase Mather**'s version of the war against "savages" and instead called Metacomet a "son of the forest" who withstood the injustices of the English colonists. The English colonists who practiced their own savagery put Metacomet's head on public display for the next twenty years and sold his ten-year-old son into slavery.

Throughout all his autobiographical writing, Apess criticized the hypocrisy of white Christians, bluntly stating that the missionaries had injured Native Americans more than they had helped them. He accused white Christians of degrading Native Americans, breaking up their own governments, thus leaving them with no recourse but to fight for their legal rights.

REFERENCES

Apess, William. *A Son of the Forest and Other Writings.* 1829. Amherst: University of Massachusetts Press, 1997.

———. *On Our Own Ground: The Complete Writings of William Apess, a Pequot.* Ed. Barry O'Connell. Amherst: University of Massachusetts Press, 1992.

Dannenberg, Anne M. " 'Where, Then, Shall We Place the Hero of the Wilderness?': William Apess's *Eulogy on King Philip* and Doctrines of Racial Destiny." *Early Native American Writing: New Critical Essays.* Ed. Helen Jaskoski. New York: Cambridge University Press, 1996.

McQuaid, Kim. "William Apess, a Pequot: An Indian Reformer in the Jackson Era." *New England Quarterly* 50 (1977): 605–625.

Murray, David. *Forked Tongues: Speech, Writing and Representation in North American Indian Texts.* Bloomington: University of Indiana Press, 1991.

Renate W. Prescott

ATHERTON, GERTRUDE (1857–1948). Gertrude Horn was born in San Francisco, where she would live periodically throughout her life. She married George Atherton in 1876 and had two children. After her husband's death in 1887 she traveled and lived in New York, London, and Munich. She started her writing career with short stories about California; her writings would include novels, short stories, newspaper articles, editorials, essays, and an autobiography, *Adventures of a Novelist* (1932). Her writings are generally marked by an interest in history and a concern with social and economic class.

Atherton spent most of World War I in France as a reporter for the *New York Times* and *The Delineator*. She also performed charity work and edited the *American Woman's Magazine*, a war propaganda publication. Her novels about the war include *Mrs. Balfame* (1916), in which the title character rationalizes killing her husband by contrasting one murder against the atrocities and mass killings committed by men in war, and *The White Morning: A Novel of the Power of German Women in Wartime* (1918), in which German women stage a revolution to overthrow the aristocratic, war-hungry government and replace it with a republic. In order to carry out the revolution, the heroine must confront the power of romantic love, finally killing her war-mad lover. *The Living Present* (1917) is a collection of Atherton's essays on French women's activities during the war. Atherton saw in the war an opportunity for a male-dominated society to give way to one that allowed women greater freedom and placed emphasis on the rights and intellect of women: "Never, prior to the Great War, was such an enormous body of women awake after the lethargic submission of centuries, and clamoring for their rights."

In the years between the two world wars, Atherton showed increasingly conservative and even fascist tendencies; she suggested at one time that Franco would be better than Communist rule in Spain. She did, however, speak out against Hitler in a rally at Carnegie Hall in 1938, calling him "the curse of the world." She felt that Hitler's attack on the Jews was an attack on civilization itself.

REFERENCES

Leider, Emily Wortis. *California's Daughter: Gertrude Atherton and Her Times.* Stanford: Stanford University Press, 1991.

McClure, Charlotte S. *Gertrude Atherton.* Boston: Twayne Publishers, 1979.

Jennifer A. Haytock

B

BAILEY, TEMPLE (188?–1953). Born in Petersburg, Virginia, Irene Temple Bailey grew up in Washington, D.C. She was educated in private schools in Virginia and lived in St. Louis and Washington as an adult. She wrote sentimental short stories and novels for serial publication in magazines, and much of her work was extremely popular when it was first published.

Bailey's *The Tin Soldier* (1919) is a domestic novel about the ideology behind American participation in World War I. A reviewer for the American Library Association *Booklist* described the book as "Too long and too sentimental, but full of good principles." In the course of the novel, the characters reevaluate their emotional and ideological priorities. The story centers on the romance of a young woman, Jean MacKenzie, and Derry Drake, "the tin soldier"—a man who has stayed out of the war for mysterious reasons. In the end, Derry breaks a promise to his dead mother in order to respond to his country's greater claim on him. Jean MacKenzie grows out of a good-hearted but nevertheless selfish, isolated view of the world. She must learn to love Derry enough to let him leave for the war; she becomes, as her nickname "Jean-Joan" reflects, a point of connection between the military attitude and domestic spirit.

The novel shows a range of women's attitudes toward the war. Alma Drew believes the war a silly distraction from parties, whereas Hilda Merrit goes to France because she is a nurse and feels she can work there, though she has no patriotic spirit with which to make her endeavor or her relationships with the wounded noble. In contrast, Drusilla Gray gives up a comfortable life in order to live in the mud like the soldiers and to give them the spiritual comfort of her glorious singing voice. Drusilla also offers a liberated view of life for women after the war: "When the Tommies come marching home again they will find comrades, not clinging vines."

REFERENCE

Goldman, Dorothy. " 'Eagles of the West?' American Women Writers and World War I." *Women and World War I: The Written Response*. Ed. Dorothy Goldman. New York: St. Martin's Press, 1993.

Jennifer A. Haytock

BALABAN, JOHN (1943–   ). One of the most significant American poets to emerge from the Vietnam War, Balaban was born in Philadelphia and converted to the Quaker faith while still in high school. His principled stand against war led him to refuse military service. Instead, after graduating from Harvard with an M.A. in 1967, conscientious objector status was officially granted by his draft board, a grimly comic episode described in his 1991 memoir *Remembering Heaven's Face: A Moral Witness in Vietnam*. He performed his alternative service in Vietnam with the International Voluntary Services, the largest private volunteer agency under contract to the U.S. Agency for International Development (USAID). As a college teacher and hospital charity worker, Balaban witnessed the suffering and endurance of the Mekong Delta's civilian population at first hand, and his experiences in Vietnam as a pacifist, humanitarian, and translator have provided the foundation for all his books beginning with *After Our War*, which won the Lamont Selection of the Academy of American Poets and a nomination for the National Book Award in 1974. His subsequent books, critically recognized as an important canon of work about Vietnam, have included a novel set in Southeast Asia, *Coming Down Again*. (1985, revised in 1989); the 1991 memoir; several volumes of poetry, most notable of which are *Blue Mountain* (1982), *Words for My Daughter* (1991), and *Locusts at the Edge of Summer* (1997); as well as his translations of *Vietnamese Folk Poetry* (1974) and in *Ca Dao Vietnam: A Bilingual Anthology of Vietnamese Folk Poetry* (1980). He also provided the text for Geoffrey Clifford's photographs in *Vietnam: The Land We Never Knew* (1989).

Balaban's poetry is insistently moral and intensely imagistic. The title of his first volume enunciates the plurality of those who caused, experienced, and suffered the conflict in Southeast Asia. Balaban's own selection of poems from his first volume for his midlife retrospective *Locusts at the Edge of Summer* reflects his desire to remember, thirty years after the fact, the violence and destruction wreaked upon a verdant and paradisiacal landscape and its inhabitants. There is palpable rage in such poems as "Mau Than," which indicts the scene of American soldiers voyeuristically taking pictures of the mutilated genitalia of a wounded girl. But much of his poetry subtly avoids precise attribution of agency to one side or the other, a deliberate ambiguity that implicitly blames all combatant forces. A sophisticated and horrific poem drawing on the conventions of Elizabethan revenge tragedy, "Carcanet: After Our War," powerfully equates the Four Horsemen of the Apocalypse to the ruthless generals on all sides who blight Vietnam, making all that is solid a deliquescent morass of muck and decay. Other poems are less explicitly critical and allow images in arrested moments in time to convey the implicit critique. "The Guard at the Binh Tuy Bridge" has the seemingly arbitrary power over life and death as he aims at a woman leaning over the side of a boat. The force of the poem originates in the dreamlike and misty setting poised between earth and water, and the bridge connecting the two elements. The source of the potential violence in the poem, the soldier, is conspicuous by his godlike suspension over the tension-filled, elemental scene Balaban depicts.

Balaban's poetry about the Vietnam War published since the 1974 collection is marked by memorably supernatural and surreal imagery, exemplifying the estranging experience of Vietnam. "After Our War," anthologized in *Blue Mountain*, is a nightmare vision of the disembodied organs and limbs of Vietnam's victims inching their inexorable way back to America, the source of their desecration. In a bitterly ironic version of the immigrant experience, Vietnam's victims arrive en masse to haunt and reproach America's desire to forget the tragic fiasco. The poem ends in a flurry of unanswered questions about how America's comforting myths will be adequate to justify the trauma of this war. The spectral presence of the dead is also the focus of the 1990 Pushcart Prize–winning poem "For the Missing in Action." The setting, in contrast to "After Our War," is the Vietnamese rural landscape, forever pocked by the destruction of aerial bombardment and haunted by a weird kind of topiary: the vegetal body of the dead combatant, the "green creature" whose trace is marked by the weeds forming the shape of the fallen soldier. Mindful of war's lasting effects on future generations, Balaban's recent poetry is marked by the presence of children on both sides of the war, like the boys who discover the "viny man" in "For the Missing in Action." And the screaming Vietnamese boy on the operating table in "Words for My Daughter" is a pain-filled rebuke to the symbol of our perpetuation of militarism and violence in the American boy dressed as a Green Beret for Halloween trick-or-treating, an "evil midget" who is unselfconsciously aping his father in fatigues standing outside the door.

Balaban's body of work about the lasting traumas of the Vietnam War for the American and Vietnamese people is a powerful advocacy of moral thought and action as an antidote to the blind forces of war and destruction. He succeeds in his self-defined role of "moral witness" to the Cold War's most painful and divisive episode.

REFERENCES

Balaban, John. *Locusts at the Edge of Summer: New & Selected Poems*. Port Townsend, WA: Copper Canyon Press, 1997.

Smith, Lorrie. "Resistance and Revision by Vietnam War Veterans." *Fourteen Landing Zones: Approaches to Vietnam War Literature*. Ed. Philip K. Jason. Iowa City: Iowa University Press, 1991. 49–66.

Walsh, Jeffrey. " 'After Our War': John Balaban's Poetic Images of Vietnam." *Vietnam Images: War and Representation*. Ed. Jeffrey Walsh and James Aulich. New York: St. Martin's Press, 1989. 141–152.

David A. Boxwell

BECKER, STEPHEN (1927–). Born in Mount Vernon, New York, Stephen David Becker was a wunderkind, reading fluently at age three, entering Harvard on a scholarship at age sixteen (where he studied Chinese), and graduating in 1947. He served in the U.S. Marine Corps in 1945. By twenty-one, he was a professor in Peking. His family life in Massachusetts, where he taught and wrote, was interrupted by teaching stints at Brandeis, the University of Alaska, Bennington, and several other colleges. Later, the Beckers moved to Tortola in the British Virgin Islands. Apart from writing his eleven novels, two nonfiction works, and a film adaptation, Becker has translated works by André Malraux and Elie Wiesel, among others.

When the War Is Over (1969) is the fictionalized story of a historical incident: In 1865, Lieutenant Marius Catto of the Union army was shot by Thomas Martin, a sixteen-year-old boy fighting with Colonel Jesse's riflemen. Catto recovered, but the boy was tried and sentenced to death. A year after the sentence had apparently been commuted, the boy was executed by order of General "Fighting" Joe Hooker. Martin is thought to be the last official casualty of the Civil War.

The novel, which contains both historical and fictional people, is told from Catto's point of view. Together Catto and the regimental surgeon, Jack Phelan, discuss the purposes of power and the ethics of war; the soldier is always responsible: "Here I am, then. Like a weed," Catto says, and Phelan replies, "But a thinking weed." Thomas Martin's murder is caused partly by Hooker's rage for power, partly by Lincoln's assassination. Catto sees in the "tale of Thomas Martin . . . that life had no meaning but what we brought to it, and [Catto] considered himself the last truly free man in a world careering toward universal slavery."

Dog Tags (1973) is the story of Benny Beer, a Jewish soldier who, at the end of World War II, is wounded, found naked in Germany, and interrogated by his own army before being returned to New York. He attends medical school on the G. I. Bill, meets his wife-to-be, and simultaneously falls in love with another woman. Posted to Korea, Beer is taken prisoner while working in a forward MASH (mobile army surgical hospital) unit. He refuses to collaborate, but holding the Hippocratic oath above all others, he doctors both Americans and Koreans, for which he is again later interrogated. After three years in a prisoner of war (POW) camp, Benny returns home to become, as Jack Phelan does in *When the War Is Over*, an obstetrician ("They're all mine," Benny says of the children he delivers). The final episode in the novel involves a Vietnam veteran who has beaten his wife and child. The day after his forty-sixth birthday, the day after he saves the veteran and his family, Benny dies of a heart attack.

Despite its ending, *Dog Tags* is a more hopeful book than *When the War Is Over*, in part because it follows the healer, not the soldier. Catto cannot excuse the soldier's acts; Phelan and Beer try to compensate for humanity's murderousness. In the face of the Korean camp commander's bleak note that "[a]ll war is now total war," Benny tells the men to eat weeds, because "weeds beat scurvy!"—the smallest things can make life possible. Benny "pondered war and decided that men liked it. Statistically. In a large population the number of men who love to kill is sufficient to form a modern army. War was here to stay." His conclusion hardens Benny's belief that murder is never right: "I do not believe in killing anyone today for the sake of some maybe-if-we're-lucky better world tomorrow. Because that automatically makes it a worse world tomorrow, right there." The characters in both novels share each other's beliefs: *Dog Tags* continues the philosophical trajectory of *When the War Is Over*. Becker's novels are equally full of hope and love, pain and disappointment.

REFERENCES

Becker, Stephen. "Stephen Becker." *Contemporary Authors Autobiography Series*. Vol. 1. Detroit: Gale, 1984. 33–46.
Rev. of *Dog Tags*, by Stephen Becker. *New York Times Book Review* 23 September 1973: 7.
Rev. of *Dog Tags*, by Stephen Becker. *Time* 19 November 1973: 111.
Rev. of *When the War Is Over*, by Stephen Becker. *Saturday Review* 17 January 1970: 40.

Tim Blackmore

BEERS, ETHYL LYNN (1827–1879). Born in Goshen, New York, Ethelinda Eliot began contributing poetry to magazines under the pseudonym Ethyl Lynn. After she married William H. Beers in 1846, she added her married name. *Harper's Weekly Magazine* published her most famous poem, "The Picket Guard," in November 1861. The poem's audience spread quickly, and several Southern authors tried to claim it as their own. The myths about the poem increased when the *London Times* printed it, claiming the poem was written by a young Confederate soldier who died in battle (Beers 349). Set to music by a Richmond music publisher in 1864, the poem is often found in Civil War music collections. Despite being written by a Northern woman, the poem has found its way into several anthologies of Southern war poems, including *War Songs and Poems of the Southern Confederacy*, whose editor, H. M. Wharton, a "private in General Lee's Army," claims that "no poem written during the war had a wider popularity."

The majority of Beers's war poems rely on pathos to achieve their effect. In "The Picket Guard," retitled "All Quiet Along the Potomac" for her collection, Beers tells the story of a "lone sentry" who is slain by "a rifleman hid in the thicket" as he guards the camp, thinking of his wife and children "in the low trundle-bed / Far away in the cot on the mountain." The imagery of the poem has a Wordsworthian quality: There is a "blasted pine tree" and a "tremulous . . . night-wind," but here the sudden "flashing" is not one of inspiration. Rather, it brings a quick death with the "red life-blood . . . ebbing and plashing." Beers had other successes, notably "Company K," "Which Shall It Be?" and "The Baggage Wagon." Her collected poems were published in October 1879, and she died the next day.

REFERENCES

Beers, Ethyl Lynn. *All Quiet Along the Potomac and Other Poems*. Philadelphia: Porter and Coates, 1879.

Wharton, H. M., ed. *War Songs and Poems of the Southern Confederacy*. Philadelphia: John C. Winston, 1904.

James M. Dubinsky

BELASCO, DAVID (1853–1931). David Belasco, born in San Francisco when the Gold Rush was still in full swing, had a long career as a playwright, director, and producer. A major figure in the development of the American theater, Belasco was a pioneer in the rise of naturalism. His dramatic approach included a natural acting style, detailed stage settings, a more thorough integration of music into the production, and subtle lighting effects combined with emotionalism and dramatic incident.

War, although only one of countless topics presented in the plays with which Belasco was associated, was the basis for some of his most popular productions. Belasco cowrote with Franklyn Fyles a play called *The Girl I Left Behind Me*. Produced in 1893, the play drew upon the American Indian wars and such incidents, still in the public mind, as the battle of Little Bighorn in 1876, the insurrection by Sitting Bull in 1890, and the excursions of General Nelson Miles against the Sioux in 1890–1891. The play is heavy with action as Sioux attack an outlying army post in Montana and places considerable stress on love and honor.

Belasco was approximately twelve years old when the Civil War drew to a close and not surprisingly turns to that war for such plays as *The Heart of Maryland* (1895) and *The Warrens of Virginia* (1907)—the former written by Belasco, the latter by William C. De Mille but revised and produced by Belasco. The plots of these plays feature lovers struggling to overcome both the forces of war and the intrigues of villains. Both plays qualify as melodramas in an age when melodrama was both popular and critically respectable.

REFERENCES

Marker, Lise-Lone. *David Belasco: Naturalism in the American Theatre*. Princeton, NJ: Princeton University Press, 1975.
Winter, William. *The Life of David Belasco*. 2 vols. New York: Moffat, Yard, 1918.

Edward J. Rielly

BENÉT, STEPHEN VINCENT (1898–1943). The son of a career officer in the U.S. Army, Stephen Vincent Benét grew up on army bases throughout the country and attended military academies in Georgia and California. Upon his graduation from Yale in 1918 he enlisted in the army, only to be discharged three days later when his poor eyesight, which he had tried to conceal, was finally discovered. Thereafter, his military interests could find expression only in his writing; the ultimate result is *John Brown's Body* (1928), a 15,000-line epic poem in eight books that he called a "cyclorama" of the Civil War. Like most of Benét's work, it was an immediate popular success and went on to become one of the all-time best-selling American poems. Although there was some grumbling from Southern Fugitive-Agrarians such as **Allen Tate**, critics agreed that it presented a version of the war that North and South alike could appreciate. After all, according to Benét, both sides were fighting for, as one of his characters puts it, "Something beyond you that you must trust," and both Lincoln and Lee are portrayed as heroes.

John Brown's Body is structured around actual military and political events, including John Brown's raid on Harper's Ferry, the firing on Fort Sumter, First Bull Run, Shiloh, Vicksburg, Gettysburg, the Wilderness, Sherman's march to the sea, Appomattox, and the death of Lincoln. These events are enacted and described by a wide array of historical and fictional characters representing a cross section of both the Union and Confederacy, slaves and freemen. Benét's panorama shifts fluidly from battlefield to drawing room, from slave quarters to headquarters. The feeling throughout is of one continuous action, an implacable flow of history in which both characters and reader are caught up.

Nevertheless, the poem suffers in the end from Benét's efforts to make it palatable to all. In his attempt to be representative, he too often resorts to regional and racial stereotypes, and rather than explore the individuality of such figures as Grant, Lee, Lincoln, and Davis, he is content to work within the myths in which their worshippers had already cloaked them. Similarly, his considerations of the causes and conduct of the war now seem somewhat superficial and romantically naive. Still, *John Brown's Body* remains an important literary work about the Civil War and a noteworthy achievement in modern narrative poetry.

Although *John Brown's Body* is Benét's principal contribution to American war literature, several of his poems of the 1930s are strong and disturbing expressions of the prewar anxiety so many Americans were beginning to feel. "1939," for example, features an army of skeletons marching to war; "Nightmare for Future Reference" has all humanity rendered sterile by war; and "Nightmare at Noon" is the dramatized panic attack of a modern American in 1940 who is contemplating the likelihood of his country's involvement in the war in Europe.

REFERENCES

Selected Works of Stephen Vincent Benét. 2 vols. New York: Farrar and Rinehart, 1942.
Stroud, Parry. *Stephen Vincent Benét.* New York: Twayne, 1962.

Lucas Carpenter

BERGER, THOMAS (1924–). Born in Cincinnati, Ohio, Thomas Berger is an important writer of American comic fiction. He has written over a dozen satiric novels on a wide variety of subjects, including the American West in his best-known novel *Little Big Man* (1964) and Camelot in *Arthur Rex* (1978).

Berger's experiences in the U.S. Army surfaced in his first novel, *Crazy in Berlin* (1958). The protagonist of the novel is Carlo Reinhart, a soldier in the occupation forces in Germany at the end of the World War II. He is an average man in intellect and morality when he enlists in the army. Once in the army, he discovers he likes it because "the petty decisions were provided and the major ones ignored." However, while in Berlin, the German American Reinhart struggles with issues of morality covering a wide range of ideologies. He is forced to confront his own heritage, the events of the war, communism, Nazism, Americanism, and Judaism. In an attempt to reconcile these issues, Reinhart unsuccessfully tries to save a Jewish Communist traitor, Schild. After Schild dies, Reinhart is injured and taken to the psychiatric ward because of his feelings of guilt. He recovers and is sent home. Carlo Reinhart is the protagonist in three other Berger novels, *Reinhart in Love* (1962), *Vital Parts* (1970), and *Reinhart's Women* (1981).

Little Big Man is the fictional life story of 111-year-old Jack Crabb, who claims to be the sole white survivor of the Battle of Little Bighorn. Berger frames Crabb's story with a forward and epilogue by Ralph Fielding Snell, an emotionally distressed narrator who has recorded Crabb's tale. Although the reader should question the reliability of the narrative, Crabb gives what seems to be an accurate description of his adventures with General **Custer**, the cavalry, and the Old West. The novel is Berger's meditation on the creation of history and America through language. Like his other novels, Berger has reworked a popular genre of fiction, in this case, the Western. Of interest is how Crabb describes, through his first-person narrative, the role of the army in the conquest of the West and the Native Americans.

REFERENCES

Crews, Robert. *Thomas Berger*. New York: Morrow, 1994.
Landon, Brooks. *Thomas Berger*. Boston: Twayne, 1989.
Madden, David W., ed. *Critical Essays on Thomas Berger*. New York: G. K. Hall, 1995.

Sean C. F. McGurr

BERRY, WENDELL (1934–). Except for brief periods of study at Stanford and in Italy (as a Guggenheim fellow) and teaching at New York University, Berry has lived his life close to his Port Royal, Kentucky, birthplace. An essayist, poet, novelist, small farmer, and professor at the University of Kentucky, Berry's chief concern lies in exalting simplicity, agrarianism, and independence and in bemoaning a culture that, he argues, has lost contact with the land and is too dependent on merchandise, ownership, and centralization. Berry's attitude toward militarism was formed, in part, through experiencing the conformist ideals of the military high school he attended—an experience that only fueled his rebelliousness and sent him deeper into the solace of the Kentucky River wilds. In step with his ecological philosophy, Berry holds that the modern militaristic mind-set is both a cause and an effect of the dwindling American individualism.

In "Property, Patriotism, and National Defense" (collected in his *Home Economics*), Berry writes that he is "not by principle a passive man, or by nature a pacific one." He believes that there are honorable causes for fighting, but that modern war is consistently carried out to protect the pecuniary interests of a few under forged principles. In nuclear age warfare, "we allow our technology to propose for us the defense of Christian love and justice (as we invariably put it) by an act of perfect hatred and perfect injustice."

While warfare is not a running preoccupation in Berry's poetry and fiction, it plays a major role in some of his work. The title of his short poem "Against the War in Vietnam" (1968) bluntly encapsulates his view of that conflict, and in his dialogic poem "The Long Night" (1978) a black and a white woman find common ground in nature against the backdrop of the Civil War. The faceless, destructive nature of war is a theme in his second novel, *A Place on Earth* (1967), which dramatizes the tragic effects of World War II on a small Kentucky community, especially farmer Mat Feltner, who loses a son to the war. The title character of his novel *The Memory of Old Jack* (1974) recalls his childhood in the Civil War era with longing for its pastoral life and regret for the suffering it produced.

REFERENCES

Angyal, Andrew J. *Wendell Berry*. New York: Twayne, 1995.
Merchant, Paul, ed. *Wendell Berry*. Lewiston, ID: Confluence, 1991.
"Wendell Berry." *1986 Current Biography Yearbook*. Ed. Charles Moritz. New York: Wilson, 1986.

Bryan L. Moore

BESSIE, ALVAH (1904–1985). Alvah Cecil Bessie, born in New York City, attended De Witt Clinton High School and graduated from Columbia University. After working in publishing and journalism, he wrote short stories and became drama reporter for *New Masses*. Bessie served with the Lincoln Battalion from 1937 until the end of the Spanish Civil War and fought in the bloody Aragon retreat. His uncompromising *Men in Battle* (1939) and an edited anthology, *The Heart of Spain* (1952) by American veterans, are his principal works on the Spanish conflict, although he also wrote of the war through flashbacks in his angry novel *The Un-Americans* (1957) after he was blacklisted as a Communist.

Men in Battle records the fate of the Fifteenth International Brigade after the Republican victory at Teruel and through the tragic Ebro defensive campaign. Although the memoir outlines wider military operations, it concentrates upon the experience of the author's fellow soldiers facing loss and defeat. By also describing his own fear at being bombed and under fire, Bessie achieves credibility as a narrator. *Men in Battle* reports unflinchingly on the conduct of a beaten army, its confusion, loss of morale, and terror. Particularly harrowing are the descriptions of death and wounding such as that of Bessie's blinded comrade, Aaron.

What differentiates *Men in Battle* is its insider's consideration of motive and ideology, although the political passages of the memoir are not usually intrusive. Thus, the book is more than the portrayal of a doomed expedition because the author seeks to explain why the volunteers chose to dedicate their lives to the fight against fascism. Generally Bessie's prose is functional, but at such moments it becomes rhetorically dignified. He suggests that men from all walks of life enlisted to "achieve self integration," as they believed "that love must come alive in the world."

REFERENCES

Bessie, Alvah. *Men in Battle: A Story of Americans in Spain.* New York: Charles Scribner's Sons, 1939.

Juste, John M. *Say That We Saw Spain Die; Literary Consequences of the Spanish Civil War.* Seattle: University of Washington Press, 1996.

Jeff Walsh

BIERCE, AMBROSE (1842–1914). Bierce is best known for his tales of the macabre and supernatural and the biting aphorisms of his *Devil's Dictionary*; however, in a number of memoirs and short stories about the Civil War, he also provides some of the most graphic and powerful depictions in American literature of the physical and psychological carnage that war wreaks upon the individual.

Born in Ohio and raised in rural Indiana, Bierce at the age of eighteen enlisted in the Ninth Indiana Infantry when the Civil War began. An excellent soldier, working his way up from private to brevet major, he saw a great deal of action throughout the war, including the battles of Stones River, Missionary Ridge, Kennesaw Mountain, where he sustained a severe wound, Franklin, and Nashville. Following service on a military expedition through the West in 1866–1867, Bierce resigned from the army in San Francisco to begin his writing career. He remained there for the next twenty-nine years, except for a sojourn in England from 1872–1875, becoming one of the most accomplished newspaper columnists and short story writers in the country.

Most of Bierce's stories and reminiscences about the war appeared in the 1890s, in the collections *Tales of Soldiers and Civilians* (1892) and *Can Such Things Be?* (1893) and his columns for the *San Francisco Examiner*. The two most famous of these pieces depict what happens when a civilian with a romanticized view of war encounters its actuality. "Chickamauga" presents a deaf-mute child whose play takes him to the edge of a battlefield, where he sees thousands of wounded men whom he does not recognize for what they are, regarding them as playmates in his imaginary parade; only when he returns home to find his mother dead as a result of stray shots does he understand what has happened and collapses in despair. "An Occurrence at Owl Creek Bridge," which has won great praise for its insight into the workings of the human consciousness, focuses on a Southerner who believes that engaging in espionage is a glorious act of patriotism but winds up in the unromantic situation of being hanged by Federal troops. Still resisting grim reality, he imagines himself escaping and returning home in the instant between the opening of the trapdoor beneath his feet and his fall to the end of the rope.

Many of Bierce's lesser-known war stories likewise deal with the effects of the realities of war on a naïf; however, in most of these the character in question is a soldier rather than a civilian. "A Son of the Gods," "Killed at Resaca," "George Thurston," and "One Officer, One Man" depict the deaths by various means of men who refuse to abandon the illusion that they ought to behave heroically under fire, that any feeling of fear or even self-preservation is a sign of unworthiness. "A Horseman in the Sky," "The Coup de Grace," and "The Affair at Coulter's Notch" deal with soldiers' confrontations with the literally fratricidal nature of the Civil War when their duty requires them to kill members of their own families or close friends. "Jupiter Doke, Brigadier-General" is the story of an officer who twice flees in terror from the battlefield but nonetheless manages to rise in the ranks due to his political connections and his ability to make his cowardice look like leadership in his official reports—a subject Bierce also takes up in a number of his nonfiction pieces, including "What I Saw of Shiloh" and "The Crime at Pickett's Mill," which, respectively, indict Union generals U. S. Grant and O. O. Howard for ineptitude and pusillanimity.

Not surprisingly, given the content of his stories, Bierce's memoirs, including "A Little of Chickamauga" and "On a Mountain" in addition to the two mentioned above, similarly concentrate on the horrors of war, particularly the line soldier's lack of understanding of his strategic and tactical position and the gruesomeness of the dead and wounded, which evokes not compassion but revulsion. The soldier in this situation, Bierce implies, survives by discarding all of his prior illusions about combat and simply concentrating, in a manner that might be called proto-existential, on the tasks that lie immediately before him.

Despite the harrowing picture that most of his stories and memoirs present, Bierce apparently remained personally ambivalent about war. Three circumstances lead to this conclusion. The first is the tour of the battlefields on which he had served that Bierce took in 1913, in the course of which he implied to an interviewer that his Civil War service had been the most significant feature of his life. The second is the story "A Resumed Identity," in which the protagonist, like Bierce himself, revisits a battlefield of his youth; there he is exhilarated to find himself transported back in time to the battle and then falls dead when he realizes that this return to the past has been an illusion. The third is the fact that following his own tour the seventy-one-year-old Bierce journeyed into Mexico to observe the war being waged by Pancho Villa against the government forces of Victoriano Huerta. His fate cannot be confirmed, but what evidence there is suggests that he died in the battle of Ojinaga, on January 14, 1914.

REFERENCES

Bierce, Ambrose. *Ambrose Bierce's Civil War*. Ed. William McCann. Los Angeles: Gateway, 1956.

Davidson, Cathy N., ed. *Critical Essays on Ambrose Bierce*. New York: G. K. Hall, 1982.
———. *The Experimental Fictions of Ambrose Bierce: Structuring the Ineffable*. Lincoln: University of Nebraska Press, 1984.
Fuentes, Carlos. *The Old Gringo*. New York: HarperCollins, 1986.
O'Connor, Richard. *Ambrose Bierce: A Biography*. New York: Little, Brown, 1967.
Schaefer, Michael W. *Just What War Is: The Civil War Writings of De Forest and Bierce*. Knoxville: University of Tennessee Press, 1997.

Michael W. Schaefer

BINNS, ARCHIE (1899–1971). Born and raised on the Pacific coast of Washington, Archie Fred Binns belonged to one of the first families of western Washington and became known primarily as a novelist and historian of the Northwest. The grandson of a Confederate blockade runner killed at sea in the Civil War, Binns himself served on a lightship off the coast of Washington before enlisting in the U.S. Army in 1918, from which he retired as a second lieutenant in 1922. After stints as a sailor, newspaper reporter, and book editor, he published his first novel, *Lightship*, in 1934.

A semiautobiographical work, *Lightship* treats the sometimes claustrophobic world of the continually anchored lightship as a microcosm of the disparate elements of society, pitting personalities against one another in the cramped quarters of the vessel. Eventually, despite their differences, they are forced to work together in a fierce storm in order to save not only themselves but also the passenger ship heading toward the reef by which the lightship is stationed. A second novel, *The Laurels Are Cut Down* (1937), follows a young man and his brother from Washington into military service during World War I. After surviving the Germans, both are sent to Siberia, where one is killed and the other is left lonely and embittered. Upon returning to the Northwest, the surviving brother discovers the land they once knew is changed forever.

The majority of Binns's works, both fictional and nonfictional, is less concerned with the larger struggles of armies than with the implications of the regimented lifestyle on the spirits of those largely unknown individuals that make up the majority of each side. Many of his protagonists are men of simple character who find themselves increasingly uncomfortable with the complications of the worlds they are unwillingly thrust into, whether by warfare or the vagaries of society itself.

REFERENCES

Bone, D. W. Rev. of *Lightship*, by Archie Binns. *Saturday Review of Literature* 25 August 1934: 64.
Marsh, F. T. Rev. of *The Laurels Are Cut Down*, by Archie Binns. *New York Times Book Review* 18 April 1937: 7.

Patrick Julian

BISHOP, JOHN PEALE (1892–1944). Bishop's writings respond not only to the wars of his lifetime but also to the American Civil War. The military history of Charles Town (now Charleston), West Virginia, where Bishop was born and raised, particularly influenced his literary work. Charles Town, a late eighteenth-century battlefield and the site of John Brown's 1859 trial and execution, appears most significantly in Bishop's 1931 volume of interconnected stories *Many Thousands Gone* as the imaginary town of Mordington. The title story's examination of the Civil War as it influenced the lives of Mordington civilians won Bishop the *Scribner's Magazine* prize as well as enduring admiration from readers of Civil War fiction.

Bishop attended Princeton University, where he participated in the campus literary scene along with writers F. Scott Fitzgerald and **Edmund Wilson**, and his poems, essays, and short stories won many prizes. After graduating in 1917, Bishop became a first lieutenant of infantry, in the 84th Division, eventually serving in France during the final months of World War I. His experiences escorting prisoners of war and carrying out the disinterment and reburial of American soldiers became sources for works like "In the Dordogne" and "Resurrection."

Bishop's early poem of World War I, "February 1917," predates the writer's war service. Published in Bishop's first volume of poetry, *Green Fruit* (1917), the poem foregrounds the conflicted assertions of its speaker, who anticipates answering the call to "go down with the rest" in war despite the necessary fall from romantic self-possession of his thoughts and dreams to dehumanization amid broken bodies and the dreamless dead. In contrast, Bishop's postwar poem "In the Dordogne," from *Now With His Love* (1933), casts the experience of loss during war not in terms of an individual speaker's thoughts and dreams but through a collective speaker's courage and endurance. "In the Dordogne" uses Christian imagery and repetition to suggest the daily deterioration, yet mysterious persistence, of the soldiers' hope that "courage would avail something" and the terrible waste of young lives would not be in vain. The uneasy resignation about death found in "In the Dordogne" transforms into a passionate need to embrace life in "Resurrection." A short story that concludes the collaborative volume written by Bishop and Edmund Wilson entitled *The Undertaker's Garland* (1922), "Resurrection" traces the physical and psychological reactions of a young, lonely lieutenant, in command of a prisoner of war camp, to the disinterment of an American soldier who will reburied in a soldiers' graveyard.

After marrying Margaret Grosvenor Hutchins in 1922, Bishop lived in Europe for much of the 1920s, returning to the United States in 1933. During World War II, he served for a year as Director of Publications, Bureau of Cultural Relations of the Council of National Defense, a post offered to him by close friend and then Librarian of Congress **Archibald MacLeish**. Around this time, Bishop's deep concern about the fall of France to the Germans found poetic voice in his 1941 "Occupation of a City" and its haunting descriptions of a besieged city's silences. His talent for evoking the frightening collapse of civilizations ranged from such directly contemporary poems to more historical meditations like "The Return," which Bishop described as set somewhere in the

Roman empire but paralleling nonetheless the state of twentieth-century Europe. The poem recalls a fearful atmosphere of coming apocalypse in which people wish to die and even vultures starve as they loom overhead. Known as an elegiac, sensitive writer on war and a dedicated father of three sons, Bishop died of heart disease in 1944.

REFERENCES

Bishop, John Peale. *The Collected Essays of John Peale Bishop*. Ed. Edmund Wilson. New York and London: Scribner's, 1948.
————. *The Collected Poems of John Peale Bishop*. Ed. Allen Tate. New York and London: Scribner's, 1948.
Spindler, Elizabeth Carroll. *John Peale Bishop: A Biography*. Morgantown: West Virginia University Library, 1980.
Tulloss, Thomas. "Et Ego in Arcadia: Death in 'Resurrection': John Peale Bishop's World War One Fiction." *Focus on Robert Graves and His Contemporaries* 1.7 (June 1988): 18–23.

Catherine J. Tramontana

BISHOP, THOMAS BRIGHAM (1835–1905). A native of Wayne, Kennebec County, Maine, Thomas Brigham Bishop was one of the most popular composers during the Civil War era. His name has been virtually forgotten, but his songs, such as "John Brown's Body," "When Johnny Comes Marching Home," and "Sweet Evelina," have not. Although he worked variously as a musician, music teacher, soldier, publisher, and banker, Bishop's overriding passion was music and songwriting, and he devoted all available time to it.

According to MacIntyre, as commander of Company G, a colored company within an unnamed Union regiment, Bishop wrote "Shoo, Fly!"—a song inspired by a saying his soldiers used, exemplifying the typical Bishop characteristics of memorable simplicity and tunefulness. Nevertheless, the melody that brought him the greatest fame is "The Battle Hymn of the Republic." The author of its lyrics, **Julia Ward Howe**, reportedly wrote them as a poem one evening with Bishop's song "John Brown's Body" in her mind. This was not an unusual occurrence with Bishop's music.

Because many of Bishop's songs expressed universal patriotic sentiments, during the Civil War they encouraged civilians and soldiers on both sides of the Mason-Dixon Line. Thus, if one did not know the correct words to one of Bishop's songs, one could easily change them. This happened often, making Bishop's work popular and the task of accounting all songs connected to him difficult. After the war, Bishop continued composing songs that brought him fame and renown, enabling him to live a life of quiet comfort. He died on May 15, 1905, in his Philadelphia, Pennsylvania, home.

REFERENCE

MacIntyre, John J. *The Composer of "The Battle Hymn of the Republic."* New York: William H. Conklin, 1917.

Sandra Alagona

BLACK HAWK [MA-KA-TAI-MI-SHE-KIA-KIAK] (1767–1838). In a desperate attempt to protect his people's ancestral lands, Black Hawk led a group of Sauk in the Upper Mississippi Valley conflict of 1832, which is known by his name. The Black Hawk War lasted fifteen weeks, costing the lives of roughly 450 to 600 Indians and seventy settlers and soldiers. Among the figures involved were Abraham Lincoln, who served as a volunteer, and Jefferson Davis, who escorted Black Hawk to prison.

Beginning with intertribal fighting in the time of early French and Spanish exploration, *The Life of Black Hawk* provides insight into the tactics and motives of warring peoples indigenous to North America. As a young warrior, Black Hawk distinguished himself among the Sauk for his bravery in battles with the Osage and Cherokee. His narrative relates the tears of his people when the Spanish settlement in St. Louis gave way to the American colonizers. Soon, the Sauk were swindled out of their lands east of the Mississippi with the treaty of 1804, and when the War of 1812 broke out, Black Hawk fought briefly for the British, who promised the Sauk that their lands would not be taken from them. Black Hawk's confusion over the tactics of British and American forces is surpassed only by his misunderstanding of the significance of writing; signing his mark for the first time, in 1816, he unwittingly ceded his village to settlers. Although he sought to remain on the land through passive resistance, in 1832 Black Hawk and other Sauk were driven forcibly from their village. Black Hawk was further deceived into believing an alliance with the Winnebago, Pottawatomi, and the British in Canada would provide a fighting force to reclaim their land. With merely 400 warriors, Black Hawk was cornered into fighting an army of thousands. After a few successful skirmishes, the lack of supplies and the difficulty of the terrain took their toll. At the Battle of Wisconsin Falls, Black Hawk masterminded a difficult river crossing amid the attack of numerically superior forces. With his people exhausted from travel and dying of starvation, Black Hawk surrendered himself into the custody of the Winnebago. After a brief imprisonment, he was taken to Washington to see Andrew Jackson, who refused to release him. Instead, Black Hawk was taken on a tour of the major American cities to impress upon him the might of his conquerors.

Upon his return to his people, Black Hawk summoned the interpreter Antoine LeClaire, wishing to give an account of his life that would explain the causes of the conflict and the principles that guided his leadership. LeClaire then turned to John B. Patterson, a newspaper editor, for help in taming the narrative into a publishable manuscript. Doubts persist as to the authenticity of the text, fueled by the substantive revisions by Patterson in the 1882 edition. Although it is difficult to determine how literal the translation is, the original 1833 version remains the standard. The first of the narrated autobiography genre in Native American literature, *The Life of Black Hawk* offers a unique perspective on the armed struggle against the westward expansion efforts of the United States.

REFERENCES

Black Hawk, Antoine LeClaire, and John B. Patterson. *Black Hawk, an Autobiography*.
    1833. Ed. with new intro. by Donald Jackson. Urbana: University of Illinois Press,
    1955.
Ruoff, A. LaVonne Brown. *American Indian Literatures: An Introduction, Bibliographic
    Review, and Selected Bibliography*. New York: Modern Language Association,
    1990.

David Kilpatrick

BLEECKER, ANN ELIZA (1752–1783). The poems of Ann Eliza
Bleecker form an early example of the sentimental narrative. Her poems are
reactionary and politically complicated, expressing a maternal grief and a desire
to stop time to cope with her loss in the midst of the American War for Independence. Born in 1752 into a prosperous New York merchant family, she began
her career as an author at the age of seventeen after her marriage to John J.
Bleecker, a wealthy lawyer, who encouraged his wife to preserve her poems.
The Bleeckers moved to Tomhanick, a small town twelve miles north of Albany,
where she was geographically isolated from her family and friends. Her lone-
liness prompted her to write both letters and poems, and her melancholy deepened with the approaching war. She wrote her poems in the midst of interactions
among the Six Nations of the Iroquois, and the tone is one of rage and a fear
of Indian attacks, thus expressing the influence of the captivity narrative.

Such literary influences became more evident as the war became inevitable.
Her writing darkened after the assaults of Iroquois and British forces near Tomhanick in 1777, and the threat of the approaching British forces led by General
John Burgoyne, "the infatuated Burgoyne," forced her to flee Albany with her
two daughters. After this flight, she wrote *History of Maria Kittle*, published in
1779 and three times posthumously in the 1790s. Using mythological descriptions—such as "Ceres presides over fields through which screaming Indians run,
killing and tearing off scalps"—and the time period of the French and Indian
War of 1754–1763 as a basis, Bleecker conveys the terror of the unknown. She
treats the unnamed native tribes as instigators of violence against women, particularly mothers, an attitude enhanced in 1781 when she had to flee Albany
again when her husband was captured by a raiding party. At this time, she also
lost her mother, her sister, and her youngest daughter, Abella, whose death she
contributed to her forced flight from her home.

After 1781, Bleecker's poetry corresponded directly to the loss of the three
important females in her life. Her poems narrated the progress toward American
independence and included her personal chronicles of the war. Perhaps her most
distressing poem, "Lines Written in Retreat from Burgoyne"—which began with
the rhetorical question, "Was it for this?"—called attention to a mother's loss:
"Was it for this, with thee a pleasing load, / I sadly wander'd thro' the hostile
wood; / When I thought fortune's spite could do no more, / To see thee perish

on a foreign shore?" (Faugeres 215). In a subsequent poem, "On Reading Dryden's Virgil," she compared her own loss to the epic loss and relates the history of war to the history of family: "Shall Aeneas for lost Creuse mourn, / And tears be wanting on Abella's urn?" (230).

Her poems evidence her own political and emotional biases. On one hand, the poem "Peace" celebrated the end of war in the lines "Echo is no longer plaintively mourning / But laughs and is jocund as we; / . . . carve 'Washington' on every tree" (252). In the poem "Another," she meditates on her approaching death and her "grief" that she has "indulged her silent woe" at the expense of her surviving daughter, Margaret Faugeres. The latter continued the work of her mother, collecting her mother's letters, poems, and articles into one collection, *The Posthumous Works of Ann Eliza Bleecker, in Prose and Verse. To Which Is Added a Collection of Essays, Prose and Political, by Margaretta Faugeres.*

REFERENCES

Ellison, Julie. "Race and Sensibility in Early America." *American Literature* 65.3 (September 1993): 445–474.

Faugeres, Margaretta. *The Posthumous Works of Ann Eliza Bleecker, in Prose and Verse. To Which Is Added a Collection of Essays, Prose and Political, by Margaretta Faugeres.* New York: T. & J. Swords, 1793.

Giffen, Allison. " 'Till Grief Melodious Grow': The Poems and Letters of Ann Eliza Bleecker." *Early American Literature* 28 (1993): 222–241.

Jennifer Harrison

BOUDINOT, ELIAS (1740–1821). Born in Philadelphia to a family of Huguenot ancestry, Boudinot began attending the Philadelphia Academy in 1751. After moving to Princeton, New Jersey, where his father was the postmaster, he chose the law as his profession, receiving a license in 1760 and establishing a successful practice in Elizabethtown.

During the Stamp Act controversy, Boudinot quietly supported efforts to resist royal authority. By 1774 he had joined the Essex County Committee of Correspondence and was elected to New Jersey's Provincial Congress. After briefly serving as aide-de-camp to William Livingston (commander of the New Jersey militia), Boudinot was made Commissary General of Prisoners in 1777. He later resigned in order to take a seat in the Continental Congress, where he served from 1778 to 1779 and from 1781 to 1784. Elected President of the Congress in 1782, he officially signed the Treaty of Paris in 1783.

Following the war, Boudinot became an ardent Federalist and was elected to the House of Representatives for three terms. He later served as Director of the Mint and was active in causes such as abolition and Indian education.

As an author, Boudinot is known primarily for his religious writing. However, he also prepared his *Journal or Historical Recollections of American Events during the Revolutionary War*, which was initially circulated among family and friends during his lifetime and was eventually published in 1894. It includes vignettes and details that Boudinot claimed "are likely to be lost to posterity" unless recorded by those who participated in "the eventful crisis." Arranging material "without any attention to order," he relied primarily on his own memory, old letters, and short anecdotes related by other leading figures. The *Journal* includes discussion of congressional proceedings, the treatment of prisoners, military strategy, cases of espionage, and major turning points during the war.

Boudinot also made a significant contribution to the literature of the Revolution as an orator and prolific letter writer. Portions of his addresses and correspondence were collected and published in 1896: *The Life, Public Services, Addresses and Letters* is especially valuable because of the insight it provides into the relationship between George Washington and Congress.

REFERENCES

Boudinot, Elias. *Journal or Historical Recollections of American Events during the Revolutionary War*. Ed. Frederick Bourquin. 1894. New York: New York Times & Arno Press, 1968.
———. *The Life, Public Services, Addresses and Letters of Elias Boudinot*. Ed. Jane J. Boudinot. Boston and New York: Houghton Mifflin, 1896.
Boyd, George Adams. *Elias Boudinot: Patriot and Statesman, 1740–1821*. Princeton, NJ: Princeton University Press, 1952.
Clark, Barbara Louise. *E. B.: The Story of Elias Boudinot IV, His Family, His Friends, and His Country*. Philadelphia: Dorrance, 1977.

Robert D. Sturr

BOURJAILY, VANCE (1922–   ). "We were war-born," says Vance Bourjaily's Skinner Galt. "The war made us." The same can be said of Bourjaily's writing. Vance Nye Bourjaily, born in Cleveland, Ohio, served in the American Field Service as an ambulance driver (1942–1944), and in the U.S. Army (1944–1946). He graduated from Bowdoin in 1947, cofounded the literary journal *Discovery*, and began teaching in the Iowa Writer's Workshop in 1957. Bourjaily's first four novels—*The End of My Life* (1947), *The Hound of Earth* (1955), *The Violated* (1958), and *Confessions of a Spent Youth* (1960)—trace World War II's effects on his generation.

The End of My Life (1947) is the story of Thomas "Skinner" Galt, a college man who, with three friends, Freak (a young innocent), Rod (a failed musician), and Benny (a Marxist), join an ambulance service in the Middle East during World War II. They are all changed by war: Freak loses his faith in Skinner; Rod struggles with his homosexuality, learns to play the Arab pipes, and goes AWOL; and Benny becomes a soldier. Through flashbacks, Bourjaily depicts Skinner's love affair with a young actress, Cindy—a relationship he will later destroy. Skinner's carelessness at the front results in the death of an American nurse. He is last seen in prison.

Bourjaily's novel, while burdened by its hardboiled **Hemingway** style, is a gentle portrayal of the "war-born" Skinner refers to. Rod's music has been perverted in America ("America means about as much to me as the snot in my nose," he says); Freak has not had a chance to grow up; and Benny can't stand the army's sadism. Skinner is a "destroyer": Unable to bear the idea of beauty being ruined, Skinner pulls down ideals before they can be established. Yet Skinner is not a nihilist: "Identity is a funny thing, and I'm losing it. Skinner Galt is on the way out. He's had his day, now he's going. When I get out of [prison] I'll be someone else. . . . I'll be Tom Galt." The end of Skinner means the beginning of the true Tom Galt.

In *Old Soldier* (1990), the narrative of Joe McKay (a tough but loving man who's been a top sergeant since World War II) and his brother Tommy (fiddler, bagpiper, and DOG ["Dean of Gays"] in New York) unwinds. The novel opens with the end of Joe's marriage and his reacquaintance with Tommy, who tells Joe the decimation caused the gay community by AIDS is like combat: "Maybe I'm starting to know how you felt in the war," a parallel the Old Soldier accepts. In the second half of the novel Joe goes on a fishing trip with Tommy. Tommy's admission he has AIDS causes Carl, an eavesdropping young fool who believes he's caught AIDS from a toilet seat, to burn Joe's camper, shoot out his car tires, and wound Tommy. Returning from making a stretcher, Joe finds that his brother has drowned himself. The novel closes with Little Joe, effectively the son of both brothers, being raised lovingly and tolerantly by Joe.

Music is central to both novels. Rod, ashamed of his homosexuality but delighted by the Arab pipes, would be relieved to meet Tommy, a musician happy in a gay community. Where World War II has shaped Skinner's generation, the war on AIDS, about which Tommy plays a pibroch ("Lament for the Children"), is the battlefield in *Old Soldier*. Bourjaily connects war with the hatred of beauty, music, and ways of loving that are other than heterosexual. Benny reflects on the damage done by the war:

We've all been involved in this war unconsciously, ever since we were old enough to know what the word inevitable meant. It was so clear it was coming. All of us are pre-war neurotics to some extent. . . . [E]very time we read a book about the last war, we were fighting this one.

The task facing the postwar generation is to find some purpose in peace. These five novels sketch an arc from war and neurosis (**Eliot**'s "Hollow Men" that Skinner loves so much) to music and nature (most of Bourjaily's recent writing is about the natural world).

REFERENCES

Bourjaily, Vance. "A Certain Kind of Work." *Afterwords*. Ed. Thomas McCormack. New
        York: Harper & Row, 1969. 176–191.
———. *The End of My Life*. New York: Charles Scribner's Sons, 1947.
———. *Old Soldier*. New York: Donald I. Fine, 1990.
Muste, John. M. "The Second Major Subwar: Four Novels by Vance Bourjaily." *The
        Shaken Realist*. Ed. Melvin J. Friedman and John B. Vickery. Baton Rouge:
        Louisiana State University Press, 1970. 311–326.

                                                              Tim Blackmore

BOURNE, RANDOLPH (1886–1918). Born in Bloomfield, New Jersey, Randolph Bourne was an influential essayist—a part of the literary renaissance that swept Greenwich Village in the 1910s, and arguably the most significant of the young antiwar intellectuals during World War I. Bourne was badly disfigured at birth as a result of a forceps delivery and further deformed after suffering spinal tuberculosis at age four. Extremely self-conscious about his appearance, he never appeared publicly without wearing a large cape. Bourne received his bachelor's and his master's degrees at Columbia University where he was exposed to progressive political thinkers such as John Dewey. He contributed essays to *The Atlantic Monthly* while a student and while traveling Europe on a fellowship from Columbia. When the *New Republic* was founded in 1914, Bourne joined its staff. He also contributed to *The Dial* and *Seven Arts* magazines.

Bourne's travels in Europe had interested him in different forms of government and inspired him to write his first publication, a pamphlet for the American Association for International Conciliation, which proposed international arbitration as an alternative to war. *Arbitration and International Politics* was published in 1913. The following year he authored another, *The Tradition of War*, a study of the social conditions that lead to war, for the same organization. Next, he compiled *Towards an Enduring Peace: A Symposium of Peace Proposals and Programs, 1914–1916*, which briefly discussed antiwar propositions from peace activists in America and Europe. These early works are important to Bourne's development as an antiwar spokesman and author, allowing him to move from the prowar progressivism expressed at the *New Republic* to the pacifist beliefs espoused by *Seven Arts* that Bourne was eventually to adopt himself, making a firm break from Dewey and many other prowar radicals.

In July 1916, Bourne published two of his most important essays. "Trans-National America," appearing in *The Atlantic Monthly*, argues, "No reverbatory effect of the great war has caused American public opinion more solicitude than the failure of the 'melting-pot.'" He proposes that Americans hold on to their cultural heritage rather than attempting to assimilate themselves, thus creating a truly cosmopolitan society. "A Moral Equivalent for Universal Military Service" was published in the *New Republic*. Here Bourne proposes that in lieu of military conscription all American youths should serve two years in community service. Though neither of these two articles can be considered war literature per se, they do examine social conditions that Bourne felt led to war.

Bourne began increasingly to disagree with the editors of the *New Republic*, and while he wrote for that magazine until his death, his significant antiwar articles appeared in *Seven Arts*. In "The War and the Intellectuals," Bourne criticizes those whom he felt had rationalized their support for American intervention in Europe. Reminding his readers that the prowar forces in America were largely upper class, he states that "it was the least liberal and least democratic elements among whom . . . the war sentiment was found," and therefore by supporting war America's intellectuals "have identified themselves with the least democratic forces in American life." Bourne concludes that "the real enemy is War rather than imperial Germany" and urges intellectuals to resist attempts to rationalize and even romanticize the war. "A War Diary" predicts the long-term effects of World War I on American culture. "Twilight of Idols" attacks the prowar stance of John Dewey, as had an earlier piece for *The Dial*, "Conscience and Intelligence in War."

Randolph Bourne died in 1918 during an influenza epidemic. At the time of his death he was working on a history of conscientious objection in America. Van Wyck Brooks edited *History of a Literary Radical*, a collection of Bourne's most important essays, in 1920. Bourne remained an important influence on such authors as Dwight MacDonald, Lewis Mumford, and Noam Chomsky. The League of American Writers established a Randolph Bourne Memorial Award for "distinguished service for culture and peace" in 1941.

REFERENCES

Bourne, Randolph. *The Radical Will: Randolph Bourne, Selected Writings*. Ed. Olaf Hansen. New York: Urizen, 1977.
————. *War and the Intellectuals: Collected Essays*. Ed. Carl Resek. New York: Harper and Row, 1964.
Vitelli, James R. *Randolph Bourne*. New York: Twayne, 1981.

Randall Clark

BOYD, JAMES (1888–1944). Despite his limited corpus, Boyd has had much influence on the development of the American historical novel due to his keen eye for authentic detail and his polished style. Born on July 2, 1888, to a wealthy family in Harrisburg, Pennsylvania, Boyd spent much of his life in Southern Pines, North Carolina, a region in which he set several of his novels. After earning a bachelor's degree from Princeton and a master's in literature from Cambridge, Boyd worked as a teacher, cartoonist, and editor. In February 1918, despite health problems, he went to Europe as a volunteer in the American Expeditionary Force (AEF) ambulance service. After the war he returned to America and embarked on a writing career.

Boyd's first novel, *Drums* (1925), was an instant success. Praised by one reviewer as "the finest novel of the American Revolution which has yet been written" (Beckwith 3) and selling 50,000 copies in its first year, it has remained in print ever since. *Drums* is the story of Johnny Fraser, a young Scots immigrant to North Carolina whose adventures take him to London and then to service with John Paul Jones on the warship *Bonhomme Richard*, where he is wounded. After convalescing in North Carolina, he joins the forces of Daniel Morgan that in 1781 trap and destroy the British troops under the command of Banastre Tarleton at the battle of the Cowpens, South Carolina, a crucial American victory in the southern theater.

Boyd's next novel, *Marching On* (1927), often rated his best, centers on James Fraser, a descendant of the hero of *Drums*, during the era of the Civil War. A young man of a good but impoverished North Carolina family, Fraser falls in love with Stewart Prevost, the daughter of a wealthy planter who considers Fraser too plebeian to marry into his family. When the war breaks out Fraser joins the Confederate army and endures great hardship, including two years in a Northern prison camp. Ultimately, Union soldiers destroy the Prevost plantation, and this leveling effect of the war brings Fraser and Stewart together in marriage. The novel is notable for the acute realism of its battle scenes, the authenticity of its historical elements, and its perceptive look at the characters' inner conflicts. However, most critics found the happy ending too contrived and sentimental, and Boyd agreed.

In addition to writing several more novels—*Long Hunt* (1930), *Roll River* (1935), and *Bitter Creek* (1939)—Boyd gave considerable artistic energy to war-related activities during World War II. In company with Sherwood Anderson, **Stephen Vincent Benét, Archibald MacLeish,** Burgess Meredith, William Saroyan, and others, he formed the Free Company of Players to produce radio dramas designed to counteract Axis propaganda. He also edited and published *The Pilot*, a weekly newspaper in Southern Pines, from 1941 until his death in 1944.

REFERENCES

Bain, Robert, Joseph M. Flora, and Louis D. Rubin, Jr., eds. *Southern Writers: A Biographical Dictionary*. Baton Rouge: Louisiana State University Press, 1979.

Beckwith, E. C. Rev. of *Drums*. *Literary Review* of the *New York Evening Post* 11 April 1925: 3.

Whisnant, David E. *James Boyd*. New York: Twayne, 1972.

Randal W. Allred

BOYD, THOMAS (1898–1935). Best known for his first novel, *Through the Wheat* (1923), Thomas Boyd was born in Defiance, Ohio, and left high school to join the Marine Corps in World War I. Barely in his twenties by the time of the Armistice, Boyd served with the Marine Brigade of the Second Division, which suffered a higher casualty rate than any other unit in the American Expeditionary Force (AEF), and participated in the battles of Belleau Wood, Soissons, St. Mihiel, and Blanc Mont (all vividly presented in *Through the Wheat*). He was gassed at Blanc Mont and awarded the Croix de Guerre.

After the war, Boyd edited the book page of the *St. Paul Daily News* before becoming a full-time novelist and biographer in 1925. Recommended to Scribner's by F. Scott Fitzgerald, Boyd's first novel instantly secured his reputation as an artist who excelled in the rendering of war experience. His subsequent work includes another war novel, *The Dark Cloud* (1924), an important collection of short stories, *Points of Honor* (1925), and a sequel to *Through the Wheat, In Time of Peace* (1935). Thomas Boyd died in 1935 of a stroke—at age thirty-six.

A hair-raising snapshot of modern warfare, *Through the Wheat* follows its nondescript protagonist, Private Hicks, from one bloodbath to another during

the Allied counteroffensives of 1918. The novel does not emphasize characterization (we learn little about Hicks's background or personality); instead, Boyd
uses Hicks's sleep-deprived consciousness as a camera lens, one that records
the sensations of battle in all their blurred, at times hallucinatory, horror. At the
same time, the third-person narrator employs images of remarkable power:
Dampness descends on Hicks "like a heavily draped ghost that wanted to kiss
[his] entire body" (24), while a barrage resembles "a huge black animal with
fiery eyes and hoofs of brimstone that were kicking and prancing all over the
woods" (140). Throughout, the novel offers a unique blend of numbed reportage
and poetic intensity.

Through the Wheat is also a novel of protest. At the beginning, embittered
by months of pointless physical labor, Hicks looks forward to proving himself
against the Germans; on the final page, four excruciating battles later, he is a
worn-out zombie who wears the "thousand yard stare" seen, a generation later,
on the faces of Marines at Iwo Jima or Okinawa. Even Hicks's climatic action—
his single-handed attack on a German position—stems not from heroic resolve
but from suicidal apathy. Boyd also demonstrates how American propaganda
led to the wanton killing of surrendering Germans and portrays the incompetence
that was all too common among the volunteer officers of the AEF.

The short story collection *Points of Honor* provides a more expansive vision
of American participation in World War I, rejecting the "romance" of war
through a variety of grotesque situations: A soldier is sentenced to five years in
Leavenworth for a minor infraction; an officer who has avoided combat receives
an award for valor; a French widow hides the crosses marking American graves
so that she may grow vegetables above the decomposing corpses; and so on. In
both *Through the Wheat* and *Points of Honor*, Boyd offers a haunting portrait
of the doughboy's war.

REFERENCES

Cooperman, Stanley. *World War I and the American Novel*. Baltimore: Johns Hopkins
    University Press, 1967. 159–165.
Matsen, William E. *The Great War and the American Novel*. New York: Peter Lang,
    1993. 89–96.
Noverr, Douglas A. "A Midwesterner in the Maelstrom of History: Thomas Boyd's
    Characterization of William Hicks." *Midamerica: The Yearbook of the Society
    for the Study of Midwestern Literature* 10 (1983): 99–109.

Steven Trout

BOYLE, KAY (1902–1992). Minnesotan Kay Boyle received little formal
schooling, traveling around America and Europe from her first year and then
for much of her long and prolific life. At seventeen by her own admission she
had penned hundreds of poems, short stories, a novel, and an outline of history
"tinged with pacifism." Some of the earliest published novels treat semiautobiographical Jamesian themes revolving around the unworldly young American

woman who seeks romance in Europe. From the mid-1930s through the mid-1950s, however, Boyle is at her mature peak with the overtly political short novels and stories set in prewar, wartime, and postwar France and Germany. There a somewhat wider range of characters find dignity through a personal commitment to principles of democracy and liberalism rising above the war, which serves as a contemporary context for highlighting those more permanent values.

Boyle lived in France, Austria, England, and again France from 1922 to 1941. With her O. Henry Prize–winning story "The White Horses of Vienna" (1935), she warned of the rise of Nazism, vividly evoking that city's lost past and uncertain future. Her personal favorite was another O. Henry winner, "Defeat" (1941), which provides a chilling perspective on France's complacent collapse the year before. These and related stories, among them the devastatingly ironic "They Weren't Going to Die," are now reunited in her collected *Fifty Stories*. Successive groups in this collection cover Austria and England on the eve of the war, France during the war, and occupied Germany afterward.

Among her novels, *Primer for Combat* (1942) takes the form of an American woman's diary spanning the period from June 20 to October 2 of 1940 and chronicling the first hundred days of Nazism in France. The popular *Avalanche* (1944) is an early representation of the Resistance through the eyes of a girl, half French, half American, in France. In *A Frenchman Must Die* (1946), a young Franco-American engineer survives a German prison camp, joins the French underground movement, and hunts down a notorious collaborationist. *1939, A Novel* (1948, but written much earlier) is a suite of Dallowayesque interior monologues recounting twenty-four hours in the life of a French American woman and her Austrian lover, who volunteers for the French army but is interned as an enemy alien. In these and some of her other works (totaling some forty volumes), Boyle's prose and judgments are crisp and penetrating. As William Shirer has said in introducing her German Occupation stories, "No writer going to live and work among the Germans for the first time has been more frank and honest about her feelings."

During her tenure as teacher of creative writing at San Francisco State College (1963–1979), she continued her political activism in favor of civil and human rights, including the anti–Vietnam War movement. She had spoken out against McCarthyism in the 1950s and would speak up in support of Amnesty International in the 1980s. Some of the political writings are reprinted in *Words That Must Somehow Be Said: Selected Essays, 1927–84* (1985).

Over six decades Kay Boyle played a front-line role in protests against accepted wisdom and convention in America and Europe: on campus, in jail, and everywhere in her writings, which will endure.

REFERENCES

Bell, Elizabeth S. *Kay Boyle: A Study of the Short Fiction*. New York: Twayne, 1992.
Mellen, Joan. *Kay Boyle: Author of Herself*. New York: Farrar, Straus & Giroux, 1994.

Spanier, Sandra Whipple. *Kay Boyle, Artist and Activist*. Carbondale: Southern Illinois
    University Press, 1986.
Uehling, Edward M. "Tails, You Lose: Kay Boyle's War Fiction." *Twentieth-Century
    Literature* 34.3 (Fall 1988): 375–383.

Roy Rosenstein

BRACKENRIDGE, HUGH HENRY (1748–1816). Born in Kintyre, near
Campbellstown, Scotland, Brackenridge immigrated to Pennsylvania with his
family in 1753 and lived through Indian depredations on the frontier following
Gen. Edward Braddock's defeat (1755) near present-day Pittsburgh. Brackenridge studied from 1768 to 1771 at the College of New Jersey [Princeton] and
was a classmate of James Madison and **Philip Freneau**. Following his formal
education, Brackenridge served variously as a chaplain in the Continental Army,
an editor, attorney, and judge. A prolific writer, Brackenridge penned several
books and dozens of plays, poems, and articles, including *Father Bombo's Pil-
grimage to Mecca in Arabia*, in collaboration with Philip Freneau (1770); *The
Rising Glory of America*, also in collaboration with Philip Freneau (1771); *The
Battle of Bunkers-Hill* (1775); *The Death of General Montgomery at the Siege
of Quebec* (1777); "Before the Battle of Brandywine," *United States Magazine*
(1779); *Incidents of the Insurrection in Western Pennsylvania in the Year 1794*
(1794); and *Modern Chivalry* (1792–1815).

Brackenridge's war literature is historically based and expresses the patriotic
sentiments of a man who was both fascinated and appalled by the experience
of war. The theme of America's rising glory runs throughout much of the author's work. Brackenridge envisioned an America whose course was predestined
by divine providence. America and its citizenry were exemplars to the world of
a new and glorious order. Ultimately, Brackenridge aimed to inform his readers
while he entertained and inspired them. The attitudes informing all of the works
trace the author's intellectual evolution and the political issues that affected him
most at the time of their publication. Thus, Brackenridge's war literature is an
insight into intellectual and cultural history during the formative period of the
United States.

Salient works dealing with the Revolution—*The Battle of Bunkers-Hill, The
Death of General Montgomery at the Siege of Quebec*, and "Before the Battle
of Brandywine"—focus on the element of American valor to wring moral victory from defeat. Writing in the vein of the "heroic bard," young Brackenridge
hoped alternately to inspire and to outrage his readers. In these three works,
America and its republican soldiery represent the culmination of a divinely inspired plan for human liberty. Britain, on the other hand, has forsaken its enlightened heritage for brutality in its efforts to suppress the rising glory of the
young republic.

One of the results of the American Revolution was an increased tempo in
western settlement. Brackenridge followed the migration into the western coun-
ties of Pennsylvania. While there, he successfully took part in the efforts of

local leaders to quiet the Whiskey Insurrection of 1794. Brackenridge's *Incidents* clearly reflects western concerns in the 1790s. As the narrator moves through the varied scenes, he voices the concerns and fears of insurrectionists. Attorney Brackenridge is sympathetic to western issues of whiskey excises, the use of force to suppress the rebellion, and the threat these actions pose to the stability of the fragile union of states. In many ways the narrator is symbolic of the collective psyche of the greater population of the republic. The character's confusion and wishes are really those of a people attempting to found a new nation as they define themselves for the world and for one another.

REFERENCES

Brackenridge, Hugh Henry. *A Hugh Henry Brackenridge Reader, 1770–1815*. Ed. with intro. by Daniel Marder. Pittsburgh: University of Pittsburgh Press, 1970.
————. *Incidents of the Insurrection*. Ed. Daniel Marder. New Haven, CT: College & University Press, 1970.
Marder, Daniel. *Hugh Henry Brackenridge*. New York: Twayne, 1967.

Ricardo A. Herrera

BROOKS, ALDEN (1883–1964). Born in Cleveland, Brooks attended schools in France and England before he graduated from Harvard University in 1905. A teacher in the United States before the First World War, he later established himself as newspaper correspondent in France, writing for such periodicals as the *New York Times* and *Collier's*. As World War I progressed, Brooks took a more active role in the war effort, first by driving an ambulance for American troops. Later he went to a French artillery school and, in 1918, became a lieutenant of field artillery in the French army, where he served out the remainder of the war.

Brooks first received attention as a writer of fiction with his 1917 collection of short stories, *The Fighting Men*. Full of the horrors of war, the six stories in *The Fighting Men* focus on soldiers of six different nationalities (English, Slavic, American, French, Belgian, and Prussian) whose involvement in the war is colored by the peculiar cultural and psychological characteristics of their race. These stories were praised for their ability to render the typical fighting men of the Eastern and Western Fronts with accuracy and economy of means. Brooks's only other published short story, "Out of the Sky," appears two years later in an anthology called *War Stories* (Roy J. Holmes and A. Starbuck, eds.).

In 1929, Brooks sold a nonfiction account of his experiences in the French army to a French publisher, which appeared under the title *Battle in 1918, As Seen by an American in the French Army*. A year later the same account was published in America under the title *As I Saw It*. Told in an objective and dispassionate manner, *As I Saw It* is generally considered an important record of military maneuvers. Brooks's unwavering objectivity can at times become "exasperating" (as one reviewer put it), but his manifold digressions and insights into the conditions, perceptions, and expertise of soldiering in the French artillery make it an important document of the military "middle class."

Brooks also published a novel (*Escape*, 1924) and several book-length critical perspectives on Shakespeare.

REFERENCES

Adler, Elmer. "An Artilleryman's Account of the War's Last Phase." Rev. of *As I Saw It*, by Alden Brooks. *New York Times* 21 September 1930: sec. 4:2.

Boynton, H. W. Rev. of *The Fighting Men*, by Alden Brooks, *A.L.A. Booklist* December 1917: 94.

Coyle, William, ed. *Ohio Authors and Their Books*. Cleveland: World Publishing Co., 1962.

Rev. of *The Fighting Men*, by Alden Brooks. *New York Times Book Review* 2 September 1917: 325.

Eric Weitzel

BROWN, HARRY (1917–1986). Born in Portland, Maine, Brown attended Harvard University from 1936 to 1938 but did not graduate. Instead, he worked as a copyboy at *Time* and as a copy editor for *The New Yorker*. His first poetry collection, *The End of a Decade*, was published in 1940 and was followed a year later by *The Poem of Bunker Hill*, which uses heroic and epic language to narrate this historic battle against the British. After his induction into the U.S. Army in 1941, Brown published another collection, *The Violent: New Poems* (1943), but attracted more attention as a humorist of army life. He coauthored *It's a Cinch, Private Finch* (1943) and then wrote (under the pseudonym Artie Greengroin) a series of comic stories for the weekly army magazine *Yank* about a wisecracking G.I. from Brooklyn stationed in England.

However, it was Brown's first novel, *A Walk in the Sun* (1944), that established his reputation as one of the foremost writers of realistic war fiction. In less than 200 pages, *A Walk in the Sun* tells the seemingly simple story of an American infantry platoon landing in Italy, then slowly advancing on an isolated farmhouse roughly six miles away. Cut off entirely from communication with the outside world and gradually losing its chain of command, the platoon nevertheless perseveres, intent on accomplishing its mission, no matter what the cost.

Just before leaving the army in 1945, Brown contributed to the script of *The True Glory* (1945), a documentary film detailing the battle for Europe, from D-Day to V-E Day. In November 1945, Brown's only play, *A Sound of Hunting*, opened in New York; the action concerns a squad of eight men holed up in a bombed-out house near Cassino, Italy.

After *A Walk in the Sun* was made into a successful film in 1946, Brown found work as a Hollywood screenwriter on three minor movies, none of them war related. However, Brown soon returned to the topic of World War II with *Sands of Iwo Jima* (1949), for which he wrote the original story and shared the screenplay credit. Starring John Wayne as a tough Marine sergeant, *Sands of Iwo Jima* was enormously popular and influential and earned Brown an Academy Award nomination. That same year, Brown wrote his final book of poetry, *The Beast in His Hunger* (1949), which concluded with six war poems, placing World War II in a more ancient context.

Over the next ten years, Brown wrote or cowrote the screenplays for another fifteen films, including *Eight Iron Men* (1952), based on his play *A Sound of Hunting*; *D-Day, the Sixth of June* (1958) about the Normandy invasion; *Between Heaven and Hell* (1956) and *The Deep Six* (1958), both about combat in the Pacific; and *Ocean's Eleven* (1960), Brown's final screenplay, about a group of World War II veterans who use their wartime skills to rob the casinos of Las Vegas.

Brown wrote three more novels between 1960 and 1973, including one, *The Stars in Their Courses* (1960), that sets the story of *The Iliad* in 1870s Colorado. He died of emphysema at the age of sixty-nine.

REFERENCES

Agte, Lloyd Mark. "Harry Peter McNab Brown: Classical Stylist and Hollywood Screenwriter." Diss. Kent State University, 1980.

Breit, Harvey. Rev. of *A Walk in the Sun*, by Harry Brown. *New York Times Book Review* 25 June 1944: 3.

Mayberry, George. Rev. of *A Walk in the Sun*, by Harry Brown. *New Republic* 3 July 1944: 14.

Redman, B. R. Rev. of *A Walk in the Sun*, by Harry Brown. *Saturday Review of Literature* 1 July 1944: 1.

James I. Deutsch

BROWN, LARRY (1951–). Born in Oxford, Mississippi, where he still resides, Brown held numerous positions before becoming a writer, including those of housepainter, retail worker, carpenter, and University of Mississippi student. After the publication of a collection of stories, *Facing the Music* (1988), which received a literary award in 1990 from the Mississippi Institute of Arts and Letters, and his first novel, *Dirty Work* (1989), which he later adapted as a play, Brown quit his sixteen-year career as a firefighter in 1990 to turn to writing full-time.

In *Dirty Work*, Brown combines one of his favorite subjects, the rural south, with that of the Vietnam War. The novel, which is set in a veteran's hospital, focuses on two Vietnam veterans, Braiden Chaney and Walter James, both Marines, both from Mississippi, one black, the other white. Reminiscent of Joe Bonham, Dalton Trumbo's protagonist in *Johnny Got His Gun*, Braiden returned from Vietnam as a quadruple amputee and has spent the past twenty-two years in a hospital bed. Walter came home with all limbs intact but with his face horribly disfigured and part of his brain tissue destroyed. In chapters that primarily alternate between the two as narrators, Braiden and Walter tell the stories of their lives and the war's impact on them. Part flashback, part dialogue, part monologue, *Dirty Work* is a powerful antiwar novel. While at times humorous, the novel examines the sacrifices that Vietnam has demanded from the two veterans, its power deriving from the depiction of a single day and night in which Braiden and Walter converse, their hospital beds side by side, revealing, both physically and emotionally, how the war has devastated their lives. The horror of the war is brought to the forefront, especially when Braiden reveals he wishes to die and counts on Walter to end his suffering. Walter at first resists Braiden's request but eventually acquiesces after learning that he and his war injuries have inadvertently caused the death of another friend. Brown shows a side of the war frequently ignored—that of seriously wounded, forgotten veterans who lead tragically restricted, isolated, and unproductive lives through no choice of their own. The closing image of Jesus weeping ensures that *Dirty Work*, unlike the war victims it portrays, will not be forgotten.

A second collection of short fiction, *Big Bad Love* (1990), two novels, *Joe* (1991) and *Father and Son* (1996), and one nonfiction work, *On Fire* (1994), attest to Brown's continued success as a writer.

REFERENCES

Dean, Michael P. "Larry Brown's Southern Novel." *Notes on Mississippi Writers* 23 (June 1991): 75–83.
Ketchin, Susan. "An Interview with Larry Brown." *Southern Quarterly* 32 (Winter 1994): 95–109.

Catherine Calloway

BROWNELL, HENRY HOWARD (1820–1872). Although Henry Howard Brownell has largely been forgotten in the twentieth century, his Civil War poetry was highly regarded in his own day. Dr. Oliver Wendell Holmes called him "our battle laureate," and scholars have debated whether **Herman Melville** plagiarized Brownell's "The River Fight" in "Battle for the Mississippi," and whether **Walt Whitman** plagiarized phrases from Brownell's "Down!" in "O Captain, My Captain!"

Born in Providence, Rhode Island, Henry Howard Brownell grew up in East Hartford, Connecticut, where he graduated from Washington (now Trinity) College in 1841. After a year of teaching in Mobile, Alabama, he returned to Hartford, studied law, and was admitted to the bar in 1844. Despite his legal practice, his main interests were literary: Between 1847 and 1855 he published two volumes of poetry and two of history.

In 1862 Brownell published a poem in the Hartford *Evening Press* based on the general orders issued by David G. Farragut, commander of the Union Navy's West Gulf Blockading Squadron. Farragut was impressed enough to begin a correspondence with its author. This eventually led Farragut to appoint Brownell his personal secretary aboard his flagship, the USS *Hartford*, with the rank of ensign. In this post Brownell was required to take notes of any action in which his ship was engaged, a duty he "performed with coolness and accuracy," according to Farragut. This work provided him with material for his two volumes of war poetry: *Lyrics of a Day* (1864) and *War-Lyrics and Other Poems* (1866).

Although some of the poems in these collections are trite and derivative, in the best of them Brownell draws on his firsthand battle experiences, giving his poetry vividness and vitality and an overwhelming feeling of place rarely found in Civil War poetry. The reader is transported aboard the *Hartford* and witnesses the carnage, tastes the smoke of gunfire, and feels the heat of burning ships. Perhaps also because of his naval experiences, Brownell romanticizes the war less than his noncombatant contemporaries, leavening his patriotic prose of the Union cause with an awareness of the defeats and death that cause entailed.

After the war, Brownell was recommissioned into the navy and accompanied Farragut on his 1867 European trip. In 1871, he developed cancer of the cheek and died a bachelor on October 31, 1872, in his Hartford, Connecticut, home.

REFERENCES

Burton, Richard. *Literary Likings*. 2nd ed. Boston: Lothrop, Lee & Shepard Co., 1903.
————. *Lyrics of a Day, or Newspaper Poetry by a Volunteer in the U.S. Service*. New York: Carleton, 1864.
————. *War-Lyrics and Other Poems*. Boston: Ticknor and Fields, 1866.
Wilson, Edmund. *Patriotic Gore: Studies in the Literature of the American Civil War*. 2nd ed. New York; London: W. W. Norton & Company, 1994.

Sandra Alagona

BURDICK, EUGENE. *See* **Lederer, William J. and Burdick, Eugene**.

BURNETT, W. R. (1899–1982). William Riley Burnett, creator of crime fiction's gangster and "caper" genres, was born in Springfield, Ohio, to a family long active in state politics. Rejected for service with the U.S. Army Balloon Corps in 1918, the young man spent the next several years at a dull government job, then "escaped to Chicago" to become a writer. His first published novel, *Little Caesar* (1929), was an immediate best-seller; subsequent efforts, including *High Sierra* (1940) and *The Asphalt Jungle* (1949), solidified his literary reputation.

Burnett preferred to write about things he knew: machine politics, dance halls, boxing, the fringes of the underworld. As he had no firsthand military knowledge, his war writings focused on home-front or peripheral issues. The novelette *The Goodhues of Sinking Creek* (1988, written 1980) is based in part on the experiences of Burnett's grandfather, who during the Civil War had suffered abuse from his Ohio neighbors for speaking out in support of the Confederacy. *The Dark Command* (1940), set in the 1860s, is not concerned with the North–South conflict but rather with a parallel struggle in "Bleeding Kansas." The book has a distinctly 1940s sensibility: Villain Polk Cantrell (William Quantrill) is depicted not as a standard Old West outlaw but as a nineteenth-century Fascist.

The Quick Brown Fox (1942), reworking themes first explored in the peacetime novel *King Cole* (1936), traces the rise to power of a charismatic con-man who dazzles American voters with Hitler-inspired rhetoric.

Burnett was an equally effective propagandist in short story form. In "The Ivory Tower" (*Good Housekeeping*, March 1945), a man decides to move as far as he can from the "civilization" that drove him to a nervous breakdown. He settles alone on a beautiful island in the South Pacific; for years, M's only contact with the outside world is a periodic supply ship. One morning in 1945, he is rocked awake by an explosion and shot at when he runs outside to investigate: Japanese soldiers have taken over his Eden. Although wounded, he efficiently stalks and kills the invaders one by one, then returns to civilization with a new appreciation of what it means to be American.

W. R. Burnett is best known as an author of fiction, but some of his most accomplished war writings are in screenplay form. Two of these earned him Academy Award nominations: *Wake Island* (1942), cowritten with Frank Butler; and his 1968 adaptation, with James Clavell, of Paul Brickhill's prison camp memoir *The Great Escape*.

REFERENCES

Mate, Ken, and Pat McGilligan. "W. R. Burnett: The Outsider." *Backstory: Interviews with Screenwriters of Hollywood's Golden Age.* Ed. Pat McGilligan. Berkeley: University of California Press, 1986. 49–84.

"William Riley Burnett." *Authors Today and Yesterday.* Ed. Stanley Kunitz. New York: H. W. Wilson, 1988. 225–226.

Katherine Harper

BURNS, JOHN HORNE (1916–1953). Born in Andover, Massachusetts, Burns was educated there at Phillips Academy before graduating from Harvard and becoming a schoolteacher in Windsor, Connecticut. After being inducted into the infantry in 1942, he served as an intelligence officer until 1946 in North Africa and Italy. During a brief postwar literary career, he published three novels, of which only *The Gallery* in 1947 was critically acclaimed. Burns died of a cerebral hemorrhage in Leghorn, Italy, in 1953.

The Gallery is set in August 1944, within the Galleria Umberto in Naples. Its self-conscious narrative comprises chapters called "Portraits" juxtaposed against more meditative "Promenade" interludes located in Casablanca, Algiers, and Naples. The contrapuntal narration situates the self-contained stories of Americans and Italians against a wider background of cultural breakdown. Burns writes elegantly of this turmoil, what the narrator calls "the riddle of war," although his fastidious prose is sometimes marred by ornateness and overuse of metaphor.

The novel generates a powerful mood of discontent and nervous energy. Its American characters are broadly divided into the emotionally insecure, such as Hal, a charismatic officer with "a great emptiness within," who are restlessly driven to question everything; and those opportunists who are out to exploit others, such as Motes, a sycophantic captain who surrounds himself with similar toadies. *The Gallery*'s scrupulous treatment of latent homosexuality reinforces this frenetic sense of repression and anxiety.

While the Americans reveal themselves to be "very poor spiritually" and to have "bankrupt souls," the Italians are more favorably treated, as in the story of "Giulia," which illustrates the virtues of the traditional Neapolitan family. *The Gallery* suggests that, among the ruins of war, a Mediterranean culture shaped by simpatico or sympathy toward people and by respect for art offers a model for spiritual renewal.

REFERENCES

Aldridge, John W. *After the Lost Generation: A Critical Study of the Writers of Two Wars.* New York: McGraw-Hill, 1951.
Mitzel, J. *John Horne Burns: An Appreciative Biography.* Dorchester, MA: Manifest Destiny Books, 1974.

Jeff Walsh

BUTLER, ROBERT OLEN (1945–). Born in Granite City, Illinois, and raised in an academic family, Robert Olen Butler graduated from Northwestern University summa cum laude with a degree in oral interpretation (B.A., 1967) and went on to study playwriting at the University of Iowa (M.A., 1969). A draftee, Butler served in the U.S. Army from 1969 to 1972, achieving the rank of sergeant. Fluent in Vietnamese (trained by the army), he served his tour in Vietnam as an interpreter for military intelligence. He was also an interpreter for U.S. advisers.

Although Butler has written on topics other than Vietnam, his strongest work reflects his experience in the war. His fiction, however, doesn't emphasize the details of combat; instead he writes about people dealing with their problems in a world that war creates. Also, he successfully presents his Vietnamese characters as human beings, not as story backdrops. Presumably, his language training assisted him in coming to a sympathetic understanding of the Vietnamese and their culture.

After the army, Butler was an editor for *Energy User News* while he worked on his "Vietnam Trilogy," novels with interlocking characters. The earliest of the three (and considered the strongest) is *The Alleys of Eden* (1981). The central character, Clifford Wilkes, an army deserter, finds refuge with Lanh, a Saigon prostitute. He hides out in her apartment for several years, enjoying an erotic interlude that Butler graphically describes. Clifford leaves only when the South Vietnamese government has fallen and North Vietnamese troops are on the verge of entering Saigon. He and Lanh manage to escape to the United States, but ironically, the stress of the new situation drives them apart—they have lost their Eden.

Second in the trilogy, *Sun Dogs* (1982) is set largely in Alaska. The central character, Wilson Hand, remains haunted by his experience in Vietnam, where he was briefly a prisoner of the Viet Cong before his commanding officer (who appears in *On Distant Ground*) rescues him. This captivity leaves him with a sense of powerlessness that is magnified by his ex-wife's suicide and the dangers he confronts working in Alaska.

In *On Distant Ground* (1985), the last work in the trilogy, Butler attempts to bridge the conflicting cultures. David Fleming is tried by court-martial for setting free a Viet Cong officer. Though found guilty, he is not sent to prison. Believing that he has a son living in Vietnam, he returns to Saigon just before the city's fall in 1975. He finds his son but is arrested by the North Vietnamese, who are now in control of the country. He and his son are allowed to return to the United States by the Viet Cong officer he had himself freed years before. Though thematically positive, *On Distant Ground* is the least successful novel in the trilogy, as its characters are not convincingly drawn.

The Deuce (1989), with its theme of dual ancestry, follows logically from *On Distant Ground*. Tony, a child of an American father and Vietnamese mother, isn't happy in his comfortable middle-class life in New Jersey. Traveling to Montreal to join a Vietnamese community, he is robbed and stranded in New York City, where he must come to terms with his complex heritage.

In 1993, Butler was awarded the Pulitzer Prize for *A Good Scent from a Strange Mountain* (1992), a collection of stories concerning Vietnamese emigrants living in the area of Lake Charles, Louisiana. These skillfully written stories deal with their pain of dislocation and loss, their determination to survive in an alien land, and their wartime memories. Written from surprising perspectives (a Saigon bar girl is one narrator), these stories supply a necessary complement to the American memory of the Vietnam War. In "The American Couple," Butler pointedly juxtaposes two veterans—one American, one Vietnamese—with intertwining wartime experiences but different ways of coping in postwar America.

Only a short portion of *They Whisper* (1994) involves Vietnam, specifically the narrator's account of his sexual experience there. But *The Deep Green Sea* (1998) is devoted to Butler's familiar locales and themes. Veteran Ben Coles— middle aged and divorced—returns to Vietnam to recapture the sense of life that he experienced in combat many years before. Although Ho Chi Minh City is not the Saigon of old, he finds compensation in his affair with Le Thi Tien, a young Vietnamese working for the Tourist Authority. The story moves to a disastrous end as together they search for Tien's mother, a bar girl whom Ben may have known. Although the scenes of Vietnam are well written, the basic story may strike some readers as unlikely.

REFERENCES

Beidler, Philip D. *Re-Writing America: Vietnam Authors in Their Generation*. Athens:
        University of Georgia Press, 1991.
Christopher, Renny. *The Vietnam War/The American War: Images and Representations*

in Euro-American and Vietnamese Exile Narratives. Amherst: University of Massachusetts Press, 1995.

Myers, Thomas. *Walking Point: American Narratives of Vietnam*. New York: Oxford University Press, 1988.

Steve Anderson

BUTTERWORTH, WILLAM E. *See* **Griffin, W.E.B**.

C

CABLE, GEORGE WASHINGTON (1844–1925). Cable was born in New Orleans, Louisiana. At fourteen, following his father's death, he left school and worked to help support his family. When New Orleans fell to Union troops, Cable left the city, and by October 1863, he enlisted in the 4th Mississippi Cavalry. After being wounded during Sherman's march to Meridian, Mississippi, Cable served as a clerk to General Wirt Adams and then to General Nathan Bedford Forrest. Following the war, Cable's views changed regarding Southern secession; he believed that the South fought the war merely to preserve an unjust slave system.

Cable's depiction of war varies in his fiction. In " 'Sieur George" (1873), the mysterious 'Sieur George returns from the Mexican War with a saber wound. Yet Cable omits the details of George's war experience. He also never mentions the Civil War, which should be concluding as the story ends. In 1880, Cable published his most critically acclaimed novel, *The Grandissimes*. However, his first novel representing the Civil War is *Dr. Sevier* (1884). The story concerns the struggles of a young married couple, John and Mary Richling. John is a disinherited son of a slave-owning family; Mary is a poor Northern girl. Together they endure illness, imprisonment, poverty, and separation. When the war begins, Mary and her daughter attempt to rejoin John in New Orleans. Their encounters with both Northern and Southern soldiers offer the novel's most memorable war images. Cable does depict the fall of New Orleans briefly; however, he seems hesitant to portray war's brutality. He conveys his changed view of the North when he declares: " 'Go marching on,' saviors of the Union; your cause is just. Lo, now, since nigh twenty-five years have passed, we of the South can say it!" This comment regarding the Northern soldiers angered many Southerners. *John March, Southerner* (1894) also upset Southern readers. The novel depicts a struggle for the soul of the postbellum South between John March and the villainous ex-Confederate John Wesley Garnet. With March's victory, Cable replaces a corrupt slaveholding class with an industrialized, democratized New South.

Cable's most financially successful novel, *The Cavalier* (1901), uses the Civil War as the background for a romance. Richard Thorndyke Smith, a youthful version of Cable, narrates the story. Assigned to Lieutenant Ned Ferry, Smith participates in several skirmishes during July and August 1863. Although Cable presents a fairly realistic depiction of the preparation, fighting, and bloody aftermath, it is important only in regard to the love story between Ferry and Charlotte Oliver. *Kincaid's Battery* (1908) is Cable's other wartime romance. Like *Dr. Sevier*, Cable sets the novel in New Orleans but largely avoids portraying the suffering experienced during the Union occupation. Rather, the war functions as the background for another romance—this time between artillery captain Hillary Kincaid and Anna Callender.

Because of his Civil War military service, Cable is a unique American writer. Yet he was rarely willing or able to represent the brutality of war in his fiction.

REFERENCES

Cleman, John. *George Washington Cable: Revisited.* New York: Twayne, 1996.
Rubin, Louis D., Jr. *George W. Cable: The Life and Times of a Southern Heretic.* New York: Pegasus, 1969.
Turner, Arlin. *George W. Cable: A Biography.* Durham, NC: Duke University Press, 1956.

Paul R. Cappucci

CAPUTO, PHILIP (1941–   ). Born in Chicago, Illinois, Philip Caputo served in the U.S. Marine Corps from 1964 to 1967. Arriving overseas in 1965, he was an officer in the first combat unit sent to Vietnam, the 9th Marine Expeditionary Brigade. A successful career at the *Chicago Tribune* from 1969 to 1972 brought him and William Hugh Jones the Pulitzer Prize in 1972 for their coverage of election fraud. While on assignment in Beirut for the *Tribune* in 1975, Moslem gunmen opened fire on Caputo, and he spent six weeks recovering from both foot and ankle wounds. During this time, he completed work on what was originally a novel, his memoir *A Rumor of War* (1977).

This first book begins with Caputo's patriotic ROTC days at Loyola and his six-week stint at Officer Candidate School at Quantico in the summer of 1961. While suffering the psychological and physical abuse of boot camp, he observes an atmosphere of brainwashing, machismo, and masochism. After arriving in Vietnam, his company engages in exhausting search-and-destroy missions in the thick rainforests of the Annanese Cordillera. The company learns the savagery of battle, and Caputo succumbs—beginning a cycle of killing frenzies followed by remorse, guilt, and degradation. As the numbers in his company decline, he must contend with recurring dream hallucinations, an increasing sense of psychic numbing, and the clarity of becoming indifferent to the reality of his own death. The culminating irony in *A Rumor of War* brings Caputo and five members of his patrol to face charges of murdering citizens thought to be Viet Cong. While there are no resulting convictions, Caputo clearly blames his complicity on the U.S. government.

Departing from autobiography, Caputo wrote *Horn of Africa* (1981), a novel in which three U.S. intelligence agents are engaged in arms smuggling to an Islamic tribe fighting against the Ethiopian government. Norstrand, the central figure, is a savage killer inclined to torture and efficient with the mechanics of modern warfare. *DelCorso's Gallery* (1983) is a novel balanced with heavy moral and aesthetic issues. It centers on the rivalry between Nicholas DelCorso, a Vietnam veteran, and the man who mentors his career as a combat photographer, P. X. Dunlop. Set in Vietnam and Lebanon, we see DelCorso's endorsement of untouched photos contrasted to Dunlop's work that is altered for effect and appeal. In his third novel, *Indian Country* (1987), Caputo provides an in-depth look into the psychological aftershocks and emotional trauma left over from the Vietnam War. Christian Starkmann suffers from flashbacks triggered by seemingly inconsequential events, and he devolves into a gun-carrying obsessive paranoiac who strings his home with barbed wire and becomes suspicious of the people around him.

Caputo's *Means of Escape* (1991) returns to memoir as he recounts (with imaginative liberties) his life as a war correspondent in Vietnam, Lebanon, Israel, and Afghanistan. Signaling a departure from memoir and war narrative, *Equation for Evil* (1996) is a thriller centered on a forensic psychologist who strives to expose the evils of a modern-day mystic. *Exiles* (1997) is a collection of three short novels questioning cultural conflicts and colonialism: A chance encounter joins separated family from disparate class positions, a shipwreck survivor upsets the racial power on a fishing island, and four U.S. soldiers hunt a tiger in Vietnam.

REFERENCES

Bonn, Maria S. "A Different World: The Vietnam Veteran Novel Comes Home." *Fourteen Landing Zones: Approaches to Vietnam War Literature*. Ed. Philip K. Jason. Iowa City: University of Iowa Press, 1991.

Durham, Marilyn. "Narrative Strategies in Recent Vietnam War Fiction." *America Rediscovered: Critical Essays on Literature and Film of the Vietnam War*. Ed. Owen W. Gilman, Jr., and Lorrie Smith. New York: Garland, 1990.

McInerney, Peter. " 'Straight' and 'Secret' History in Vietnam War Literature." *Contemporary Literature* 22.2 (1981): 187–204.

Myers, Thomas. "Dispatches from Ghost Country: The Vietnam Veteran in Recent American Fiction." *Genre* 21.4 (1988): 409–428.

Styron, William. "A Farewell to Arms." *New York Review of Books* 23 June 1977: 3.

Brad E. Lucas

CATHER, WILLA (1873–1947). Born in Virginia and raised in Nebraska after age ten, Willa Sibert Cather moved to Pittsburgh, then New York, upon graduating from the University of Nebraska in 1895. She was an editor at *McClure's Magazine* until 1912 when she left to write full-time. Cather is best known for stories representative of Nebraska pioneer farm life like *O Pioneers!* (1913) and *My Antonia* (1918). She won the Pulitzer Prize for fiction for her only war novel, *One of Ours* (1922).

When *One of Ours* was first published, critics had objected to Cather writing a story that depicted men in combat. This novel was also devalued for its romantic view of war, a stance antithetical to much of the war literature from this period. It has been acknowledged that this was not Cather sentimentalizing the war but the thoughts of her naive protagonist, Claude Wheeler. Besides some well-documented mistakes in military procedure and organization, there is also an inaccuracy in the language used by the soldiers; but this may also be attributed to Claude's romantic nature. *One of Ours* is a broad view of war: The text examines the psychology necessary to send men to war and to rally noncombatants to support that war.

Cather's protagonist, Claude Wheeler, is modeled on the experience and death, in 1918, of a young cousin to whom she felt bonded by their mutual feelings of frustration toward Nebraska farm life. Claude is an overly sensitive young man. His land-grabbing father, Nat, is a cruel man who thinks his son a fool; and his mother, Evangeline, is an intelligent woman restricted by her narrow adherence to religion. Evangeline forces Claude to attend a second-rate religious college in Lincoln instead of the University of Nebraska, where he thinks he would be challenged. He surreptitiously takes a history course at the university, but he is soon called home to run the farm. Faced with farm life, Claude decides to marry Enid Royce, an avid Prohibitionist and religious zealot who is passionless and indifferent to marriage. Thus, Claude is ripe for excitement and romance when World War I breaks out. After Enid runs off to join her missionary sister in China, Claude returns to his parents' house where Evangeline and Mahailey fervently argue and map out the war's progress with newspapers and atlases. These women construct a romantic ideal of genteel Europe under destruction by the vicious "Hun"—an image Claude finds hard to reconcile to his kindly immigrant neighbors. Claude joins the American Expeditionary Force as a lieutenant, making friends at camp who "shared his Quixotic ideas." During transport to France, Claude flourishes while caring for men dying from an influenza outbreak. Once in France, he is inspired by the French acceptance of the war and by their noble struggle. He views their efforts as heroic and looks to emulate their ideals. Shortly thereafter, Claude dies by drawing enemy fire, and his thoughts express his contentment that he had led his men well. Evangeline is comforted that her idealistic son had "beautiful beliefs to die with," despite her bitter feelings that the war was useless and men died for ideals that could not be realized.

Many features of this novel may be indebted to the writings of **Dorothy Canfield Fisher**.

REFERENCES

Cooperman, Stanley. "The War Lover: Claude." *Critical Essays on Willa Cather.* Ed. John J. Murphy. Boston: G. K. Hall, 1984. 169–176.

O'Brien, Sharon. "Combat Envy and Survivor Guilt: Willa Cather's 'Manly Battle Yarn.' " *Arms and the Woman: War, Gender, and Literary Representation.* Ed. Helen M. Cooper, Adrienne Auslander Munich, and Susan Merrill Squier. Chapel Hill: University of North Carolina Press, 1989. 184–204.

Schwind, Jean. "The 'Beautiful' War in *One of Ours.*" *Modern Fiction Studies* 30.1 (Spring 1984): 53–71.

Stout, Janis P. "The Making of Willa Cather's *One of Ours*: The Role of Dorothy Canfield Fisher." *War Literature & the Arts* 11.2 (Fall-Winter 1999): 48–59.

Woodress, James. *Willa Cather: A Literary Life.* Lincoln: University of Nebraska Press, 1987.

———. *Willa Cather: Her Life and Art.* New York: Pegasus, 1970.

Donna L. Pasternak

CHAMBERLAIN, WILLIAM (1903–1966). Born Edwin William Chamberlain in Challis, Idaho, Chamberlain studied for two years at the University of Idaho before accepting appointment to the U.S. Military Academy with the class of 1927. During his West Point years, he showed his literary inclinations by working on the cadet literary magazine. Upon graduation, Chamberlain began a twenty-year career that included service in the G3 Division of the War Department General Staff during World War II. He retired as a brigadier general in 1946.

Soon after his disability retirement, Chamberlain began a successful career as a short story writer and novelist. His specialties were western, combat, and Cold War narratives. Some of his novels were written specifically for young adults. Typical Chamberlain titles are *Trumpets of Company K* (1954), *Combat General* (1963), *Red January* (1964), and *China Strike* (1967). During the 1950s and early 1960s, Chamberlain's stories were featured regularly in *The Saturday Evening Post*. In all, he published some sixty stories, and his strengths are more evident here than in his longer fiction.

His best combat stories are collected in two volumes: *Combat Stories of World War II and Korea* (1962) and *More Combat Stories of World War II and Korea* (1964). Many of these action-filled pieces pose problems of command involving a clash of personalities or motives. Chamberlain usually provides a cross section of American types and a range of attitudes about the situation at hand. His work tends toward the sentimental; with good-natured tough guys gutting it out for their country. Most of his Korean War stories, like "The Trapped Battalion," were written during the war and designed to be inspirational and supportive. "Star Over Korea" pushes this tendency to an extreme. Chamberlain also wrote many stateside stories of military life.

Though Chamberlain did not write for posterity, his narratives are entertaining and skillful. A longtime military man and eyewitness to the European Theater, Chamberlain brings both his expertise and his love of the military to this substantial body of neglected work.

REFERENCE

Ehrhart, W. D., and Philip K. Jason, eds. Introduction. *Retrieving Bones: Stories and Poems of the Korean War.* New Brunswick, NJ: Rutgers University Press, 1999.

Philip K. Jason

CHESNUT, MARY BOYKIN (1823–1886). "Of necessity a rebel born" into a proud South Carolina family, Chesnut breathed maverick politics; her father was a U.S. congressman and then a fervent states' rights governor of South Carolina, whereas her husband, James Chesnut, Jr., helped establish the Confederacy and ordered the bombardment of Fort Sumter in April 1861. To weather the ensuing social and political melee in the Confederacy, Chesnut turned to her private journal and there captured the essence of those fractious times.

Chaos is her theme as the consumptive upheaval of the Civil War parallels the internecine politics within the Confederacy. Petty squabbling and incessant maneuvering within the Davis administration kindle an explosive atmosphere already rife with false rumors, class tension, and family estrangement. As supplies grow more scarce and hope more desperate, Chesnut's cherished Southern ideals jockey with fear of slave violence, Northern raids, and Sherman's warpath, as well as the heartache of a stormy marriage and an inability to bear children. Ending her journal shortly after Lee's surrender at Appomattox, Chesnut reveals a South looking to a bleary future tasked by a ruined economy, wasted cropland, and Northern exultation.

Until the early 1980s, the version of her material most familiar to historians had been *A Diary from Dixie*, published in two different editions in 1905 and 1949. Both editions, however, were cavalierly cut and bore little resemblance to the text Chesnut had written between 1881 and 1884—an extensive work, cast in diary form, based upon her intensely private Civil War journal. Since Chesnut left neither title for this text nor explanation about its genesis, *The Saturday Evening Post* assumed it to be the one composed during the war and entitled the excerpts it published *A Diary from Dixie*. This misnomer stuck until C. Vann Woodward edited and published the 1880s version as *Mary Chesnut's Civil War* (1981) and then joined Elisabeth Muhlenfeld to edit and publish for the first time *The Private Mary Chesnut: The Unpublished Civil War Diaries* (1984). More recently, Chesnut's daily accounts gained an even wider audience from their use within Ken Burns's successful documentary on the Civil War.

REFERENCES

Muhlenfeld, Elisabeth. *Mary Boykin Chesnut: A Biography.* Baton Rouge and London: Louisiana State University Press, 1981.

Woodward, C. Vann, ed. *Mary Chesnut's Civil War.* New Haven and London: Yale University Press, 1981.

Woodward, C. Vann, and Elisabeth Muhlenfeld, eds. *The Private Mary Chesnut: The*

Unpublished Civil War Diaries. New York and Oxford: Oxford University Press, 1984.

Sandra Burr

CHILDRESS, WILLIAM (1933–   ). Born in Hugo, Oklahoma, Childress grew up in a family of sharecroppers and migrant cottonpickers. He enlisted in the army in 1951, serving in Korea in 1952 and 1953 as a demolitions expert and secret courier. After receiving two college degrees, Childress has had a long and varied career as a teacher, editor, and writer. His Korean War experience is reflected in a dozen powerful poems appearing in two collections, *Burning the Years* (1971) and *Lobo* (1972), later consolidated into *Burning the Years and Lobo: Poems 1962–1975* (1986).

Interestingly, the Vietnam War seems to have been a catalyst for Childress. While several of his Korean War poems were written prior to the American buildup in Vietnam ("The Soldiers" and "Shell Shock"), his poems become more pointed, cynical, and bitter as the 1960s—and the Vietnam War—advance. In one of his finest poems, "Korea Bound, 1952," he compares soldiers on a troopship—ostensibly free men in a democracy—with Pharoah's slaves, and in the poem's final irony, they sail past Alcatraz Island, then a federal prison, where the prisoners' "lack of freedom guarantees their lives."

Childress writes movingly about the travails of soldiers and the costs of war in poems such as "The Soldiers" and "Shell Shock," and his empathy for comrades is matched by his contempt for the generals who command them. Both "Combat Iambic" and "Death of a General" are scathingly unrelenting, reminiscent of Siegfried Sassoon at his best. And "The Long March," a poem that begins with the words "North from Pusan," concludes: "the General / camps with the press corps. / Any victory will be his. / For us there is only / the long march to Viet Nam."

In "The Long March," Childress makes explicit his rising horror at yet another futile and unwinnable Asian war like his own. And "For My First Son" is as bitter as bitter gets. After enumerating the "future of steel" toward which his son's "tiny fingers grope"—a flamethrower's blast, trenchfoot, worms, gangrene, shrapnel, empty eyes—Childress concludes: "these are / the gifts of male birthdays, / the power and glory, and / the lies of leaders send them."

REFERENCE

Ehrhart, W. D. "Soldier-Poets of the Korean War." *War, Literature & the Arts* 9.2 (Fall–Winter 1997): 7–11.

W. D. Ehrhart

CHURCH, BENJAMIN (1639–1718). Born in Duxbury, Massachusetts, Benjamin Church became the most famous soldier and Indian fighter of seventeenth-century New England. When King Philip's War broke out in 1675, Church was commissioned a captain. He took part in the Great Swamp Fight against the Narragansetts in December of 1675, but his biggest contribution came the next year when he raised a number of companies of friendly Indians to fight against Philip's warriors. Church fought alongside his Indian allies, learning their ways of frontier warfare. After eliminating most of the hostile Indian war chiefs, on August 12, 1676, Church and his Indian company caught up with King Philip and killed him, thus ending the war. Church was called back into military service often and continued to be active in public and private affairs until January 1718, when he died, aged seventy-eight, after falling from his horse.

Church kept a journal of his military exploits, edited and published after his death by his son Thomas. *The Entertaining History of King Philip's War* was first published in 1716 and subsequently reprinted with expanded coverage of Church's later campaigns under the new title *The History of Philip's War*. The main thesis of the book details that Church's capability to respect the Indians, their knowledge, and their ways of life and war allowed him to become their most feared enemy. His respect for the Indians also allowed Church to become a skilled diplomat and recruiter of Indian warriors against Philip.

Church wrote the book, in part, to ensure his reputation in the face of later "armchair" critics of his exploits. The narrative often shifts from a conversational, natural language to a formal style that suggests that the writing of the book was a collaboration between father and son. Like all such journals, this one must be read with a skeptical eye, for Church's ego has a way of skewing some facts. For instance, the battles Church participates in are recounted as the most important of the war, while those he missed are glossed over, no matter what their real significance. However, the book is captivating and instantly made Church a model of the prototypical American frontier hero. There are numerous humorous anecdotes, usually aimed at the Puritan government and church, institutions Church rarely agreed with. Church's ego is also at odds with the orthodox Puritan view of history as the story of God's workings on earth. Church, despite his name, makes the reader know that it was his skill and bravery that defeated Philip; Providence had little to do with it.

REFERENCES

Church, Benjamin. *Diary of King Philip's War, 1675–76*. Tercentenary ed. Chester, CT: Pequot Press, 1975.

Church, Thomas. *The History of Philip's War, Commonly Called the Great Indian War of 1675 and 1676*. 1829. Facsim. ed. Ed. Samuel G. Drake. Bowie, MD: Heritage Books, 1989.

Slotkin, Richard, and James K. Folsom. "Benjamin Church: King of the Wild Frontier." *So Dreadfull a Judgment: Puritan Responses to King Philip's War 1676–1677*. Middletown, CT: Wesleyan University Press, 1978.

Kyle F. Zelner

CHURCHILL, WINSTON (1871–1947). Born and raised in St. Louis, Winston Churchill, American novelist, essayist, politician, editor, and historian, may have been the most popular novelist of the American middle class in his time. Mainly known for his early historical romances, Churchill focused his later novels on current social and political themes.

His war novels were part of a scheme to produce five historical novels that would span American history; he only produced three of these. The first was *Richard Carvel* (1899), which chronicles the fortunes of the title character, a young Marylander who goes through a series of episodic adventures during the American Revolution. Carvel joins the crew of the *Bonhomme Richard*, is wounded in battle with the *Serapis*, and ends up in London being nursed by his lady love, Dorothy Manners, whom he eventually marries. Another Revolutionary War novel, *The Crossing* (1904), follows young David Ritchie, who joins George Rogers Clark's force as a drummer boy in the Vincennes campaign. As a young man, he volunteers to serve his country by investigating secession intrigues in the post-Revolutionary West. He ultimately marries a New Orleans aristocrat and settles in Louisville.

Churchill is best known for his Civil War novel *The Crisis* (1901). Although perhaps the best of the war romances, *The Crisis* remains transitional in its style due to its mix of sentimental romance with realistic technique; it likewise employs the conventional romantic plot of a Southern spitfire falling in love with a Union officer. The story follows Stephen Brice, a Bostonian blue blood, and his recently widowed mother, who come to St. Louis in 1858 for young Brice to study the law with his father's friend Judge Whipple. Brice meets Virginia Carvel and her father the colonel, both ardent secessionists. Brice competes with Virginia's cousin Clarence Colfax for her affections, but she spurns the morally stolid Yankee in favor of her dissipated and reckless cousin. As the events of the coming war unfold in the divided city, Brice meets Lincoln and becomes a confirmed Republican. Eventually entering the Union army, Brice twice saves the life of his rival Colfax, now a Confederate officer. After spirited resistance, Virginia finally admits her love for Brice in rather sentimental colors. The story ends abruptly, with Colonel Carvel dead in battle (in one sentence), Colfax pardoned, Brice and Virginia married, and Lincoln assassinated. Half a dozen other essential characters are left unaccounted for, including Eliphalet Hopper, the unscrupulous Yankee who buys out Colonel Carvel's store and tries to force Virginia to marry him. But Churchill's rich narrative style and wit preserve this novel as a fine read. *The Crisis* also fosters the traditional view of the sainted Lincoln and the North's righteous fund of virtue.

Churchill's critical reputation has suffered over the years. Often acknowledged as a fine historian with a keen eye for detail in his novels, he is nevertheless criticized for his stereotyped fictional characters. He was not an innovator; rather, his work reflected his own age. As Warren I. Titus puts it, "Churchill recalls the Victorian era, not the fiction of Crane or Norris or Dreiser" (37).

REFERENCES

Hofstadter, Richard, and Beatrice Hofstadter. "Winston Churchill: A Study in the Popular
     Novel." *American Quarterly* 2 (Spring 1950): 12–28.
Titus, Warren I. *Winston Churchill.* New York: Twayne, 1963.
Schneider, Robert W. *Novelist to a Generation: The Life and Thought of Winston Chur-
     chill.* Bowling Green, OH: Bowling Green State University Popular Press, 1976.
Walcutt, Charles C. *The Romantic Compromise in the Novels of Winston Churchill.* Ann
     Arbor: University of Michigan Press, 1951.

Randal W. Allred

CIARDI, JOHN (1916–1986). Born of Italian immigrant parents in 1916
in the North End of Boston, Ciardi was raised by his mother in Medford after
his father died in an auto wreck when he was three. He grew up within sight
of Tufts, where he earned his A.B. degree in 1938. He took an M.A. degree
from the University of Michigan and there won the prestigious Avery Hopwood
Prize for poetry. In 1940, he published his first book, *Homeward to America.*
In 1942, not long after the war broke out, he entered the U.S. Army Air Corps.
According to biographer Edward Cifelli, Ciardi trained to be a navigator, was
denied a commission on charges he called "phony," busted to private, and re-
trained to be a gunner on a B-29. As a gunner, he flew fifteen bombing missions
from Saipan in the "one unit in which [he] felt mortally enlisted."

Ciardi achieved much fame as a poet and critic, publishing forty books of
poetry and criticism. From 1955 to 1972, he was director of Middlebury College's Bread Loaf Writers Conference. His translation of Dante's *Inferno* won
worldwide acclaim, and he spent many years as poetry editor of the *Saturday
Review.*

His first major work after World War II was *Other Skies* (1947), which contained several award-winning poems (e.g., "Poem for My 29th Birthday" won
Poetry magazine's prize in 1946). Containing forty-two poems, the book is
arranged in four sections, depicting the transformation of a young man into a
"gunner for our tribe" ("Autobiography of a Comedian"). The irony, irreverence,
and seriousness in this volume are hallmarks of his style (both as an airman and
poet). The first section describes the eve of war, beginning with the poet watching for signs of storms and ending with a pronouncement that, above all, he and
his friends must survive. The second section portrays the future airman's training. Evident is Ciardi's uncertainty about whether or not he has mastered his
military skills and what such mastery means to his identity. The last two sections
describe the poet's war experiences and return to civilian life. In poems such as
"Elegy Just in Case," his playfulness and clever use of metrics shine as he has
fun with letters of condolence that are hewn out of his own experience of having
to write such letters.

In "On a Photo of Sgt. Ciardi a Year Later," the last poem in this collection
and one of his most widely known, Ciardi clarifies the differences between the

preconceptions and stereotypes of the photographer and the realities of the airman. Cifelli quotes John Frederick Nims's claim that the poem demonstrates Ciardi's knowledge of "the difference between the heroic and the heroics."

Throughout his other books, but particularly in *39 Poems* (1959), he often returns to the subject of war and the human responses to it. His war diary, *Saipan*, published posthumously, presents the narrative voice that later sang in the poems. In it, we see him watching "the mechanical men [who] would never fully grasp their pointlessness." In it, we see questioning, bitterness, and the longing to understand mortality and immortality. Most important, we come to understand a man who learned that "writing cannot be made to take the place of the world. The world will remain in its own sprawl."

REFERENCES

Ciardi, John. *Ciardi Himself: Fifteen Essays on the Reading, Writing, and Teaching of Poetry*. Fayetteville: University of Arkansas Press, 1989.
————. *Saipan: The War Diary of John Ciardi*. Fayetteville: University of Arkansas Press, 1988.
Cifelli, Edward. *John Ciardi: A Biography*. Fayetteville: University of Arkansas Press, 1997.
Krickel, Edward. *John Ciardi*. Boston: Twayne, 1980.

James M. Dubinsky

CIVIL WAR. Two truisms pervade the majority of critical studies of Civil War literature. The first is that more has been written about this conflict in every genre—history, biography, memoir, prose fiction, poetry, drama—than any other in American history (in 1957, Robert Lively counted 500 novels alone). The second is that, despite this tremendous volume of material, comparatively little of it in the genres traditionally regarded as "literature," particularly fiction and poetry, ranks among the greatest American work.

The most frequently advanced explanation for this circumstance is that, for various reasons, the most gifted writers of American literature in the post–Civil War years—Henry James, **Mark Twain, William Dean Howells**, and Henry Adams—did not serve in the war (Mark Twain did join a Confederate militia company, but he deserted after only three weeks, as he explains in his memoir "The Private History of a Campaign that Failed" [1865]) and as a result, they rarely addressed it directly. **Edmund Wilson**, Daniel Aaron, and John Limon have all written insightfully about this fact, noting that the war reverberates in various ways through the work of these men but is never given center stage. However, these and other critics also posit a number of other explanations besides lesser talent for the failure of those who did serve to write the epic masterpieces that the great national drama of the war should conceivably have evoked. One problem, as Aaron points out, was that many who might have written powerfully from firsthand experience were too traumatized to do so, either by the war itself or by the ideological and racial issues that prompted it and that it failed to settle. A nearly insurmountable obstacle for those who did wish to write about such matters, as Aaron, Wilson, Limon, Thomas Beer, and Bernard De Voto all discuss, was the literary marketplace of the period. In their fiction, veterans such as **Henry Morford** (*Shoulder-Straps* [1863], *The Days of Shoddy* [1864]), James K. Hosmer (*The Thinking Bayonet* [1865]), **John W. De Forest** (*Miss Ravenel's Conversion from Secession to Loyalty* [1867]), **Sidney Lanier** (*Tiger-Lilies* [1867]), **Albion W. Tourgée** (*Figs and Thistles* [1879], *A Fool's Errand* [1879], *Bricks without Straw* [1880]), Wilbur F. Hinman (*Corporal Si Klegg and His "Pard"* [1889]), **Joseph Kirkland** (*The Captain of Company K* [1891]), and **Ambrose Bierce** (*Tales of Soldiers and Civilians* [1892], *Can Such Things Be?* [1893]) sought to tell the truth about the horrors of combat, the miseries of army hospitals, the mixed and often ignoble motives that impelled men to fight, the cynical manipulation of the public's war spirit by politicians and journalists, the profiteering engaged in by army officers and civilian contractors, and the corruption and failure of Reconstruction. These efforts were vitiated, however, by the unwillingness of editors and publishers to present the full, graphic reality of such matters to a genteel reading public and by the authors' own desires to appeal to this public by interlarding their realistic accounts with the conventional elements of popular fiction. The result was that even the most honest of these works, with the sole exception of those by Bierce, give over a good deal of their length to contrivances such as sentimental love stories and melodramatic intrigues involving pure heroines, noble heroes, and dastardly villains.

Despite such efforts to both please and educate their audience, these authors met with little success, as reflected by their generally scant sales. Most readers did not want their mixture of realism and romance; what they wanted was more or less pure romance, as first provided by Southern writers such as the Confederate veteran **John Esten Cooke** (*Surry of Eagle's Nest* [1866], *Hilt to Hilt* [1869], *Mohun* [1869]) and the younger **Thomas Nelson Page** (*Two Little Confederates* [1888], *Meh Lady* [1893], *Red Rock* [1899]) and **Thomas Dixon** (*The Leopard's Spots* [1902], *The Clansman* [1905], *The Man in Gray* [1921]). These authors paint a falsified picture of the antebellum South as a land of gracious plantations populated by noble cavaliers, beautiful and gentle ladies, and happy, docile slaves—a land that is brutally swept away by the war and its Reconstruction aftermath. The reading public both North and South, weary of sectional conflict and the seemingly insoluble problems of race, eagerly devoured these tales. Such novels were characterized by their idolatry of Confederate leaders such as Robert E. Lee, Jeb Stuart, and Stonewall Jackson; their stereotyped depictions of African Americans as irredeemably inferior to whites; their concomitant approval of the actions of the Ku Klux Klan; and their frequent plot device of lovers ideologically divided by the war and reunited as its conclusion. Most often, the Unionist member of the couple comes to appreciate the virtues of the Confederate cause (if not always of slavery), and the marriage of this couple epitomizes the reconciliation of the white North and South. So popular over many years was this type of romance, which reached its apogee in **Margaret Mitchell**'s 1936 novel *Gone with the Wind* and its 1939 film version, that it became the dominant form of Civil War fiction, with many Northern writers adopting all or part of its melodramatic machinery. These include **Winston Churchill** (*The Crisis* [1901]), **James Boyd** (*Marching On* [1925]), **Joseph Pennell** (*The History of Rome Hanks and Kindred Matters* [1944]), and Ross Lockridge (*Raintree County* [1947]). The great popular success during this period of **Stephen Crane**'s highly realistic *The Red Badge of Courage* (1895), often rated as the best American war novel of all time, was anomalous. It is perhaps explicable by the unmatched power of Crane's insight into the psychology of the individual facing battle and his concomitant ignoring of the ideological and sectional issues that provoked the war.

A more thoughtful and technically accomplished if not always less tendentious counterweight to such popular romance was the work in the 1920s, 1930s, and 1940s of the group of Southern writers originally known as the Agrarians. These writers and their followers sought in both fiction and social criticism to debunk the "plantation myth" of the Page and Mitchell school and substitute their own myth of the yeoman white Southern farmer. They considered this figure the ideal repository of the original American virtues destroyed by the war and replaced by the values of industrial capitalism in its aftermath. This group includes **Stark Young** (*So Red the Rose* [1934]), **Caroline Gordon** (*None Shall Look Back* [1937]), **Allen Tate** (*The Fathers* [1938]), and **Robert Penn Warren** (*Band of Angels* [1955]). Comparably serious and well written but less partisan work came in the same period from **Evelyn Scott** (*The Wave* [1929]), **MacKinlay Kantor** (*Long Remember* [1934], *Arouse and Beware* [1936], *Andersonville* [1955]), and **Ben Ames Williams** (*House Divided* [1947]), among others, but critics generally agree that the most insightful and powerful fictional studies of the effects of the war upon the South are **William Faulkner**'s *The Unvanquished* (1934) and *Absalom, Absalom!* (1936).

More recent Civil War novels of considerable literary merit are **Michael Shaara**'s *The Killer Angels* (1974) and **Charles Frazier**'s *Cold Mountain* (1997).

Edmund Wilson argues that one of the consequences of the failure of veterans of the war to write first-rate fiction about it is due to the constraints of their literary culture. The greatest eyewitness accounts of the conflict itself and of its effects on the home front are the memoirs and diaries of participants both famous and obscure. Less concerned about the literary market than the professional writers were, or totally unconcerned in the case of private diarists, these men and women presented their views in their own voices, without the clutter of romance and melodrama. (It should perhaps be noted that a number of the professional novelists wrote equally frank and uncluttered memoirs but were unwilling or unable to publish them. De Forest's *A Volunteer's Adventures* and *A Union Officer in the Reconstruction* were not published until 1946 and 1948, respectively, while Morford's *Red-Tape and Pigeon-Hole Generals as Seen from the Ranks* did not appear until 1964.) Among the most gifted memoirists in the ranks of the war's major figures are William T. Sherman (*Memoirs* [1875]) and Ulysses S. Grant (*Personal Memoirs* [1886]) on the Union side and Richard Taylor (*Destruction and Reconstruction* [1879]) and John Mosby (*Mosby's War Reminiscences* [1887]) on the Confederate. **Samuel Watkins**'s *Co. Aytch* (1882) and John Haley's *The Rebel Yell and the Yankee Hurrah* (1985) provide the enlisted man's view, presented with sharp detail and clarity of style, as a counterpoint to the perspective of these commanders. The most skilled diarists, most of whose work was not published until the twentieth century, are women who wrote with honesty and verve about the lives of those far from the battle lines. Charlotte Forten Grimke (*The Journals of Charlotte Forten Grimke* [1988]), Caroline Seabury (*The Diary of Caroline Seabury* [1991]), Sarah Morgan (*The Civil War Diary of a Southern Woman* [1992]), and Kate Stone (*Brokenburn: The Journal of Kate Stone* [1995]) are significant members of this group. However, the most accomplished and best known is **Mary Boykin Chesnut** (*Mary Chesnut's Civil War* [1982]), whose power of insight and command of language are so striking that Daniel Aaron has speculated that she might have written the greatest war novel of all had she turned her talents to fiction. (For further discussion of this subject, see **Civil War—Women's Diaries**.)

Not surprisingly, the outbreak of the war prompted a flood of poetry that did not abate during the ensuing four years. Perhaps equally unsurprisingly, most of this verse is sentimental partisan doggerel, the most famous examples being Thomas R. Randall's "Maryland, My Maryland" (1861) and **John Greenleaf Whittier**'s "Barbara Frietchie" (1864). More accomplished and generally less strident works came from **Henry Howard Brownell** (*Lyrics of a Day* [1864], *War-Lyrics and Other Poems* [1866]), **James Russell Lowell** (*Biglow Papers, Second Series* [1867]), and Nathaniel Southgate Shaler (*From Old Fields* [1882]) in the North and **Henry Timrod** ("The Cotton Boll," "Ethnogenesis" [1861]), Paul Hamilton Hayne (*The Battle of Charleston Harbor* [1865]), and Abram Joseph Ryan (*Father Ryan's Poems* [1879]) in the South. The greatest poetry of the war years and those immediately following is that of **Herman Melville** (*Battle Pieces and Aspects of the War* [1866]), who frequently expresses misgivings about the human cost of the war and the future of democracy in a militarized and industrialized culture, and **Walt Whitman** (*Drum-Taps* [1865], *Sequel to Drum-Taps* [1865–1866]), whose faith in the war's rightness and the future of democracy is hard-won in such poems as "The Wound-Dresser" and "A March in the Ranks Hard-Prest, and the Road Unknown," meditations inspired by the wounded men whom he tended in Washington, D.C., hospitals, and "When Lilacs Last in the Dooryard Bloom'd," his elegy for Abraham Lincoln. Much less poetry than fiction about the war has appeared in the years since its conclusion, and still less of significance. **Stephen Vincent Benét** attempted, with considerable success, to write the great epic poem of the war, sympathetic to both sides, in *John Brown's Body* (1928). The Agrarians' ideals are advanced in Donald Davidson's *Lee in the Mountains* (1938) and Allen Tate's "Ode to the Confederate Dead" (1959), while **Robert Lowell** takes a more skeptical view of the way contemporary society memorializes the war and its casualties in "For the Union Dead" (1960).

REFERENCES

Aaron, Daniel. *The Unwritten War*. New York: Knopf, 1973.
Beer, Thomas. *Stephen Crane*. New York: Knopf, 1923.
De Voto, Bernard. "Fiction Fights the Civil War." *Saturday Review of Literature* 18 December 1937: 3–4.
Diffley, Kathleen. "The Roots of Tara: Making War Civil." *American Quarterly* 36 (1984): 359–372.
Limon, John. *Writing After War: American War Fiction from Realism to Postmodernism*. New York: Oxford University Press, 1994.
Lively, Robert. *Fiction Fights the Civil War*. Chapel Hill: University of North Carolina Press, 1957.
Sweet, Timothy. *Traces of War*. Baltimore: Johns Hopkins University Press, 1990.
Thompson, Lawrence S. "The Civil War in Fiction." *Civil War History* 2 (March 1956): 83–95.
Wilson, Edmund. *Patriotic Gore: Studies in the Literature of the Civil War*. 1962. Boston: Northeastern University Press, 1984.

Michael W. Schaefer

CIVIL WAR—WOMEN'S DIARIES. Until the advent of social historical and feminist studies, a large portion of the written record of the Civil War, women's journals, remained unexamined—though not unpreserved or unpublished. Many writers recognized the significance of their diaries and preserved their records in libraries and published through small private presses. Additionally, many published versions of original diaries and journals were maintained throughout the war, particularly during the late nineteenth and early twentieth centuries. Civil War–era diaries, however, remained difficult to obtain until recently. Renewed attention in the Civil War period has resulted in a resurgent interest in these texts, which provide vivid personal accounts and insight into the period. Now, many volumes are readily available in editions by both popular and academic presses. Though diaries of Union women are available, many published diaries provide accounts by Confederate women.

Perhaps the most famous diary of the period belongs to **Mary Boykin Chesnut** (1823–1886). Her husband, James Chesnut, resigned from the U.S. Senate upon secession to serve in the Confederate Senate. Mary Chesnut's ties to political leaders and her social connections provided extraordinary access to historically significant information. Originally published as *A Diary from Dixie* in 1905 and 1949, Chesnut's "diary" was actually a retrospective account of Chesnut's experiences during the war that she had revised, edited, and expanded for publication. Chesnut returned to the diary from after attempting to produce a novel based on her experiences. After her death, the untitled manuscript was retitled and published as an "authentic" Civil War diary. In 1981, C. Vann

Woodward published *Mary Chesnut's Civil War* (Yale University Press), an expanded critical edition that restored expurgated passages. This Pulitzer Prize–winning text raised questions about Chesnut's textual authenticity. In 1984, C. Vann Woodward and Elisabeth Muhlenfeld published *The Private Mary Chesnut: The Unpublished Civil War Diaries* (Oxford), which includes the text of the extant versions of Chesnut's original diaries and provides critical insight into her experiences and interpretation of the events she would further examine in her longer work.

Four other significant diaries of Confederate women are *Sarah Morgan: The Civil War Diary of a Southern Woman* (Simon and Schuster, 1992); *The Secret Eye: The Journal of Ella Gertrude Clanton Thomas, 1848–1889* (University of North Carolina Press, 1990); *The Diary of Emma LeConte* (University of Nebraska, 1987), which also provides detailed accounts of Sherman's march through the Carolinas; and *The Diary of Emma Holmes, 1861–1866* (Louisiana State University Press, 1994). Morgan's diary covers the Federal occupation of New Orleans and the writer's escape from Baton Rouge into northern Louisiana and provides critical insight into her changing perception of the war. While she began her journal as an ardent Confederate, Morgan begins to question the nobility and viability of the Confederate cause as the war drags on. Thomas's journal, edited by Virginia Burr, is a greatly condensed version of the original text housed at Duke University Library. The diary explores the years preceding the war and the writer's experiences of life in Confederate Georgia. Holmes's journal records life in Charleston, South Carolina.

The University of South Carolina Press's important series Women's Diaries and Letters of the Nineteenth Century South offers several significant diaries by Confederate women: *Lucy Breckinridge of Grove Hill: The Journal of a Virginia Girl, 1862–1864*; *A Plantation Mistress on the Eve of the Civil War: The Diary of Keziah Goodwyn Hopkins Brevard, 1860–1861*; *A Northern Woman in the Plantation South: Letters of Tryphena Blanche Holder Fox, 1856–1876*; *A Confederate Lady Comes of Age: The Journal of Pauline DeCaradeuc Heyward, 1863–1888*; and *A Rebel Came Home: The Diary and Letters of Floride Clemson, 1863–1866*. These texts provide significant details of the political and personal actions of women during the conflict.

Two interesting diaries complicate the Confederate view of the war. Written from the perspective of a Northerner, *The Diary of Caroline Seabury* (University of Wisconsin Press, 1991) traces Seabury's experiences as a schoolteacher in Columbus, Mississippi, and her eventual escape from behind the Confederate lines in 1863. *The Journals of Charlotte Forten Grimke* (Oxford University Press, 1988) provides the rare insights of an African American woman and her experiences as educator.

As well as serving as teachers, women worked in field hospitals as nurses and doctors. *Kate: The Journal of a Confederate Nurse* (Louisiana State University Press, 1959), *A Confederate Nurse: The Diary of Ada W. Bacot, 1860–1863* (University of South Carolina Press, 1994), and *Civil War Nurse: The*

Diary and Letters of Hannah Ropes (University of Tennessee Press, 1993) reveal the significant contributions made by women to the war effort. *A Woman Doctor's Civil War: Esther Hill Hawks' Diary* (University of South Carolina Press, 1992) provides the unique experience of a nineteenth-century woman physician.

The experience of the war refugee is vividly recounted in two interesting diaries. *Brokenburn: The Journal of Kate Stone, 1861–1868* (Louisiana State University Press, 1995) offers the writer's commentary of her retreat into Texas during the invasion and occupation of Louisiana, while *A Woman's Civil War: A Diary with Reminiscences of the War from March 1862* (University of Wisconsin Press, 1992) explores Cornelia Peake McDonald's refugee life in the Shenandoah Valley of Virginia. Several other compelling diaries that provide information on particular regions of the Confederacy are Eliza Andrew's *Diary of Georgia Girl, 1864–1865* (University of Nebraska Press, 1997), Ellen Renshaw House's *A Very Violent Rebel* (University of Tennessee Press, 1996), *The Diary of Dolly Lunt Burge, 1848–1879* (University of Georgia Press, 1996), *The Civil War Diary of Clara Solomon: Growing Up in New Orleans, 1861–1862* (Louisiana State University Press, 1995), *A Lost Heroine of the Confederacy: The Diary and Letters of Belle Edmondson* (University of Mississippi Press, 1990), and *Shadows on My Heart: The Diary of Lucy Rebecca Buck of Virginia* (University of Georgia Press, 1997).

In addition to these published texts, many unpublished diaries are housed in library collections, historical society archives, and genealogical research centers around the United States. These texts have provided considerable insight into the personal experiences of women during the Civil War, illuminating historical, literary, and social research with vivid accounts of one of the nation's critical periods.

REFERENCES

Attie, Jeanie. *Patriotic Toil: Northern Women and the American Civil War*. Ithaca, NY: Cornell University Press, 1998.

Bunkers, Suzanne L., and Cynthia A Huff. *Inscribing the Daily: Critical Essays on Women's Diaries*. Amherst: University of Massachusetts Press, 1996.

Clinton, Catherine, and Nina Silber, eds. *Divided Houses: Gender and the Civil War*. New York: Oxford University Press, 1992.

———. *The Other Civil War: American Women in the Nineteenth Century*. New York: Hill and Wang, 1984.

———. *The Plantation Mistress: Women's World in the Old South*. New York: Pantheon, 1982.

———. *Tara Revisited: Women, War and Plantation Legend*. New York: Abbeville Press, 1997.

Culpepper, Marilyn Mayer. *Trials and Triumphs: Women of the American Civil War*. East Lansing: Michigan State University Press, 1991.

Faust, Drew Gilpin. *Mothers of Invention: Women in the Slaveholding South in the American Civil War*. Chapel Hill: University of North Carolina Press, 1996.

Forbes, Ella. *African-American Women during the Civil War*. New York: Garland Press, 1998.

Fox-Genovese, Elizabeth. *Within the Plantation Household: Black and White Women in the Old South*. Chapel Hill: University of North Carolina Press, 1988.
Rable, George. *Civil Wars: Women and the Crisis of Southern Nationalism*. Urbana: University of Illinois Press, 1991.
White, LeeAnn. *The Civil War as a Crisis in Gender: Augusta, Georgia 1860–1890*. Athens: University of Georgia Press, 1995.

Amy L. Wink

CLEMENS, SAMUEL LANGHORNE. *See* **Twain, Mark.**

COBB, HUMPHREY (1899–1942). Cobb was born in Florence, Italy, to American parents who returned the family to the United States when he was thirteen. In 1916, seventeen-year-old Cobb joined the Canadian Army so that he might serve in World War I; he was sent to France the next year. His letters home contained such vivid descriptions of the war that they were published in his local newspaper. Cobb decided to remain in Europe for several years after the Armistice, working on a freighter and traveling throughout the Continent. During these years he wrote two novels that he never submitted for publication and ultimately destroyed. In 1934 Cobb moved to New York, where he worked as a copywriter before publishing *Paths of Glory* in 1935.

Set during World War I, the novel draws its title from a line in Thomas Gray's "Elegy Written in a Country Churchyard" (1750): "The paths of glory lead but to the grave." Dax, a colonel in the French army, is ordered to take a German stronghold nicknamed "the Pimple," even though his commanding officers realize that such a maneuver is almost impossible. When the French fail to take the hill, three men are chosen to be executed for cowardice; one is chosen by lot, one is chosen because he has a criminal record, and one is selected by his lieutenant whom he has seen panic and accidentally kill a fellow soldier. Dax defends the men at their court-martial, but it is obvious that the trial is unfair and the outcome has been predetermined. The trial has been staged to deflect attention from the irresponsible decisions of the commanders. All three men are executed. Though *Paths of Glory* is entirely fictitious, Cobb based it on several published accounts of similar incidents that occurred during World War I. *Paths of Glory* addresses not just the unfairness and brutality of war but also the indifference of many officers to the plight of those in combat and the arbitrary manner in which some men survive war while others are killed.

Cobb published no other books but did write a serial about the American military entitled "None But the Brave" for *Collier's* magazine in 1938. He also completed an unpublished manuscript titled "November 11, 1918: The Story of the Armistice." *Paths of Glory* remains the cornerstone of Cobb's reputation. It was adapted into a successful play in 1935 and was the source for Stanley Kubrick's highly acclaimed 1957 film in which Kirk Douglas plays Dax.

REFERENCES

Bowen, Elizabeth. Rev. of *Paths of Glory*, by Humphrey Cobb. *New Statesman and Nation* 14 September 1935: 345.

Cohn, L. H. Rev. of *Paths of Glory*, by Humphrey Cobb. *Saturday Review of Literature* 1 June 1935: 5.

Ferguson, Otis. Rev. of *Paths of Glory*, by Humphrey Cobb. *New Republic* 10 July 1935: 257.

McWilliams, C. "Tribute." *New Republic* 22 May 1944: 710.

Tabachnick, Stephen E. "Afterword." *Paths of Glory*, by Humphrey Cobb. Athens: University of Georgia Press, 1987.

Randall Clark

COHAN, GEORGE M. (1878–1942). A versatile, gifted vaudevillian professional, Cohan embodies the golden era of entertainment and one-man showmanship. Concurrently actor, composer, librettist, playwright, director, manager, and producer, the original Song and Dance Man (title of his 1923 hit in which he starred) appeared as an infant with the family team that became the Four Cohans. By 1901 he graduated to Broadway with his first full-length drama, a musical comedy. For forty years he wrote, adapted, or produced over fifty plays and musicals and controlled five to seven theaters, in addition to starring in many of his shows and his three moving pictures. He composed music and lyrics for more than 500 songs, including "Give My Regards to Broadway," "Mary," and "The Yankee Doodle Boy," which described himself.

Anticipating Ron Kovic by seventy years, Cohan made much of his birth on the Fourth of July. (He was really born on July 3). From the early "You're a Grand Old Flag" (originally "Rag") to the ever-popular "Over There," Cohan indulged his unabashed patriotism and flag-waving skills. Sometimes several such songs are conflated into a patriotic medley, as in *George Washington, Jr.*, which begins with a flag-raising. The most famous militaristic composition by the author of "American Born" was inspired by the keynotes of "Taps." When President Woodrow Wilson declared war on Germany on April 6, 1917, Cohan read the headlines and scribbled the chorus to his mobilizing show *Johnnie, Get Your Gun*. (Dalton Trumbo later replied with the grisly World War I novel and Vietnam-era film *Johnny Got His Gun*.) Just a "bugle call," said Cohan dismissively, "Over There" was heard 'round the world within a month. First performed professionally by Nora Bayes, World War I's most famous song was recorded also by Enrico Caruso. Much later, Cohan received a gold Congressional Medal of Honor, the first granted a songwriter. Five years before America entered a new war, Congress hailed "Over There" and "You're a Grand Old Flag" as national victory hymns. "We Must Be Ready" was composed six months before Pearl Harbor.

REFERENCES

Cohan, George M. *Twenty Years on Broadway and the Years It Took to Get There*. New York: Harper, 1925.

Glann, Frank Warren. "An Historical and Critical Evaluation of the Plays of George M. Cohan, 1907–1920." Diss. Bowling Green State University, 1976.

McCabe, John. *George M. Cohan: The Man Who Owned Broadway.* 1973. New York: Da Capo, 1979.

Moorehouse, Ward. *George M. Cohan: Prince of the American Theater.* Philadelphia: Lippincott, 1943.

Roy Rosenstein

COOKE, JOHN ESTEN (1830–1886). Cooke seems to have been familially destined for his dual careers as writer and soldier: His older brother and cousin, Philip Pendleton Cooke and **John Pendleton Kennedy**, were both well-regarded authors; his uncle, Philip St. George Cooke, was a general in the Union army during the Civil War; and the Confederate cavalry commander Jeb Stuart was his nephew by marriage. A member of an old and prominent Virginia clan, Cooke early on decided on writing as his profession; by 1861 he had published stories, poems, historical essays, and ten novels, mostly historical romances in the manner of James Fenimore Cooper and Sir Walter Scott and most depicting exploits of the Virginia aristocracy of the eighteenth century.

Though not a vehement defender of slavery, Cooke was an ardent Virginia patriot, and so when the Civil War began, he immediately joined the Confederate army. He served throughout the war, most notably as an aide to Stonewall Jackson and Jeb Stuart. His participation in many battles left Cooke with no illusions about the nature of war, which he privately characterized as "the fit work of brutes and brutish men" with "nothing really heroic or romantic or in any way calculated to appeal to the imagination." However, his dedication to the Southern cause during and after the war led him to present a very different picture in his writings on this subject. In 1863 he produced an adoring biography of the recently slain Stonewall Jackson, and throughout the war he published many idealized articles about battles and camp life, collected in the book *Wearing of the Gray* in 1867, emphasizing Southern glory and chivalry rather than the realities of bloodshed and misery.

Cooke continued in this vein after Lee's surrender, essentially ignoring slavery as one of the issues of the war and becoming one of the first and most prolific proponents of the myth of the Lost Cause. In 1867, he published *Surry of Eagle's Nest*, his first historical romance about the war, a combination of his own experiences with Stonewall Jackson and other actual figures with a melodramatic plot involving knightly Southern officers, pure Southern damsels, and devious Northern villains. Cooke repeated this formula in 1869 in the novels *Hilt to Hilt*, in which the central historical figure is John Singleton Mosby, and *Mohun*, which focuses in its historical sections on Jeb Stuart. In all these works Cooke occasionally adverts to the horror of battle, but his overriding concerns are illustrating the gallantry of the outnumbered and poorly supplied Confederate army and burnishing the reputations of its leaders, often providing footnotes to attest to the factuality of the noble statements that he puts in the mouths of Jackson, Stuart, and others.

Cooke takes the same approach in his works of supposedly straightforward history, which include, in addition to *Wearing of the Gray, Hammer and Rapier* (1870) and *Life of General Robert E. Lee* (1871). Many of the same passages describing battles and campaigns that he uses in his novels turn up in these volumes; more surprisingly, so do a number of the novels' fictional characters.

REFERENCES

Beaty, John Owen. *John Esten Cooke of Virginia*. New York: Columbia University Press, 1922.

Bratton, Mary Jo. "John Esten Cooke and His 'Confederate Lies.'" *Southern Literary Journal* 13 (Spring 1981): 72–91.

Michael W. Schaefer

COOPER, JAMES FENIMORE (1789–1851). As a practicing historian, James Fenimore Cooper carefully researched the historical settings of the novels that were to bring him his fame. Cooper served as a naval officer on the Great Lakes but resigned his commission before the hostilities of the War of 1812 began. He remained close friends with his former colleagues including James Lawrence, who was killed on the deck of the *Chesapeake* in 1813, and William Branford Shubrick, who became one of the earliest admirals in the U.S. Navy. Cooper was a prolific commentator on the Somers affair of 1842 and the subsequent court-martial of Alexander Slidell Mackenzie, who also was Cooper's literary rival in the realm of naval history and biography.

In addition to the narrative version of his *History of the Navy of the United States of America* (1841), Cooper set somewhat more than a third of his thirty-two novels in a period of well-defined warfare. In most of these works, Cooper uses warfare to parallel nature as a threatening environment for a double cast of protagonists—one usually the center of the love interest, the other a rustic but highly competent savior figure. The first internationally successful American novel, *The Spy; a Tale of the Neutral Ground* (1821) exhibits the ambiguity of action and intention in two protagonists who are noncombatants. In a few works, the psychology of warfare becomes a theme itself. These include *Lionel Lincoln; or, The Leaguer of Boston* (1825), in which the twin themes of madness and war elucidate each other, and *The Deerslayer: or, The First Warpath* (1841), in which Natty Bumppo is transformed from woodsman to warrior.

As a historical novelist Cooper's range was enormous. It makes some sense to list his primary war fiction according to the conflicts represented:

- King Philip's War: *The Wept of Wish-Ton-Wish* (1829)
- War of Austrian Succession (Jacobite Rebellion): *The Two Admirals* (1842)
- French and Indian Wars: *The Last of the Mohicans* (1826), *The Pathfinder* (1840)
- Revolutionary War: *The Spy* (1821), *The Pilot* (1823), *Lionel Lincoln* (1825), *The Red Rover* (1827), *Wyandotte* (1843)
- Wars of the French Revolution: *The Wing-and-Wing* (1842)

- War of 1812: *The Oak Openings* (1848)
- Mexican War: *Jack Tier* (1848)

Cooper's reputation as inventor of the genre of the Indian novel rests on several of the works mentioned, as well as *The Prairie* (1827), whose background is a fictionally stylized conflict between the Sioux and Pawnee nations during the development of the Louisiana Purchase. *The Deerslayer* (1841), though the least assignable to a specific conflict (it is set on the eve of the French and Indian War), is perhaps the most susceptible to a post-Vietnam psychological analysis of war and the individual. About a third of Cooper's nonfictional *Ned Myers; or, A Life before the Mast* (1843; rpt. Annapolis: Naval Institute Press, 1989, with an introduction and notes by William S. Dudley) is devoted to the War of 1812 and its aftermath as experienced by a common sailor and prisoner of war. The State University of New York Press has published several titles in an ongoing scholarly edition of Cooper's fiction and nonfiction.

REFERENCES

Beard, James Franklin. "Cooper and the Revolutionary Mythos." *Early American Literature* 11 (1976): 84–104.

Egan, Hugh, ed. *Proceedings of the Naval Court Martial in the Case of Alexander Slidell Mackenzie*. Delmar, DE: Scholars Facsimiles & Reprints, 1992.

Peck, Daniel H. "A Repossession of America: The Revolution in Cooper's Trilogy of Nautical Romances." *Studies in Romanticism* 15 (Fall 1976): 589–605.

Philbrick, Thomas. *"The Last of the Mohicans* and the Sounds of Discord." *American Literature* 43 (1971): 25–41.

Williams, John, ed. *The Last of the Mohicans*. New York: Oxford University Press, 1990.

Robert D. Madison

CORRIDOS. Traditionally sung in Spanish, the *corrido* is a Mexican American folk ballad, usually of anonymous origin, that flourished between 1865 and 1915 in the Southwest. The most significant folk genre for Mexican Americans during this time, the *corrido* derives its name from *correr*, a Spanish word meaning "to run," and the Spanish *romance corrido*, a medieval romance distinguished by its lack of refrain. An early form of news reportage, the *corrido* related information important to the Spanish American culture, especially the people's version of historical events where heroes were immortalized, in poetic form. Most frequently, the *corrido* reflected the cultural conflict between the Anglo-Americans and Mexican Americans who inhabited the southernmost regions of Texas along the Mexican-American border. The Mexican-American War of 1846–1848 and the Mexican Revolution of 1910–1920 particularly influenced the composing of *corridos*.

The *corrido*, like the traditional ballad form, usually consists of quatrains, narrates a single dramatic episode in the first or third person, includes dialogue, takes courage as its theme, and recounts the exploits of the hero. In addition, the typical *corrido* invokes the attention of the audience, includes specific geographical locations, names characters, lists dates, focuses on male protagonists, reflects a patriarchal society, and bids the audience farewell. In early revolutionary *corridos*, the heroes generally die. Sometimes called a "Border ballad," the *corrido* is also known by a number of Spanish terms: *versos, tragedia, historia, mañanitas, romance,* and *narración*.

"El corrido de Gregorio Cortez," which narrates a conflict between Texas Rangers and Mexican Americans around the turn of the century, is among the most celebrated. The subject of numerous *corridos*, Cortez, a farmer of Mexican descent, became an outlaw while defending his brother, Roman, who was shot by a sheriff after being accused of stealing a mare from an American. Forced to flee from Texas after shooting the sheriff who wounded his brother, Cortez crossed the Mexican-American border, where he killed or wounded other law enforcement officers, or "cowardly *rinches*," whenever surrounded. Cortez finally surrendered after realizing that other Mexican Americans had lost their lives as a result of his flight and the Anglo-Americans' revenge. For singlehandedly outwitting hundreds of men, Cortez has been immortalized as a folk hero, not only in the *corrido* but also in the film industry. In 1982, "The Ballad of Gregorio Cortez" was made into a movie.

A conflict with Texas Rangers is also related in the *corridos* of Jacinto Trevino, another Mexican American, who eluded arrest after a saloon brawl. Unlike Cortez, Trevino did not surrender to the "cowardly *rinches*" pursuing him. Such *corridos* especially celebrate Mexican nationality as can be seen in "Jacinto Trevino": "The chief of the *rinches* said, even though he was an American, / Ah, what a brave man is Jacinto; you can see he is a Mexican!"

Other *corridos* immortalize such heroic figures as Valentin Mancera, Joaquin Murrieta, Pancho Villa, and Emiliano Zapata. However, not all *corridos* focus on Mexican American disputes or revolutionaries. "El Hijo Desobediente" ("The Disobedient Son"), for instance, deals with the conflict between a father and a son, and "Kiansis I" ("Kansas I") with a cattle drive from Texas to Kansas. The preservation of the *corrido* as a folk and literary form owes much to Americo Paredes, a University of Texas folklorist, who collected and recorded several hundred *corridos* in the 1950s.

REFERENCES

Herrera-Sobek, Maria. *The Mexican Corrido: A Feminist Analysis.* Bloomington: Indiana University Press, 1990.
Paredes, Americo. *Folklore and Culture on the Texas-Mexican Border.* Ed. and intro. Richard Bauman. Austin, TX: CMAS Books, 1993.
Werner, Louis. "Singing the Border News (Mexican Corrido)." *Americas* 1 November 1994: 48+.

Catherine Calloway

COZZENS, JAMES GOULD (1903–1978). James Gould Cozzens was born in Chicago and attended Harvard College. He did not graduate but was awarded an honorary degree in 1952. Although he started writing early—his first published work appeared in *The Atlantic Monthly* when he was just sixteen—Cozzens's other jobs included teaching the children of American engineers in Cuba, spending a year in Europe as a traveling tutor, and working in both advertising and publishing. Some of these experiences provided the material for his early novels *Confusion* (1924), *Cock Pit* (1928), *The Son of Perdition* (1929), and *Ask Me Tomorrow* (1940). Other early works include *S. S. San Pedro* (1931), a fictionalized account of an actual shipwreck; *The Last Adam* (1933), about a physician; *Castaway* (1934), a psychological fantasy; *Men and Brethren* (1936), a character study of an Episcopal clergyman; and *The Just and the Unjust* (1942), a tale about lawyers.

Cozzens spent three years during World War II in the Army Air Force, and out of this experience comes his finest novel, *Guard of Honor* (1948), for which he earned the Pulitzer Prize in 1949. *Guard of Honor* is a product of Cozzens's mature period, and it is a "war novel" only in the sense that it is about the military as bureaucracy and takes place during World War II. There are no combat scenes or depictions of the movements of great armies as in other works that were inspired by the war. Rather, the substance of the work comes from a detailed diary Cozzens kept while assigned to the Training Literature Section of the Army Air Forces School of Applied Tactics.

The action of *Guard of Honor* covers three days in 1943 at a large Florida air-training base. The events of those days include, among others, a near race riot and the accidental death of a group of paratroopers. Cozzens attempts to identify and dramatize the limitations that inhibit human conduct and thereby create difficult moral choices for those involved. Therefore, the issue in *Guard of Honor* is not so much General Beal's particular crisis of having to deal with the challenge to segregated clubs on the part of black pilots but rather the overwhelming complexity of the mammoth social organism known as the Army Air Force. Each of two of the more significant other characters in the novel— Colonel Ross, the professional soldier, and Captain Hicks, the citizen soldier— come to realize and understand the intricacies of cause and effect that, along with the inevitable operations of good and bad fortune, work to limit human moral action. As Colonel Ross believes: "A man must stand up and do the best he can with what there is."

The theme of average men finding themselves in situations that require that they confront crucial moral dilemmas is a recurring one in Cozzens's work. Although examined in his two late novels—*By Love Possessed* (1957) and *Morning Noon and Night* (1968)—it is perhaps nowhere better promulgated than in *Guard of Honor*.

Cozzens succumbed to cancer in 1978.

REFERENCES

Bracher, Frederick. *The Novels of James Gould Cozzens*. New York: Harcourt, 1959.
Bruccoli, Matthew J. *James Gould Cozzens: A Descriptive Bibliography*. Pittsburgh: University of Pittsburgh Press, 1981.

————. *James Gould Cozzens: A Life Apart.* New York: Harcourt, 1983.

                                                                             Peter Katopes

CRANE, STEPHEN (1871–1900). Born in Newark, New Jersey, Crane spent his early years in upstate New York. After a year each at Lafayette College and Syracuse University, he moved to New York City to make his career as a writer. City life suggested the subject, and Crane's occasional work as a reporter may have contributed to the realistic style for his first novel, *Maggie: A Girl of the Streets*, which he had privately published in 1893. That same year, deriving his knowledge of war only from his reading, he completed his war masterpiece, *The Red Badge of Courage.*

A sense of isolation, a style heavily laden with images and symbols used in a manner akin to the French Symbolist poets and the literary practitioners of Impressionism, and a fatalistic view of man's attempts at finding self-worth and happiness inform Crane's prose and poetry. Crane established his reputation with *The Red Badge of Courage* (1895), a magnificent evocation of an innocent Union soldier's responses to the boredom, violence, and confusion of war. Henry Fleming's attempts to measure himself against shifting notions and models of heroism allow Crane to delineate the flux of instinct, will, physical sensation, and spirit that both drives and circumscribes human behavior. An early classic of American war literature, this compact novel was written by a man who had no experience of war. Crane's ironic juxtaposing of scenes and his narrator's sometimes ironic tone cannot mask Crane's affection for the imaginary subject of his experiment.

Early in the story, Henry considers flight, and when his regiment is attacked, he runs off and hides in a wood, festering in a mix of self-reproach and self-pity. He is soon reunited with Jim Conklin, the horribly wounded "tall soldier," whose eerie death Henry witnesses. Henry then encounters and abandons a "tattered" man whose mind is gone. Caught up in the flight of panicked troops, Henry is struck with a rifle and then attended to by the "loud youth" who bandages his wound. For a while, his shame is masked by his fallacious red badge of courage. The next day, however, sees Henry transformed. Perhaps undeserved praise has inspired him. He shows courage, even daring, on the battlefield. No longer battlesick, Henry is ambiguously positioned by Crane: He may be a true hero reborn out of failure, or he may be a mere automaton driven by group pressure and hysteria.

Such ambiguities have appealed to Crane's critics, as has the richness of the novel's symbolic texture and the firm accommodation of theme, style, and structure. Crane's focus keeps oscillating between the individual and the group (the column, regiment, procession, or "ragged line"), insisting on the pressure that subordinates the former to the latter. The many instances of synesthesia, such as "crimson roar," establish the confused bombardment of the senses in combat. In the twentieth century, almost every important American novelist of war has acknowledged Crane as an influential literary ancestor.

The success of *The Red Badge of Courage* gave a second life and first commercial publication to *Maggie* and guaranteed publication of *The Little Regiment* (1896), a collection of six short stories about the Civil War noteworthy as examples of naturalistic style. The grouping of stories known as the "Spitzbergen tales" has special significance as Crane's most mature fictional treatment of war. Crane's other imaginative treatments of war include selections in his second volume of poems, *War Is Kind* (1899), whose title poem manages a blend of passion and irony:

> Mother whose heart hung humble as a button
> On the bright splendid shroud of your son,
> Do not weep.
> War is kind.

Viewed by many critics (along with *The Black Riders*, 1895) as an example of early modernist manner, Crane's war poetry, like all his poetry, is notable for its organic rhythms and its ability to freeze moments charged with strong emotion.

Before writing *War Is Kind*, Crane had reported on the Greco-Turkish War and the Spanish-American War. His journalistic writings are found in *Wounds in the Rain* (1900). These include "War Memories," a piece of personal journalism on the Spanish-American War that has won the praise of influential critics. Crane's experiences in Greece are the basis for his satirical novel *Active Service* (1899). The posthumously published historical effort *Battles of the World* (1901) adds nothing to Crane's reputation. After living off and on in England, Crane died in a German sanitarium while attempting to recover from tuberculosis.

REFERENCES

Crane, Stephen. *The Works of Stephen Crane.* Ed. Fredson Bowers. 10 vols. Charlottesville: University Press of Virginia, 1969–1975.

Meredith, James H., ed. *Stephen Crane in War and Peace.* A Special Edition of *War, Literature, and the Arts.* USAF Academy, CO: 1999.

Mitchell, Lee Clark, ed. *New Essays on "The Red Badge of Courage."* Cambridge: Cambridge University Press, 1986.

Stallman, Robert. *Stephen Crane: A Biography.* New York: Braziller, 1968.

Philip K. Jason

CUMMINGS, E. E. (1894–1962). e. e. cummings's (he preferred the lower case) responses to the wars of the twentieth century trace his evolution from conscientious objector in his twenties to contrarian isolationist during World War II to McCarthyite Cold War hawk in the final decade of his life. While best known as an experimental, yet popular, modernist poet, cummings made his first mark on the world of letters for a startlingly original autobiographical novel, *The Enormous Room* (1922), which detailed his experiences in the First World War as a detainee of the French government from September to December 1917. Regardless of his shifting political stances, cummings was a consistent and cantankerous advocate of the individual's right to self-determination, a right that state systems, he believed, threatened most in times of war. In a 1944 letter he observed, "War means that true individuals show their true individuality: it also means that all unreally human beings become really unhuman."

Edward Estlin Cummings's upbringing in the household of a Harvard professor and Unitarian clergyman prepared him for a life of independent thinking and hostility to state authority. After graduating from Harvard (with an M.A. in 1916) and embarking on a full-time career as a poet in New York City, cummings refused to be swept up in America's sudden wartime fervor. Instead, on April 7, 1917, the day after the United States declared war on Germany, cummings followed the lead of his friend **John Dos Passos** and volunteered for noncombatant duty in the Norton-Harjes Ambulance Service, a Red Cross unit serving with the French army.

As he fictionalizes the experience in his captivity narrative *The Enormous Room*, cummings soon discovered he detested the management of the Service and many of his xenophobic American compatriots. Instead, cummings bonded with a fellow driver, William Slater Brown, developing an even more skeptical attitude to the war. Guilty by association, cummings was forced to follow Brown to a detention center in the northwestern French town of La Ferté-Macé, on charges of sending disloyal missives critical of the French government and insufficiently hostile to Germany. Their three months of internment at La Ferté-Macé were marked by Kafkaesque confrontations with petty bureaucratic overseers and their stupid, sadistic, and corrupt henchmen, the prison guards. La Ferté-Macé emerges in the novel as an absurdist modern hell. In cummings's modernist reinscription of Bunyan's *The Pilgrim's Progress*, the only redeeming characters are the so-called "Delectable Mountains." Social outcasts and racial outsiders, these characters (Josef Demestre, Zulu, Surplice, and Jean le Négre) are those few who heroically maintain their individual wills and incorruptible natures in the face of oppressive government power structures. The novel's stinging attack on mass conformity in the face of such adversity is conveyed in cummings's hallmark style: sardonically inventive and playfully ironic.

Much of cummings's poetry for the forty years following the publication of his only novel is similarly driven by a satiric impulse to condemn state control over individuals. Above all, cummings detested cant justifying war. In Part Two of the 1926 volume *is 5*, the poet mercilessly satirizes bloviating politicians and families who send young citizens and sons to war to die for ideals that have been falsified into cliché and empty apothegm. "my sweet old etcetera," "come, gaze with me upon this dome," and "next to of course god america i" are significant for the ferocity of cummings's sallies against those who romanticize suffering and death in combat, thereby perpetuating war. If cummings identifies most with anyone it is the heroic conscientious objector of his most savage and profane antiwar poem, "i sing of Olaf glad and big" (in the 1931 volume *W[ViVa]*). Olaf fiercely opposes the coerced patriotism necessitated by war, as well as such specious symbolism as kissing the flag to demonstrate love for one's country.

cummings's loathing of the New Deal's increase in federal authority came to a head during the Second World War, which cummings distanced himself from for the duration, bitterly considering it President Roosevelt's war. He was especially critical of America's anti-Japanese racism, best expressed in "ygUDuh" (in *1 X 1* [1944]). A clutch of poems in *XAIPE* (1950) articulates the poet's rejection of the glorification of even a noble anti-Fascist war: "why must itself up of every park," "neither awake," and "where's Jack Was." The soldier's voice from beyond the grave in poem 40 ("I'm") insists that war is not what people imagine it to be, while the unimaginable scale of destruction unleashed by bombing Hiroshima and Nagasaki prompted the poem titled "whose are these (wraith a clinging with a wraith)." In this sonnet cummings argues that militarism and perversion of the scientific imagination have conjoined to make "chaos absolute." While cummings alienated many in the 1950s when his anti-Roosevelt sentiments evolved into McCarthyite antileftism, he was applauded for his liberal position on the Hungarian Uprising in a poem written for the Boston Arts Festival. "Thanksgiving (1956)" castigates America's ineffectual response to the Soviet invasion of Hungary and sourly observes how "uncle sam" (refigured as a lisping, effeminate homosexual) has become unfit for moral leadership of the world.

cummings, to the end, was predictable in one way in his response to war: He always went his own cranky, romantic individualist's way against the conventional political wisdom and the surge of popular patriotic hysteria. He created a body of antiwar work born of the satirist's idealistic rage against the "really unhuman" in war.

REFERENCES

cummings, e. e. *Complete Poems: 1904–1962.* Ed. George J. Firmage. New York: Liveright, 1991.

———. *The Enormous Room: The Typescript Edition.* Ed. George James Firmage. New York: Liveright, 1978.

Friedman, Norman, ed. *E. E. Cummings: A Collection of Critical Essays.* Englewood Cliffs, NJ: Prentice-Hall, 1972.

Kennedy, Richard S. *Dreams in the Mirror: A Biography of E. E. Cummings.* New York: Liveright, 1980.

David A. Boxwell

CUSTER, GEORGE ARMSTRONG (1839–1876). An 1861 graduate of the U.S. Military Academy, Custer was born in New Rumley, Ohio, and educated in Monroe, Michigan. A poor student, Custer proved an adept cavalry commander. He quickly rose in rank because of his skill and audacity, as well as through the favor of his superiors. Under the pseudonym "Nomad," Custer penned fifteen descriptive letters from 1867 to 1875 in the sporting journal *Turf,*

Field and Farm. Nomad's letters reveal the life, interests, and amusements of the post–Civil War frontier army officer corps. Horses, racing, and hunting were popular diversions for frontier soldiers, and thus Custer's letters are telling relations of soldiers' off-duty tastes and the frequent monotony of soldiering.

First published as twenty serialized articles for the magazine *Galaxy*, *My Life on the Plains* (1874) is a classic account of military operations against various tribes of Plains Indians in Kansas, Oklahoma, and Texas from 1868 through 1869. Custer wrote the articles while commanding a two-company post in Elizabethtown, Kentucky (1872–1874). For Custer, as for many officers on the frontier or in garrison, writing was a release from drudgery. *My Life* is as much a history of the Indian Wars as it is a memoir of Custer's early frontier days. Throughout the book Custer portrays himself as a decisive and confident commander with highly developed tactical skills, personal leadership, and field craft. Custer's views on Indians are mixed. While Custer plainly considered the Indian "a savage" possessed of "a hostility so deep-seated and inbred" that he was incapable of willingly adopting the "modes and habits of civilization," he also openly admired the spirit of resistance. Indeed, Custer conjectured that he too would have fought against the encroachments of white America in the West.

Custer's life and literary career came to an end on June 25, 1876, at Little Bighorn in Montana. His literary achievements, while not stunning examples of prose or history, are important contributions to the social and cultural history of the frontier army and are important insights into the mind of late nineteenth-century Americans.

REFERENCES

Barnett, Louise. *Touched by Fire: The Life, Death, and Mythic Afterlife of George Armstrong Custer*. New York: Henry Holt, 1996.

Custer, Elizabeth B. *Boots & Saddles, or Life in Dakota with General Custer*. 1885. Norman: University of Oklahoma Press, 1961.

Custer, George Armstrong. "From West Point to the Battlefield." *The Custer Reader*. Ed. Paul Andrew Hutton. Lincoln: University of Nebraska Press, 1992.

———. *My Life on the Plains*. 1874. Chicago: Lakeside Press, 1952.

———. *Nomad: George A. Custer in Turf, Field and Farm*. The John Fielding and Louise Lasater Maher Series. Ed. Brian W. Dippie. Austin: University of Texas Press, 1980.

Ricardo A. Herrera

D

DAVIS, RICHARD HARDING (1864–1916). Davis was born in Philadelphia, Pennsylvania, the son of novelist Rebecca Harding Davis. After spo-
radically attending Swarthmore College, Lehigh University, and Johns Hopkins
University (1880–1886) without obtaining a degree, he became a reporter and
got his first taste of military action when in 1892 he accompanied an army unit
pursuing a Mexican bandit in Texas. Thereafter, he was a freelance author.

Soldiers of Fortune (1897), his most popular novel, tells how Robert Clay,
an American civil engineer, who fought in Egypt and Algeria, is hired by New
York businessman Langham to manage his Valencia Mining Company (i.e.,
Juragua Iron Company, which Davis saw in Cuba in 1886) in Olancho (i.e.,
Venezuela, which Davis visited in 1895). After improving mine operations, Clay
successfully leads loyalist Olanchans against revolutionists headed by Mendoza,
who has murdered the president. Romance appears when Langham inspects his
property and brings his daughter along. The success of *Soldiers of Fortune*—
$5,000 for serial rights and 100,000 book copies its first year—indicate public
approval of the Manifest Destiny philosophy it espouses. In 1913 Davis super-
vised a movie version of his novel filmed in Cuba. Modern critics deplore its
comic-opera hero and his jingoism.

Davis was a daring war correspondent during the Cuban insurrection (after
which he repudiated William Randolph Hearst's yellow journalism), the Greco-
Turkish War (working alongside **Stephen Crane**), the Spanish-American War,
the Boer War, Belgian Congo outbreaks, the Russo-Japanese War, and World
War I. Out of his dispatches grew several books. *Cuba in War Time* (1897)
advocates American intervention. *A Year from a Reporter's Note-Book* (1898)
is hasty and brash but informative. The *Cuban and Puerto Rican Campaigns*
(1898) details battles, criticizes several generals, but praises the navy. *With Both
Armies in South Africa* (1901) criticizes British ineptitude and praises Boers as
defeated crusaders. *With the Allies* (1914) excoriates German savagery and urges
American preparedness and involvement. *With the French in France and Sa-*

lonika (1916) describes the British and French in Serbia and Bulgaria and challenges the United States to intervene.

Though once regarded as the best war correspondent of his era, Davis now seems facile and flamboyant, his reporting more impressionistic than detailed. At his best, however, he is arrestingly graphic.

REFERENCES

Davis, Richard Harding. *The Novels and Stories of Richard Harding Davis.* 1916. New York: Charles Scribner's Sons, 1919.
Downey, Fairfax. *Richard Harding Davis: His Day.* New York: Charles Scribner's Sons, 1933.
Lubow, Arthur. *The Reporter Who Would Be King: A Biography of Richard Harding Davis.* New York: Scribner's, 1992.
Osborn, Scott Compton, and Robert L. Phillips, Jr. *Richard Harding Davis.* Boston: Twayne, 1978.

Robert L. Gale

DE FOREST, JOHN WILLIAM (1826–1906). Journalist, poet, historian, and author of fourteen novels, De Forest is esteemed largely for just one book, his Civil War novel *Miss Ravenel's Conversion from Secession to Loyalty* (1867), generally regarded as the most realistic account of Civil War combat prior to **Stephen Crane**'s *The Red Badge of Courage* and sometimes cited as an influence on Crane's novel. Born in Connecticut of well-to-do parents, De Forest intended to go to Yale but because of chronic bronchitis was instead sent to Europe and the Near East to recover his health. Deciding upon a writing career during this extended sojourn, De Forest on his return to America began by publishing a history of Connecticut's Indians in 1851. Over the next ten years he produced several novels on various subjects and two travel books based on his overseas experiences.

Shortly after the outbreak of the Civil War, De Forest volunteered for the Union army and was commissioned a captain in the 12th Connecticut Volunteers. Over the next three years (1862–1864) he served in Louisiana, seeing action in several engagements, including the protracted Union siege of Port Hudson, and in Philip Sheridan's Shenandoah Valley campaign, taking part in the battles of Winchester, Fisher's Hill, and Cedar Creek. During this service, De Forest wrote a number of precisely observed and lucid descriptions of his experiences, detailing not only the sights and sounds of battle but also how it felt to be under fire. He forthrightly notes that any such encounter entails confusion, since one knows little about the battle except that one is being shot at, and fear—at least when one is familiar enough with combat to understand its dangers. He emphasizes that these emotions are ordinarily counterbalanced by a preoccupation with one's practical duties as a soldier.

The success of these excellent pieces, most of which were published in *Harper's New Monthly Magazine*, encouraged De Forest to write *Miss Ravenel's*

Conversion, which draws heavily, especially in its battle scenes, on the events he reported in his autobiographical essays. The novel's main characters are Lillie Ravenel, a Southerner transplanted to New England who undergoes the shift in sympathies indicated in the title; her husband, Colonel Carter, an able and courageous but venal career soldier in the Union army; Captain Edward Colburne, a younger and more gentlemanly volunteer in Carter's command who quietly loves Lillie from a distance and, after Carter's death in battle, eventually marries her; and Mrs. Larue, an impoverished Southern widow who seeks to improve her economic status by any means available, including seducing Carter and abetting his profiteering schemes.

William Dean Howells and other contemporary critics praised De Forest's realism in his depiction of the mixture of bravery and degeneracy in Carter's nature and of Mrs. Larue's powerful sexuality and the uses to which she is willing to put it, but what has won the book still more admirers from De Forest's own day to the present is the frankness with which the author depicts, from Colburne's point of view, the chaos and bloodshed of combat, the horrors of medical treatment for the wounded both on the field and behind the lines, the mixture of monotony and sudden danger that comprised siege operations, the boredom of camp life, and the means by which the neophyte Colburne copes with these ordeals and thus attains veteran status. As in the autobiographical essays, the main method is sustained attention to the practical obligations of being a soldier as prescribed and implied by army regulations.

In addition to novels and poems on many subjects, De Forest continued to publish essays and book reviews on military matters throughout the rest of his long career. The most extensive of these pieces, "Our Military Past and Future," is in accord with the realistic approach of his wartime essays and *Miss Ravenel's Conversion* in its emphasis on the realities of battle and the necessity of giving recruits an accurate picture of these realities so they will be able to behave with equanimity when they first go into combat. De Forest also collected his wartime essays into a book of memoirs, but he died before he could see this volume through to publication. It was not finally published until 1946, under the title *A Volunteer's Adventures*.

De Forest occasionally doubted whether he had lived up to his own principles of realism in his battle writing. Upon reading *War and Peace* for the first time, he wrote to Howells that "nobody but [Tolstoy] has written the whole truth about war and battle. I tried and told all that I dared, and perhaps all I could, but there was one thing I did not dare tell, lest the world should infer that I was naturally a coward, and so could not know the feelings of a brave man. I actually did not dare state the extreme horror of battle and the anguish with which the bravest soldiers struggle through it." Other critics have judged De Forest more generously and perhaps more justly. Their opinion is encapsulated in the title of an essay on *Miss Ravenel's Conversion* that appeared in *American Heritage*: "Best Novel of the Civil War."

REFERENCES

De Forest, John William. *Miss Ravenel's Conversion from Secession to Loyalty*. 1867.
    Ed. Gordon S. Haight. San Francisco: Rinehart, 1955.
———. *A Volunteer's Adventures*. Ed. James H. Croushore. New Haven, CT: Yale
    University Press, 1946.
Light, James F. *John William De Forest*. New York: Twayne, 1965.
Limon, John. *Writing After War: American War Fiction from Realism to Modernism*.
    New York: Oxford University Press, 1994.
Schaefer, Michael W. *Just What War Is: The Civil War Writings of De Forest and Bierce*.
    Knoxville: University of Tennessee Press, 1997.
Stone, Albert E., Jr. "Best Novel of the Civil War." *American Heritage* June 1962: 84–88.

Michael W. Schaefer

DELL, FLOYD (1887–1969). Floyd Dell, a novelist, essayist, playwright, editor, and social critic, was born and reared in the rural Midwest, worlds away from the cities where he would make his mark as one of the foremost intellectuals of his generation. The son of a butcher and a schoolteacher, Dell saw firsthand the effects of the depressions of the 1890s on the struggling middle class, a memory that would shape his political disposition forever after. After a series of jobs at small-town newspapers in Iowa and Illinois, Dell moved to Chicago in 1908, where in five years at the *Chicago Evening Post's Friday Literary Review* he became one of the foremost book reviewers and literary editors in the nation. Among his accomplishments, he, along with Sherwood Anderson and Maurice Brown, was a formative influence in the local arts movement now known as the Chicago Renaissance. In 1913, Dell brought his prodigious talents to New York's bohemian center, Greenwich Village, where he began work on the radical literary journal *The Masses* and helped found the seminal little theater company the Provincetown Players.

In August of 1917, Dell and five others involved with the publication of *The Masses* were indicted under the recently passed Espionage Act, charged with "conspiring to obstruct recruiting and enlistment to the injury of the service." Dell's part in said conspiracy consisted of an unsigned introduction to a series of letters from imprisoned British conscientious objectors published in the August 1917 issue. The comments included an outline of the rights of conscientious objectors, one of which, incidentally, Dell was not. A part of the article read, "There are some laws which the individual feels he cannot obey, and which he will suffer any punishment, even that of death, rather than recognize them as having authority over him. This . . . constitutes a conscientious objection, whatever its original sources may be in political or social opinion." The trial lasted nearly two weeks before a hung jury temporarily freed the defendants. Two months later Dell himself was drafted and reported to basic training, where he was discharged after it was learned he remained under indictment. A second jury was convened in 1918, and it, too, reported back deadlocked. All charges were dropped in January 1919.

In the following decade, Floyd Dell would go on to become a successful novelist, shaping his personal experiences into fictional accounts of characters that became that much more alive for his insight. His writing, quick, witty, and precisely detailed, found an audience in those readers in the 1920s searching for answers to the larger questions about life, love, and the place of the idealist in an increasingly faceless and mechanized society. Only on one occasion did Dell approach the subject of war again, in his 1926 novel *An Old Man's Folly*. The title character, Mr. Windle, is a quietly radical individual who discovers himself late in life when confronted with a group of young idealists protesting World War I. Dell's descriptions of the other side of the home front's frenzied patriotism ring authentic, providing a touch of social history amidst the fiction. As his novels grew less and less popular, Dell finally ceased writing in 1934, dedicating his time to the Works Progress Administration and later compiling his voluminous works for a collection at the Newberry Library. Floyd Dell died in July 1969.

REFERENCES

Douglas, Clayton. *Floyd Dell: Life and Times of an American Rebel*. Chicago: I. R. Dee, 1994.

Hatcher, Harlan. *Creating the Modern American Novel*. New York: Farrar & Rinehart, 1935.

O'Neill, William L., ed. *Echoes of Revolt: "The Masses" 1911–1917*. Chicago: Quadrangle, 1966.

Patrick Julian

DEL VECCHIO, JOHN M. (1947–   ). Born in Bridgeport, Connecticut, John M. Del Vecchio graduated from Lafayette College in 1969 with a B.A. From 1969 through 1972, he served in the U.S. Army as a correspondent, including a tour in Vietnam during which he was awarded the Bronze Star for valor. After leaving the military, he worked at real estate, construction, and carpentry, but his preoccupation was writing on the Vietnam War (he describes his first three novels as a "trilogy about America's Southeast Asia era").

While his long, sprawling novels seem to support the Vietnam War, his sympathy is for the American soldiers (and Asian allies) who were, in his view, sacrificed and finally betrayed by fickle national policy during that long conflict and its aftermath. The larger vision of his work suggests that threats from a dark and violent world are counterbalanced by glimpses of the possibility of utopian harmony.

The 13th Valley (1982), the first novel in the trilogy, is based on an actual campaign and includes maps, reports, and other documents to lend credibility and verisimilitude. He develops the narrative around three characters, each representing a different response to armed conflict. Lieutenant Rufus Brooks attempts to explain warfare intellectually. Sergeant Daniel Egan accepts it as a primal physical contest. James "Cherry" Chelini is the draftee who does not want to be there, yet he manages to survive. To provide perspective and scope, Del Vecchio introduces other characters who read historical and political accounts of Vietnam. Forming a kind of "think tank," they fight the brutal, ugly war as they discuss its merits, causes, and issues. These devices, along with the rich detail, result in a complex and multileveled narrative, which some critics consider the best novel based on the Vietnam War.

For the Sake of All Living Things (1990) follows the story of one family during the Cambodian holocaust. At the center of the novel is Chhuon, an educated man (an agronomist), thus among that population that the Khmer Rouge seeks to exterminate. Remaining alive by subterfuge, he holds true to the Buddhist tenet that all life is sacred. Consistent with that philosophy, his daughter Vathana serves selflessly in refugee camps, thereby earning the name "Angel." But his son Samnang falls into the hands of the Khmer Rouge, who transform him into one of their most vicious adherents. Despite the horrific vision of life inherent in its subject matter, the novel leaves the hope that good will survive.

Carry Me Home (1995), last in the trilogy, focuses on three Vietnam veterans and their subsequent traumas in resuming life in postwar America. Time after time, Tony Pisano seems to have his life under control, only to regress into self-destruction. Tyrone Blackwell, an African American, finds that in a racist culture his service in Vietnam gains him no more respect than he had before. Robert Wapinski, finding that society is not ready for his progressive ideas, founds a commune for veterans trying to work through their problems. Although Robert dies from the effect of his wartime exposure to Agent Orange, the veterans continue his experimental community, affirming his sacrifice and vision.

REFERENCES

Herzog, Tobey C. *Vietnam War Stories: Innocence Lost*. New York and London: Routledge, 1992.
Myers, Thomas. *Walking Point: American Narratives of Vietnam*. New York: Oxford University Press, 1988.

Steve Anderson

DICKEY, JAMES (1923–1997). Born in Atlanta, Georgia, to Eugene Dickey, a lawyer, and Maibelle Swift Dickey, James Lafayette Dickey as a youth was more interested in sports (especially football) than in literature. In 1942, after briefly attending Clemson A & M College (now Clemson University), Dickey enlisted in the Army Air Corps. While serving in the Pacific as a navigator on bombers, Dickey developed a passion for literature in his spare time. Upon being discharged from the military in 1946, he enrolled at Vanderbilt University, where he earned his bachelor's and master's degrees in English.

In 1950, Dickey began teaching at Rice University, but he was quickly summoned by the air force for the Korean War. In 1952, he returned to Rice, then won a *Sewanee Review* fellowship, which allowed him to travel in Europe. In 1956, after teaching a year at the University of Florida, he worked briefly as an advertising copywriter. By the late 1950s, Dickey's poetry was appearing widely in literary magazines; collections soon followed. His growing reputation brought fellowships, temporary "poet-in-residence" positions at several colleges and universities, and prestigious awards (his fourth collection, *Buckdancer's Choice*, won the National Book Award for Poetry). In 1969, he accepted a professorship at the University of South Carolina, a position he occupied until shortly before his death from lung disease.

Most of Dickey's published poems about war can be found in his early poetry collections; some of these poems rank among his finest literary efforts. "The Jewel" (1960) concerns the inability of a former American pilot during peacetime to forget his terrifying yet thrilling wartime experience. In "The Performance" (1960), the narrator, a former pilot, remembers a fellow pilot who was killed as a prisoner of war during World War II; the narrator regards that pilot as having been more courageous than himself, if less lucky. "Between Two Prisoners" (1962) depicts the beheading of captured American pilots in a schoolyard by a Japanese guardsman, who is likewise executed one year later, the narrator acknowledges; the poem asserts that people condemned to death speak a common language that to the living remains a "foreign tongue." "Drinking from a Helmet" (1964) explores a young soldier's deepening awareness of death and his increasing empathy toward the plights of other soldiers. "The Firebombing" (1965), one of Dickey's most acclaimed poems, also reflects the perspective of a former World War II pilot. This narrator lives comfortably in the suburbs yet needs to reconcile himself to past deeds, as he recognizes that the measure of heroism he received through serving his country came at the expense of Japanese civilians who died innocently from bombs he dropped from an airplane. The narrator resolves to accept responsibility for his actions but also to view those actions as inevitable wartime behaviors.

Two of Dickey's three published novels are explicitly about war. Set during World War II, *Alnilam* (1987) concerns a blind man's quest to locate his son, an Air Corps pilot allegedly killed in a training accident. The father's search for truth leads him into a top-secret "higher military" group that demands among its members a code of heroism and fanatical dedication to flying; the son proves to be this group's central figurehead. *Alnilam* interpolates passages of conventionally presented narrative with highly symbolic sections in which the text is divided into two adjacent columns on the page, one column printed in a bold typeface under the heading "dark," the other in a fainter typeface under the heading "light."

To the White Sea (1993) depicts the ordeal of a World War II air force gunner shot down by the Japanese during an air raid of Tokyo. Parachuting into enemy territory, the gunner eludes capture by heeding the survivor's "instinct" he learned growing up in the wilderness of Alaska. The novel contrasts the violence of the larger war (which is portrayed as an impersonal and unnatural force of destruction) with the violence of the gunner during his journey northward toward freedom (which is represented as a force of nature, since, like the animal predators he observed in the Alaskan wilderness, the gunner must draw on his own strength to survive in a harsh environment).

Although not overtly about war (in its famous plot, urban/suburban men take a canoe trip down a soon-to-be dammed wild river), Dickey's other novel, *Deliverance* (1970), projects an archetypal situation in which people test the boundaries of their morality under extreme circumstances—a predicament that is certainly applicable to soldiers in battle.

Writing about war, which he did frequently during his long career, not only helped Dickey to come to terms with his own military experience but also to assess the meaning of war.

REFERENCES

Baughman, Ronald. *Understanding James Dickey*. Columbia: University of South Carolina Press, 1985.

Calhoun, Richard J., and Robert W. Hill. *James Dickey*. Boston: Twayne, 1983.

Dickey, Christopher. *Summer of Deliverance: A Memoir of Father and Son*. New York: Simon & Schuster, 1998.

Dickey, James. *The Whole Motion: Collected Poems, 1945–1992*. Middletown, CT: Wesleyan University Press, 1992.

Goldstein, Laurence. "The Poetry of Firebombing: The Case of James Dickey." *The Flying Machine and Modern Literature*. London: Macmillan, 1986.

Ted Olson

DIXON, THOMAS (1864–1946). In addition to his careers as an actor, playwright, screenwriter, filmmaker, lawyer, state legislator, and minister, Thomas Dixon was one of the best-selling novelists of the early twentieth century, especially in the realm of Civil War fiction. Born in Shelby, North Carolina, Dixon attended college at Wake Forest, earning a master's degree in 1883, and then did further graduate work at Johns Hopkins University and the University of North Carolina at Greensboro, receiving an L.L.B. from the latter school. Although he did not turn to writing until midlife, he nevertheless produced a large body of work, running to more than twenty volumes.

Dixon's most famous book is his racist Civil War novel *The Clansman* (1905). Subtitled *A Romance of the Ku Klux Klan*, the novel follows the Stonemans of the North and the Camerons of the South, who are drawn together at the war's end by friendship and romance between children of the two families. The newfound love between Elsie Stoneman and Ben Cameron symbolizes reconciliation between the regions. After the war, the Stonemans come South with the carpetbaggers to the town of Piedmont, where the Camerons live. Father Stoneman (a thinly veiled Thaddeus Stevens), who leads the Radicals in Congress bent on punishing the South, is held in thrall by a thirst for personal revenge and by his mulatto housekeeper: a "strange brown woman of sinister animal beauty and the restless eyes of a leopardess." Under Stoneman's direction, the Negro-dominated legislature plots to take property from the disenfranchised whites, as well as to legalize miscegenation and mixed marriages. The long-suffering whites endure this threat only so long. When the animalistic Negro Gus (in Federal uniform) breaks into the home of Mrs. Lenoir and her daughter Marion, the sweetheart of all Piedmont, brutally beating them both, Dixon sensationalizes the inevitable rape of Marion and the subsequent racial outrage. To escape the shame of the cruel rape, mother and daughter choose to throw themselves off Lover's Leap in a joint suicide. The noble Klan rises up and executes vengeance on Gus and his partners and disarms the Negro troops. A racial war erupts, and Stoneman's conspiracy unravels in the face of white solidarity, black corruption, and Klan gallantry. Stoneman himself relents only when his son Phil is arrested by Negro troops and is nearly executed. (He is saved at the last minute, of course, by the Klan.) Elsie relents and marries Ben, his sister Margaret marries Phil, and whites resume control of their beloved land.

Ten years later, when the Southern-born D. W. Griffith released his groundbreaking film *Birth of a Nation*, based on *The Clansman* and *The Leopard's Spots* (1902), public controversy intensified. Like the novel, the film unabashedly condemns Reconstruction and its excesses, in the process demonizing the Negro as the rapacious dupe of Yankee carpetbaggers and the savage defiler of Southern white womanhood. In a departure from the novel's plot, Silas Lynch, the salacious mulatto right-hand carpetbagger to Stoneman, designs to have Elsie for himself. She spurns Lynch, who then assaults her, as blue-coated Negro soldiers run rampant in the streets. Father Stoneman comes to his reconciliatory sense in the nick of time when Elsie is about to be ravished by the evil Lynch. The noble Clan rides to the rescue, saving the lives of Stoneman, his son Phil, and daughter Elsie (winning her heart for the gallant Clan leader, young Colonel Cameron). However, in another departure from the novel, they are too late to save the little sister of Ben Cameron, who is raped by the Northern Negro Gus— but only symbolically, since she throws herself off the cliff rather than submit to Gus's black desires.

Everett Carter estimates that more than 3 million people saw the film in the first ten months in New York alone. The film caused quite a stir in 1915 and prompted President Woodrow Wilson, Griffith's fellow Virginian, to say that "it was like writing history with lightning" (quoted in Carter). It still causes a stir, prompting protests and demonstrations when it is shown. The influence of the overt racism of this novel and film on American culture cannot be fully measured. Besides furthering the cause of separation of the races as the principle that will save the South and American culture, *Birth of a Nation* led directly to the resurgence of the Klan in the 1920s, especially in the Midwest.

Other titles among Dixon's published novels are *The Traitor* (1907), *The Fall of a Nation* (1916), *A Man of the People* (1920), *The Man in Gray* (1921), *The Black Hood* (1924), and *The Flaming Sword* (1930). He wrote a play, *The Sins of the Father* (1912), and the photo play for *Birth of a Nation* (1915). He also wrote a theological work entitled *What Is Religion? An Outline of Vital Ritualism* (1892).

REFERENCES

Carter, Everett. "Cultural History Written with Lightning: The Significance of *The Birth of a Nation* (1915)." *Hollywood as Historian: American Film in a Cultural Context.* Ed. Peter C. Rollins. Lexington: University Press of Kentucky, 1983. 9–19.

Cook, Raymond Allen. *Thomas Dixon.* New York: Twayne, 1974.

Oliver, Lawrence J. "Writing from the Right during the 'Red Decade': Thomas Dixon's Attack on W.E.B. Du Bois and James Weldon Johnson in *The Flaming Sword.*" *American Literature* 70 (March 1998): 131–152.

Randal W. Allred

DOS PASSOS, JOHN (1896–1970). Raised in America and Europe, John Dos Passos was the product of a long-term affair between a Washington, D.C., widow and a prominent New York lawyer. In the summer of 1917, a year after his graduation from Harvard, Dos Passos volunteered for the Norton-Harjes Ambulance Service in France. He served as an ambulance driver on the Verdun front and later, under the auspices of the American Red Cross, in northern Italy.

Dos Passos was one of the most prolific and outspoken antiwar writers to emerge in the post–World War I era. Between 1920 and 1932 he published three war novels, and his innovative literary technique and bold attack upon traditional notions of warfare helped establish his reputation as a daring young writer. In *Men at War*, **Ernest Hemingway** exclaimed of Dos Passos's seminal novel *Three Soldiers* that "the writing of it was as valuable a pioneering feat in American letters as some minor Lewis or Clark's expedition into the North West."

Despite his service in the ambulance corps, Dos Passos was no eager warbacker. He had strong pacifist leanings and scornfully dismissed the idea that the war was being fought to protect democracy or to achieve some other lofty goal. In August 1917, Dos Passos wrote a friend, "The war is utter damn nonsense—a vast cancer fed by lies and self seeking malignity on the part of those who don't do the fighting. . . . [E]verything said & written & thought in America about the war is lies—God! They choke one like poison gas." In another letter to the same friend, Dos Passos added, "If people could only realize the inanity of it—or if they had the courage to stop being dupes . . . I am convinced that it is through pure cowardice that the war continues."

The first of his war novels, the brief and highly autobiographical *One Man's Initiation—1917* (1920) is the work of a novice, ideologically clunky and lacking the finesse of Dos Passos's later novels. Though it draws upon Dos Passos's own experience on the French front in 1917, the characters are never quite fully developed. However, the novel includes a memorable scene in which the protagonist, Martin Howe, comes across a tilting, roadside crucifix. Someone has replaced Christ's crown of thorns with a crown of barbed wire, and as Howe looks on, a passing soldier kicks the crucifix so that it falls face down into the mud. The symbolism—that the war destroyed old pieties—is hard to miss. Despite its shortcomings, *One Man's Initiation* provides early evidence of Dos Passos's efforts to use fiction to convey his sense of the futility and tragedy of the war.

In 1921 Dos Passos's second war novel, *Three Soldiers*, immediately sparked a controversy. The lengthy work traces three American soldiers from their days in training camp to their days in postwar France. None of the trio achieves anything like traditional military glory. The Harvard aesthete, Andrews, goes AWOL after the armistice and on the novel's final page is arrested by the military police. The gun-happy Midwesterner, Chrisfield, kills an officer, but his dirty deed goes undetected and unpunished. The shop clerk from San Francisco, Fuselli, dreams of rising through the ranks, but he is court-martialed for contracting venereal disease and ends up on permanent KP (kitchen patrol) duty in a labor battalion.

Making overt use of machine imagery throughout *Three Soldiers*, Dos Passos none too subtly suggests that modern war turns soldiers into "automatons" who engage in "industrialised slaughter." Despite the outcry of indignant war supporters who accused Dos Passos of maliciously slandering the rank and file of the American Expeditionary Forces, the novel was a great popular success.

After a decade-long hiatus, Dos Passos returned to the commanding theme of World War I in his novel *1919*, published in 1932. The work, which ultimately would become the second volume in Dos Passos's *U.S.A.* trilogy, makes use of a variety of innovative literary techniques. Interspersed with passages of straight narrative are "Newsreel" sections (composites of news headlines, song lyrics, and other ephemeral snippets of the era), brief biographical sketches of famous men (Wilson, Morgan, etc.), and "The Camera Eye" sections (stream-of-consciousness passages expressing Dos Passos's own point of view). The five main fictional characters in the novel are Joe Williams (a sailor), Dick Savage (a self-centered Harvard man), Eveline Hutchins (a Red Cross worker), "Daughter" (a relief worker), and Ben Compton (a Jewish radical from New York). The novel concludes with a bitterly sardonic section, "The Body of an American," describing the burial of John Doe (the unknown soldier) in Arlington National Cemetery.

Less well known in Dos Passos's 1939 *Adventures of a Young Man*, a novel of the Spanish Civil War, which reflects the author's disillusionment with communism. His hero, Glenn Spottswood, becomes a labor organizer whose efforts are crippled by the interference of the Communist Party. Imprisoned in Spain for Trotskyite sympathies, Spottswood, facing execution, dies instead on a suicide mission that is the cost of his freedom.

Dos Passos's works of nonfiction include *Tour of Duty* (1946), based upon his experiences as a correspondent in World War II; *Mr. Wilson's War* (1962), a study of Woodrow Wilson and U.S. history in the early twentieth century; and his memoir *The Best Times* (1966).

REFERENCES

Carr, Virginia Spencer. *Dos Passos: A Life*. New York: Doubleday, 1984.
Dos Passos, John. *The Fourteenth Chronicle: Letters and Diaries of John Dos Passos*.
    Ed. Townsend Ludington. Boston: Gambit, 1973.
Ludington, Townsend. *John Dos Passos: A Twentieth Century Odyssey*. New York: Dutton, 1980.
Maine, Barry, ed. *Dos Passos: The Critical Heritage*. New York: Routledge, 1988.

Cynthia Wachtell

DUNBAR, PAUL LAURENCE (1872–1904). Poet, novelist, and short story writer Paul Laurence Dunbar was born the son of ex-slaves in Dayton, Ohio, in 1872, a town that later served as the setting for some of his most significant works of fiction. Educated at Dayton's Central High, Dunbar would publish his first war poem, "Our Martyred Soldiers," in 1888, three years before his graduation. Given that Dunbar's father enlisted in the Union army in 1863, it seems natural that Dunbar would be drawn to war as a literary theme. Although he did go on to write a handful of poems protesting the forgotten heroics of black soldiers, it is not until *The Fanatics* (1902), his third novel, that Dunbar gives the subject of the Civil War an in-depth analysis. By then, his concerns had changed dramatically. Dunbar self-published his first book of poems, *Oak and Ivy*, in 1892. His second volume, *Majors and Minors* (1896), was reviewed favorably by **William Dean Howells**, who would write the introduction to his third volume, *Lyrics of a Lowly Life* (1896). Two years later, Dunbar produced his first collection of short stories, *Folks from Dixie*, and his first novel, *The Uncalled*. His finest novel, *The Sport of the Gods*, was published in 1902, only two years before his death. The author of five volumes of poems, four collections of short stories, and four novels, Dunbar remains one of the most influential and prolific figures in African American literature.

Set in the small town of Dorbury, Ohio (a fictionalized Dayton), *The Fanatics* is the story of three white families ripped apart by their differing allegiances during the Civil War. Dunbar takes the theme of a "house divided" and offers it in dizzying triplicate: Stephen Van Doren, a staunch Democrat, rejects his "copperhead" son Robert for refusing to align himself with the either the Northern or the Southern cause. Bradford Waters, an equally ardent Republican, lauds his son's choice to join the Union army but disowns his daughter for her unwillingness to break off her romance with Robert. Colonel Alexander Stewart, a displaced Southerner, denounces his Unionist son as a traitor to his heritage. Waters loses his son; Van Doren returns with an arm missing after having joined the war to assuage his father. At the close of the conflict, the families reconcile, recognizing the unnecessary price all paid for their "fanaticism." While it may appear that Dunbar's novel falls into the most obvious traps of sentimental fiction, Dunbar overtly mocks the characters' melodrama and, with it, the melodramatic postwar narratives that emerged to heal the psychological wounds left by a long, massive, brutal war. The characters repeatedly refer to "their principles," yet their principles are unconvincingly articulated; the war, one character says, is "for the Union and State's rights and all of that." The "all of that," Dunbar implies, is slavery—the issue the nation only belatedly acknowledged as the underlying cause of the war. The one black character in the novel, the town crier "Nigger Ed," is ridiculed as a "dog" until after he joins the war, nursing the dying and wounded of Dorbury. Although the town still considers him less than a man, he becomes their "pet," valued not for his own humanity but for the stories he relays of their lost sons' deaths in the battlefield. A stinging criticism of both national and racial conflict, *The Fanatics* stands as an invaluable contribution to American war literature.

REFERENCES

Martin, Jay, ed. *A Singer in the Dawn: Reinterpretations of Paul Laurence Dunbar.* New York: Dodd Mead, 1975.
Revell, Peter. *Paul Laurence Dunbar.* Boston: Twayne, 1979.

Jennifer C. James

DUNBAR, RUTH (1882–1963). Little is known about Ruth Dunbar today. During her lifetime, she wrote two novels, one, *The White Tide*, published posthumously in 1993, on the thirtieth anniversary of Dunbar's death. Her only other known published work, *The Swallow: A Novel Based Upon the Actual Experiences of One of the Survivors of the Famous Lafayette Escadrille* (1919), is an unsentimental story of the human side of war.

The narrator of the novel, Richard Byrd, leaves his home and his fiancée in El Paso, Texas, in order to fight as an aviator in World War I. Having been turned down for enlistment in the British fighting forces, he makes his way to France and joins the Foreign Legion, despite his having failed the vision test. Dunbar suggests the expendability of human life in combat by noting that anyone can join the Legion, even if unfit for service. The narrator, however, describes joining the Legion as being "born again": "[I]t is the international revival meeting, the great chance to start life clean." Dunbar's religious imagery captures the fervent zeal and blind faith that lead Byrd and others like him to seek adventure without thought of the sacrifices of family, the potential for death, or the purpose of the fight.

Dunbar does not focus on battle scenes or politics of war. Instead, she draws attention to the human consequences of war that go by unnoticed or addressed. The discussion of aviator training is marked by the juxtaposition of the eagerness for battle and the high death rate for pilots during training. In the battle of Verdun, Byrd is shot, and Dunbar's criticism of war heightens. The inhumanity of war takes on a personal face when those who administer to the sick and dying do so with routinized impersonality. Despite a young man calling out for comfort, a priest refuses to offer comfort until he is convinced the soldier is Roman Catholic. The field hospital and personnel, ill-equipped to attend to the continuing stream of wounded soldiers, allow soldiers to linger in the midst of death without attention; some, like Byrd, lie for days "without moving an inch in a reeking mass of blood, pus, and perspiration." Because of incompetence, drug addiction develops. Despite a discussion of some of the medical techniques used to save lives and limbs, the novel suggests these advancements come at too high a price.

REFERENCE

Rev. of *The Swallow*, by Ruth Dunbar. *New York Times Review of Books* 1 June 1919: 306+.

Pamela Monaco

DUNNE, FINLEY PETER (1867–1936). Finley Peter Dunne was born in Chicago, Illinois. After serving on the editorial staffs of the *Evening-Post* and *Times-Herald* from 1892 to 1897, he became editor of the Chicago *Journal*, acting in that capacity from 1897 to 1900. A member of the second generation of nineteenth-century American humorists who were influenced by Artemus Ward, Petroleum V. Nasby, and **Mark Twain**, Dunne is best known as the author of a series of essays featuring an alter ego, "Mr. Dooley," an Irish saloon keeper in Chicago.

Mr. Dooley's (and Dunne's) widespread popularity among readers rested on the barkeep's thick brogue, his shrewd outlook on life and society, and his biting commentary on contemporary events and leaders. Dismay and anger at social and political injustice, as well as sympathy for the downtrodden and the unprivileged, infused all of Dunne's works.

In 1898, spurred by the outbreak of the Spanish-American War, to which—as with all wars—he had an inherent and ironic aversion, Dunne put together some of his clippings from the *Post* and the *Journal* in a volume he called *Mr. Dooley in Peace and War* (1898). Encouraged by the success of this volume, Dunne followed with *Mr. Dooley's Philosophy* (1900), which included essays on the Boer War, and *Dissertations by Mr. Dooley* (1906) and *Mr. Dooley Says* (1910), each of which offered up some of Dunne's biting commentary on the Russo-Japanese War. Looking backward in 1899, Dunne included one essay on the Civil War in *Mr. Dooley in the Hearts of His Countrymen*.

Somewhat jaded by the persistence of war during his lifetime, Dunne had a tendency to shy away from commenting on the First World War. However, he did manage a few essays on this international catastrophe in *Mr. Dooley on Making a Will and Other Necessary Evils* (1919).

REFERENCES

Ellis, Elmer. *Mr. Dooley's America: A Life of Finley Peter Dunne*. New York: Knopf, 1941.
Fanning, Charles. *Finley Peter Dunne and Mr. Dooley: The Chicago Years*. Lexington: University Press of Kentucky, 1978.

Filler, Louis, ed. *The World of Mr. Dooley*. New York: Collier, 1962.
Schaaf, Barbara, C. "The Man Who Invented Mr. Dooley." *Chicago Magazine* 26.3
       (March 1977): 116–217.

Peter Katopes

E

EASTLAKE, WILLIAM (1917–1997). Brooklyn-born William Derry Eastlake spent four years in the U.S. Infantry and was wounded at the Battle of the
Bulge. As a young man, he knew Theodore Dreiser, Nathaniel West, and Clifford Odets. Between 1948 and 1950, he studied at the Alliance Française in
Paris. He settled on a working ranch in New Mexico, where he wrote four of
his seven novels about the fictional "Checkboard" region. His war novels, *Castle
Keep* (1965), *The Bamboo Bed* (1969), and *The Long Naked Descent into Boston*
(1977), are intricate texts that belong with the surreal work of **Joseph Heller,
Kurt Vonnegut, Thomas Pynchon, Mark Twain**, and **Herman Melville**.

In *Castle Keep*, the one-eyed Major Falconer and his scruffy band of shell-
shocked soldiers find their way through the Ardennes to the castle of Maldorais,
an art treasure-house owned by the Comte de Maldorais and Thérèse, his wife-
niece-daughter (it is never clear how they are related). The novel is episodic:
The men visit the whorehouse in town, take a gondola out into the nearby
swamp to find Americans and Germans, sell each other postwar tract housing,
and listen to lectures on art, the Bhagavad Gita, and Freudian psychoanalysis.
Finally the Germans attack the castle and kill everyone except Pfc. Alistair
Benjamin, a would-be novelist, and Thérèse, now pregnant with Falconer's
child; their escape has been ensured by the obsessed Major.

The novel is a satirical discussion of war, art, and culture. Pfc. Benjamin
writes, "the people moved about the streets with Utrillo-like stiffness, and the
castle was by Rembrandt, the king, Major Falconer, a Roualt, and all the whores
were by Modigliani. The war was by us." Art historian Captain Beckman is
determined to save Maldorais, just as Falconer is convinced it must be destroyed
if the German line is to be broken. Their struggle parallels the one in *Moby
Dick* between Ahab (Falconer) and Starbuck (Beckman), observed by Ishmael
(Benjamin). Despite dark loomings (Sergeant Rossi asks, "Did you hear a
scream? . . . It sounded like a woman or an eagle or a world coming to an end.
Everything I've never heard"), Benjamin concludes hopefully, "We had the castle within us. We carried it away."

Castle Keep is a postmodern text: Beckman gives Benjamin the title of East-lake's book and cautions the reader to "remember, despite the ancient castle, this cannot be a Gothic tale because it was the Second World War." The nar-rative is shared by the squad members, all of whom prove eloquently insightful.

Eastlake's 1965 somewhat hopeful, if cool, assessment of America's cultural illnesses had become a hot rage by 1969 as he watched America immolate itself (and Asia) in Vietnam. *The Bamboo Bed*'s spiraling narrative moves back and forth in time, giving us an account of Captain Clancy, a **Custer**-like figure whose military successes are ended by his disastrous assault on Ridge Red Boy. As with *Castle Keep*, the novel is episodic. There are four bamboo beds: the one slept in by Clancy and Madame Dieudonné (a French rubber plantation owner); a search and rescue helicopter nicknamed the *Bamboo Bed*; the bed where Nurse Jane and Captain Knightbridge sleep; and the stand of bamboo the dying Clancy lies in throughout the novel. Other characters include Peter (a deserter) and Bethany (a hippie) who offer flowers to the troops and sing folks songs; Mike, Clancy's oldest friend, who's sent by army intelligence to find and kill Clancy; and the crazed, apparently armless Colonel Yvor who fires a ma-chine gun by pulling a lanyard with his teeth, whose greatest pleasure is prowl-ing the jungle in an attack helicopter. Ultimately the groups are united by the bamboo beds and kill each other or are killed by the Vietnamese.

Angrier and less ironic than *Castle Keep, The Bamboo Bed* is an indictment of colonialism (French and American) and an attack on American racism and on the devaluation of sex and love in the face of war. Eastlake suggests that Nazism is never far away, specifically accusing Westmoreland and McNamara. "Love is a lot of Christian shit that went on all over Germany while the Germans were burning people in ovens," Clancy thinks. "And now love goes on all over America while Americans are burning people in villages." Eastlake frets about sex and militarism: "When you get out of West Point you don't even know what to do with your pecker," says Knightbridge, "excepting to point it at the enemy . . . and get it blown off." America is better at murder and castration than life and creation (Knightbridge has a vision of "millions of gallons of red blood" used as a defoliant in Vietnam). Colonel Yvor, one of Dr. Strangelove's rela-tions, "was the war all by himself." Once more war is personified: deformed, mutilated, obsessed, murderous—Ahab.

In his collection of poetry and articles *A Child's Garden of Verses for the Revolution* (1970) Eastlake cannot contain his rage with America. He sees the same forces of colonialism operating in Asia as in the American Southwest. During an address to West Point cadets Eastlake noted that "responsibility is non-transferable. You cannot say after wiping out a village, 'My superior told me to do it.' You're big boys now. Behave yourselves. Don't blame all your sins on General Westmoreland." His early discussions of art and castles give way to caustic ire about humanity's propensity for evil: "You don't think man is smart? You don't think man will prevail?" one of his characters asks. "You should see him behave in Asia."

Eastlake's last novel, *The Long Naked Descent into Boston* (1977), is another postmodern narrative, this time about America's Revolutionary War, told from the vantage point of a group of journalists who observe the Battle of Breed's Hill from a hot-air balloon. The novel is considered by most critics to be a failure.

REFERENCES

Eastlake, William. "William Eastlake." *Contemporary Authors Autobiography Series.* Vol. 1. Detroit: Gale, 1984. 201–214.

Haslam, Gerald. *William Eastlake.* Austin: Steck-Vaughn Company, 1970.

McPheron, William. "The Critical Reception of William Eastlake." *Review of Contemporary Fiction* 3.1 (1983): 84–92.

Mottram, Eric. "The Limits of Survival with the Weapons of Humour: William Eastlake." *Review of Contemporary Fiction* 3.1 (1983): 68–83.

Tim Blackmore

EASTMAN, CHARLES ALEXANDER (1858–1939). Charles Eastman, a Dakota Sioux, was born as Ohiyesa in Minnesota during the Indian wars of the later part of the nineteenth century. He was reared by his grandparents in Canada, where they fled from U.S. soldiers after the 1862 Dakota uprising. His father, Many Lightnings, whom the family believed was hanged after the Dakota uprising, returned when Ohiyesa was fifteen years old and insisted his son receive "the white man's education" after he himself had been converted to Christianity, taking the name Jacob Easton. Ohiyesa was baptized as Charles Alexander Eastman, and after studying at Dartmouth and earning his medical degree from Boston University Medical School, he practiced medicine at the Pine Ridge Reservation, where his people referred to him as the "Indian white doctor." In his autobiography, he wrote of the Wounded Knee Massacre (1890) in which U.S. soldiers attacked a village and then tracked down and killed scores of fleeing women and children. Although he believed that the massacre was started by a few "hot-headed" Indians, he was shaken by the callousness with which they were killed. Eastman registered his complaints, thereby earning the disfavor of his employers and being fired. He moved back East with his wife and children and began writing books for young people, celebrating a rather idealistic view of the Native American way.

In *From the Deep Woods to Civilization: Chapters in the Autobiography of an Indian* (1916), Eastman described how he organized a small rescue party to go out onto the freezing plains to look for survivors of the Wounded Knee Massacre. Many of the dead were found frozen in the snow, sometimes huddled together where they were shot trying to escape the soldiers. The wounded and dying were scattered about, crying and singing their own death songs. Some members of the rescue party recognized their own kinsmen, which excited even more grief among them. Although Eastman was appalled by the massacre, he differentiated between the Native Americans who succumbed to the "Ghost

Dance Craze" and those who came to the fort for safety as "Christian Indians." The children who survived the massacre, he reported, were placed with "kind Christian families."

A major theme throughout all of Eastman's writing is the civilizing influence of Christianity. This theme is continued in *Wigwam Evenings* (1909), a collection of stories in which young warriors, wise grandfathers, and animals offer important lessons about how to live in harmony within the "Great Mystery." In *Indian Boyhood* (1902) and *The Soul of the Indian* (1911), the "Great Mystery" is compared favorably as being very much like Christianity, inferring an innate goodness that Native Americans already possess. *Old Indian Days* (1907) contains a curious story of a "Chief Soldier" who marries a white woman who eventually returns to her own people. By mutual agreement, the parentage of the children is kept secret, but one will grow up to become a "minister of the Christian gospel" and thus be saved from his coarser heritage. Although these stories and autobiography bear witness to a period of great upheaval for Native Americans, the theme of Christianity from the "deep woods" of dark wilderness to the light of "civilization" lends an unsteady picture of one of the most bloody periods of American history. Many of Eastman's works have been reissued by the University of Nebraska Press.

REFERENCES

Eastman, Charles. *From the Deep Woods to Civilization: Chapters in the Autobiography of an Indian*. New York: Little, Brown, 1916.
Flood, Renée Sansom. *Lost Bird of Wounded Knee: Spirit of the Lakota*. New York: Scribner's, 1995.
McLaird, James D. "The Writings of Ohiyesa—Charles Alexander Eastman, M.D., Santee Sioux." *South Dakota History* 6 (1975): 55–73.
Wilson, Raymond. *Ohiyesa: Charles Eastman, Santee Sioux*. Urbana: University of Illinois Press, 1983.

Renate W. Prescott

EDMONDS, WALTER D. (1903–1998). Born in Boonville, New York, Edmonds took a degree from Harvard, where he edited the *Advocate* and began writing fiction. He published stories in *Scribner's, The Atlantic Monthly*, and *McCall's* before finishing his first novel, *Rome Haul* (1929), an account of life along the Erie Canal during the 1850s. With this book, Edmonds began a series that chronicled American life in the Mohawk Valley in central New York from the American Revolution to the start of the twentieth century. *The Big Barn* (1930), *Erie Water* (1933), and *Chad Hanna* (1940) all deal with life in this region.

Edmond's most successful book, critically and commercially, was *Drums along the Mohawk* (1936), set on the New York frontier during the Revolution. Mixing fictional characters like Gilbert and Lana Martin with historical ones like General Nicholas Herkimer, he gives a vivid account of events there between 1776 and 1784, including the Battle of Oriskany and the massacre at Cherry Valley. His account of military action between the Mohawk Valley farmers and British and Indian forces provides both an accurate historical account and a fast-paced story. As in other novels, Edmonds focuses on events in the daily lives of his fictional characters and undertakes little analysis of the military or political forces at work in the Revolutionary period. John Ford directed a movie version in 1939.

Twice married, to Eleanor Stetson and Katherine Baker-Carr, Edmonds received the Newbery Medal for his juvenile novel *The Matchlock Gun* (1941) and the National Book Award for *Bert Green's Barn* (1975), another book for younger readers. In 1995, he published a book about his own childhood, entitled *Tales My Father Never Told*. Edmonds, who died January 24, 1998, received honorary degrees from Union College, Rutgers, Colgate, and Harvard, and he was a member of the National Academy of Arts and Sciences.

REFERENCE

Wyld, Lionel D. *Walter D. Edmonds, Storyteller*. Syracuse: Syracuse University Press, 1982.

Robert C. Petersen

EHRHART, W. D. (1948–   ). Born and raised in small Pennsylvania towns, William Daniel Ehrhart enlisted in the Marine Corps immediately following his graduation from high school in 1966. He served in Vietnam with an infantry battalion from 1967 to 1968 and was wounded in the battle for Hue during the Tet Offensive of 1968. Released from active duty in 1969, Ehrhart went on to graduate from Swarthmore College (1973) and to earn an M.A. in creative writing from the University of Illinois at Chicago (1978).

Ehrhart first gained national recognition as a poet in *Winning Hearts and Minds* (1972), a collection of Vietnam War poetry dedicated to the cause of ending America's involvement. Eight of Ehrhart's early poems appeared in this collection. His poems have since appeared in a number of venues, including literary journals and national newspapers. His poetry collections include *A Generation of Peace* (1975), *The Samisdat Poems* (1980), *To Those Who Have Gone Home Tired* (1984), *The Outer Banks and Other Poems* (1984), *Just for Laughs* (1990), *The Distance We Travel* (1993), and *Beautiful Wreckage: New and Selected Poems* (1999). Some of Ehrhart's most widely excerpted and commented upon poems are "The One That Died," "A Relative Thing," "Making the Children Behave," and "Letter"—all of which have been praised for their "precision and control" as well as their provocative challenge to the American sense of identity and purpose (Beidler 159–160). Ehrhart has also edited two collections of Vietnam War poetry, *Unaccustomed Mercy: Soldier-Poets of the Vietnam War* (1989) and *Carrying the Darkness: The Poetry of the Vietnam War* (1985, 1989), and, along with Jan Barry, coedited a third, *Demilitarized Zones: Veterans after Vietnam* (1976). Companion enterprises are his *Soldier-Poets of the*

Korean War, which appeared as a special issue of *War, Literature, and the Arts* (1997) and the anthology *Retrieving Bones: Stories and Poems of the Korean War* (with Philip K. Jason, 1999).

Ehrhart established himself in prose with *Vietnam-Perkasie* (1983), an artful memoir of his Vietnam experience written in the form of a nonfiction novel. Following *Vietnam-Perkasie*, Ehrhart wrote a second memoir, *Passing Time* (1986, 1995), centered on his postwar experiences as a G.I. Bill student at Swarthmore. Not simply a sequel, *Passing Time* is a self-contained nonfiction novel that features well-realized dramatic flashbacks to his Vietnam experiences skillfully interwoven between comic episodes of undergraduate life. Ehrhart's third major prose work, *Busted: A Vietnam Veteran in Nixon's America* (1995), is an essentially realistic account of Ehrhart's ironic efforts to avoid federal prosecution on a minor marijuana charge while the country at large was grappling with the Watergate scandal. *Busted*, however, melds fact and fiction. The ghosts of three former friends killed in Vietnam appear at regular intervals and function like a Greek chorus throughout the narrative. The exchanges between the narrator and these ghosts seem calculated to make the reader aware of just how far America in the 1970s had devolved from the innocent ideals of the generation it sent into Vietnam.

A veterans' activist as well as a writer, Ehrhart in 1987 published *Going Back*, a book-length account of his 1985 trip to Vietnam in the company of fellow writers **John Balaban** and **Bruce Weigl**. He is also featured in episode 5, "America Takes Charge," of the PBS series *Vietnam: A Television History*. In 1999, Ehrhart published *Ordinary Lives: Platoon 1005 and the Vietnam War*, a series of profiles that follows, through Vietnam and beyond, the lives of those young Marines with whom Ehrhart trained at Parris Island in 1966. While Ehrhart's commercial success remains limited, critics have long recognized him to be one of the most distinctive and influential voices to emerge from the American experience in Vietnam. A special issue of the journal *War, Literature & the Arts* (Smith 1–30) is dedicated to his contribution.

REFERENCES

Beidler, Philip D. *Re-Writing America: Vietnam Authors in Their Generation*. Athens: University of Georgia Press, 1991.

Smith, Lorrie. "Against a Coming Extinction: W. D. Ehrhart and the Evolving Canon of Vietnam Veteran's Poetry." *War, Literature & the Arts* 8.2 (1996): 1–30.

Tal, Kali. *Worlds of Hurt: Reading the Literatures of Trauma*. New York: Cambridge University Press, 1996.

Edward F. Palm

ELIOT, THOMAS STEARNS (1888–1965). Born in St. Louis, Missouri, T. S. Eliot was educated in St. Louis until 1906 when he entered Harvard University. After graduation, he spent a year at the Sorbonne and then returned to Harvard for doctoral work. In 1914, he received a Traveling Fellowship to Marburg, Germany. Due to the outbreak of World War I, however, he went to London. Although Eliot did not write extensively about war, his desire to serve the war effort and his expression of the times in his verse illustrate the effect war had on his life.

Eliot made several attempts to volunteer during World War I. Prior to the United States' entrance into the war, he tried enlisting in the U.S. Navy but was rejected because of a hernia. In August–September 1918, he then tried joining the Intelligence services of both the U.S. Navy and Army, but red tape prevented his enlistment. Although he did not create poetry specifically about World War I, Eliot's work reflects the desolation of the period. "Gerontion," which he wrote between 1917 and 1919, expresses an atmosphere of isolation and sterility. The poem opens with the speaker declaring himself a thirsty old man awaiting the rain in a typically drought-ridden month while a boy reads to him. The speaker then confesses that he has had no personal experience at the "hot gates" of battle. In 1922, Eliot published *The Waste Land*. This landmark poem expresses the loss of belief and sense of disillusionment that pervaded the postwar period. For many of this generation, the war had shattered meaning and reduced the world to a pile of fractured bits. As Eliot declares, in the section entitled "What the Thunder Said," that the once vibrant survivors of the war era endure, but gradually they die fitful deaths.

By the start of World War II, Eliot had converted to Anglicanism and gained British citizenship. Because of the German bombings, Eliot served as a fire watcher on the roof of the Faber and Faber offices during the winter of 1940–1941. His observations from these rooftops appear in Part II of the "Little Gidding" section of the *Four Quartets*. He likens the aftermath of destruction that lingered after a bombing as literally a dust inhaled, symbolizing the air of death and despair wrought by Nazi raids. Eliot also generated other works regarding World War II. "Defense of the Islands," which he hesitates to describe as verse, commemorates the sacrifices of those who defended Britain. He speaks to future generations so they understand the events of the prior as duties fulfilled on command and through obedience. The other short work inspired by the war is "A Note on War Poetry." In this work, war becomes a series of circumstances that cannot be avoided but must be met head-on instead through appropriate military tactics.

REFERENCES

Ackroyd, Peter. *T. S. Eliot: A Life*. New York: Simon and Schuster, 1984.
Alldritt, Ken. *Modernism in the Second World War: The Later Poetry of Ezra Pound, T. S. Eliot, Basil Bunting, and Hugh MacDiarmid*. New York: Peter Lange, 1989.
Eliot, T. S. *The Complete Poems and Plays, 1909–1950*. New York: Harcourt, 1971.
Kenner, Hugh. *The Invisible Poet: T. S. Eliot*. New York: McDowell Oblensky, 1959.

Paul R. Cappucci

EMERSON, GLORIA (1929–   ). Gloria Emerson began her career as a journalist at age twenty-one when she began doing editorial work for *Prome-*

nade, a magazine distributed to New York hotel guests. Never having attended university, Emerson learned her craft in the field. She first went to Vietnam in 1956 as a freelancer. She began her work for the *New York Times* in 1957 as a writer of women's features and was allowed to return to Vietnam in February 1970. She remained until the end of the war. Profoundly affected by her experiences in Vietnam, Emerson won the 1971 Polk Award for foreign reporting on the effects of the war on the people of South Vietnam.

She quit the paper to write *Winners & Losers: Battles, Retreats, Gains, Losses, and Ruins from the Vietnam War* for which she won the 1978 National Book Award, the same year **Michael Herr**'s *Dispatches* was nominated for the award. Emerson used her notes and tapes from Vietnam and interviews from people in twenty-four states to write *Winners & Losers*. Written in the style of New Journalism, the book is a woven composite of what the war did to people on all sides of it, including veterans, deserters, draft evaders, former prisoners of war, bereaved parents, members of various antiwar movements, and defenders of U.S. intervention in Indochina. Through it all, she portrays herself as a woman haunted—even obsessed—by what she has seen and heard. The underlying message throughout her book is not to forget. Her tone is self-righteous at times but always frank as she chooses to allow her readers to experience the results of the war through its effects on individuals.

Emerson's more recent writings include *Some American Men* (1985), a book that focuses, in part, on the lives and practices of Vietnam veterans; "The Children in the Field" (*TriQuarterly* [Winter 1986]), an article on various relationships between children and war; and *Gaza: A Year in the Intifada: A Personal Account from an Occupied Land* (1991). Her continuing scholarly interest in American war experiences is evidenced by her 1994 and 1995 reviews in *The Nation* of Peter Arnett's *Live from the Battlefield: From Vietnam to Baghdad: 35 Years in the World's War Zones* and the Library of America's *Reporting World War Two.*

REFERENCES

Bonn, Maria S. "The Lust of the Eye: Michael Herr, Gloria Emerson, and the Art of Observation." *Papers on Language and Literature*, (Winter 1993): 28–47.

Edwards, Julia. *Women of the World: The Great Foreign Correspondents.* Boston: Houghton Mifflin, 1988.

Samantha J. Ward

EMERSON, RALPH WALDO (1803–1882). One of the central figures in American literature, Emerson was born in Boston and educated at Boston Latin School, Harvard College, and Harvard Divinity School. Following the ministerial heritage of his forebears, Emerson became a Unitarian minister. But disillusioned with the ceremonial practices of the church, thirsty for a more emotional, subjective spirituality, and emotionally crushed by the death of his wife, Ellen Louise Tucker, he resigned his position in 1831 and sailed for Europe. On returning, he moved to Concord (where he lived the rest of his life), and in 1835, he married Lidian (Lydia) Jackson and started a family. A year later he published *Nature*, which delineates the basic tenets of most of his succeeding work and established him as the leading spokesperson for New England Transcendentalism.

Emerson's most famous contribution to war literature is the first quatrain of his "Concord Hymn," written for the 4th of July 1837 unveiling of the North Bridge Battle Monument, which commemorated one of the American Revolution's opening battles:

> By the rude bridge that arched the flood,
>   Their flag to April's breeze unfurled,
> Here once the embattled farmers stood
>   And fired the shot heard round the world.

Before and during the Civil War, Emerson's contributions to the Union were realized much more through speech making and activism than through rhetorical prose or poetry. Though decidedly opposed to slavery at least as early as the mid-1820s, he was not an abolitionist per se. In 1838 he presented a lecture sponsored by the American Peace Society entitled "The Peace Principle" (which appears under the seemingly contradictory title "War" in his collected works). Characteristic of Emerson's essays, the speech bespeaks a complex, philosophical view of warfare. War is useful, he writes, to "educate the senses, call into action the will, and perfect the physical constitution," but, he continues, "sympathy with war is a juvenile and temporary state." Always the meliorist, Emerson foresees a future in which war is unnecessary.

By 1844, influenced by wide reading and the antislavery beliefs of Lydia, Emerson began giving speeches in opposition to slavery. Still, lectures such as "New England Reformers" (1844) posit a belief in reform but not as a means of coercing "the private man" or immolating self-government. Emerson disliked politics, its fixed, artificial, partisan language (which is at odds with his belief in the organic nature of language as discussed in *Nature* and elsewhere). But the Fugitive Slave Law (1851) moved him even closer to a Republican abolitionist position. "The last year has forced us all into politics," he wrote in an 1851 lecture specifically on the Law; and in his writings and public speeches leading up to Fort Sumter, Emerson espoused civil disobedience as a means of protesting such unjust laws. The depth of that conviction was realized in 1854, when he joined the Underground Railway. By championing, financing, and entertaining John Brown before his attack on Harper's Ferry, Emerson actively altered his own earlier belief in "compensation." His support of Brown indicated a shift to the view that sometimes evil prevails and that the direct, militant, Puritanical activism of Brown and his cohorts was the best means for ending the great evil of slavery.

Emerson wrote infrequently in the war years. His chief work in this period was his eulogy to his friend Thoreau, who died in May 1862. In his journals, however, he expressed contempt for the mindlessness of the South in general. In the first three years of the war, Emerson entertained the belief that the conflict would lead to an intellectual and moral regeneration in the country. But as the war dragged on, these beliefs were held in check by his skepticism toward politics, New England politics included. He had mixed views toward Lincoln, and he would later call Johnson "our mad President."

In addition to antislavery speech making, Emerson was appointed a member of the Board of Visitors by Secretary of War Edwin Stanton, and he inspected the cadet corps at West Point. The war was mentally hard on Emerson, and by 1864, he had turned his concerns away from it and back to the realm of the intellectual. After the war, he was unable to recapture the richness that characterizes much of his work in the 1840s and 1850s.

REFERENCES

Aaron, Daniel. *The Unwritten War: American Writers and the Civil War*. Madison: University of Wisconsin Press, 1987.
Baker, Carlos. *Emerson among the Eccentrics: A Group Portrait*. New York: Penguin, 1996.
Neufeldt, Leonard. "Emerson and the Civil War." *Journal of English and German Philology* 71 (1972): 502–513.
Richardson, Robert D., Jr. *Emerson: The Mind on Fire*. Berkeley: University of California Press, 1995.

Bryan L. Moore

EMPEY, ARTHUR GUY (1883–1963). Best known for his war memoir *Over the Top* (1917), Arthur Guy Empey served in the U.S. Cavalry and the National Guard before joining the British Army in 1915. Despite his citizenship in a then-neutral nation, he fought as a machine gunner on the Western Front and returned to the United States only after being seriously wounded during a trench raid. Empey subsequently made the American war effort his personal crusade: He exploited his war experience for its propaganda potential in *Over the Top* (published in England as *From the Fire Step*), promoted Liberty Bonds at public rallies (a period photograph shows Empey wearing a life preserver from the *Lusitania* as he harangues the audience), and produced a guide to trench warfare, *First Call* (1918).

A runaway success (by 1918, the book had passed through twenty-two printings), *Over the Top* is one of the most influential examples of a literary genre that thrived during the Great War—the propaganda memoir. Typically written by soldiers too maimed to return to the front, such texts purport to describe the war, in all its ugliness, from an "authentic" perspective; in addition, they inevitably endorse the Allied cause or contend that comradeship and excitement offset the discomforts of war. Very much of this pattern, *Over the Top* follows Empey from New York (where he learns of the sinking of the *Lusitania* and decides to fight) to England, where he manages to secure a combat post despite his nationality, then on to France. The bulk of the book describes his initiation into the monotony, nervous tension, and fatigue of trench warfare, and it is often surprisingly candid. Confronted by a decomposing corpse, for example, Empey feels a "sort of helpless hopelessness and a mad desire to escape it all" (101). Gloom and nausea dominate many of the battlefield scenes.

Nevertheless, *Over the Top* seldom strays far from its implicit objective of inspiring the reader to emulate the author. Though Empey's animosity toward the Hun is subdued in comparison with many other wartime writers', *Over the Top* still reinforces the image of a cruel and devious enemy. "The Saxons," Empey writes, "though better than the Prussians and Bavarians, have a nasty trait of treachery in their make-up" (156). And, to illustrate the point, he describes how a group of Saxons once arranged a gift exchange with the British soldiers opposite them (à la the Christmas Truce of 1914), then prepared a booby trap for the hapless Tommies. Equally effective, as propaganda, is Empey's assertion that "anticipation is worse than realization"—despite the horrors that *Over the Top* describes. Once at the front, a man discovers that "he finds relief in the fun and comradeship of the trenches" (280).

Whatever subtlety Empey incorporated into his war memoir disappears in the bombastic *First Call*. A collection of tips for Western Front novices, the book opens with the author's personal exhortation to "Sammy": "Just give old Kaiser Bill and his 'wonderful efficiency stuff' such a Yankee walloping that there won't be enough gas left to fill the envelope of one of his baby killing gas bags called Zeppelins" (iii).

REFERENCE

Quinn, Patrick. "The Experience of War in American Patriotic Literature." *Facing Armageddon: The First World War Experienced*. Ed. Hugh Cecil and Peter H. Liddle. London: Leo Cooper, 1996.

                                                                    Steven Trout

EVERSON, WILLIAM (1912–1994). Born in Sacramento to Louis Waldemar Everson, a Norwegian immigrant, and his Minnesota-born wife, Francelia Marie Herber Everson, William Oliver Everson grew up in California's San Joaquin Valley. After graduating from high school in 1931, Everson briefly attended Fresno State College, joining the Civilian Conservation Corps in 1933. Later, back at Fresno State, he began to write poems after discovering the work of **Robinson Jeffers**. In 1938, Everson married and started farming near his parents' house; his earliest poetry reflected his strong identification with nature.

In 1940, with World War II spreading across Europe, Everson registered for the draft, requesting conscientious objector status. In 1942, he defended his unorthodox belief system (which combined Western humanism and Buddhism) before a draft board, stating his conviction that all life is sacred. Upon being drafted in 1943, Everson was sent to a Civilian Public Service camp in Waldport, Oregon.

During these years, Everson wrote numerous antiwar poems, some of which were published in chapbooks printed at the Waldport camp. One chapbook, *X War Elegies* (1943), includes elegiac poems authored by Everson before arriving at Waldport. In this collection the poet bemoans the war's widening swath of destruction and explores his personal reasons for refusing to fight. Another chapbook, *The Waldport Poems* (1944), features the poet's recounting of his difficult transition from civilian life to the conscientious objector camp. In a sequence of poems composed while at Waldport but not published until 1948, Everson discusses his wife's adultery, presenting her behavior as a metaphor for the faithlessness among humans in wartime.

Released from Waldport in 1946, Everson moved to the San Francisco Bay area, divorced, and embarked on a career as a handpress printer. In 1948, after reading St. Augustine's *Confessions*, the poet converted to Catholicism, eventually joining the Dominican Order as a lay monk. During the 1950s and 1960s, Everson, now known as Brother Antoninus, wrote poetry that addressed his spiritual and religious concerns as a monk. In 1969, wanting to remarry, Everson left the Dominican Order. His later secular poems rarely deal with war.

REFERENCES

Bartlett, Lee. *William Everson: The Life of Brother Antoninus.* New York: New Directions, 1988.

Everson, William. *The Residual Years: Poems 1934–1948.* New York: New Directions, 1948.

Hall, James B., Bill Hotchkiss, and Judith Shears, eds. *Perspectives on William Everson.* Grants Pass, OR: Castle Peak Editions, 1992.

Ted Olson

F

FAST, HOWARD (1914–). Howard Melvin Fast, a New York City high school dropout, is known as the prolific author of historical novels that present a fresh, individualistic perspective. For some critics, his later works are marred by his association with the Communist Party, propaganda, and sentimentality. Fast's uncluttered and vivid writing style is his strength, along with his versatility and wide range of interests. Although he held a few odd jobs as a youth and attended the National Academy of Design, Fast has supported himself as a writer and lecturer throughout his long career, despite being ostracized for his loyalty to communism.

Fast's war-related novels include *Conceived in Liberty: A Novel of Valley Forge* (1939), notable for its stark, realistic portrayal of the downtrodden American army's grim winter at Valley Forge; *The Unvanquished* (1942), a vastly sympathetic account of George Washington's military losses and retreats from the Battle of Long Island to his first crossing of the Delaware; and *Citizen Tom Paine* (1944), not a war novel per se but rather a "fictional biography" that provides a startlingly original portrait of the great rabble-rouser and revolutionary pamphleteer who energized the American Revolution. Fast returned yet again to the American Revolution in *April Morning* (1961), a sophisticated portrait of the first day of the fighting. This novel is characterized by moderation and balance—what Andrew Macdonald calls a "virtually perfect relationship between literary character and research, with the sights and sounds of April 19, 1775, effectively integrated into the narrative" (102). Fast also address the American Revolution in *The Crossing* (1971), *The Hessian* (1972), and *Seven Days in June* (1994).

In *Freedom Road* (1944), Fast explores the aftermath of the Civil War, particularly the effects of the war on those whose lives were most changed, the former slaves of the American South. Rather than dealing with the war itself, Fast focuses on the immediate postyears of the Civil War, during the years of Reconstruction, "a period that is considered unromantic and ultimately shameful, when many of the high hopes and aspirations of the war years were sacrificed in an effort to reinstitute prewar 'normalcy' " (MacDonald 68).

The circumstance of war influences several other Fast novels, including *The Last Frontier* (1941), about an Indian campaign of the late 1870s, and *The Winston Affair* (1959), which details aspects of World War II. Fast's poetry includes the small collection *Korean Lullaby* (undated, but 1951 or 1952), a series of poems that questions U.S. involvement in the Korean War. In one segment, servicemen speak from beyond the grave.

Foremost among Fast's works are the five novels that make up the *Immigrants* series. These novels do not emphasize war actions but rather, in their span of a century (from the 1880s to the 1980s), trace the rise, interaction, and occasional decline of several families of newcomers to California. The effects of several wars are woven into the overall tapestry of causes and effects, the happenstances, of the central family's individual and collective lives.

Fast is also well known for *Spartacus* (1951), his novel about the slave revolt in ancient Rome led by the title character. Many critics read this work as a metaphor for the American Revolution, the war that has captivated Fast's imagination for over sixty years.

REFERENCES

Fast, Howard. *Being Red*. Boston: Houghton Mifflin, 1990.
MacDonald, Andrew. *Howard Fast: A Critical Companion*. Westport, CT: Greenwood Press, 1996.
Rideout, Walter B. *The Radical Novel in the United States, 1900–1954: Some Interrelations of Literature and Society*. 1956. New York: Columbia University Press, 1992. 275–285.

Julianne White

FAULKNER, WILLIAM (1897–1962). William Cuthbert Falkner was born on September 25, 1897, in New Albany, Mississippi. He later added the "u." In 1902 his family moved from Ripley to Oxford, and except for occasional absences, he lived there for sixty years. His career in fiction writing is notable for radical modernist experiments in form and an almost complete absorption with the mythical Yoknapatawpha County. Faulkner's reputation is based on his unique bifocal vision combining the history and legends of his own "little postage stamp of native soil" in northern Mississippi with, as he revealed in his 1950 Nobel acceptance speech, "love and honor and pity and pride and sacrifice."

He began his career writing Lost Generation–inspired texts about the Great War. He had recognized that World War I was an event for his generation commensurate with the Civil War. Rejected by the U.S. Army, he enlisted in the Royal Air Force, but his service was limited to flight training in Toronto. However, he returned to Mississippi in a uniform, with a cane, a limp, and a "steel plate" in his skull. Faulkner's war texts—two novels, "The Waste Land" section of *Collected Stories*, and a few fugitive sketches and poems—concern postwar malaise and veterans whose tragedy was that they had *not* died. Faulkner was affected by the romantic legend of air war, its intensity of violence, and the glamorous knighthood of pilots.

A poem "The Lilacs" (one manuscript dated "Jan. 1 1920") portrays a gravely wounded veteran that verbally anticipates Donald Mahon, the maimed, blind, and isolated protagonist of Faulkner's first novel, *Soldiers' Pay* (1926). Helped by another veteran, Donald returns to his Georgia hometown, his minister-father, and his fiancée. Through the shock of his injury, he has lost all remembrance of the past. He exists only for the recollection of one moment, the air battle that left him a living corpse. With the traumatic "repetition" of his injuring, he can die.

Faulkner's third novel, *Sartoris* (1929), is partly the story of Bayard Sartoris, a returning World War I veteran, and partly the story of the family and community to which he returns. In addition, Faulkner relates postwar despair to Sartoris's "doom" and "fatality." Paralleling Bayard and his dead brother John are their Civil War ancestors. Faulkner thus compares the war in a heroic age fought in defense of a homeland with a technological war fought overseas for abstract notions.

A decade later with *The Unvanquished* (1938) Faulkner returns to the Sartoris family during the Civil War and Reconstruction. The narrator Bayard (the grandfather in *Sartoris*) is a boy of twelve at the beginning of the action. All events, however, are seen in retrospect with a man looking for meaning in the past—personal, familial, and regional. The setting is not the battlefield but the home front where the women and children must assume masculine responsibilities. Faulkner further distances events by having Bayard remember his cousin Drusilla telling the story of a past event, the "Great Locomotive Chase," but with the historical opponents reversed, the Confederate engine outrunning the Union.

The story of Sutpen in *Absalom, Absalom!* (1936), the grandest of Faulkner's novels, epitomizes the story of the South as an extreme but representative example of the vicious elements in the plantation system. Here the social and personal converge with Faulkner's alignment of the South's defeat with the destruction of a family and a plantation. The last shot in a fratricidal war is Henry Sutpen's killing his half brother, whom he loves, to stop him marrying their sister, whom they both love, preventing not the incest but the miscegenation. A Mississippi Götterdämmerung occurs when Wash Jones, a poor white, realizes that his idol Sutpen is the exploiter of the land and of people (slaves and poor whites). In despair, he kills Sutpen because he now understands how and why the South lost the war. Published with a map locating sites of his Yoknapatawpha fictions, *Absalom, Absalom!* culminated Faulkner's ruminations on the Civil War's meaning in the moral panorama of history.

Spending eleven years working on *A Fable* (1954), Faulkner began with some of the literary properties of the Great War, a troop-initiated cease-fire, the "Unknown Soldier," and the appearance of a Christ-figure on the battlefield. The book's central conflict is not between nations but between the dualities of human nature, personified by the Supreme General (military hierarchy and power) and his son (peace and unity). To preserve military discipline, the general must order his son's execution. Usually described as abstract and didactic, *A Fable*, nevertheless, combines the realistic and the mythic in one of Faulkner's most elaborate plottings of parallels between "present" events and those of Holy Week.

Finally, as Faulkner reveals in his Nobel Prize speech, his fictional world centers on the human heart in "conflict with itself which alone can make good writing because only that is worth writing about."

REFERENCES

Bradford, M. E. "The Anomaly of Faulkner's World War I Stories." *Mississippi Quarterly* 36 (1983): 243–262.

Faulkner, William. *Absalom, Absalom! "The Corrected Text"* and *The Unvanquished. Novels 1936–1940*. New York: The Library of America, No. 42, 1990.

———. *A Fable. Novels 1942–1954*. New York: The Library of America, No. 73, 1994.

———. *Flags in the Dust*. New York: Random House, 1973. Rpt. of *Sartoris*, 1929.

Gray, Richard. *The Life of William Faulkner: A Critical Biography*. Oxford: Blackwell, 1994.

Gresset, Michel. "Faulkner's War with Wars." *Faulkner and History*. Ed. Javier Coy and Michel Gresset. Salamanca: Ediciones Universidad de Salamanca, 1986.

Kartiganer, Donald M. " 'So I, Who Had Never Had a War . . . ': William Faulkner, War, and the Modern Imagination." *Modern Fiction Studies* 44.3 (Fall 1998): 619–648.

Robert M. Slabey

FIRST WORLD WAR. Although the United States was late in entering the 1914–1918 war and only did so in 1917, the conflict proved crucial in shaping the 1920s as a decade of artistic experiment and intellectual scepticism. For an emergent cohort of writers including **Dos Passos,** Fitzgerald, **Hemingway**, and **Faulkner**, often referred to as the postwar "Lost Generation," the war marked out a psychological barrier between a defunct, older culture in which they were raised and radically new ways of thinking, feeling, and behaving.

During the war years a number of American authors responded actively to appeals that America's duty was to help "make the world safe for democracy" by choosing to serve in war-torn Europe: Dos Passos, Hemingway, and **cummings**, for example, volunteered to be ambulance drivers; several notable women novelists of an older generation, including **Edith Wharton, Willa Cather**, and **Dorothy Canfield Fisher**, carried out charity and relief work; and most influentially, the charismatic poet **Alan Seeger** joined the French Foreign Legion in 1914, wrote francophile poems exhorting Americans to defend "civilization" (including the famous "I Have a Rendezvous with Death," which prophesied his own death), and died heroically in 1916.

When American troops began to fight in 1917, the actualities of mass technological warfare were brought home. Although losses were fewer than during the Civil War, and more soldiers died from diseases than from enemy fire, the conflict irrevocably changed the cultural consciousness of war. Because Allied casualties, by today's standards, were high, a number of writers were inevitably killed or wounded: The religious poet **Joyce Kilmer**, who was one of the first American soldiers to engage in combat, died in battle in 1917; the novelist and dramatist **Laurence Stallings** had his leg amputated at Belleau Wood, which he drew upon in his angry novel *Plumes* (1924), about a war veteran who was badly treated by the postwar government; and dramatist **Robert Sherwood**, who later wrote extensively of the war in a series of plays, including *Waterloo Bridge* (1930), was gassed while fighting with the Canadians at Vimy Ridge. In response to the realities of mechanized war, literary representation largely abandoned the earlier rhetoric of sacrifice and trust for a more critical discourse.

The pervasive sense of malaise and rootlessness evident in the work of younger writers who had voluntarily served in Europe, like Hemingway or Cowley, or been subjected to the harsh routines of military discipline, such as Fitzgerald, Faulkner, **John Peale Bishop, Edmund Wilson**, and **Archibald MacLeish**, helped to set the tone of postwar "disillusionment" in which the values of small-town America were comprehensively challenged. The war acquired potent symbolic value as a spiritual catalyst in novels such as Hemingway's *The Sun Also Rises* (1926): As a literary theme it thus contributed to a new kind of creative sensibility, extending vision and stimulating formal innovation. Among such experimental war writing two modes predominated: the realist or naturalist and the modernist.

The 1920s war novel aimed for authenticity in portraying military life. To achieve this a series of controversial issues were treated, some of which shocked contemporary readers; those addressed included mental breakdown, loss of morale, desertion, class conflict, bureaucratic incompetence and corruption, and what has been called "the psychology of slavery"—how the army oppresses the individual soldier and destroys his identity. Such themes were communicated through a literary technique that emphasized fidelity to detail, a practice deriving indirectly from the sociological and quasi-scientific theories of naturalism. Dos Passos's *Three Soldiers* (1921) is the founder-text of this genre, whose influence is seen later in such works as **Thomas Boyd**'s *Through the Wheat* (1923), which depicts the battles of Chateau-Thierry and Soissons, and **William March**'s interesting, composite novel *Company K* (1933).

Broadly speaking, the conventions of realism became dominant in World War I writing. This is illustrated through an unlikely source, Laurence Stallings and **Maxwell Anderson**'s comedy *What Price Glory?* (1924). At first glance this comic drama, which employs ribald dialogue and exaggerated humor, seems to have little in common with the historical pessimism of *Three Soldiers*. However, on closer inspection, its air of troublesome defiance is seen to echo the central Dos Passos motif of how the army brainwashes its men. *What Price Glory?* displays affinities with other realist texts also in its accurate and bawdy use of formerly taboo language, of pithy soldiers' slang, oaths, and obscenities.

American modernism was well advanced when the foremost war writers began to publish, and Dos Passos, cummings, Hemingway, and Faulkner absorbed its impact. *Three Soldiers*, for example, a novel without easily recognizable transitions, may be understood as an experimental fiction whose simultaneous method of narration and integral patterns of imagery combine both documentary and symbolism in avant-garde fashion.

A major modernist, **Ezra Pound**, not usually considered a war poet, wrote of the conflict in a series of oblique, allusive works. The *Cathay* poems correlatively evoke lonely frontiers, exiled soldiers, and dislocation of family life; *Propertius* mocks the rhetoric of patriotism by exalting love above war; and *Hugh Selwyn Mauberley* laments the tragic waste of a high principled generation. Pound's technical innovations influenced the war poems written by e. e. cummings, who similarly deconstructed orthodox verse, subverted established rules of syntax and grammar, and was anarchic and rebellious in a formal sense. cummings's imprisonment in a French internment camp for insubordinate attitudes was the source for his novel *The Enormous Room* (1922). Whereas Dos Passos explored how the military machine turned men into automatons, cummings emphasized the opposite, that such attempts at behaviorist indoctrination could be defeated by the spark of divinity within human beings. As the United States moved further toward pacifism and isolationism after the war, this insight was in rapport with wider public attitudes. *The Enormous Room* dispenses with chronology, sequential plotting, and traditional characterization and has much in common with the techniques of Cubism or Symbolism.

Although cummings has usually received critical acclaim for his iconoclastic writing, Hemingway is more closely associated with World War I than any other writer. Images found in his fiction such as those of "a separate peace" or "a farewell to arms" have passed into common usage. Like cummings, Hemingway reclaimed the war from cliché and "made it new," defamiliarized, shorn of heroic virtue and martial rhetoric. A foretaste of this method occurs in some of the vignettes within *In Our Time* (1925), which demonstrate minimalism, austerity of language, and purity of diction. These passages anticipate his mature fiction by capturing what are essentially fleeting states, thereby recreating what Krebs, one of his characters in the short story "Soldier's Home," called "the cool, valuable" quality of combat.

In *A Farewell to Arms* (1929) Hemingway gave definitive articulation to the myth of a lost generation at war, created in Frederick Henry, its most representative hero, and constructed a legendary fable of personal survival. Henry's experiences closely parallel Hemingway's own when the author was wounded on the Austrian front driving ambulances for the Italian army, and war teaches him to rely upon his primal instincts, to live empirically and be suspicious of abstract formulations of all kinds. No institutions can provide shelter in *A Farewell to Arms* against the larger, destructive forces of upheaval, and only love, friendship, and the intactness of the physical world survive the chaos. With its aura of betrayal and emphasis upon the psychology of individual preservation, this has become the core World War I narrative, best expressed in the novel's magnificent account of desertion, defeat, and anarchy in the Caporetto retreat. Historians have estimated that in excess of 8 million men died in World War I, which lends added imaginative relevance to Hemingway's primitivist myth of getting out alive.

Compared with Hemingway's, William Faulkner's copious war writing often seems stilted and overliterary. His two novels that treat World War I directly, *Soldiers' Pay* (1926) and the Pulitzer Prize–winning *A Fable* (1955), both lack immediacy, narrative action, and characters that engage the reader. Faulkner, who served with the British air force but did not fight, usually wrote about the war in a philosophical, meditative, and elegiac tone, which tends to make it remote. Only in some of his short stories did he capture the conflict's imaginative resonances, as in "Crevasse," "Victory," "All the Dead Pilots," and "Turnabout."

Literature reflected how the war affected the lives of women. Its effects upon female sexual behavior were addressed in **Amy Lowell**'s poem "Patterns" and **Eugene O'Neill**'s play *Strange Interlude* (1928). Lula Vollmer's play *Sun Up* (1923) explored its impact upon bereaved mothers. Most interesting of all are those novels about the consequences of the conflict written by women, including **Edith Wharton**'s *The Marne* (1918) and *A Son at the Front* (1923); Willa Cather's *One of Ours* (1922); **Gertrude Atherton**'s *The Living Present* (1917); **Ruth Dunbar**'s *The Swallow* (1919); Ann Sedgwick's *Adrienne Toner* (1921), and Dorothy Canfield Fisher's *The Deepening Stream* (1930). *See also* **Vigilantes**.

REFERENCES

Cooperman, Stanley. *World War I and the American Novel*. Baltimore: John Hopkins University Press, 1967.
Cowley, Malcolm. *Exile's Return: A Literary Odyssey of the 1920s*. New York: Norton, 1934.
Matsen, William E. *The Great War and the American Novel*. New York: Peter Lang, 1993.
Quinn, Patrick, and Steven Trout, eds. *New Perspectives on the Literature of the Great War*. New York: St. Martin's Press, 1999.

Jeff Walsh

FISHER, DOROTHY CANFIELD (1879–1958). Although Dorothy Canfield Fisher was born and raised in Kansas, she spent her summers in Vermont and considered the state her true home; consequently, the largest portion of her work centered on Vermont. She traveled extensively in France, and her interest in France would later lead to her involvement in both world wars, as well as to novels that attacked materialism, social and racial discrimination, and brutality. When World War I broke out, she and her husband, John Fisher, frustrated by the inaction of the U.S. government, were eager to assist in the war effort. She first worked with blind soldiers, counseling them on how to accept their limitations, a tale chronicled in "The First Time After." She wrote stories to send back to America, which were published from September 1917 to October 1918 in *Harper's* and other journals. They comprised her first collection of war tales, *Home Fires*, published in 1918, which put a face to the tales of human suffering, thus showing that war affected all people.

Her story "On the Edge" recounts the tale of a typical French mother, Jeanne Bruneau, who had to create a cheerful atmosphere for her children during the war with a diet lacking vital nutrients and the emotional scars of both wartime and an absent father. In the first story in the *Home Fires* collection, "Notes from a French Village in the War Zone," the narrator, an American knowledgeable about the history of France, notes of American soldiers, "You could almost see their brilliant, shadowless New World youth deepened and sobered by the past." Dorothy Canfield Fisher is most effective in these tales showing the ravages of war on this society and the contrasts between prewar and wartime societies. In one sense, her tales are the perfect example of propaganda. Not only does she recount the horror of the trenches, but she shows appreciation for the private aid given by Americans. Her tales were attempts to introduce the French to American audiences, and since *Home Fires* went through six printings, there is every indication Dorothy Canfield Fisher was successful.

Fisher's concern for the war cause continued as it became evident that the world was heading toward another world conflict. Her final novel, *Seasoned Timbers*, represents her effort to discuss the threat to human freedom presented by fascism. Even though the setting was rural Vermont, specifically the small town of Clifford, the setting for all of her Vermont novels, the theme was that this could happen anywhere. Eager to help end fascism in Spain, at the age of sixty, she was too old to participate actively. To help out in the war effort, she formed the Children's Crusade in 1940, focusing on having children in America contribute a penny for each year of their life to the war cause. Considered controversial, this project still raised $140,000 to assist the children of war-ravaged Europe. However, unable to do more for the war cause, Fisher turned her focus toward a subject about which she had always been passionate, education. She wrote *Our Young People* to warn children about the problems of the past, the unpredictability of the future, and the dangers of too much leisure time. Although Dorothy Canfield Fisher herself cannot be accused of wasting time, she has somehow escaped lasting recognition.

REFERENCES

McCallister, Lois. "Dorothy Canfield Fisher: A Critical Study." Diss. Case Western Reserve University, 1969.
Price, Alan. "Writing Home from the Front: Edith Wharton and Dorothy Canfield Fisher Present Wartime France to the United States: 1917–1919." *Edith Wharton Newsletter* 5.2 (Fall 1988): 1–8.
Washington, Ida H. *Dorothy Canfield Fisher: A Biography.* Shelburne, VT: New England Press, 1982.

Jennifer Harrison

FISHER, VARDIS (1895–1968). In his more than thirty works, Vardis Alvero Fisher explored the cultural heritage of the western American frontier, as well as his own past. Born on March 31, 1895, in rural southeastern Idaho, Fisher led a life of hardship. Formal schooling was impossible until he was able to work to pay for his education. Raised a Mormon, he soon began to question his beliefs, a soul-searching that would become the focus of twelve of his books, known as the "Testament" novels, in which Fisher attempts to comprehend how Christian beliefs have influenced the modern world. In these novels, Fisher searches for a connection between myth and history, which influenced his belief that unless man understood the past, he could not understand himself. In his autobiographical tetralogy, actually a case study of an individual, Vridar Hunter, Fisher uses Hunter to illustrate that man's failure is due to his inheritance of the burdens of the past.

Although Fisher's work does not lend itself to smooth categorizations, his work roughly falls into three categories: the autobiographical novels, such as those centering on Vridar Hunter and on the history of the individual on the western frontier; the anthropological novels, which deal with the history of the human race, such as *My Holy Satan* and *Intimations of Eve*; and the Americana novels, such as *Children of God*, which concern the history of certain key events in history, such as the advent of Mormonism. Fisher devoted much of his life to searching for the connections between man and society, beginning with his studies at the University of Utah in 1915. He briefly joined the air corps in 1915, then resigned, only to be drafted into the army in 1917, and his brief stints in the military no doubt affected his writing.

His "Testament" novels, part of the anthropological categorization of his work, again continue the discussion of history versus myth. His questions concerning self-identity and motive for actions are integral to understanding Western literature. Increasingly concerned with the human psyche, Fisher uses his characters to observe the perceived corruption in the U.S. government, the rise of fascism, and the approach of World War II. He focused his attention on understanding why man had become so intent on conflict. His first novel in the series, *Darkness and the Deep*, describes humanity's earliest ancestors Wuh and Murah, thus setting up his contention that human history is separate from natural history. In *The Island of the Innocent*, he describes the war of the Maccabees, concentrating on the love between a Greek man and a Jewish woman, thus setting the tone that historical actions allowed human beings to understand themselves. Therefore, Fisher would argue that psychology is central to explaining the importance of myth in relation to history. Human vulnerability, he argued, led to war, misery, and fanatical currents such as fascism.

In addition to seeking answers to the timeless questions of the modern era, Fisher also sought to provide explanations. The Americana novels attempt to ascertain why man acted as he did under certain circumstances, and the frontier is the basic setting for all of these novels. He focused on the Mormon movement in *Children of God* and on the Lewis and Clark expedition in *Tale of Valor*, in which he used the description of Indian-white animosity to discuss the nature of man. *Tale of Valor* is written using the point of view of the omniscient third-person narrator, but much of the narrative focuses on the historical figure of Meriwether Lewis. In *Children of God*, which won the Harper prize for fiction in 1939, he used his personal history to explain Mormonism, or at least the early history of the Mormon movement, since he stopped his discussion with the 1890 manifesto officially outlawing polygamy. The main character, Vridar Hunter, left his Mormon environment in Idaho for urban New York only to discover that life in the East was not as idyllic as originally dreamed, a cataclysmic event that paralleled Fisher's own life. In turn, these novels also reflect a certain distrust of what Fisher termed "the Eastern establishment," a criticism later expressed in his essay "Critics and the Reviewers" in his textbook for new writers, *God or Caesar?* The novelists' task, Fisher argued, was to perceive "the past which produced the child." Such reflections mirror Fisher's own doubts about the increasing role of the government, as well as contribute to the overwhelming tone of skepticism surrounding much of his work. This skeptical tone is similar to his own personal conflict and therefore is pertinent for explaining the connection between myth and history that had become the central focus of Fisher's work.

REFERENCES

Lyon, Thomas J., ed. *A Literary History of the American West*. Fort Worth: Texas Christian University Press, 1987. 854–870.

Strong, Lester. *The Past in the Present: Two Essays on History and Myth in Vardis Fisher's Testament of Man*. Brooklyn: Revisionist Press, 1979.

———. "Vardis Fisher Revisited." *South Dakota Review* 24.3 (Autumn 1986): 25–37.

Jennifer Harrison

FOOTE, SHELBY (1916–   ). Shelby Foote was born in 1916 in Greenville, Mississippi. Foote's literary career was influenced by his childhood friendship with schoolmate Walker Percy and his association with Percy's uncle, the noted Southern author Alexander Percy. After attending the University of North Carolina for two years, Foote left school in 1937 to begin writing his first novel. Although a highly acclaimed writer of novels and short stories dealing with the American South, Foote is best known for his massive three-volume narrative history of the Civil War.

In 1952, Foote published *Shiloh*, which signified his arrival as a novelist. In this historical novel, Foote recounts the events of the Civil War battle through the eyes of five soldiers whose paths cross at critical junctions. *Shiloh* achieved critical acclaim for his extensive research, realism, and blend of fictional and historical characters. Critics often compared *Shiloh* to **Crane**'s *Red Badge of Courage* and considered Foote's treatment of the fortunes of war, with its root within the character of men, to be more complex.

In 1954, Foote began a three-volume narrative of the Civil War that took over twenty years to complete. Foote combined the historian's standards of scholarship with lively writing to "tell us how it was, to recreate it and make it live again." Many critics agree that Foote accomplished his goal, as his convincing characterizations and use of narrative to develop suspense and anticipation create the illusion that the reader is not so much reading a book as sharing an experience. Foote also received praise for his extensive research, attention to detail, objectivity, and balance; in particular, he was lauded for redressing the symmetry between the Eastern and Western Theaters of war. Many scholars, however, find Foote's historical account lacking because he focused primarily on military issues, overlooking economic, political, and social themes. They also note that his narrative account lacked an overarching thesis, relied upon secondary and published sources instead of primary documents, and made sweeping judgments. Accepting the work's shortcomings, most academic historians praise it as well written and an outstanding narrative history of the war.

REFERENCES

Mississippi Quarterly 24.4 (Fall 1971). A special issue on Shelby Foote.

Phillips, Robert L. *Shelby Foote: Novelist and Historian*. Jackson: University of Mississippi Press, 1992.

White, Helen, and Reddings S. Sugg, Jr. *Shelby Foote*. Boston: Twayne, 1982.

William T. Hartley

FORBES, ESTHER (1891–1967). Esther Forbes, born in Westborough, Massachusetts, spent two years studying history at the University of Wisconsin and in the 1920s worked on the Houghton Mifflin editorial staff. Her interest in the American Revolution and the life of Paul Revere is reflected in books she wrote for both adults and children. They include Pulitzer Prize–winning *Paul Revere and the World He Lived In* (1942), 1943 Newbery Award winner *Johnny Tremain: A Novel for Young and Old*, and, also for children, *America's Paul Revere* (1948). She also wrote several historical novels for adults, including *Paradise* (1937), an epic of colonial Massachusetts that ends with King Philip's War, and *The General's Lady* (1938), set during the American Revolution.

Forbes's works reflect several aspects of her own background, including her New England ancestry, her mother's accomplishments as a regional historian, and her brief tenure as a history student studying under Frederick Jackson Turner. In 1926, she published her first novel, *Oh Genteel Lady!*

Both *Johnny Tremain* and *Paul Revere and the World He Lived In* are reflective of Forbes's interest in and concern for the questions of human freedom provoked by World War II. Concerning *Johnny Tremain*, Forbes originally planned for the title character to adopt a neutral position in regard to the looming conflict between Britain and America. However, the attack on Pearl Harbor changed her mind about the nature of neutrality. When she began writing *Johnny Tremain* in earnest on December 8, 1941, the title character was a patriot.

Conflict in *Johnny Tremain* is virtually bloodless until the end, when a friend's death in the revolution's first battle prompts the protagonist to abandon all doubts about the American cause. The war begins as the novel closes, and Johnny, an apprentice to a Boston silversmith, watches in horror as British soldiers flood Boston "like a river of blood." He concludes that "hundreds would die, but not the thing they die for." It is against this backdrop that Johnny moves from adolescence into manhood.

The title character of *Paul Revere and the World He Lived In* is driven exclusively by a quest for liberty and honor—the only motivations necessary for fighting Britain. Conflict in the book is described in terms of the repressive Old World menacing the New because it craves freedom.

REFERENCES

Balcs, Jack. *Esther Forbes: A Bio-Bibliography of the Author of Johny Tremain*. Lanham, MD: Scarecrow Press, 1998.
Mainiero, Lina, ed. *American Women Writers*. New York: Frederick Ungar, 1980.
Van Gelder, Robert. "An Interview with Esther Forbes." *Writers and Writing*. New York: Scribner's, 1946. 291–295.

Laura M. Chmielewski

FOSDICK, CHARLES AUSTIN (1842–1915). As one of the pioneers of the American adventure serials genres, Charles Austin Fosdick, writing under the pen name Harry Castlemon, published upward of sixty books for boys in the latter half of the nineteenth century, including many set during the Civil War. Born and raised in western New York, Fosdick traveled to Cairo, Illinois, at the outbreak of the Civil War to enlist in the U.S. Navy. As a member of the Mississippi Squadron, he served on a gunboat patrolling the river and took part in the siege of Vicksburg, experiences that would become the basis for a number of his books, among them *Frank on a Gunboat* (1864), *Frank before Vicksburg* (1865), *Frank on the Lower Mississippi* (1867), *Rodney the Partisan* (1890), *Marcy the Blockade Runner* (1891), *Marcy the Refugee* (1892), and *A Rebellion in Dixie* (1897).

The Castlemon books, written specifically for schoolboys, were developed in series of three to six volumes around a central character, an adventurous boy the age of Fosdick's readers. In addition to the Frank and Marcy series listed above, other groupings included *George in Camp* (1879), *George at the Fort* (1881), *George at the Wheel* (1881), and the six-volume *Sportsman's Club* series (1873–77). The format of the stories varied little from series to series; usually the protagonist takes part in a number of thrilling exploits while learning the manly virtues necessary for survival. Each narrative was fairly realistic in tone, written in a brisk, almost spare style intended to keep the pages turning, and the adventures were not "fantastic" in the sense that each was within the realm of possibility, however slight.

For a time, the Castlemon books were among the most popular children's books in the nation, comparing favorably with those of William Taylor Adams

("Oliver Optic") and Horatio Alger. As the century waned, however, Fosdick's increasingly formulaic work became less popular, and other writers began dominating the field of serial adventures. The final Castlemon work, *A Struggle for a Fortune*, was published in 1902, and by the time of his death in 1915, Charles Austin Fosdick was a nearly forgotten figure.

REFERENCES

Blanck, Jacob. *Harry Castlemon, Boy's Own Author: An Appreciation and Bibliography.* New York: R. R. Bowker, 1941.
Owen, Maurice. "Harry Castlemon (Charles A. Fosdick): Chronology of Books." *The Boys Book Collector 1* (Spring 1970): 75–78.

Patrick Julian

FOX, JOHN, JR. (1862/1863?–1919). While accounts vary as to the year of his birth, the location and day of John Fox's birth are certain, Stony Point, Kentucky, on December 16. After spending his freshman year at Transylvania College in nearby Lexington, Fox transferred to Harvard, where he graduated cum laude with a Bachelor of Arts degree in 1883. Upon graduation, Fox gave thoughtful consideration to a career in law but chose instead to work as a newspaper reporter in New York City, a more cosmopolitan locale than his home in eastern Kentucky.

Fox's brief stint as a journalist in the mid-1800s made him a logical choice to cover the Spanish-American War for both *Harper's Weekly* and *Scribner's* in 1898. Besides forging a friendship with **Richard Harding Davis**, the conflict allowed Fox to mythologize the exploits of **Teddy Roosevelt** and his Rough Riders, a friend Fox made while giving public lectures to recoup money lost in failed mining and real estate ventures in the early 1890s. Ultimately, the author's time in Cuba gave him the idea to write the fictional war novel *Crittenden: A Kentucky Story of Love and War* (1900), which continued the sentimentality and local color of Fox's early short fiction. Ultimately, Fox used the novel to show how the Spanish-American War brought citizens together to fight for a common cause, thus laying to rest the old animosities of the Civil War.

For his next novel, Fox chose to expand on his earlier treatment of America's Civil War. In *The Little Shepherd of Kingdom Come* (1903), Fox's hero, Chad Buford, has difficulty deciding whether to fight for the Union or Confederate army. By book's end, Buford chooses to fight for the Union and becomes a courageous soldier. Because of the novel's overwhelming success, *Scribners'* asked Fox to cover the Russo-Japanese War in 1904. After this final, brief excursion into the fray of war, Fox returned home to Kentucky in 1905, where he spent his remaining years writing the melodramatic fiction for which he is now famous. Upon his death of pneumonia in 1919, Fox was working on *Erskine Dale—Pioneer* (1920), a historical novel set during the Revolutionary War.

REFERENCES

DeEulis, Marilyn. "Primitivism and Exoticism in John Fox's Early Work." *Appalachian Journal: A Regional Studies Review* 4 (1977): 133–43.

Holman, Harriet R. "John Fox, Jr.: Appraisal and Self-Appraisal." *Southern Literary Journal* 3.2 (1971): 18–38.
Titus, Warren I. *John Fox, Jr.* New York: Twayne, 1971.

Shawn Holliday

FRANK, PAT (1907–1964). Born in Chicago as Harry Hart, Pat Frank attended the University of Florida before commencing a substantial career as a newspaperman. Journalistic positions in Jacksonville, Florida, and New York City preceded a much longer stay in Washington, D.C., where he worked for the *Washington Herald*, eventually as chief of its Washington Bureau. World War II took him abroad—first with the Office of War Information and then with the Overseas News Agency—to Italy, Austria, Germany, Turkey, and Hungary. His interest in international affairs and the state of the postwar world found expression in his successful first novel, *Mr. Adam* (1946), a best-seller that enabled him to shift his career focus. Seven other books would follow—four of them novels—to include *Hold Back the Night* (1951), his skillful and enduring novel of the Korean War.

The novel memorializes the Marines' legendary winter withdrawal from the Chosin Reservoir in North Korea at the end of 1950. Frank's fiction admirably reflects the harrowing nature of that experience and the heroism of those Marines who fought their way southward to evacuation through forbidding terrain and the most brutal weather conditions imaginable. Although the book has value simply as a written monument to that chapter of Marine Corps history, it is also a well-written and engaging story. The protagonist is Captain Sam Mackenzie, commander of Dog Company, a World War II veteran who embodies the best qualities of the career Marine. He displays both immense tactical and technical proficiency and an intense humanity. While Mackenzie's primary focus is clearly the welfare—indeed, the survival—of his troops, he does not suffer bad behavior gladly. His disdain for a malingering lieutenant is nearly palpable, and at one point he admonishes one of his men for referring to a Korean woman as a "gook." Through such fictional moments, Frank rightly suggests that even the most heroic units and operations are not made up entirely of heroes.

An interesting aspect of the plot, even mentioned in Frank's *New York Times* obituary, concerns a totemic bottle of Scotch whisky that Mackenzie carries with him throughout. Originally given him by his then-fiancée (later his wife) before he left for Guadalcanal, the unopened bottle serves as a good-luck charm that sees the Marines of Dog Company through the Chosin ordeal. Like the distinctive shoulder patch of the First Marine Division that Mackenzie has worn in both conflicts, the Scotch also links one war with another in the context of the larger Marine tradition, a continuity in which Frank the novelist seems particularly interested.

The predominant theme in most of Frank's other published work is the threat of nuclear disaster in the Cold War world, a theme even mentioned briefly in *Hold Back the Night*. His *Alas, Babylon* (1959) is considered a classic of speculative fiction. It concerns a small Florida town that somehow escapes destruction when a nuclear holocaust ravages the United States overnight, and a thousand years of civilization is undone. This concern also found nonfiction expression in his *How to Survive the H-Bomb, and Why* (1962).

REFERENCES

Kupferberg, Herbert. Rev. of *Hold Back the Night*, by Pat Frank. *New York Herald Tribune Book Review* 16 March 1952: 5.
Lee, Charles. Rev. of *Hold Back the Night*, by Pat Frank. *Saturday Review* 8 March 1952: 13.

James R. Kerin, Jr.

FRAZIER, CHARLES (1950–   ). Born and raised in the Appalachian country so memorably portrayed in his first novel, *Cold Mountain*, Charles Frazier, a sometime literature professor, now writes and raises horses. Hailed as the greatest Civil War novel since **Michael Shaara**'s *The Killer Angels, Cold Mountain* was a monumental best-seller for much of 1997. It has been amply praised also for its humane and hopeful vision of healing and love in the midst of chaos and destruction.

The story follows a traumatized and shell-shocked Confederate soldier named Inman who, late in 1864, leaves the military hospital in Raleigh, North Carolina, where he has been recovering from a grievous neck wound and begins to walk home to Cold Mountain, far to the west in the Appalachians. His odyssey becomes spiritual as well as physical: He is returning home to rediscover himself and to resume a romance with Ada Monroe, a cultivated Charleston woman who remains in the mountains after the death of her minister father, struggling to make a life with the help of a woods-wise mountain girl named Ruby. Chapters about Inman alternate with chapters about Ada; she finds a new life in the land, and he moves closer to home and healing, both geographically and spiritually. His journey is violent and mythic through a forlorn landscape peopled with grotesques, spiritual orphans, vigilantes, and other wounded souls. The Civil War itself is portrayed with nightmarish irony, as brutalizing mass murder rather than noble crusade. The lyrical style of the novel's language is strongly flavored with the piquant texture of regional speech.

The novel was made into a United Artists film by Academy Award–winning director Anthony Minghella.

REFERENCES

Bell, Millicent. "Cold Mountain." *Partisan Review* 65 (Fall 1998): 635–648.
Giles, Jeff. Rev. of *Cold Mountain*, by Charles Frazier. *Newsweek* 28 July 1997: 64–65.
Gussow, Mel. "A Civil War Deserter Reaches No. 1." Rev. of *Cold Mountain*, by Charles Frazier. *New York Times* 27 August 1997: C1, C12.
Kazin, Alfred. "The Long Journey Home." Rev. of *Cold Mountain*, by Charles Frazier. *New York Review of Books* 20 November 1997: 18.

Randal W. Allred

FREDENBURGH, THEODORE (1897–1975). A lifelong Boston resident, Theodore Fredenburgh enlisted with the Massachusetts Infantry at age fifteen, obtaining the rank of first sergeant by the time of his discharge at age eighteen. He enlisted again when the United States entered World War I, serving overseas with the 101st Field Artillery, where he eventually acquired the rank of second lieutenant.

Upset with how authors often portrayed soldiers from World War I as victims of neurosis, Fredenburgh drew on his own experiences to write *Soldiers March!* (1930), a realistic look at an infantry soldier during the war. *Soldiers March!* is the story of Eddie Zorn, a young man who enthusiastically goes to France to serve in the war, work hard, and be promoted while serving his country, whether that means glory or a noble death. However, he comes to realize the anonymity he has in the war machine. As he crosses the sea, "somewhere in Zorn's consciousness a doubt stirred. Patriotism—the flag, bands, ideals of service—here at sea meant only iron and blood." The army is merely steel and human flesh sacrificed for the war machine, and "he was in it; a part, a tiny part, of a great cold system." The war is not merely combat but also the long waiting periods between battles in which soldiers live in squalor and sickness. Zorn fights not only Germans but illness, lack of medicine, lice, and the bureaucracy of the army. The novel ends with Zorn departing for officers' training camp, not being broken by the war but surviving, despite the fact that his ideals have been destroyed.

Although Fredenburgh's writing style is not as notable as many other American authors who served in World War I, he has many of the same concerns as contemporaries such as **Hemingway** and **Dos Passos**: the mechanization of man and the inhumanity of war on the individual. Fredenburgh didn't return to the subject of the war in his only other book, *Sow the Wind* (1936).

REFERENCES

Cooperman, Stanley. *World War I and the American Novel*. Baltimore: Johns Hopkins University Press, 1967. 137–141.
Warren, Dale. "Boston Booktrade News." *Publishers' Weekly* 20 September 1930: 1282–1283.

Sean C. F. McGurr

FREDERIC, HAROLD (1856–1898). Harold Frederic's 1896 review of *The Red Badge of Courage* in the *New York Times* was largely responsible for bringing **Crane**'s novel to public attention, and like his friend Crane, Frederic was a native of upstate New York and a foreign correspondent who often wrote war fiction in the new naturalistic style. In fact, Frederic's first known story, written while he was starting out as a journalist in Utica, New York, has a Revolutionary War setting, and his first novel, *In the Valley* (1890), is also set during the Revolution. Although basically a historical romance, *In the Valley* is also a realistic and historically accurate account of the political situation in the Mohawk Valley leading up to the Battle of Oriskany in 1777.

In *The Copperhead* (1893), a novella, Frederic turns his attention to the home front during the Civil War, realistically depicting the intolerance of dissent that festers during war, even in communities far from the battlefields. Abner Beech, the copperhead of the title, finds that his belief in states' rights makes him the target of ostracism and attacks by the abolitionists who dominate his rural New York village. Ultimately, however, Beech is readmitted to the community and granted a measure of respect as a man who holds to his principles in the face of a tyrannous majority. To capitalize on the success of *The Copperhead*, Frederic republished it in 1894 along with several other stories set in upstate New York during the Civil War as *The Copperhead and Other Stories of the North during the American War* (1894).

Frederic's next book, *Marsena and Other Stories of the Wartime* (1894), continues his exploration of war, but his hitherto realistic style gives way to a full-blown naturalism. In *Marsena*, the title novella, a beautiful but vain and shallow young woman makes her male admirers show their love for her by enlisting. She later becomes a nurse in an army hospital, and in a patently ironic ending, one of her boyfriends, a young private, dies while trying to get her attention as she cares for a slightly wounded officer.

Frederic continued to write war stories throughout his career, and even though he will always be primarily remembered as the author of *The Damnation of Theron Ware* (1896), his war fiction deserves comparison with that of Crane and **Ambrose Bierce**. Much of his war fiction has been collected in a modern edition entitled *Stories of York State*.

REFERENCES

Brigos, Austin, Jr. *The Novels of Harold Frederic*. Ithaca: Cornell University Press, 1969.

Frederic, Harold. *Harold Frederic's Stories of York State*. Ed. Thomas F. O'Donnell. Syracuse: Syracuse University Press, 1966.

O'Donnell, Thomas F., and Hoyt C. Franchere. *Harold Frederic*. New York: Twayne, 1961.

Lucas Carpenter

FRENEAU, PHILIP (1752–1832). Philip Morin Freneau is known as the "Poet of the Revolution," an epithet popularized during his lifetime. Born in New York City and educated at the College of New Jersey (Princeton), Freneau contemplated or tried numerous careers (everything from clergyman to seaman) while attempting to carve a place for himself in the newly emerging American literary culture. His early poetry mingles satire with sentimentalism and admiration for America's rural tradition, with these elements feeding into patriotic fervor after 1775. After enduring six weeks of incarceration on a British prison ship (the experience that provided both the material and title of one of his most famous poems), Freneau became a passionate advocate of the cause of American

revolutionaries. Out of this incident grew his commitment to republican principles. His works appeared in pamphlets and newspapers during the course of
the Revolution.

In 1786, he published a collection entitled *The Poems of Philip Freneau,
Written Chiefly During the Late War*. The collection contains 111 poems, of
which only 13 do not have explicitly "American" themes. The "battle poems"
that comprise a sizable portion of the volume are recapitulations of the bravery
and suffering of patriot Americans. These poems also reflect the author's persistent belief that civilization was "moving west" and that times of drama and
conflict in America's present were a much more valuable literary source than
anything that had happened in Europe's past.

The drama and conflict of the American Revolution provided plenty of material for testing this theory. Freneau's poems catalog British atrocities, the arrival of Hessians, details of battles, and seemingly arcane incidents like
Franklin's departure for France. Poems like "American Independent" show that
the poet considered the country's success in battle as moral, predestined triumph:
"America! The work of peace be thine, Thus shalt thou gain a triumph more
divine."

Stylistically, the most interesting and successful war poems are satires of key
British figures. Poems like "General Gage's Soliloquy," "The Midnight Con-
sultations," and "General Gage's Confession" use ridicule and irony to render
their subjects ridiculous. However, the serious aspects of the conflict are not
neglected in these poems: Freneau believed that Britain's high command was
populated with cowards who hid behind the foot soldiers they employed to
murder Americans. Poems like the elegy "On Walking over the Ground of Long
Island, near New-York, where many Americans were interred from the Prison
Ships, during the War with Great Britain" and "The Tomb of the Patriots"
balance the glory of battle with war's starkest reality—casualties. This sentiment
is underscored in "The American Soldier," in which the poet exhorts his reader
to be forever mindful of "He, who once warred on Saratoga's plains, sits musing
o'er his scars and wooden leg." This theme is present even in works written at
the height of the war. "On the Memorable Victory of John Paul Jones" describes
in detail the famous naval victory and lauds its leader but also laments the loss
of life among heroic men on both sides of the conflict. Such praise as " 'T was
Jones, brave Jones to battle led / As bold a crew as ever bled" does not undermine the tragic by-product of the battle itself ("Alas! That e'er the god decreed
/ That brother should by brother bleed").

Freneau continued to write poetry throughout the rest of his life, but much
of his postwar fame is owed to his position as newspaper editor. He founded
the *National Gazette* in 1791 and used it as a pulpit to champion his friends
Jefferson and Madison. This enterprise lasted only two years, and after 1793 he
sold books, continued to serve in the merchant marine, and prepared volumes
of poetry that capitalized on his reputation as "Poet of the Revolution." However, the topics of his poems moved away from war and favor reflection on the

benign side of nature. Ironically, Philip Freneau met his death in a snowstorm in 1832.

REFERENCES

Elliott, Emery. *Revolutionary Writers: Literature and Authority in the New Republic, 1725–1810.* New York: Oxford University Press, 1986.
Freneau, Philip. *Poems of Freneau.* Ed. Harry Hayden Clark. New York: Hafner Publishing, 1960.
Litz, A. Walton, ed. *American Writers: A Collection of Literary Biography.* Supplement II, Part 1. New York: Scribner's, 1981.
Marsh, Philip M. *Philip Freneau: Poet and Journalist.* Minneapolis: Dillon Press, 1967.

Laura M. Chmielewski

FROST, ROBERT (1874–1963). From his earliest juvenilia to his final volume, *In the Clearing*, published in 1962 when he was eighty-eight, Robert Lee Frost wrote poems about human nature and the inevitability of conflict. He lived through three of the twentieth century's major wars and the times that bred them, but he never fought in one. Born in 1874, he was forty years old and living "under thatch" in England when World War I broke out. When World War II erupted, Frost was sixty-five. Although he did not fight, some of his best friends did, including Edward Thomas, the British poet and writer, who died at Vimy Ridge in France in 1917. Several of his finest war poems, "To E. T." and "The Soldier," are tributes to Thomas. Frost admired Thomas's noble nature and his willingness to go to battle knowing he would probably not return. According to Frost biographer Lawrance Thompson, Frost said of Thomas that "of the three ways out of [life], . . . he [chose] the greatest way."

Named for Robert E. Lee, Frost paid tribute to bravery such as Thomas's his entire life, going so far as to state on his deathbed that he'd "rather be taken for brave than for anything else" (*Selected Letters*). His fascination with bravery surfaces continually in his work, as does his belief in the inevitability of conflict. As one "acquainted with the night," he believed war and violence were ingrained in the human condition. In "The Flood," for instance, he describes the sheer force of violence that is always waiting to overflow any controls humans may impose. Frost felt that we cannot dam the flow of blood for long; it will find its release in implements of war and peace.

The inevitability of war, often portrayed by Frost as a battle between man and nature, led him to look for ways to score points, to elevate the human spirit. For Frost, courage and sacrifice seem to have been saving graces. Both are aptly described in "The Gift Outright," a poem he recited at Kennedy's inauguration. In this poem, Frost couples the act of "giving" with acts performed on the battlefield. Such giving leads to salvation. Despite many poets who voiced contrary opinions, particularly after the world wars, Frost believed in glory and in finding something of value in the pain and loss accompanying war. For him, the value lay in the gift of sacrificing oneself, of being a "fallen lance," a spirit that can transcend time and space. He develops this theme in "A Soldier."

Frost also addressed the larger political issues associated with war. In *Steeple Bush*, published in 1947, Frost reacted to the atomic bomb and the looming Cold War, focusing on his concern about whether or not humans will survive their latest technological innovations. In "One Step Backward Taken," he depicts a world on the brink of nuclear war. He argues for caution in the tongue-and-cheek poem "The Planners," while poking fun at the "Federation of Mankind" in "The Courage to Be New." Yet despite the impending doom, he offers his characteristic counterpoint by providing hope for our redemption. In "Directive," the speaker holds out an appropriately broken goblet, directs us to cold brook water, and tells us to drink and become "whole again beyond confusion."

REFERENCES

Dubinsky, James M. "War and Rumors of War in Frost." *Robert Frost Review* (1995): 1–22.

Frost, Robert. *The Poetry of Robert Frost*. Ed. E. C. Lathem. New York: Holt, 1969.

Newdick, Robert. "Robert Frost Looks at War." *South Atlantic Quarterly* 38 (January 1938): 52–59.

Thompson, Lawrance Roger. *Robert Frost: The Years of Triumph, 1915–1938*. New York: Holt, 1970.

James M. Dubinsky

FULLER, CHARLES (1939–   ). Born and raised in Philadelphia, Charles Fuller is one of the most important contemporary African American playwrights. He attended Roman Catholic High School and went on to attend Villanova (1956–1958) and LaSalle (1965–1968). For four years in between these college stints, Fuller was in the army as a petroleum laboratory technician in Japan and Korea. Two of his best-known plays, *The Brownsville Raid* and *A Soldier's Play*, were influenced by his army experiences.

A Soldier's Play (1981) won the Pulitzer Prize for Drama in 1982. The play's central themes revolve around racism, power, and relationships between blacks and whites. The action occurs during World War II on an army base in Louisiana. A black sergeant, Waters, has been murdered, and Captain Richard Davenport, the first black officer at Fort Neal, is sent to investigate. In a series of flashbacks, the identity of the killer, as well as that of the victim, is uncovered, revealing Waters to be a man with many motivations. Despite his rank, Davenport, as a black officer and lawyer, faces many forms of discrimination in a U.S. Army that is still segregated. In this play, Fuller is able to create complex characters whose interactions avoid becoming formulaic.

The Brownsville Raid (1976) is based on historical incident that occurred in Brownsville, Texas, in 1906. All 167 soldiers from the all-black 25th Infantry unit were dishonorably discharged after no one confessed to starting a riot that ended up killing two men, a white and a Mexican. Like *A Soldier's Play, The*

Brownsville Raid is successful because of its portrayal of characters without typecasting, as well as showing how America treated black soldiers whose job it was to defend her.

Sally (1988) is the first play in a cycle titled *We: A History in Five Plays*. It focuses on black soldiers during the Civil War who are upset by the reneging of the Union army's promise of equal pay. The play also explores possibilities of love and compassion during times of war.

REFERENCE

Anadolu-Okur, Nilgun. *Contemporary African American Theater: Afrocentricity in the Works of Larry Neal, Amiri Baraka, and Charles Fuller*. New York: Garland, 1997.

Sean C. F. McGurr

FUSSELL, PAUL (1924–   ). Born and raised in Pasadena, California, Fussell attended Pomona College and participated in ROTC before being called to active duty in 1943. He completed Officer Candidate School and served as an infantry lieutenant in France, where he was seriously wounded on March 15, 1945. Upon his release from active duty in 1946, he returned to Pomona College, earning a B.A. (1947) and going on to Harvard, where he completed M.A. (1949) and Ph.D. (1952) degrees in English. Fussell went on to Rutgers, where he earned tenure as a professor of eighteenth-century British literature before drawing on his personal experience and turning to war as a literary and personal theme in his writing. He is now the Donald T. Regan Professor of English Literature (emeritus) at the University of Pennsylvania.

Fussell's first foray into war literature was *The Great War and Modern Memory* (1975), a landmark work that still stands as the definitive account of the ways in which World War I has colored our perceptions and conditioned our responses to life ever since. Fussell's principal focus throughout the book is on the "intersections of literature with life," particularly what he terms the "simultaneous and reciprocal process by which life feeds materials to literature while literature returns the favor by conferring forms upon life." He demonstrates not only how the Edwardian generation's literary and cultural models were found to be woefully inadequate in the face of the world's first sustained experience with modern mass warfare, leading to wholesale disillusionment, but also how the literary responses to that disillusionment have established a pervasive irony as the dominant literary response to life in the modern age. A popular and a critical success, *The Great War and Modern Memory* won the 1976 National Book Award for Award for Arts and Letters, the National Book Critics Circle Award for Criticism, and the **Ralph Waldo Emerson** Award of Phi Beta Kappa.

Wartime: Understanding and Behavior in the Second World War (1989) reflects Fussell's very personal concern, as one who had been there, for the ways in which the World War II experience "has been sanitized and romanticized almost beyond recognition by the sentimental, the ignorant, and the bloodthirsty." In an attempt to "to balance the scales," Fussell reminds the reader at every turn of the horrific nature and the unprecedented scale of the carnage and of the unnecessary waste occasioned by widespread mismanagement and incompetence throughout that war. The result has been widely criticized as a cynical and personally bitter defamation of an effort others would prefer to remember as a "Good War" or "Great Crusade."

Fussell's latest book, a first-person memoir titled *Doing Battle: The Making of a Skeptic* (1996), forms both a personal coda and capstone to the work he began with *The Great War and Modern Memory*. An unflinchingly honest and self-ironic account of his life to date, including his wartime experiences and their lasting influence on him, *Doing Battle* is perhaps closest in tone to Wilfred Owen's poem "Dulce et Decorum Est." Fussell reveals himself to be not a pacifist or even an idealist where war is concerned. He acknowledges the sad necessity of fighting and winning the Second War World War, but he steadfastly rejects all attempts at romanticizing or glorifying that experience.

Wartime and *Doing Battle* both grew out of occasional essays that Fussell had published in various journals and that were reprinted in a collection entitled *The Boy Scout Handbook* (1982). In the title piece to his later collection *Thank God for the Atomic Bomb* (1988), Fussell expresses his unregenerate faith in the conventional view of the atomic bombings of Hiroshima and Nagasaki as expedients that shortened the war and ultimately saved more lives than they took. Fussell is also the editor of *Norton Book of Modern War* (1991), a comprehensive anthology of the acknowledged best war writing from World War I through Vietnam.

REFERENCES

Hynes, Samuel. Rev. of *Wartime*, by Paul Fussell. *New Republic* 13 November 1989: 34.

Kermode, Frank. Rev. of *The Great War and Modern Memory*, by Paul Fussell. *New York Times Book Review* 13 August 1975: 2.

Rev. of *The Great War and Modern Memory*, by Paul Fussell. *The New Yorker* 20 October 1975: 171.

Sherry, Michael. Rev. of *Doing Battle*, by Paul Fussell. *New York Times Book Review* 19 September 1996: 18.

Tylee, Claire M. " 'The Great War in Modern Memory': What Is Being Repressed?" *Women's Studies Quarterly* 23 (Fall–Winter 1995): 65–77.

Edward F. Palm

G

GELLHORN, MARTHA (1908–1998). Born in St. Louis, Missouri, Martha Ellis Gellhorn attended her mother's coeducational school, then began studies at Bryn Mawr. After dropping out her junior year, she married Marquis de Jouvenal in 1933 and became a writer for *Vogue* magazine. During this time, she penned her first novel, *What Mad Pursuit?* and she met **Ernest Hemingway**.

In 1935, Hemingway convinced *Scribner's Magazine* to publish Gellhorn's short story "Exile," which details the struggles of a German refugee fleeing his country because he fears Hitler has disrupted the German way of life. Gellhorn's perceptions of war and keen sense of detail led editors at *Collier's Weekly* to hire her on as war correspondent for the Spanish Civil War. Unlike other reporters who documented the historical and factual information, Gellhorn focused on the war's emotional and psychological impact, writing about wounded soldiers, orphaned children, and people whose lives were forever altered by war.

In 1940, Gellhorn married Hemingway and published *A Stricken Field*, which depicts a historical overview of the invasion of Czechoslovakia through the eyes of Gellhorn's protagonist, Mary Douglass. Douglass, a war correspondent, reports the injustices perpetuated by the Nazi regime and warns England of the tragic implications resulting from its indifference to Hitler. During World War II, Gellhorn served as a war correspondent in England and, during the D-Day invasion, hid on a hospital ship headed for the Normandy beaches. While serving as a stretcher bearer, she became the only writer to prepare unauthorized reports on the invasions.

After the war, Gellhorn published *The Wine of Astonishment* (1948) and *The Honeyed Peace* (1953), both of which identify the psychological torment experienced by the tragic loss of innocence and guilt of survival. Characters in these novels, whose lives have been defined by war, refuse to forget what war has done to them.

Of all her writings, Gellhorn's collection of war dispatches in the *Face of War* (1959) proves to be her most poignant observations of the casualties of war. In the introduction, Gellhorn writes that "war is a malignant disease, an idiocy, a prison, and the pain it causes is beyond telling or imagining." After working in Vietnam, Gellhorn revised the first edition to include six more reports.

Well into her eighties, Gellhorn continued to serve as a war correspondent. She covered the Arab-Israeli conflicts, and at eighty-one, she worked in Panama when Noriega was ousted. The last years of her life, Gellhorn remained in London and died at the age of eighty-nine.

REFERENCES

Elwood-Aikers, Virginia. *Women War Correspondents in the Vietnam War, 1961–1975.* Metuchen, NJ: Scarecrow Press, 1988.
Lassner, Phyllis. " 'Camp Follower to Catastrophe': Martha Gellhorn's World War II Challenge to the Modernist War." *Modern Fiction Studies* 44.3 (Fall 1998): 792–812.
Rollyson, Carl E. *Nothing Ever Happens to the Brave.* New York: St. Martin's Press, 1990.

Mary Hricko

GHOST DANCE SONGS. Inspired by the visionary teachings of the Paiute prophet Wovoka (ca. 1856–1932), also known as Quoitze Ow and Jack Wilson), the Ghost Dance movement spread to many of the Native American tribes in the Great Basin and on the plains in 1889–1890. At the core of Wovoka's teachings, a mixture of Christian and traditional Native American elements inspired by a vision he experienced while suffering from scarlet fever, was the belief that the Native American world was soon to be regenerated by a messiah, with the return of the buffalo and other game animals and the resurrection of ancestors. All Native Americans would then live in a paradise on earth, free from death, disease, and the policies of white people.

Wovoka's followers believed that this new age would come into being through the regular performance of the Ghost Dance, each time for five successive days. The ceremony involved communal singing and dancing in a circle, as in traditional tribal "round dances"; in the Ghost Dance, this performance would ideally induce a trance state in which the participants would travel to the spirit world. Upon regaining consciousness, those who had had this experience would communicate it to others in song. Thus, there was no limit to the number of Ghost Dance songs, though several became favorites; each tribe had certain songs that were a regular part of its version of the ceremony, with many of these blending the tribe's particular mythology with that of the Ghost Dance religion. Like most Native American ceremonial literature, the songs utilize repetition and syllables that have no meaning beyond the power of their sound.

Despite the fact that Wovoka's messianic message was peaceful, as the movement grew, so too did the concerns of the U.S. government, partly because some groups, especially among the Lakota (Sioux), ignored the pacifistic aspects of the religion and regarded it as a call for renewed warfare. While many Ghost

Dancers believed the coming paradise would include all races living in harmony, these more warlike groups interpreted the prophecy as foretelling the obliteration of the white race by warriors wearing bullet-proof Ghost Dance shirts, as recounted in *Black Elk Speaks*. Attempts by the Bureau of Indian Affairs to suppress the Ghost Dance led to the massacre of 150 Lakota by the Seventh Cavalry at Wounded Knee, South Dakota, on December 28, 1890, which effectively put an end to the Indian Wars.

Although most tribes abandoned the Ghost Dance after Wounded Knee, the religion continued to be practiced well into the twentieth century. Ghost Dance songs offer the most direct expression of the beliefs and experiences of the religion's adherents, making their study central to an understanding of one of the darkest chapters in American history. The most comprehensive collection of Ghost Dance songs, including those of the Arapaho, Cheyenne, Comanche, Paiute, Lakota, Kiowa, and Caddo, was gathered at the end of the nineteenth century by James Mooney, a sympathetic ethnologist who found the Arapaho songs to be the most important and beautiful in both idea and expression. More recent works, such as that of Judith Vander, explore the complex cultural and individual meanings of the songs' lyrics.

REFERENCES

Mooney, James. *The Ghost-Dance Religion and the Sioux Outbreak of 1890*. 1896. Lincoln: University of Nebraska Press, 1991.

Neihardt, John G. *Black Elk Speaks*. Lincoln: University of Nebraska Press, 1932.

Ruoff, A. LaVonne Brown. *American Indian Literatures: An Introduction, Bibliographic Review, and Selected Bibliography*. New York: Modern Language Association, 1990.

Vander, Judith. *Shoshone Ghost Dance Religion: Poetry, Songs and Great Basin Context*. Chicago: University of Illinois Press, 1997.

David Kilpatrick

GILLETTE, WILLIAM HOOKER (1855–1937). More famous as an actor than as a writer, Gillette was nevertheless a prolific playwright, director, and successful theater impresario. He is possibly the most well-known American actor of the latter half of the nineteenth century. Born in Hartford, Connecticut, to U.S. Senator Francis Gillette and Elizabeth Daggett Hooker, Gillette was educated at Yale, Hartford, Harvard, and the Massachusetts Fine Arts Institute before making his stage debut in 1875 in New Orleans. He wrote twenty-five plays, many of them adaptations of popular novels and stories, including *The Professor* (1881), *Held by the Enemy* (his first successful Civil War drama, 1886), *A Legal Wreck* (1888), *All the Comforts of Home* (1890), *Too Much Johnson* (1894), *Clarice* (1905), *The Red Owl* (1907), *Samson* (1908), *Among Thieves* (1909), and *Electricity* (1910). Gillette scored his most notable triumphs with *Sherlock Holmes* (1899), his dramatization of Arthur Conan Doyle's stories, in which he played the title role to great acclaim, and *Secret Service* (1895), a Civil War drama he wrote as a starring vehicle for himself.

In *Secret Service*, Gillette's hero is Captain Alexander Dumont, an agent for the United States Secret Service, who infiltrates the Confederate Telegraph Service under the assumed name of Captain Thorne. As Captain Thorne, a southern officer, Dumont has the mischance of falling in love with Edith Varney, the daughter of the rebel General Varney, commander of the Telegraph Service. Thorne is faced with a dilemma: he knows that if he uses the rebel telegraph to send vital data to the Northern army, he will implicate Edith in the eyes of her own people. As a man of honor, he refuses. Edith tries to help him escape, but he refuses such help because it would bring scandal upon her family and subject her to arrest. Ultimately, Dumont is arrested by Confederate troops, and he is about to be shot when General Randolph arrives with the news confirming that Thorne/Dumont indeed did not send the message to the Yankees, thus saving his life. Instead, he is imprisoned for the duration of the war. *Secret Service* was the most popular war play of the period, having 1,700 performances by 1915. At that point, it was the most popular drama on the New York stage. It has enjoyed many revivals, including two unremarkable films, although modern audiences find it distinctly melodramatic.

A new edition of Gillette's collected plays was issued in 1983.

REFERENCES

Cook, Doris E. *Sherlock Holmes and Much More, or, Some of the Facts about William Gillette*. Hartford: Connecticut Historical Society, 1970.
Cullen, Rosemary, and Don B. Wilmeth. Introduction. *Plays*. By William Hooker Gillette. Cambridge: Cambridge University Press, 1983.
Vinson, James, and D. L. Kirkpatrick. *Dramatists*. New York: St. Martin's Press, 1979.

Randal W. Allred

GLASGOW, ELLEN (1873–1945). Born in Richmond, Virginia, in 1873, Ellen Glasgow was raised in the sheltered tradition thought proper for Southern women. She was kept from school and therefore was mainly self-educated. As she states in her autobiography, *The Woman Within* (1954), she rebelled early against "the pattern of society, as well as the scheme of things in general." In 1942 she received the Pulitzer Prize for Fiction, and her work is noted for its focus on Southern social history and its attention to the role and definition of Southern women.

Glasgow's fourth novel, *The Battle-Ground* (1902), takes place in Virginia in the time around the Civil War. In her characters, Glasgow contrasts various attitudes toward the South, slavery, and secession. Dan Montjoy grows from a boy who approaches the battle as if it were a foxhunt to a man who endures the starvation, sickness, and endless marching of war. This growth makes him worthy of the love of the heroine, Betty Ambler, through whom Glasgow addresses the difficulties of war for women: poverty, starvation, the loss of beloved men, and the extended, helpless waiting. The war also makes prominent the South's complex relationships of race and class, especially between blacks and poor whites. Glasgow's next novel, *The Deliverance* (1904), describes the period of Reconstruction in the South. In this novel, an old blind woman spends her days living on lies, believing that the Confederacy has never been defeated.

World War I was an important event in Glasgow's life and a strong influence on her writing. The war meant changes in personal relationships; both her lover, Henry Anderson, and her friend Anne Virginia Bennett, a Red Cross nurse, left for the war. Further, the war itself showed that humans have a strong instinct for violence, changing Glasgow's and the world's faith in civilization. *The Builders* (1919) explores the relationship of Caroline Meade, a nurse to the wealthy Blackburn family, with David Blackburn, a political radical who believes that the nation must enter World War I in order to show the world a society that is neither socialist nor autocratic. The important issue, for the characters and their ideology, is a balance between personal responsibilities and desires and a commitment to the larger good; America must grow beyond regionalism and even nationalism to internationalism. World War I is an important marker of changes in American manners and thinking in several other Glasgow novels as well, including *Barren Ground* (1925), *The Romantic Comedians* (1926), and *Virginia* (1935).

The Sheltered Life (1932) describes the decay of Southern aristocratic society in the years leading up to the First World War. In her critical work *A Certain Measure: An Interpretation of Prose Fiction* (1943) Glasgow says she wrote *The Sheltered Life* to show the connection between the suffering caused by idealism in the Civil War and the same kind of misery brought about by the idealism of World War I. General Archbald, a veteran of the Civil War, secretly dislikes violence and the Southern code but has sacrificed his life to it, and he helps transform his granddaughter Jenny Blair from a spirited girl to a young woman blinded by personal responsibility by the Southern aristocratic way of life, leading to the novel's final tragedy. John Welch, a young doctor, believes in the possibility of a better society and leaves to fight in World War I.

Glasgow continued to associate war with a cycle of changing idealisms. In 1941 she wrote: "War has come. . . . Another age of Disenchantment is ending. Another age of illusion is beginning."

REFERENCES

Dillard, R.H.W. "On Ellen Glasgow's *The Battle-Ground.*" *Classics of Civil War Fiction.* Ed. David Madden and Peggy Bach. Jackson: University Press of Mississippi, 1991.

Goodman, Susan. *Ellen Glasgow: A Biography.* Baltimore: Johns Hopkins University Press, 1998.

Matthews, Pamela R. *Ellen Glasgow and a Woman's Traditions.* Charlottesville: University Press of Virginia, 1994.

Jennifer A. Haytock

GORDON, CAROLINE (1895–1981). Born in Todd County, Kentucky, Caroline Gordon was raised near Clarksville, Tennessee, and educated at Bethany College in West Virginia. She married poet and novelist **Allen Tate** in 1924 and was divorced from him in 1959. Gordon worked as typist for British novelist Ford Madox Ford in New York and Paris, and Ford advised Gordon during the writing and publication of her first novel, *Penhally* (1931). A family chronicle, it traces the Llewelyn family from before the Civil War to the start of the twentieth century. Gordon focuses less on actual military and political events than on her thesis about the essential link between traditional values and the ownership of land.

In *None Shall Look Back* (1937), however, Gordon does deal directly with the events of the Civil War. Chiefly focusing on military action in Tennessee, Mississippi, and Georgia, the book introduces U. S. Grant and Robert E. Lee as characters, but it is Nathan Bedford Forrest who plays the chief role in the life of Gordon's protagonist, Lucy Churchill. In action at Fort Donelson, Nashville, Franklin, and other places, he embodies a code of selfless bravery and devotion to duty that Gordon sets up as an ideal and that inspires Rives Allard, Lucy's future husband. Nevertheless, this devotion is to a losing cause. And neither Forrest nor Rives is spared suffering because of heroism. *None Shall Look Back* ends with the wedding trip of Lucy and Rives, at the end of the Civil War, to the grim, dark Allard family home in Georgia. Gordon implies here that their future lives will be played out in a much less heroic, even more constraining, environment than that of the war.

Gordon's connections with the Southern Agrarians can be seen in her treatment of a man's relationship to land in *Aleck Maury, Sportsman* (1934), *The Garden of Adonis* (1937), and *Green Centuries* (1941), the last of which deals with Kentucky at the time of the American Revolution. After these novels, Gordon began to turn from examination of history in her fiction. While she continues to be interested in the hero and his quest, her focus becomes spiritual, as is suggested by the novels *The Women on the Porch* (1944), *The Forest of the South* (1945), *Strange Children* (1951), and *The Malefactors* (1956). Only in *The Glory of Hera* (1972) does she revert to the purely heroic, telling the story of the twelve labors of Heracles.

Gordon was also the author of distinguished short stories and of the critical texts *The House of Fiction* (1950), edited with Allen Tate, and *How to Read a Novel* (1957). She died in Cristabel de las Casas, Mexico.

REFERENCES

Fraistat, Rose Ann C. *Caroline Gordon as a Novelist and Woman of Letters*. Baton Rouge: Louisiana State University Press, 1984.
Jonza, Nancylee N. *The Underground Stream: The Life and Art of Caroline Gordon*. Athens: University of Georgia Press, 1995.
Makowsky, Veronica A. *Caroline Gordon*. New York: Oxford University Press, 1989.

Robert C. Petersen

GRAYDON, ALEXANDER (1752–1818). Born in Bristol, Pennsylvania, Graydon studied the law as a young man but had not completed his training when the American Revolution began. Commissioned as a captain in the Continental Army in early 1776, he raised a company of Pennsylvania troops. Taken prisoner during the loss of Fort Washington in November of 1776, he was held in New York for eight months. He was then paroled to Philadelphia where he stayed until his formal exchange in 1778.

Following the war, Graydon worked to ratify the Constitution in Pennsylvania and served as prothonotary of Dauphin County. When his Federalist views caused him to lose political influence in the late 1790s, he retired from public life. Declaring that he had "no pretensions to fame or distinction in any kind, neither as soldier, nor statesman, nor traveler, nor author," Graydon anonymously published an autobiography in 1811: *Memoirs of a Life, Chiefly Passed in Pennsylvania, within the Last Sixty Years; with Occasional Remarks upon the General Occurrences, Character and Spirit of that Eventful Period* was divided into roughly equal parts covering his early life, military service, and postwar political career.

Graydon's section on the war is of historical interest because of the details he provides concerning the treatment of prisoners. He describes his own mild captivity as an officer but also attacks British officials for the inhumane conditions that existed on the prison ships where common soldiers and sailors were kept.

In broader terms, Graydon's examination of the war is noteworthy because his account stands in contrast to the romanticized narratives of the Revolution that increasingly appeared in the early nineteenth century. Graydon does not narrate glorious victories or repeat patriot propaganda. Instead, he presents himself as a detached observer of the way the war was conducted and uses personal anecdotes and satire to offer a conservative warning against the democratic spirit unleashed by the struggle. With political villains like Thomas Jefferson in mind, Graydon echoed the views of many disaffected Federalists in charging that the war's noble aims had been manipulated by ambitious and self-serving men.

REFERENCES

Arch, Stephen Carl. "Writing a Federalist Self: Alexander Graydon's *Memoirs of a Life.*" *William and Mary Quarterly* 52 (1995): 415–432.
Graydon, Alexander. *Memoirs of His Own Time*. 1846. Ed. John Stockton Littell. New York: New York Times, 1969.
Sanderlin, Robert Reed. "Alexander Graydon: The Life and Literary Career of an American Patriot." Diss. University of North Carolina at Chapel Hill, 1968.

Robert D. Sturr

GRIFFIN, W.E.B. (1929–). "W.E.B. Griffin" is the most prominent of the several pen names employed by William Edmund Butterworth III, a prolific best-selling writer who has published more than 100 books on a variety of subjects ranging from stockcar racing to skyjacking. Born in Newark, New Jersey, Butterworth served in the U.S. Army as a combat correspondent during the Korean War, winning the Expert Combat Infantryman's Badge, and then embarking on a writing career that would eventually win him the title of "Most Prolific Alabama Author of All Time." As W.E.B. Griffin, he is the author of no fewer than 19 war novels, chief among them the eight-volume *The Brotherhood of War* series consisting of *The Lieutenants* (1983), *The Captains* (1985), *The Majors* (1984), *The Colonels* (1985), *The Berets* (1985), *The Generals* (1986), *The New Breed* (1987), and *The Aviators* (1988); and the seven-volume *The Corps* series composed of *Semper Fi* (1986), *Call to Arms* (1987), *Counterattack* (1990), *Battleground* (1991), *Line of Fire* (1992), *Close Combat* (1992), and *Behind the Lines* (1993).

The *Brotherhood of War* is a cross section of the U.S. military in action, from privates to generals to presidents, from World War II to Vietnam. However, even though the experience of combat plays a prominent role in each of these novels, the primary perspective employed is the romantic world of military intelligence and covert operations. Indeed, *The Brotherhood of War* is an extended examination of how military intelligence affects strategy and spawns a wide array of "special" operations, and its locale wanders around the globe to wherever U.S. interests are being threatened by the godless Soviets. Butterworth creates a cast of four or five principal male soldiers, almost invariably white officers, of various ages, ranks, and socioeconomic backgrounds whose lives intersect at key points in the narrative. They are alike, however, in that they are all versions of the All-American Boy who becomes the ideal American soldier: courageous, patriotic, intelligent, resourceful, and, when necessary, absolutely ruthless. When not protecting our national security, their major interests, like those of warriors throughout history, are alcohol and women. Their women, too, are also everything an American warrior could want: sexy, devoted, and faithful.

Butterworth's rendering of the world of the career officer corps at one of the critical periods of the Cold War is idealized but generally convincing; however, his almost exclusive focus on the professional military results in a highly unbalanced depiction of the actual history of the Vietnam era. For example, it is almost impossible to determine from Butterworth's narrative that the Vietnam War was a deeply divisive national undertaking that the United States did in fact lose. In fact, *The Brotherhood of War* suggests a version of American history as told by the Pentagon, and in this and many other respects, Butterworth strongly resembles Tom Clancy.

Similarly, *The Corps* is a multigenerational patriotic saga of the U.S. Marine Corps from shortly before World War II to its glory days in the Pacific. Butterworth begins in China in 1938, where there had been a substantial U.S. Marine and Navy presence alone the Yangtze River ever since the Boxer Rebellion was crushed by European and American forces at the turn of the century. When the Japanese invaded China in 1937, American and Japanese troops were in close proximity for the first time, and Marine intelligence was instructed to find out as much as possible about the military capability of this growing threat from the east, information that, according to Butterworth, was responsible for the rapid Marine buildup in the Pacific in anticipation of war with the Japanese.

The cast of *The Corps* is a representative cross section of those Marine officers who were instrumental in the massive reorganization and expansion of the Corps after Pearl Harbor, a process that culminated in the first Marine offensive action at Guadalcanal. Butterworth is primarily a writer of patriotic action-adventure-romance, which is generally accomplished at the expense of intellectual and emotional complexity. On the other hand, the breadth, detail, and accuracy of his military historical research are impressive, whether the subject be water-cooled machine guns, uniform insignia, or company-level personnel policies. Some of the most intriguing parts of *The Corps* deal with how the M-1 came to be adopted as the standard Marine infantry weapon and why the Marine Raiders were formed.

As W.E.B. Griffin, Butterworth is also the author of *Honor Bound* (1995) and *Blood and Honor* (1996), both of which are set in Argentina during World War II and involve American and Nazi espionage and intrigue. He is presently at work on another multivolume series recounting the creation and history of the Office of Strategic Services (OSS).

REFERENCES

Caton, Bill. "Bill Butterworth." *Fighting Words: Words on Writing from 21 of the Heart of Dixie's Best Contemporary Authors*. Ed. Bill Caton. Montgomery, AL: Black Belt, 1995.

Murray, David. Rev. of *The New Breed*, by W.E.B. Griffin. *New York Times Book Review* 20 December 1987: 17.

Rev. of *The Lieutenants*, by W.E.B. Griffin. *West Coast Review of Books* March 1983: 52.

Lucas Carpenter

H

HALBERSTAM, DAVID (1934–   ). Born in New York City, David Halberstam served as a foreign correspondent for the *New York Times* in Vietnam from 1962 to 1963 and received the Pulitzer Prize for International Reporting in Vietnam in 1964. He also reported from the Congo (1961–1962) and Poland (1965–1966).

Halberstam's *One Very Hot Day* (1968) is often considered one of the best novelistic accounts of the Vietnam War. Set in the early days of the American involvement in Vietnam, the novel traces the journey of two American "advisors" as they accompany a group of Vietnamese soldiers and officers through the Mekong Delta. One of the few American novels to treat Vietnamese as full characters, the novel's strength is its ability to articulate the cultural barriers between Americans and the South Vietnamese. Captain Beaupre (a cynical veteran of battles in Korea, Germany, and Normandy) is impatient with the allies and must constantly restrain himself to be polite to Captain Dong (an official consumed with his personal safety and political advancement). The relationship between Lieutenant Anderson (an eager West Pointer) and his counterpart Lieutenant Thuong is perhaps the more interesting one. Anderson has learned Vietnamese, but it is clear that his efforts have not managed to bridge the gaps between the two cultures.

With his background as a journalist, Halberstam is more prolific in his nonfiction work. His earliest book, *The Making of a Quagmire* (first published in 1965 and reissued in 1987 under the title *The Making of a Quagmire: America and Vietnam*) tells the story of the "quagmire" that was to become full-blown American participation in the Vietnam War. As a reporter in Vietnam, Halberstam loved the country and its people and deplored the thought of Communist conquest. Thus, in *The Making of a Quagmire*, he supports the U.S. presence in the country but speaks out against the methods he sees Americans taking. In *Ho* (1971) Halberstam clearly admires Ho Chi Minh as a subject, and he sees (as is made even more clear in *The Best and the Brightest*) American underestimation of Ho Chi Minh as a beginning point for disastrous results for Americans in Vietnam. The title of *The Best and the Brightest* (1972) refers to the intellectual and corporate elite who came to Washington with Kennedy in 1961. Halberstam blames "the best and the brightest" for U.S. involvement in Vietnam. Kennedy is portrayed more favorably than the men who worked for him, but he is still described in *The Best and the Brightest* as "too cool, too hard-line in his foreign policies, too devoid of commitment." Part journalistic history, part psychological analysis, part political commentary, the book contains the deep research and detailed reporting that mark all of Halberstam's work.

Halberstam's recent works reflect varied interests. *The Summer of '49* (1989) and *October 1964* (1994) are about the sport of baseball. He also wrote *The Fifties* (1993), a look at American life in the 1950s; *The Reckoning* (1994), about economic relations between Japan and America; and *The Amateurs: The Story of Four Young Men & Their Quest for Olympic Gold* (1996).

REFERENCES

Emery, Michael. *On the Frontlines: Following America's Foreign Correspondents Across the Twentieth Century*. Washington, D.C.: American University Press, 1995.
Prochnau, William. *Once Upon a Distant War*. New York: Random House, 1995.

Samantha J. Ward

HALDEMAN, JOE (1943–   ). Born in Oklahoma, Haldeman earned a B.S. in astronomy from the University of Maryland before spending most of 1968 in Vietnam as a combat engineer attached to the Fourth Infantry Division. Haldeman, who earned an M.F.A. from the University of Iowa, has written two memorable novels directly about the war, *War Year* (1972) and *1968* (1995), and many shorter works in which the war plays a prominent part. In dozens of other works, his imaginary worlds are transformations of the American 1960s and 1970s.

War Year reads like a first (largely autobiographical) novel. It conveys a grim, matter-of-fact, battlefield realism but allows little perspective on the horrors it records. The theme of physical and spiritual wounding, which runs through much of Haldeman's work, makes an early appearance here.

With his prizewinning *The Forever War* (1975), Joe Haldeman made his mark in the world of science fiction. "There are parallels between the Vietnam War and *The Forever War*," Haldeman wrote in 1988. Both wars "drag on and on and when the soldiers come back, they find that the country they were supposedly fighting for has radically changed. And most people don't much care about what happened to them." Other parallels between Haldeman's imagined thousand-year war and the one he knew in Vietnam include an unhealthy pride in superior technology and a need to see the enemy as an inferior species.

In 1997, Haldeman published *Forever Peace*, a sequel (of sorts) to *The Forever War*. Set in the year 2043, *Forever Peace* takes place during a twelve-year war fought by automated, armor-plated American "soldierboys." The soldierboys work in hunter/killer, H&I, and psy-ops teams (all Vietnam War terms). Haldeman's imagined war is a hellish one, especially after the protagonist and his significant other battle more than the enemy in this tautly written novel.

Haldeman's *None So Blind* (1996) is a Vietnam War–heavy collection of ten short stories, a novella called "The Hemingway Hoax," and four of what he labels "story poems." The pieces with the strongest Vietnam War connections— "The Monster," "Graves," "DX," "Images," and "The Hemingway Hoax"—all contain fantasy/science fiction elements. In the story "Images," a Vietnam vet turned community theater actor discovers that the best performer in his group actually is an alien who gives new meaning to the term "getting into character." In the poem "DX," which originally appeared in the anthology *In the Field of Fire* (1986), Haldeman evokes the incident that was responsible for his war wounds. The poem has parallels with characters and events in *War Year*.

In "The Hemingway Hoax," the protagonist is a **Hemingway** scholar who was wounded during his Vietnam tour. As the story evolves, the character meets Hemingway's ghost and, on several occasions, reexperiences parts of his own past. Each time he does so, the gory battlefield details are significantly different. The scholar–veteran assesses Hemingway's wounds from World War I in the light of his own experience with similar ones. This work, which was published separately as a novel in 1990, shares with *The Forever War* the distinction of winning both the Hugo and Nebula awards.

1968 (1995) is a biting novel set in Vietnam and on the home front in which Haldeman depicts a most unglamorous view of war and its aftermath. Haldeman's story centers on John "Spider" Spiedel, an everyman college dropout who gets drafted and undergoes a nightmarish Vietnam combat tour in which he is first mentally unbalanced by graves registration work and later becomes the sole survivor of an ambush. The novel's parallel story involves Spider's prewar girlfriend, Beverly, and her journey from naive college student to counterculture veteran. Through her story, Haldeman puts readers at key antiwar events as well as at the King and Robert Kennedy assassinations.

Haldeman spits out Spider and Beverly's stories in short, biting paragraphs grouped into brief chapter bursts. This bluntly straight-ahead style works well in conjuring up Spider's nightmarish world and Beverly's not exactly smooth coming-of-age adventures. Haldeman spices up the narrative with some science fiction–like passages. Perhaps no author has captured the surreal nature of Vietnam War combat more intimately than has Joe Haldeman.

REFERENCE

Franklin, H. Bruce. "The Vietnam War as American Science Fiction and Fantasy." *Science Fiction Studies* 17.3 (November 1990): 341–359.

Marc Leepson

HALE, EDWARD EVERETT (1822–1909). This prolific writer, born in Boston in 1822, was one of nineteenth-century New England's grand old men of letters. A Harvard graduate and an ordained Unitarian minister, Hale channeled his deep beliefs in morality and ethics into his writing, which embraced everything from history to religion to classical mythology to social welfare. Although well known for his roles as editor, reviewer, or contributor for periodicals as varied as *The Christian Examiner, North American Review*, and *The Youth's Companion*, he gained fame with his vastly popular short story "The Man without a Country," published in the December 1863 issue of *The Atlantic Monthly*.

Frederic Ingham, a retired navy officer, narrates the tale of Philip Nolan, a passionate southwestern army officer who in 1807 joins Aaron Burr's ill-fated Western conspiracy. Convicted of treason, Nolan is sentenced to exile at sea and prohibited from hearing the name of or learning information about the United States in accordance with his wish to "never hear of the United States again." Perpetually estranged, Nolan eventually realizes the depth of his folly. The allure of "separate sovereignty" turns into nightmares as Nolan's immature desire for secession metamorphoses into a fervent adult patriotism. Reading and studying only intensify his intellectual and emotional torment, for they torment the keen sense that secession from the Union robs him of the very roots of his identity.

Written for a Northern audience emotionally drained by the Civil War, this story seeks to reinvigorate the "just" patriotism of those who chose the Union over the Confederacy by illustrating the dangers of secession and egocentrism. It also criticizes slavery as a gutting of true identity; Hale's comparison of Nolan's situation to that of illegally seized Africans who desire to return home— the heartland of their identities—reveals the utter destitution of a man who, unlike the Africans, has no homeland and therefore no real sense of self.

Hale's service as a director for the Sanitary Commission resulted in his memorialization in the Soldiers' Monument on Boston Common, also the site of B. L. Pratt's statue dedicated in 1913 to this "Prophet of Peace" and "Patriot."

REFERENCES

Adams, John R. *Edward Everett Hale*. Boston: Twayne, 1977.
Hale, Edward Everett. *The Works of Edward Everett Hale*. Library edition. 10 vols. Boston: Little, Brown, 1898–1900.
Holloway, Jean. *Edward Everett Hale: A Biography*. Austin: University of Texas Press, 1956.

Sandra Burr

HALL, JAMES NORMAN (1887–1951). Hall was born in Colfax, Iowa, and educated there and at the college later renamed Grinnell. Touring Wales on holiday when World War I broke out, the young woodshed poet joined up as private 690 in the Ninth Battalion, Royal Fusiliers, among Lord Kitchener's First Hundred Thousand. Discharged late in 1915 after service as a machine-gunner at various points on the British front, he recounted his experiences in his first autobiographical work, serialized in *The Atlantic Monthly* and collected as *Kitchener's Mob* (1916). Hall then enlisted in a squadron of volunteer American airmen serving in the French army, the famous Lafayette Escadrille. In January 1918, Sergeant Hall was transferred to the U.S. Army with the rank of captain in the 103rd Pursuit Squadron. As combat pilot and then flight commander in the 94th Pursuit Squadron, he had a brilliant and daring record alongside Eddie Rickenbacker. A survivor of three crashes, credited with five kills, Hall became a much admired and decorated Ace. On a sortie in May, he was shot down in a dogfight inside German lines. Interned in the prisoner of war (POW) camp at Landshut in Bavaria, he was allowed to escape after the Armistice.

At twenty-nine, Hall met his close contemporary and near look-alike, Charles Bernard Nordhoff (1887–1947), a fellow American (though London-born) who had crossed the Atlantic to fly with the Lafayette Escadrille. Following Hall's book *High Adventure* (1918), telling of his exploits as a *pilote de chasse*, Nordhoff published his own Lafayette experiences as *The Fledgling* (1919), which was serialized in *The Atlantic* much as Hall's *Kitchener's Mob* had been published there a few years earlier. After demobilization in 1919, the new team of Nordhoff and Hall launched their collaboration with a two-volume history of *The Lafayette Flying Corps*, written in Martha's Vineyard and published the following year, when the two authors settled in Tahiti. After several travel books written independently or jointly, Hall turned to fiction in collaboration with Nordhoff. The first fictional product of their partnership was a juvenile, *Falcons of France* (1929), in which the American hero, Charles Selden, sees much action, is captured by the enemy, and escapes from a German prison camp. Writing solo, Hall also penned *Flying with Chaucer* (1930), which tells how a battered *Canterbury Tales* accompanied him during his months as a POW. The two authors' collaboration peaked with the immensely popular historical fiction that is *The Bounty Trilogy (Mutiny on the Bounty*, 1932; *Men against the Sea,* 1934; and *Pitcairn's Island*, 1934), followed by other, less successful novels set also in the South Sea Isles. *Men without Country* (1942), mostly Hall's work, was the inspiration for Michael Curtiz's film *Passage to Marseille*, intended to capitalize on the success of the same director's *Casablanca,* featuring essentially the same cast. Finally, Hall's own *Lost Island* (1944) treats the impact of the war on a Polynesian island, and his *A Word for His Sponsor* (1949) addresses the growing threat of nuclear holocaust.

Hall modestly defined himself as a journalist. After the thrilling narrative of the mutiny against Captain Bligh and his miraculous survival with a handful of loyal crewmen, Hall's most readable books remain his autobiographical, historical, and fictional works transcribing aerial adventures in the open-cockpit Blériot and Spad planes of World War I.

REFERENCES

Hall, James Norman. *My Island Home*. Boston: Little, Brown, 1952.
Johnson, Robert Leland. *The American Heritage of James Norman Hall*. Philadelphia: Dorrance, 1969.
Roulston, Robert. *James Norman Hall*. Boston: Twayne, 1978.

Roy Rosenstein

HARRIS, JOEL CHANDLER (1848–1908). A journalist, short story writer, and novelist, Harris is best known for his humorous Uncle Remus stories, which made him almost as famous as his contemporary **Mark Twain**. Among his lesser-known works are a number of pieces dealing with the Civil War.

Harris was raised by his mother, a seamstress, in the small Georgia town of Eatonville, following her abandonment by his father before the boy's birth. His lifelong career in journalism began when he was apprenticed at thirteen to Joseph Addison Turner, the owner of a newspaper published at Turnwold plantation. During this period, Harris formed lifelong friendships with older slaves who told him the tales that he eventually collected into the Uncle Remus stories. He published the first of these in the Atlanta *Constitution* in 1879 to critical and public acclaim; many others followed and were collected in a series of popular books beginning with *Uncle Remus: His Songs and His Sayings* (1880).

In addition to the Uncle Remus stories and other pieces for children, from the late 1880s until his death, Harris wrote short stories, novelettes, and novels that included social realism, local color, and ethnic dialect, balanced by sentimentalism, tragedy, and Gothic elements. A teenager during the Civil War, Harris was mostly sheltered from it in rural Georgia, but it figures prominently in many of these works. Several stories in his two early collections—*Free Joe and Other Georgian Sketches* (1887) and *Balaam and His Master and Other Stories and Sketches* (1890)—are set during the war, with an emphasis on reconciliation between North and South, symbolized by marriage of a Yankee and a Southerner. In *Tales of the Home Folks in Peace and War* (1889) and *On the Wing of Occasions* (1900), the majority of the stories are directly about the war and include not terribly realistic scenes of battles. Five of the stories in *On the Wing of Occasions* deal with the Confederate secret service, and in these Harris's lack of battle experience and superficial understanding of military history are apparent. In the last and probably the best tale, "The Kidnapping of President Lincoln," two men sent by the South to kidnap Lincoln are so impressed by his wisdom and compassion that they abort the mission. The war is also used as a backdrop to family problems, frequently involving themes of seduction, abandonment, and illegitimate birth that seem to reflect Harris's consternation over his own origins.

The emphasis is again on romance and reconciliation in Harris's 1904 novelette *A Little Union Scout*, in which the narrator discovers that a famous Union spy is actually an attractive woman with whom he falls in love and marries.

The Shadow between His Shoulder-Blades, published posthumously in 1909, is more realistic, somewhat in the vein of **Stephen Crane's** *The Red Badge of Courage*. Here, Harris undercuts wartime heroics and shows the absurdity and confusion of battle, as when the protagonist is praised for accidentally capturing two Union soldiers and barely escapes being hanged as a spy.

Harris died in 1908 just after being baptized a Catholic.

REFERENCES

Bickley, R. Bruce, Jr. *Joel Chandler Harris*. Boston: Twayne, 1978.
Cousins, Paul. *Joel Chandler Harris: A Biography*. Baton Rouge: Louisiana State University Press, 1968.

Ymitri Jayasundera

HARRISON, CHARLES YALE (1898–1954). Although an American, Charles Yale Harrison will always be associated with the Canadian experience of World War I, the subject of Harrison's first novel, *Generals Die in Bed* (1930). Born in Philadelphia, Harrison served with the Canadian Army on the Western Front until he was wounded in 1918. After the war, Harrison worked as a reporter in Montreal, then moved to New York, where he began his writing career. In addition to *Generals*, Harrison produced a biography of Clarence Darrow and several other novels, none of which matched the success of his first book.

Illustrative of the antiwar mood that swept through European and North American literature in the late 1920s and early 1930s, *Generals Die in Bed* can best be described as a Canadian *All Quiet on the Western Front*—only without the memorable imagery of Remarque's masterpiece. Complete with a bitterly ironic title, a virtual convention at the time, Harrison's novel shares a number of features with Remarque's, including the same style of first-person, present-tense narration and many of the same thematic emphases. Only the uniforms are different. Like Paul Baumer's narrative, the book follows a group of enlisted men (in this case, Canadians) from one seemingly pointless battle to the next, all the while stressing their transformation into brutal creatures of instinct. However, Harrison's vision of the war, as presented through the eyes of an anonymous private soldier, is, if anything, bleaker than Remarque's. While the German novelist presents comradeship as the one great positive to emerge from the battlefield, Harrison ruthlessly denies its existence: In one scene, we see the narrator's comrades fight among themselves for a scrap of bread; in another, the narrator leaves a wounded friend behind while fleeing from the front line.

Episodes in which Harrison's enlisted men shoot their own officers, butcher hordes of surrendering Germans, and drunkenly pillage a French town complete a representation of World War I that comes, at times, dangerously close to parody.

REFERENCES

Nielsen, Robert F. Introduction. *Generals Die in Bed*. By Charles Yale Harrison. Hamilton, Ontario: Potlatch, 1975.

Thompson, Eric. "Canadian Fiction of the Great War." *Canadian Literature* (Winter 1981): 81–96.

Steven Trout

HASFORD, GUSTAV (1947–1993). Born in Haleyville, Alabama, Hasford served in the U.S. Marine Corps from 1966 to 1968 and was a combat correspondent in Vietnam. He briefly attended Santa Monica City College after military service and also worked as a hotel clerk. Hasford may well have been radicalized by his military service: He once listed his political preference as "socialist" and his religion as "beer." *The Short-Timers* (1979), which was the basis for the 1987 Stanley Kubrick film *Full Metal Jacket*, is certainly the product of that radicalization. Hasford was a member of the Vietnam Veterans against the War and in 1988 was charged by police with grand theft for taking more than 700 books from American and English libraries. He was ultimately convicted of the lesser charge of possessing stolen property.

The Short-Timers is certainly Hasford's attempt to depict the horrible cruelty of war, and the extremely violent novel is a study of the brutalization that occurs when men must be trained to fight and kill.

The Short-Timers draws on Hasford's military experiences in Vietnam as a combat correspondent. One of the main themes has to do with the development of the soldier's callousness conditioned by the brutal training in Marine boot camp and then reinforced by the horrible cruelty of battle. The main voice in the novel is that of William "Joker" Doolittle, a Marine combat reporter. Joker's view is dark and ironic as he describes the various events of the book. For instance, he narrates the actions of Pvt. Pyle, who robotically assassinates his drill sergeant in boot camp before killing himself; and Rafterman, who hungrily cannibalizes one of his own dead comrades in Vietnam. And there is Joker himself who recounts the horrors of war—and his own mercy killing of a best friend—through a mask of black humor and cold indifference that enables him to survive the colder and darker reality of the war.

The novel received mixed critical reviews. While one reviewer called it the "best work of fiction about the Vietnam War I've read," another cited it for its violence, remarking that the novel may work as "purgation, but . . . it not only fails to move but to interest."

Hasford also wrote *The Phantom Blooper* (1990), a sequel to *The Short-Timers* that follows Joker's further adventures in Vietnam as he becomes a prisoner of war and eventually confronts the Phantom Blooper, the mythical renegade "White VC," who symbolizes the dark collective conscience of the American G.I. in Vietnam. Dedicated to the 3 million Vietnam veterans "who were betrayed by their country," *The Phantom Blooper* is another angry yet compelling expression of Hasford's darkly upsetting cynicism.

Hasford's final work, *A Gypsy Good Time* (1992), is a satire on contemporary Hollywood and is narrated by a character who is a Vietnam veteran. Hasford died in Greece of complications from diabetes.

REFERENCES

Beidler, Philip D. *American Literature and the Experience of Vietnam*. Athens: University of Georgia Press, 1982.
Herzog, Tobey C. *Vietnam War Stories: Innocence Lost*. New York and London: Routledge, 1992.
Los Angeles Times 3 February 1993: A12.
Melling, Philip H. *Vietnam in American Literature*. Boston: Twayne, 1990.

Peter Katopes

HAYSLIP, LE LY (1949–). Phung Thi Le Ly was born in the peaceful rice-farming village of Ky La (later named Xa Hoa Qui) in the Quang Nam province of central Vietnam. She was the sixth child in a devout Buddhist family that revered its traditions, ancestors, and land. Born during French colonial rule, Hayslip attended a local school until the Vietnam War escalated, and her life continued amidst combat. Although her village labored for the government by day, she aided the Viet Cong in their fight against South Vietnamese (Army of the Republic of Vietnam [ARVN]) and American forces by working as a lookout, digging tunnels, and tending to the wounded. Suspected of treason by the Viet Cong, Hayslip was sentenced to death, only to be raped and then released by the men assigned to execute her. As a result, her village shunned her and southern forces suspected her activities with the Viet Cong. She fled to Da Nang and then Saigon at the age of fourteen.

This turbulent childhood is the catalyst for memoirs *When Heaven and Earth Changed Places* (1989) and *Child of War, Woman of Peace* (1993). The first account, written with Jay Wurts, chronicles the first twenty years of her life in Vietnam, interwoven with journals from her 1986 return to Vietnam from the United States. She narrates the years of her brutal childhood and life as a teenage refugee working as a servant in Saigon. Leaving Saigon pregnant with her master's child, she works the streets of Da Nang by dealing in black market merchandise, serving as a drug courier, and maneuvering through relationships with American military men—some are brutal and others are simply exchanges of sex for money. She eventually emigrates to the United States in 1970 and begins a lifelong transformation from war victim to political activist. These postwar years comprise *Child of War, Woman of Peace* (written with son James Hayslip) as Hayslip emerges from failed relationships and marriages to build rehabilitation centers in Vietnam through the East Meets West Foundation. Hayslip's two memoirs were developed into the film *Heaven and Earth* (1993), the third film in Oliver Stone's Vietnam trilogy.

REFERENCES

Christopher, Renny. *The Viet Nam War/The American War: Images and Representations in Euro-American and Vietnamese Exile Narratives*. Amherst: University of Massachusetts Press, 1995.

Hayslip, Le Ly. "We Vietnamese Can Finally Heal If We Want To." *Los Angeles Times*
        12 September 1994: B4.
Kempley, Rita. "Nine Questions for . . . Le Ly Hayslip." *Washington Post* 2 January
        1994: G2.

Brad E. Lucas

HEGGEN, THOMAS (1919–1949). Born in Fort Dodge, Iowa, Thomas
Orlo Heggen was inclined toward a literary life by the influence of his older
cousin and lifelong friend Wallace Stegner. Heggen attended several colleges,
graduating from the University of Minnesota in 1941. Here he met Chuck Roberts, whose surname he borrowed for his famous character, and Max Shulman,
his unofficial rival as campus writer and wit. After graduation, Heggen worked
for *Reader's Digest* until he enlisted in the navy a week after Pearl Harbor but
just before he would have been drafted. Heggen served briefly as a yeoman;
then, after attending the wartime Midshipman School at Northwestern University, he was commissioned in August 1942. Heggen served on several ships: a
gasoline tanker, a cargo ship, and finally the USS *Virgo*, which carried fighting
men to the enemy islands. Discharged in December 1945, Heggen finished the
task of transforming his experiences into fiction.

Published in 1946, *Mr. Roberts* was an instant success. Though critics did
not regard it a literary masterpiece, they recognized its originality and accuracy
in portraying shipboard life, especially the debilitating effects of boredom, grind-
ing routine, and small-minded enforcement of regulations. The book sold
100,000 copies in hardback and well over a million in paperback. More a series
of vignettes than a carefully plotted narrative, *Mr. Roberts* provides the back-
water view of the Pacific Campaign. Readers follow the USS *Reluctant* as it
transports supplies from one tiny island to the next: islands named Tedium,
Apathy, and Ennui. A classic of wartime support operations, it has spawned
many imitations. A special area of interest is the portrait of Roberts, the ship's
first lieutenant and cargo officer, as the epitome of the natural leader. Against
him, the shortcomings of others are measured. Heggen's greatest achievement
is the book's tragicomic tone, the humor that both recognizes and makes bear-
able the absurdities of life. Mr. Roberts, Ensign Pulver, Doc, and the ignomin-
ious Captain are permanent contributions to military lore.

The somber aspects of the novel are diminished and the farcical accentuated
in the highly successful dramatic version (1948), scripted by Heggen and Joshua
Logan, and in the unforgettable film starring Henry Fonda as Roberts and Jack
Lemmon as Ensign Pulver.

Heggen did not survive the success of his only novel. He could never find
the resources to sustain the literary career he so earnestly sought. In May 1949,
he was found dead in the bathtub of his New York apartment, a nearly empty
bottle of sleeping pills nearby.

REFERENCES

Leggett, John. *Ross and Tom: Two American Tragedies*. New York: Simon and Schuster,
        1974.

Smith, David P. Introduction. *Mr. Roberts*, by Thomas Heggen. Annapolis: Naval Institute Press, 1992.

Philip K. Jason

HEINEMANN, LARRY (1944–). A product of working-class Chicago, Larry Heinemann served with the 25th Infantry Division armored reconnaissance in Vietnam from March 1967 to March 1968. Lacking the funds to stay in school, he was drafted when he graduated from a two-year college. After serving in Vietnam, Heinemann took writing courses and began teaching. His first novel, *Close Quarters* (1979), fictionalizes his Vietnam War experience. His second novel, *Paco's Story* (1986), won the National Book Award for fiction and depicts a Vietnam War combatant's return home. Besides these two novels, he has published shorter fiction and nonfiction plus a third novel, *Cooler by the Lake*, a slapstick story about Chicago.

Heinemann's war novels are chillingly realistic portrayals of the evil and senselessness implicit in Vietnam War service—an experience that cemented his own often-voiced contempt for the military and its leadership. Heinemann's soldiers view their tours as menial labor, albeit violent and unsatisfying. These are men who know they were sent to Vietnam because their families could not afford to keep them out of it. Heinemann's narrators are war-savvy combatants who ascribe to the Puritan beliefs of fate and destiny. These soldiers do not mourn their postmodern, deterministic situations; they merely survive an experience strictly controlled by chance. Heinemann's characters show little remorse or regret for the evil they witness or perpetrate in a Vietnam that is claustrophobic and congested. In Heinemann's Vietnam, the American trash heap clutters the countryside with material but no native people: Only whores and profiteers abound, and Vietnam becomes a macabre place for American soldiers merely to die. Heinemann experiments with tense in *Close Quarters* and voice and narration in *Paco's Story* to express an urgency to the telling of these episodic stories.

Close Quarters is a realistic combat story that follows Philip Dosier through his Vietnam tour of duty and his return home. The novel opens on Dosier's first day with the Reconnaissance Platoon armored personnel carriers where he is assigned to the seven-three "track" and meets his mentor, Cross. As Cross introduces Dosier to the evils of Vietnam, the reader witnesses this corruption at a rate equal to Dosier's own acquiescence to that evil. This is particularly apparent when, at the beginning of the novel, Dosier can politely refuse an experience with the local prostitute, Claymore Face, to his forced degradation of her toward its end when he threatens to shoot her if she does not publicly perform fellatio on a group of soldiers. Dosier is an attentive war participant and earns the nickname Deadeye, a name both suggestive of his military and sexual prowess. With Cross's rotation home, Dosier establishes a friendship with the equally cruel but ill-fated Quinn: a relationship rooted in their contempt for the war, military leadership, and Vietnam. This is a horrific combat story, both graphic and sinister. Despite the numerous misogynistic and xenophobic episodes, the reader is left with empathy toward Dosier and his corruption. At Quinn's grave in Terre Haute, Dosier reconfirms that no one comes home from Vietnam, and *Close Quarters* ends.

Paco Sullivan is Alpha Company's only survivor when they are hit by a friendly fire artillery barrage while at Fire Base Harriette. These "collective" dead graphically tell *Paco's Story* from the time he is with their platoon in Vietnam to the time he leaves Boone, Texas, where the real time of the story takes place. The novel follows Paco's arrival in Boone, his attempts to find employment, his work as a dishwasher at the Texas Lunch, and his eventual escape to parts west. Events in Boone spark flashbacks to events from the war. The evils of Vietnam are present back in Boone as Paco attempts to reconcile to a life after Fire Base Harriette. Paco's history begins in Vietnam: There are no prewar events to identify with in *Paco's Story*. Paco does not interact with the reader or the residents of Boone: He is more specter than the collective dead who tell his story and who reinforce the idea that life and death are randomly predetermined. Paco is not a sympathetic character though. His own cruelty is evident as a participant in the violent gang rape of a Viet Cong prisoner and in his own voyeuristic dealings with the college student Cathy whose cruelty to him points back to his own behavior in Vietnam. Paco is powerless to overcome his Vietnam war experience. When confronted with his victimization by Cathy, Paco leaves his job and moves his "collective" dead in the hopes of finding less interference elsewhere.

REFERENCES

Beidler, Philip D. *Re-Writing America: Vietnam Authors in Their Generation.* Athens: University of Georgia Press, 1991.
Cronin, Cornelius A. "Historical Background to Larry Heinemann's *Close Quarters*." *Critique: Studies in Contemporary Fiction* 24.2 (Winter 1983): 119–129.
Schroeder, Eric James. "Larry Heinemann." *Vietnam, We've All Been There: Interviews with American Writers.* Westport, CT: Praeger, 1992.
Scott, Grant F. "*Paco's Story* and the Ethics of Violence." *Critique: Studies in Contemporary Fiction* 36 (Fall 1994): 69–80.

Donna L. Pasternak

HELLER, JOSEPH (1923–1999). Heller was born in Brooklyn and raised in the seaside neighborhoods of Coney Island. He came of age as America entered World War II, and in 1942, he enlisted in the Army Air Corps. As a bombardier with the 340th Bombardment Group, Heller flew sixty combat missions over Italy and France in B-25 medium bombers based on Corsica. After the war, Heller's study of literature culminated in a master's from Columbia (1949), a Fulbright scholarship to Oxford (1949–1950), and two years teaching at Penn State. His first published work appeared in the fall 1945 issue of *Story*, an issue dedicated to short fiction by returning servicemen. As an undergraduate at New York University, he placed stories about Jewish life in depression-era

Brooklyn with *Esquire* and *The Atlantic Monthly*, but he published no new fiction until 1955, when "Catch-18" (published in *New World Writing* 7) previewed the first chapter of a work-in-progress that, six years later, would become the enduring classic *Catch-22*.

Catch-22 is perhaps the most uncharacteristic of World War II novels. Heller confronts the attitudes of postwar America in general and in particular those of the big business world of promotion and advertising where he worked after returning to New York in 1952. His settled form—a grotesque blending of the comic and tragic—reflects the dark humor influences of Waugh, Nabokov, and Celine in ways that seriously question traditional views of heroism. The plot draws on Heller's own wartime experiences, but it is loaded with anachronisms from life in Cold War America that reinforce the novel's satiric bite.

The novel cycles recursively through the wartime adventures of Yossarian, a B-25 bombardier who is determined to live forever or die trying. The narrative is periodically punctuated by self-initiated stays in hospital—Yossarian's only recourse in a war where both sides are apparently determined to kill him. As his commanders continue to raise the number of missions each airman must fly, more and more of Yossarian's zany comrades are killed. Others simply disappear. All live under the watchful eyes of ambitious commanders, shadowy Criminal Investigations Division (CID) men, and the burgeoning M & M Enterprises of Milo Minderbinder, an entity that slowly takes control of events on both sides of the war. Initially, "catch-22" is simply the double paradox imposed by regulation on Heller's aviators—they must fly more missions even if they don't want to, because resistance is the reflex of a sane man; they can only be grounded if they are insane enough to want to fly combat missions, and no one that sick requests to be grounded anyway. During his last furlough in Rome, Yossarian discovers that M & M Enterprises has taken over the entire war, transforming "catch-22" into a chillingly McCarthyesque rationale: "they have a right to do anything we can't stop them from doing."

Heller's "catch" was controversial, but widespread acceptance at home and abroad combined with unfolding events in Vietnam to make the novel a perennial campus classic and the title a part of the language. In the mid-1960s, Heller adapted his brand of comedy to the Pacific war, developing (as Max Orange) pilot episodes for the television series *McHale's Navy*. But in his 1967 antiwar play *We Bombed in New Haven*, Heller discarded all historical context and presented a nameless war where everyman can be a casualty, anywhere a target.

Heller's other war literature is derivative: a two-act dramatization of *Catch-22* (1971); *Clevinger's Trial* (1973), a one-act play developed from chapter 8 of the novel; and two deleted *Catch-22* chapters revised as stories, "Love, Dad" (*Playboy*, December 1969) and "Yossarian Survives" (*Playboy*, December 1987). His five subsequent novels move away from war fiction. In *Something Happened* (1974), Heller refines the paranoia, fear, and sense of alienation developed in *Catch-22* but does so in a corporate version of the American dream-turned-nightmare that represents his finest achievement in fiction. Heller's late-career sequel to *Catch-22* continues this pattern; *Closing Time* (1994) catches up with Yossarian and other fugitives from the earlier novel as their civilian careers (and their lives) draw to a close.

REFERENCES

Heller, Joseph. *Now and Then: From Coney Island to Here*. New York: Knopf, 1998.
Kiley, Frederick, and Walter MacDonald, eds. *A "Catch-22" Casebook*. New York: Crowell, 1973.
Merrill, James. *Joseph Heller*. Boston: Twayne, 1987.
Nagel, James. *Critical Essays on "Catch-22."* Encino, CA: Dickenson, 1974.
Potts, Stephen W. *Catch-22: Antiheroic Antinovel*. Boston: Twayne, 1989.

Jonathan R. Eller

HELLMAN, LILLIAN (1905–1984). Lillian Hellman was born in 1905 in New Orleans and lived there until her family moved to New York in 1911. She wrote plays, short stories, and screenplays, often working closely with the production of her plays and films. Hellman's anti-Fascist and pro-Communist political views caused trouble for her with the American government in the McCarthy era, and she was called before the House Un-American Activities Committee (HUAC) in 1952. She wrote three autobiographies: *An Unfinished Woman* (1969), about her personal life; *Pentimento* (1973), about people she knew; and *Scoundrel Time* (1976), about her experiences with McCarthyism and the HUAC.

In the mid-1930s Hellman worked on a documentary (*The Spanish Earth*, released 1937) about the war in Spain with **Archibald MacLeish** and **John Dos Passos**, with **Ernest Hemingway** writing and speaking the narration. In 1937 Hellman traveled to Spain to see the fighting, and when she returned, she wrote an article about her experiences called "Day in Spain." Here she describes soldiers from different countries united in the fight for democracy: "these foreigners from everywhere were noble people."

In *Watch on the Rhine* (1941), which won the Drama Critics' Circle Award for the best American play, Hellman portrays the confrontation of an anti-Nazi activist with a pro-Fascist mercenary in the home of the Farrellys, an upper-middle-class American family. The Farrelly daughter Sara has married a German, Kurt. Kurt's work against Hitler and fascism has left him weakened and tired, but he knows that he must leave his family and return to continue the fight: "The world is out of shape," he explains to his children, "when there are hungry men. And until it gets in shape, men will steal and lie and—kill." Sara's mother and brother are forced out of their self-centered world by the political realities their European visitors represent, and they become a small but active part of the resistance to fascism in Europe. *The Searching Wind* (1944) continues themes from *Watch on the Rhine*; the weakness of a career diplomat, Alexander Hazen, in not having opposed fascism strongly enough brings upon him a degree of responsibility for World War II. Through flashbacks the characters discuss the significance of world events, such as Mussolini's takeover of Italy and the rise of the Nazis.

Written at the end of World War II in anticipation of postwar cultural changes, *Another Part of the Forest* (1946) shows the lingering effects of the Civil War on two Southern families. The Bagtrys, an aristocratic family, are genteelly starving, and John Bagtry, never having recovered from losing the war, plans to leave for another war in Brazil. The Hubbards have become wealthy from the money Marcus Hubbard earned from war profiteering, and his children scheme and backstab to get money from their father for their own plans.

In 1949 Hellman adapted Emmanuel Roblès's *Montserrat* for the stage in New York. The play takes place in Valencia, Venezuela, during the Spanish Occupation in 1812. Montserrat is a supporter of the rebel Bolivar, and in order to force him to reveal Bolivar's plans for escape, the Spanish government tortures Montserrat by putting him in a room with six innocent people and then executing those people one by one. Montserrat, with the help of one of the victims, refuses to break, and though he is killed, Bolivar safely joins his followers.

REFERENCES

Moody, Richard. *Lillian Hellman: Playwright*. New York: Bobbs-Merrill Company, 1972.
Rollyson, Carl. *Lillian Hellman: Her Legend and Her Legacy*. New York: St. Martin's Press 1988.

Jennifer A. Haytock

HELPRIN, MARK (1947–   ). Mark Helprin is notorious for making up fictitious stories about his life. While some details about his biography are questionable, we do know that he was born in New York City and that he spent many of his teenage years living in the British West Indies, where he served briefly in the British Merchant Navy in 1967. After receiving a Bachelor of Arts degree from Harvard University in 1969, he enrolled at the Harvard Center for Middle Eastern Studies, where he received his M.A. in 1972. Bored with academic life, Helprin left the United States to join the Israeli armed forces later that year.

While an undergraduate at Harvard, Helprin sold his first short story to *The New Yorker*. Subsequently, in 1975, he published his first book, *A Dove of the East and Other Stories*. The volume's title story possibly derives from Helprin's own military experiences. Although set during World War II, the story shows how survivors of tragic circumstances become heroic by coping with the loss of loved ones. In his second book, *Refiner's Fire; The Life and Adventures of Marshall Pearl, a Foundling* (1977), Helprin draws more heavily on his time spent in the Israeli army. Now an Israeli citizen, the author used the novel to draw parallels between America's Civil War and Israel's continual Middle Eastern conflicts. As the story's hero, Marshall Pearl, lies dying on the Israeli war front in 1973, he comes in and out of consciousness; at times, he reminisces about the happier events of his life, while, at others, he hallucinates that he is a Civil War soldier dying on an American battlefield. Ultimately, Helprin employs the novel's flashback structure to present the circularity of time, highlighting common patterns of past, present, and future human existence.

After spending much of the late 1970s in a counterinfiltration unit that patrolled the Israel-Lebanon border, Helprin returned to the literary scene in 1981 with *Ellis Island and Other Stories*. In one of the volume's best stories, "Martin Bayer," Helprin depicts the carefree summer adventures of the protagonist's life before he leaves for World War I.

In 1991, the author published his fifth book, *A Soldier of the Great War*, which fuses the structure of *Refiner's Fire* with the themes of "A Dove of the East" and "Martin Bayer." Set in Italy in 1964, the novel presents an old man's reminiscences about the events of his life before, during, and after World War I, which works to reaffirm the cycle of life for the protagonist and readers alike. Alessandro Giuliani, the protagonist, is a professor of aesthetics who believes that reflecting the beauty of God's work in art is the only way he can redeem his tragic life of suffering. Although he recounts the terrible events of his life throughout the novel, toward the end of the bildungsroman he reaches an epiphany: Life is worth living. Ironically, while he yearned for death as a young man, at old age, he fears it. Many critics consider this Helprin's finest and most mature work.

Since the late 1980s, Helprin has become known as one of the country's leading conservative intellectuals. Besides having published articles against nuclear disarmament and America's military downsizing, Helprin also serves as a senior fellow of military and strategic issues at the Hudson Institute, a right-wing think tank. In the mid-1990s, Helprin gained more political leverage by penning Robert Dole's retirement speech from the U.S. Senate. Even though some think Helprin's literary and political aspirations may be inherently at odds, his dual interests fit him in with such other American writers as Washington Irving, Nathaniel Hawthorne, and **Herman Melville**, all of whom held important political posts during the most productive period of their literary careers.

REFERENCES

Field, Leslie. "Mark Helprin and Postmodern Jewish-American Fiction of Fantasy." *Yiddish* 7.1 (1997): 57–65.
Keneally, Thomas. "War and Memory." *New York Times Book Review* 5 May 1991: 1–2.
Linville, James. "Mark Helprin: The Art of Fiction CXXXII." *The Paris Review* 35 (1993): 160–199.

Shawn Holliday

HEMINGWAY, ERNEST (1899–1961). In introducing his anthology *Men at War* (1942), Hemingway writes, "I have seen much war in my lifetime and I hate it profoundly. But there are worse things than war; and all of them come with defeat." While Hemingway is often depicted as one who glorified war, he would find his greatest success depicting individuals traumatized by their experiences in war.

Born in conservative Oak Park, Illinois, Hemingway learned to hunt and fish in the woods of northern Michigan. After high school, Hemingway worked as a reporter in Kansas City. In 1918 he signed up as an ambulance driver for the American Red Cross. In July on the Italian front, he was wounded by mortar and machine gun fire, though the extent of his wounds is uncertain. Recovering in Milan, Hemingway fell in love with a nurse, Agnes von Kurowsky, who later ended the relationship.

The wartime experience and fractured romance served as sources for *A Farewell to Arms* (1929), perhaps Hemingway's greatest achievement in war fiction. Notable for its vivid description of the retreat at Caporetto, *A Farewell to Arms* is also a powerful register of the spiritual malaise consequent upon war. The personal tragedy of Lieutenant Henry is subsumed in the larger tragedy of the war itself.

In 1922, Hemingway covered the Greco-Turkish war for the *Toronto Star*. As a correspondent, Hemingway observed many important statespeople, including Benito Mussolini, whom he interviewed. His first book, *Three Stories and Ten Poems* (1923), published in Paris, was followed by his first major success, the story collection *In Our Time* (1925). "Big Two-Hearted River," "Soldier's Home," and several untitled prose vignettes reflect Hemingway's experiences as participant in and observer of war. "Big Two-Hearted River" tells of Nick Adams, who has returned from the war and is trying to regenerate his spirit in the northern woods of Michigan through the act of trout fishing. Adams defines for himself a "separate peace" through his experience in the wilderness and his return to writing. The story omits the seemingly essential element (Nick's war experiences) and, like much of Hemingway's work, fuses autobiography and fiction.

Traveling to Spain, Hemingway discovered the bullfight, the Pamplona bull run, and the San Fermin Fiesta. These experiences inspired *Death in the Afternoon* (1932) and *The Dangerous Summer* (1985), as well as one of his best novels, *The Sun Also Rises* (1926). The last portrays a World War I veteran and journalist, rendered impotent by combat service, trying to negotiate "Jazz Age" Europe.

In 1927, Hemingway married Pauline Pfeiffer, a fashion editor for *Vogue*. The following year he moved to Key West, Florida. Travels to Africa led to the publication of *Green Hills of Africa* (1935), a safari narrative. In 1937, Hemingway, supporting the Loyalists, covered the Spanish Civil War for the North American Newspaper Alliance. From this experience, he wrote the play *The Fifth Column* (1938) and *For Whom the Bell Tolls* (1940).

The Fifth Column, a minor artistic achievement, manages to convey the damage war does to a community and its inhabitants. It is a drama of wartime counterespionage in a city (Madrid) under siege. In a 1969 edition, it is combined for the first time with four stories about the war. These supplement his "Old Man at the Bridge," first collected in *The First Forty-Nine Stories* (1938).

For Whom the Bell Tolls, one of Hemingway's most attractive and compelling novels, tells of an American, Robert Jordan, who joins the Loyalist army and becomes involved with a guerilla unit charged with destroying a bridge. The novel has been praised for its honesty in describing the human frailties that undermine effective, principled action. Few individuals live up to the nobility of their causes. Another tragic romance of men and women at war, this relatively late work shows a Hemingway, as Lionel Trilling puts it, "wholly aware of the moral and political tensions which existed in actual fact" (quoted in Meyers, 340).

After marrying **Martha Gellhorn** in 1940, Hemingway spent much of World War II hunting Nazi submarines off the Cuban coast in his fishing boat. In 1944, he resumed work as a war correspondent and traveled with American troops in France and Germany, participating in the Allied liberation of Paris. In 1946, he married Mary Welsh and made several more trips to Africa. Hemingway eventually settled in Cuba, but toward the end of his life, in the wake of revolution, he moved to Ketchum, Idaho, where, suffering from disease and depression brought on by the advanced stages of alcoholism, he committed suicide.

During the 1950s, he produced several novels that are considered failures, many published posthumously: *Across the River and into the Trees* (1950), *Islands in the Stream* (1970), and *The Garden of Eden* (1986). Yet he also produced some of his most popular and enduring work: *The Old Man and the Sea* (1952), which received the Pulitzer Prize in 1953 and helped Hemingway secure the Nobel Prize in 1954, and *A Moveable Feast* (1964). His other works include *The Torrents of Spring* (1926), *Winner Take Nothing* (1933), and *To Have and Have Not* (1937). *By-Line: Ernest Hemingway* (1967) collects his dispatches as a war correspondent along with other reportage.

REFERENCES

Baker, Carlos. *Hemingway: The Writer As Artist*. 4th ed. Princeton: Princeton University Press, 1972.
Donaldson, Scott, ed. *New Essays on "A Farewell to Arms."* New York: Cambridge University Press, 1990.
Meyers, Jeffrey. *Hemingway: a Biography*. New York: Harper, 1985.
Monteiro, George, ed. *Critical Essays on Ernest Hemingway's "A Farewell to Arms."* New York: G. K. Hall, 1994.
Reynolds, Michael S. *Hemingway: The American Homecoming*. New York: Blackwell, 1992.
————. *Hemingway: The Final Years*. New York: Norton, 1999.
————. *Hemingway: The Paris Years*. New York: Blackwell, 1989.
————. *Hemingway: The Thirties*. New York: Norton, 1997.
————. *Hemingway's First War: The Making of "A Farewell to Arms."* Princeton: Princeton University Press, 1976. Rpt., New York: Blackwell, 1987.
————. *The Young Hemingway*. New York: Blackwell, 1986.

Dean Rehberger

HERGESHEIMER, JOSEPH (1880–1954). Born to a middle-class family in Germantown, Pennsylvania, Joseph Hergesheimer dallied with painting until a meeting with Lucas Cleeve turned him to writing. Known as one of the early twentieth-century's foremost aesthetes, Hergesheimer enjoyed a literary popularity that has since fallen off dramatically. The most notable of his novels are *The Three Black Pennys* (1917), *Java Head* (1918), *Linda Condon* (1919), *Balisand* (1924), and *The Limestone Tree* (1929). He also wrote a number of short stories and critical essays. Hergesheimer's public speaking received less acclaim, as his caustic statements were wont to offend. His infamous comment "Literature in the United States is being strangled with a petticoat" is one such example.

Hergesheimer uses American involvement in wars as a character-shaping background for many of his novels. For example, the American Revolution informs the conflicting political beliefs of Federalist Richard Bale and Republican Gawin Todd throughout *Balisand*, culminating in their deaths. Hergesheimer responded to criticism about his main character, Bale, by noting that he himself was "a Federalist in temperament." He also explained that Bale's character is informed by a "satirical bitterness" caused by the United States' recent involvement in World War I.

The American Civil War is the background for *The Limestone Tree*, where the emotional strain of the war affects the Kentucky families whose lives Hergesheimer charts. As with *Balisand*, political loyalty drives many of the events of the novel, as characters struggle to maintain an affiliation with the Federal government.

In one of his minor novels, *Cytherea*, Hergesheimer's characters are victims of the social and moral fragmentation following World War I. Lee, for example, has been stripped of religious conviction and feels he is emptily going through the ritual motions of worship.

Hergesheimer also wrote an unsuccessful biography, *Sheridan: A Military Narrative*, disappointing many readers with an objective portrayal of the general that pleased neither those who thought him a hero nor those who thought him a villain. In addition, Sheridan's personality is underdeveloped, most likely a result of Hergesheimer's lack of interest in the general and the difficulty he had in accessing primary material.

REFERENCES

Gimmestad, Victor E. *Joseph Hergesheimer*. Boston: Twayne Publishers, 1984.
Martin, Ronald E. *The Fiction of Joseph Hergesheimer*. Philadelphia: University of Pennsylvania Press, 1965.

Cristie L. March

HERNE, JAMES A. (1839–1901). Born James Ahern in Cohoes, New York, to an Irish immigrant father, James A. Herne was drawn to stage acting in his youth. He remained best known as a character actor until he began writing plays in his forties. He initially wrote stage adaptations of popular novels, like

Oliver Twist, and cowrote others with David Belasco, their first success being *Hearts of Oak* (1879). Later, influenced by Ibsen, he turned to continental realism, which often met with resistance from audiences and theater owners. His most notable plays are *Margaret Fleming* (1890), *Shore Acres* (1893), *Griffith Davenport* (1899), and *Sag Harbor* (1899).

One of Herne's first original plays was *The Minute Men of 1774–5* (1886), which covers the conflicts during the American Revolution and culminates in the battle of Lexington. The heavily overplotted romantic melodrama was a failure, and Herne's future successes came from avoiding melodrama and concentrating on realist theater.

Herne's *Griffith Davenport*, based on Helen Gardener's novel *An Unofficial Patriot*, is considered by some to be the best military drama of the American nineteenth century. Herne's play follows Reverend Griffith Davenport during the Civil War and reveals the agony of a family and nation divided on the issue of slavery. One of the most striking scenes occurs when Beverly Davenport's mother reads his letter from the front, displaying the weary tragedy of the war to the audience. In Act V, Davenport has become a prisoner of the South, held captive by his own son. The play ends with him bidding farewell to his wife, as they plan for their lives after the war ends. Herne revised the play to fit chronologically with the events in Lincoln's political career, permeating the play, as his wife Katherine suggested, "with the spirit of Lincoln." The play was a failure, since it displayed anti-South sentiment during a time when the South was being hailed for its participation in the Spanish-American War. Critics, however, have praised *Griffith Davenport* as being the first Civil War drama to deal with the issue of slavery and the first to treat the war as a militarily and emotionally complex event.

REFERENCES

Denison, Patricia. "The Legacy of James A. Herne: American Realities and Realism." *Realism and the American Dramatic Tradition*. Ed. William W. Demastes. Tuscaloosa: University of Alabama Press, 1996. 18–36.

Edwards, Herbert J., and Julie A. Herne. *James A. Herne: The Rise of Realism in the American Drama*. Orono: University of Maine Press, 1964.

Perry, John. *James A. Herne: The American Ibsen*. Chicago: Nelson-Hall, 1978.

Cristie L. March

HERR, MICHAEL (1940–   ). British-born Michael Herr had moved to New York City by the time he was twenty and began his career as a writer. Although not formally trained in journalism, he is regarded as one of the premier journalists of the Vietnam War. After approaching *Esquire* magazine in 1967 for accreditation to Vietnam, he received a visa and a $500 advance to do whatever work necessary to write about the war. Before leaving Indochina in 1968, Herr published war accounts in *Esquire, Rolling Stone*, and *New American Review*.

His memories and notebooks from Vietnam were later compiled and refined into *Dispatches* (1977).

Herr's book was labeled as nonfiction, and he was nominated for the National Book Award for nonfiction, but *Dispatches* clearly defies genre classifications, ushering in the period of New Journalism. Truly a novel text in its experimental and complex approach, it conveys the madness of war and the dynamics of rock and roll psychedelia. Herr brings us the photojournalist Sean Flynn, the daredevil son of Errol, and a group of footsoldiers high on LSD and Jimi Hendrix. With great accuracy, Herr captures the language of American soldiers in Vietnam, and through their dialogue we can better understand what is often called an incomprehensible war. Elements of autobiography, journalism, interview, war narrative, minidrama, and metafiction comprise Herr's book, creating a collage of multiple information modes. This metafictional approach to writing about Vietnam creates an incomprehensible narration at times, and readers are urged to understand that appearances in Vietnam are rarely consistent with their underlying reality.

The collage style of Herr's account is further complicated by its nonlinear, associative narrative. As John Hellmann comments, "[Herr] makes the objective goals of the conventional journalist irrelevant by constructing his book not as a direct report on the Vietnam War, but rather as an exploration of his *memory* of the war. As such, *Dispatches* consists of a series of fragments, ranging from the briefest snapshots to fully dramatized episodes, arranged in nonchronological juxtaposition" (142). This approach foregrounds the cultural, political, and personal reactions to the wars in Vietnam and elsewhere, for many people receive only inaccurate representations of warfare and cannot truly reach a full understanding of the repercussions of Vietnam. Donald Ringnalda writes, "The book is a deep 'recon' probe (without fire support) into murky questions such as who we are and how we know what we think we know" (70). For Herr, these questions plagued him in Vietnam and afterwards while he composed *Dispatches*. Herr's literary interests have extended into film as well. Based on his work in *Dispatches*, Francis Ford Coppola contracted Herr to write the narration for *Apocalypse Now* (1979). Herr later received Writers Guild and Academy Award nominations for his screenplay adaptation for Stanley Kubrick's *Full Metal Jacket* (1987).

Departing from war themes, Herr's second book, *Walter Winchell: A Novel* (1986), was labeled a novel, but it is really a screenplay–biography focused on the life and times of Walter Winchell, whose syndicated daily gossip column reached millions. With Michael Peellaert, Herr cowrote a book about Las Vegas history and culture in *The Big Room* (1990). They bring together a cast of famous figures ranging from Franklin D. Roosevelt to Bugsy Siegel and Liberace.

REFERENCES

Bonn, Maria S. "The Lust for the Eye: Michael Herr, Gloria Emerson, and the Art of Observation." *Papers on Language & Literature* 29.1 (1993): 28–48.

Hellmann, John. "The New Journalism and Vietnam: Memory as Structure in Michael Herr's *Dispatches.*" *South Atlantic Quarterly* 79.2 (1980): 141–151.

Ringnalda, Donald. "Unlearning to Remember Vietnam." *America Rediscovered: Critical Essays on Literature and Film of the Vietnam War.* Ed. Owen W. Gilman, Jr., and Lorrie Smith. New York: Garland, 1990. 64–74.

Stewart, Matthew C. "Style in *Dispatches*: Heteroglossia and Michael Herr's Break with Conventional Journalism." *America Rediscovered: Critical Essays on Literature and Film of the Vietnam War.* Ed. Owen W. Gilman, Jr., and Lorrie Smith. New York: Garland, 1990. 189–204.

Brad E. Lucas

HERSEY, JOHN (1914–1993). Born in Tientsin, China, John Richard Hersey returned to the United States in 1924 when his father, a missionary, became seriously ill. Educated at Yale University (B.A., 1936), his work as a correspondent with *Time* and *Life* magazines during World War II provided him with material for his six major novels about war.

Men on Bataan (1942), written from his research and interviews while in the United States and clearly apprentice work, provides a pastiche of experiences of those who suffered the Japanese attack on the Philippine Islands in early 1942. Interspersed with reflections about General Douglas MacArthur are descriptions of the many men, Americans as well as Filipinos, who served valiantly on the Bataan Peninsula. More successful is *Into the Valley* (1943), which details the experiences of a Marine company sent into battle on Guadalcanal in the Solomon Islands. Hersey, who accompanied the operation, uses vignettes to develop his characters and strong imagery to create the sound and feel of jungle warfare. The narrator (clearly Hersey) and Captain Rigaud develop a mutual respect for each other as they suffer the rigors of the mission.

Hersey's first fictional coverage of the European Theater, *A Bell for Adano* (1944), portrays the American occupation of a small Italian village. Major Joppolo, the town's assigned American governor, becomes enmeshed in a struggle to recover a bell for the town while concurrently fighting General Marvin's inappropriate and oppressive orders. Not directly a combat novel, this work portrays a good but ineffectual hero in conflict with an unthinking military bureaucrat. Based on Hersey's brief visit to Italy, this popular wartime book was awarded the 1945 Pulitzer Prize.

Hersey's most famous journalistic writing, *Hiroshima* (1946), first appeared in *The New Yorker* a year after the atomic bomb leveled this Japanese city. Hersey bases his short work—an early example of the "nonfiction novel"—on interviews conducted in 1945 with about thirty survivors. He describes the minutes, hours, and days following the blast. The book's impact comes from Hersey's unironic understatement. With passages such as "the clouded air was giving off a thick dreadful miasma" and "Altogether, Miss Sasaki was left two days and two nights under a piece of propped-up roofing with her crushed leg," Hersey creates a sense of immediacy without sentimentality. He allows readers to draw their own conclusions. However, in his 1985 "Aftermath" appended to the novel, Hersey is more cynical and judgmental about this apocalyptic event.

As *Hiroshima* tells of one of the endings of World War II, his next narrative, *The Wall* (1950), chronicles one of the beginnings. Set in the Warsaw ghetto from November 1939 to May 1943, the novel fictionalizes Hersey's extensive research on the fate of the ghetto's 500,000 Jews. The narrator, Noach Levinson, a cultural historian and an idiosyncratic recorder of and participant in the events, gains authority because of the immediacy of his experiences. Of the numerous characters whose stories Levinson tells, three—Levinson himself, Rachel Apt, and Derek Berson—evolve as the central figures in this exploration of survival in, and attempted escape from, the totalitarian rule imposed on the wartime ghetto.

Hersey's final World War II novel, *The War Lover* (1959), plunges the reader into the trauma of battle as experienced by Bo Boman, a B-17 Flying Fortress copilot, and his pilot, Buzz Marrow. Boman, the narrator of this psychologically tense narrative, tells his story in alternating chapters that focus on "The Tour" and "The Raid." The former chapters examine in realistic detail the disorientation of a twenty-five-mission combat tour, the lives of the pilots and their crews, the weather, and the tensions and friendships that develop among the men. Interspersed chapters dealing with Bo's twenty-fourth mission, a raid deep into Germany, develop the consequences of Bo's new knowledge: that Buzz earned his Distinguished Flying Cross only because of Bo's bravery and that Buzz's love of war is debilitating rather than empowering. Because of this knowledge, Bo survives to return to Daphne, his English lover and a life-giving force in the novel, while Buzz, trapped by his fear, must die, drowning as their battle-damaged aircraft crash-lands and sinks into the English Channel.

Hersey does not again return to World War II in an extended manner, but his moral vision about war and survival, on both a personal and a political level, reverberate through his many later narratives. In his foreword to *Images of War*, a 1989 volume dedicated to visual art generated during World War II, Hersey writes that war, in its "astonishing complexity," is "fought by human beings. The cost is in human values and human lives." These words provide a simple coda for one of the messages in the six narratives that Hersey himself writes about war, its causes and its consequences.

REFERENCES

Hudspeth, Robert N. "A Definition of Modern Nihilism: *The War Lover.*" *University Review* 35 (Summer 1968): 243–249.
Huse, Nancy L. *The Survival Tales of John Hersey*. Troy, NY: Whitson Publishing, 1983.
Sanders, David. *John Hersey Revisited*. Boston: Twayne, 1990.

Charles J. Gaspar

HIGGINS, MARGUERITE (1920–1966). Born in Hong Kong and raised in California, Marguerite Higgins rose to prominence during World War II for her *New York Herald Tribune* reports of the London Blitz and the Allied invasion of Europe. Present at the liberation of Buchenwald and Dachau, her graphic reports confirmed the horrors of the Holocaust. Higgins's autobiography, *News Is a Singular Thing* (1955), traces her experiences as a "lone woman correspondent among all those men" (11). Her other books include *War in Korea—The Report of a Woman Correspondent* (1951); *Red Plush and Black Bread* (1955); *Jessie Benton Fremont* (1962); *Our Vietnam Nightmare* (1965); and *Overtime in Heaven: Adventures in the Foreign Service*, with Peter Lisagor (1964). She published numerous articles for *Mademoiselle, Saturday Evening Post, Newsweek, Time*, and *U.S. News and World Report*. Her biography, Antoinette May's *Witness to War*, was published in 1983 by Beaufort Books.

Higgins intended her autobiography, *News Is a Singular Thing*, as a "personal account of a career of covering world crises and of some of the heroes and villains of those crises" and is what she "[chose] to tell" of her experiences (13). An unflinching and exciting account of her life as a correspondent, *News* offers critical insight into Higgins's life and career from the author's perspective. May's biography, *Witness to War*, offers a somewhat dated perspective of Higgins's experiences, focusing more on her personal than professional life. *War in Korea* won critical acclaim upon publication and provides a candid account of U.S. involvement in Korea as well as the difficulties Higgins faced and surmounted as a female correspondent. A combination of autobiography and critical reporting, *War in Korea* advocates U.S. involvement to halt Communist expansion. Similarly, *Our Vietnam Nightmare* warns against complacency toward the "Red" invasion but recognizes the complexity of the Vietnam conflict. Higgins urges U.S. responsibility toward Vietnam and the "obligation to bring it to an end" (314).

At the height of her career, Higgins succumbed to the rare tropical disease leishmaniasis and died after a protracted and painful illness. She is buried in Arlington National Cemetery.

REFERENCES

Higgins, Marguerite. *News Is a Singular Thing*. Garden City, NY: Doubleday, 1955.
———. *Our Vietnam Nightmare*. New York: Harper and Row, 1965.
———. *War in Korea: The Report of a Woman Combat Correspondent*. Garden City, NY: Doubleday, 1951.
Lisagor, Peter, and Marguerite Higgins. *Overtime in Heaven: Adventures in the Foreign Service*. Garden City, NY: Doubleday, 1964.
May, Antoinette. *Witness to War: A Biography of Marguerite Higgins*. New York: Beaufort Books, 1983.

Amy L. Wink

HIGGINSON, THOMAS WENTWORTH (1823–1911). The fame of Thomas Wentworth Higginson is inextricably intertwined with the twentieth-century explosion in popularity of the poems of Emily Dickinson. And Higginson indeed was instrumental in her growth as a poet—first through his essays in *The Atlantic Monthly* during the Civil War; second, through his correspondence with her; and finally, through his editing of her posthumously published poems and his early criticism of her work in the 1890s. But his association with Dickinson is only the most well-known aspect of a very remarkable life.

Higginson, a militant abolitionist and confederate of John Brown, interrupted his literary life in 1862 when he received an offer from Brigadier General Rufus Saxton to command a regiment of freed slaves in South Carolina. The 1st South Carolina Volunteers (later the 33rd U.S. Colored Troops) saw action in a variety of riverine engagements on the southeast coast, contributing to the success of the experiment of arming black troops so vociferously urged by Frederick Douglass and others. The unit was appropriately mustered out early in 1866 at Fort Wagner, the site of the graves of Colonel Robert Gould Shaw and many of the men of the 54th Massachusetts, another early black regiment. But Higginson was not with them at the end: After a brush with a cannonball on the Edisto in 1864, a literally and spiritually shell-shocked Higginson had determined to resign his commission and resume his literary life in New England.

On his return, Higginson—who had deliberately refrained from journalizing publicly while in uniform—began a series of sketches for *The Atlantic* based on the South Carolina experiment. Finding them difficult to continue (probably for psychological reasons) he turned to writing fiction and essays unrelated to the war. His output was enormous, and Higginson unsurprisingly began to suffer literary as well as military burnout. Nevertheless, in 1868 he decided to collect his existing war essays and some additional material in a volume that he published late in 1869, *Army Life in a Black Regiment*.

Despite Higginson's difficulty in writing it, *Army Life* emerged as something of a black Walden: a local-color masterpiece that uses the brave-new-worldness of the Sea Islands to balance the material and psychological invasiveness of the war. It is a book of many tones, ranging from the sentimental in "The Baby of the Regiment" to the existential in "A Night in the Water," with the optimism of the early war in "Up the St. Mary's" balanced by the disillusion of "Up the Edisto." And the book is always a paean to the freed slave as a fighting man and, eventually, as citizen: "Till the blacks were armed, there was no guaranty of their Freedom," Higginson wrote. "It was their demeanor under arms that shamed the nation into recognizing them as men."

REFERENCES

Higginson, Thomas Wentworth. *Army Life in a Black Regiment and Other Writings*. Ed. R. D. Madison. New York: Penguin, 1997.
Wells, Anna Mary. *Dear Preceptor: The Life and Times of Thomas Wentworth Higginson*. Boston: Houghton Mifflin, 1963.

Robert D. Madison

HIMES, CHESTER (1909–1984). Chester Himes's fiction describes what he calls the "absurdity" of African American identity in a culture defined in principle by democracy and in practice by racism and institutional segregation. Unlike *Native Son* author Richard Wright, whose naturalist fiction focuses on the sources of African American social determination, Himes's often autobiographical work is more concerned with the individual's response to those conditions. Nowhere is this theme more apparent than in his first two novels, *If He Hollers Let Him Go* (1945) and *Lonely Crusade* (1947), which draw heavily from Himes's own experience in the California shipyards during World War II. The war overseas, a battle for democracy fought against white supremacists but ignited by racial hatred after Pearl Harbor and soldiered by segregated armies, serves as a backdrop for the embattled position of the African American at home.

Bob Jones of *Hollers* and Lee Gordon of *Crusade* are two well-educated black men given positions of authority in the labor vacuum created by the war, then ruined by white men unwilling to recognize their authority and white women looking to seduce them. When management supports their attackers, Bob and Lee are forced to see their authority for what it is: a token meant to curry favor with blacks in the community. The novels investigate the internal conflicts these crises of knowledge and disempowerment ignite, manifest in the men's fear and rage. Bob's story is told over the course of five days and nights, alternating between nightmares of white subjugation and still worse waking realities; Lee's plays out largely in paranoid dialogues between himself, Marxist ideologues, and the white ruling class. Both men express their rage in elaborate murder schemes against their accusers and oppressors, though neither is able to carry out his plans, perhaps implying further impotence or fear. But while these emotions reflect the absurdity in which the men live, as expressions of will and desire they relentlessly assert individual existence. Bob Jones's last words, even as he's being led away to enlist in the military in order to escape prosecution for a rape he did not commit, say it best: "I'm still here." His survival in the war of race is tenuous but not token.

REFERENCES

Himes, Chester. *My Life of Absurdity: The Autobiography of Chester Himes*. Vol. II. Garden City, NY: Doubleday, 1976.
———. *The Quality of Hurt: The Autobiography of Chester Himes*. Vol. I. Garden City, NY: Doubleday, 1972.
Margolies, Edward. *The Several Lives of Chester Himes*. Jackson: University Press of Mississippi, 1997.
Milliken, Stephen. *Chester Himes: A Critical Appraisal*. Columbia: University of Missouri Press, 1976.

Dean DeFino

HINOJOSA, ROLANDO (1929–). Born in Mercedes, Texas, of mixed Chicano-Anglo parents, Hinojosa served two years in the army in the late 1940s, then was recalled in 1950, serving in the Korean War as a tank crewman in a reconnaissance unit. After the war, he went on to successful simultaneous careers as a university professor and administrator and as a writer. Writing mostly in Spanish, Hinojosa is not well known among English-speaking readers, but in the Spanish-speaking community in the United States, Latin America, and Europe, he has a large following. Many of his characters are Korean War veterans, including his recurring protagonist Rafe Buenrostro, and both *Korean Love Songs*, a 1978 novel-in-verse, and his 1993 *The Useless Servants* deal with the war directly.

Korean Love Songs differs from most of Hinojosa's work in two ways: It is in verse and in English. "I had originally tried to write about Korea in Spanish," he explained, "but that experience wasn't lived in Spanish." The narrator of the thirty-eight-poem sequence is Buenrostro, and the action moves from Pusan to North Korea, then south again with the Chinese in pursuit, and finally north once more to the 38th parallel.

While Anglo-Chicano conflict—a major thread in most of Hinojosa's writing—is present here, the main focus of the book is on the war itself, its ugly reality, and its terrible cost. "Christ, / What am I doing here?" asks Buenrostro in "Incoming," while in "A Matter of Supplies" he seems to answer himself: "It comes down to this: we're pieces of equipment / To be counted and signed for. / On the occasion some of us break down, / And the parts which can't be salvaged / Are replaced with other GI parts, that's all."

The Useless Servants covers much the same ground as *Korean Love Songs* but is written in the form of a diary kept by Buenrostro. In these detachable, separately titled vignettes, Rafe tells his story in a way that emphasizes the bonding of soldiers who have trained and suffered together. However, the tone is oddly flat, as if the horrors that are being recorded cannot be allowed to register emotionally. Perhaps the fictional journal-keeper has already built a defense against being in constant despair. Perhaps he is in a state of shock. In any case, the eerie discrepancy between content and tone forces the reader to make compensations and to wonder about Rafe's shrunken range of feeling and response.

REFERENCES

Ehrhart, W. D. "Soldier-Poets of the Korean War." *War, Literature & the Arts* 9.2 (Fall–Winter 1997): 12–19.
Saldivar, Jose David, ed. *The Rolando Hinojosa Reader: Essays Historical and Critical.* Houston: Arte Publico Press, 1985.

W. D. Ehrhart

HOOKER, RICHARD (1924–1997). H. Richard Hornberger was born in Trenton, New Jersey, and graduated from Bowdoin College and Cornell University Medical School. In 1952 he served with the 8055th Mobile Army Surgical Hospital in Korea. His experiences, the people he met, and the stories he heard became the basis for the novel *M*A*S*H* (1968), which he wrote under the pseudonym of Richard Hooker. The novel only faintly resembles the film and television series it inspired, and Hooker's writing style is not the sort admired by most literary critics. Nevertheless, having achieved the status of popular culture icon and being firmly placed in the antiauthoritarian tradition of comic war literature, *M*A*S*H* can hold the interest of readers.

Unlike most war literature, combat is not a major feature of the novel. Instead, it focuses on those who are confronted with the consequences of combat—medical personnel engaged in the physically and emotionally exhausting duty of treating casualties. Hooker demonstrates through his characters—mainly Hawkeye Pierce, Duke Forrest, and Trapper John McIntyre—the skill and dedication required for such work. Yet through these characters Hooker also demonstrates how the stresses created by this work produce very unmilitary behavior, as much of the novel concerns itself with the pranks, schemes, and general hell-raising of Hawkeye, Duke, and Trapper. Unlike combatants, the surgeons fight no climactic battle but cope day in and day out with whatever circumstances arise—a fact reflected by the novel's episodic structure.

Yet *M*A*S*H*'s most significant feature may be in the way it can be read as a Cold War document. At the conclusion, Hawkeye and Duke leave Korea neither because the war is over nor because they have accomplished some great deed. Rather, their tours of duty have ended, so they are transferred out of Korea and discharged from the army. In this way the novel reflects the static nature of the Cold War in the 1950s: It is a continuous conflict with no satisfactory ending in sight. Thus, while *M*A*S*H* seems to be no serious contender as a major work of American war literature, it nevertheless lends itself to serious cultural commentary.

Hornberger wrote twelve sequels to *M*A*S*H*, several as sole author and others with **William E. Butterworth**, featuring *M*A*S*H* characters both in the United States and abroad. He lived in Bremen, Maine, and practiced thoracic surgery at Thayer Hospital in Waterville, Maine. His death, on November 4, 1997, was caused by leukemia.

REFERENCES

Axelsson, Arne. *Restrained Response: American Novels of the Cold War and Korea, 1945–1962*. Westport, CT: Greenwood Press, 1990.

Gilliard, Fred. "Richard Hooker's *M*A*S*H*: Affirmation of Chaos." *Rendezvous: Idaho State University Journal of Arts and Letters* 9.1–2 (1974): 15–21.

Joe Sarnowski

HOPKINSON, FRANCIS (1737–1791). Born in Philadelphia, Francis Hopkinson was among the first students to attend Benjamin Franklin's Academy of Philadelphia. After studying law, traveling to England, and serving as a customs collector, he eventually married and settled in Bordentown, New Jersey. Despite connections to the English political establishment, he became an ardent supporter of independence and used his varied talents as a writer, poet, musician, and artist to the support the cause. He is most often remembered as a signer of the Declaration of Independence and for designing the American flag. He also held two important administrative posts during the war by serving as head of the newly formed Navy Board and as Congress's treasurer of loans.

Among his literary efforts, Hopkinson wrote *A Pretty Story* (1774), an influential allegory that attacked the repression of Boston in the aftermath of the tea party. It presented the story of settlers who are given undeveloped land by a nobleman who later attempts to force them to pay a tax on "water gruel." The villain of the piece was the nobleman's steward, who was meant to represent Lord North. Hopkinson also produced a widely read essay ("The Prophecy") in early 1776 that advocated the declaring of independence.

In addition to political allegory, Hopkinson wrote popular ballads as a way to improve morale during the war. While in charge of the navy, he was responsible for an incident in January 1778 that inspired his most famous song, "The Battle of the Kegs." He arranged to send waterproofed kegs of gunpowder down the Delaware River to serve as makeshift mines in Philadelphia harbor. British commanders overreacted and ordered their men to fire on the kegs. In mocking the bumbling efforts of "The conqu'ring British troops," Hopkinson drew attention to their fear and panic. His song emphasized the fact that although the city was in the possession of the enemy, it might one day be retaken.

After the British withdrew, Hopkinson aimed his later satires at Loyalists who remained in Philadelphia. Following the war, he became embroiled in state politics and wrote pamphlets in favor of the Constitution.

REFERENCES

Andrews, William D. "Philip Freneau and Francis Hopkinson." *American Literature, 1764–1789: The Revolutionary Years.* Ed. Everett Emerson. Madison: University of Wisconsin Press, 1977. 127–144.

Hastings, George Everett. *The Life and Works of Francis Hopkinson.* Chicago: University of Chicago Press, 1926.

Zall, Paul M. *Comical Spirit of Seventy-Six: The Humor of Francis Hopkinson.* San Marino, CA: Huntington Library, 1976.

Robert D. Sturr

HOWARD, BRONSON (1842–1908). One of the most commercially successful American playwrights of the late nineteenth century, Bronson Howard wrote comedy and drama with equal facility, including, in the latter category, one of the most popular Civil War plays of the era, *Shenandoah*. The son of a prosperous Detroit merchant, Howard attended Yale but was forced to withdraw before graduating due to problems with his eyes. Returning home, he took a job as drama critic for the *Detroit Free Press*. He began his career as a playwright with *Fantine* (1864), an adaptation of Victor Hugo's *Les Misérables*.

Soon after *Fantine* completed its run in Detroit, Howard moved to New York to serve as drama critic for the *Tribune*. Beginning in 1870, he wrote a string of plays that proved hugely successful on both New York and European stages and enabled him to abandon journalism, becoming the first American dramatist to earn his living entirely from his plays. These include the comedies *Saratoga* (1870) and *Diamonds* (1872) and the melodramas *Moorcroft* (1874), *The Banker's Daughter* (1878), *Young Mrs. Winthrop* (1882), *One of Our Girls* (1885), and *The Henrietta* (1887).

Shenandoah (produced in 1889, published 1897) was the last of these successes. Here Howard uses the time-honored Civil War melodrama plot device of friends and lovers separated by their regional loyalties: New Yorker Kerchival West and Virginian Robert Ellingham are best friends as cadets at West Point and are in love with one another's sisters, but the outbreak of war severs these relationships, with West becoming a colonel in the Union army and Ellingham a colonel in the Confederate. After many convolutions of plot, including trials for espionage, accusations of infidelity, and revelations of long-lost children, the lovers and friends are reconciled at the close of the war.

Although his commercial fortunes declined following *Shenandoah*, Howard continued to write and to work on behalf of the interests of other American playwrights. The most significant of these efforts was his 1891 founding of the American Dramatists Club, which ultimately became the Society of American Dramatists and Composers.

REFERENCES

Bordman, Gerald. *The Oxford Companion to American Theatre*. New York: University Press, 1984.
Quinn, Arthur Hobson. *A History of the American Drama from the Civil War to the Present Day*. New York: F. S. Crofts, 1945.

Michael W. Schaefer

HOWE, JULIA WARD (1819–1910). An active feminist, reformer, and a poet, Julia Ward Howe was born to a prosperous and well-regarded New York family descended from early Puritan stock. She helped her husband, Dr. Samuel Gridley Howe, produce an abolitionist newspaper in Boston and was acquainted with the leading figures of the movement during the 1840s and 1850s.

Howe published several volumes of fairly conventional poems, but she is best known for "The Battle Hymn of the Republic," first published in February 1862 in *The Atlantic Monthly*. This perhaps most famous of all Civil War lyrics was set to the tune of the abolitionist marching song "John Brown's Body Lies a-Mould'ring in the Grave," which in turn was originally a Methodist camp song ("Say, brothers, will you meet us on Canaan's happy shore?"). After reviewing Federal troops outside of Washington in November 1861, Howe was riding back into the city with friends when they began singing "John Brown's Body." (This review, ironically, had been broken up by a daring Confederate attack, which sent soldiers and civilian spectators fleeing across the bridge into the city.) According to Debbie Williams Ream, the soldiers on the road cheered, and a friend asked why she did not write better words for "that stirring tune" (59–64). That night, Howe watched the army campfires out on the Mall in Washington. Unable to sleep, she arose and wrote the lines that had been forming in her mind as if by revelation:

Mine eyes have seen the glory of the coming of the Lord:
He is trampling out the vintage where the grapes of wrath are stored;
He hath loosed the fateful lightning of His terrible swift sword:
His truth is marching on.

Recently, scholars have suggested that Howe may also have been influenced by the poetry of **Whittier** and Macaulay, as well as by the militant battle songs of seventeenth-century Puritan England, which employ the eschatological tropes of the Apocalypse, the Second Coming, and the earthly vengeance on the wicked carried out by God's servants. In Howe's second verse, Christ walks among the Union camps; in the third, bayonets are the instruments of spreading the gospel, and the hero means to "crush the serpent with his heel"; in the fourth verse, one's worthiness to stand before God at the last day is equated with one's alacrity in joining the crusade against the South. In the last verse, all are enjoined to emulate Christ and sacrifice their lives to free the slaves.

Although the piece was written to "John Brown's Body," Howe meant it as a poem. By April 1862, however, Oliver Ditson published it with the stirring marching tune, and its popularity spread across the nation. The powerful Christian imagery did its work: The war had become the work of salvation. When President Lincoln first heard the song in 1863, he is reported to have begged, "Sing it again!"

REFERENCES

Clifford, Deborah Pickman. *Mine Eyes Have Seen the Glory: A Biography of Julia Ward Howe*. Boston: Little, Brown, 1979.
Ream, Debbie Williams. "Mine Eyes Have Seen the Glory." *American History Illustrated* (January–February 1993): 59–64.
Richards, Laura E., and Maud Howe Elliott. *Julia Ward Howe: 1819–1910*. Boston: Houghton Mifflin, 1915.

Randal W. Allred

HOWELLS, WILLIAM DEAN (1837–1920). Born in small-town Ohio, Howells's career took him to Boston and then New York. He was the most influential editor of his era and a versatile author who published novels, short fictions, poetry, plays, and essays.

Howells was raised with abolitionist and pacificist views. The Civil War brought these values into conflict, as it did for many intellectuals of his generation. Howells had written a campaign biography of Abraham Lincoln, enabling the young journalist to lobby successfully for an appointment as consul in Venice, where he spent the war years. Howells's biographers agree that he was troubled in after years by this escape from combat. His novels contain several veterans of the Union army, including Silas Lapham (in the novel of that name, 1885) who rose to the rank of colonel, and Lindau (in *A Hazard of New Fortunes*, 1890) who lost a hand in combat. Descriptions of Civil War battles appear only obliquely, in reminiscences of such characters.

Like his friend **Mark Twain**, Howells was appalled by the Spanish-American War. His story "Editha" (1905) is set at this time, though the war itself is not named, presumably to generalize its antiwar message. In this tale, the title character is a young woman who is swept up in war fever and persuades her reluctant fiancé George to enlist. He does, and he is killed in his unit's first engagement. Visiting George's mother, Editha is denounced by the older woman, who thanks God that her son did not live to kill others—"the sons of those miserable mothers and the husbands of those girls that you would never see the faces of." While Editha is able to dismiss these views as the ravings of a "vulgar" woman, and to return to her realm of the "ideal," Howells clearly endorses the "vulgar" sentiments of the mother.

REFERENCES

Cady, Edwin H. *The Realist at War.* Syracuse: Syracuse University Press, 1958.
————. *The Road to Realism.* Syracuse: Syracuse University Press; 1956.
Howells, W. D. *A Selected Edition of W. D. Howells.* Bloomington: Indiana University Press, 1968.

Charles L. Crow

HUBBARD, ELBERT (1856–1915). Born and raised in central Illinois, Hubbard began his career as a traveling salesman, capitalizing on his charm, striking appearance, and shrewd understanding of American consumers. By the mid-1880s, he had become a partner in a Buffalo soap company but sold his share in 1892 to pursue a new career as an author, eventually founding a popular monthly magazine called *The Philistine*. The articles written by Hubbard were filled with aphorisms and sentiments that championed hard work, personal loyalty, and individual initiative. These qualities found their greatest expression in his best-known publication, "A Message to Garcia," which first appeared in the March 1899 issue of *The Philistine*. Supposedly written by Hubbard in one hour, this 1,500-word essay became an immediate sensation and was reprinted by the millions.

Composed like a sermon, "A Message to Garcia" begins with the accomplishments of Lieutenant Andrew Rowan during the early weeks of the Spanish-American War. Ordered by President William McKinley to deliver an important message to General Calixto Garcia, leader of the Cuban insurgents "somewhere in the mountain fastnesses of Cuba—no one knew where," Rowan quietly did as he was told, "without asking any idiotic questions," without going "on a strike for higher wages," without seeking someone else to do the job for him. What the world needed, according to Hubbard, were more individuals like

Rowan, willing and able to "do the thing" that needs to be done and carry a message to Garcia.

Shortly after the outbreak of World War I, Hubbard wrote an antiwar pamphlet, "Who Lifted the Lid Off of Hell?" The answer, according to Hubbard, was "William Hohenzollern. . . . Hell was made in Germany." Less than one year later, Hubbard was one of the 128 Americans who died onboard the British steamship *Lusitania*, torpedoed by a German submarine in May 1915.

REFERENCES

Champney, Freeman. *Art and Glory: The Story of Elbert Hubbard*. New York: Crown, 1968.
Hamilton, Charles F. *As Bees in Honey Drown: Elbert Hubbard and the Roycrofters*. South Brunswick, NJ: A. S. Barnes, 1973.
Hubbard, Elbert. *The Complete Writings of Elbert Hubbard*. 20 vols. East Aurora, NY: Roycroft, 1908–1915.

James I. Deutsch

HUBBARD, WILLIAM (1621–1704). Born in England, William Hubbard came to Massachusetts during the Great Migration of the 1630s. A member of Harvard University's first graduating class, he was later the town minister of Ipswich and its representative to the General Court. In 1677, Hubbard was appointed the official historian of King Philip's War by the legislature. He died in 1704 at the age of eighty-three.

King Philip's War, which raged throughout New England from 1675 to late 1676, was the deadliest war per capita in all of American history. Hubbard chronicled the actions of the Native Americans and English colonists in his history *A Narrative of the Troubles with the Indians in New England*. Published in 1677, the history was so well received by the Massachusetts General Court that they ordered it imprinted "as being of Publick Benefit."

The brutality and scope of the war stunned New Englanders. Many wondered why God's chosen "City on a Hill" was being made to withstand such a violent assault that threatened its very existence. Led by **Increase Mather**, many conservative Puritans saw the war as God's punishment for a decline in religiosity taking place as the second generation of Puritans rose to power. In stark contrast, Hubbard places the war in a much more modern context and sees it as a conflict between civilized and barbarous human beings, not as a sign of God's anger. In keeping with the modern nature of his history, Hubbard minimizes allusions to God's direct intervention in the war in order to present New Englanders as the war's true heroes, not only as tools of God. The modernist Hubbard employed a light writing style and even humor at times when describing events, as opposed to the tragic, almost Gothic writing of first-generation historians. Although a member of the second generation, Hubbard was still very much a Puritan and saw the war as a magnificent battle between right and wrong, good over evil. The Puritan victory highlighted the heroic sacrifice of God's chosen people. Taken in context with the book's appointment as the colony's official account, it is clear that Hubbard's modern view of history prevailed over the antiquated views of Mather and others because it was much more in touch with the reality of a New England undergoing transformation from a religious example into a dynamic, market-driven society.

REFERENCES

Hubbard, William. *A Narrative of the Troubles with the Indians in New England*. 1677. Facsim. rpt. of 1864 ed. published by Samuel G. Drake. 2 vols. Bowie, MD: Heritage Books, 1990.
Nelsen, Anne Kusener. "King Philip's War and the Hubbard-Mather Rivalry." *William & Mary Quarterly* 3rd ser., 27.4 (October 1970): 615–629.
Perry, Dennis R. " 'Novelties and Stile Which All Out-Do': William Hubbard's Historiography Reconsidered." *Early American Literature* 29.2 (1994): 166–182.

Kyle F. Zelner

HUGHES, LANGSTON (1902–1967). Langston Hughes was born in Joplin, Missouri, and attended Columbia University for one year (1921–1922) but earned his A.B. from Lincoln University (1929). His writings first appeared in the 1920s and received a wide readership during that decade's Harlem Renaissance. By celebrating African American culture and by addressing social and political inequalities both at home and abroad, while writing in every literary form, Hughes became the most renowned African American author of his time as well as one of America's most distinctive voices.

While he produced no single volume devoted to the subject of war, as a socially engaged author of the twentieth century Hughes's attentions periodically fell upon warfare and military institutions. An early piece, "Poem to a Dead Soldier," takes issue with society's tendency to honor the fallen without facing the total reality of death, while "The Colored Soldier" points out how the First World War's "fight to save democracy" did not conquer race prejudice in the United States.

As with many intellectuals, Hughes rallied to the republican cause in the Spanish Civil War. While serving as a news correspondent in that conflict, Hughes also wrote some of his most moving war poetry. "Letter from Spain" identifies race prejudice as a facet of colonialism as well as fascism, while "Postcard from Spain" expresses the belief that the fight against fascism is the start of a wide-ranging fight against racism. "Air Raid: Barcelona" captures the horror and death of an air raid (for both defenders and attackers). "Moonlight in Valencia: Civil War" looks past the propaganda of war to face the violence done to human bodies. And "Madrid—1937" links the defeat of fascism not only to the progress of liberty but to the progress of all humanity. Also rooted in the ideals of this period, poems such as "Good Morning, Stalingrad," "Salute to Soviet Armies," and "When Armies Passed" demonstrate Hughes's hope that the egalitarian promise of communism will be realized. A large portion of

Hughes's prose work, *I Wonder as I Wander: An Autobiographical Journal* (1956), treats this period of his career.

Hughes continued to address issues raised by the Second World War and its aftermath. Both "Jim Crow's Last Stand" and "Will V-Day Be Me-Day Too?" express the continued hope that the moral battle against fascism will be fought on the home front as well as abroad, while "Mother in Wartime," "War," "Official Notice," and "Total War" are skeptical about any redeeming features in war. Also from this period come many of the popular Simple stories, some of which deal with the impact of war and military institutions (for example, "A Veteran Falls," "Simple on Military Integration," and "Serious Talk about the Atom Bomb"). Hughes continued as a socially engaged author up to his death, which resulted from complications following prostate surgery.

REFERENCES

Hughes, Langston. *The Collected Poems of Langston Hughes*. Ed. Arnold Rampersad and Daniel Roessel. New York: Knopf, 1994.

Miller, R. Baxter. *The Art and Imagination of Langston Hughes*. Lexington: University Press of Kentucky, 1989.

Rampersad, Arnold. *The Life of Langston Hughes. Vol. I: 1902–1941; I, Too, Sing America*. New York: Oxford University Press, 1986. *Vol. II: 1941–1967; I Dream a World*. New York: Oxford University Press, 1988.

Joe Sarnowski

HUNTER, EVAN (1926–). Born in New York as Salvatore Albert Lombino, Hunter served in the U.S. Navy from 1944 to 1946, graduated from Hunter College, and taught at a vocational high school. He has written over 100 books, including works under the pseudonyms Curt Cannon, Hunt Collins, Ezra Hannon, and Richard Marsten; and as Ed McBain, he writes a very popular series of detective novels. His best-known work under his legally adopted name is *The Blackboard Jungle* (1954), based on his teaching experiences in New York City. He also wrote the screenplay for Alfred Hitchcock's *The Birds* (1963). He has been married twice and has four children.

His novel *Sons* (1969), written as Evan Hunter, traces three generations of men from an American family who serve in three wars. Bert Tyler serves in France in World War I; his son Will serves in Italy in World War II, and Will's son, Wat, serves in Vietnam, a draftee. The novel is told in first-person chapters, alternating among the three men. The novel attempts to chronicle generational changes but is filled with clichés. The family has worked its way up the economic ladder; Bert starts as a lumberjack, then works his way up in a paper mill, Will owns his own publishing firm, and Wat grows up a privileged middle-class child who rebels by playing in a rock band. There are historical errors, such as Will joining the "United States Air Force," rather than the Army Air Corps, in 1943. Grandfather and grandson have more in common than either with Will, member of the World War II generation; Bert was sympathetic to unions and was called a "Bolshevik" and became conscious of American Indian issues; Wat works with the civil rights movement. The war service serves mostly as a plot device; Bert's disillusioning experience is gone over very lightly, and Will's World War II experience consists more of picking up girls than flying. Although grandfather and father survived their wars, Wat dies in Vietnam, an event that requires a break from the first-person narrative.

REFERENCE

Rev. of *Sons*, by Evan Hunter. *New York Times Book Review* 28 September 1969: 54.

Renny Christopher

I

INDIAN CAPTIVITY NARRATIVES. Known collectively as Indian captivity narratives, stories of non-Indians held captive by Indians have fascinated readers from the time of their first publication through to the close of the frontier in the late nineteenth century. Scholarly attempts to catalog the canon indicate that literally thousands of such narratives were told, retold, chronicled, and published. Throughout their long and complex history, Indian captivity narratives have served Euro-American culture in a variety of cultural, historical, and literary ways, and they have been studied, scrutinized, and analyzed by anthropologists, sociologists, historians, and literary scholars who find in their texts a wealth of information and insight into American myths, fears, and culture. Warfare between European newcomers to the New World and the indigenous inhabitants of North America both inspired and was in turn significantly shaped by the writing and publication of captivity literature that from colonial times to the present provides an uninterrupted chronicle of the Euro-American military imagination.

During the seventeenth and eighteenth centuries, captivity narratives were written to foment public opinion in the colonies against what were perceived as the enemies of national expansion into the western wilderness. The first of these enemies was the French, who are vilified in dozens of colonial captivities for challenging British hegemony in North America by inciting their native allies to commit war crimes and depredations against the British. In the popular account of his captivity titled *A Faithful Narrative* (1758), for example, Robert Eastburn capitalizes on the war spirit of the times by taking every opportunity to incite hatred against the French by listing numerous instances of French-inspired Indian atrocities. "Even in Time of *Peace*," states Eastburn, the French governor of Canada "gives the *Indians* great Encouragement to *Murder* and *Captivate* the poor Inhabitants of our Frontiers." According to Eastburn, the French are so *barbarous* that "contrary to the *Laws* of *War* among all *civilized Nations*," they train the young men their Indian allies captured from the English as recruits for the French military who are then "employed in *Murdering* their Countrymen; yea, perhaps their *Fathers* and *Brethren*."

At the time of the American Revolution, captivity narratives hurl similar accusations against the British. In *A Narrative of the Capture of Certain Americans at Westmoreland by the Savages* (ca. 1780), for example, the British are excoriated for having used their Indian allies to perpetrate war crimes. By offering the Indians a reward for scalps but not for prisoners, the British are said to encourage the Indians to keep their captives alive "for the purpose of carrying the baggage" until they reach the British garrison at Niagara, where the captives were then tomahawked "and their scalps, not themselves," redeemed.

Throughout the seventeenth, eighteenth, and nineteenth centuries, most captivity narratives make every possible literary effort to vilify Native Americans. The typical narrative portrays all Native Americans as cruel and diabolical. Writing a military history (*Decennium Luctuosum*, 1699) about Indian captivity during the early French and Indian Wars, the seventeenth-century Puritan cleric and collector of captivity stories Cotton Mather refers to Indians as "Barbarous Opressors," "merciless *Tyrant*[s]," "Diabolical Master[s]," and "furious Tawnies." According to Mather, "no words can Sufficiently describe the Cruelty undergone by our *Captives*" who "must ever now and then have their Friends made a *Sacrifice of Devils* before their Eyes." "In fine," continues Mather, "when the *Children* of the *English Captives* Cryed at any Time, so that they were not presently quieted, the manner of the *Indians* was, to dash out their Brains against a *Tree*."

By the middle of the nineteenth century, the image of the Indian portrayed in the typical captivity narrative remained essentially unchanged from that in Mather's time. According to Mary Smith's *Affecting Narrative* (1815), Indians are "monsters of barbarity" who "ought certainly to be excluded from all the privileges of human nature, and hunted down as wild beasts, without pity or cessation." The same view of Indians appears in the *Narrative of the Captivity and Providential Escape of Mrs. Jane Lewis* (1833), where it is argued that the "character of the savage mind, naturally fierce, revengeful and cruel, will not receive and cherish the introduction of the arts and sciences: but on the contrary renders it more debased and inveterate—therefore, the policy of a great nation ought to be, and is, to overawe and intimidate." By 1867 captivity narratives such as *General Sheridan's Squaw Spy and Mrs. Clara Blynn's Captivity* summarize the military intent behind more than three centuries of captivity stories: "Any parleying with the Savages . . . is worse than folly . . . for the Indians are bloodthirsty, and cannot be tamed." "Thus," states the author, "in the war of races extermination must certainly be the fate of the Indians."

Virtually every major Indian tribal group, every region of the United States, and every war between Indian Americans and Euro-Americans are represented in the canon of captivity narratives. Together these narratives constitute a provocative military history of Indian and Euro-American contact on the westering frontier of the United States. *The Remarkable Adventures of Jackson Johonnot*

(1791), for example, tells the story of a captivity among the Kickapoo Indians in the Ohio Territory. The setting of *A Narrative of the Life and Sufferings of Mrs. Jane Johns* (1837) is east Florida during the Second Seminole War while other narratives such as Royal B. Stratton's *Captivity of the Oatman Girls* (1857) and Fanny Kelly's *My Captivity among the Sioux Indians* (1871) tell of captivities among the Indians of the West during the latter part of the nineteenth century. Indeed, one much overlooked aspect of the captivity tradition was the incorporation of captivity narratives into American military histories. From the time of the Cotton Mather, through the early nineteenth-century historical works of George Bancroft and **Francis Parkman**, and through late nineteenth-century military histories such as Thomas Dawson's *The Ute War* (1879), captivity narratives become a means for justifying a white colonial policy of military aggression and expansionism toward the native peoples of the Americas.

Research into the historicity of many narratives has shown them to be only loosely based on fact. The primary reason why American Indians took captives was not to torture them but to adopt them into the tribe, so most captives were treated with considerable humanity. As a consequence of warfare and the introduction of European diseases, Indian tribal numbers had been drastically reduced. Captives were one means of replenishing those numbers, and most captives soon adjusted to the lifestyle of their captors to the point that when given the opportunity to return to the culture of their birth, they preferred to remain among their adopted families. Nonetheless, truth was of less importance to the writers and promoters of captivity narratives than sensationalism and military propaganda, and as a consequence the intent of the vast majority of narratives was to horrify white audiences into hating what the novelist **Hugh Henry Brackenridge** referred to as "the animals, vulgarly called Indians" (*Narratives of a Late Expedition against the Indians*, 1782).

The *Narrative of the Capture and Providential Escape of Misses Frances and Almira Hall* (1832) illustrates the vast discrepancy between historical truth and military propaganda that characterized most captivity narratives. Replete with tortures, scalpings, murders, and barbarities "too shocking to be presented to the public," the Hall narrative was published to recruit militia for service in the so-called Black Hawk War (1831–1832). In this narrative, Euro-American men living in Illinois territory are encouraged to enlist in the army and thus help "to revenge the cruelties perpetrated" by the Indians "on the infant, the mother, and the defenceless." Specifically, this narrative demands the capture and execution of the Sauk chief **Black Hawk**, who is said to have ordered the execution of all white captives.

In his autobiography published in 1833, Makataimeshikiakiak (Black Hawk), by this time a celebrity who had toured the United States and been entertained by numerous government dignitaries including President Andrew Jackson, repudiates such charges as those made against him in the Hall narrative. In the words of Makataimeshikiakiak himself, "Before I take leave of the public, I must contradict the story of some village criers, who (I have been told) accuse me of 'having murdered women and children among the whites!' " "This assertion," states the great Sauk chief, "is false! I never did, nor have I any knowledge that any of my nation ever killed a white woman or child." "I make this statement of truth," continues Makataimeshikiakiak, "to satisfy the white people among whom I have been travelling . . . that when they shook me by the hand so cordially, they did not shake the hand that had ever been raised against any but warriors."

REFERENCES

Burnham, Michelle. *Captivity and Sentiment: Cultural Exchange in American Literature, 1882–1861.* Hanover, NH: University Press of New England, 1997.

Derounian-Stodola, Kathryn Zabelle, and James A. Levernier. *The Indian Captivity Narrative, 1500–1900.* New York: Twayne, 1992.

Ebersole, Gary L. *Captured by Texts: Puritan to Postmodern Images of Indian Captivity.* Charlottesville: University Press of Virginia, 1995.

Levernier, James A. "The Captivity Narrative as Regional, Military, and Ethnic History." *Research Studies* 45 (1977): 30–37.

Levernier, James A., and Hennig Cohen, eds. *The Indians and Their Captives.* Westport, CT: Greenwood Press, 1977.

Namias, June. *White Captives: Gender and Ethnicity on the American Frontier.* Chapel Hill: University of North Carolina Press, 1993.

Pearce, Roy Harvey. "The Significance of the Captivity Narrative." *American Literature* 19 (1947): 1–20.

Slotkin, Richard. *Regeneration through Violence: The Mythology of the American Frontier, 1600–1860.* Middletown, CT: Wesleyan University Press, 1973.

VanDerBeets, Richard. " 'A Thirst for Empire': The Indian Captivity Narrative as Propaganda." *Research Studies* 40 (1972): 207–215.

———, ed. *Held Captive by Indians.* Knoxville: University of Tennessee Press, 1994.

James A. Levernier

J

JAKES, JOHN (1932–   ). Sometimes referred to as "America's history teacher," sometimes as the "acknowledged master of the family saga," John Jakes is best known for two series of novels, the eight-volume *The Kent Family Chronicles* and the *North and South* trilogy. Although he had published a great deal before the phenomenal success of the *Kent* series, the enormity of the success of that series led to his "overnight sensation" status and reputation. Born on March 31, 1932, in Chicago, he credits the movies, legitimate theater, and reading as his early influences, influences that can be easily seen in the cinematic flair of his prose. He graduated from DePauw University in 1953 with a degree in creative writing and holds an M.A. in American literature from Ohio State, which he earned the following year. He made his living as an advertising copy-writer for many years, while writing on the side, before devoting all of his time to writing.

The Kent Family Chronicles, which was originally named The American Bi-centennial Series, was conceived by Lyle Kenyon Engel as an unapologetically commercial venture to capitalize on the celebratory mood of the country's bi-centennial. The series follows the Kent family from the Revolutionary War to the close of the nineteenth century. Throughout the *Kent* novels, Jakes uses the Kent family, individually and collectively, as a metaphor for the nation itself. They participate in America's major historical events, such as the writing of the Declaration of Independence; they debate major political issues; and they inter-act with major historical figures such as Benjamin Franklin, **Theodore Roose-velt**, Andrew Carnegie, and Frederick Douglass. The entire series contains Jakes's unshakable belief in the principles upon which the United States was founded: democracy, freedom, and unalienable human rights. Specifically, *The Bastard* (1974) and *The Rebels* (1975) are set before, during, and immediately after the American Revolution; *The Seekers* (1975) and *The Furies* (1976) depict the War of 1812, the Western expansion, and the pre–Civil War era; *The Titans* (1976) and *The Warriors* (1977) follow the Civil War and Reconstruction; and *The Lawless* (1978) and *The Americans* (1980) conclude the series.

Jakes returns to the Civil War for his second major series, which consists of *North and South* (1982), *Love and War* (1984), and *Heaven and Hell* (1987). This trilogy shows the effect of the war on two families, the Mains of South Carolina and the Hazards of Pennsylvania. Thus, as he did in the *Kent* saga, Jakes uses family as a metaphor for the nation. The entire series explores the causes and consequences of the War between the States. The historical significance of the Civil War—the dissolution of the unity of the nation, the upheaval of change and the carnage of this war, and the hope of reconciliation represented by Reconstruction—binds the three books together, presenting insights as revelations that unfold slowly across generations and over time, rather than as brief flashes of immediate understanding. This series conceives of the Civil War as an archetypal experience for the nation: the loss of innocence and idealism as a nation, the biblical opposition of good and evil, and the inevitability of personal, as well as national, dilemmas.

Jakes is an incredibly prolific writer who has published many more novels other than the ones discussed here, as well as novels under two other pseudonyms. However, *The Kent Family Chronicles* and the *North and South* trilogy are the novels for which he will be best, and most fondly, remembered.

REFERENCES

Hawkins, Robert. *The Kent Family Chronicles Encyclopedia*. New York: Bantam, 1979.
Jones, Mary Ellen. *John Jakes: A Critical Companion*. Westport, CT: Greenwood Press, 1996.
Salvatore, Nick, and Ann Sullivan. "From Bastard to American: The Legitimization of a Fictional Family." *Radical History Review* 26 (1982): 140–150.

Julianne White

JARRELL, RANDALL (1914–1965). Born in Nashville, Tennessee, Randall Jarrell was educated at Vanderbilt University, where he enjoyed the guidance and friendship of several writers in the Fugitive Movement. After finishing an M.A. in 1939, he taught at the University of Texas, Austin, and had published two volumes of poetry by the time the United States entered World War II. Although he enlisted to train as a ferry-pilot, he did not qualify for the program. He remained in the Army Air Force as an enlisted man, serving as a control tower operator and later as a flight instructor. He spent the war years in the States; he experienced no direct combat, a fact few readers could guess from his work alone. In a period of a few years, he wrote and published nearly fifty poems in two volumes—*Little Friend, Little Friend* (1945) and *Losses* (1948)—that dealt in some way or other with World War II. By all critical accounts, Jarrell—an influential poet and critic in postwar America— came to artistic maturity during the war years.

He is perhaps best known for his five-line poem "The Death of the Ball Turret Gunner," an unforgettable statement on the horrors of aerial combat in World War II (or on any combat in any war). In the poem's powerful imagery, suggestive of abortion, the doomed gunner falls from the symbolic innocence of prenatal existence into the service of his country. After huddling fetuslike in the belly of an aircraft, he awakens, paradoxically, to the dream reality of war—a nightmare of darkness and instruments of death. The poem ends with troubling understatement, as the speaker is efficiently cleaned from the turret "with a hose."

This short piece presents or suggests several major themes amplified elsewhere in his war poetry: the dream reality of war, the essential innocence of the combatants, the indifference of technological warfare, the cold abstraction of the war state, and the certainty of death in combat. For example, "Eighth Air Force" presents fighting men not as murderers but as the inevitable victims of war. "Losses" is about the loss of life as well as the loss of innocence of the young men who wake up to the reality of their situation as warriors flying over England. "Siegfried" speaks of the irrational but inevitable events of war. In "Transient Barracks," a returning serviceman is astonished at the simple fact that home is "real." Jarrell's war poems reveal a dark, deterministic world in which men pursue an ultimately unsuccessful quest for transcendence—a theme evident in much of his work before and after the war.

In addition to war poetry, he wrote other verse as well as one novel, three children's books, translations, and literary criticism. He was killed in an automobile accident in 1965.

REFERENCES

Ferguson, Suzanne. *The Poetry of Randall Jarrell*. Baton Rouge: Louisiana State University Press, 1971.

Jarrell, Randall. *The Complete Poems*. New York: Farrar, Straus, & Giroux, 1969.

Pritchard, William H. *Randall Jarrell: A Literary Life*. New York: Farrar, Straus, & Giroux, 1990.

Steve Anderson

JEFFERS, ROBINSON (1887–1962). Born John Robinson Jeffers to William Hamilton Jeffers and Annie Robinson Jeffers, Jeffers was raised in western Pennsylvania and schooled there and in Europe. He attended the University of Pittsburgh and then, after his father retired and moved his family to suburban Los Angeles, Occidental College. Upon graduating from Occidental in 1905, Jeffers took graduate courses in European languages and literatures at the University of Southern California (USC) and the University of Zurich. Next, Jeffers studied medicine at USC (1907–1910), but despite outstanding work as a medical student, he left USC to study forestry at the University of Washington. That profession displeased him. Wanting to concentrate on poetry, he returned to California. By 1912, he had produced his first book, a privately published collection of derivative verse. In 1913, Jeffers married Una Call Kuster, recently divorced, with whom he had been in an illicit relationship since 1906.

Robinson and Una were planning to move to England when World War I broke out. Forced to remain in the States, they settled in seaside Carmel, California, where Jeffers built a house out of rocks gathered from the beach. There, isolated from the High Modernist aesthetics being promoted in European literary circles, he began to compose highly individualistic poetry that stylistically and thematically reflected his identification with that rugged coastal environment.

Although he never served in the military, Jeffers frequently grappled with the meaning of war; indeed, it might be said that war galvanized his poetic imagination. The destruction in Europe during World War I shocked him into believing that Western civilization was endangered and that its Judeo-Christian morality had become bankrupt. The prospect of America's inevitable involvement in the European war disgusted Jeffers (he stated, "The only war that is morally defensible is a war of defense"), yet he considered war "A natural condition of the race. . . . [A]n unavoidable spectacular madness." Thus, Jeffers did not seek conscientious objector status; instead, he volunteered for the U.S. Balloon Corps (though the war ended before he was called to service).

Jeffers's first mature poems date from the end of World War I. His ambivalence toward that war finds fullest expression in "The Truce and the Peace," a sonnet cycle written shortly after the Armistice of November 1918 (though first published in 1924). In "The Truce and the Peace," the poet acknowledges the war's devastation, the screams of the men and bugles, and the destruction of the landscape, then notes that such horrors lead to the realization that God exists. Jeffers recalls World War I in such other lyric poems as "Woodrow Wilson" (1925) and "The Dead to Clemenceau: November, 1929" (1931), both of which critique the actions and attitudes of wartime political leaders.

In the mid-1930s, disturbed by Hitler's rise to power in Germany, Jeffers began to compose numerous lyric poems prophesying the coming international calamity, including "Rearmament," "Air-raid Rehearsals," "Hellenistics," and "Contemplation of the Sword" (all first published in 1938). "Going to Horse Flats" (also 1938) proposes an escape from certain warfare by a turn to God. Jeffers's disillusionment deepened after the onset of World War II, a fact evident in numerous lyric poems (noteworthy more for their strident political views than for their artfulness) published in 1941. In "The Day Is a Poem," for instance, Jeffers attacks Hitler, while in "Shine Empire" the poet castigates the United States for moving toward involvement in the European power struggle.

After America's entry into World War II, Jeffers wrote some of the most effective antiwar poems of his career, including lyric poems like "Ink-sack," "The Eye," and "Historical Choice." One longer narrative poem from this period, "The Inhumanist," is particularly striking for its evocation of Cold War hysteria and its apocalyptic speculations regarding the impact of a full-scale nuclear war (the poem refers to it as the third in a succession of world wars). These and related poems were published in *The Double Axe and Other Poems* (1948). In a notorious act of censorship, Jeffers's publisher, Random House, chose to exclude nearly a dozen poems from that volume and to publicly disagree with the poet's nonconformist political views by inserting a written disclaimer within the volume. Despite featuring some of Jeffers's finest political poetry, *The Double Axe* angered many Americans, who felt that the poet's individualism and isolationism—qualities that before World War II had interested both readers and critics—had gone too far. Thereafter, postwar America ignored him and his work.

More recently, Jeffers's poetry is again receiving recognition for its stylistic originality and for its unflinching exploration of controversial political, social, and environmental themes.

REFERENCES

Bennett, Melba Berry. *The Stone Mason of Tor House: The Life and Works of Robinson Jeffers*. Los Angeles: Ward Ritchie, 1966.
Jeffers, Robinson. *The Collected Poetry of Robinson Jeffers*. Ed. Tim Hunt. 3 vols. to date. Stanford: Stanford University Press, 1988–
Shebl, James. *In This Wild Water*. Los Angeles: Ward Ritchie, 1976.

Ted Olson

JOHNSTON, MARY (1870–1936). Born in Buchanan, Virginia, Mary Johnston received her education largely through private tutors and her own reading due to illness throughout most of her childhood. At nineteen, after her mother's death, she assumed the responsibility of hostess and companion for her father. Financial need and desire for therapeutic relief from continuing illness prompted her to write *Prisoners of Hope* (1898), a historical romance about seventeenth-century Virginia plantations. The phenomenal success of her second book, *To Have and to Hold* (1900), about the Jamestown settlement, encouraged her to write mostly similar romances for the next ten years.

Johnston's Civil War novels represent her most serious attempt at historical fiction. *The Long Roll* (1911) and its sequel *Cease Firing* (1912) pay tribute to the heroic South and her father, John William Johnston, a former major of artillery. They weave together historical details and fictional plots to dramatize the experiences of war. *The Long Roll* begins with the outset of the war in a small Virginia town in 1860 and contains a love triangle, involving villainous Maury Stafford, Virginia gentleman Richard Cleave, and Judith Cary. The conventional romantic plot loosely parallels the progression of the war: The initial optimism and victories of the Confederates fade into elemental struggles in savage battles as Stafford sabotages the romance between Cleave and Cary and later passes a wrong order to Cleave during the battle of the Seven Days. Cleave unknowingly leads his regiment into an ambush at White Oak Swamp and faces court-martial. Military campaigns, with episodes told from different perspectives and with General Stonewall Jackson as an egocentric but heroic commander, give the most vivid moments of action and emotion in the novel. The accidental death of Jackson at the hands of his own troops at the Battle of Chancellorsville in 1863 and Richard's dismissal foreshadow the darker years to come.

In *Cease Firing* the battles in Vicksburg, the Mississippi Valley, Tennessee, and West Virginia and in the Wilderness are portrayed with the same intensity. A second romantic plot, involving Judith Cary's brother Edward and Desiree Gaillard, adds melodramatic qualities to the increasing hardship of the South. They fall in love at first sight, suffer separations after marriage, and eventually die together under the assaults of drunken Northern soldiers. The happier ending of Richard and Judith brings hope, but only for these two individuals. They are married after Stafford confesses his crime and Richard resumes command of his regiment. The novel ends with the Army of Northern Virginia on its way to Appomattox. The South faces inevitable defeat, but the soldiers march on. Johnston's most successful character in both novels is Stephen Dagg, a cowardly mountain man whose major concerns in battles are his safety and comfort. He lies, robs, and does not hesitate to desert. His survival principle serves as a contrast to the moral principle and heroism of the major characters.

These historical novels mark the beginning of Johnston's interest in social and political problems and philosophy in the second half of her career. She became involved in the women's suffrage movement and prison reform, but her novels from this period, suffused with mystical and supernatural philosophy, attracted only a modest readership. In her last three novels Johnston returned to Virginia historical romances, the genre for which she is most remembered.

REFERENCES

Cella, C. Ronald. *Mary Johnston*. Boston: Twayne Publishers, 1981.
Johnston, Mary. *Cease Firing*. Baltimore: Johns Hopkins University Press, 1996.
———. *The Long Roll*. Baltimore: Johns Hopkins University Press, 1996.

Chih-Ping Chen

JONES, JAMES (1921–1977). Jones was born in Robinson, Illinois. Jones's father ruined his dental practice by excessive drinking, while his mother became an obese diabetic. Profits from oil on a family farm were lost in the 1929 crash. In 1939 Jones graduated from high school and soon enlisted in the U.S. Army. He served in the Army Air Corps at Hickham Field and Wheeler Field, Hawaii, and was a welterweight boxer at Pearl Harbor. His mother died in March 1941. In September he transferred to the infantry and was assigned to Schofield Barracks. He often visited Honolulu's Hotel Street strip and relished drinking and whoring with many enlisted men there.

When the Japanese attacked Pearl Harbor on December 7, 1941, Jones ran headquarters messages and later that day helped build and man Makapuu Point pillboxes. In March 1942, his father committed suicide. In May, Jones made corporal and soon attended writing and American literature classes at the Manoa campus of the University of Hawaii. His Twenty-Fifth Infantry Division landed on January 1, 1943, at Guadalcanal, in the Solomon Islands. His F Company, Twenty-Seventh Infantry Regiment, went into combat January 11. Jones killed a Japanese soldier in hand-to-hand fighting, was wounded in the head by Japanese mortar fragments on January 12, and was briefly hospitalized. He then participated in the capture of Kokumbona village on January 23, mangled his right ankle, and required surgery in New Hebrides. He was transferred to San Francisco, then Memphis, arriving in May. After hospitalization and designation to limited service, he was incorrectly assigned to full infantry duty instead. He went AWOL in November. In December, demoted to private, he did latrine duty and the following March made sergeant. He became a psychiatric-ward patient in the army hospital at Camp Campbell, Kentucky, was diagnosed as psycho-neurotic, and was honorably discharged in July 1944.

Jones, impressed by Thomas Wolfe and long interested in a writing career, attended classes at New York University in 1945, wrote in North Carolina until August, then returned home to Illinois. In 1948 he published his first war story, "Temper of Steel," in *The Atlantic Monthly*, a tale of the knifing to death of a Japanese enemy. *From Here to Eternity*, his best-selling blockbuster, followed in 1951. While book sales were reaching 4 million, film rights brought him $82,000. The novel was translated into eleven foreign languages. Jones's second best-seller, *Some Came Running* (1958), film rights for which earned $250,000, dramatizes a soldier's efforts to understand his hometown's postwar narrow-minded materialism.

Married in 1957, Jones and his wife established their residence in Paris the following year, partly for income-tax and foreign-royalty advantages. Jones's minor novel *The Pistol* (1959) concerns a soldier clinging to a .45, as a talisman, immediately after the bombing of Pearl Harbor. Jones was a consultant-writer for Darryl Zanuck's war movie *The Longest Day* (1961). A year later Jones published *The Thin Red Line*—the second part of a war trilogy beginning with *From Here to Eternity*. Some of the thirteen pieces in his *The Ice-Cream Head-ache and Other Stories* (1968) concern war and reveal his skill in keeping fiction short and vivid. Jones was a *New York Times Magazine* special reporter in South Vietnam from February 26 to March 28, 1973. His *Viet Journal* (1974) makes it clear that he opposed American involvement in Southeast Asia, reviled South Vietnam's corrupt leaders, esteemed U.S. Army enlisted men, and despised North Vietnamese duplicitous cunning and savagery.

In 1974 Jones and his family left Paris and soon located on Long Island. For *WWII: A Chronicle of Soldiering* (1975), which features grim war art, Jones provided textual material combining history, casualty figures, and reminiscence. Desperately ill, he wrote and dictated what became *Whistle* (1978), the third part of his war trilogy.

From Here to Eternity features men in the regular army in Hawaii just before Pearl Harbor. Idealistic Private Robert E. Lee Prewitt and cynical First Sergeant Milton Anthony Warden are sharply contrasted. Both career soldiers, they si-multaneously love and hate the army. Prewitt has an affair with a prostitute, while Warden is in love with his captain's wife. Jones bitterly presents enlisted men hurt by rank consciousness, dehumanizing discipline, favoritism, and cor-ruption. Evil seeps down from the commanding general to the captain, a sadistic sergeant, and even a private feigning insanity to be discharged. The graphic novel is riddled with obscene language. In *The Thin Red Line* an infantry unit rushes into combat on Guadalcanal. Some eighty named soldiers are dehumanized so that the outfit, a machine with replaceable parts, can grind on, in the process rendering both heroism and cowardice equally meaningless. *Whistle* takes four infantrymen who are wounded in 1943 back home where they feel guilty for having survived combat, fear future duty, and are troubled by women and disgusted at civilians enjoying the good life. Climactically, a sergeant, transferred to the European Theater, cannot face more slaughter and slips quietly into the cold ocean on the way over.

In his naturalistic and technically traditional war fiction, Jones depicts swarms of males in a brutal world where bureaucracy demeans and females distract and where the individual is hopelessly lost in a world of chance.

REFERENCES

Garrett, George. *James Jones*. New York: Harcourt Brace Jovanovich, 1984.
Giles, James R. *James Jones*. Boston: Twayne, 1981.
Jones, James. *To Reach Eternity: The Letters of James Jones*. Ed. George Hendrick. New York: Random House, 1989.
McShane, Frank. *Into Eternity: The Life of James Jones, American Writer*. Boston: Houghton Mifflin, 1985.
Morris, Willie. *James Jones: A Friendship*. Garden City, NY: Doubleday, 1978.

Robert L. Gale

JONES, JAMES ATHEARN (1791–1854). Born at Tisbury, Massachusetts, Jones was best known as a folklorist. He interacted with Native Americans, specifically the Gayhead tribe, who worked in his family's house on Martha's Vineyard. Jones studied law with local attorneys, taught school, and edited newspapers.

Jones's first novel was the two-volume work *The Refugee, a Romance* (1825), which he published using the pseudonym Captain Matthew Murgatroyd of the Ninth Continentals. Protagonist Gilbert Greaves attempts to recruit Tories around New York City to fight in the American Revolution. When his commander acts immorally, Greaves switches allegiances and dramatically, and unrealistically, presents his sword to George Washington. Captured at the Battle of White Plains, Greaves is predictably rescued from execution as a traitor. Jones penned vivid images of New York and military leaders. Perhaps he was inspired by **James Fenimore Cooper**'s popular novel *The Spy* (1821), a fictionalized account of a true story about a Revolutionary War soldier who saved George Washington's life and which shared many of the same themes such as patriotism and heroism as Jones's work.

Jones's three-volume *Haverhill; or Memoirs of an Officer in the Army of Wolfe* (1831) follows the adventures of hero Lynn Haverhill, the son of an oysterman, who must impress the father of the woman he loves. Swept out to sea during a gale, Haverhill is rescued by a ship carrying British soldiers to

Quebec and personally commissioned an ensign by General Wolfe. Haverhill undergoes stereotypical adventures and hardships, including being responsible for alerting Wolfe to how to capture Quebec. Because of his military prowess, Haverhill is considered worthy to marry his sweetheart. Although providing better dialogue and description than his first novel, Jones's work is unoriginal, overly sentimental, artistically flawed with a rigid style of dialogue interrupted by unrelated exposition, and imitative of romantic novels about war written in the early nineteenth century by such authors as James Fenimore Cooper and Sir Walter Scott.

Jones's best-known work, the three-volume *Tales of an Indian Camp* (1829), was probably the first collection focusing on aboriginal folklore published in America. Jones includes tales about Native American conflicts with white settlers and other tribes. He created romanticized images, exclamatory statements, and embellishments to present his tales. His manuscript "Warfare of the North American Indians" (1830) describes past occurrences of tribal warfare, emphasizing bravery and perseverance of combatants. Many of Jones's stories are told from a European perspective, such as an unnamed English captain describing the capture of Fort William Henry during the French and Indian War in which French-allied Indians massacred English soldiers and civilians.

REFERENCES

Flanagan, John T. "A Pioneer in Indian Folklore; James Athearn Jones." *New England Quarterly* 12 (September 1939): 443–453.

McNeil, W. K. "James Athearn Jones: Pioneer American Folklorist." *Folklore on Two Continents: Essays in Honor of Linda Dégh.* Ed. Nikolai Burlakoff, Carl Lindah, and Harry Gammerdinger. Bloomington, IN: Trickster Press, 1980. 321–327.

Pease, Richard L. "James Athearn Jones." *Memorial Biographies of the New England Historic Genealogical Society.* 2 vols. Boston: New England Historic Genealogical Society, 1881. 204–222.

Elizabeth D. Schafer

JUST, WARD (1935–). Born in Michigan City, Indiana, Just attended Trinity College in Hartford, Connecticut, and, after graduating, worked as a journalist with the *Waukegan News-Sun* in 1957. After stints with *Newsweek* and *Reporter*, he joined the *Washington Post* as a correspondent in South Vietnam from 1965 to 1967. He has won numerous awards for both his fiction and nonfiction and was a contributing editor for the *Atlantic* from 1972 to 1984.

After being seriously wounded in 1967 while accompanying a reconnaissance patrol near the Cambodian border, Just returned home and wrote the well-received *To What End: Report from Vietnam* (1968). Just describes with his acute reporter's eye the horrible chaos of the war in Vietnam, the various political factions, the entrenched Vietnamese bureaucracy, and its American overlay. *Military Men*, a study of the character of the American professional soldier and of the army as it existed during the Vietnam era, appeared in 1970. Just wonders whether an organization, which like the military is so steeped in discipline, can continue to be effective in a culture that continuously devalues discipline.

Using his experiences as a correspondent, Just increasingly turned to fiction as his medium of preference. His books explore the serious personal and political dilemmas that war creates in the modern era. In 1974, he published *Stringer*, his first major novel about Vietnam.

Stringer is a civilian intelligence operative partnered with a regular army officer named Price. Their mission is to plant electronic sensors near trails used by the enemy. When the sensors alert them to enemy movement, they coordinate bombing runs by radio. Stringer and Price are characters whose personalities and individual ideas of duty are in opposition, and Price is eventually killed because of his inability to deviate from his own rigid adherence to military form and discipline. Stringer is left alone, without supplies, to survive in the jungle and is himself driven mad by the madness of war.

In 1984 *The American Blues*, Just's second major work of fiction about Vietnam, appeared. Semiautobiographical in nature, *The American Blues* is narrated by a journalist obsessed with Vietnam, an obsession that causes both intellectual and emotional paralysis preventing him from completing his book about the war and thus putting it behind him once and for all.

Leaving his wife and son just after the fall of Saigon in 1975, he visits the home of a well-known writer friend where he tries to work out his feelings about the war and his life. He has a brief affair with a younger woman who does not share his sense of history, and he discovers through this liaison that he cannot return home feeling as he does. The novel concludes with the narrator returning to Vietnam, where he somewhat uncomfortably reconnects with his past. The narrator's final words, "Listen . . . Everything's going to work out fine," are ambiguously ironic, suggesting perhaps his own belief that the past and Vietnam will haunt him—and us—forever.

Just includes some short fiction about Vietnam in two of his collections— *The Congressman Who Loved Flaubert and Other Stories* (1973) and *Honor, Power, Riches, Fame, and the Love of Women* (1979)—and his novel, *In the City of Fear* (1983), is set during the Vietnam War.

REFERENCES

Beidler, Philip D. *Re-Writing America: Vietnam Authors in Their Generation.* Athens: University of Georgia Press, 1991.
Just, Ward. "Vietnam: The Camera Lies." *Atlantic* (December 1979): 63–65.

Peter Katopes

K

KANTOR, MacKINLAY (1904–1977). Born in Webster City, Iowa, MacKinlay Kantor worked at various periods as a reporter, war correspondent, and screenwriter, but he is best known for his short stories and novels, particularly those dealing with the American Civil War and World War II, which are marked by meticulous research and accurate detail.

Long Remember (1934), generally considered Kantor's best historical novel, describes the impact of the Civil War on several civilians caught up in the battle of Gettysburg. *Arouse and Beware* (1936) is the story of two Union soldiers who escape the horrific Confederate prison at Belle Island and encounter dangerous Union stragglers, courageous Underground Railroad members, and compassionate Southern home guardsmen.

Kantor's best-known work, the Pulitzer Prize–winning *Andersonville* (1955), is a long, rambling, but powerful story about those who lived in and around the Confederate prison of the title, primarily focused on what happens in a world of limited resources when all authority breaks down. Although much of the horror in the prison stockade stems from the Confederate captors' failure to provide adequate provisions, a good deal of the violence is caused by the prisoners themselves, especially a group of raiders made up primarily of immigrants and New York slum dwellers, who harass and steal from the new prisoners until they are stopped by a group of Midwesterners who call themselves Regulators.

Although Kantor considered himself a pacifist, he had a lifelong fascination with the military, which led to his becoming a war correspondent for the *Saturday Evening Post* during World War II. Attached to the British Royal Air Force and the American Eighth Air Force, Kantor sought to get as close as possible to the front lines; ignoring rules restricting correspondents to observer status, he trained as a gunner and flew eleven combat missions. Out of these and other experiences came two novels of World War II: *Happy Land* (1943), the story of a young sailor killed in the Pacific and of his grief-stricken father, and *Glory for Me* (1945), an account in verse of the return of several veterans to postwar civilian life, which in 1946 formed the basis of the highly regarded William Wyler film *The Best Years of Our Lives*.

In 1951, Kantor published *Don't Touch Me*, one of the earliest novels of the Korean War. In it, he examines the unusual domestic circumstances, for American servicemen, of a commuter war in which pilots attack the Korean enemy from a large U.S. air base in occupied Japan. The base, a transplanted American town, is home to the pilots and their families, and the mounting tensions of a mission to attack Pyongyang, the North Korean capital, further aggravate marital discords.

His novel *Spirit Lake* (1958) about an 1857 Indian massacre of white settlers in northern Iowa, although moderately successful, marked the beginning of his slide into obscurity. Kantor's later years were marked by a decline in his creative powers brought about in part by a battle with alcoholism. Although he tried to recapture his form with his novel *Valley Forge* (1975), most of his later works lacked control or were reworked versions of earlier stories he kept in his files.

REFERENCES

Hibbs, Ben. Preface to *Story Teller, MacKinlay Kantor*. New York: Doubleday, 1967.
Kantor, MacKinlay. *The Historical Novelist's Obligation to History*. Macon, GA: Wesleyan College, 1967.
Kantor, Tim. *My Father's Voice: MacKinlay Kantor, Long Remembered*. New York: McGraw-Hill, 1988.

Dean Rehberger

KARLIN, WAYNE (1945–   ). Born in New York City, Wayne Karlin attended White Plains High School before enlisting in the Marine Corps. Transferred to Vietnam in December 1965, Karlin was initially assigned to an air control squadron as a clerk, but later he voluntarily extended his tour for combat duty as a helicopter door gunner. Following his release from active duty in 1967, he briefly attended Pierce College in Los Angeles. In 1969, he moved to Israel and attended the American College there. After earning his B.A., Karlin worked as a journalist in the United States and Israel and began writing fiction. He went on to complete an M.A. in creative writing at Goddard College in 1976 and now teaches at the Charles County Community College in Maryland.

As a member of the First Casualty Press, a veterans' project formed to protest through literature U.S. Vietnam involvement, Karlin, along with Basil T. Paquet and Larry Rottmann, edited *Free Fire Zone: Short Stories by Vietnam Veterans* (1973) and also contributed five stories.

Karlin has since written five novels about war or war-related themes. *Crossover* (1984), a spy thriller about two Israeli agents assigned to save a dissident Russian scientist from the PLO (Palestine Liberation Organization), posits a hidden agenda counter to the Jewish state's most basic sense of national identity. *Lost Armies* (1988), set in Maryland in a Vietnamese refugee community, involves an English teacher (himself a veteran of the war), a young Vietnamese woman who is his student, and her brother. A distinctive terrorist act suggests the secret return of the teacher's fellow veteran and friend, long classified as missing in action (MIA) and now assumed to be bent on revenge for the betrayal of his platoon in Vietnam. The surprise ending speaks to the difficulties of cultural projection and misunderstanding that plagued both sides during the war. *The Extras* (1988), a story of star-crossed lovers set amidst the ongoing Arab-Israeli conflict, revolves around an Israeli man, himself the veteran of two wars, and a Palestinian woman, his former childhood friend. The two meet again and fall in love on a movie set, but entangling alliances prevent them from achieving a separate peace. The protagonist of Karlin's *US* (1993) is a Vietnam veteran and expatriate Bangkok bar owner named Loman who is forced to assist an American congressman in a mad scheme to prove the existence of live MIAs in the Southeast Asia of the 1980s. The "US" of the title is rumored to be a group of renegade former MIAs now smuggling opium in the Golden Triangle. In a surprise twist, this group is indeed found to exist but also to consist of the "missing" we on the "U.S." side were largely responsible for dislocating. *Prisoners* (1998), a polyvocal novel set mostly in the early 1990s, involves several people profoundly touched by the Vietnam War. The various threads are tied together by the story of a teenage Vietnamese American girl who has run away in search of the black G.I. who had fathered her in Vietnam. The novel culminates in a haunted veteran's healing trip back to Vietnam.

Essentially a nonfiction novel, *Rumors and Stones* (1996) reconstructs a journey Karlin took in 1993 to rediscover his own roots as a writer and person. The literal destination was the Jewish village of Kolno in eastern Poland, from which his mother had long ago emigrated and whose inhabitants in July 1941 were all killed by the Germans. The journey occasions Karlin's reflections on his own Vietnam experiences and on certain parallels between the American war in Vietnam and the Holocaust.

Also noteworthy are Karlin's efforts on behalf of the "Voices from Vietnam" series of Curbstone Press. He has joined Le Minh Khue and Truong Vu in editing *The Other Side of Heaven: Post-War Fiction by Vietnamese and American Writers* (1995). The stories are juxtaposed to suggest and challenge the cultural constructions both sides held concerning the righteousness of their respective causes. Karlin has also edited two collections of translated Vietnamese stories representative of the war and its continuing effects on Vietnam: Le Minh Khue's *The Stars, the Earth, the River* (1997) and Ho Anh Thai's *Behind the Red Mist* (1998). These collections stem from Karlin's concern for the unfortunate fact that the Vietnamese experience has been largely unavailable to American readers seeking to understand the American war in Vietnam.

REFERENCE

Christopher, Renny. *The Viet Nam War/The American War: Images and Representations in Euro-American and Vietnamese Exile Narratives.* Amherst: University of Massachusetts Press, 1995.

Edward F. Palm

KENNEDY, JOHN PENDLETON (1795–1870). Born and raised in Baltimore, Kennedy was significantly influenced by his mother, Nancy Clayton Pendleton, who was descended from a distinguished Virginia family with a history of service in the American Revolution. After graduating from Baltimore College, he fought in the War of 1812 with the Fifth Regiment of the Maryland Militia and participated in the battles of Bladensburg and North Point. He then became a lawyer and achieved notoriety as a politician, serving as both a state legislator and congressman.

Kennedy also earned fame as a writer of historical fiction. His first book, *Swallow Barn* (1832), included sketches of Virginia society in the period after the Revolution. Three years later he wrote *Horse-Shoe Robinson*, the first novel to depict the Revolution as it was fought in the South. Finally, in 1838 he published *Rob of the Bowl*, a tale set in colonial Maryland.

As a war story, *Horse-Shoe Robinson* is not original. Kennedy relied heavily on the formula of the historical romance and imitated **James Fenimore Cooper**'s *The Spy* in constructing his story around the situation of a family's divided loyalties. However, because it is set in Carolina in 1780, it offers a unique description of the Southern theater of the war, as well as comic scenes that rely on the region's dialect and colorful local characters. In detailing events surrounding the fall of Charleston, the novel also dramatizes what is described in the subtitle as "The Tory Ascendancy," the uncertain period that followed the conquest of the Southern colonies by the British (a theme later used by **William Gilmore Simms**).

While the plot of the novel is organized around a conventional love story between Major Arthur Butler (a Continental officer) and Mildred Lindsay (the daughter of a Loyalist), Kennedy's most engaging character is Horse-Shoe Robinson, Butler's scout and friend. Like Cooper's Natty Bumppo, he is a plain-spoken hero who defies the aristocratic pretensions of his Tory antagonists. The conclusion of the novel is also noteworthy because of its vivid depiction of the battle of King's Mountain.

Although he wrote no other novels, Kennedy continued to be a prominent politician and literary celebrity until his death in 1870.

REFERENCES

Bohner, Charles H. *John Pendleton Kennedy: Gentleman from Baltimore*. Baltimore: Johns Hopkins University Press, 1961.

Kennedy, John Pendleton. *Horse-Shoe Robinson*. Ed. Ernest Leisy. 1937. New York: Hafner, 1962.

Ridgely, Joseph V. *John Pendleton Kennedy*. New York. Twayne, 1966.

Robert D. Sturr

KEY, FRANCIS SCOTT (1779–1843). Best-known as the author of the poem that supplied the American national anthem's lyrics, Francis Scott Key left a body of work that includes speeches, translations, and pamphlets as well as verse. However, most of his professional life was spent practicing law, and he neither considered himself nor aspired to be a literary luminary.

For the most part, his poems concentrate on pastoral and classical themes, reflecting a lifelong interest in nature. Despite its prominence as the ultimate American patriotic ode, "The Star-Spangled Banner" (originally titled "Defense of Ft. M'Henry") is actually more of a prayer of thanksgiving than an exaltation of patriotism and is thus consistent in theme and form to much of his other verse. Written in 1814 when Key spent several hours as a prisoner on a British ship, "The Star-Spangled Banner" chronicles a night of fearful uncertainty in which the narrator questions *if* the republic, represented by the flag, can prevail over the tyrannical forces that seek to destroy it. In the end, the "Heav'n rescued land" is justified as a nation through the help of God, symbolized by the flag's triumphant survival. The poem also illustrates that Key shared the popular sentiment that religion and patriotism were deeply intertwined.

This belief persists in other patriotically themed verse. "Song," "Hymn for the Fourth of July, 1832" and "Sunday School Celebration July Fourth 1833" all assert Key's conviction that the preservation of freedom is dependent on the "light of salvation."

Key's belief that God's favor was a prerequisite for American military victories also appears in his speeches. His 1796 address to the Washington Society asserts that Americans should "acknowledge and praise the Power that defended them." One of twelve "managers" of the American Colonization Society and an advocate of restricting the slave trade, Key's 1842 speech to Congress both outlines his sentiments for "just war" and evokes his status as author of "The Star-Spangled Banner." "When that standard flings forth its folds over the destitute and abandoned . . . then does it achieve a higher triumph than its proudest battles have ever won." Key died of pleurisy in 1843.

REFERENCES

Bercovitch, Sacvan, ed. *The Cambridge History of American Literature: Volume One: 1590–1820.* Cambridge: Cambridge University Press, 1994.

Key, Francis Scott. *Poems of the Late Francis Scott Key, Esq.* Ed. Henry V. D. Johns. New York: Robert Carter and Bros., 1857.

Meyer, Sam. "Religion, Patriotism, and Poetry in the Life of Francis Scott Key." *Maryland Historical Magazine* 84.3 (1989): 267–274.

Laura M. Chmielewski

KILMER, JOYCE (1886–1918). As a poet, journalist, lecturer, and critic, Alfred Joyce Kilmer was well established in his literary career when in the spring of 1917 he left behind his wife and four young children and volunteered for the American Expeditionary Force. Preferring to enlist as a private, rather than to join the Officers' Reserve Training corps, Kilmer did not shun danger, and on July 30, 1918, he died in action during the Second Battle of the Marne.

For his bravery, Sergeant Kilmer—he had been promoted prior to his death—was posthumously awarded the Croix de Guerre.

Born in New Brunswick, New Jersey, Kilmer graduated from Rutgers College in 1904 and received his A.B. from Columbia in 1906. Between 1911 and 1917 he published three volumes of poetry; in addition, he wrote and served as an editor for such notable publications as the *New York Times, The Churchman,* and *The Literary Digest.* His most famous piece of writing, the simple yet elegant poem "Trees," appeared in *Poetry* in 1913.

Although Kilmer was an enthusiastic supporter of the Allies' cause, he completed only a handful of war poems before his death. However, two of these works—"The White Ships and the Red" and "Rouge Bouquet"—were frequently anthologized and established Kilmer's reputation as a popular war poet.

Written for the *New York Times,* "The White Ships and the Red" was first published in May 1915 and expresses Kilmer's indignation over the sinking of the *Lusitania.* Invoking the age-old convention of describing ships in feminine terms, Kilmer describes the *Lusitania* as a wounded and bleeding woman. More specifically, he imagines the conversation that takes place between two recently sunken ships: the *Titanic* and the *Lusitania.* As the crimson *Lusitania* explains to the icy-pale *Titanic,* "My wrong cries out for vengeance."

"Rouge Bouquet," composed in a dugout in France, is a touching tribute to a group of American soldiers who were buried alive by the blast of an enemy shell. In the tidily rhymed verses of the poem, Kilmer builds upon traditional notions of comradeship, bravery, and heroism. The second stanza begins:

> There is on earth no worthier grave
> To hold the bodies of the brave
> Than this place of pain and pride
> Where they nobly fought and nobly died.

Death, in Kilmer's verses, is not gruesome or grisly; it is instead conceived of as a long "slumber."

A convert to Catholicism, Kilmer was inclined to interpret the war in religious terms and hoped that others would do the same. Consequently, in his poem "Prayer for a Soldier in France," Kilmer envisions the suffering of the soldier as a reenactment of the suffering of Christ on the Cross. In another war work, a sonnet titled "The Peacemaker," Kilmer describes Christ in military terms as a Captain who smiles "from the Cross upon a conquered world."

REFERENCES

Cargas, Harry J. *I Lay Down My Life: Biography of Joyce Kilmer.* Jamaica, NY: St. Paul Editions, 1964.

Kilmer, Joyce. *Complete Works.* Ed. Robert Cortes Holliday. New York: George H. Doran, 1929.

———. *Joyce Kilmer: Poems, Essays, and Letters.* Ed. Robert Cortes Holliday. 2 vols. New York: George H. Doran, 1918.

Smaridge, Norah. *Pen and Bayonet: The Story of Joyce Kilmer*. New York: Hawthorn, 1982.

Cynthia Wachtell

KILPATRICK, JUDSON (1836–1881) and MOORE, J. OWEN (n.d.).

Born in northwestern New Jersey, Hugh Judson Kilpatrick first won fame as a Union general, earning the nickname "Kill-Cavalry" for his reckless campaigning style during the Civil War. After the war, Kilpatrick failed at electoral politics but enjoyed celebrity as an orator and diplomat, serving as an ambassador to Chile at his death. His sole literary effort is *Allatoona* (1874), one of the earliest plays about the Civil War and a quintessential example of a once highly popular American literary genre, the Civil War melodrama. His coauthor was J. Owen Moore, an attorney from Orange County, New York, who also wrote *Strife* and *Tempted*.

Allatoona is based on an actual episode that took place during Sherman's Atlanta campaign, the defense of Allatoona, Georgia, on October 5, 1864, by Union troops under the command of Major General John M. Corse. The play is dedicated to Corse, who wrote a preface confirming its accuracy. However, this historical accuracy is leavened with the sentimentalism and exaggerated emotion of nineteenth-century melodrama, including a plot that features a noble hero in conflict with a deceitful villain. These characters first appear as cadets at West Point on the eve of secession: Harry Estes, a Northerner, embarrasses Charles Dunbar, the dastardly Southern brother of his beloved Helen, in a fist-fight. Helen then breaks off her engagement with Estes and leaves for the Confederacy with her brother. The paths of these three cross again during the war, with Estes and Dunbar squaring off in battle three times before General Corse shoots Dunbar at the climax of the play, the action-packed scene of the battle at Allatoona. The play ends with the Union forces triumphant and Helen in the arms of Estes.

The first known performance of *Allatoona* was at the Eagle Theatre, New York, in October 1877. It was staged again for an audience of 1,500 at an August 1878 grand reunion of Civil War veterans held on Kilpatrick's New Jersey farm. Some fifty years later Christopher Morley revived and rewrote the play under the title *The Blue and the Gray*; this version was performed at the Old Rialto in Hoboken, New Jersey, in 1930.

REFERENCES

Kilpatrick, (Hugh) Judson, with J. Owen Moore. *Allatoona*. New York: Samuel French, 1875.

Martin, Samuel J. *"Kill-Cavalry," Sherman's Merchant of Terror*. Cranbury, NJ: Fairleigh Dickinson University Press, 1996.

Mason, Jeffrey D. *Melodrama and the Myth of America*. Bloomington: Indiana University Press, 1993.

Morley, Christopher. *The Blue and the Gray, or War Is Hell*. Revised and edified from

an old script by Judson Kilpatrick and J. Owen Moore. Garden City, NY: Doubleday, 1930.

Quinn, Arthur Hobson. *A History of the American Drama from the Civil War to the
Present Day*. New York: F. S. Crofts, 1945.

David Kilpatrick

KIM, RICHARD E. (1932–   ). A native of northern Korea, Richard E. Kim
served in the Republic of Korea Army throughout the Korean War. At various
times he was a liaison officer to different U.S. commands and an aide-de-camp
to high-ranking officials, both Korean and American. After the war, he came to
the United States to continue his formal education—first at Middlebury College,
next at Johns Hopkins, then at Iowa (where he studied creative writing along
with Philip Roth, among others), and finally at Harvard. The focus of his studies
having become writing, he combined this interest with his cultural heritage and
military experience to produce a novel called *The Martyred* (1964). The critical
and commercial success of this first work, set in the first year of the Korean
War, was especially remarkable for the fact that its author, like Joseph Conrad,
wrote it in a language not his native tongue.

Noteworthy for its Korean perspective, *The Martyred* is part war novel, part
mystery, part moral, and part philosophical inquiry. Like some of his later work,
this book is concerned with the ways in which war can affect personal morality.
Its plot revolves around the fate of fourteen Christian ministers arrested by the
Communists in Pyongyang. Of the group, twelve have died—executed, it turns
out—while two survived: one gone mad and the other very reluctant to talk.
The latter, a Mr. Shin, is the central figure of the story along with Captain Lee,
the novel's narrator. Lee and two other military officers—Colonel Chang and
Captain Park—are involved for different reasons in the attempt to determine
what happened, how, and why. Kim's unraveling of the tale deals masterfully
with ambivalence and ambiguity as it considers some fundamentally opposing
forces within the human condition: good and evil, truth and illusion, hope and
despair, physical death and spiritual immortality. All three of the Korean officers
undergo some kind of change from a simpler to a more complex state of mind
as the novel explores the nature of human suffering and the purpose of religious
belief. The latter portion of the book also contains a nicely written description
of the retreat from Pyongyang after the Chinese intervention in the war late in
1950.

Kim wrote another military novel, *The Innocent* (1968), that has to do with
a coup d'état in Korea after the war. Not as successful as *The Martyred*, it
suffers to some degree from an excessively complex plot and lacks the powerful
thematic import of its predecessor. After teaching English at a variety of American universities throughout the 1960s and 1970s, Kim started a literary agency
in Massachusetts and became particularly active in an effort to have South Korean publishers begin paying royalties to foreign authors for the publication of
their work in Korea. He was a Fulbright Scholar at Seoul National University

(1981–1983). Kim has written and narrated several documentaries for Korean television. His *Lost Names* (1998), while published as a memoir, in the author's view can just as easily be read as fiction. Its focus is the later years of Japanese occupation of Korea (1932–1945).

REFERENCES

Kim, Richard E. *Lost Names: Scenes from a Korean Boyhood.* 1988. Berkeley: University of California Press, 1998.

Lynch, W. S. "A Strange Form of Love." Rev. of *The Martyred,* by Richard E. Kim. *Saturday Review* 22 February 1964: 58.

Rev. of *The Martyred,* by Richard E. Kim. *The New Yorker* 18 April 1964: 20.

Walsh, Chad. Rev. of *The Martyred,* by Richard E. Kim. *New York Times Book Review* 1 February 1964: 1.

James R. Kerln, Jr.

KING PHILIP'S WAR. The 1675–1676 conflict between English colonists and Algonquians known as King Philip's War established colonial dominance in southern New England. The devastating loss of life to both sides during the fourteen months of war is amply recorded in the twenty-one accounts written within the eight years that passed since the conflict began (along with the more than 400 letters written during the fighting that survive in archives). All of these accounts reflect the perspective of the victor and, as such, portray the conquered natives as evil savages, especially the Wampanoag leader Metacom, whom the English settlers nicknamed King Philip. However, the literary works these accounts inspired often adapted the perspective of the defeated Native Americans, in an effort to foster a still-unformed American identity.

Among the twenty-one accounts printed in thirty editions from 1675 to 1682, three stand out as most significant in the history of American literature: **Increase Mather**'s *A Brief History of the War with the Indians in New-England* (1676), **William Hubbard**'s *Narrative of the Troubles with the Indians in New-England* (1677), and **Mary Rowlandson**'s *The Sovereignty and Goodness of God* (1682). Both Puritan ministers, Hubbard's title suggests the difference between his and Mather's narratives. For Hubbard, the tactics of the defeated enemy didn't fit the dignity implied by the term "war." What they share in common is an emphasis on providing a "true" account that likewise justifies atrocities inflicted upon the natives. Rowlandson's account of her three-month captivity at the hands of Nipmuck Indians was America's first best-seller. Widely anthologized, it remains a popular classic of the American literary canon. Another important account, that of King Philip's killer, **Benjamin Church**'s *The Entertaining History of King Philip's War*, was published by Church's son in 1716. With their descriptions of torture and massacre, these accounts became popular on both sides of the Atlantic, establishing the stereotypes of natives as inhuman savages and the conquering colonists as brave champions of civilization, their bravery rooted in unshakeable faith.

The overly unsympathetic, remorseless, and self-gratified bias of those accounts left from the English colonists provoked Washington Irving to compose "Philip of Pokanoket" (1814), an essay included in his *Sketchbook*. In contrast to the barbarous villain of the Puritan accounts, Irving's character is more noble than savage, a hero whose patriotism should be embraced. This prompted a revaluation of the conflict and provided a new basis for the construction of American identity, based on a mythical appropriation of the (absent) noble savage. *Yamoyden: A Tale of the Wars of King Philip* (1820), an epic poem by James Eastburn and Robert Charles Sands, provoked controversy with its negative depiction of English settlers. **James Fenimore Cooper**'s novel *The Wept of Wish-ton-Wish* (1829) was considered a failure by its author, though it achieved popularity in dramatic adaptation. In **John Greenleaf Whittier**'s "Metacom" (1830), the Wampanoag leader laments the loss of his people's lives and lands in swift lyrical verse.

This revaluation of the conflict and the elevation of King Philip to the status of mythical icon reached its most popular expression with *Metamora; or, the Last of the Wampanoags*. Written by John Augustus Stone, the play was made famous through the performance of Edwin Forrest (the first American-born theater star), who performed the title role for forty years, beginning in 1829. The five-act tragedy follows the hero to his doom as he refuses to submit to his, his people's, and the emerging nation's fate. Having plunged a knife into his wife to prevent her from living as a slave, Metamora delivers a final curse upon his white oppressors before he is shot. The overwhelming popularity of the play spawned numerous imitations, leading eventually to parodies such as John Brougham's burlesque *Metamora; or, The Last of the Pollywogs* (1847). A later dramatic revival of the legend, Robert Caverly's *King Philip* (1884), lacks the eloquence of Stone's *Metamora*, the awkward syntax and broken speech of the title character rendering the play an exercise in limited vocabulary, which denies the protaganist the nobility of tragic speech.

With the exception of Rowlandson's autobiographical account of captivity, the literature of King Philip's War has received surprisingly scant critical attention in the late twentieth century. Jill Lepore's *The Name of War: King Philip's War and the Origins of American Identity* (1998) is a notable exception, which makes a strong case for the conflict and its literary representations as central to the formation of an American sense of nationhood.

REFERENCES

Leach, Douglas Edward. *Flintlock and Tomahawk: New England in King Philip's War.* New York: Norton, 1966.

Lepore, Jill. *The Name of War: King Philip's War and the Origins of American Identity.* New York: Knopf, 1998.

Lincoln, C. H., ed. *Narratives of the Indian Wars, 1675–1699.* New York: Barnes and Noble, 1941.

Page, Eugene R., ed. *Metamora and Other Plays.* Princeton, NJ: Princeton University Press, 1941.

David Kilpatrick

KIRKLAND, JOSEPH (1830–1893). By profession a businessman and attorney, Kirkland was by avocation an editor, historian, literary critic, and author of three novels, including a semiautobiographical Civil War story, *The Captain of Company K.* Raised in Michigan and New York, Kirkland was inspired by the successful literary career of his mother, Caroline, who introduced him to the literary circles of New York City, where he received an informal education in writing. He became a clerk and reader for *Putnam's Monthly Magazine* in 1852; however, in 1855 he decided on a career in business and moved to central Illinois, and eventually to Chicago, to work for railroads and mining operations.

When the Civil War began, Kirkland enlisted and was elected a lieutenant in the Twelfth Illinois regiment, which was sent to Cairo, Illinois, to secure the Union's hold on the junction of the Mississippi and Ohio Rivers. Kirkland saw only limited action during this assignment, consisting of a few skirmishes, before transferring to the staff of George McClellan, commander of the district. When McClellan took command of the Army of the Potomac, Kirkland accompanied him to Washington; there he transferred to Fitz-John Porter's staff and served with distinction in the battles of the Peninsula campaign and at Antietam and Fredericksburg. When Porter was cashiered in 1863, Kirkland resigned his commission and resumed his business career in Illinois.

Kirkland began dabbling in journalism in the 1860s, but he did not start writing novels until the 1880s. He espoused the principles of realism articulated by his literary mentor, **William Dean Howells**, and won critical praise for his realistic treatment of rural midwestern life and speech patterns in *Zury: The Meanest Man in Spring County* (1887) and *The McVeys* (1888). However, *The Captain of Company K* (1891), tracing the wartime life of Union volunteer William Fargeon, is a lesser achievement. Kirkland models the early part of this story on his own career: Chicago businessman Fargeon enlists and is elected an officer in a regiment that is sent to Cairo and fights in several skirmishes. At this point Kirkland departs from personal experience, for Fargeon remains in the west after McClellan's departure, serving under Ulysses Grant during the capture of Fort Donelson and the battle of Shiloh, where he loses a leg, leading to his being invalided out of the army.

As long as Kirkland focuses on the war the novel is quite realistic, for he vividly captures the native enthusiasm of recruiting drives; the reliance of the army's many neophyte officers on the few veterans in their ranks for guidance; the confusion and gore of battle and the anguish it creates in the combatants; the frequency of death and serious wounds and the grim conditions of military hospitals; the eagerness of senior officers to claim credit for the achievements of their subordinates and the readiness of newspaper reporters to abet those officers' efforts; and the nation's indifference toward veterans after the war. Unfortunately, Kirkland's saccharine handling of Fargeon's courtship of a young Chicago woman offsets these strengths, rendering half the novel hopelessly sentimental.

REFERENCES

Henson, Clyde E. *Joseph Kirkland*. New York: Twayne, 1962.
Kirkland, Joseph. *The Captain of Company K*. 1891. New York: Irvington, 1968.

Michael W. Schaefer

KIRSTEIN, LINCOLN (1907–1996). Best known as the founding director
of the New York City Ballet and its companion institution, the School of American Ballet, Lincoln Kirstein was also a notable art critic and dance historian.
Born in Rochester, New York, Kirstein was raised in Boston and educated at
Harvard University. There he founded *Hound and Horn*, an influential literary
magazine, and began his comparatively less distinguished career as a poet and
novelist.

Already established as an arts impresario when World War II broke out,
thirty-six-year-old Kirstein joined the army in 1943, serving as a private in such
duties as courier, interpreter, and chauffeur with General Patton's Third Army.
These experiences inspired the bulk of Kirstein's poetry from that time forward.
His work was first collected in *Rhymes of a Pfc.*, published by New Directions
in 1964. Expanded two years later as *Rhymes and More Rhymes of a Pfc.*, this
version was republished by Godine, under the earlier title, in 1981. Kirstein's
body of war poems is among the most sizable to be produced by anyone who
saw World War II service. There are approximately 100 of them, and they make
up the bulk of his 1987 *The Poems of Lincoln Kirstein*.

Kirstein's work is that of an accomplished formalist. He enjoys solving the
problems of intricate stanzaic structures, and he often builds carefully developed
narratives that incorporate the rich vernacular of men at war. While some of his
poetry would be classified as light verse, much of it is witty without being
lighthearted. Kirstein's themes are not trivial. Poems like "Barracks," "Cadets,"
"Gloria," "P.O.E.," "Black Joe," "Tent-Mates," "Air-Strike," "Rank," "4th Armored," and "The Chosen" show Kirstein's keen social awareness. Taken together, his "rhymes" present an elaborate, novelistic record of an unusual tour
of duty.

In a note to the first edition, W. H. Auden praised Kirstein's virtuosity and
his ear for common speech. In his *Wartime* (1989), **Paul Fussell** notes Kirstein's
forging of "demotic-ironic idioms" to reflect an "understanding of the war as
virtually co-terminous with error."

REFERENCES

Kirstein, Lincoln. *The Poems of Lincoln Kirstein*. New York: Atheneum, 1987.
Vaughn, David K. "Snapshots in the Book of War: Lincoln Kirstein's *Rhymes of a PFC*."
    Visions of War: World War II in Popular Literature and Culture. Ed. M. Paul
    Holsinger and Mary Anne Schofield. Bowling Green: Bowling Green State Uni-
    versity Popular Press, 1992.

Philip K. Jason

KOMUNYAKAA, YUSEF (1947–   ). Born in Bogalusa, Louisiana, Yusef Komunyakaa was a correspondent for army publications in Vietnam, where he was awarded the Bronze Star. After military service, he studied at the University of Colorado (B.A., 1975), Colorado State (M.A., 1979), and the University of California, Irvine (M.F.A., 1980). He was poet-in-the-schools in New Orleans from 1984 to 1985. He has won numerous prizes for his work, including the Pulitzer Prize in 1994 for *Neon Vernacular* (1993). The author of several volumes of poetry, he is professor of English and African American Studies at Indiana University.

The bulk of his poetry dealing with warfare is collected in *Dien Cai Dau* (1988), Vietnamese for, literally, "off the wall," or crazy—pronounced "dinky dow" by G.I.s. In tone, his verse catches the anger, despair, and resignation of men fighting a pointless war. Most poems in the collection are free-verse lyrics, usually shorter than a page, focusing on archetypal Vietnam War subjects: the Red Cross girls ("Donut Dollies"), hangouts in Saigon ("Tu Do Street"), customs and superstitions ("Short Timer's Calendar"), the guy back home who steals a G.I.'s girlfriend ("Combat Pay for Jody"), men planning to kill their "gung ho" commander ("Fragging"), and so on; it is a bleak but lyric encyclopedia of the Vietnam experience. One of his methods is to begin with topics that only the veteran would be familiar with (those just mentioned, for example), then reveal their impact and meaning to veteran and nonveteran alike. As an interpreter of the Vietnam War experience, Komunyakaa takes the war home to everybody.

Further, as an African American, he brings an awareness of the racial conflict within the military. Although black and white are mutually hostile at one level, the conditions of warfare reconcile them at another. In "Tu Do Street," he metaphorically suggests the embrace or connectedness of soldiers of both races as they visit the same prostitutes, "minutes apart," and thus combine not only breath and bodily fluids but also their nightmares and desperate escapes.

In *Thieves of Paradise* (1998), Komunyakaa devotes a section ("Debriefing Ghosts") to poems that recount, among other things, a visit to Vietnam after the war. In "The Hanoi Market," the speaker visits a stall that sells T-shirts silkscreened with a portrait of Marilyn Monroe. The narrator asks if this is why he and others went to war.

REFERENCES

Gotera, Vince. *Radical Visions: Poetry by Vietnam Veterans.* Athens: University of Georgia Press, 1994.
Stein, Kevin. "Vietnam and the 'Voice Within': Public and Private History in Yusef Komunyakaa's *Dien Cai Dau.*" *Massachusetts Review* 36 (Winter 1995–1996): 541–561.

Steve Anderson

KOPIT, ARTHUR (1937–   ). Born in New York City, Arthur Kopit spent his youth in a wealthy suburb. He attended Harvard on a scholarship for electrical engineering but decided instead to become a playwright. At Harvard, he wrote such plays as *The Questioning of Nick* (1957) and *Sing to Me Through Open Windows* (1959), and in 1959, he received a great deal of attention for *Oh Dad, Poor Dad, Mamma's Hung You in the Closet and I'm Feelin' So Sad*. Nine years later, Kopit premiered his next major play, *Indians* (1968), which received much critical acclaim. For the next eight years, he wrote little for the stage, but in 1977 he produced *Wings* for radio, the stage version of which earned him the Pulitzer Prize.

The year 1984 saw Kopit's *End of the World*, in which Trent is commissioned to write a play about nuclear war. As Trent immerses himself in nuclear war culture, he becomes bewildered by the paradoxes of deterrence strategy. "NO one can write a play from this material!" he announces, stymied by the peculiar logic of the "war-gamers" he interviews. In the end, Trent comes to understand the allure of nuclear apocalyptic power and why its thrill has so complicated nuclear world affairs.

Despite *End of the World*'s ironic address of the nuclear arms race, *Indians* remains Kopit's more thought-provoking treatment of the way America approaches war situations. *Indians* bridges two troubling periods of armed conflict in American history: the Caucasian settlement of the Wild West, and the Vietnam War. The connection between the two lies in General Westmoreland's 1966 comment about the Vietnamese civilians killed by U.S. troops: "Of course our hearts go out to the innocent victims of this." Kopit incorporates this line into *Indians* and structures the play so that the relationship between Indian and "American" echoes (and is, as Kopit pointedly notes, a historical precedent for) the relationship between Vietnamese and American.

In addition, by using Buffalo Bill, the well-known western "hero," as the pivotal character in the play, Kopit questions the American tradition of mythologizing those historical figures who, by becoming legends, justify American policy toward "inconvenient" ethnic groups. In juxtaposing a contemporary situation with a mythohistorical one, Kopit charts American conflict trends in a way that is shamefully thought-provoking.

REFERENCES

Gross, Karl. " 'The Larger Perspective': Arthur Kopit's *Indians* and the Vietnam War." *Modern War on Stage and Screen/Der Moderne Krieg auf der Buhne*. Lewiston, NY: Mellen, 1997.

O'Neill, Michael C. "History as Dramatic Present: Arthur L. Kopit's *Indians*." *Theatre Journal* 34.4 (December 1982): 493–504.

Zins, Daniel L. "Waging Nuclear War Rationally: Strategic 'Thought' in Arthur Kopit's *End of the World*." *The Nightmare Considered: Critical Essays on Nuclear War Literature*. Ed. Nancy Anisfield. Bowling Green, OH: Bowling Green State University Popular Press, 1991.

Cristie L. March

KOREAN WAR. Addressing the literary legacy of the Korean War, **Paul Fussell** notes that Korea "generated virtually no literature, perhaps one reason it seems to be, as Clay Blair has called it, The Forgotten War" (651). Fifteen years earlier Peter G. Jones made a similar observation in his study of the American war novel: "The literature of the Korean War is slight in both volume and quality, a situation probably explained to a large degree by the absence of a national commitment to that war" (185). Whatever the cause-and-effect relationships suggested by critics with respect to the quantity or quality of Korean War literature, there is more of it than is generally realized. There are dozens of published novels written by American authors that depict, describe, or significantly allude to the U.S. experience in the Korean War. There are also several plays and numerous short stories, many of the latter having been incorporated into at least one of several anthologies. Even in the realm of poetry, the charge of literary vacuity does not hold true.

The novel constitutes the principal imaginative response to the Korean conflict, beginning with **MacKinlay Kantor**'s *Don't Touch Me* in 1951. In the nearly five decades since, there have appeared a variety of novels that include some relatively well-written books like Curt Anders's *The Price of Courage* (1957), Francis Pollini's *Night* (1960), Charles Bracelen Flood's *More Lives Than One* (1967), George Sidney's *For the Love of Dying* (1969), Michael Lynch's *An American Soldier* (1976), James Hickey's *Chrysanthemum in the Snow* (1990), Susan Choi's *The Foreign Student* (1998), as well as many other works of lesser quality.

If these titles are unfamiliar, they are in that sense representative of Korean War fiction as a whole. Even a versatile student of twentieth-century American literature would likely respond with only a few names if asked to list novels that involve the Korean War. That list might include **James Michener**'s *The Bridges at Toko-ri* (1953), **William Styron**'s *The Long March* (1952), and perhaps Richard Condon's *The Manchurian Candidate* (1957). It is notable that of these, only Michener's novel features fictional action occurring during the war itself and involving the depiction of combat. **Richard Hooker**'s *M*A*S*H* (1968) is a special case, a work better known for its film and television adaptations than for itself.

To describe the novels of the Korean War in terms of their provenance and general content is to make three points. First, most of the fiction was written during the decade in which the war began and in that which followed; several novels were published during the war itself. The period of least apparent interest was the 1970s, the decade that saw the painful climax, denouement, and immediate aftermath of the American involvement in its second "limited" Asian war. The past two decades have seen a slight resurgence of interest, a trend possibly connected to an increase in awareness and memorialization reflected by the development of the Korean War Veterans Memorial in Washington, D.C. Probably the finest work of this resurgent period is Chaim Potok's *I Am the Clay* (1992). Next, the great majority of texts are concerned with ground forces—army and Marine actions—as opposed to those fighting the sea or air war; while there are many more army novels than Marine ones, the Marines' share of the fictional corpus is still disproportionately large—and the Marine image conspicuously more visible—when measured against the size of their force in Korea. Finally, most of the novels address either the entire period of the war or, more commonly, some period within its latter two years. Relatively few novels are primarily concerned with events that occurred in 1950, during the manic half-year that contained most of the war's maneuvering. Accordingly, that early period seems significantly underrepresented in terms of fictional treatment. One powerful exception here is **Rolando Hinojosa**'s *The Useless Servants* (1993), which chronicles the early mayhem in diary format.

In the conclusion to his study *Restrained Response: American Novels of the Cold War and Korea, 1945–1962*, Arne Axelsson discusses his perception of a "particular stress on historical accuracy and general authenticity in war and military novels." (166). Relating this emphasis to the authors of such novels, Axelsson establishes three categories of Korean War novelists: the "military professionals"; others—such as reservists and draftees—with military experience; and professional writers of one kind or another. He argues that novelists in each of these categories have found it especially important to achieve realism or verisimilitude.

A fair number of Korean War novels were indeed written by authors who served in that conflict; and, of course, they wrote fiction that has much to do with their own experience. Hence, **James Salter**, a West Point graduate who served in both the Army Air Corps and its separate-service successor, depicts in *The Hunters* (1956)—one of the best Korean War novels—the same kind of fighter unit and pilots that he must have encountered at his base in Kimpo during the war. Many of the ground-combat novels were also written by Korean War veterans. Among them is Curt Anders, an army captain and company commander in Korea, whose *The Price of Courage* (1957) reflects infantry life during the stalemated latter phase of the war. Another veteran-author is **Thomas Anderson**, whose worthwhile *Your Own Beloved Sons* (1956) reflects his own experience with a reconnaissance company during the war's first year. Styron qualifies as both a Marine veteran of the Korean War period (though not the war itself) and as one of the "professional writers"; Michener is otherwise the most recognizable name within the latter category. His contribution to the Korean War bibliography is not limited to *The Bridges at Toko-ri*; he also wrote *Sayonara* (1953), which—though set almost entirely in Japan—is a novel of the Korean War period and features airmen who have fought in the ongoing conflict. Journalist-turned-novelist **Pat Frank** had already written a best-seller by the time he published his Korean War novel *Hold Back the Night* (1951)—an excellent fictional treatment of the Marines' legendary fighting withdrawal from the Chosin Reservoir. And followers of popular fiction in the 1950s would recognize also the name of Frank G. Slaughter, a most prolific novelist known for his emphasis on the medical profession. Thus *Sword and Scalpel* (1957) is a novel that manages to combine the medical interest with the prisoner of war/ collaboration motif as well as the reservist-regular contrast, two fairly common thematic interests. The former motif figures prominently in such later novels as *Dog Tags* (1973) by **Stephen Becker** and *War Babies* (1989) by Frederick Busch.

The African American experience during the Korean War is well-represented by Wilbert L. Walker's *Stalemate at Panmunjon* (1980).

There is more short fiction that emerged from the Korean War than "the forgotten war" rubric might suggest but also much less than was written about World War II. It plays a minor role in the fictional legacy of the conflict as well since relatively few stories made their way into anthologies. The most prolific author was **William Chamberlain**, who published dozens of stories in the 1950s, many about the Second World War and Korea. Along with such other writers as Jacland Marmur, who concerned himself mainly with naval tales, Chamberlain was a frequent contributor to the *Saturday Evening Post*, and much of his work was republished in book form. Several stories appeared in the only collection devoted exclusively to the short fiction of the Korean War, Albert B. Tibbets's 1962 anthology *Courage in Korea: Stories of the Korean War*. Many others are available in **Ehrhart** and Jason's *Retrieving Bones: Stories and Poems of the Korean War* (1999).

The response of playwrights has been meager. Among the very few plays that concern the Korean War, the two most significant take as their subject the problem of the returning American officer accused of collaboration with the Communist enemy. *The Rack* was created by Rod Serling for a 1955 live television production, then made into a 1956 film by Metro-Goldwyn-Mayer. *Time Limit!*, written by Henry Denker and Ralph Berkey, had a short run on Broadway in early 1956, then became a United Artists film the following year. Neither of these plays is great drama, and each profited from the translation into film. Their chief interest lies in their approach to the problematic prisoner of war situation. Like most novels that handle this theme, they refrain from either simple condemnation or easy acceptance of collaborative behavior. And like many Americans then and probably even now, neither the novelists nor the playwrights are comfortable with either "the code" per se or the idea that its violation is a matter of no real significance.

The Korean War is different from its predecessor wars of this century in that it has inspired exceptionally little formally published verse. Moreover, little of that is worthy of attention. A most helpful study by W. D. Ehrhart has unearthed Korean War poems by a half-dozen poets; perhaps most notable among them is Rolando Hinojosa, whose 1978 collection *Korean Love Songs: From Klail City Death Trip* constitutes, in Ehrhart's words, "the largest group of poems about the Korean War by a single author" (13). Also noteworthy is the major sequence in **Keith Wilson**'s *Graves Registry* (first published in 1969). Poems like those by Hinojosa, Wilson, and **William Childress** convey the grim reality of the combat experience; and, as is true of most war poetry, the best moments are those that reflect some kind of irony. Aside from collections by Hinojosa and Wilson and the scattering of poems written by a handful of others (including

William Meredith, William Wantling, and Reg Saner), verse inspired by the Korean experience seems to be limited in both quantity and quality.

The two most engaging memoirs of the Korean War are **Martin Russ**'s *The Last Parallel* (1957) and James Brady's *The Coldest War* (1990), while **Marguerite Higgins**, in *War in Korea—The Report of a Woman Combat Correspondent* (1951), has provided the most vivid reportage.

REFERENCES

Axelsson, Arne. *Restrained Response: American Novels of the Cold War and Korea, 1945–1962*. New York: Greenwood Press, 1990.

Edwards, Paul M., comp. *The Korean War: An Annotated Bibliography*. Westport, CT: Greenwood Press, 1998.

Ehrhart, W. D. "Soldier-Poets of the Korean War." *War, Literature & the Arts* 9.2 (1997): 1–47.

Ehrhart, W. D., and Philip K. Jason, eds. *Retrieving Bones: Stories and Poems of the Korean War*. New Brunswick, NJ: Rutgers University Press, 1999.

Fussell, Paul, ed. *The Norton Book of Modern War*. New York: Norton, 1991.

Jones, Peter G. *War and the Novelist: Appraising the American War Novel*. Columbia: University of Missouri Press, 1976.

Miller, Wayne Charles. *An Armed America: Its Face in Fiction—A History of the American Military Novel*. New York: New York University Press, 1970.

James R. Kerin, Jr.

L

LANIER, SIDNEY (1842–1881). Composer, critic, flutist, Lanier was a Renaissance man and the South's premier poet of the nineteenth century. Best known today for his poems "The Symphony" (1875) and "The Marshes of Glynn" (1878), as well as his first work of literary criticism, *The Science of English Verse* (1880), in his time Lanier was also renowned for his forays into various genres of war literature. His experiences as a Confederate soldier during the battles of the Seven Days and Chancellorsville and his imprisonment at Point Lookout, Maryland, over the winter of 1864–1865 so scarred him that he turned to poetry, essays, public addresses, and the one novel, *Tiger-Lilies* (1867), to explore his reactions to those cataclysmic times.

Two thirds of *Tiger-Lilies* takes place in the months leading up to the fall of Richmond in 1865, during which time the stark realities of warfare reveal the true characters of a group of young soldiers. Philip Sterling, humanist lover of music and poetry, embodies gentlemanly virtues by remaining true to the Confederacy, to his beloved, and to Southern honor despite imprisonment in a Union camp. Yankee John Cranston, however, shows his corrupt, crassly commercial nature by pursuing a personal vendetta instead of being a true patriot. Lanier also underscores the importance of family honor and pride in the Southern underclass with his portrait of the Smallin brothers; Cain confronts his brother Gorm, a deserter, and in a blistering attack strips from him the honor of bearing his family name—leaving Cain, ironically, to carry on the family line.

The most striking image of the Civil War in *Tiger-Lilies* lies in Book II, where Lanier casts the consuming combat as "the blood-red flower of war, which grows amid thunders," an ironic juxtaposition of the pacific and the savage that encapsulates Lanier's ambivalence about war's value to humanity. Critics have noted Lanier's debt to the red blossom found in Alfred Tennyson's poem "Maud" (1856)—"flames / The blood-red blossom of war with a heart of fire" (III, ll. 52–53)—but they have not been as keen to notice Lanier's possible influence on **Stephen Crane**'s *The Red Badge of Courage* (1895), in which red, flaming flowers pervade the naturalistic environment: "Camp fires, like red, peculiar blossoms, dotted the night": exploding shells "looked to be strange war flowers bursting into fierce bloom."

During Reconstruction Lanier also attempted to reconcile Southern uncertainty and despair under Northern subjection with an optimism necessary for regional survival. His early poetry, including "Laughter in the Senate" and "Raven Days," vented his frustrations at the Union; he excoriates Northern senators in "Steel in Soft Hands" for standing by while real men faced each other in physical combat. He skewered as well the ubiquity of Southern arrogance in essays like "Bombs from Below: Wanted, Engineers!" (1867). Yet as time passed, Lanier saw wisdom in achieving a noble moral character and in his "Confederate Memorial Address" (1870) pleaded with Southerners to bear egregious wrongs with "the calmness and tranquil dignity that becomes men and women who would be great in misfortune." That Lanier, at the end of his life, was able to write a series of children's books that resurrected the glorious warriors of European legend in *The Boy's Froissart* (1879), *The Boy's King Arthur* (1880), *The Boy's Mabinogion* (1881), and *The Boy's Percy* (1882) reveals, perhaps, his moral resolution in a warrior code commensurate with Southern honor.

REFERENCES

De Bellis, Jack. *Sidney Lanier*. New York: Twayne, 1972.
Lanier, Sidney. *The Centennial Edition of the Works of Sidney Lanier*. 10 vol. Baltimore: Johns Hopkins University Press, 1945.
Mims, Edwin. *Sidney Lanier*. Boston and New York: Houghton Mifflin, 1905.
Starke, Aubrey Harrison. *Sidney Lanier: A Biographical and Critical Study*. Chapel Hill: University of North Carolina Press, 1933.

Sandra Burr

LEDERER, WILLIAM J. (1912–) and BURDICK, EUGENE (1918– 1965).

Born and raised in New York City, William Lederer dropped out of high school and worked as an assistant to the noted newspaper columnist and novelist Heywood Broun before enlisting in the navy in 1930. Appointed from the ranks to the U.S. Naval Academy, he graduated and was commissioned in 1936. He saw combat in World War II and rose to the rank of captain before his retirement from the navy in 1958.

Eugene Burdick was born in Sheldon, Iowa, but grew up in Los Angeles. He graduated from Stanford University and served as a naval officer in World War II. A Rhodes Scholar, Burdick earned an Oxford Ph.D. in 1950. In 1952, he joined the political science faculty at the University of California, Berkeley, where he taught until his death in 1965.

Lederer and Burdick first met in 1948 at the Breadloaf Writers' Conference in Vermont. Their collaboration resulted in numerous articles and two political novels—*The Ugly American* (1958), a popular and influential indictment of our foreign aid and diplomatic efforts, and a less successful sequel entitled *Sarkhan* (1965).

The Ugly American is set in a fictional Southeast Asian country that the authors call "Sarkhan" and that they offer as an illustration of how America in real life was losing the Cold War. The book targets our entire foreign service effort, ranging from pampered secretaries and bureaucrats to a crass, politically appointed ambassador ignorant of the country's language, culture, and customs. The most prominent exception to the prevailing ugly Americanism in the novel is the title character himself, a retired engineer named Homer Atkins, whose physical appearance ironically belies his willingness to live and work in a remote village for the betterment of the people. Other exemplary characters include Father John Finian, a Jesuit priest who immerses himself in the culture, and a Colonel Edwin Hillendale, an intelligence operative who uses his knowledge of Sarkhanese manners and mores to ingratiate himself with the people.

The Ugly American remains one of the most popular and influential political novels ever written. It was serialized in the *Saturday Evening Post* and in short order became both a best-seller and a Book-of-the-Month Club selection. It prompted President Dwight D. Eisenhower to order a thorough investigation of our Foreign Service effort, and it was read and admired by other prominent politicians, including then-Senator John F. Kennedy. A film adaptation, starring Marlon Brando, but blunting the book's message, appeared in 1963.

Lederer and Burdick's sequel to *The Ugly American*, *Sarkhan*, centers on a plot by a renegade Sarkhanese general to exploit America's fear of communism for his own ends. His plan is to manufacture a threat of communist invasion, thus forcing a massive American buildup and ultimately justifying his seizing power from Sarkhan's monarch. Two Americans—a retired navy captain and an academic—learn of the plot and attempt to expose it. Both die in the attempt, and it is revealed that a high-ranking CIA (Central Intelligence Agency) official had been behind the general's machinations all along.

While it is primarily a political novel, Burdick's *The Ninth Wave* (1956) contains chapters loosely based on his real-life combat experiences aboard a navy destroyer. Burdick, along with Harvey Wheeler, also wrote the novel *Fail-safe* (1962), an alarming vision of how a nuclear war could inadvertently be triggered by a simple failure in our communications technology. Burdick's post-humous collection, *A Role in Manila: Fifteen Tales of War, Postwar, Peace, and Adventure* (1966), includes five war stories. Lederer went on to write *Our Own Worst Enemy* (1968), a nonfiction examination of why the massive American buildup in Vietnam, particularly the indiscriminate use of our overwhelming firepower, was proving to be self-defeating. Instead, Lederer recommended a people-to-people approach akin to that which he and Burdick had prescribed in *The Ugly American*.

REFERENCES

Christie, Clive. *"The Quiet American" and "The Ugly American": Western Literary Perspectives on Indo-China in a Decade of Transition, 1950–1960*. Occasion

Paper 10. Canterbury, England: University of Kent Centre of South-East Asia Studies, 1989.

Drinnon, Richard. *Facing West: The Metaphysics of Indian-Hating and Empire-Building.* Norman: University of Oklahoma Press, 1997.

Hellmann, John. *American Myth and the Legacy of Vietnam.* New York: Columbia University Press, 1986.

Lederer, William J. *All the Ships at Sea.* New York: Norton, 1950.

Edward F. Palm

LONGFELLOW, HENRY WADSWORTH (1807–1882). Longfellow's clarity, metrical facility, and melodious ease made him one of the most popular poets of the nineteenth century. After graduating from Bowdoin College in 1825, Longfellow spent three formative years in Europe, returning to become professor of modern languages; after more travel, he held a similar chair at Harvard from 1836 to 1854. Longfellow's first wife, Mary Rotter, died in 1835. In 1843 he married Frances (Fanny) Angleton, who died in a fire at their home in 1861; Longfellow's efforts to rescue her left him with permanent scars. He gained international fame with his narrative poems: *Evangeline* (1847), *The Song of Hiawatha* (1855), *The Courtship of Miles Standish* (1858), and *Tales of a Wayside Inn* (1863), a collection modeled on Chaucer's *Canterbury Tales.*

Longfellow's boyhood in Portland, Maine, fostered his appreciation of ships, seacoasts, and sea travel. "My Lost Youth" (1855) recalls the War of 1812, when young Henry could hear and see, from "the bulwarks by the shore / And the fort upon the hill," the battle between the British *Boxer* and the American *Enterprise.* "The Building of the Ship" (1849) gained fame for its last stanza ("Thou too, sail on, O ship of State! / Sail on, O UNION, strong and great!"), appropriate to the controversy of 1850 and again in the civil war, when Lincoln reportedly admired them.

Longfellow's abolitionist 1842 *Poems on Slavery* are atypically direct engagements with contemporary politics; in them frankly sentimental ballad-poems like "The Slave in the Dismal Swamp" are juxtaposed against the powerful, Miltonic "The Warning":

> There is a poor blind Samson in this land
>> Shorn of his strength and bound in bonds of steel,
> Who may, in some grim revel, raise his hand,
>> And shake the pillars of this Commonweal,
> Till the vast Temple of our liberties
>> A shapeless mass of wreck and rubbish lies.

Despite his interests in sagas, folk poetry, and naval lore—and his antislavery politics—Longfellow is usually more pacific or elegiac than martial: He downplays conquest and aggression and amplifies hopes for peace. He began "The Arsenal at Springfield" (1843) after Fanny remarked that the massed gun barrels the couple saw there resembled an organ. The poem combined Longfellow's pacifistic instincts with his historical awareness. Longfellow recites a history of warfare, then prays for an end to war:

> Were half the power that fills the world with terror,
>   Were half the wealth bestowed on camps and courts,
> Given to redeem the human mind from error,
>   There were no need of arsenals or forts:
> The warrior's name would be a name abhorred!

The Courtship of Miles Standish depicts its titular "Puritan Captain" as a boastful yet valiant soldier whose virtues suit him to defend settlements but not to woo "the Puritan maiden Priscilla": "I can march up to a fortress and summon the place to surrender, / But march up to a woman with such a proposal I dare not."

Longfellow's antiwar sentiments did not outlast the attack on Fort Sumter. His only poem on a Civil War battle, "The Cumberland," depicts the sinking of that Union ship on March 8, 1862, after she refused to surrender to the Confederate ironclad *Merrimack*. Longfellow's eight stanzas try to mimic the pace and force of the encounter:

> Then, like a kraken huge and black,
>   she crushed our ribs in her iron grasp!
> Down went the Cumberland all a wrack,
>   With a sudden shudder of death,
>   And the canon's breath
> For her dying gasp.

Longfellow also wrote two undistinguished poems on the Northern dead, "Killed at the Ford" and the sonnet "A Nameless Grave."

Longfellow's best-known war-related work is surely "Paul Revere's Ride" (1860), the landlord's first tale in *Tales of a Wayside Inn*: "Listen, my children, and you shall hear / of the midnight ride of Paul Revere." A century of American schoolchildren have verified the prediction by reciting the poem, which also contributed to the vernacular the phrase "One if by land and two if by sea." The story of Revere's ride to Concord on April 18, 1775, warning the Minutemen that Redcoats were advancing "by sea"—thus preparing American troops for the battles of Lexington and Concord—entered American folk memory largely through Longfellow's poem.

Longfellow sank severely in repute with the rise of modernism, though W. H. Auden in 1950 reminded American readers never to "underestimate . . . Longfellow's attempt to secure democratic respect for smoothness, correctness, and craftsmanship" and praised his many translations.

REFERENCES

Arvin, Newton. *Longfellow: His Life and Work*. Boston: Little, Brown, 1962.
Longfellow, Henry Wadsworth. *Works of Henry Wadsworth Longfellow*. 1886. 11 vols. New York: Oxford University Press, 1979.

Wagenknecht, Edward. *Henry Wadsworth Longfellow: His Poetry and Prose.* New York: Ungar, 1986.

———. *Longfellow: A Full-Length Portrait.* New York: Longmans, Green & Co., 1955.

Stephen Burt

LOWELL, AMY (1874–1925). Amy Lowell wrote about war in the same manner that she participated in the world of modern literature: with verve and outspoken conviction. Born in Boston, Massachusetts, to Augustus and Katherine Lowell, she was a member of the well-known Lowell family; poet–critic **James Russell Lowell** was her grandfather's cousin. Sevenels, her parents' Brookline estate, remained Lowell's home throughout her life, a home she shared with actress Ada Dwyer Russell, her longtime companion. Lowell tackled many roles and became a prolific poet, biographer of Keats, editor of Imagist anthologies, and galvanizing spokesperson for modern poetry.

Drawn by her interest in the Imagist poets, Lowell traveled to London in 1913 to meet the group's professed leader, **Ezra Pound**. Lowell soon assumed a leadership role herself and published, in America, poets like H. D., John Gould Fletcher, and D. H. Lawrence in *Some Imagist Poets* (1915, 1916, 1917). Lowell's zeal drew Pound's anger, and he disparagingly dubbed Lowell's efforts the "Amygist" movement. If her relationship with Pound was thus tainted, Lowell's connections with other prominent writers were more successful, as evidenced by her sustained correspondence with Lawrence.

Lowell's most famous contribution to American war literature is the poem "Patterns," which opens her 1916 volume *Men, Women and Ghosts*. The poem's speaker walks among garden paths, concealing a letter that announces her fiancé's death in action. As her monologue goes from the patterns of the mazelike garden and her "stiff, correct" brocaded gown to the related pattern of restrictive social customs, the speaker's meditations culminate in an angry condemnation of war:

> For the man who should loose me is dead,
> Fighting with the Duke in Flanders,
> In a pattern called a war.
> Christ! What are patterns for?

Although "Patterns" is set in the eighteenth century, its passionate antiwar sentiment resonated strongly with readers during and after World War I.

In the same volume, five poems arranged under the heading "War Pictures" further demonstrate Lowell's bold statements about war as well as her stylistic range. The poems are written in short-lined free verse, heroic couplets, and the polyphonic prose for which Lowell is known. In "The Allies," her description of "the long snail-slow serpent of marching men" concludes emphatically that "[t]his is the war of wars, from eye to tail the serpent has one cause: PEACE!" Lowell's conviction demonstrated itself as well when she read "The Bombardment," accompanied by a friend who pounded a bass drum each time the poet pronounced the word "Boom!" Lowell extended the scope of her war literature in *Can Grande's Castle* (1918) with poems that describe historical events, such as the opening of trade relations between the United States and Japan, but are inspired by the contemporary scene of World War I.

In addition to her poems and performances, Lowell initiated poetry libraries for military training camps and hospitals in Massachusetts and elsewhere after the United States entered World War I. Thus, through her writing and actions, Lowell contributed her energies to the promotion of poetry's importance in society during wartime.

REFERENCES

Benvenuto, Richard. *Amy Lowell*. Boston: Twayne Publishers, 1985.

Damon, S. Foster. *Amy Lowell: A Chronicle*. Boston and New York: Houghton Mifflin, 1935.

Gould, Jean. *Amy: The World of Amy Lowell and the Imagist Movement*. New York: Dodd, Mead, & Company, 1975.

Healey, E. Claire, and Keith Cushman, eds. *The Letters of D. H. Lawrence and Amy Lowell, 1914–1925*. Santa Barbara, CA: Black Sparrow Press, 1985.

Lowell, Amy. *The Complete Poetical Works of Amy Lowell*. Intro. by Louis Untermeyer. Boston: Houghton Mifflin, 1955.

Catherine J. Tramontana

LOWELL, JAMES RUSSELL (1819–1891). Admired in his time as critic, essayist, satirist, editor, statesman, and orator, and as the serious lyric poet he aimed from his youth to be, Lowell is now remembered mostly for his comic and dialect poetry. He grew up in Cambridge, graduating from Harvard in 1838. In 1843, he helped set up the short-lived journal *The Pioneer*, which combined literary goals with antislavery politics; in the same year he married Maria White, who died in 1853. In 1855 he took over **Longfellow**'s chair of modern languages at Harvard. Lowell married his daughter's governess, Frances Dunlap, in 1857; the same year saw him take the reins of the new *Atlantic Monthly*, where he remained as editor until 1861, continuing to publish political essays there and in the *North American Review*, which he coedited with Charles Eliot Norton from 1864 to 1868. Lowell served as U.S. minister to Spain from 1877 to 1880 and minister to England from 1880 to 1885, where his social and oratorical skills were well received.

Lowell opposed the Mexican War and commented on Union policy during that conflict and the Civil War in the first and second series of *Biglow Papers* (1848 and 1861–1866), which purport to collect the work of untutored Yankee poet Hosea Biglow of Jalaam, annotated, corrected, and introduced by the effusively well-meaning, mock-scholarly local parson, Homer Wilbur. Like many New England Whigs and abolitionists, Lowell regarded the Mexican War as unjust and unprincipled. "Biglow's" first verses express his indignation at a "cruetin Sarjunt":

Thrash away, you'll *hev* to rattle
  On them kettledrums o'yourn,—
'Taint a knowin' kind of cattle
  Thet is ketched with mouldy corn;
Put in stiff, you fifer feller,
  Let folks see how spry you be,—
Guess you'll toot till you are yeller
  'Fore you git ahold o' me!

Biglow in turn satirically impersonates a bevy of other characters, from Jefferson Davis himself to the "pious editor" who exclaims, "I *don't* believe in princerple / But, O, I *du* in interest." Other *Papers* versify letters back to Jalaam from its errant native son Birdofredum Sawin. Having enlisted, Sawin finds that the Southwest has too many insects, the American officers are mean, and the Mexicans

        aint much diff'rent from wut we be,
An, here we air ascrougin' 'em out o'thir own dominions,
Ashelterin' 'em, as Caleb says, under our eagle's pinions,
Wich means to take a feller up jest by the slack o' 's trowsis
And walk him Spanish clean right out o' all his homes and houses;
Wall, it doos seem a curus way, but then hooraw for Jackson!
It must be right, for Caleb sez it's reg'lar Anglo-Saxon.

Sawin later loses a leg, an arm, an eye, and a rib, proposes to run for president, and finds himself held prisoner by a fugitive slave. "Mason and Slidell: A Yankee Idyll," among the most celebrated of the Second Series, attacks Britain's tacit support of the South but explains Lincoln's 1862 decision to release two Confederate envoys seized when Union troops boarded a British vessel.

The last of the *Papers*—an address to a mock-congress of garden cabbages, with interpolations by other characters—scalds Andrew Johnson's pro-Southern bias while taking a moderate position on Reconstruction:

My frien's, you never gathered from my mouth
No, nut one word ag'in the South ez South,
Nor th' ain't a livin, man, white, brown nor black,
Gladder 'n wut I should be to take 'em back;
But all I ask of Uncle Sam is fust
To write up on his door, "No goods on trust"; [. . .]
make 'em Amerikin, an' they'll begin
To love their country ez they loved their sin;
Let 'em stay Southun, an' you've kep' a sore
Ready to fester ez it done afore.

Lowell wrote in 1866 that the *Biglow Papers'* success "soon began not only to astonish me, but to make me feel . . . I held in my hand a weapon . . . I found the verses of my pseudonym copied everywhere."

Lowell became a prolific, respected, political commentator whose geniality and patience suited him for explaining nuanced arguments. His 1864 essay on Lincoln lauds the president's moral and political wisdom, his ability to listen to the country and make haste slowly: "Never was ruler so absolute as he, nor so little conscious of it; for he was the incarnate common-sense of the people." Among his few poems about the Civil War, Lowell's attempts to commemorate the Union's war dead, the "Ode Recited at the Harvard Commemoration" in July 1865, gained immediate accolades for its twelve sections, stately periods ("Lofty be its mood and gravel"), but its sententious abstractions, stentorian confidence, and sheer length do not commend it to modern taste. Lowell eulogizes Lincoln ("our Martyr-Chief"), then describes the Union victory as a triumph of democratic principles and instructs the Republic: "Bow down, dear Land, for thou hast found release. . . . No poorest in thy borders but may now / Lift to the juster skies a man's enfranchised brow!"

REFERENCES

Duberman, Martin. *James Russell Lowell*. Boston: Houghton Mifflin, 1966.
Lowell, James Russell. *Complete Poetical Works of James Russell Lowell*. Ed. H. E.
   Scudder. Boston: Houghton Mifflin, 1925.
Wagenknecht, Edward. *James Russell Lowell*. New York: Oxford University Press, 1971.

Stephen Burt

LOWELL, ROBERT (1917–1977). Two decades apart, the poet Robert Lowell made the front pages of the New York and Boston dailies for his principled opposition to war. In 1943, Lowell wrote to President Roosevelt asserting his status as a conscientious objector to a war the poet believed was no longer purely defensive. The saturation bombing of Hamburg was especially appalling to Lowell, who spent a year and a day in the Federal Correctional Center in Danbury, Connecticut. In 1965, Lowell made headlines again by refusing the commander in chief. Declining an invitation to participate in a White House arts festival, Lowell wrote a condemnation of President Johnson's escalation of the war in Vietnam, which was printed on the front page of the *New York Times*. This high degree of public visibility was a measure of Lowell's cultural authority as a poet whose life and works were inextricably bound up with the history of warfare.

Son of a career naval officer and descended from eminent military officers on both sides of his illustrious family, Lowell spent a childhood, as recorded in his memoir "91 Revere Street" (in *Life Studies*, 1959), surrounded by the artifacts of war: toy soldiers and imposing portraits of his military ancestors. Also playing notable parts in the Lowell family drama were his father's friends like the larger-than-life character Commander Billy "Battleship Bilge" Harkness. His mother's snobbish loathing of the military lifestyle, coupled with her Napoleon complex, was also crucial in forming Lowell's ambivalent preoccupation with war and its power to compel, destroy, and regenerate, all of which permeate the fabric of his poetry.

Significant in Lowell's vast body of work for sustained attention to war and militarism are poems that are directly autobiographical and personal, such as "Memories of West Street and Lepke" and "Commander Lowell" (in *Life Studies*), as well as poems that are critical meditations on the familial and ancestral experiences of war, like "At the Indian Killer's Grave" and the magnificent Melvillean elegy for his cousin Warren Winslow, a naval officer killed in World War II, "The Quaker Graveyard in Nantucket" (both of which first appeared in the Pulitzer Prize–winning *Lord Weary's Castle*, 1946). Lowell uses the direct effects of war and violence on himself or specific members of his family as a point of departure for analysis of the role of individuals in the history of nationalist violence, the persistence of war's legacy from generation to generation, and the extent to which Western civilization has depended upon armed conflict. By contrast, when Lowell considers outsiders and victims, such as "A Mad Negro Soldier Confined at Munich" and Colonel Robert Shaw and his African American soldiers in "For the Union Dead," the poet demonstrates that heroism in the face of oppression is made possible only by war.

Attuned to the persistent universality of warfare, Lowell reflected on a myriad number of specific conflicts in history, ranging from the heroic exploits of the Trojan War (the dramatic monologue "Falling Asleep Over the Aeneid" in *The Mills of the Kavanaghs*, 1951) to the terrifying possibility of nuclear annihilation in the Cold War ("Fall, 1961" in *For the Union Dead*, 1964) to the thuggish militarization of the response to Vietnam protesters ("The March 1" and "The March 2" in *Notebook*, 1970). In all of these works, Lowell goes far beyond the purely personal and confessional for which he is best known. Lowell's body of work, in sum, is one of the most significant responses in all of American literature to the actual events and the mythic ramifications of war.

REFERENCES

Axelrod, Steven Gould. *Robert Lowell: Life and Art*. Princeton, NJ: Princeton University Press, 1978.

Hamilton, Ian. *Robert Lowell: A Biography*. London: Faber and Faber, 1983.

Lowell, Robert. *Selected Poems*. New York: Farrar, Straus and Giroux, 1977.

Mariani, Paul. *Lost Puritan: A Life of Robert Lowell*. New York: W. W. Norton, 1994.

Perloff, Marjorie. *The Poetic Art of Robert Lowell*. Ithaca, NY: Cornell University Press, 1973.

David A. Boxwell

M

MacLEISH, ARCHIBALD (1892–1982). Born in Glencoe, Illinois, Archibald MacLeish graduated from Yale in 1915 and postponed his studies at Harvard to serve eighteen months in the army, where he fought in the second battle of Marne. Although MacLeish was promoted to captain, his war experience was met with personal tragedy when his brother Kenneth was killed in action one month before the Armistice. This loss forever shaped MacLeish's view of war, prompting him to write poetry such as "Memorial Rain," which contrasts the poet's personal remembrance of his brother's death with the rhetoric of a politician's postwar tribute.

MacLeish's fourth volume of poetry, *Streets in the Moon* (1926), includes war poetry that reflects the disillusionment of the war experience. "The Silent Slain" offers an analogy between the men of Roland trapped at Roncevaux and the soldiers killed in World War I. In a "Belgian Letter," MacLeish presents the anguish of an old man who is reminded of his sons killed in the war when he finds the body of a young American soldier. "The End of the World," "Mistral over Graves," and "Interrogate the Stones" all reflect MacLeish's anger toward the futility of war.

MacLeish's longer poems, such as his Pulitzer Prize–winning *Conquistador* (1932), present old soldiers who express their reality of war. In *Conquistador*, an eighty-year-old soldier criticizes the way in which "beautiful battles" are recorded to glorify the war. Though it follows sixteenth-century Mexican history, this narrative is clearly meant to address the condition of war and warriors on universal terms and is colored by MacLeish's own experience of battle.

In addition to poetry, MacLeish wrote plays that reflected his sociopolitical views of war. In *Fall of the City* (1937) and *Air Raid* (1938), the characters accept their fates willfully rather than fight against military oppression. In *The Fall of the City*, MacLeish depicts a city that falls victim to Nazi Germany's authoritarian rule. Although MacLeish does not name the city in the play, *The Fall of the City* was written three months before Nazi Germany invaded Czechoslovakia.

From 1939 to 1945, MacLeish served as the Librarian of Congress, the assistant director of the Office of War Information, and the assistant secretary of state. During this time, he published a collection of poetry, *America Was Promises* (1939), and a controversial pamplet, *The Irresponsibles* (1940), which criticized the leading intellectuals of his generation as being indifferent to the war crisis. MacLeish wrote several essays to assist with the preparation of war: "The American Cause" (1941), "American Opinion and the War," and "A Time to Act" (1942).

In 1953, MacLeish won his second Pulitzer Prize for *Collected Poems 1917–1952* and received the National Book Award for Poetry. During the 1960s and 1970s, MacLeish wrote a series of articles criticizing the government's response to Vietnam and solidified his position as the war dragged on. In his last years, MacLeish continued to write essays and give radio lectures, redirecting his focus from his criticism of politics to the value of patriotism. He died in 1982 and was buried near his home in Conway, Massachusetts.

REFERENCES

Donaldson, Scott. *Archibald MacLeish: An American Life*. Boston: Houghton Mifflin, 1992.
Drabeck, Bernard A., and Helen E. Ellis. *Archibald MacLeish: Reflections*. Amherst: University of Massachusetts Press, 1986.
MacLeish, Archibald. *Collected Poems, 1917–1972*. Boston: Houghton Mifflin, 1985.
———. *Letters of Archibald MacLeish 1907–1982*. Ed. R. H. Winnick. Boston: Houghton Mifflin, 1983.

Mary Hricko

MAHAN, ALFRED THAYER (1840–1914). Alfred Thayer Mahan, a captain in the U.S. Navy for most of his adult life, was one of the most influential authors of the late nineteenth century. His naval career spanned forty years, beginning in 1856 with his entry into the U.S. Naval Academy at Annapolis and ending with his retirement from the service in 1896. Mahan's real significance, however, came through his writing on naval subjects. This alternative career began in 1886 when he became Lecturer on Naval Tactics and History at the newly established Naval War College in Newport, Rhode Island. His lectures at the college became the basis for his first and most important book, *The Influence of Sea Power Upon History*. In this treatise, Mahan argued that history contained lessons demonstrating the significance of sea power. Despite changes over time, Mahan explained, there are strategic and tactical principles that are rooted in the "essential nature of things." Mahan continued writing on this important topic for the rest of his life, producing an enormous body of work relating to the subject of sea power.

Mahan's arguments had a significant impact on the thinking of his fellow citizens and on readers from around the world. But, as Mahan himself admitted, *The Influence of Sea Power Upon History* was not an original piece of work from either an intellectual or a conceptual standpoint. The study of naval power and its significance was ages old. Any claim to originality for Mahan rests upon his treatment of the material. The doctrine of sea power, as conceptualized by Mahan, was an understanding of history that linked patriotism, politics, and economics. It was a philosophy of empire that seemingly was confirmed by a study of the past. Mahan's formulation came in an era ready and waiting for such an exposition. By studying power in this manner, however, Mahan created the first historically based international security studies. He was without peer as a historian and journalist of his era, buttressing the imperial aspirations of many nations. Enormously influential itself, *The Influence of Sea Power Upon History* supported the growth of the U.S. Navy and the flowering of American imperialism.

Mahan was also a successful biographer, writing lives of Nelson (1897) and Farragut (circa 1892), as well as his own memoir, *From Sail to Steam* (1907).

REFERENCES

Livezy, William E. *Mahan on Sea Power*. Norman: University of Oklahoma Press, 1981.
Mahan, Alfred Thayer. *From Sail to Steam: Recollections of a Naval Life*. 1907. New York: DeCapo Press, 1968.
———. *Letters and Papers*. Annapolis: Naval Institute Press, 1975.
Seager, Robert. *Alfred Thayer Mahan: The Man and His Letters*. Annapolis: Naval Institute Press, 1977.
Sumida, Jon Tetsuro. *Inventing Grand Strategy and Teaching Command: The Classic Works of Alfred Thayer Mahan Reconsidered*. Baltimore and London: Johns Hopkins University Press, 1997.

Michelle C. Morgan

MAILER, NORMAN (1923–). Norman Mailer was born in Long Branch, New Jersey, and grew up in Brooklyn, New York. Mailer entered Harvard University in 1939 at the age of sixteen. During his undergraduate years, his first published short story, "The Greatest Thing in the World," appeared in the *Harvard Advocate* and was awarded a college fiction prize by *Story* magazine.

Mailer graduated with honors from Harvard in 1943 with a B.S. degree in aeronautical engineering. He was drafted into the army in March 1944 and served as an artillery surveyor, intelligence clerk, and a rifleman with a reconnaissance unit in the Philippines. His World War II experience was the fodder for Mailer's autobiographical novel *The Naked and the Dead*, which he wrote while enrolled at the Sorbonne in Paris. The book was published to widespread critical and popular acclaim in 1948. "There is a fine authenticity" in *The Naked and the Dead*, **John P. Marquand** said in his *Book of the Month Club News* review. "His realism never conceals his sensitive understanding, and his skillful character delineation gives his battle scenes a significance that is never reportorial."

Written in a gritty, realistic style and filled with G.I. profanities, *The Naked and the Dead* follows a group of soldiers as they storm Anopopei, a tiny, tropical Japanese-held Pacific Island. In this long, ambitious work, Mailer takes the reader through a hellish combat assault filled with vivid scenes that include a tropical storm, a night attack, and a reconnaissance squad's treacherous mission into the jungle. *The Naked and the Dead* is widely regarded as one of the two or three finest American literary novels of World War II. The book was a best-seller, and following its publication, Mailer gained a reputation as one of the nation's most promising young writers. His literary stature dimmed when his second and third novels, *Barbary Shore* (1951) and *The Deer Park* (1955), were published to largely negative reviews. In 1954, Mailer was one of the founders of *The Village Voice*, for which he wrote a weekly column. His *Advertisements for Myself* (1959), a collection of unfinished stories, letters, essays, and notebook entries, restored his literary reputation.

Mailer regained widespread critical and popular success in the late 1960s. His vocal opposition to the Vietnam War is reflected in *Why Are We in Vietnam?* (1967), a brilliant topical novel told in the voices of a young macho Texan and a crippled Brooklyn genius. On the surface the book deals with an Alaskan hunting trip, but its main themes are the panoply of 1960s social and political issues and an examination of the propensity for institutionalized violence and rites of passage. The war is mentioned only once, on the novel's final page when the young hunter and his buddy crow about going "off to see the Wizard . . . Vietnam, hot damn."

The war also was a theme in Mailer's nonfiction: *Miami and the Siege of Chicago* (1968) and *The Armies of the Night* (1968), which Mailer described as "history as a novel; the novel as history." Called a major attempt at "the quintessential sixties book" by critic Philip Beidler, *The Armies of the Night* is written in the third person and describes the activities of "Norman Mailer," whom the author characterizes as the book's "protagonist." The protagonist takes part in the 1967 march on the Pentagon and is arrested in the process. He philosophizes about the war and about the state of the nation. The war, the protagonist says, "was bad for America because it was a bad war, as all wars are bad if they consist of rich boys fighting poor boys when the rich boys have an advantage in the weapons." As for the country, the protagonist "had come to decide that the center of America might be insane." *The Armies of the Night* won the Pulitzer Prize for general nonfiction and the National Book Award for Arts and Letters.

Norman Mailer has written twenty-seven books of fiction and nonfiction, including *Of a Fire on the Moon* (1971), which deals with the Apollo 11 moon landing; *The Prisoner of Sex* (1971), an essay that challenged some tenets of the then-nascent feminist movement; *The Executioner's Song* (1979), a "nonfictional novel" based on the life of Gary Gilmore, the convicted murderer, which won his second Pulitzer; and the novels *Ancient Evenings* (1983), *Harlot's Ghost* (1991), and *Oswald's Tale* (1995). Mailer also has written, produced, directed, and acted in several films, including *Maidstone* (1971), which was based on *The Armies of the Night*. Mailer, who has been married six times, has nine children.

REFERENCES

Beidler, Philip D. *Scriptures for a Generation: What We Were Reading in the Sixties.* Athens: University of Georgia Press, 1994.
Lennon, J. Michael, ed. *Critical Essays on Norman Mailer*. Boston: G. K. Hall, 1986.
Mills, Hilary. *Mailer: A Biography*. New York: McGraw-Hill, 1984.
Poirier, Richard. *Norman Mailer*. New York: Viking, 1972.

Marc Leepson

MARCH, WILLIAM (1893–1954). Born in Mobile, Alabama, William March (the pen name for William Edward Campbell) served in the Marine Corps in World War I and was decorated for heroism at Blanc Mont. After his discharge in 1919, March went to work for the Waterman Steamship Company in Mobile and remained with the company until 1938, when he became a full-time writer. In his portraiture of the American South—contained in books such as *Come in at the Door* (1934) and *The Tallons* (1936)—March arguably rivals **Faulkner**. However, he remains best known for his last novel, *The Bad Seed* (1954), and his first, *Company K* (1933), an ironic commentary on American participation in World War I.

Reflecting the influence of literary modernism, *Company K* presents a collective protagonist—one company in a Marine regiment of the American Expeditionary Force (AEF)—through 113 vignettes, each narrated by a different soldier and arranged in chronological order. Initially, this technique seems a mere gimmick. Yet the novel has an impressive cumulative effect (akin to that of **Dos Passos**'s *U.S.A.* trilogy) as pettiness and disillusionment pervade its multiple perspectives, replacing the boyish energy and high spirits displayed by the men when they enlisted. Of the many horrors witnessed by March's Marines, one in particular underscores the gap between home-front enthusiasm and the reality "over there": the Malmedy-like massacre of a group of *German* prisoners. Ordered by the martinet Captain Matlock, this atrocity stands at the center of the text and reverberates through to the end, as the surviving members of the unit— now broken, haunted men—return to a hopelessly ignorant America. Equally chilling is the vignette in which Boyd imagines the Unknown Soldier (interred in Arlington National Cemetery in 1921) as an anonymous Marine: Eviscerated by a shell fragment and impaled on barbed wire, the soldier flings away his dogtags as an act of protest; a compassionate German finally ends his misery.

Even more than **Thomas Boyd's** *Through the Wheat* or **Laurence Stallings**'s *Plumes, Company K* denies any value in the Great Adventure.

REFERENCES

Matsen, William E. *The Great War and the American Novel*. New York: Peter Lang, 1993.

Simmonds, Roy S. *The Two Worlds of William March*. University: University of Alabama Press, 1984.

Steven Trout

MARQUAND, JOHN P. (1893–1960). Born in Delaware, raised in Newburyport, Massachusetts, Marquand graduated from Harvard (1914). A *Lampoon* staffer, then a journalist, he served with the National Guard in west Texas (1916), contributing dispatches to the Boston *Transcript*. Called back to duty in 1917, he went to France in 1918 and saw considerable action as an artillery officer. After the war, he wrote successful popular magazine fiction, light novels, and the first of his Mr. Moto series (1935–1957). In 1938, his first serious fiction, *The Late George Apley*, won the Pulitzer, and he followed with nine more novels. During World War II, he worked on an investigatory panel studying biological warfare; resigning in 1944, he went to the Pacific as a war correspondent.

Marquand published a Boston trilogy (1937–1941: *Apley, Wickford Point*, and *H. M. Pulham, Esquire*), a World War II trilogy (1942–1946: *So Little Time, Repent in Haste*, and *B. F.'s Daughter*), a postwar business trilogy (1948–1955: *Point of No Return, Melville Goodwin, USA*, and *Sincerely, Willis Wayde*), and a final novel (1958: *Women and Thomas Harrow*). *Thirty Years* (1954) includes fiction and essays on war.

In Marquand's mature fiction, wartime experiences guide his protagonists, though the settings are usually urban America. For example, in *So Little Time*, protagonist Jeffrey Wilson suffers flashbacks to World War I combat, tolerates his wife's America First Committee campaign work, and is disappointed when unable to reenlist after Pearl Harbor. Yet the novel is largely set in New York and Hollywood. *B. F.'s Daughter* tells of World War II through Polly Fulton's view in wartime Washington. She deals with men changed by battle, always trying somehow to be "normal." Charles Gray's postwar banking world successes in *Point of No Return* all seem to hinge, subtly, on the veteran's "ruptured duck" on his lapel. *Melville Goodwin, USA*, describes a military officer's career from West Point and World War I through the "long weekend" and World War II to the Cold War beginnings. Yet even this work is a study not of war but the business of the American military.

In peacetime or war, Marquand's characters reflect, in their day-to-day lives, the unsettled, combative world of the twentieth century's first half. The scars of war never disappear from their minds. Marquand's focus on the combatant's experience is held at a distance, however; he writes not of combat but of war's effect on the individual and society. Yet war's effect is no less present, providing crucial background to the lives of major characters in all his novels.

REFERENCES

Bell, Millicent. *Marquand: An American Life*. Boston: Atlantic–Little Brown, 1979.
Birmingham, Stephen. *The Late John Marquand*. Philadelphia: Lippincott, 1972.

Mark D. Noe

MASON, BOBBIE ANN (1940–   ). Born in Mayfield, Kentucky, Mason grew up on her family's dairy from near Paducah, Kentucky. After receiving a B.A. from the University of Kentucky, she wrote for fan magazines, then returned to school, earning an M.A. from the State University of New York at Binghamton and a Ph.D. from the University of Connecticut. After teaching journalism at Mansfield State College in Pennsylvania and publishing two works of literary criticism, *Nabokov's Garden: A Nature Guide to Ada* (1974) and *The Girl Sleuth: A Feminist Guide to the Bobbsey Twins, Nancy Drew, and Their Sisters* (1975), Mason left teaching to pursue a career as a fiction writer.

Aside from her first collection of short fiction, *Shiloh and Other Stories* (1982), the 1983 recipient of the PEN/**Ernest Hemingway** Award for First Fiction, Mason is perhaps best known for her first novel, *In Country* (1985). Framed by a journey to the Vietnam Vetcran's Memorial in Washington, D.C., most of the novel's action is set in Hopewell, Kentucky, where seventeen-year-old Samantha (Sam) Hughes is on a quest to learn more about her father (who was killed in Vietnam before her birth), the war he fought in, and herself. Mason's approach is unusual in that her protagonist is the child of a dead soldier and not a returning veteran. However, Mason does address the subject of the returning veteran and his readjustment to postwar society as well as that of the health hazards of Agent Orange through her portrayal of Emmett, Sam's uncle, and his friends, Vietnam veterans who suffer from posttraumatic stress disorder.

Mason is well known for her interest in language, especially that of popular culture, which is reflected in *In Country* in the allusions to Bruce Springsteen, Pepsi, *M*A*S*H*, MTV, and *People* magazine. Language is also important in *In Country* in its focus on the inadequacy of language to convey the Vietnam War experience. Sam's quest to know her father and his war takes her to history books, her father's war diary and letters home, and the stories of returning veterans, none of which can capture the war in words. Phrases such as "blown away," "humping the boonies," "walking point," and "in country" fascinate Sam, to the point where she tries to live language in order to understand what Vietnam was like, but what Sam learns is that words cannot even begin to substitute for the real experience. As her Uncle Emmett states of Vietnam, " 'There ain't no way to tell it.' " Sam's quest skillfully provides the focal point for an often overlooked aspect of the war—its effect on children, women, and other family members who were emotionally wounded on the home front. Through such characters as Sam, her mother, Sam's grandparents, and Emmett, Mason concerns herself with the scarred legacy of the Vietnam War, its aftermath, and its effect on future generations. *In Country* was made into a movie in 1989, starring Bruce Willis and Emily Lloyd.

A Vietnam War combat veteran is also the focus of Mason's "Big Bertha Stories," included in her second short story collection, *Love Life* (1989). In depicting the posttraumatic stress disorder of Donald, the protagonist, who insists on telling his war stories to his wife, Mason again shows the effects of the war on not only the returning veteran but also his family.

Two other novels, *Spence + Lila* (1988) and *Feather Crowns* (1993), demonstrate Mason's continued success as a writer. Many of her short stories have appeared in prestigious periodicals such as *The New Yorker* as well as in numerous anthologies.

REFERENCES

Durham, Sandra Bonilla. "Women and War: Bobbie Ann Mason's *In Country.*" *Southern Literary Journal* 22 (Spring 1990): 45–52.
Lyons, Bonnie, and Bill Oliver. "An Interview with Bobbie Ann Mason." *Contemporary Literature* 32 (1991): 449–470.

Catherine Calloway

MATHER, INCREASE (1639–1723). Born in Dorchester, Massachusetts, to the Reverend Richard and Katherine Mather, Increase Mather was trained from his earliest days to be the perfect Puritan. He was educated first at Harvard University and later traveled to Ireland to attend Trinity College in Dublin. Back in Boston, he married the daughter of the influential preacher John Cotton and became the leader of Boston's Second Church. While still attending to his duties as minister, he became the president of Harvard College in 1681. Along with his son Cotton, Increase was a major figure in Massachusetts politics and government for the next twenty years. Mather served as Massachusetts's ambassador to two kings in England, but he returned home in political disfavor and was removed from power. He spent the rest of his years heavily involved in the intellectual debates of the colony, but he never again held any real position of power. Increase Mather died in August 1723 at the age of eighty-five.

Increase Mather's contributions to American war literature come in the form of two histories of King Philip's War. His first book appeared just after the death of King Philip in 1676 and was entitled *A Brief History of the War with the Indians in New England . . . Together with a Serious Exhortation to the Inhabitants of that Land.* The second book, *A Relation of the Troubles Which Have Happened in New England . . .* was published in 1677. As a traditional Puritan, Increase Mather saw the war as both divine punishment for New England's sins and God's test of the colonists' righteousness. At the heart of New England's sinfulness was the lax attitude toward religion shown by the second and third generations of Puritans coming to power in New England. Concerned more with earthly transactions than those of the soul, these new generations had lost the spirit of the revered first generation that had undertaken the Great Migration and established the "new Israel" of the Bible Commonwealth.

Seeing the war as a punishment by God aimed at the purification of His people, Mather's history treats God as the main actor in both his histories of the war. God is credited for both Indian victories, as a chastisement for the wayward and sinful colonists, and Puritan victories, which show His compassion to a people starting to turn back to the righteous ways of their forefathers. The histories are thus reduced to three actors, God as the driving force, the Indians as instruments of His anger, and the colonists, objects of His anger and later His mercy. Individuals have little standing in these histories, but God and the churches, after they lead the people toward a renewal of Christian spirit, are the real heroes of the war. The English victory, according to Increase Mather, had nothing to do with military prowess and everything to do with a realization of sin and a renewal of faith.

REFERENCES

Hall, Michael G. *The Last American Puritan: The Life of Increase Mather*. Hanover, NH: Wesleyan University Press, 1988.

Mather, Increase. *The History of King Philip's War*. Facsim. rpt. of the 1862 Samuel G. Drake ed. of *A Brief History of the War with the Indians in New England . . . Together with a Serious Exhortation to the Inhabitants of that Land*. Bowie, MD: Heritage Books, 1990.

———. *A Relation of the Troubles Which Have Happened in New England, by reason of the Indians there, . . .* 1677. New York: Arno Press, 1972.

Nelsen, Anne Kusener. "King Philip's War and the Hubbard-Mather Rivalry." *William & Mary Quarterly*, 3rd ser., 27.4 (October 1970): 615–629.

Slotkin, Richard, and James K. Folsom. "Increase Mather: Puritan Mythologist." *So Dreadfull a Judgment: Puritan Responses to King Philip's War, 1676–1677*. Middletown, CT: Wesleyan University Press, 1978.

Kyle F. Zelner

MAULDIN, BILL (1921–). William Henry Mauldin was born in Mountain Park, New Mexico. He was a sickly child who turned his attention to drawing. After completing a correspondence course in drawing, he left high school before graduation to study at the Chicago Academy of Fine Arts. In 1940, he enlisted in the Arizona National Guard, which was called into active service shortly after he joined. As a cartoonist for the 45th Infantry Division *News*, Mauldin covered the fighting in Sicily, where he was wounded, Italy, France, and Germany. His cartoons reached a wide audience as they were published in *Stars and Stripes*, as well as seventy-nine domestic newspapers, earning him a Pulitzer Prize in 1945.

Mauldin is best known for his cartoon characters of Willie and Joe. These two infantrymen were irreverent toward rank, cynical about the war, never shaved, and were always dirty, yet they were the most admired faces of the war. Mauldin's characters portrayed army life realistically with all its jokes, gripes, and tragedy, leading one critic to call him "the pen and brush counterpart of Ernie Pyle." Mauldin was able to portray the life of soldiers on the front lines accurately because he ate, slept, marched, and fought with them. Mauldin displayed a sardonic humor that helped to make men in constant peril laugh at the torment of their existence; his cartoons offered an escape valve for the soldier's frustrations. Mauldin served as an ombudsman for the regular soldiers, conveying their complaints about bureaucratic red tape, shelling, c-rations, civilians, and rear-echelon brass. Mauldin's textual commentaries were in keeping with the spirit of his drawings and showed him to be a keen observer and discerning thinker. Although immensely popular with the troops, Mauldin's cartoons drew criticism from general readers and high-ranking officials, such as General George Patton. Collections of his Willie and Joe cartoons have been published as *Star Spangled Banter* (1944), *Mud, Mules and Mountains* (1944), and *Up Front* (1945).

Although known primarily for his cartoons, Mauldin has also written several works of prose. In *Back Home* (1947), Mauldin provides an autobiographical account of his activities since leaving the army. Mauldin offers insightful criticism on the treatment of returning veterans, race relations, the domestic political scene, and international relations. Critics praised *Back Home* for its wit, humor, and thought-provoking commentary. For *Bill Mauldin in Korea* (1952), the characters of Willie and Joe were resurrected as a series of letters from Joe, now a war correspondent in Korea, to his former buddy Willie. Mauldin's use of Joe as a war correspondent allowed him not only to discuss the action along the front lines but also the commanders in the rear and the ongoing peace talks. Although Mauldin was complimented for his eye for detail and thoughtful commentary, critics noted that Mauldin was at his best with his illustrations and his discussion of the front-line troops. Mauldin has also written two autobiographical works—*A Sort of Saga* (1949), which describes his childhood, and his memories, *The Brass Ring* (1971). Mauldin has worked as a cartoonist for the St. Louis *Post-Dispatch* and Chicago *Sun-Times* and an actor in the film *The Red Badge of Courage*.

REFERENCES

Painton, Frederick C. "Up Front with Bill Mauldin." *More Post Biographies.* Ed. John E. Drewry. Athens: University of Georgia Press, 1947.
"Willie and Joe." *Time* 31 January 1972: 70–71.

                                                                    William T. Hartley

McCARTHY, CORMAC (1933–   ). As a preschooler, Rhode Island–born Charles Joseph McCarthy, Jr., moved with his family to his longtime home and literary region, near Knoxville, Tennessee. An enlistee who served in the U.S. Air Force from 1953 to 1957, in the mid-1970s McCarthy made an important physical and literary move to El Paso, Texas.

All of McCarthy's published works to date, eight novels and two plays, include elements of physical violence. Yet only his disturbing and richly suggestive historical novel *Blood Meridian* (1985) directly deals with warfare. Its major martial focus—undeclared warfare against Mexico and Native American nations in the years immediately following the 1846–1848 Mexican War—begins with a fictional 1849 filibustering expedition into Mexico. This historical activity was spurred by the desire of many U.S. citizens to extend their country deeper into Mexico than the treaty of Guadalupe-Hidalgo provided. Ironically, in one of the novel's several vivid and graphic (albeit never clinical) battle scenes, Indians all but wipe out the American force before it fights any Mexicans.

From this point, the novel proceeds to a fuller-scale "military" focus, scalp hunting. Relative to this activity in the novel, numerous characters, incidents, and details are historically verifiable. Among the many historical figures employed by McCarthy are scalp hunter John Joel Glanton and Mexico's governor of the state of Chihuahua, Angel Trias, who hired Glanton's marauders. The novel's most memorable character, Judge Holden, may have been a historical figure as well, though his existence has recently come into doubt.

Many of the scalp hunters' bloody exploits, including their murdering peaceful Mexicans for their scalps in order to sell them as Indian ones, are also historically based, as is the poetically just 1850 Yuma Crossing slaughter of most of the scalp hunters at the hands of Yaqui Indians. But McCarthy's extensive literary gifts make the novel his own. Particularly important is his handling of Holden's relationship with "the kid," another of the novel's central characters. Among the many levels the book operates on, both inside and outside of this pair's relationship the protean judge at once espouses and incarnates a sort of metaphysics of violence, of war, one incomplete until 1878 when these last two survivors of Glanton's party collide for the final time.

REFERENCES

Sepich, John. *Notes on Blood Meridian.* Louisville: Bellarmine College Press, 1993.
Woodward, Richard B. "Cormac McCarthy's Venomous Fiction." *New York Times Magazine* 19 April 1992: sec. 6: 28–31+.

David N. Cremean

McCARTHY, MARY (1912–1989). Seattle-born Mary Therese McCarthy was raised by various relatives after being orphaned as a young girl. She graduated from Vassar in 1933 and quickly began an association with *Partisan Review.* Beginning as a drama critic, she moved on to explore a range of social issues. McCarthy was well established as a novelist, travel writer, and essayist before venturing into Vietnam War reportage. *The Company She Keeps* (1942), *The Groves of Academe* (1952), *Venice Observed* (1956), and *The Group* (1963) are among her better-known early works.

McCarthy took two trips to North and South Vietnam in the mid-1960s to witness firsthand the effects of American military involvement. Her observations came out in three slim volumes: *Vietnam* (1967), *Hanoi* (1968), and *Medina* (1972). These were republished along with other related essays in the sturdy collection *The Seventeenth Degree* (1974). In what Gordon O. Taylor considers "a continuous sequence," McCarthy's narrative fuses her roles of critic, polemicist, autobiographer, and reporter.

Although many of McCarthy's observations about Vietnam are compelling, they are often marked by nostalgia and idealization. She laments, for instance, seeing English displacing French as the language of the educated class in Vietnam, and she contrasts the present state of the landscape with what she imagines it must have been like before the war. "Before the Americans came," she muses, "there could have been no rusty Coca-Cola or beer cans or empty whiskey bottles." She objects to "this indestructible mass-production garbage floating in swamps and creeks, lying about in fields" and making the once-beautiful country hideous.

McCarthy, then, writes less about combat (she never visited the front line) than about cultural imperialism. She contrasts the "naked [American] power and muscle" and the crass commercialization and conspicuous consumption of Saigon with a fastidious and tenacious Hanoi, a city in which, "as far as [she] can judge, everybody under forty was in peak physical condition." Though her sympathies are evident, McCarthy's detailed observations of conditions in the cities, villages, and refugee camps of Vietnam during the war are of lasting historical and cultural interest.

REFERENCES

Brightman, Carol. *Writing Dangerously: Mary McCarthy and Her World.* New York: Clarkson Potter, 1992.

Gelderman, Carol, ed. *A Glance: Conversations with Mary McCarthy.* Jackson: University Press of Mississippi, 1991.

Taylor, Gordon O. "The Word for Mirror: Mary McCarthy." *Chapters of Experience: Studies in Twentieth Century American Autobiography.* New York: St. Martin's Press, 1983.

James Kelley

McDONALD, WALTER (1934–   ). Born, raised, and educated in Lubbock, Texas, McDonald joined the Air Force Reserve Officer Training Corps (ROTC) in college, during the Korean Conflict. After completing pilot training, McDonald chose a teaching assignment at the Air Force Academy. Following his second tour at the Academy, McDonald went to Vietnam for brief assignments at Tan Son Nhut and Cam Ranh Bay air bases from late 1969 to early 1970. While not assigned to a flying unit during those months, McDonald returned home with enough material to fuel his imaginative fires.

Medically retired in 1971 after fourteen years of service, McDonald began writing poems that examined familiar regions: flight, family, Vietnam, the military, and his homeland, Texas. His first collection, *Caliban in Blue* (1976), contains poems that are powerfully evocative, conveying a sense of immediacy in lines like "Off again, / thrusting up at scald / of copper in orient west" (from "Caliban in Blue"), "The tiger sways again // The flesh it finds / on sudden trails is pungent // sprinkled with explosives" (from "The Jungles of Da Lat"), and "Incoming rockets blast memory / with fresh concussions" (from "Night at Cam Ranh Bay"). Reverberant with echoes of Yeats, **Eliot**, and Conrad, these passages convey the almost visceral excitement of combat flight along with an understanding of the larger implications of such emotions.

McDonald's subsequent collections deal primarily with life on the tough, hardscrabble west Texas plains. Even here, themes of flight recur: "I jockey the throttle behind planes," he says in "Taking Off in Winter" (from *Rafting the Brazos*, 1988), just as he "used to ride round-ups / down canyons." In three collections of the late 1980s—*The Flying Dutchman* (1987), *After the Noise of Saigon* (1988), and *Night Landings* (1989)—images of flight and war become more prominent, as if shards of a painful, if imagined memory. In "Storm Warning" (from *The Flying Dutchman*) his persona sees a funnel cloud, remembers Vietnam, and calls himself a "slow twister in hot unstable air." Similarly, in "The Food Pickers of Saigon" and "Crashes Real and Imagined" (both from *After the Noise of Saigon*) the personae express a stoic fatalism that conveys an unstated will to survive amidst harsh landscapes of memory and imagination.

This tone continues in the early 1990s collections about the Texas plains. In *Counting Survivors* (1995), however, McDonald's personae seem more willing to confront the terror of surviving. In "What If I Didn't Die Outside Saigon" and "War in the Persian Gulf," the speaker reflects on his own and his friend's potential death. In "Out of the Stone They Come," chronicling McDonald's visit to the Vietnam Veterans Memorial, this muted emotion is even more poignantly evoked:

> I saw my son's own image in the stone
> but found no other face,
> only a wide black wall
> and names, names blurring together.

Staring at the memorial, with tears blurring his vision, the persona recognizes the bleak inevitability of war and admits to the pain of his guilt at having survived.

In addition to his poetry about the Vietnam War, McDonald has worked in other genres. He has written critical articles on a variety of subjects; he has coedited a casebook on **Joseph Heller**'s *Catch-22*; and he has written *A Band of Brothers: Stories about Vietnam* (1989). He lives and writes in Texas.

REFERENCES

Gotera, Vince. *Radical Visions: Poetry by Vietnam Veterans*. Athens: University of Georgia Press, 1994.

Hudgins, Andrew. "From First Books to Collected Poems." *Hudson Review* 4 (Winter 1989): 737–744.

Woods, Christopher. "An Interview with Walter McDonald." *Re: Artes Liberales* 13 (Fall 1986): 1–6.

Charles J. Gaspar

McHENRY, JAMES (1785–1845). Born at Larne, County Antrim, Ireland, McHenry studied medicine before emigrating to Pennsylvania in 1817, where he was fascinated by patriotic themes. His narrative poem *Waltham: An American Revolutionary Tale* (1823) consists of three cantos: "Love," "Patriotism," and "Victory." The poem's hero, a soldier called Henry, loves a Quaker woman named Ellinore Waltham, whose father plots against George Washington until awareness of Henry's sense of duty to Washington convinces him otherwise. McHenry's text is flawed by being too melodramatic and static with minimal character development. His contemporary descriptions of Pennsylvania, however, are admirable.

Using the pseudonym Solomon Secondsight, McHenry wrote several novels featuring warfare in western Pennsylvania. *The Wilderness: or, The Youthful Days of Washington* (1823)—also published as *The Wilderness; or, Braddock's Times. A Tale of the West*—discusses the role of Protestant Ulstermen living near Fort Duquesne during the French and Indian War. In this romantic novel, George Washington chooses his country instead of a woman named Maria whom he loves. Maria is wooed by men fighting on both sides, and Washington chivalrously rescues the man she loves most. In depiction of themes and characters, McHenry's work was similar to **James Fenimore Cooper**'s novel *The Spy* (1821), which was a fictionalized account about a Revolutionary War soldier saving George Washington's life.

The Betrothed of Wyoming: An Historical Tale (1830) pits honorable colonists against dishonorable Tories and depicts the events leading to the 1778 Wyoming massacre. McHenry shows the extremes of good and evil as characters manipulate each other with falsehoods and threats. Redemption is possible only for the righteous who have suffered from the actions of their antagonists. The Gothic *Meredith; or, The Mystery of Meschianza* (1831) reveals conflicts and betrayals between family and friends during the American Revolution. British soldiers are cast as unscrupulous villains. Honor is lauded as the most important virtue. Disguised individuals seek revenge for wrongs, and mistaken identities and supernatural apparitions are crucial to plot resolution.

McHenry also wrote criticism, plays, and epic poems and contributed to *The Jackson Wreath, or National Souvenir* (1829), commemorating Andrew Jackson's victory at the Battle of New Orleans. His writing about Ulster Americans is considered his best work.

REFERENCE

Blanc, Robert E. "James McHenry (1785–1845), Playwright and Novelist." Diss. University of Pennsylvania, 1939.

Elizabeth D. Schafer

MELVILLE, HERMAN (1819–1891). Best known as author of *Moby-Dick* (1851), Melville was born into a prosperous New York family that declined after the business failure and death of Herman's father. Unable to obtain the education or career that his family's status once promised, Melville went to sea as a merchant seaman, then as a whaler. He found himself in Honolulu after adventures in the South Seas and enlisted for a voyage home on the U.S. Navy frigate *United States*, which had seen service in the War of 1812. From this cruise Melville learned the harsh discipline of naval life and heard stories from older sailors who had seen combat in the U.S. and British navies. He thus gained an enlisted man's perspective on naval glory, as bought by the blood of sailors for the benefit of officers and politicians. Later, in *Moby-Dick*, Ishmael envisions a scene of wooden warships locked in battle, the sailors swarming over decks, the sharks swarming below, feasting on sailors' bodies. Turned upside down, the picture remains about the same, a "sharkish" business either way. War would remain for Melville proof of an ineradicable savagery in human society.

Melville recreated his cruise on the *United States* in his slightly fictionalized *White-Jacket* (1850). He looks backward to the Revolutionary War in *Israel Potter* (1855), a retelling of an autobiography by an American who fought at Bunker Hill and then entered the navy and was by ill fortune stranded for decades in Britain after being separated from his ship. Melville imaginatively extends Potter's wartime role, making him a revolutionary Everyman. As John Paul Jones's quartermaster, he participates in the victory of the *Bonhomme Richard* over the *Serapis*. Another twist of fate allows Potter to observe **Ethan Allen** as a captive in England. Melville drew on Allen's own *Narrative* (1779), for this portrait, and makes Allen a grander version of Potter, an American hero undone by fortune's whimsies.

The middle-aged Meville played no active role in the Civil War, though he visited the front, met Grant, and in April 1864 accompanied a military kinsman on a three-day cavalry raid into northern Virginia. By this time Melville was writing the poems that would become *Battle-Pieces and Aspects of the War* (1866), his comprehensive evocation of the conflict from John Brown's execution to Lee's surrender. Melville dramatizes many voices and perspectives: It is a mistake to read any single poem as an expression of the author's views. Nonetheless, the war is shown as "the terrible historical tragedy of our time" (as he says in a prose "Supplement"), requiring a national rebirth. Among memorable poems, "The Scout toward Aldie," based on his tag-along cavalry experience, describes a raid against the forces of Confederate guerrilla leader Col. John Mosby, here envisioned as a trickster hero.

In his last years, Melville returned to the era of wooden ships for *Billy Budd, Sailor* (posthumous, 1924). The setting is the British navy in the interval between the Great Mutiny at Nore and the victory of Admiral Nelson at Trafalgar. But the novella draws also on the "Somers Affair" of 1842, in which three American sailors, including the son of the secretary of war, were hanged at sea for allegedly plotting mutiny. The justice of the event was debated in the press, and the captain and his officers maligned. One of these officers was Melville's cousin.

Billy Budd poses the question of whether justice can exist in the context of war. The hero is impressed from the significantly named merchant ship *Rights-of-Man* to the British warship *Bellipotent* (the "power of war"). Falsely accused of mutiny by the ship's master-at-arms, Billy strikes his tormentor dead in the presence of his captain, Edward Vere. Though he understands the higher truth of the situation (as his nickname, "Starry Vere," or "heavenly truth," suggests), the captain instructs his drumhead court to condemn Billy to death. Billy is hanged. Melville surrounds the event with images of Christ's Crucifixion.

This narrative is one of the most interpreted in American literature, and radically different readings have been offered. *Billy Budd* is a profound antiwar statement, a meditation on the eternal betrayal and sacrifice of youth to the god of war. Yet Vere also has been viewed as a sympathetic portrayal of the dilemma of command. Understanding the injustice of Billy's death, sympathizing with him like a father, he still must enforce the discipline of the fleet, which will be wielded by his kinsman, Lord Nelson, to save Britain.

REFERENCES

Adler, Joyce Sparer. *War in Melville's Imagination*. New York and London: New York University Press, 1981.

Garner, Stanton. *The Civil War World of Herman Melville*. Lawrence: University Press of Kansas, 1993.

Howard, Leon. *Herman Melville: A Biography*. Berkeley: University of California Press, 1951.

Melville, Herman. *Battle-Pieces and Aspects of the War*. Ed. Sidney Kaplan. Gainesville: Scholars' Facsimiles & Reprints, 1960.

———. *Billy Budd, Sailor: An Inside Narrative*. Ed. Harrison Hayford and Merton M. Sealts, Jr. Chicago: Chicago University Press, 1962.

———. *The Writings of Herman Melville*. Ed. Harrison Hayford, Hershel Parker, and G. Thomas Tanselle. Evanston: Northwestern University Press, 1968– .

Charles L. Crow

MEREDITH, WILLIAM (1919–   ). Born in New York, William Meredith grew up in Darien, Connecticut. He attended Princeton University, where he began writing poetry. After graduation, he worked for a year with the *New York Times* before World War II brought him to the Aleutians and the Hawaiian Islands. He served as a naval aviator in the Pacific Theater from 1942 to 1944, later reenlisting as a carrier pilot in the Korean War. His wartime experiences became important subjects in his first two collections: *Love Letter from an Impossible Land* (1944) and *Ships and Other Figures* (1948). The first collection, which won the Yale Series of Younger Poets competition, was published while Meredith was still in the navy.

The war poems in *Love Letter from an Impossible Land* and *Ships and Other Figures* express, with emotional honesty, humane concerns about the horrors and meaning of war. Such concerns and a personal voice distinguish many of Meredith's successful poems in which the poet struggles to comprehend the life and death of soldiers. Questions about human worth arise as he reflects on the overwhelming battle actions and hovering destruction. The intensity of physical actions, as in "Navy Field" and "Carrier," tends to diminish the importance of individual identity. Often a simple willingness to face death, like in "Airman's Virtue," is behind what other people see as a soldier's bravery. Belief in God's love can console a troubled and lonely mind like his in "Love Letter from an

Impossible Island." Yet the waste of lives, like the death of a fellow pilot in a training flight in "Notes for an Elegy," throws shadows on this faith.

Meredith has taught at Princeton, the University of Hawaii, and Connecticut College. His many literary distinctions include his appointment as the Library of Congress poetry consultant (1978–1980) and the Pulitzer Prize in Poetry for his *Partial Accounts: New and Selected Poems* (1988). A stroke in 1983 forced Meredith to retire from teaching and left him with expressive aphasia. But Meredith continues to write. His 1997 collection *Effort at Speech* won the National Book Award.

REFERENCES

FitzGerald, Gregory, and Paul Ferguson. "The Frost Tradition: A Conversation with William Meredith." *Southwest Review* 57 (1972): 108–117.

Howard, Richard. "William Meredith." *Alone with America: Essays on the Art of Poetry in the United States since 1950.* Rev. ed. New York: Atheneum, 1980.

Meredith, William. *Effort at Speech: New and Selected Poems.* Evanston: TriQuarterly, 1997.

———. *Poems Are Hard to Read.* Ann Arbor: University of Michigan Press, 1991.

Rotella, Guy. " 'A Dark Question Answered Yes': The Poems of William Meredith." *Three Contemporary Poets of New England.* Boston: Twayne, 1983.

Chih-Ping Chen

MICHENER, JAMES (1907?–1997). Although some accounts state he was born circa 1907 probably in New York, James A. Michener was the foster son of Mabel Haddock Michener, who raised him in Bucks County, Pennsylvania. After earning a B.A. degree at Swarthmore College in 1929, Michener taught and worked as a textbook editor. From 1944 to 1946, he served with the navy in the Pacific Theater as a historian. His wartime experiences became the basis for his first novel, *Tales of the South Pacific* (1947), which received wide acclaim. In 1948, Michener won a Pulitzer Prize for *Tales of the South Pacific*, which was adapted by Rogers and Hammerstein into a hit Broadway musical. With the financial freedom that came from the musical adaptation of *Tales of the South Pacific*, Michener has become one of America's most commercially successful writers of historical fiction.

Although a collection of short stories, Michener considered *Tales of the South Pacific* a novel because of its strong theme, limited setting, and recurring characters involved in the anti-Japanese operation "Alligator." Michener adeptly utilized history, local color, and characterization to juxtapose the native and American cultures, portraying the romanticism of the islands alongside the arrival of the American bulldozers. Through this comparison Michener highlighted the brotherhood of all men and that warfare often hastens this revelation. Through the preparation and participation in operation "Alligator," Michener conveys the flavor of the Pacific War by giving a glimpse of the men and women in the South Pacific at play or on operations. Although Michener's tales are inclusive, showing the different branches of the services, allies, natives, and the lush landscape of the jungle, he doesn't claim to present the war in its entirety, arguing that "if you were not the man at the end of it . . . you didn't know what war was." "Romantic, nostalgic, tragic—call it what you will," as one reviewer stated, it was "the finest piece of fiction to come out of the South Pacific War."

After spending eight days aboard an aircraft carrier, Michener wrote his second war novel, *The Bridges at Toko-ri* (1953), arguably the most successful novel of the Korean War. Michener describes in detail the difficult mission of the fighter pilots and the bravery they exhibit, developing the novel's central theme that through all history warriors of freedom have had to fight the wrong war at the wrong place and that civilization depends upon the sacrifices of such men. Although well received, some reviewers considered Michener's characterizations to be nothing more than stereotypes, such as the mad anti-Communist admiral or the hero who does not like the war and sees no reason for it. Originally published in *Life* magazine, *Bridges at Toko-ri* was later adapted for film.

The Michener formula of historical fiction involves a big old-fashioned narrative of successive generations of fictional families living through documented historical events, celebrating all-American virtues. Many of Michener's works of historical fiction have dealt in part with war or war-related themes, notably *Sayonara* (1954), which, though essentially a love story, is set against the background of the Korean War. Others include *Bridge at Andau* (1957), *Kent State* (1971), *Texas* (1985), *Legacy* (1987), and *The Eagle and the Raven* (1990). Although much of his earlier work received critical acclaim, these later works have been criticized for their unrealistic characters and long, plodding narratives. In 1977, President Gerald Ford awarded Michener the Medal of Freedom.

REFERENCES

Becker, George J. *James A. Michener*. New York: Ungar, 1983.
Day, Arthur Grove. *James A. Michener*. New York: Twayne, 1964.
Hayes, John Phillip. *James A. Michener: A Biography*. Indianapolis: Bobbs-Merrill, 1984.
Severson, Marilyn S. *James A. Michener: A Critical Companion*. Westport, CT: Greenwood Press, 1996.

William T. Hartley

MILLER, ARTHUR (1915–). Arthur Miller was born in Manhattan on October 17, 1915, to Isidore Miller, a women's coat manufacturer, and Augusta Barnett Miller, a schoolteacher. Despite a financially comfortable childhood, Miller's life drastically changed as a teenager when his father lost assets during the Great Depression. After the family's move to less-fashionable Brooklyn, Miller attended James Madison and Abraham Lincoln High Schools, where teachers remember him as an inauspicious student. Without the grades or money to attend college, Miller worked as a stock clerk in an automobile parts warehouse for two years until his acceptance at the University of Michigan. While there, he began his playwriting career, winning two Avery Hopwood awards for

Honors at Dawn (1936) and *No Villain* (1937), autobiographically based plays about striking workers that first publicly exhibited the author's Marxist sympathies.

After receiving his B.A. in 1938, Miller worked briefly writing radio scripts until he gained employment gathering research for **Ernie Pyle**'s feature-film *Story of GI Joe* (1945). Miller's experiences touring Fort Dix, Camp Croft, and Fort Benning awakened his first interest in war writing. He became especially concerned with the ordinary soldier's views on the aims of war. While conducting research for the film, Miller kept a journal of his observations on military life, which he published under the title *Situation Normal* (1945). During that same year, Miller also released a novel condemning anti-Semitism, entitled *Focus*. In the book, Newman, a gentile, buys a new pair of glasses, which make him look Jewish to others. The novel's ensuing plot presents the hero's slow recognition of his own anti-Semitism and his resulting empathy with the Jewish race. At book's end, the protagonist runs to the defense of a Jewish grocer, Finklestein, whose shop is being raided by an outraged group of Jew-haters.

While Miller's subject matter in *Focus* was spurred by the genocidal treatment of Jews at Nazi hands, Miller's outrage at the capacity for human evil reached its peak twenty years later when he attended a Nazi war crimes trial in 1964. Besides resulting in the *New York Herald Tribune* article "How the Nazi Trials Search the Hearts of All Germans," Miller's courtroom observations also served as the inspiration for his 1964 play *Incident at Vichy*. In this work, Miller tests the morality of seven characters, which include a Communist, a Catholic, and a Jew, to see if they will act to defy a Nazi interrogator who carries out the regime's racial policies. At play's end, only one character, Von Berg, accepts his complicity in the human race. Unlike Quentin in *After the Fall* (1964), who experiences overwhelming guilt for escaping the Nazi death camps but fails to turn his torment into positive social action, Von Berg signs his own death warrant by turning down his pass for freedom in order to suffer with the Jews. By writing *After the Fall* before *Incident at Vichy*, Miller uses the earlier play to present the problems of ignoring responsibility that the later play tries to resolve.

In 1980, Miller fictionally returned to Nazi concentration camps in his television screenplay *Playing for Time*. In this work, Miller once again explores the theme of complicit guilt. In the story, Fania Fenelon escapes death at Auschwitz by participating in the camp's female orchestra. Her realization that talent alone prevented her death causes her to examine her beliefs about murder and her responsibility to other suffering human beings. Such important philosophical questions on war and suffering cause many to consider Arthur Miller the most moral American playwright of the twentieth century.

REFERENCES

Bloom, Harold, ed. *Arthur Miller*. New York: Chelsea House, 1987.
Carson, Neil. *Arthur Miller*. New York: Grove, 1982.

Lowenthal, Lawrence. "Arthur Miller's *Incident at Vichy*: A Sartrean Interpretation."
    Modern Drama 18 (1975): 29–41.
Miller, Arthur. *Timebends: A Life*. New York: Grove, 1987.

Shawn Holliday

MITCHELL, MARGARET (1900–1949). Margaret Mitchell was born in
Atlanta, Georgia, a city that was to figure prominently not only in her own life
but also in that of her great heroine, Scarlett O'Hara. Having spent only one
year in college, Mitchell in 1922 joined the staff of the *Atlanta Journal Sunday
Magazine*, which she left in 1926 to begin work on what became her only novel,
Gone With the Wind (1936). The book won a Pulitzer Prize, and in 1939 a film
version was released to great acclaim.

   Gone With the Wind follows the development of Scarlett O'Hara, a coy Southern belle, as she faces the horrors of the American Civil War and its aftermath.
Scarlett begins young, naive, and secure in the antebellum world of her father's
estate, Tara, courted by numerous local youths but pining away for Ashley
Wilkes, the son of a neighboring plantation owner. Devastated by Ashley's
marriage to his cousin Melanie, Scarlett marries Melanie's brother, Charles
Hamilton, whose quick death in the war leaves Scarlett a young widow and her
child by Charles fatherless. Scarlett waits out the war in Atlanta, until the Union
army's burning of that city forces her to flee. She is rescued by Rhett Butler, a
charming outcast whose profiteering has made him both hero and scourge. Scarlett returns to Tara to find the home intact but her family shattered by the strains
of war. Faced with poverty, Scarlett must work in the fields and take charge of
the house; when the war ends, she marries her sister's fiancé, Frank Kennedy,
and builds a lumber empire with his money, taking full advantage of the postwar
demand for building materials. After Frank's death in an attempt to avenge an
attack upon her, Scarlett accepts the marriage proposal of Rhett Butler, but that
marriage collapses after the death of their child, Bonnie. Scarlett returns to Tara
as a woman hardened by war and its consequences, for whom the estate represents the solace of a past that cannot return.

   Compared to the works of such writers of the New South as **William Faulkner** and Flannery O'Connor, *Gone With the Wind* may seem to lack subtlety.
Its themes are broad—love, war, and the struggles involved in facing both. And
Mitchell's novel is concerned not with the New South but with the Old South
and its demise during and after the Civil War. Scarlett's trials reflect those of
the culture to which she belongs, and it is easy to become distracted by the fact
that the novel romanticizes social customs that are difficult to justify by contemporary standards. Its heroine is a member of the slaveholding class, and her
struggles, with which Mitchell invites us to sympathize, signify the struggles of
that culture against the changing tide of racial and social relations that irrevocably altered it. The novel has survived its author, who died in 1949, as an
emblem not only of a culture long defunct but also of a conflict of values that
has yet to be completely resolved.

REFERENCES

Edwards, Anne. *Road to Tara: The Life of Margaret Mitchell*. New Haven: Ticknor & Fields, 1983.

Hanson, Elizabeth I. *Margaret Mitchell*. Boston: Twayne, 1990.

Pyron, Darden Asbury. *Southern Daughter: The Life of Margaret Mitchell*. New York: Oxford University Press, 1991.

Taylor, Helen. *Scarlett's Women*: Gone With the Wind *and Its Female Fans*. New Brunswick, NJ: Rutgers University Press, 1989.

Thomas March

MITCHELL, WEIR (1829–1914). By profession, Silas Weir Mitchell was a physician, one of the leading neurologists of the second half of the nineteenth century, author of myriad pioneering publications in his field and a precursor to Freud in his psychological studies. By avocation, he was also a prolific writer of poetry and fiction, including many works dealing with the Civil War.

After education at the University of Pennsylvania, Jefferson Medical College in Philadelphia, and in Europe, Mitchell, a lifelong resident of Philadelphia, settled in 1851 into private practice and clinical research. At the outbreak of the Civil War, he refused an appointment as a field surgeon in the Union army due to family considerations; instead, he worked from 1862 through 1864 under contract to the army in Philadelphia hospitals, caring for the wounded brought back from the front lines. This experience led Mitchell to contribute to a number of significant works on the treatment of gunshot wounds and nerve paralysis, and it also formed the background, to a greater or lesser degree, for a short story, "The Strange Case of George Dedlow" (1866), and five novels: *In War Time* (1884), *Roland Blake* (1886), *Circumstance* (1901), *Constance Trescot* (1905), and *Westways* (1913).

Despite his lack of firsthand observation, Mitchell handles battle scenes realistically, emphasizing the chaotic and bloody nature of the fighting in the Wilderness in *Roland Blake* and at Gettysburg in *Westways*, but such scenes are rare; Mitchell's main interest in all five novels are the social, emotional, and psychological effects of the war on those who remain behind the lines and on veterans who return to resume their lives with their families and friends, rendered in line with **William Dean Howells**'s dicta regarding literary realism. *In War Time*, for instance, is chiefly focused upon the social and personal disintegration of a dissolute contract surgeon for the Union army in Philadelphia, while *Westways* primarily depicts the home front conflicts the war creates among the members of a small-town Pennsylvania family whose loyalties are divided between North and South.

Mitchell's fiction was widely read in its own day and esteemed by many literary figures, including his good friends Howells and **James Russell Lowell**. However, most modern critics regard it as second-rate, lauding Mitchell's often acute renderings of individual psychology but noting as well his frequent reliance on sentimentality and melodrama.

REFERENCES

Earnest, Ernest. *S. Weir Mitchell, Novelist and Physician.* Philadelphia: University of
    Pennsylvania Press, 1950.
Lovering, Joseph P. *S. Weir Mitchell.* New York: Twayne, 1971.

Michael W. Schaefer

MOORE, J. OWEN. See **Kilpatrick, Judson and Moore, J. Owen**.

MOORE, MARIANNE (1887–1972). Born in St. Louis, Missouri, Moore
grew up in Carlisle, Pennsylvania, with her mother and brother. She graduated
from Bryn Mawr College in 1909, and in 1915, her poems began to appear in
literary magazines like *Egoist, Others,* and *Poetry.* Moore settled in Manhattan
in 1918, participating in New York City's dynamic modernist art scene and
serving as editor of the influential *The Dial* magazine from 1925 to 1929.
Moore's innovative syllabic verse, characterized by uniquely patterned stanzas,
light rhyme, and quotations from diverse sources, brought high praise from her
modernist contemporaries throughout her career and unprecedented recognition
from the literary world in 1952, when she received the Bollingen Award, the
National Book Award, and the Pulitzer Prize.

    In her poetry, Moore responded to both World War I and World War II, often
by examining the intersection of war and ethics. World War I–era poems, like
"To Military Progress" (first published in 1915 with the title "To the Soul of
'Progress' ") and "To Statecraft Embalmed" (1915), satirically address the states
of mind that make war possible. For example, the speaker of "To Military
Progress" condemns the mind's regimented disregard for the body and chides
the ironic lack of progress made through military progress and, more emblem-
atically, through self-destructive vanity.

    Moore incorporated World War II events into poems like "Light Is Speech"
(1941), which praises then-occupied France, and "A Carriage from Sweden"
(1944), which lists among Sweden's virtues its sanctuary status for Danish Jews.
But it was Moore's 1943 poem "In Distrust of Merits" that accorded her a
controversial place in the history of twentieth-century American war literature.
The poem was hailed by W. H. Auden and others as the premier poem of World
War II, denounced by **Randall Jarrell** as failing to understand the real nature
of war, and continues to garner mixed assessments from critics.

    "In Distrust of Merits" not only protests against the merits of outward vio-
lence, as its title suggests, but also against the inward "contagion" within each
person that erodes trust, faith, and peace. Yet the poem's protest oscillates between polemic certitude and ethical uncertainty, representing what Moore saw
as both the need to object to war and the simultaneous need to suspect a too-
certain sense of rightness. Such conflicted protest is evident in the poem's concluding stanza, in which the speaker dramatizes the tension between the need
to conquer the causes of war within herself and her simultaneous reluctance to

admit that need. Like "In Distrust of Merits," Moore's 1944 " 'Keeping Their World Large' " demonstrates the poet's engagement with the moral dilemmas of external war and its symbolic counterpart, what Moore considered the internal war within each person. Specifically, the speaker of " 'Keeping Their World Large' " laments the overwhelming number of deaths wrought by war, but with the sober knowledge that civilians, who merely "fight fat living and self-pity," are protected by soldiers who act as their physical and spiritual shields. That Moore's brother, John Warner Moore, served as a naval chaplain and fleet captain in the Pacific during World War II influenced her thinking about the ethical responsibilities of citizens on the home front.

Moore also explored her ideas about war in prose. In a 1943 review of Wallace Stevens, entitled "There Is a War That Never Ends," she praises the poet's formulation of a violence within the individual that guards against external violence (*Complete Prose* 382). And in a 1949 essay entitled "Humility, Concentration, and Gusto," Moore proposes that the three qualities named in the essay's title are poetry's "foremost aids to persuasion" (*Complete Prose* 420), even, and especially, in a time of war.

REFERENCES

Molesworth, Charles. *Marianne Moore: A Literary Life*. New York: Atheneum, 1990.
Moore, Marianne. *Complete Poems*. 1967. New York: Macmillan, 1981.
———. *The Complete Prose of Marianne Moore*. Ed. Patricia C. Willis. New York: Viking Penguin, 1986.
———. *The Selected Letters of Marianne Moore*. Ed. Bonnie Costello, Celeste Goodridge, and Cristanne Miller. New York: Knopf, 1997.
Schweik, Susan. "Writing War Poetry 'Like a Woman': Moore (and Jarrell)." *A Gulf So Deeply Cut: American Women Poets and the Second World War*. Madison: University of Wisconsin Press, 1991. 31–58.

Catherine J. Tramontana

MOORE, MILCAH MARTHA (1740–1829). Moore was born on the island of Madeira, where, as a child, she copied verses to improve her penmanship. After her mother's death in 1751, Moore moved to Philadelphia. She married Dr. Charles Moore in 1767, but the Quaker church disowned the couple because they were cousins. During the American Revolution, Moore retreated to the safety of the Delaware Valley outside British-occupied Philadelphia.

Moore collected poems and prose from newspapers and unpublished works written by Revolutionary leaders and colonists. Like many educated colonial women who circulated handwritten manuscripts, Moore copied work in a commonplace book that she loaned to friends and relatives. Her collection reveals details about eighteenth-century society and culture, particularly the ideological conflicts debated by Quakers. Also, her book documents the diversity of Philadelphia when it was a crucial colonial center.

Although she was not an author, Moore deliberately chose the writing she copied into her book. She carefully transcribed work for readers, organizing material by author, subject, and chronology. Dating as early as 1704, selected pieces were written through the period ending in 1788 and chronicled the time and place in which they were created. Moore included pieces about such Revolutionary issues as taxation, politics, and military maneuvers that revealed such myriad attitudes as pacifism, patriotism, and loyalism.

Approximately 100 of Moore's 126 commonplace book entries were written by women authors, including Susanna Wright (1697–1784), Hannah Griffitts (1727–1817), and Elizabeth Graeme Fergusson (1737–1801). Moore's book gives voice to pre-Revolutionary women and their literary and intellectual culture. Her collection book proves that many eighteenth-century American women were intellectually active as readers and writers and interested in more than domestic topics, involving themselves in political matters and communicating about contemporary issues. Moore also credits Griffitts as author of "The Female Patriots, Address'd to the Daughters of Liberty in America, 1768," a poem often attributed to Moore. Moore's commonplace book is valuable as a source of works for which no other known copies exist.

Moore managed a school for poor girls and wrote the book *Miscellanies, Moral and Instructive* (1787), which was reprinted in numerous editions in the United States and Great Britain. She died in New Jersey. Moore's commonplace book was donated to Haverford College in 1966 by a relative.

REFERENCES

Blecki, Catherine La Courreye, and Karin A. Wulf, eds. *Milcah Martha Moore's Book: A Commonplace Book from Revolutionary America*. University Park: Pennsylvania State University Press, 1997.
Stabile, Susan Marie. " 'By a Female Hand': Letters, Belles Lettres, and the Philadelphia Culture of Performance, 1760–1820." Diss. University of Delaware, 1996.

Elizabeth D. Schafer

MORFORD, HENRY (1823–1881). Born at New Monmouth, New Jersey, Morford worked as a storekeeper and postmaster before he began his writing career. He founded and edited the *New Jersey Standard*. Morford moved to New York, where he managed a bookstore and travel office, publishing popular travel guidebooks. He also performed editorial work for the *New York Atlas* and *Brooklyn New Monthly Magazine*.

Morford penned a variety of writing—poetry, novels, plays, and journalistic essays and editorials. He wrote three Civil War novels during the 1860s. *Shoulder-Straps: A Novel of New York and the Army* (1863), *The Days of Shoddy: A Novel of the Great Rebellion in 1861* (1863), and *The Coward: A Novel of Society and the Field in 1863* (1864) reveal Morford's attitude toward war and opinion of military leaders. A fourth book, *Red-Tape and Pigeon-Hole Generals as Seen from the Ranks During a Campaign in the Army of the Potomac* (1864), is a narrative of Morford's alleged Civil War experiences, although official sources do not list him as having enlisted. During the Civil War, Morford was clerk of the court of common pleas in New York City. He probably also printed wartime materials, dedicating *The Coward* to "Patriot Printers of America."

In these works, he presented officers in the Northern army as incompetent, corrupt, and cowardly, questioning their facades of bravery. Morford also cynically depicted contractors as being greedy and more interested in personal profit than military goals. A major theme in Morford's books is how soldiers misinterpret their own strengths and flaws of character during war and thus are misunderstood by their superiors, peers, and community. Contemporary critics suggested that the poor quality of Morford's work was because of his journalistic tendencies to produce superficial stories quickly based on current events. Morford's plots rely on coincidences, mistaken identities, and secrets. Duels, quests, heroic actions, reconciliations, and mysteries are often used as literary devices.

In 1876, Morford addressed the American Revolution for the centennial. In *The Spur of Monmouth; or, Washington in Arms* (1876), he tells of a romance between a Quaker woman named Catharine Trafford and Colonel George Vernon, who is actually George Washington in disguise. Again confused identities facilitate plot twists. Morford also prepared patriotic poems for Fourth of July programs and *The Great Rebellion: Grand National Allegory and Tableaux, written expressly for J. M. Hager's Concerts* (1863).

REFERENCE

"Morford, Henry." *Dictionary of American Biography.* Vol. 7. Ed. Dumas Malone. New York: Charles Scribner's Sons, 1934.

Elizabeth D. Schafer

MURFREE, MARY NOAILLES (1850–1922). Growing up mostly during the Civil War and Reconstruction, Mary Noailles Murfree received her formal schooling at Nashville Female Academy and Chegary Institute in Philadelphia. Encouraged by the intellectual environment of her home, with parents devoted to art, reading, and music, Murfree started writing short stories and became popular for her realistic mountain tales of mystical landscapes and rustic folk, especially *In the Tennessee Mountains* (1884) and *The Prophet of the Great Smoky Mountains* (1885). Writing mostly under the pseudonym of Charles Egbert Craddock, Murfree often drew inspirations from her life and experiences in Tennessee and Mississippi.

In her Civil War novels, Murfree focuses on individual struggles during and after the war. The central plot of *Where the Battle Was Fought* (1884) concerns a cannon-shattered mansion (based on the author's memory of the ruined Murfree Grantland estate) near an old battlefield in Fort Despair; its aging owner, General Vayne; his daughter Marcia; and her suitor, Captain John Estwicke, a Southerner in the Union army. The Gothic battlefield embodies the South's failure and loss in the war, while Estwicke's loss of his father due to the war, his alienation from the community, and his unexpected inheritance provide a dramatic center for the "battles" in the novel. The bitterness between Vayne and Estwicke underlines the clash between the old code of honor and the emerging factual approach to life. Reconciliation is reached after Estwicke risks his life for two locals, thereby winning the respect of the townspeople and the hand of Marcia. Their union symbolizes a new beginning for a new generation. The minor plots of estate schemes and townsfolk add interesting dramatic tension, though not much thematic development.

The Storm Centre (1905) presents a similarly romantic plot but a more integrated structure. Fluellen Baynell, a Federal captain, is a patient in the house of Judge Roscoe and his widowed niece, Leonora Gwynn, in occupied Roanoke City. Also under the roof but hiding is Julius, the judge's Confederate son. The war serves as a background to bring out a spectrum of personal conflicts. Loyal to the South, Roscoe nevertheless tries to be a gentleman host for Baynell and other Federal officers. Baynell struggles between his official position in the house and his desired role as Leonora's suitor. With her painful memory of her abusive husband vivid in her mind, Leonora discourages Baynell but is aware of his kindness toward Julius's children under Roscoe's care. The novel's most interesting character is Uncle Ephraim, a black slave and trickster figure who lies and acts to help Julius escape. The dramatic but forced happy ending reiterates Murfree's theme of reconciliation: Court-martialed and sentenced to death for abetting Julius's hiding, Baynell is miraculously released and marries Leonora.

Three of Murfree's short stories of individual moral growth also involve the Civil War as background: "The Bushwhackers" (1899), "The Raid of the Guerilla" (1909), and "The Lost Guidon" (1911). After her popularity declined in the mid-1890s, Murfree became active in social and community affairs and tried writing about colonial frontiersmen, Indian wars, and Mississippi culture, but local-color fiction remains her most acclaimed genre.

REFERENCES

Cary, Richard. *Mary N. Murfree*. New York: Twayne, 1967.
Parks, Edd Winfield. *Charles Egbert Craddock*. 1941. Port Washington, NY: Kennikat Press, 1972.

Chih-Ping Chen

MYRER, ANTON (1922–1996). Born in Worcester, Massachussetts, in 1922, Anton Myrer attended Harvard University, where his academic career would be interrupted by the United States' entrance into World War II and his own enlistment in the Marine Corps, in which he served from 1942 to 1946. He returned to Harvard to complete his education after the war, but those four years would forever imprint his life and work with the indelible stamp of the war experience. His best fiction arose from that experience, and the best passages of that fiction, by all critical accounts, are the passages describing the hellish warfare only firsthand experience can offer.

The Big War (1957) concerns American Marines in the South Pacific and is considered a self-contained trilogy, since it is divided into three parts. The first section begins with the last days of training camp and the last furloughs home for the young Marines; the second part of the book is in the form of a long letter home from one of the soldiers to his girlfriend. The third and final section of the book describes the battle on the beach, which became the grave for many of the Marines. This last section of the book is not only indicative of the poetic style Myrer would eventually perfect in *The Last Convertible*; it is also written with the authority of one who has experienced such horrors and would endear Myrer to readers and critics, veterans and nonveterans alike, for its gritty realism and poignancy. This novel was filmed in 1958 and renamed *In Love and War*.

Once an Eagle (1968), which was made into a television miniseries, contrasts two military men: Sam Damon, an enlisted man, and Courtney Massengale, who only views war as a game and soldiers as chess pieces to be sacrificed for the "greater good" of winning the game. In 1996, *Once an Eagle* was reprinted by the Army War College Foundation Press with a foreword by John W. Vessey, Jr. (General, U.S. Army, Ret.). Vessey calls this a "classic novel of soldiers and soldiering" but also remarks that at the same time it is "a consummate anti-war book" (xvii). This novel confirms Myrer's gift for creating compelling, charismatic characters and for drawing readers inexorably into the total war experience.

The Last Convertible (1978) is by far Myrer's most romantic and nostalgic work, but it is also the novel that concerns itself most directly with the very real consequences of the war on ordinary people's lives. This is also Myrer's most autobiographical novel, as it chronicles the lives of five disparate Harvard classmates. What bonds these men, besides their academic lives at Harvard and their war experiences, is a 1938 Packard convertible they dub "The Empress," which becomes a symbol of a lost age, their lost innocence, and the changes an entire country undergoes as a result of those losses. This novel, too, was made into a television miniseries in the late 1970s.

Although he wrote other works not relating to war, he is best known for these three novels that center directly on World War II. These novels show the growth of a writer coming to terms with his own experience, which then becomes a metaphor for the experience of an entire generation of men and women for whom the war became a Defining Moment. Myrer's place in American war literature is characterized by a keenly developed sense of both the tragic and poetic in warfare that "mark him as a true member of his decent, romantic, stunted generation" (Ansen 88), a generation defined by a world at war.

REFERENCES

Ansen, David. "Class of '44." *Newsweek* 1 May 1978: 83+.
"Myrer, Anton." *Contemporary Authors: New Revision Series*. Vol. 3. Detroit: Gale, 1997. 390.

Julianne White

N

NASON, LEONARD H. (1895–1970). Leonard Hastings Nason seldom kept his opinions to himself, either in print or in person. As a student at Vermont's Norwich University, his quick tongue led to his ejection and reacceptance on a repeated basis. (During one of the "out" periods, he served with General Pershing's troops along the Mexican border.) In 1917, the Somerville, Massachusetts native joined the army's officer training program, where he promptly sassed a superior and was just as promptly expelled. In the summer of 1918, while serving with the 76th Field Artillery in France, he was wounded in action; on returning to the front, he suffered a second wound. For these, he received a Purple Heart, a sergeant's stripes, and two citations for gallantry. After his discharge, Norwich University reaccepted the hero long enough for him to earn his degree.

Nason's first writings were poems, which he published in the "A Line o' 'Type or Two" column of the *Chicago Tribune* under the pen name "Steamer." War fiction was the natural next step. His first novel, *Chevrons* (1926), and its sequel, *Sergeant Eadie* (1928), follow the adventures of the author's alter ego, an impudent, unconventional, but ultimately dedicated front-line fighter. As in most of Nason's writings, the narrative tone in these early books zigzags between the clinical and the flippant: In *Chevrons*, Sergeant Eadie is repeatedly challenged for wearing a wound stripe when he had "only" been gassed, a situation that is treated not as tragic but as a running gag.

Buoyed by success, Nason continued to turn out war-related books. In the tension-filled *The Man in the White Slicker* (1929, serialized 1928), a machine gun unit searches for the American officer who approached them in midbattle and ordered them to fire on their own troops. *A Corporal Once* (1930) is a largely comic account of an army orderly's failed attempts to earn a promotion; unlike most of Nason's work, it could not be first be published serially because of the highly suggestive final scene. Nason's interwar novels include *The Top Kick* (1928), *The Incomplete Mariner* (1929), *The Fighting Livingstons* (1931), plus the nonfiction account *Approach to Battle* (1941) and the story collections

Three Lights from a Match (1927) and *Among the Trumpets: Stories of War Horses and Others* (1932).

But November 1918 had not signaled the end of Leonard H. Nason's military career. During his rise to literary success, he had remained active in the Cavalry Reserves; after the bombing of Pearl Harbor, the forty-six-year-old writer returned to active duty in the Mediterranean Theater. His armored unit was the first to enter Morocco, and Nason himself, now a lieutenant colonel, served as Military Governor of the Rabat District in 1942. The unit took part in the Tunisian campaign and in the liberation of Paris in 1944.

Following the war, Colonel Nason returned to family life in Centerville, Massachusetts. He continued to write, but at a much slower pace; his book-length postwar output consisted only of *Contact Mercury* (1946) and one other minor volume. He died in 1970 at the age of seventy-four and was buried in Arlington National Cemetery.

REFERENCE

"Leonard Hastings Nason." *Twentieth-Century Authors*. Eds. Stanley Kunitz and Howard Haycraft. New York: H. W. Wilson, 1955. 1006–1007.

Katherine Harper

NEIHARDT, JOHN GNEISENAU (1881–1983). John Neihardt developed his lifelong reverence for the American West when his mother, abandoned by John's father, moved her family in 1892 to the Great Plains of Nebraska. When Neihardt was eleven years old, he experienced a vision during an illness, summoning him to his vocation as a writer. In 1921 he was named Nebraska's poet laureate for writing about the mood of courage with which our pioneers explored and subdued our plains, but he quickly turned to the focus of his life's work: the drama of the Plains Indians at their most perilous time in American history, chronicled in the last two parts of *A Cycle of the West* (1949) and *Black Elk Speaks* (1932). These key works have been reissued, along with other Neihardt titles, by the University of Nebraska Press.

A Cycle of the West recounts the period between 1822, when white fur trader expeditions encroached onto Indian lands, to the official closing of the frontier in 1890 after the massacre of Wounded Knee. The five-part *A Cycle of the West* begins with the story of the fur traders: *The Song of Hugh Glass* (1915), *The Song of Three Friends* (1919), and *The Song of Jed Smith* (1941). The final and most dramatic parts of the *Cycle, The Song of the Indian Wars* (1925) and *The Song of the Messiah* (1935), are epic poems that tell of the heroic efforts of the Sioux to save their way of life. *The Song of the Indian Wars* is a creation in epic poetry of the fight of the Sioux for the sacred Black Hills, culminating with the vivid description of the Battle of the Little Bighorn in which the Sioux were victorious over General **George Armstrong Custer**.

In *The Song of the Messiah*, the Paiute prophet Wovoka teaches the Indians a Ghost Dance that reputedly holds the power to return to the Indians their rightful lands and rid them of the white invaders. The poem ends with the final defeat in 1890 at Wounded Knee in which the Minneconjous Sioux Big Foot is killed, signaling the end of any hope the Sioux might have had to become autonomous among a powerful white nation.

Black Elk Speaks (1932) is an oral history of the life of medicine man Nicholas Black Elk, an Oglala Sioux and second cousin of Crazy Horse, who witnessed the Battle of the Little Bighorn as well as the massacre at Wounded Knee. Central to the book, however, is the vision Black Elk experienced when he was nine in which he saw the Six Grandfathers sitting in a rainbow teepee in the sky. They foretold the loss of their sacred lands, the destruction of the bison, and the breaking of the sacred hoop that held the Indian Nations together. However, they also gave Black Elk symbolic gifts that would give him the power to heal the Indian Nation. Although Black Elk interpreted his center of the earth as Harney Peak, located in the Black Hills, he stated that the center was "wherever one stands," elevating his message from a local vision to a universal one.

Some critics have disputed the chronological order that Neihardt imposed onto Black Elk's oral history. Others have pointed out that Neihardt was too far removed from Black Elk's narrative voice. Black Elk, who did not speak English, spoke in Sioux to his son, who in turn interpreted his father's words to Neihardt's daughter. She acted as stenographer, and Neihardt edited the transcription. However, Neihardt claimed that the voice of Black Elk "came close to what he said, and exactly what he meant." *The Sixth Grandfather* (1984) was published to make available to scholars of western history the complete interview materials. Despite these criticisms, *Black Elk Speaks* remains an important oral history document, as faithfully recorded as it could be, of a man who witnessed two of the greatest and most tragic events of Native American history, the Battle of the Little Bighorn and the Wounded Knee Massacre. Neihardt tells his own story in *All Is But a Beginning* (1972).

REFERENCES

Aly, Lucile Folse. *John G. Neihardt: A Critical Biography*. Amsterdam: Rodopi, 1977.
Neihardt, John G. *All Is But a Beginning*. New York: Harcourt Brace Jovanovich, 1972.
———. *The Giving Earth: A John G. Neihardt Reader*. Ed. Hilda Neihardt Petri. Lincoln: University of Nebraska Press, 1991.
Richards, John Thomas. *John G. Neihardt: A Selected Bibliography*. Metuchen, NJ: Scarecrow Press, 1983.
Whitney, Blair. *John G. Neihardt*. Boston: Twayne, 1976.

Renate W. Prescott

NEMEROV, HOWARD (1920–1991). Born in New York City to wealthy and cultured parents, Howard Nemerov attended the exclusive Fieldstone School and Harvard, graduating just in time for World War II. Romantically attracted to flying, Nemerov enlisted in the Royal Canadian Air Force in 1941 and earned his commission as a flying officer with the RAF Coastal Command. In 1944 he transferred to the U.S. Army Eighth Air Force, where he rose to rank of first lieutenant by the end of the war.

Nemerov is the author of twenty-six books including novels, collections of short stories, books of essays, and numerous volumes of poetry. His many awards include the National Medal of Arts, the Bollingen Prize, the Pulitzer Prize, the Theodore Rothke Memorial Prize, and honorary degrees from thirteen colleges and universities. He was also a Guggenheim fellow and Poet Laureate of the United States from 1988 to 1990.

In a 1967 letter to Kay Boyle, Nemerov wrote in defense of his lack of political involvement, "Maybe my trouble with history was that at first I didn't believe in it; from my boyhood in the Depression history was separated by the deep and absolute trench of the First War; then when the Second War brought it to my compulsory notice, and when we got through that viciously necessary orgy, I guess I accepted—and was not alone in doing so—a rather simplified story of how with the passing of Hitler evil itself had gone out of the world; a story so incredible it need only be summarized to be smiled at." His participation in the war deepened his skepticism and prevented him from taking subsequent events seriously. As he said, "If my poetry does envision the appearance of a new human nature, it does so chiefly in sarcastic outrage, for that new human nature appears in the poetry merely as a totalitarian fixing of the old human nature, whose principle products have been anguish, war, and history." As do most war veterans, Nemerov remains skeptical even in his own affirmations.

His fiction explores the problems romantic people face when they clash with reality and does not deal directly with war as a major theme. If it is mentioned at all, war is a distant backdrop that sweeps away the decay of the old order. War, however, is a primary theme in his first two volumes of poetry—*The Image and the Law* (1947) and *Guide to the Ruins* (1950)—and, tellingly, in his last poetry collection: *War Stories* (1987). Critics focus on Nemerov's divided personality, his duality of vision, and the tension found in his work between romantic and realist, belief and unbelief, his heart and his mind. A favorite illustration of the "opposed elements" of his personality are the proud veteran's thirty-three poems depicting the madness of war. Befitting a pilot's perspective of battle, his war poems are restrained and distant. "For a saving grace, we didn't see our dead, / Who rarely bothered coming home to die, / But simply stayed away out there / In the clean war, the war in the air."

REFERENCES

Bartholomay, Julia A. *The Shield of Perseus: The Vision and Imagination of Howard Nemerov*. Gainesville: University of Florida Press, 1972.

Labrie, Ross. *Howard Nemerov*. Boston: Twayne, 1980.

Meinke, Peter. *Howard Nemerov*. Minneapolis: University of Minnesota Press, 1968.

Nemerov, Howard. *A Howard Nemerov Reader*. Columbia: University of Missouri Press, 1991.

Potts, Donna. *Howard Nemerov and Objective Idealism.* Colombia: University of Missouri Press, 1994.

Joseph T. Cox

NOAH, MORDECAI MANUEL (1785–1851). Noah was born in Philadelphia but grew up in Charleston, South Carolina, after his father abandoned the family and his mother died. In 1808 Noah helped Simon Snyder become governor of Pennsylvania and was made a major in the Pennsylvania militia for his efforts. Although he never saw any active combat, for the rest of his life he was known as "Major Noah."

Noah wrote a number of plays dealing with military themes. Several of these plays deal with the Revolutionary War, such as *Marion, or the Hero of Lake George* (1821); *Oh Yes! or, The New Constitution* (1822); and *The Siege of Yorktown* (1824), whose first production was notable with Lafayette in the audience. Noah served as U.S. consul to Tunis from 1813 to 1815, during the height of Barbary coast piracy. From this firsthand knowledge, Noah wrote *Yusef Caramalli, or the Siege of Tripoli* (1820), which ended in a grand ballet that, upon the second performance, resulted in the destruction of the Park Theater by fire. *The Grecian Captive, or the Fall of Athens* (1820) concerns itself with the struggle for Greek independence.

Noah's most popular play focuses on the War of 1812. *She Would Be a Soldier, or the Plains of Chippewa* (1819) was performed over eighty times by 1868. Christine, the main character, falls in love with a soldier about to be engaged at the Battle of Chippewa (July 5, 1814). Feeling that he has thrown her over for another, Christine disguises herself as a man and, because of her prowess with a rifle, is able to enlist in the American army, only to be court-martialed and almost executed before she is found out. Noah creates a character known as the "Indian Chief" who exhibits remarkable conscience and cultivation. He sides initially with the British, but after his capture by the Americans, who try to befriend him, he says: "Think you I would be your enemy unless urged by powerful wrongs? No, white man, no! the Great Spirit whom we worship, is also the God whom you adore." For the time period, Noah demonstrates a surprising sensitivity for gender and cultural issues, while staying close to historical events.

REFERENCES

Moody, Richard, ed. *Dramas from the American Theatre 1762–1909.* New York: Houghton Mifflin, 1969.

Sarna, Jonathan D. *Jacksonian Jew: The Two Worlds of Mordecai Noah.* New York: Holmes and Meier, 1981.

Brian Adler

NORDHOFF, CHARLES BERNARD. *See* **Hall, James Norman**.

O

O'BRIEN, TIM (1946–   ). Born in Austin, Minnesota, O'Brien grew up in Worthington, Minnesota. In 1969 and 1970, after graduating from Macalester College with a degree in political science, he served as a foot soldier in Vietnam. O'Brien worked on a graduate degree in government at Harvard University and reported on national affairs for the *Washington Post* before making writing his career. He began his first book, *If I Die in a Combat Zone* (1973), while in Vietnam, publishing excerpts in magazines before returning home from the war. This book reflects O'Brien's own military service, from boot camp to war zone and after, including the inner turmoil he experienced while debating going to Canada and deserting the war, a notion that he eventually explores in his other literary works. O'Brien has frequently stated, "I was a coward. I went to war."

While much of O'Brien's writing deals in some way with the Vietnam War, he has repeatedly objected to being labeled a war writer. His works transcend Vietnam to encompass such important universal issues as the meaning of existence, imagination, truth, memory, courage, death, love, moral ambiguity, the ongoing process of reality, and the mystery of the unknown. In a Hemingway-esque style full of sentences that often rely heavily on pronouns and easy-to-follow subject-verb patterns, O'Brien poses significant epistemological and ontological concerns that force the reader to continually question the problematic nature of knowing a reality that is objective and absolute and that stress the impossibility of finding definite answers and resolutions. His writing is characterized by an emphasis on what is asked rather than what is known.

O'Brien's second novel, *Going After Cacciato* (1978), the 1979 recipient of the National Book Award, has frequently been termed the definitive Vietnam War novel. Throughout the work, O'Brien examines the tension resulting from the counterpoint of desertion versus moral commitment through a squad's pursuit of Cacciato, a soldier who departs Vietnam without leave to go to Paris. Supposedly the real Cacciato walks away from the war in Chapter One, and an imagined pursuit of him begins in Chapter Three, but due to the interweaving of the theme with a three-part structure, the reader cannot know which events, if any, are real and which are imaginary. Because the fantasy sections merge with a supposedly actual scene in Vietnam (where the terrified protagonist, Paul Berlin, prematurely fires his rifle and alerts the real Cacciato, allowing him to escape the squad's pursuit of him in the Vietnamese mountainside), the novel leads the reader to question whether the journey to Paris is only imagined and, if so, to wonder if the other events of the war also take place and if Paul Berlin actually stands guard duty in an observation post by the sea. Through recounting specific atrocities that take place in the war, O'Brien goes beyond the ambiguities raised by the novel's structure to call attention to the ambiguous nature of the Vietnam War itself, where polarities of right and wrong, of good and evil, become impossible to distinguish.

In *The Things They Carried* (1990), O'Brien's fifth book and the recipient of the Chicago Heartland Tribune Award, O'Brien focuses on the physical and emotional burdens carried by the soldier in Vietnam, both during the war and after the soldier returns home. Part collection of stories, combat novel, nonfiction, narrative fragments, and metafiction, the book resists easy classification. Its twenty-two chapters, some only a few pages in length, others many pages, consist of part "story-truth," part "happening-truth." Because O'Brien names his narrator Tim O'Brien and blends factual details of the real Tim O'Brien with those of the fictional one, the reader is led to question the autobiographical nature of the work. Implicit in O'Brien's ambiguity is the impossibility of telling a "true" war story, a theme that is repeatedly illustrated through metafictive strategies, where stories are told and retold in various versions by questionable narrators.

Vietnam also appears in O'Brien's sixth book, *In the Lake of the Woods* (1994), a novel about a failed political race, the mystery of love, and the existence of evil. John Wade, the protagonist, is a Vietnam veteran whose political career crumbles after the revelation of his participation in the My Lai massacre. O'Brien details the massacre, which haunts Wade's postwar life, in numerous passages. When Wade's wife, Kathy, disappears during the couple's postelection retreat, Wade becomes a suspect of foul play. The mystery of Kathy's disappearance is never solved, and as in other O'Brien works, the questions are more important than any answers or resolutions. O'Brien focuses on the "maybes," the many possibilities of what could have happened, not actualities, while showing how the war and its atrocities have impinged upon the characters' lives, even years later.

O'Brien's first novel, *Northern Lights* (1975), the story of two brothers, one a Vietnam veteran, and his third novel, *The Nuclear Age* (1985), an account of a young man's growing up during the Cuban missile crisis and the Vietnam War era, have received the least critical attention. *Tomcat in Love* (1998) is a comic novel in which the protagonist's Vietnam War background plays a part. In addition to his seven books, O'Brien has published numerous short stories, nonfiction essays, and book reviews in periodicals, newspapers, and anthologies.

REFERENCES

Calloway, Catherine. " 'How to Tell a True War Story': Metafiction in *The Things They Carried.*" *Critique* 36 (1995): 249–257.

Herzog, Tobey C. *Tim O'Brien.* New York: Twayne, 1997.

Kaplan, Steven. *Understanding Tim O'Brien.* Columbia: University of South Carolina Press, 1995.

Catherine Calloway

O'HARA, THEODORE (1820–1867). Born in Kentucky, O'Hara graduated from St. Joseph's College in Bardstown, Kentucky, by 1839. He served in the Mexican War, being brevetted a major and honored for his gallantry in battle. In 1850, O'Hara was wounded in an expedition attempting to liberate Cuba from Spain. When O'Hara traveled to Frankfort, Kentucky, to recuperate, he began writing tributes to soldiers killed in action.

O'Hara's elegies timelessly memorialize veterans of all wars. His verses contain similar motifs such as rust and blood stains, weapons, and graves. Themes of honor, valor, and glory accentuate his focus on rituals involved in the death and burial of heroes. O'Hara's first public verse was "The Old Pioneer" (1850) a dirge about Daniel Boone. His best-known elegy, "The Bivouac of the Dead" (1850), written in honor of Kentucky soldiers killed during the Battle of Buena Vista and reinterred in Frankfort Cemetery, is considered one of the greatest martial elegies. As a soldier–poet, O'Hara knew his subject well. This dirge originally consisted of ninety-six lines arranged in twelve stanzas written in hymn meter common at that time, which consisted of stanzas like those in hymns with four lines rhyming *abab*. O'Hara continued to revise his elegy, and various versions appeared in contemporary newspapers and anthologies.

Representative of the sentimental Victorian era, "The Bivouac of the Dead" was compared to Thomas Gray's "Elegy Written in a Country Churchyard." O'Hara's staccato syllables ("The muffled drum's sad roll has beat / The soldier's last tattoo; / No more on life's parade shall meet / That brave and fallen few.") creates a militaristic imagery representing the hazards, discomforts, and grief soldiers accept and depicts the satisfaction of duty and final exile and community of death. In 1867, Congress passed an act to establish national cemeteries and by the 1880s selected "The Bivouac of the Dead" to commemorate Union dead. Called "Uncle Sam's Official Poet," O'Hara's verses appear on a gate at Arlington National Cemetery and on plaques in military cemeteries in the United States and Europe.

O'Hara also edited John A. Scott's Mexican War memoir *Encarnación Prisoners* (1848) and several newspapers. He served as a captain in the 2nd United States Cavalry and sided with the Confederacy during the Civil War. "The Bivouac of the Dead" is carved on O'Hara's tombstone.

REFERENCES

Hughes, Nathaniel Cheairs, Jr., and Thomas Clayton Ware. *Theodore O'Hara: Poet–Soldier of the Old South.* Knoxville: University of Tennessee Press, 1998.

Hume, Major Edgar Erskine. *Colonel Theodore O'Hara, Author of the Bivouac of the Dead.* Charlottesville, VA: Historical Publishing Co., 1936.

Ware, Thomas C. " 'Where Valor Proudly Sleeps': Theodore O'Hara and 'The Bivouac of the Dead.' " *Markers: The Journal of the Association for Gravestone Studies* 11 (1996): 82–111.

Elizabeth D. Schafer

O'NEILL, EUGENE (1888–1953). Born in New York City, Eugene Gladstone O'Neill was the son of James O'Neill, whose dramatic career helped to shape O'Neill's development as a playwright. O'Neill attended Princeton University briefly and, between 1913 and 1916, worked closely with the Provincetown Players. Generally considered America's premier playwright, O'Neill received three Pulitzer Prizes and, in 1936, was awarded the Nobel Prize. Writing from 1916 through 1943, from one war to another, he created many characters whose lives were directly affected by war.

When his characters anticipate the impact of their actions on future wars, they emphasize the interrelatedness of life, a recurring interest in O'Neill's plays. In *Marco Millions* (1925), to advance his standing with Kublai, Marco Polo reasons that since the powder in a firecracker can maim a child, it can revolutionize war, extending the Kublai's power and influence. In "The Personal Equation" (1915), members of the International Workers Union argue that a worldwide labor strike might diminish patriotic support of an expected war with Mexico.

In three early plays, personal, political, and military concerns complicate the lives of characters directly involved in war-related circumstances. In *The Sniper* (1917), a peasant named Rougon, having learned that the Germans killed his wife and son and destroyed his entire farm, fires at passing German soldiers, who return his fire and kill him. In *In the Zone* (1916–1917), their nerves strained because they occupy a British steamer loaded with ammunition on a sea full of German submarines, seamen convince themselves that one of their number, Smitty, is a spy. Searching his personal belongings, they find letters that reveal not that he is employed by the Germans but rather that because he is a drunk, Smitty's girl has left him. *The Movie Man* (1914) is set in Mexico during a revolution. The title character negotiates with the commander in chief of the Constitutionalist Army for the release of a condemned political prisoner.

In his major plays, O'Neill introduces characters who look back on war experiences, often in an attempt to repair or regain a reputation for heroism. In *Mourning Becomes Electra* (1931), O'Neill uses Greek mythology to enrich a realistic drama of one family's tragic fall following the American Civil War. Specifically, he draws on the *Oresteia* for the basic plot in which Agamemnon, a homecoming soldier, is murdered by Clytemnestra, his unfaithful wife. As O'Neill's play opens, the Civil War ends and the central male characters, all military men, return to their New England homes. Educated at West Point and a veteran of the Mexican War, Ezra Mannon has served as a brigadier general in the Civil War. Having been encouraged by his sister Lavinia to emulate his father, Ezra's son Orin also joins the army and is wounded while serving as first lieutenant of the Infantry. Under attack, Orin's momentary insanity is misunderstood to be an act of courageous aggression. After the war, Orin complains of being haunted by memories of the men he killed. Peter Niles, a friend of Orin's and a suitor to Lavinia, serves as captain of Artillery. Niles, too, is wounded.

A *Touch of the Poet* (1942) takes place on June 27, the nineteenth anniversary of the Duke of Wellington's victory over Napoleon's army during the Peninsular War (1808–1814). Having distinguished himself during this battle, Cornelius Melody celebrates by dressing in his uniform and drinking with friends, including Jamie Cregan. Having served under Melody, Cregan knows that had Con not resigned, he would have been court-martialed for killing a Spanish noble whose wife he had seduced.

In *The Iceman Cometh* (1939), regular customers at Harry Hope's bar drink to forget their inability to realize their dreams. Among them are two soldiers who have forgotten an earlier enmity—and the commitment it represents. Cecil Lewis was a British army captain. In the Boer War (1899–1902), Lewis fought against Piet Wetjoen, a general. Both earned bad reputations during their service, Lewis for misappropriating funds and Wetjoen for cowardice. Like the others at the bar, these ex-soldiers fantasize about a future in which their pasts are forgotten and they can go home as heroes. O'Neill feared that audiences would be unreceptive to the nihilism portrayed in *The Iceman Cometh*.

World War I provides the dramatic occasion for *Shell Shock* (1918) and for *Strange Interlude* (1927). In the first, Major Jack Arnold blames himself for having retrieved Lieutenant Herbert Roylston's body in order to take his cigarettes. Discovering that Roylston is alive cures Arnold of his shell shock. *Strange Interlude* (1927) begins with the death of Gordon Shaw, a character based on the real-life Hobart Amory Hare Baker, a Princeton athlete killed in the World War I. At the start of the play, Shaw has already been killed in action and his fiancée, Nina Leeds, plans to become a nurse in a hospital for wounded soldiers.

For O'Neill's characters, war sparked creativity as well as destruction. It increased both solidarity and jealousy. It could inspire or destroy self-esteem. Whatever its larger political consequences, war simply could not be separated from the ordinary lives of individuals.

REFERENCES

O'Neill, Eugene. *Eugene O'Neill: Complete Plays*. New York: Library of America, 1988.
Ranald, Margaret Loftus. *The Eugene O'Neill Companion*. Westport, CT: Greenwood Press, 1984.
Sheaffer, Louis. *Eugene O'Neill: Son and Artist*. Boston: Little, Brown, 1973.
———. *O'Neill: Son and Playwright*. Boston: Little, Brown, 1968.

Mary S. Comfort

P

PAGE, THOMAS NELSON (1853–1922). Page was the granddaddy of Southern literature, the first writer to appear boldly and peculiarly Southern in print as American regional literature became a widespread genre. Hugely popular with Northern and Southern audiences during Reconstruction and beyond, Page's writing formed the fountainhead of the plantation tradition, in which the Old South—particularly Tidewater Virginia—was resurrected with glorious nostalgia, complete with the noblest aristocratic heroes and heroines; the happiest loyal slaves; and the staunchest Confederate warriors. These character types, cast in melodramatic contours, featured in sentimental plots that paid homage to the great heart and spirit of the South, especially as they were embodied in her soldiers.

The Civil War plays a central role in Page's first and perhaps best-known work, the short story "Marse Chan: A Tale of Old Virginia," which appeared in *Century Magazine* (1884) and three years later in his first volume of short stories, *In Ole Virginia* (1887). A dashing Southern heir, whose story is narrated in dialect by an old Negro bodyservant, duels for the sacred honor of family and friends but is spurned by his longtime love; wounded to the soul, he throws himself into the war and covers himself with glory through a succession of rash exploits. Sufficiently chastened over time, the heroine relents and writes him a love letter just in time for him to read it before he is killed in battle. That letter, tucked into his pocket, becomes a symbol of all the hopes and dreams of the South that are dashed with the outcome of the war.

Not all Page's war stories, however, were steeped in pathos. Indeed, crucial to his stated desire to use his literature to regenerate good feelings between postbellum North and South was a brisk, energetic treatment in many stories of the universal worth of Southern folks. Thus, in "The Burial of the Guns," a Confederate battery of men old and young prove themselves soldiers' soldiers, devoted to their commander, their cannons, and their cause even after Lee's surrender at Appomattox. Detailing the pride and fortitude of idealized warriors amid wonderfully concrete images of battle—for example, the cannon named

The Cat "jumped as she spat her deadly shot from her hot throat"—Page suggests the indomitable and manly spirit of Southern men, especially in defeat, characteristics vital to the health of the reunited States. In his efforts at healing, Page also penned children's books to impress upon upcoming generations the need for national unity. In *Two Little Confederates* (1888), a Southern family protects Northern soldiers from the Confederates, giving a higher priority to close friendship with good people than to the dictates of warfare. After the war is over, a daughter marries one of those Northerners, thereby linking bloodlines, regions, and values in a commitment that is a microcosm of the restored Union.

Although Page was too young to participate in the Civil War, he did become the U.S. ambassador to Italy during World War I and wrote about his experiences in *Italy and the World War* (1920). In addition, he was an essayist, social commentator, novelist, and biographer whose works included *The Old South: Essays Social and Political* (1892), *Social Life in Old Virginia* (1897), *Red Rock* (1899), and *Robert E. Lee: Man and Soldier* (1911).

REFERENCES

Baro, Gene, ed. *After Appomattox: The Image of the South in Its Fiction 1865–1900.* New York: Corinth Books, 1963.
Gross, Theodore L. *Thomas Nelson Page.* New York: Twayne, 1967.
Page, Thomas Nelson. *The Novels, Stories, Sketches, and Poems of Thomas Nelson Page.* Plantation Edition. 18 vols. New York: Scribner's, 1906–1912.

Sandra Burr

PAINE, THOMAS (1737–1809). Born the son of a corset maker in Thetford, England, Paine was apprenticed to his father's craft but went to sea before settling into a checkered career as corset maker and excise officer. In 1772, he wrote his first serious polemic, a pamphlet urging reform of Britain's Excise Service. This effort attracted the notice of Benjamin Franklin, who apparently encouraged Paine's emigration to America. In October 1774, carrying a letter of introduction from Franklin, Paine arrived in Philadelphia and became editor of *Pennsylvania Magazine.*

Paine's most famous polemic, *Common Sense*, debuted on January 10, 1776—the same day the colonies received a speech signaling the king's intransigence. *Common Sense*, published as "by an Englishman," galvanized public opinion and may even have dashed any residual hopes for reconciliation between the American colonies and Great Britain. The pamphlet's heart is its middle section, "Thoughts on the Present State of American Affairs," in which Paine's axiomatic appeals and clever analogies present American independence as a rational, evolutionary process. After a forceful reminder of Britain's recent unparental conduct at Lexington and Concord, Paine brilliantly exploits the commonplace metaphor of Britain as mother country. He points out that while a child initially subsists on milk, it must progress to meat in order to thrive. He then exposes the essential irrationality of the union itself, observing that nature holds no examples of brutes devouring their young or of a satellite larger than its primary planet. Such examples, Paine maintains, argue for America's natural independence from Great Britain. Paine concludes with an effective fashioning of the Enlightenment conviction that legitimate power derives only from popular sovereignty, a sentiment soon echoed in the Declaration of Independence.

Not immediately evident is Paine's habit of heightening his arguments with emotional appeals and associations that verge on demagoguery. King George III, for instance, is variously termed the "Pharaoh of England" and the "Royal Brute of Great Britain."

Common Sense was a phenomenal success. Over 120,000 copies were sold by March 1776 alone, making its author, whose identity soon became known, a household name throughout Colonial America. For the next several years, Paine revised and expanded *Common Sense* through nineteen editions in America, seven in Great Britain, and one (in French) on the Continent.

Paine's next contribution to the American cause was *The American Crisis* series, written while Paine was serving in the Continental Army. The first in this series—released on December 19, 1776—is famous for its stirring, memorable opening:

These are the times that try men's souls: The summer soldier and the sunshine patriot will in this crisis, shrink from the service of his county; but he that stands it Now, deserves the love and thanks of man and woman.

Paine once again plays on popular prejudices and fears in urging colonists to stay the course: Britain intends, he argues, not simply to enforce its laws but also to reduce the colonies to slavery. British loyalists are cowards motivated by "servile, slavish, self-interested fear." Worse yet, he suggests, a British victory would turn the colonists' homes into "barracks and bawdy-houses for Hessians," and colonial men would be raising children of doubtful paternity.

Despite its excesses, the stirring rhetoric and patriotic appeal of *The American Crisis* have been credited with bolstering the resolve and morale of the Continental Army during the difficult winter of 1776–1777. Washington reportedly ordered the pamphlet read to the troops just before their victorious surprise attack against Hessian troops on December 26, 1776. Paine continued his *Crisis* series throughout the course of the war, the sixteenth and final number appearing on December 9, 1783.

In 1787, Paine traveled to France, where he would write his final revolutionary polemic, *The Rights of Man*. Essentially a defense of the French Revolution, *The Rights of Man* (1791, 1792) holds up the American Revolution as a model. The American experience, Paine suggests, exposed monarchy as an irrational and outmoded institution and established the movement toward representative government as a reasonable process and a universal human right. While this pamphlet was a popular success, Paine's suggestion that the British too should overthrow their monarch got him convicted in absentia for seditious libel in England. In France, Paine's opposition to the execution of Louis XVI so angered

France's Committee of Public Safety that he was arrested and imprisoned for ten months.

The American government—for which Paine had presumably had done so much—failed to protest Paine's imprisonment. Especially hurt by the indifference of his former patron George Washington, Paine published a bitter personal attack on the popular Washington—a rash step that cost Paine political and popular favor. Returning to America in 1802, Paine was repudiated as a radical and vilified as an atheist for *The Age of Reason* (1793, 1795), the deistic treatise he had also published while in France. Paine died in obscurity in New Rochelle, New York.

REFERENCES

Aldridge, Alfred Owen. *Man of Reason: The Life of Thomas Paine*. New York: Lippincott, 1959.
Paine, Thomas. *The Complete Writings of Thomas Paine*. Ed. Philip S. Foner. 2 vols. New York: Citadel Press, 1969.
Wilson, Jerome D., and William F. Ricketson. *Thomas Paine*. Boston: Twayne, 1978.

Edward F. Palm

PARKMAN, FRANCIS (1823–1893). As a freshman at Harvard College in 1840, Boston native Francis Parkman decided to embark upon what was to become his life's work, a history of the colonial struggle for supremacy in North America. The series, eventually titled *France and England in America*, became a classic of American history and literature. Indeed, Parkman is hailed as one of the greatest historians the New World has produced. He combined depth and accuracy of research, literary skill, and sensitivity to his work, achieving all despite a lifetime of serious medical handicaps.

The series Parkman wrote began with the dawn of French colonization in America and ended with its eclipse. Warfare was the main element of many of the volumes. For example, *A Half-Century of Conflict*, the sixth volume in the series, covered the years between 1700 and 1748, a time filled with the border strife that marked the start of the final struggle between New France and the English colonies. The seventh and last volume, *Montcalm and Wolfe*, arguably Parkman's best work, examined the culminating war itself, the French and Indian War. Parkman's choice of focusing upon the two leaders of that struggle, which ended with the downfall of New France on the Plains of Abraham in 1759, made possible a gripping story of determination and willpower. Parkman also wrote *The Conspiracy of Pontiac*, which completed the history of the English conquest and focused upon the subsequent great Indian uprising against the new rulers of North America. With his series, Parkman wrote the complete history of the contest between two great European systems in the colonial field and explained how the conflict in America was intricately involved with the struggle for power in Europe. Parkman's greatest contribution was to demonstrate that seemingly obscure events in America had a vital effect on the course of world history.

REFERENCES

Boorstin, Daniel J. *The Creators*. New York: Random House, 1992.
Morison, Samuel Eliot, ed. Introduction. *The Parkman Reader*. By Francis Parkman. Boston and Toronto: Little, Brown, 1955.
Schama, Simon. *Dead Certainties: Unwarranted Speculations*. New York: Knopf, 1991.
Wade, Mason. *Francis Parkman: Heroic Historian*. New York: Viking Press, 1942.

Michelle C. Morgan

PAUL, ELLIOT (1891–1958). Although raised in Boston, Elliot Paul's writing was more influenced by his European experiences, first as a soldier in World War I and then as an expatriate in Paris. *Impromptu* (1923) is the story of Irwin Atwood, a private whose "senses were being deadened" by the war machine. However, when he returns disillusioned to find his fiancée driven to prostitution, Atwood can only find solace by returning to the army that had used him. Paul experiments stylistically in this novel, applying his knowledge of musical composition to the novel, telling the story in brief vignettes and half sentences. *Imperturbe* (1924) is the story of Lester Davis, who, like Paul, worked many jobs before going to the war. He eventually finds a troubled peace similar to that of the poet in **Walt Whitman**'s poem "Me Imperturbe," thus the title.

After these early novels, Paul moved to Paris, working as a journalist and editor of the little magazine *transition*. There he wrote *The Amazon* (1930), a comic novel of a young woman who desires to go to war. Alberta Snyder organizes a signal corps unit made of women and contrives to get to France and the front lines. Once again Paul managed to draw on his own life; the narrator of the book is a foreign correspondent, like Paul, who hears of Alberta's unit and puts together the pieces of her story.

Using his journalistic and novelistic skills, Paul wrote two nonfiction books about the effects of upcoming wars in cities he had lived in. *The Life and Death of a Spanish Town* (1937) is considered his most important work because of the powerful voice in which he condemns fascism, which destroys the community of Santa Eulalia del Rio during the Spanish Civil War. *The Last Time I Saw Paris* (1942) tells how the beginning of World War II encroaches on a small section of Paris while also portraying some of the feel of Paris for expatriates. Paul's expatriate status allowed him a unique perspective on the cultures that were involved in wars during his lifetime. The destruction of these societies is a major concern of his war literature.

REFERENCE

Ford, Hugh. *Published in Paris: American and British Writers, Printers, and Publishers in Paris, 1920–1939*. New York: Macmillan, 1975.

Sean C. F. McGurr

PENNELL, JOSEPH STANLEY (1908–1963). Born on July 4, 1908, in Junction City, Kansas, and educated at Kansas University and Pembroke College of Oxford University, Pennell worked as a teacher, news reporter, editor, radio announcer, and actor before turning to fiction writing. His first and best novel, *The History of Rome Hanks and Kindred Matters* (1944), the product of five years' work, was set during the American Civil War and focused on the title character's efforts to understand himself by coming to grips with his divided heritage. This subject was close to Pennell's heart, since he himself came from a family that had sent sons to both the Union and Confederate armies; he drew heavily on family materials and stories for the novel. While some critics found the story vulgar, others praised its stark realism and experimental technique, such as the use of flashbacks. Hamilton Basso exemplified this division in his review for *The New Yorker*, calling the novel "chaotic, undisciplined, and formless, . . . extravagant and sentimental," yet also praising it as "a work of unusual talent, and . . . the best novel about the Civil War I have read, with the natural exception of *The Red Badge of Courage*" (66).

After the publication of *Rome Hanks* Pennell joined the U.S. Army as a private and served in the final year of World War II, rising to the rank of second lieutenant and command of an antiaircraft battery. After the war he married and settled at Tillamook Head, Oregon, where he continued his writing career with novels such as *The History of Nora Beckham* (1948), which is generally regarded as his only work of significance besides *Rome Hanks*, and *The History of Thomas Wagnal* (1951).

REFERENCES

Basso, Hamilton. Rev. of *Rome Hanks*, by Joseph Stanley Pennell. *The New Yorker* 15 July 1944: 66.

Mayberry, George. Rev. of *Rome Hanks*, by Joseph Stanley Pennell. *New Republic* 14 August 1944: 195.

Prescott, Orville. Rev. of *Rome Hanks*, by Joseph Stanley Pennell. *Yale Review* 34 (Autumn 1944): 34.

Randal W. Allred

PHELPS, ELIZABETH STUART (1844–1911). Born to Reverend Austin Phelps and nineteenth-century writer Elizabeth Stuart Phelps, Mary Gray Phelps assumed her mother's name after the latter's death in 1852. While this sometimes confuses researchers, the younger Elizabeth Stuart Phelps married Herbert Dickinson Ward in 1888 and is often differentiated from her mother by this second, and parenthetical, last name. A prolific author, Phelps published fifty-five books—both novels and collected short fiction—countless short stories, poems, and articles on the conditions of women.

The Civil War plays a significant role in many of Phelps's works, including her first short story "A Sacrifice Consumed" published in *Harper's New Monthly Magazine* (ca. 1863). Mirroring Phelps's own experience, this story explores a young woman's loss of her fiancé in the battle of Antietam. Her novel *Mercy Glidden's Work* (1865) examines a young woman's service in a Civil War hospital. While primarily concerned with the conditions of mill girls, *Up-Hill; or Life in the Factory* (1865) reveals the disenfranchising effects of war on those powerless to prevent it. Phelps's most popular work, *The Gates Ajar* (1868), likewise examines the consequences of a war that left countless women widowed and bereaved. The novel focuses on the spiritual death and renewal of Mary Cabot who, in mourning her brother's death, searches for meaning outside traditional theology and for a way to live with loss. In her powerful novel *The Story of Avis* (1877), Phelps explores the choices facing a woman artist who must choose between a career and life as a wife and mother. In an attempt to force Avis to alter her decision not to marry him, Philip Ostrander enlists because "war offered the quickest and most incisive road to a glorious solution of inglorious personal difficulties" (164–165). His resulting war injuries and return influence Avis's disastrous decision to marry him.

In addition to her novels, Phelps used the Civil War in her short stories "The Oath of Allegiance" (1909), "Annie Laurie" (1891), "Comrades" (1911), "An Hour with Gwendolyn" (1879), and "Margaret Bronson" (1865). Though it was never staged, her play *The Veteran: A Drama of the Streets* focuses on a blind Civil War veteran ignored by the society he served.

REFERENCES

Bennett, Mary Angela. *Elizabeth Stuart Phelps*. Philadelphia: University of Pennsylvania Press, 1939.
Kessler, Carol Farley. *Elizabeth Stuart Phelps*. Boston: Twayne, 1982.
Phelps, Elizabeth Stuart. *The Story of Avis*. Ed. Carol F. Kessler. New Brunswick, NJ: Rutgers University Press, 1985.

Amy L. Wink

PIERCY, MARGE (1936–). Born into a working-class family in Detroit, Piercy received a scholarship to attend the University of Michigan. She began writing while studying there, but her first six novels were rejected. Finally, Piercy published *Going Down Fast* in 1969, and she has been a productive, often best-selling novelist ever since. She lives in Massachusetts with her third husband.

Piercy has received many awards and honors, including a PEN New England award and an honorary doctorate from Bridgewater State College. She has written twelve volumes of poetry, thirteen novels, and various nonfiction works. Her best-known novel is *Woman on the Edge of Time* (1976), a speculative work in which the fate of a twentieth-century woman in a mental institution will help determine whether the future is utopian, or dystopian and perpetually at war.

Her novel *Vida* (1980) details the life of a 1960s leftist activist who has gone underground after committing a protest bombing. A major character in the novel, Vida's fellow fugitive and lover, is a man who deserted in order not to serve in Vietnam after being denied conscientious objector status. *Vida* is one of a very few novels to deal in detail with the anti–Vietnam War movement. Piercy, who was herself an SDS (Students for a Democratic Society) organizer, has continued to be involved in feminist causes. The novel speaks with the voice of experience.

In *Gone to Soldiers* (1987), Piercy moves to World War II, creating a large canvas with ten main characters: Bernice, a Civil Air Patrol pilot; her brother Jeff, involved with the French resistance; Ruthie, a factory worker; her brother Duvey, a member of the merchant marine; Murray, a Jewish Marine in the Pacific war; Louise, a journalist; Daniel, a cryptographer; Jacqueline, a French Jew in Paris; Naomi, her sister, sent to live safely in Detroit; and Abra, a WASP leftist recruited into the Office of Strategic Services (OSS). All of them have chapters from their points of view, a mosaiclike structure attempting a picture of both European and Pacific Theaters and the U.S. home front, in the manner of **Herman Wouk**'s *Winds of War*, but Piercy's encyclopedic novel tries to focus more on the experiences of women.

REFERENCES

Doherty, Patricia. *Marge Piercy: An Annotated Bibliography*. Westport, CT: Greenwood Press, 1997.
Walker, Sue, and Eugenie Hammer, eds. *Ways of Knowing: Essays on Marge Piercy*. Mobile, AL: Negative Capability, 1991.

Renny Christopher

POUND, EZRA (1885–1972). Born in Hailey, Idaho, Pound spend most of his early life in Pennsylvania. He earned a bachelor's degree from Hamilton College in 1905 and a master's from the University of Pennsylvania in 1906. After moving to London in 1908, Pound worked as a literary editor, published poems and articles, and emerged as the leading spokesperson for Imagism and Vorticism. Although Pound did not write what can be described as war poetry, his use of specific war images and his political activism during World War II show the significant impact that war had on his life and writings.

Pound did not volunteer in World War I. *Cathay* (1915), a collection of Imagist translations, has been characterized as his response to the war. According to Hugh Kenner, Pound's images of dislocation, devastation, and distant glories reveal "a sensibility responsive to torn Belgium and disrupted London" (202). For example, in "Homage to Sextus Propertius" (1919), Pound explores the causes of war and criticizes its glorification in art. *Hugh Selwyn Mauberley* (1920) also alludes to war, specifically the carnage of World War I. Parts IV and V describe the war as a waste of young lives for the profit of the bungled cultural and political establishment ruled by old men. Moreover, Pound treats World War I in his *Cantos* (finally collected in 1970), specifically Canto 16, which comments on the death of Henri Gaudier, symbolic of the deadly effect of war on art.

Pound left England for France in 1920 and then moved to Rapallo, Italy, in 1924. After this move, Pound became a fervent supporter of Benito Mussolini's Fascist government. During World War II, his broadcasts on Rome Radio supporting Italian Fascists were accompanied by anti-Semitic commentary and attacks on President Franklin Roosevelt. In response, in 1943, U.S. government indicted Pound for treason. As early as 1944, Pound expressed his devotion to Italy's failed war effort in Cantos 72 and 73. In Canto 73, according to J. J. Wilhelm's translation, a peasant girl triumphantly leads twenty Canadians to their death in a mine field for the glory of the Italian homeland (209).

Arrested in 1945, the U.S. Army imprisoned Pound for six months in Pisa, a contributor to his psychological breakdown but also a catalyst for his creation of his powerful and very personal *Pisan Cantos* (1948). The first of these cantos, Canto 74, laments the demise of Mussolini strung up by his heels in Milan, signifying the death of Pound's dream. In Canto 80, he pities Mussolini outright. Upon his return to the United States to stand trial, the court declared Pound insane, committing him to St. Elizabeth's Hospital in Washington, D.C. He was released in 1958, returned to Italy, and died in Venice in 1972.

REFERENCES

Carpenter, Humphrey. *A Serious Character: The Life of Ezra Pound*. Boston: Houghton Mifflin, 1988.
Kenner, Hugh. *The Pound Era*. Berkeley: University of California Press, 1971.
Pound, Ezra. *Cantos of Ezra Pound*. New York: New Directions, 1970.
Wilhelm, J. J. *Ezra Pound: The Tragic Years, 1925–1972*. University Park: Pennsylvania State University Press, 1994.

Paul R. Cappucci

PRESTON, MARGARET JUNKIN (1820–1897). Born in Pennsylvania, Margaret Junkin moved to Virginia when her father accepted a position as president of Washington College. A published poet and novelist who argued for the repatriation of freed slaves, she married Major J.T.L. Preston, one of the founders of Virginia Military Institute, in 1857. After the Civil War broke out, she experienced divided loyalties when her father and a sister returned to Pennsylvania following Virginia's secession. Her pain turned to sorrow during the war: Two stepsons and her famous brother-in-law, Thomas (Stonewall) Jackson, died, and another stepson lost his arm. Federal troops ransacked her home, and she watched many women lose brothers, fathers, husbands, and sons.

For her, war had little glory. In her diary she wrote, "My Very / soul is sick of carnage. I loathe / the word—*War*." To keep her spirits up, she broke a self-imposed silence and began composing poems about the suffering and sacrifice endured by Confederate soldiers, such as "A Dirge for Ashby," "Under the Shade of Trees," and "The Bivouac in the Snow," which presents Confederates

. . . devoutly kneeling
    On the frozen ground—

> Pleading for their country,
>   In its hour of woe—
> For its soldiers marching
>   Shoeless through the snow.

Despite the hardships, Preston and her adopted home, the South, endured. When the war was over, she wrote, "War has not wholly wrecked us: still / Strong hands, brave hearts, high souls are ours" ("Acceptation").

Preston's most celebrated poem is the book-length *Beechenbrook: A Rhyme of the War*. Written in the winter of 1864–1865 with a scrap of pencil on rough, Confederate-made paper, dedicated to "every Southern woman who has been widowed by the war," *Beechenbrook* was intended to be "a faint memorial of sufferings, of which there can be no forgetfulness." Sections of the poem, particularly those about a young recruit named Macpherson, seem based on her own losses. When her husband shared it with other soldiers, most shed tears. All but 50 of the original 2,000 copies were destroyed when the poem's publishing house in Richmond was burned during the evacuation in early 1865. Republished in Baltimore after the war, the book, which addressed the emotional cost of war to home and family, was a huge success and led to Preston's becoming known as the "Poetess of the South."

REFERENCES

Coulling, Mary Price. *Margaret Junkin Preston: A Biography*. Winston-Salem, NC: Blair, 1993.

Preston, Margaret Junkin. *Beechenbrook: A Rhyme of the War*. Baltimore: Kelly & Piet, 1866.

———. *Old Song and New*. Philadelphia: J. B. Lippincott & Co., 1870.

James M. Dubinsky

PYLE, ERNIE (1900–1945). Ernest Taylor Pyle was born on August 3, 1900, near Dana, Indiana. As a child, Ernie was small, shy, and timid, qualities that would later blossom into an understanding of and compassion for the little man. He majored in journalism at Indiana University but left school during his senior year. During the 1930s, Pyle was a traveling correspondent for the Washington *Daily News*, and his columns were syndicated by the Scripps-Howard chain. Pyle's columns were popular for their chatty, informal style.

In 1940, Pyle went to London to cover the war in Europe. His descriptions of the blitzkrieg were detailed, yet conversational, helping to make the war meaningful for his American readers. With America's entry into the war, Pyle joined the American forces in North Africa and followed their march through Europe. He would go to the front, meet the soldiers, live with them for days at a time, and then return to write about what he saw and whom he met. Pyle's columns focused on everyday life and the men themselves. Pyle's glimpses of people and places illuminated the vast conflict in ways that stories from headquarters and official communiqués could not. He marveled at how average folks carried out their duties, recognizing those whose contributions were usually overlooked, such as bomber repair crews or the soldiers who labored under fire to bake over thirteen tons of bread at the Anzio beachhead. Front-line troops, however, received most of Pyle's attention, "because they are the underdogs . . . and in the end they are the guys that wars can't be won without." In late 1944, he moved to the Pacific and while observing the advance of troops near Okinawa was killed by Japanese machine gun fire on April 18, 1945.

Pyle's newspaper columns earned a Pulitzer Prize for distinguished correspondence in 1944, and President Truman posthumously awarded him the Medal of Merit. His columns were collected and published as *Ernie Pyle in England* (1941), *Here Is Your War* (1943), *Brave Men* (1944), and *Last Chapter* (1946). Ernie Pyle's writing stands as an example of finely crafted journalism with an eye for detail.

REFERENCES

Lancaster, Paul. "Ernie Pyle: Chronicler of 'The Men Who Do the Dying.' " *American Heritage* 32 (February–March 1981): 30–36+.
Miller, Lee G. *The Story of Ernie Pyle*. New York: Viking, 1950.
Tobin, James. *Ernie Pyle's War: America's Eyewitness to World War II*. New York: Free Press, 1997.

William T. Hartley

PYNCHON, THOMAS (1937–   ). Thomas Pynchon was born and raised in Glen Cove, Long Island. He attended Cornell University until 1955, when he left to serve in the navy. He returned to college in 1957 and changed his major to English from engineering physics. Graduating in 1959, he began publishing short stories and novels. His third novel, *Gravity's Rainbow* (1973), set during the final year of World War II, won the National Book Award for fiction.

Gravity's Rainbow can best be described as an encyclopedic, dark comic novel: a story that deals specifically with war as bureaucratic conspiracy. There are few or no images of World War II in this text: Language of the time, military jargon, places of war, and scenes of physical conflict are more comic book stylizations than realistic battlefield encounters, although there are many scenes of graphic violence and perverse confrontations. Pynchon employs slang, jargon, and dialect to describe the historical events, fictional situations, fantasies, and dreams that challenge his vast array of characters. Pynchon's vision of war encompasses history, psychology, sociology, metaphysics, and technology. He relies on mythological and comic book characters and folktale and popular culture figures to point the way to the world's predestined extinction. For Pynchon war creates bizarre forms of order, that is, the "military-industrial complex," whose sole purpose is death.

Labyrinthine digressions aside, *Gravity's Rainbow* catalogs the American Tyrone Slothrop's journey through war-torn Europe, "The Zone," to uncover the truth about his family history and his childhood participation in Pavlovian rocket research. Slothrop works for the Psychological Intelligence Schemes for Expediting Surrender (PISCES), a British unit that learns that Slothrop's sexual liaisons are directly related to where the next V-2 rocket will fall. Aside from actual historic figures, Slothrop is pursued by characters from all countries and all societies as he searches for the elusive German Lieutenant Weissmann, alias Captain Blicero, commander of a V-2 rocket station, and his cadre of spies and henchmen. The novel ends with Pynchon's readers sitting in a darkened theater awaiting the apocalypse as a V-2 rocket falls toward them.

REFERENCES

Eller, Jonathan, and William McCarron. "A Plea for Interdisciplinary Study: A Supplement to A 'Gravity's Rainbow' Companion." *Resources for American Literary Study* 19.1 (1993): 94–106.
Tololyan, Khachig. "War as Background in *Gravity's Rainbow.*" *Approaches to* Gravity's Rainbow. Columbus: Ohio State University Press, 1983. 31–67.
Weisenburger, Steven. *A* Gravity's Rainbow *Companion*. Athens: University of Georgia Press, 1988.

Donna L. Pasternak

Q

QUINNEY, JOHN WANNUAUCON (1797–1855). Born in 1797, in the Mohican settlement of New Stockbridge, New York, Quinney was a noted diplomat and political leader who traveled to Washington, D.C., ten times to lobby in favor of the federal status and self-government of Native Americans. On July 4, 1854, he delivered his famous "Independence Day Speech" in Reidesville, New York. This moving and effective speech contrasts the independence of European Americans with the subjugation of Native Americans under European influence.

Quinney notes how America, commonly associated with freedom, progress, and equality, was founded on the division, displacement, and genocide of Native Americans. He details how the four Colonial Wars, fought between the years of 1689 and 1763, spread hostility and smallpox among the Delaware, Munsee, Mohegan, Narragansett, Pequot, and Penobscot tribes united peacefully under the "Muh-he-con-new" confederacy. According the Quinney, by the time the British had obtained control over the land between the Great Lakes and the Ohio River, the 25,000 Native Americans who "constituted the power and population of the great Muh-he-con-new Nation" had been annihilated by feuding and the "white man's diseases."

Quinney accuses the colonists of insidiously promoting hostility within the Native American tribes, while, at the same time, "transmitting to your Kings, beyond the water, intelligence of your possession 'by right and discovery' and demanding assistance to assert and maintain your hold." He also suggests that this injustice is perpetuated in the form of deeds that force the Native Americans from their territory. The forced migration of Quinney's Stockbridge tribe, which occurred in 1829, is one among many examples.

While July Fourth may signify the freedom of the great American nation, to Quinney, it held an ironic parallel to the undeserved plight of the Native American population: "the miserable weakness and dependence" of his race, handed down "from one power to another."

REFERENCES

Dyer, Louisa A. *The House of Peace*. New York: Longmans, Green, 1955.

Frazier, Patrick. *The Mohicans of Stockbridge*. Lincoln: University of Nebraska Press, 1994.

Quinney, John W. "The Speech of John W. Quinney of the Stockbridge Tribe of Indians." *Wisconsin Historical Society Report and Collections 1857–58*. Madison: Wisconsin Historical Society, 1859.

Priscilla Glanville

R

RABE, DAVID (1940–). Unquestionably the most significant dramatist to emerge from the Vietnam War, David Rabe established his reputation on plays that provocatively confront America's loss of innocence in the war. Rabe's Vietnam canon consists of *Sticks and Bones* (1969), *The Basic Training of Pavlo Hummel* (1971), *The Orphan* (1973), and *Streamers* (1976), four plays marked by satiric anger, biting black comedy, eruptions of violence, and a desire to shock audiences into an acknowledgment of America's tragic flaws. While Rabe has since written plays on other subjects like the sexual exploitation of women (*In the Boom Boom Room*, 1973) and Hollywood (*Hurlyburly*, 1984), and also written novels (*Recital of the Dog*, 1992, and *The Crossing Guard*, 1995), he is still best known for his literary engagement with the Vietnam War. He cemented his reputation with screenplays for Robert Altman's film version of *Streamers* (1983) and Brian DaPalma's *Casualties of War* (1989).

Son of a meatpacker, Rabe was educated at Loras Academy and Loras College, Catholic schools in Dubuque, Iowa, his birthplace. His graduate studies in theater at Villanova University were interrupted by the draft, and Rabe served in the army from 1965 to 1967. The final eleven months of his tour of duty were spent in Vietnam, a crucially formative episode. Assigned to the 68th Medical Group, which oversaw evacuation and surgical hospitals, Rabe never became desensitized to the suffering he witnessed. Moreover, he came to recognize the profoundly transformative effect of the war on American society. Rabe's trilogy is concerned with showing how America's involvement in Vietnam was ultimately an aggressive assertion of our comforting virtuous myths of innocence, progress, and altruism. Battling "the self-imposed national amnesia and self-exoneration" of historical and mythic revisionism, Rabe's plays and screenplays are (with one predictable exception) dedicated to illuminating the dark heart of the American national character that made the catastrophe of Vietnam possible. Only *Casualties of War* is willing to grant an upbeat ending. The female Amerasian college student's reassuring benediction is, arguably, earned only in the context of a Hollywood studio production. It is doubtful that Ericksson can so easily begin to put his combat trauma behind him. Nor can the filmgoer readily obliterate the assaultive memory of violence and rape depicted in Rabe's screenplay and realized by DaPalma's visceral direction.

By contrast, Rabe's plays make no such concessions. In terms of style, they move from the disorienting expressionism and surrealism of *Pavlo Hummel* and *Sticks and Bones* to the allegory of *The Orphan* to the veristic realism of *Streamers*. But the Vietnam plays are consistent in terms of Rabe's thematic preoccupations. The plays trace the pervasive corruption and eventual damnation of both Americans and Vietnamese on all fronts. They are marked by insistent profanity and overt performance of bloodletting. All Rabe's characters are tainted in some way by their participation in, or support for, the war. In *Sticks and Bones*, Rabe's home front play, the hollow myths of American middle-class family life are exposed in the form of television sitcom conventions. Unable and unwilling to deal with the reality of David's psychic wounding and physical blinding in Vietnam, his family (all named after the characters in the popular 1950s show *The Adventures of Ozzie and Harriet*) assist in his ritualistic suicide in the family's living room. Vietnamese women in *Pavlo Hummel* are degraded and commodified by American soldiers. For Rabe, sexual imperialism is emblematic of political imperialism, and rampant venereal disease is emblematic of everyone's spiritual corruption. Before he is grenaded to death by an American soldier who is a rival for the same whore, the fresh-faced Pavlo Hummel is transformed by his basic training into a racist killer who dehumanizes the enemy in his strenuous effort to attain mythic standards of masculinity purveyed by Hollywood war movies. The barracks of *Streamers* is a hothouse of toxic male bonding, anxious male intimacy, and primal conflict that exploded in the violent slaying of two soldiers, one of whom, Billy, is the fatal victim of his acknowledged reservoirs of racism and the unacknowledged swamps of homophobia. Recollections of Billy's boyhood desire to be a priest measure his descent into foul-mouthed and violent racism and misogyny in the army. The full import of America's tragic hubris in Vietnam is best exemplified by *The Orphan*, in which Rabe suggestively links characters from Aeschylus's *Oresteia* trilogy to the Charles Manson Family as archetypes of the uncontrolled violence inherent in a nation's claim to assert power over others.

Rabe's Vietnam works mourn all the casualties of America's longest foreign war (as in the nonsense lullaby sung at the end of *Streamers*) while also relentlessly exposing the myths of innocence, masculinity, racial equality, and beneficent expansion that have made America a destructive and self-deluded culture. Rabe's importance as an urgent and angry critic of America's involvement in Southeast Asia has been officially marked by the New York Drama Critics Circle Award (for *Streamers*), the Obie (for *Pavlo Hummel*), and the Tony (for *Sticks and Bones*). Rabe's successful plays and films have spoken to America's need to understand how the very best and worst in the national character were mired in the jungles of a disastrous overseas adventure.

REFERENCES

Kolin, Philip V. *David Rabe: A Stage History and Secondary Bibliography*. New York: Garland, 1987.
Zinman, Toby Silverman, ed. *David Rabe: A Casebook*. New York: Garland, 1991.

David A. Boxwell

REVOLUTIONARY WAR. With the possible exception of the Civil War, no single conflict had a more direct and profound impact on the definition of the American character and experience as the American War of Independence. As a result, the literature of the Revolution holds a unique position in American history, for it provides a vivid picture of the American mind during this most decisive era.

Strictly speaking, the American War of Independence began with the Battle of Lexington and Concord in April 1775 and lasted until the Treaty of Paris was signed in 1783, but the literature associated with the war began a decade earlier, as authors started responding to perceived British abuses of power, such as the Sugar Act of 1764 and the Stamp Act of 1765. From the time of these acts until the ratification of the Constitution in 1789, most writing in America reached its audience in the form of broadsides, pamphlets, or newspapers. Indeed several hundred pamphlets related to Anglo-American relations were published before the Declaration of Independence on July 4, 1776, with over a thousand more appearing during the years of the conflict. The pre-Declaration pamphlets are perhaps the more important, for in these one finds the chief arguments in favor of independence (although most of these pamphlets, prior to **Thomas Paine**, did not specifically call for independence). Most of the pre-Declaration pamphlets were written in response to some political or social action, such as the Stamp Act or the Boston Massacre in 1770. For the most part the arguments presented in these pamphlets were not original but were culled from other sources, including British and European authors and philosophers of the seventeenth and eighteenth centuries, such as Voltaire, Rousseau, and especially John Locke.

Among the many notable pamphlets appearing prior to the Declaration, standouts include James Otis's *The Rights of the British Colonies Asserted and Proved* (1764), John Dickinson's *Letters from a Farmer in Pennsylvania to the Inhabitants of the British Colonies* (1767–1768), John Allen's *Oration, on the Beauties of Liberty* (1773), Thomas Jefferson's *A Summary View of the Rights of British America* (1774), the letters and essays of Samuel and John Adams, and the orations of Joseph Warren. These pamphlets led up to the masterpiece of the genre, Thomas Paine's *Common Sense* (1776), which sold over a hundred thousand copies and did more than any other single document to move the colonists toward independence. Paine's other major contribution to the war was his series of sixteen *Crisis* papers published periodically from 1776 to 1783, which helped boost morale during the darker moments of the conflict. Influenced by Thomas Paine and other pamphleteers, as well as European natural rights theory, and in response to hostilities commenced a year earlier, in June 1776, Thomas Jefferson penned the Declaration of Independence, which was adopted by Congress on July 4, 1776, and signed by colonial representatives a month later.

Patriot literature had its counterpart in loyalist essays and sermons. Loyalist, or Tory, literature, though slower in getting started than the patriot propaganda, did help fuel the pamphlet wars prior to the conflict. Works such as Thomas Chandler's *A Friendly Address to All Reasonable Americans* (1774) and Samuel Seabury's *A View of the Controversy between Great Britain and Her Colonies* (1774) urged colonists to remain loyal to the British Parliament. During the war, true loyalist vitriol can be found in a sermon by Simeon Baxter entitled "Tyrannicide Proved Lawful" (1781). Later, toward the end of the war, Hector St. John de Crevecoeur, having abandoned his Pennsylvania farm at the outbreak of hostilities, published *Letters from an American Farmer* (1782). In the last of these letters, "Distresses of a Frontier Man," Crevecoeur's Tory sympathies can be seen in his response to the violence of the war.

Some of the more amusing literature associated with the war came in the form of satires written by Benjamin Franklin. "Rules by Which a Great Empire may be Reduced to a Small One" (1773) and "An Edict by the King of Prussia" (1773) lampoon British policy in the colonies, while "The Sale of the Hessians" (1777) comments on the British use of mercenaries.

In the field of poetry, **Philip Freneau** (1752–1832) has long been recognized as the "Poet of the Revolution." For a time a prisoner of war aboard the *Scorpion*, Freneau's "The British Prison Ship" remains one of the best poems to emerge from the Revolutionary War. Other notable poets include John Trumbull, who, in the mock-epic "M'Fingal" (1776, 1782), satirizes American Tories, and **Francis Hopkinson**, who mocked the British army in the popular "The Battle of the Kegs" (1778). Significant loyalist poets of the Revolution included Jonathan Odell and Joseph Stansbury. In "The American Times" (1780), "The Congratulation" (1779), and "The Words of Congress" (1780), Odell denounced the patriotic cause and the Continental Congress. Less virulent than Odell, Stansbury published numerous loyalist poems during the years of the conflict, including "A Pasquinade" (1780), "Invitation" (1781), "Let Us Be Happy as Long as We Can" (1782), and the conciliatory "The United States" (1783), written at the end of the war.

Both patriots and loyalists had their share of folk songs and ballads. The most renowned patriot song is "Yankee Doodle," which emerged in 1775 but went through countless revisions and spin-offs during the war. Other patriot ballads include "The King's Own Regulars" (1776), "Nathan Hale" (1776), "The Fate of John Burgoyne" (1777), and "The Dance" (1781). Not to be outdone, the loyalists countered with such ballads as "Burrowing Yankees" (1776), "The Congress" (1776), and "Yankee Doodle's Expedition to Rhode Island" (1778), which focuses on the failed American campaign against Newport in 1778.

Although the professional theater was inactive during the conflict, some dramatic literature was written during the war. The anonymous *The Battle of Brooklyn* (1776) satirizes the American army after its defeat at Brooklyn, and the British general Burgoyne's *The Blockade* (1775) was performed in British-occupied Boston. Such Tory drama was balanced against the dramatic satires of **Mercy Otis Warren** and the more even-handed *The Patriots* by Robert Munford. Meanwhile, **Hugh Henry Brackenridge** composed the patriotic *The Battle of Bunkers-Hill* (1776) and *The Death of General Montgomery* (1777), both designed more for reading than performance.

After the war, as American authors sought native materials around which to fashion a national literature, some turned to the events of the Revolutionary War for inspiration. **James Fenimore Cooper**'s *The Spy* (1821)—which centers in part around an alleged loyalist spy who is doubling as part of Washington's intelligence network—helped establish American letters on the international scene. Following the success of *The Spy*, Cooper wrote two more novels that treat war material, *The Pilot* (1823), which features an unnamed protagonist representing John Paul Jones, and *Lionel Lincoln* (1825). These efforts by Cooper notwithstanding, the most extended treatment of the war in the historical romance is the series of seven revolutionary romances by Cooper's southern contemporary **William Gilmore Simms**. Beginning with *The Partisan* in 1835 and ending with *Eutaw* in 1856, these interrelated novels take as their subject matter the conflict in the South. Later, Simms published an eighth novel based on the war, *Joscelyn: A Tale of the Revolution* (1867). Nathaniel Hawthorne also drew material from the war on occasion. "Howe's Masquerade" (1842), for example, tells of British commander William Howe on the eve of patriot victory in Boston. Other notable historical novels centered on the war include John Neal's *Seventy-Six* (1823), Lydia Maria M. Child's *The Rebels* (1825), and **John Pendleton Kennedy**'s *Horse-Shoe Robinson* (1835).

In poetry, **Longfellow** and **Emerson** both contributed efforts that reflect on the conflict. Longfellow's well-known "Paul Revere's Ride" (1861) tells of that mythic moment at the beginning of the war, while Emerson's "Concord Hymn" (1837) commemorates the "shot heard round the world" at Lexington and Concord in 1775. In the theater, one of the better early plays to emerge about the conflict was William Dunlap's blank verse *André* (1798). This sympathetic treatment of Major John André (co-conspirator with Benedict Arnold) is set entirely on André's execution day and features characters seeking pardon for André from "The General" (Washington). **James McHenry**'s *Waltham: An American Revolutionary Tale* (1823) is also a noteworthy contribution to this genre.

The American Revolution continued to engage the imaginations of writers through the later nineteenth century and throughout the twentieth. Representative works include **James A. Herne**'s drama *The Minute Men of 1774–5* (1886), **Winston Churchill**'s *Richard Carvel* (1899) and *The Crossing* (1904), **Kenneth Robert**'s *Rabble in Arms* (1933), **Walter D. Edmonds**'s *Drums along the Mo-*

hawk (1936), **Ben Ames Williams**'s *Come Spring* (1940), and several novels by **Howard Fast**, including *The Unvanquished* (1942).

Aside from the many histories of the conflict that have been written over the past two centuries, several important collections of war-related documents have been compiled. The first significant collection of such historical documents was edited together by Hezekiah Niles as *Principles and Acts of the Revolution in America* (1822).

REFERENCES

Emerson, Everett, ed. *American Literature, 1764–1789: The Revolutionary Years*. Madison: University of Wisconsin Press, 1977.

Pickering, James H., ed. *The World Turned Upside Down: Prose and Poetry of the American Revolution*. Port Washington: Kennikat Press, 1975.

Prescott, Frederick C., and John H. Nelson, eds. *Prose and Poetry of the Revolution*. New York: Thomas Y. Crowell Company, 1925.

Ringe, Donald A. "The American Revolution in American Romance." *American Literature* 49 (1977): 352–365.

Tyler, Moses Coit. *The Literary History of the American Revolution, 1763–1783*. 2 vols. 1897. New York: Frederick Ungar, 1963.

Vaughan, Alden T., ed. *Chronicles of the American Revolution*. New York: Grosset & Dunlap, 1965. [A revised version of *Principles and Acts of the Revolution in America*, complied by Hezekiah Niles.]

Eric Carl Link

REVOLUTIONARY WAR—WOMEN'S DIARIES. American women's diaries provide eyewitness civilian accounts of the American Revolution. In addition to their value as historical resources, the diaries of Margaret Morris, Sally Wister, Grace Galloway, and Mary Almy reveal these writers' interest in creating works with literary merit. Each writes to continue a relationship with a friend or relative from whom she is separated by the war, audiences whose interests the diarists share and whose opinions they value. They select incidents to interest these putative readers, they use imagery to emphasize their danger and their courage, they align setting with a dominant mood, and they create fictional characters to unify diverse entries.

The diarists begin to write when they learn, usually through rumors, of the impending arrival of soldiers or political officers near their homes. The action rises as the diarists await direct confrontation and personal involvement. Although they occasionally record the implications for the colonies of the rumors they hear, their primary concern is to characterize themselves as personally at risk, then to assure their readers that they have withstood this challenge to their identity. Thus, the primary conflict is not between Tories and Whigs, Hessians and rebels, but between the women themselves and the real and rumored dangers that threaten to change them. The climax of the diaries comes when these pressures become almost irresistible, and their stories of personal heroism conclude when they are reunited with their audiences.

Writing from her home in Burlington, New Jersey, Margaret Hill Morris (1737–1816) addresses her diary (December 1776–June 1777) to her sister Patty. Her recurring concern is to show Patty that although rumors and immediate dangers cause her neighbors to lose confidence and, in many cases, to run away, she is sustained by her Quaker faith and remains in Burlington. On December 14, 1776, she records that upon the arrival of the English fleet near Philadelphia, "the inhabitants of our little town were going in haste into the country. . . . But our trust in Providence [is] still firm, and we dare not even talk of removing our family" (December 6–8, 1776). On December 20, when a neighbor comes to her door and recounts rumors about " 'fifty of the light-horse, . . . a terrible sight to see how they all foamed at the mouth and pranced,' " Morris tries to calm him: " 'Well, but neighbor, I should suppose it was a very fine sight to see so many fine horses together, and prancing.' " The diary closes with a lengthy description of Morris's return from a visit to Philadelphia. Although she does, indeed, encounter several dangers, she returns safely and again notes her neighbors' lingering fears.

Another Quaker, Sally Wister (1761–1804) begins a diary when the British arrival in Philadelphia prompts her family to move to the Foulke farm in Gwynedd, Pennsylvania. Writing to her friend Deborah Norris, Wister records her opinions of American soldiers headquartered on the farm. Her primary concern is to assure Norris that although the dangers are real and her fear is great, she has not fallen in love with the handsome soldiers on whose protection she relies. At the same time, however, she is determined to exploit this opportunity for adventure. "When we were alone," she tells Morris, "our dress and lips were put in order for conquest" (October 19). The greatest challenge comes with the arrival of Captain Dandridge, "the handsomest man I ever beheld" (June 2). When he leaves, she proclaims her triumph: "But he is gone; and I think, as I have escaped thus far safe, I am quite a heroine, and need not be fearful of any of the lords of the creation for the future" (June 3).

Wister's diary provides insights about the social behavior of Revolutionary soldiers, but it also shows her ability to create fictional characters, for, throughout the diary, she imagines herself in dialogue with Norris. In these created conversations, she asks, then records, Norris's opinion of her behavior and of her appearance. The imagined Norris sometimes criticizes Wister's narrative digressions and asks her to return to the original subject of an entry. This created character unifies the diary, for while Wister's behavior changes with each soldier she meets, her responses to Norris remain consistent.

Grace Galloway (1730?–1782?) begins a diary (July 1778–1782) when the political climate necessitates the flight of her daughter and her loyalist husband, Joseph. Although Joseph is her first audience, she is never reunited with him and later seems to be writing to her daughter Betsy. Of uneven quality as a literary work and less entertaining than Wister's, Galloway's diary nevertheless contains several notable vignettes. For example, in what would be the climactic episode, the August 20, 1778, entry, Galloway describes her eviction, demonstrating an ability to reveal a range of emotions while recounting facts. When the agents of confiscation arrive, led by Charles Wilson Peale, she recalls advice from a friend and refuses to allow them into the house. Determined to portray herself as the lone defender of her family's wealth, Galloway frequently describes the plight of other women, similarly put out of their homes and driven to beg for food and shelter. These entries offer poignant, detailed sketches of the women as war victims. Although she loses her property, Galloway insists that she has maintained her dignity and protected her family's reputation.

The July 1778 inception of the diary of Mary Gould Almy (1735–1808) coincides with the arrival of the French fleet attempting to oust the British from Newport, Rhode Island. She documents widespread suffering, but the diary's literary interest is increased by her sympathetic use of setting. When she notes that many are confused by the lack of consistent information, for example, she also observes that fog has settled over Newport. On August 12, she describes rain on her window, creating a screen of tears through which her reader can view the situation:

No business going forward; all the shops still kept shut, nothing is to be seen in the streets, but carts and horses and some old wornout drivers, who care not who was king, or who rebelled against him. It was enough for them to know, if somebody did not conquer soon, they and their horses must soon die, and as the men were the heads of large families, so the horses were of equal consequence, their labor was to sport the whole; and let who would reign, their services must be paid for; indeed the man and the brute both claim our pity.

A Tory, Almy writes for her husband, who is fighting against the British. She wants him to know that, despite dangers and unlike this driver, she has maintained her commitment to English rule.

These diaries may be inspired initially by the diarists' awareness that their most treasured relationships depend on their emerging unchanged from extraordinary circumstances. As they continue to write, however, they take on another responsibility, a commitment to an authorial project. Personal survival and storytelling are, of course, easily reconciled; as Almy writes on August 7, if the shots all hit their targets, "there would not have been a soul left to tell the tale." Because the war threatened these diarists' very identity, it inspired them to portray themselves as heroes and to demonstrate their considerable literary talents.

REFERENCES

Almy, Mary Gould. "Mrs. Almy's Journal: Siege of Newport, R.I., 1778." *Newport Historical Magazine* 1 (1880–1881): 17–36.

Evans, Elizabeth. *Weathering the Storm: Women of the American Revolution.* New York: Scribner's, 1975.

Galloway, Grace Growdon. "The Diary of Grace Growdon Galloway." *Pennsylvania Magazine of History and Biography* 55 (1931): 32–94; 58 (1934): 152–189.

Kagle, Steven E. *American Diary Literature: 1620–1799.* Boston: Hall, 1979.

Morris, Margaret. *Private Journal Kept During a Portion of the Revolutionary War for the Amusement of a Sister.* Ed. John Jay Smith. Philadelphia: private printing, 1836. Rpt. Philadelphia, 1865. Rpt. New York: New York Times & Arno, 1969.
Wister, Sally. *Sally Wister's Journal: A True Narrative: Being a Quaker Maiden's Account of Her Experiences with the Officers of the Continental Army, 1777–1778.* Ed. Albert Cook Myers. Philadelphia: Ferris and Leach, 1902. Rpt. New York: New York Times & Arno, 1969. Rpt. Bedford, MA: Applewood, 1995.

Mary S. Comfort

RICE, ELMER (1892–1967). Born in Manhattan as Elmer Reizenstein, Rice spent most of his life in the New York area. He received a law degree from New York University but quickly realized he had no interest in becoming a lawyer. Desperate for money and knowing only that he wanted to write, Rice experimented with dramatic techniques and quickly established a reputation as an innovative, entertaining playwright. He achieved his greatest renown with *The Adding Machine* (1923), an expressionistic critique of modern technology, and *Street Scene* (1929), a working-class melodrama that won the Pulitzer Prize. Rice's career also included several years of service in the Federal Theatre Project, as well as the publication of three novels and numerous writings of social criticism.

The first of Rice's war-related plays was *The Iron Cross* (1915), set during World War I on an East Prussian farm attacked by the Cossacks. When a German veteran, missing an arm but decorated with medals, comes home to learn that his wife has been raped by the Cossacks, he believes she has dishonored him. However, after several months of being rejected by his country, the veteran returns and begs his wife to forgive him. Because of its German protagonists and antiwar theme, *The Iron Cross* was not successful when it first opened in 1917.

During the 1930s and early 1940s, Rice's plays frequently reflected his beliefs in socialism, pacifism, and antifascism. For instance, *We, the People* (1933) condemns the economic status quo and makes an issue of the mistreated veterans of World War I; *American Landscape* (1938) continues the call for workers' rights, while also introducing ghosts from previous American wars to criticize the military; *Flight to the West* (1940) focuses on World War II refugees, several of them wounded, fleeing from fascism; and *A New Life* (1943) uses a World War II hero back from the Pacific to denounce his father's wartime profiteering. The last play concludes with the veteran dedicating himself to change and "a new life" in America's postwar future.

REFERENCES

Palmieri, Anthony Francis. *Elmer Rice: A Playwright's Vision of America.* Rutherford, NJ: Fairleigh Dickinson University Press, 1980.
Rice, Elmer. *Minority Report: An Autobiography.* New York: Simon and Schuster, 1963.

Vanden Heuvel, Michael. *Elmer Rice: A Research and Production Sourcebook.* Westport, CT: Greenwood Press, 1996.

James I. Deutsch

RICHTER, CONRAD (1890–1968). Born in 1890 into the coal-mining community of Pine Grove, Pennsylvania, the novelist Conrad Richter went against his parents' wishes of his becoming a Lutheran minister and entered the journalism field. His first story was accepted for publication on September 6, 1913, and soon after he married Harvena Achenbach. They moved to New Mexico in 1928 for the sake of his wife's health, as well as to satisfy his curiosity about the Southwest. Although they remained there until 1950, only four of his twenty-one published volumes concern the Southwest. The influence of his eastern background is apparent, especially in what has been termed "the Ohio trilogy," *The Trees* (1940), *The Fields* (1946), and *The Town* (1950).

Whatever setting he chose, Conrad Richter's novels portray the pioneering American spirit. His Ohio trilogy centered on the conflicts in the fictitious town of Americus, Ohio, and chronicles the theme of town building. Although Richter wrote during the twentieth century, he depicted the effects of urbanization on eighteenth-and nineteenth-century America. Focusing on the town of Americus allowed him to highlight a problem common throughout the West, namely, that of the supercilious commercial interests. For example, in *The Sea of Grass*, published in 1937, he focused on the battle between cattleowners and homesteaders. Again, the theme of pioneers as ordinary people who accomplished the settling of a "foreign land" resurfaces, lending realism to the tales of pioneers and their traditions. The story is written as a personal conflict between cattleman Jim Brewton and his wife, Lutie, and the self-serving district attorney, Bruce Chamberlain, who campaigned for the homesteader cause. Richter explains how a conflict will carry over into succeeding generations if it remains unresolved, but in this case, the "old order" eventually rallies, as the honest Brewton is favored over the politically motivated Chamberlain.

Richter's realistic portrayal of life in the West continued with two similar novels, *The Light in the Forest* (1958) and *A Country of Strangers* (1966), both of which discussed the subject of Indian captivities, a realistic nightmare for many nineteenth-century families as the conflict in the West worsened. Perhaps most characteristic of the nightmares facing nineteenth-century America was the reality of the Civil War, expressed in *The Fields*. Here, too, the theme of Indian captivities resurfaces in the difficulties faced by the return of one child, Regina Hartman, from captivity many years after her original capture.

Conrad Richter continued to represent the enduring spirit of the pioneering American. In twelve of his sixteen novels, he used his female characters, the "Earth Mother" prototype, to represent the stabilizing forces on the frontier. Much of Richter's work is based on oral tradition, and even though few of his stories received critical acclaim, he did receive the Pulitzer Prize for Literature in 1951 for *The Town*, the last of the Ohio trilogy, as well as the National Book Award in 1960 for *The Waters of Kronos*. With his desire to create a realistic portrayal of early Americana, he deserves the label of historical novelist.

REFERENCES

Barnes, Robert J. *Conrad Richter*. SW Writers Series #14. Austin, TX: Steck-Vaughan, Co., 1968.

Friesen, Paul. "The Uses of Oral Tradition in the Novels of Conrad Richter." Diss. Texas Tech University, 1978.

Lance, Jerry Steven. "Settlement and Town Building in the Works of Four American Authors: James Fenimore Cooper, Caroline Kirkland, Herbert Quick, and Conrad Richter." Diss. University of Tennessee, 1995. Knoxville: University of Tennessee Press, 1995. 247–297.

Jennifer Harrison

RIDGE, JOHN ROLLIN (1827–1867). Also known as "Yellow Bird," and cited as the first Native American novelist, Ridge was born in Georgia, in the eastern Cherokee nation, during one of his tribe's bleakest moments. When he was twelve years old, his father, John Ridge (1803–1839), and grandfather, Major Ridge (1771–1839), were assassinated for supporting the 1835 Treaty of New Echot, which led to the forced Cherokee migration known as the "Trail of Tears." In 1849 Ridge killed a member of the antitreaty party and fled to California, where he worked as an author and newspaper editor.

In 1854 Ridge published his most notable literary achievement, *The Life and Adventures of Joaquin Murieta, the Celebrated California Bandit*, a novel that romanticizes the exploits of a real-life Spanish-American youth who is driven to lawlessness by the brutality of inexorable Anglo-Americans who covet and eventually appropriate his land. A hero in the fashion of Robin Hood, Murieta steals and murders only in response to the tyrannical, unscrupulous dominant culture.

Between 1857 and 1862, Ridge began to advocate the protection of American Indians while serving as an editor for several California newspapers: the *National Democrat*, the *San Francisco Herald*, the *Sacramento Bee*, and the *Red Bluff Beacon*. At this point he also became heavily involved in national politics. Insisting that the Union must be preserved at all costs, he protested the election of Abraham Lincoln, denounced the Emancipation Proclamation, and blamed abolitionists for the advent of the Civil War. Ridge's advocacy of equality for Native Americans did not extend to African Americans; he continued to espouse this selective policy of equality until his death in 1867. Ridge's poem "The Atlantic Cable," published posthumously in an 1868 collection, describes his vision of a unified America, a "Nation unto Nation . . . Together brought in knitted unity."

REFERENCES

Mondragon, Maria. "The Safe White Side of the Line: History and Disguise in John Rollin Ridge's *The Life and Adventures of Joaquin Murieta, the Celebrated California Bandit*." *American Transcendental Quarterly* 8.3 (1994): 173–187.

Parins, James. *John Rollin Ridge: His Life and Works*. Lincoln: University of Nebraska Press, 1991.

Ridge, John Rollin. *Poems*. San Francisco: Patot, 1868.

Yellow Bird. *The Life and Adventures of Joaquin Murieta, the Celebrated California Bandit*. Ed. Joseph Jackson. 1854. Norman: University of Oklahoma Press, 1955.

Priscilla Glanville

ROBERTS, KENNETH (1885–1957). Although he wrote prolifically in many areas, including history, autobiography, and journalism, Roberts is best known as the author of a number of well-done historical novels, most set in his native Maine and surrounding areas and featuring, among other incidents, military episodes of the American colonial and early republican periods. Following graduation from Cornell in 1908, Roberts worked as a journalist, eventually serving a nine-year stint as a staff correspondent for the *Saturday Evening Post*. In 1928, spurred by his interest in American history, he left this job to concentrate on his novels. Among the best of these are *Arundel* (1930), which deals with the American invasion of Canada in 1775–1776, led by Richard Montgomery and Benedict Arnold; a sequel, *Rabble in Arms* (1933), focusing on the efforts of the American armies led by Arnold and Horatio Gates to repel British general John Burgoyne's invasion of New York in 1777; *Northwest Passage* (1937), which includes the 1759 Anglo-American attack on the French-Indian town of St. Francis, led by **Robert Rogers** and his rangers; and *Lydia Bailey* (1947), depicting the capture in 1805, during the U.S. conflict with the Barbary pirates, of the Tripolitan town of Derna by U.S. Marines.

In all these works, Roberts follows the usual historical novel formula of involving fictional protagonists with well-known real-life people. He transcends this formula, however, through his meticulously researched, vividly detailed presentation of his chosen periods—Roberts read massively in primary sources such as soldiers' journals, in some cases turning up material unknown to professional historians—and his insightful characterizations of charismatic and complex military figures such as Arnold and Rogers, men equally capable of inspiring leadership and arrant egomania, intense patriotism and venal treachery.

As might be expected given his research into the memoirs of many participants in the conflicts he covers, Roberts handles eighteenth and early nineteenth-century American warfare realistically: His battle scenes, rendered from the combatants' point of view, emphasize confusion and bloodshed, but he also tacitly stresses that actual fighting was only one of many dangers soldiers and camp followers experienced during campaigns conducted across vast stretches of wilderness. For every page of combat, Roberts devotes dozens of pages to the extremes of climate and conditions of near-starvation that Montgomery's and Arnold's men endured in Canada, that Rogers's Rangers underwent as they journeyed to and from St. Francis, and that the Marines suffered on their march to Derna.

REFERENCES

Bales, Jack. *Kenneth Roberts: The Man and His Work*. Metuchen, NJ: Scarecrow Press, 1989.

Roberts, Kenneth. *I Wanted to Write*. Garden City, NY: Doubleday, 1949.

———. "The Truth about a Novel." *The Kenneth Roberts Reader*. Ed. Ben Ames Williams. Garden City, NY: Doubleday, Doran, 1945. 256–267.

Michael W. Schaefer

ROGERS, ROBERT (1731–1795). Born in Massachusetts, Robert Rogers became one of the most celebrated soldiers in colonial America. A master of frontier warfare, Rogers commanded Rogers's Rangers during the French and Indian War. After the English victory, Rogers went to England seeking promotion and while there wrote the three works discussed below. Rogers was later appointed a Royal Governor, was unsuccessfully tried for treason, and retired to England. During the American Revolution, he returned to America to organize loyalists, but when denied command, he returned to London and spent his final years in obscurity until his death on May 18, 1795.

While in London in 1765, Rogers, assisted by his private secretary, Nathaniel Potter, wrote two books and perhaps a play. The first volume published in 1765 was *The Journals of Major Robert Rogers*. The book was a detailed and highly readable account of Rogers's exploits during the war, which offered many English readers their first glimpse of frontier warfare. Rogers also described the Indians and the geography of America, but the journal is best known for its list of twenty-eight standing orders for Rogers's Rangers, which to this day form the basic doctrine of Rangers in the U.S. military. Frontier warfare rules such as "march in a single file, keeping at such a distance from each other as to prevent one shot from killing two men" were very different from the standard tactics used by the linear formations of the day, but they were vital to survival in the forests of America. Rogers's most important rule was that a man's common sense was always superior to any rule, and regulations would sometimes have to be broken in order to survive on the frontier.

Rogers's *The Concise Account of North America* (1765) is a detailed description of each of the colonies in America and was Rogers's attempt to attract official attention to his plan to scout the interior of North America for a Northwest Passage. *Ponteach, or The Savages of America, a Tragedy* appeared some months after Rogers left London. While the play's title page lists no author and Rogers never claimed authorship, the reviewers of London attributed it to him. The play, which focused on Chief Pontiac and the western Indian tribes, had a weak plot, dreadful dialogue, and was a complete disaster on the boards.

REFERENCES

Cuneo, John R. *Robert Rogers of the Rangers*. New York: Oxford University Press, 1959.

Morsberger, Robert E. "The Tragedy of Ponteach and the Northwest Passage." *Old*

Northwest: A Journal of Regional Life and Letters 4.3 (September 1978): 241–257.

Rogers, Robert. *A Concise Account of North America.* London, 1765. New York: S. R. Publications, 1966.

———. *Journals of Major Robert Rogers.* Facsimile reprint of 1765 ed. published for the author by J. Millan, London. Ann Arbor: University Microfilms, Inc., 1966.

———. *Ponteach, or The Savages of America, a Tragedy.* London, 1766. Chicago: Caxton Club, 1914.

Tanner, Laura E., and James N. Krasner. "Exposing the 'Sacred Jungle': Revolutionary Rhetoric in Robert Rogers' Ponteach." *Early American Literature* 24.1 (1989): 4–19.

Kyle F. Zelner

ROLFE, EDWIN (1901–1954). Born Solomon Fishman, this son of Jewish Russian immigrants and committed socialists found his passion early in poetry and politics. He started writing poems during high school and joined the Young Communist League at fifteen. After some dead-end working-class jobs in New York, he enrolled in 1929 in the University of Wisconsin; however, his commitment to socialism brought him back, one year later, to New York's leftist journalism. In 1937, he joined the International Brigades at Tarazona to fight in the Spanish Civil War until American volunteers were repatriated in fall 1938.

The subject matter of Rolfe's poetry is almost always historical and political. His first collection, *To My Contemporaries* (1936), on the depression and the exploitation of workers, won him the praise, by *The New Yorker*, of being "perhaps the most readable and sincere of the poets of the Left." Throughout his writing career, Rolfe remained loyal to his left politics.

Rolfe is one of the few American poets who did a sustained work about the Spanish Civil War. He recorded the experiences of American volunteers, including his own involvements as a radio programmer, political commissar, and a soldier, in *The Lincoln Battalion* (1939), a prose narrative. His reflections on the war were crystallized into *First Love and Other Poems* (1951). War for Rolfe reveals both the personal moments of death and devotion and the historical significances of human efforts. Such double consciousness is often achieved by the ambiguities of metaphoric language. In "City of Anguish," Madrid under bombardments contains both violence and the beauty of perseverance. The dead body of a fighter in "Epitaph" becomes a seed. The idealistic vision of "First Love" is embodied by both romantic love and the threat of death. "Elegia," written ten years later after the war, articulates triumphant lamentation over a lost community and a selfless cause.

After the war, Rolfe moved to Los Angeles and worked as a writer and translator for the film industry. He died of a heart attack in 1954. His third and last collection, *Permit Me Refuge* (1955), indicting the postwar McCarthy inquisition, was published posthumously.

REFERENCES

Nelson, Cary. "Lyric Politics: The Poetry of Edwin Rolfe." Introduction to *Trees Became Torches: Selected Poems.* Urbana and Chicago: University of Illinois Press, 1995.

Nelson, Cary, and Jefferson Hendricks. *Edwin Rolfe: A Biographical Essay and Guide to the Rolfe Archive at the University of Illinois at Urbana-Champaign*. Urbana: University of Illinois Press, 1990.

Rolfe, Edwin. *Collected Poems*. Ed. Cary Nelson and Jefferson Hendricks. Urbana and Chicago: University of Illinois Press, 1993.

———. *The Lincoln Battalion: The Story of the Americans Who Fought in Spain in the International Brigades*. 1939. New York: Random House, 1954.

Chih-Ping Chen

ROOSEVELT, THEODORE (1858–1919). Theodore Roosevelt, an American aristocrat by birth (in New York City) and training (Harvard, 1880), was brought up with a strong sense of noblesse oblige that eventually led him to the conclusion that America should take civilization to other parts of the world. Roosevelt acted on this belief by maintaining two careers throughout his life, one as a politician and the other as a writer, finding great success in both. His writing style was similar to his political style—forceful and opinionated. Nonetheless, two of his publications, *The Naval War of 1812* and the *Winning of the West* (both 1904), are considered definitive by serious historians. Roosevelt was also the author of *Rough Riders*, an important contemporary account of the 1898 Spanish-American War. Together, his writings exhibited an interest and wide-ranging knowledge of the world that helped make him an enormously popular writer.

Roosevelt's first and most scholarly work was *The Naval War of 1812*, a serious piece of academic writing supported by an imposing amount of documentation. First published in 1882, it was immediately hailed as a high water mark for naval history. Roosevelt drew on sources, such as official captains' letters and logbooks, that had not been touched by any other scholar. Reviewers were almost unanimous in their praise of the scholarship, sweep, and originality of *Naval War*. It was recognized on both sides of the Atlantic as a classic of naval history.

The longest of Roosevelt's works, *The Winning of the West*, was meant to be his masterpiece. The scope of the work was the spread of the United States across the American continent. "During the past three centuries," Roosevelt explained at the beginning of this work, "the spread of the English-speaking peoples over the world's waste spaces has been not only the most striking feature in the world's history, but also the event of all others most far-reaching in its importance." Marred by racism and a disregard for the more brutal aspects of settlement, *The Winning of the West* was, nevertheless, a dramatic and highly readable account of the nation's history.

When the United States faced war with Spain in 1898, Roosevelt volunteered for combat duty in Cuba. His courage and daring under fire made him a hero to his men and to many Americans at home who read newspaper accounts of his exploits. When he returned home, he decided to write what would be one of his best-selling and most profitable works, *The Rough Riders* (1899), an account of his battle experiences in Cuba. The book was enormously popular, remaining continuously in print since its publication.

"I have come to the conclusion," Roosevelt once wrote, "that I have mighty little originality of my own. What I do is try to get ideas from men whom I regard as experts along certain lines, and then try to work out those ideas." While Roosevelt was neither an original nor a profound thinker, his prose reflected his varied interests and attributes, and his works were rich in allusions to literary, historical, and natural phenomena. Through his writing, Roosevelt expressed some of his most dearly cherished hopes for the human race, and readers have responded ever since.

REFERENCES

Beale, Howard K. *Theodore Roosevelt and the Rise of America to World Power*. Baltimore and London: Johns Hopkins Press, 1956.
Brands, H. W. *T. R.: The Last Romantic*. New York: HarperCollins, 1997.
Harbaugh, William Henry. *Power and Responsibility: The Life and Times of Theodore Roosevelt*. New York: Farrar, Straus and Cudahy, 1961.

Michelle C. Morgan

ROOT, GEORGE FREDERICK (1820–1895). Born on August 20, 1820, in Sheffield, Massachusetts, George Frederick Root began his career in music as a teacher at Rutgers Female Academy and Union Theological Seminary. In the 1850s he attained some success as a composer of cantatas, hymns, and sentimental ballads, but it was not until the outbreak of the Civil War that he rose to national prominence as a songwriter and music publisher. This ascent was a product of several factors: a general upsurge in consumer demand for sheet music, primarily for household pianos; Root's highly efficient publishing system, which enabled him to get his songs into the market only days after the events they commemorated; and his skill at marrying stirring melodies and memorable, if often sentimental, lyrics.

Root's song "The First Gun Is Fired! May God Protect the Right!" was on sale by April 15, 1861, only three days after the Confederate bombardment of Fort Sumter. With similar rapidity, Root answered Abraham Lincoln's 1862 call for an additional 300,000 volunteers with the recruiting song "The Battle Cry of Freedom," arguably the Union army's most popular marching tune, with its stirring chorus:

> The Union forever, Hurrah boys, hurrah!
> Down with the Traitor, up with the Star;
> While we rally 'round the flag boys, rally once again,
> Shouting the Battle Cry of Freedom.

Root's "Just Before the Battle, Mother," published in 1863, became a sentimental parlor favorite thanks to its reaffirmation of the lonely soldier's moral purity even in the hellish environment of war. Its narrator declares,

Just before the battle, Mother,
I am thinking most of you;
While upon the field we're watching
With the enemy in view.
Farewell, Mother, you may never press me to your
heart again;
But, O, you'll not forget me, Mother, if I'm
numbered with the slain.

In 1864, when public concern was rising in the North about the conditions of Southern military prisons, Root provided "Tramp! Tramp! Tramp! (or The Prisoner's Hope)." Its bright marching tune is nearly belied by the despairing lyrics, in which a Union prisoner bemoans his captivity, particularly his separation from his mother, until the chorus introduces hope of liberation:

Tramp, tramp, tramp, the boys are marching,
Cheer up, comrades, they will come,
And beneath the starry flag
We shall breathe the air again,
Of the freeland in our own beloved home.

Root continued to write sentimental ballads and hymns after the war. He also joined his brother's Chicago publishing firm, Root & Cady, and promoted the careers of Henry C. Work and other composers.

REFERENCES

Epstein, Dena, J. *Music Publishing in Chicago before 1871: The Firm of Root & Cady, 1858–1871*. Detroit: Information Coordinators, 1969.
Glass, Paul, and Louis C. Singer. *Singing Soldiers: A History of the Civil War in Song*. New York: Da Capo, 1975.
Root, George Frederick. *The Story of a Musical Life*. Cincinnati, OH: J. Church, 1891.
Silber, Irwin. *Songs of the Civil War*. New York: Columbia University Press, 1960.

Randal W. Allred

ROWLANDSON, MARY (ca. 1635–1711). Born in England, Mary Rowlandson was the daughter of John White, a founder of the town of Lancaster in Massachusetts. Mary married Lancaster's first minister, the Reverend Joseph Rowlandson in about 1656. During King Philip's War, in February 1676, Lancaster was attacked by Indians who looted the town and took Mrs. Rowlandson, three of her children, and nineteen of her neighbors captive. Surviving captivity for almost three months, during which time she witnessed the death of her youngest child from wounds and exposure, Rowlandson was ransomed from the Indians and released in May. After the later release of the two remaining children, the family moved to Connecticut in 1677. Her husband died in 1678 and Rowlandson quickly remarried. She died in January 1711 around seventy-six years of age.

Mary Rowlandson's narrative of captivity, *The Sovereignty and Goodness of*

God, was published in 1682. Here is the first, most famous, and most complex of a truly American literary form, the captivity narrative. Rowlandson's work brings to the forefront of critical inquiry many crucial issues about interracial warfare and religion. Rowlandson portrays herself as the exemplary devout Puritan forced to confront and live among Indian "savages." Taken away from all that was familiar and comforting for such a long time, she felt tempted to stop resisting her captors' enticements and lead a peaceful life amid Indian society. However, in the end, Mary Rowlandson always put her faith in God and realized that her ordeal was His test of her. To resist temptation, Rowlandson turned to the one source of comfort left her—the Word of God in the Bible, which gave her the power to wait for salvation. Rowlandson's eventual redemption and return to her family and society were proof that God was all powerful and that He did reward faith with justice and mercy. Rowlandson argues that her test and ultimate reward mirrored the much bigger trial God had put New England through; and the colonial victory over the Indian "savages" was proof of the worthiness of Puritan society. Her message nicely coincided with many conservative ministers of the day, especially **Increase Mather**, who saw the war as a warning of a decline in religious feelings in the society.

REFERENCES

Logan, Lisa. "Mary Rowlandson's Captivity and the 'Place' of the Woman Subject." *Early American Literature* 28.3 (1993): 255–277.

Rowlandson, Mary. *The Sovereignty and Goodness of God by Mary Rowlandson: With Related Documents*. Ed. Neal Salisbury. Bedford Series of History and Culture. Boston: Bedford Books, 1997.

Salisbury, Neal. "Introduction: Mary Rowlandson and Her Removes." *The Sovereignty and Goodness of God by Mary Rowlandson: With Related Documents*. Ed. Neal Salisbury. Bedford Series of History and Culture. Boston: Bedford Books, 1997.

Slotkin, Richard, and James K. Folsom. "Mary Rowlandson: Captive Witness." *So Dreadfull a Judgment: Puritan Responses to King Philip's War, 1676–1677*. Middletown, CT: Wesleyan University Press, 1978.

Toulouse, Teresa A. " 'My Own Credit': Strategies of (E)Valuation in Mary Rowlandson's Captivity Narrative." *American Literature* 64.4 (1992): 655–676.

Kyle F. Zelner

RUNYON, DAMON (1880–1946). When one thinks of the literature of war, the name Damon Runyon seldom comes to mind. He is better known for three jocular story series about a young Brooklyn couple, the residents of a turn-of-the-century western town, and—his true claim to fame—the crooks and tinhorn gamblers of depression-era Broadway.

The writer was born Alfred Damon Runyan in Pueblo, Colorado, and by his early teens was turning out copy for a local newspaper. (He changed the spelling of his name at about this time, in response to a typesetter's error.) In 1898, seventeen-year-old Runyon lied about his age and joined the 18th Minnesota Volunteers, hoping to see action in the Philippines. By the time he arrived in

Manila, the conflict had ended; the boy spent the next eleven months standing guard over prisoners of war and writing fanciful accounts of his supposed "adventures" for the camp newspaper.

Back in Colorado, Runyon began publishing army-related poems in major magazines. Most were doggerel imitations of Rudyard Kipling, as exemplified by "Hikin'," published in *The Century* in October 1909:

> Gravel agitators on a long, hard hike
> —Hep!
> Kickin' up an orflfl dust along the dreary pike
> —Hep!
> Baynit scabbard draggin' o' yer foot-tracks out;
> Mouth a-pantin' open like a landed mountain trout;
> try ter lag a little, an' you hear the sergeant shout:
> "Hep!"

Runyon would later release his war poems as the book-length collections *The Tents of Trouble: Ballads of the Wanderbund and Other Verse* (1911) and *Rhymes of the Firing Line* (1912).

Hired by William Randolph Hearst's *New York American*, Runyon soon made a name for himself as a sportswriter; he also covered straight news as needed, including firsthand accounts of General Pershing's 1916 pursuit of bandit chief Pancho Villa. In 1918, he traveled to France as a war correspondent, supplying his paper with human-interest bulletins on American troops in the Argonne and, later, the occupation forces in Coblentz. The following year, he returned to the United States and began alternating top-quality sportswriting with the slang-filled short stories that would bring him worldwide fame.

The author's Second World War tales are among his grimmest, although they display his usual sardonic wit. In "A Light in France" (*Collier's*, 15 January 1944), a strongarm man, a swindler, and a gangster in self-imposed exile find themselves torn between their own self-interests and resentment toward the Nazis who have taken over their adopted home. At the story's climax, the trio douse a Gestapo man with gasoline and set him alight to serve as a beacon to Allied planes; the resulting hail of bombs kills two of the Americans and the French heroine, leaving only the gangster alive to tell the tale.

Alfred Damon Runyon died of cancer in December 1946. As per his will, air ace Eddie Rickenbacker scattered his friend's ashes over his beloved Broadway.

REFERENCES

"Damon Runyon." *Twentieth-Century Authors*. Ed. Stanley Kunitz and Howard Haycraft. New York: H. W. Wilson, 1955. 1211–1212.
D'Hri, Patricia Ward. *Damon Runyon*. Boston: Twayne, 1982.
Hoyt, Edwin P. *A Gentleman of Broadway*. Boston: Little, Brown, 1964.

Katherine Harper

RUSS, MARTIN (1931–   ). Born in Newark, New Jersey, Martin Russ left college to serve in the Marines in 1952–1953. Since that time, he has been a memoirist, a novelist, a freelance journalist, a reviewer of books, a teacher of writing, a writer about the teaching of writing, and the author of television scripts. However, his time in Korea as a combat Marine in the Korean War is the defining experience that lies behind the most important of his works, *The Last Parallel: A Marine's War Journal* (1957).

One of the best-known Korean War narratives, *The Last Parallel* is perhaps the best written. It endures because the immediacy of its contemporaneous account is nicely complemented by the author's wit and sense of humor, rare elements in the sometimes dull world of war memoirs. Noting with sardonic precision the distinguishing characteristics of his own *Sitzkrieg* world in the final year of the war, Russ establishes a parallel with World War I that is conscious, sustained, and appropriate. Perhaps reflecting a progression in self-awareness over the course of the author's experience, the narrative moves from an initial tone of something like erudite silliness to a much more subdued conclusion. Although the prose is clever, literate, and often humorous throughout, the experience of combat does occasion some somber thoughts effectively expressed. This remains a valuable book in several ways: as a literate memoir by a well-educated young Marine caught in the most egalitarian of circumstances; as a contemporaneous account of the nature of warfare in the latter phase of the Korean conflict; and, not least, through the author's sketches, diagrams, and descriptions, as an informal primer on the conduct of trench-based operations during that period.

The novel *War Memorial* (1967) is a lesser accomplishment. Somewhat odd but nonetheless interesting, the story is that of World War II Marine veteran Joe Shasta, a quirky itinerant whose life clearly reached its peak at the bloody battle of Tarawa. Shasta has difficulty accepting that the prosaic salesman's life of Barney Metraw belongs to the same person who resides in Joe's memory as the larger-than-life lieutenant of the previous war. As the novel ends, Joe seems headed off to rejoin the Marines to find another great leader. Flashbacks to action at Tarawa and even some casualty figures at the end of the book combine to make this indeed a kind of "war memorial" despite its eccentric cast of characters.

Russ's interest in the experience of combat found further expression in his nonfictional *Happy Hunting Ground* (1968), an account of a half-year's Vietnam sojourn with American, Vietnamese, and Australian troops as an accredited but freelance correspondent. In 1975, he underscored his interest in the World War II operation at Tarawa by publishing a history of the battle, *Line of Departure: Tarawa*, written for a popular audience. His other books are *Half Moon Haven* (1959), *Showdown Semester* (1980), and *Breakout* (1999), a narrative of the Chosin Reservoir campaign.

REFERENCE

Brady, James. "In Step with Martin Russ." *Parade Magazine* 25 April 1999: 18.

James R. Kerin, Jr.

S

SALTER, JAMES (1925–   ). Born in New Jersey as James Horowitz, Salter was raised in New York City and attended the Horace Mann School in Riverdale. Accepting an appointment to West Point in 1942, he graduated in 1945 with his accelerated wartime class. Salter then began a twelve-year career as an air force pilot, a career he abandoned in 1957 to pursue his literary interests. This change was made possible by the publication of his first novel, *The Hunters*, which is loosely based on Salter's six months of service in Korea in 1951. Like his hero, Salter flew 100 combat missions. The novel was made into a movie in 1958.

Salter's next novel, *The Arm of Flesh*, was less successful. However, his next four works earned critical acclaim: *A Sport and a Pastime* (1967), *Light Years* (1975), *Solo Faces* (1979), and *Dusk and Other Stories* (1988). The last won the PEN/**Faulkner** Award. Slater also wrote several film scripts, the best known of which is *Downhill Racer* (1969). A writer's writer, Salter has never won a large general readership. Considering *The Hunters* apprentice work, Salter did not permit its republication until he prepared a revised version.

First published in 1956 and reissued in a revised edition in 1997, *The Hunters* is a classic both of the Korean War and of military aviation. Salter's stunning prose captures the thrill of combat flying as well as the sights and sounds of life on the airfield. The novel's central character, Cleve Connell, is an experienced fighter pilot in his early thirties who has never before seen combat action. His deeply felt ambition to be recognized by the only means possible, shooting down MIGs, is thwarted over and over again, and with it his sense of self-worth is tested. For while bad luck plagues him, favor smiles upon Lieutenant Pell, a flashy and talented younger man whose successes, to some, are suspect. The novel examines this irrational but telling measure of a man's worth under combat conditions. Though Cleve is a finer individual and a caring leader, Pell puts more "kill" stars on his plane. Tension is raised as Cleve's chances slip away; he has a mere one kill as the end of his 100-mission tour approaches. One of his last gestures, his attribution to the downed Billy Hunter of a major kill earned by Cleve—the taking down of North Korea's ace pilot—restores a sense of emotional balance to Cleve's last days and further separates him from glory-hound Pell. Tension between these two men, its effect on those with whom they fly, and the terrain and weather of Korea are all handled with precision.

Salter's memoir, *Burning the Days: Recollection* (1997), includes many stories of his air force career. The chapter "A Single Daring Act" reprises some of the experiences that Salter transformed into *The Hunters*.

REFERENCES

Begley, Adam. "A Few Well-Chosen Words." *New York Times Magazine* 28 October 1990: 40+.

Dowie, William. "A Final Glory: The Novels of James Salter." *College English* 50 (January 1988): 74–88.

Philip K. Jason

SANDBURG, CARL (1878–1967). Carl Sandburg was born in Galesburg, Illinois, a small town near Chicago whose inhabitants were to prove rich sources of material for his poetic works. Sandburg's interest in the life of Illinois's most famous son, Abraham Lincoln, inspired his great successes as a historian and a biographer. He won two Pulitzer Prizes: one in 1940 for his *Abraham Lincoln: The War Years* (1939) and another in 1950 for his *Complete Poems* (1950). He also won a Pulitzer Special Prize in 1919 for *Cornhuskers* (1918), a collection of poems.

Sandburg's military career was brief; he served in 1898 with the Sixth Illinois Regiment during the Spanish-American War, and in 1899 he was appointed to West Point, though he left shortly thereafter. Sandburg's poetry primarily celebrates the midwestern landscapes and cityscapes that he cherished and the people who make those places come to life. But several poems about war are scattered throughout his corpus of work. In a cycle entitled "War Poems (1914–15)" published in *Chicago Poems* (1916), Sandburg turns an ironic eye upon war, lamenting the gratuitousness of death and loss in combat and revealing the complicity of ordinary citizens in the progress of war's destruction. He continues to demystify war in "Long Guns," published in *Smoke and Steel* (1920), in which he undermines the argument that guns maintain a nation, by extrapolating it to its absurd implication that guns can be the instruments for the fulfillment of all desire. In "War Time," a cycle of poems written around the time of World War II and included in the "New Section" of his *Complete Poems*, Sandburg becomes more abstract and less polemical, celebrating freedom and its reasonable defense by means of war. In "Peace between Wars," Sandburg meditates upon the ways in which war and peace define one another.

Sandburg's writing about war is not restricted to his poetry. As a follow-up to his 1926 two-volume biography *Abraham Lincoln: The Prairie Years*, Sandburg wrote *Abraham Lincoln: The War Years*, a four-volume work published in 1939. In 1942, Sandburg published *Storm over the Land*, an account of the Civil

War that includes material taken from *Abraham Lincoln: The War Years*. By combining history and biography in such a way, Sandburg's projects reveal not only the importance of Lincoln's leadership to the outcome of the Civil War but how that conflict transformed and canonized Lincoln himself in the historical imagination. A one-volume condensation of the two biographies was published in 1954 as *Abraham Lincoln: The Prairie Years and the War Years*. In 1943, he published *Home Front Memo*, a collection of essays and a few poems, some about topics related to war, others addressing such diverse subjects as political personalities, literature, and history.

Sandburg's historical novel *Remembrance Rock* (1948), the only novel he ever published, is a fictionalized account of American history from the country's beginning through World War II. Not surprisingly, Sandburg's fictional American history is, like his historical texts, a collection of the stories and experiences of those who have made this narrative possible, ordinary people upon whom the currents of history have brushed most profoundly.

REFERENCES

Callahan, North. *Carl Sandburg: His Life and Works*. University Park: Pennsylvania State University Press, 1986.

Pfennig, Gladys Zehn. *Carl Sandburg, Poet and Patriot*. Minneapolis, MN: T. S. Denison, 1963.

Sandburg, Carl. *Abraham Lincoln: The Prairie Years and the War Years*. New York: Harcourt, Brace, 1954.

———. *Abraham Lincoln: The War Years*. 4 vols. New York: Harcourt, Brace, 1939.

———. *The Complete Poems of Carl Sandburg*. Rev. and exp. ed. San Diego: Harcourt Brace Jovanovich, 1970.

———. *Home Front Memo*. New York: Harcourt, Brace, 1943.

———. *Remembrance Rock*. New York: Harcourt, Brace, 1948.

Thomas March

SCOLLARD, CLINTON (1860–1932). Poet and academician Clinton Scollard was born in Clinton, New York. He received his A.B. degree in 1881 and his A.M. in 1884, both from Hamilton College. Scollard continued his graduate studies at Cambridge and Harvard, where he met Frank Dempster Sherman, who became a lifelong friend and collaborator on one work—*A Southern Flight* (1907). Scollard taught English at Brooklyn Polytechnic Institute and at Hamilton. He was married twice, to Georgia Brown, from 1890 to 1924, and to poet and anthologist Jessie Rittenhouse, from 1924 until his death.

While not an innovative poet, Scollard was a prolific and popular one, producing over forty books during his lifetime. Even when he wrote about the brutality of war, his poetry remained optimistic: He focused on courage and sacrifice. Scollard's earliest work consisted largely of poems written in the miniature style that was then popular in America. He also wrote poetry about the open road in the manner of his Harvard classmate Bliss Carman. But by 1898, with his volume *A Man at Arms* (1898), Scollard turned his attention to poetry depicting patriotism and men at war. *Pro Patria: Verses Chiefly Patriotic* (1909) deals primarily with the Revolutionary War. In this collection, Scollard explores and exploits such symbols of patriotism as the flag in "Ballad of Old Glory." "The Flag to the Wind" explains the significance of the flag: "With my Stripes and my gathering Stars, / That I stand for a nation's weal / Supreme o'er the roar of wars." He also addresses specific battles in such poems as "At Tennent Church" and "The Way to the Neutral Ground."

The onset of World War I inspired six collections published between 1915 and 1919. Representative volumes are *The Vale of Shadows and Other Verses of the Great War* and *Ballads, Patriotic and Romantic* (both 1915). May of his poems during this period dealt with the European conflict, such as "On an American Soldier of Fortune Slain in France." In this poem Scollard acknowledges the great debt that America owes to its soldiers:

> You who sought the great adventure
> That the blind fates hold in store,
> Have beyond our mortal censure
> Passed forever evermore . . .
> We, who cling to freedom, hail you
> Son of never vanquished sires,
> Knowing courage did not fail you
> When you faced the battle fires.

Scollard also wrote about other American wars including the Civil War, the Spanish-American War, and the Revolutionary War, usually depicting the bravery of men in battle. Scollard suffered a mental breakdown in 1922 and published only two more books before his death in 1932. He was survived by his wife, Jessie B. Rittenhouse, a critic and anthologist who helped shape his career and his reputation.

REFERENCES

Benet, Laura. Rev. of *Singing Heart*, by Clinton Scollard. *New York Times Book Review* 20 May 1934: 20.

Firkins, O. W. Rev. of *Poems*, by Clinton Scollard. *Nation* 15 April 1915: 430.

Rittenhouse, Jessie B. "Memoir." *The Singing Heart: Selected Lyrics and Other Poems of Clinton Scollard*. Ed. Jessie B. Rittenhouse. New York: Macmillan, 1934.

———. *The Younger American Poets*. Boston: Little, Brown, 1904.

Randall Clark

SCOTT, EVELYN (1893–1963). Born Elsie Dunn in Clarksville, Tennessee, this author was educated at Sophie Newcombe College and Tulane University. In 1913, she ran off to Brazil with Frederick Creighton Wellman, a member of the Tulane medical faculty and a married man. The couple called themselves Cyril and Evelyn Scott, and that was the name Dunn used when she began to write poems, articles for magazines, and novels.

Scott's first published novels, *The Narrow House* (1921), *Narcissus* (1922), and *The Golden Door* (1925), comprise a trilogy examining marriage and family life in a realistic manner. Scott then produced three works of fiction dealing with American history: *Migrations* (1927), a short story collection focused on the westward movement to California; *The Wave* (1929), a novel about the Civil War; and *Calendar of Sin* (1931), a novel of American life from Reconstruction to 1914. *The Wave*, dramatizing the period from the Confederate firing on Fort Sumter in 1861 to the 1865 parade of the victorious Union army through Washington, D.C., is Scott's most critically and popularly successful work. It is notable for its experimental narrative techniques, which bring the events of the war alive in styles that range from realistic to impressionistic. Remaining objective about the Confederate cause despite her Southern heritage, Scott concentrates in an almost Marxist manner on the deterministic impact of great, impersonal historic forces upon ordinary men and women largely unable to understand what happens to them. Even unusual men, the Lincoln, Davis, Grant, and Lee of Scott's novel, cannot escape history's control, although they do sense its power.

Scott's later work had little commercial or critical success. *Eva Gay* (1932) dramatizes her years with Cyril Scott, from whom she parted in 1928. *Breathe Upon These Slain* (1934) and *Bread and a Sword* (1937) were critical of Soviet communism at a time when such criticism was not popular. Her last novel, *The Shadow of the Hawk* (1941), returns to her earlier realistic treatment of the family. The memoir *Background in Tennessee* (1937) examines her childhood and its impact on her work. In 1930, Scott married British writer John Metcalfe. Scott died in New York City in 1963 and is buried in Linden, New Jersey.

REFERENCES

Bach, Peggy. *"The Wave*: Evelyn Scott's Civil War." *Southern Literary Journal* 17.2 (1985): 18–32.
Callard, D. A. *Pretty Good for a Woman: The Enigmas of Evelyn Scott*. New York: Norton, 1985.
Welker, Robert L. *"Liebestod* with a Southern Accent." *Essays in American Literature in Memory of Richard Croom Beatty*. Ed. William E. Walker and Robert L. Welker. Nashville, TN: Vanderbilt University Press, 1964.

Robert C. Petersen

SECOND WORLD WAR. World War II saw U.S. armed forces deployed all over the globe for nearly four years—on land, on sea, in the air. According to recent estimates, about 50 million people died during the war years in combat, through bombing, in prisoner of war (POW) and concentration camps, or through famine and disease induced by the war. American G.I.s not only faced a multitude of different theaters of operation and types of military action; they also had to learn to live with the awesome destructive power unleashed by the first U.S. nuclear bombs, with the horror they found when liberating Nazi concentration camps, with prolonged POW experience, and with their new role as members of an occupation force responsible for reeducating, administrating, and reconstructing a good number of morally, socially, and economically devastated countries. Not surprisingly, the body of literature generated by this war is much greater in number, has much more variety in geographical settings and in depicted experience, and reveals considerably wider thematic variety than that of the previous world war. Most authors chose the form of the novel to tell their stories, and there are (depending on how inclusive the definition) between 1,500 and 2,000 of them, the majority published between 1945 and 1958. But there is an abundant body of poetry as well as several significant plays that reflect varied understandings of "the good war."

In contrast to the situation of World War I, the Japanese attack on Pearl Harbor on December 7, 1941, created a general consensus in the United States about the moral and political necessity of fighting the Japanese military hegemony in Asia and its fascist European allies. Attitudes toward war itself had become, due to the experience of World War I, much more pragmatic and provided little ground for the disillusionment of romantic expectations; war was seen as an unpleasant obligation rather than an opportunity for individual heroism or male initiation rituals. Moreover, military strategy had changed significantly: The command as well as the G.I.s had learned to efficiently employ high-tech weaponry in highly mobile battle structures. No longer did foot soldiers die by the tens of thousands in prolonged trench warfare, leading writers to question the meaning of it all. Now, even battles with high casualty rates, like the retaking of the South Pacific islands or the D-Day landing in Normandy, were accepted because they led to concrete military successes. Last but not least, in 1945 the United States emerged as the victorious and dominant military power, unchallenged until the 1950s.

The rich literary legacy of World War I proved adaptable to the experience of the next generation of authors who, sooner than they had expected after the "war to end all wars," were living through one of their own. In his postwar *The Literary Situation* (1954), Malcolm Cowley makes this somewhat tongue-in-cheek assessment:

One might say that a great many novels of the Second World War are based on Dos Passos for structure, since they have collective heroes in the Dos Passos fashion, and since he invented a series of structural devices for dealing with such heroes in unified works of fiction. At the same time, they are based on Scott Fitzgerald for mood, on Steinbeck for humor, and on Hemingway for action and dialogue.

In fact, the major point of criticism concerning American novels of World War II was, until the 1960s, that they were neither formally nor thematically innovative, nor did they have the wide and powerful effects on their audience that many novels about the previous war could achieve. There is some truth to this charge, as the first generation of World War II authors did not feel an immediate need to look for new and adequate forms of literary discourse. One should remember, though, that **cummings**, **Dos Passos**, **Faulkner**, Fitzgerald, and

Hemingway constituted an innovative minority among *their* contemporaries and that it was the succeeding generation of the World War II writers who widely adopted and also developed their modernist styles of writing. Yet the new war also spawned new modes of literary discourse—in fact, one can argue that novels like John Hawkes's *The Cannibal* (1948), **Joseph Heller**'s *Catch-22* (1959), **Kurt Vonnegut**'s *Slaughterhouse-Five* (1969), or **Thomas Pynchon**'s *Gravity's Rainbow* (1976) pioneered different forms of *postmodern* discourse not only in war literature but in American literature in general.

The majority of authors, though, employ modernist and psychological-realist discourse and place their heroes and events firmly into a chronologically structured historical context that includes detailed information about the characters' lives and fates before, during, and after the war; at the end, as readers we have a sense of closure and the feeling that we can explain and understand the things that happen in this fictional world. Primary subject matter includes descriptions of battle senses; the fate of a military unit and its individual members; and themes like comradeship, courage, cowardice, endurance, the experience of death and danger, as well as the often problematic relations between officers and the lower ranks.

"Combat novels" are the most numerous group: They focus on concrete missions that are rendered in detail and without much concern for a wider contextual framework and have very often become the basis for popular World War II movies. Only few of them, though, rise above the level of what John Keegan, in his 1976 *The Face of Battle*, called the "ZapBlatt-Banzai-Gott im Himmel-Bayonet in the Guts" adventure story. A notable exception is **Harry Brown**'s *A Walk in the Sun* (1944), the tersely told story of a company's mission in southern Italy. Brown reveals the existentialist underpinnings of Hemingway's factual style and also convincingly illustrates the effects of what has been called "combat numbness," that is, the prolonged exposure to the violence of war, on the soldiers. The main character, Corporal Tyne, also sets the tone for the soldiers' general attitude toward war when he contemplates, as he and his men are about to storm an ominously harmless-looking farmhouse: "What they were about to do was merely a job. . . . It was the war. It was the job. It was *their* job. Get it done and then relax, that was the thing to do." Compared to Brown's plain style, later novels often show more action, suspense, and patriotic fervor, as, for example, **Leon Uris**'s *Battle Cry* (1953), Glenn Sire's *The Deathmakers* (1960), Alistair McLean's *The Guns of Navarone* (1957), or **James Jones**'s *The Thin Red Line* (1962). Different again from these, John O. Killens, in *And Then We Heard the Thunder* (1962), presents an impressively realistic portrait of the African American experience in the U.S. armed forces.

Another identifiable group of novels expands its vision beyond the immediate horizon of combat and problematizes the role of the military as a hierarchic structure within a democratic society. Authors often employ Dos Passos's techniques of the collectivist novel, present the military as a microcosm of American society, and tend to be critical of the excessively authoritarian behavior of the military command. Such works include World War II "classics" like **Norman Mailer**'s *The Naked and the Dead* (1948), James Jones's *From Here to Eternity* (1951), **James Gould Cozzens**'s *Guard of Honor* (1948), or **Herman Wouk**'s *The Caine Mutiny* (1951). A related group of authors provides an even stronger critical focus that clearly points to its roots in the progressive and socially oriented movements of the 1930s. Their novels are examples of what Frederick J. Hoffman (in his 1964 *The Mortal No: Death and the Modern Imagination*) called "ideological melodrama"; they often feature a liberal "intellectual who must mature, the external menace or bogey, the signs of inner corruption that resembles the enemy." Among these novels are **Irwin Shaw**'s best-selling *The Young Lions* (1948), Stefan Heym's muckraking *The Crusaders* (1948), **Anton Myrer**'s *The Big War* (1958), **John Hersey**'s chilling "faction" *Hiroshima* (1946) and his psychological case study *The War Lover* (1959). The authors of both groups often filter their view of individual (military) society and the war through evolutionary models of Freudian or Marxian origin and present Nazism and fascism as a regression to lower forms of cultural/individual development.

In view of the broad prowar consensus during the war and the general climate of the Cold War years that was not very congenial to critical voices or texts, it was a clear sign of intellectual sincerity and vitality that American literature brought forth a remarkable number of novels with critical perspectives. Mailer, Shaw, Heym, Hayes, and Hersey are foremost among those who, while supporting the goals of this particular war, point to its potentially dangerous effects on the victors. However, no matter how severe the critique, those authors never attempt to discard basic American values. Rather, they warn of abuses of power and of corruption within the United States. They can thus be seen as early critics of what at the end of the Eisenhower years became generally known as the "military-industrial complex."

The fact that the war brought Americans into contact with a multitude of different cultures also yielded rich literary harvest; a good number of novels explicitly or implicitly compare American and other cultures, not always completely in favor of the American way of life. In *The Gallery* (1947), finished shortly before he died near Naples, **John Horne Burns** portrays the suffering of Italian civilians with great sensitivity and sympathy, as do John Hersey in *A Bell for Adano* (1944) and Alfred Hayes in *The Girl on the Via Flaminea* (1949). **James Michener**'s *Sayonara* (1954) and *Tales of the South Pacific* (1947) counteract prevailing negative attitudes toward Asians with tales of love and humanism.

In this category we also find many novels by women authors, based on their widespread experience of service in noncombatant units or as journalists. Cathleen Coyle's *To Hold Against Famine* (1942), Grace Hill's *Time of the Singing Birds* (1944), **Martha Gellhorn**'s *Wine of Astonishment* (1948), Susan Cooper's *Dawn of Fear* (1970), and Janet Hickman's *The Stones* (1976) offer the readers powerful stories about what happened behind the lines. A more recent imagining of women's roles is **Marge Piercy**'s *Gone to Soldiers* (1987). Perhaps the classic noncombatant novel by a male writer is **Thomas Heggen**'s *Mr. Roberts* (1946).

The postmodern novels of World War II, most of them already written under the shadow of the escalating Vietnam conflict, present quite different (fictional) realities. Most important, "war" in these novels is no longer a concrete historical event limited in space and time but becomes a complex metaphor for our contemporary industrialized society in which traditional distinctions between "peace" and "war" are rapidly losing their validity. War threatens to become a way of life, dominated by the business interests of global military-industrial corporations: As Heller puts it in *Catch-22*, "Business boomed on every battlefront." Accordingly, in novels like Hawkes's *The Cannibal*, Heller's *Catch-22*, Vonnegut's *Slaughterhouse-Five*, or Pynchon's *Gravity's Rainbow*, war is global and ever present. Peace exists, if at all, only temporarily, in the shape of ideal contrasting spaces to the fictional world of war—Sweden in *Catch-22*, Tralfamadore in *Slaughterhouse-Five*—and inevitably turns out to be but a projection of the narrator's protagonist's wishful thinking. Vonnegut's "There is nothing intelligent to say about a massacre" also indicates that to make sense of the horrors of war, to explain events and provide a sense of understanding and closure, has become impossible.

American playwrights, perhaps because of the numerous movies about the war, did not seriously respond to that historical event. **Lillian Hellman** in *Watch on the Rhine* (1941) successfully alerted Americans to the dangers of fascism and in *The Searching Wind* (1944) portrayed the failure of naive liberalism, but the plays' merits today are of the political rather than the dramatic kind. Perhaps one of the most influential comedies about the war was Donald Bevan's and Edmund Trzcinski's *Stalag 17*, based on the authors' experience in an Austrian POW camp; it was also made into a successful motion picture by Billy Wilder in 1952 and became the prototype of many other war comedies. Far less successful was Harry Brown's *A Sound of Hunting* (produced 1945, published 1946). Of the great American dramatists after the war, only **Arthur Miller** uses the war as a significant, if not central, structural element in his first successful play, *All My Sons* (1947).

Many more American poets wrote about World War II than did about World War I, though there is nothing of the heroic idealism or personal drama of **Alan Seeger** or **Joyce Kilmer**. The new style is nonchalant, cool, and laconic, with a preference for brevity and minimalism; a good example is **Randall Jarrell**'s five-line classic "The Death of the Ball Turret Gunner." Serious ethical questioning, as in Richard Eberhart's "The Fury of Aerial Bombardment" or in Phyllis McGinley's or **William Meredith**'s poetry, has become rare, and the pervasive tone is one of irony combined with matter-of-fact understatement, as in the poems by **Richard Wilbur**, W. H. Auden, Kenneth Patchen, **Louis Simpson, James Dickey, Howard Nemerov, Karl Shapiro**, and **John Ciardi**. Somewhat more engaged are the polished verses of **Lincoln Kirstein** and the book-length, free-verse narrative by Peter Bowman, *Beach Red* (1945), which was a Book-of-the-Month Club selection.

REFERENCES

Fussell, Paul. *Wartime: Understanding and Behavior in the Second World War.* New York: Oxford University Press, 1989.

Hoelbling, Walter. *Fiktionen vom Krieg im neueren amerikanischen Roman.* Tübingen: Gunter Narr, 1987.

Pisapia, Bianca Maria, Ugo Ribeo, and Anna Scacchi, eds. *Red Badges of Courage. Wars and Conflicts in American Culture.* Rome: Bulzoni Editore, 1998.

Stokesbury, Leon, ed. *Articles of War. A Collection of American Poetry about World War II.* Introduction by Paul Fussell. Fayetteville: University of Arkansas Press, 1990.

Waldmeir, Joseph. *American Novels of the Second World War.* The Hague: Mouton. 1971.

Winkler, Allan M. *The Politics of Propaganda. The Office of War Information 1942–1945.* New Haven, CT: Yale University Press, 1978.

Walter W. Hoelbling

SEEGER, ALAN (1888–1916). For some, the posthumous publication of Alan Seeger's *Poems* (1916) and *Letters and Diary* (1917) marks a significant turn in American sympathies toward the plight of the Allies in World War I, particularly the cause of France he gave his life to defend. Seeger's rhythmic style, genteel abstractions, and vivid imagery brought home for many Americans not only the import of the struggle occurring on the European continent but also the passive resolve of the soldier facing inevitable death. His poems document the epic struggle of freedom over tyranny and commemorate the individual struggles of the soldiers serving next to him in an American volunteer unit in the French Foreign Legion.

Seeger spent his early years on Staten Island until the collapse of his father's business necessitated a family move to New York City. Tutored at home, Seeger eventually attended Harvard University, graduating in 1910. The next two years saw Seeger living in Greenwich Village with bohemians and radicals, where he supported himself writing periodic freelance newspaper articles or selling the occasional poem. Convinced that New York was stifling his creative energies and jeopardizing his chances for recognition, Seeger joined a sizable group of young American intellectuals and artists in Paris in the spring of 1912. Here he completed "Juvenalia," a mixture of early poems and translations later integrated posthumously into Seeger's only published poetry collection.

When Germany swept through Belgium and into France during the early days of World War I, Seeger and other Americans rushed to defend their adopted country by forming the American Volunteer Corps. Weeks spent drilling and digging trenches gave way to a march to the front in October 1914, eventually into the Champagne region of France. Where vines should have been replete with grapes, Seeger instead saw only blackened countryside, a graveyard of human struggle. In "Champagne 1914–1915," Seeger attempts to look beyond the carnage to a time when the fertile ground of France would spring forth with life once again, fertilized by the bodies of the dead interred there and sanctified by the honor, glory, and camaraderie expended to preserve the soil. Seeger's persona longs to believe that if his blood shall be spilled in the same ground where others have shed theirs, his own memory shall be reevoked with those of his noble comrades in celebration of each year's plentiful harvest. They require little more than to be saluted in a silent toast, drunk from the wine "ripened where they fell."

June 1915 saw Seeger and his comrades billeted on the banks of the Aisne River, the inspiration for his fine war poem "The Aisne (1914–1915)." Seeger's poem is an assurance to those dead who seemed to rise from the ground in the mist that the cause for freedom for which they died has been taken up by Seeger and his comrades. The poem evokes a tone of willing sacrifice through the vivid image of a lone sentinel silhouetted against the sky waiting to ascend into heaven. Characteristically, Seeger presents the Great War as a struggle between abstract qualities such as "dull Peace," "sweet Love," and "the majesty of strife," forces that converge on the battlefield. The soldiers endure hardship to continue the struggle against tyranny begun by those sacrificed to the enemy, but the hardship comes from nature and not man.

While poems such as "Message to America" and "Ode in Memory of the American Volunteers Fallen for France" (1916) commemorate American involvement in the war before its actual declaration and attempt to hasten that formal declaration, Seeger's best-known work, "I Have a Rendezvous with Death," may be his most lasting formulation of the spirit and sacrifices displayed in the Great War. When it appeared in the *New Republic* in early 1916, Seeger rose from obscurity, having put on the lips of readers a most memorable understanding of the futility of war. The last stanza poignantly expresses what war requires of the individual and one individual's willingness to meet that obligation:

> But I've a rendezvous with Death
> At midnight in some flaming town,
> When Spring trips north again this year,
> and I to my pledged word am true,
> I shall not fail that rendezvous.

Seeger's biographer, Irving Werstein, noted the prophetic quality of the poem. Just a matter of months after its publication, on July 4, Alan Seeger was killed in a German machine gun assault on Belloy-en-Santerre (France), urging his comrades forward as he fell.

Other works Seeger left behind include his letters to his parents, a journal, and his dispatches to the *New York Sun* and *New Republic*, all published posthumously as *Letters and Diary*.

REFERENCES

Seeger, Alan. *Letters and Diary.* New York: Charles Scribner's Sons, 1917.
———. *Poems.* New York: Charles Scribner's Sons, 1916.
Werstein, Irving. *Sound No Trumpet: The Life and Death of Alan Seeger.* New York: Thomas Y. Crowell, 1967.

Mark A. Graves

SETTLE, MARY LEE (1918–). Born in West Virginia, raised in Kentucky, and educated in Virginia, Mary Lee Settle began her writing career while she was an editor for *Harper's Bazaar.* She has published twelve novels and received the National Book Award in 1978 for *Blood Tie.* Most critical attention has been paid to her *Beulah Quintet,* which explores the history and creation of American cultural identity. This series includes the prologue novel *Prisons* (1973), *O Beulah Land* (1956), *Know Nothing* (1960), *The Scapegoat* (1980), and *The Killing Ground* (1982). Her autobiography, *All the Brave Promises* (1966), focuses on her experiences in the British Women's Auxiliary of the Royal Air Force during World War II.

O Beulah Land and *Know Nothing* deal specifically with the escalating political and personal conflicts that led to the American Revolution and the Civil War. *O Beulah Land* focuses on the lives of Hannah Bridewell and Jeremiah Catlett, who both flee from bondage to struggle for freedom represented by the American wilderness in western Virginia, and the lives of Jonathan and Sally Lacey, representatives of the privileged upper class. According to Brian Rosenberg, Settle disrupts the traditional mythology by examining "the easy movement of the dispossessed to the dispossessors" (87). Similarly, *Know Nothing,* set in pre–Civil War Virginia, seeks to undermine the *Gone With the Wind* mythology of antebellum South. The descendants of the original settlers of *O Beulah Land* now face the social and cultural shifts inching the Unites States toward the divisive Civil War. In both these texts, Settle disrupts romanticizing mythologies to reveal the "seductive danger" of the impulse to "mythologize, oppress, and claim ownership" inherent in the American historical imagination (Rosenberg 98).

Also of interest is Settle's autobiography of her service in the British Women's Auxiliary of the Royal Air Force during World War II. Unable to enlist in the Unites States, Settle volunteered for service in Britain. *All the Brave Promises* (1966) is filled with "authentic and eloquently evoked personal experience" (Garrett 133) and offers insight into the creative beginnings of the author.

REFERENCES

Garrett, George P. *Understanding Mary Lee Settle.* Columbia: University of South Carolina Press, 1988.
Rosenberg, Brian. *Mary Lee Settle's Beulah Quintet.* Baton Rouge: Louisiana State University Press, 1991.

Settle, Mary Lee. *All the Brave Promises: Memories of Aircraft Woman, 2nd Class 214639*. The Mary Lee Settle Collection. Columbia: University of South Carolina Press, 1995.

————. *The Beulah Quintet*. The Mary Lee Settle Collection. Columbia: University of South Carolina Press, 1996.

Amy L. Wink

SHAARA, JEFF (1952–   ). Born in New Brunswick, New Jersey, Jeff Shaara grew up principally in Florida, graduating from Florida State University in 1974 with a degree in criminology. A small businessman, Shaara was a dealer in rare coins when his father, novelist **Michael Shaara** (*The Killer Angels*, 1974), passed away in 1988. At the suggestion of Ron Maxwell, director of *Gettysburg* (1993), the film based on *The Killer Angels*, the younger Shaara turned to writing.

He has produced two novels: *Gods and Generals* (1996) and *The Last Full Measure* (1998). Using the elder Shaara's distinctive multiple-narrator style, *Gods and Generals* is a long-awaited "prequel" to Michael Shaara's *The Killer Angels* and focuses on, principally, Robert E. Lee, Stonewall Jackson, Joshua Lawrence Chamberlain, and Winfield Scott Hancock from 1858 to the eve of the battle of Gettysburg. Shaara successfully imitates the interior monologues and introspective narrative style of his father but is less successful in capturing the eloquent realism and the authentic voices of *The Killer Angels'* characters. Too often, the younger Shaara relies upon formulas and repeated phrases ("Must not think on that now.") as well as distracting stylistic oddities, such as (in the words of one reviewer) "stringing sentence elements together without conjunctions" (Henderson B7). The reader is puzzled to find Jackson and Hancock in prominent roles, since they do not appear so in *The Killer Angels*. Thus, the sense of continuity suffers. Often, the characters tend to sound the same, all with the sensitive, reflective poetic vision that characterizes Chamberlain's voice in *The Killer Angels*. Hence, the reader finds a Stonewall Jackson who is both sensitive and unreflectivly passionate in battle. However, many of the scenes with Jackson, especially at his death, are finely rendered and compelling. There are excellent, authentic battle scenes as well.

The Last Full Measure, following the war from Gettysburg to Appomattox, is a better novel partly because the time period it covers is more compact and partly because Jeff Shaara's style is more mature and less formulaic. He treats the big themes of Death, Faith, and the meaning of the War with skill, as well as offering fine political insights. The characters all tend to be the same type of introspective observer again, even the historically ebullient Jeb Stuart. The main characters, through whose minds the story is narrated, are Robert E. Lee, James Longstreet (oddly absent in *God and Generals*), Ulysses S. Grant, Jeb Stuart, and Chamberlain. Hancock also makes his appearances but disappears after a while. Longstreet, after his wounding at the Wilderness, is also left unaccounted for.

Despite mixed reviews, both novels have been top best-sellers. Both are in early stages of film production. Shaara, at this writing, is researching a novel about the Mexican War.

REFERENCES

Henderson, Keith. "How Civil War Generals Thought and Fought." Rev. of *The Last Full Measure*, by Jeff Shaara. *Christian Science Monitor* 18 June 1998: B7.
Hooper, Brad. Rev. of *Gods and Generals*, by Jeff Shaara. *Booklist* 15 April 1996: 1395.
Kilpatrick, Thomas L. Rev. of *Gods and Generals*, by Jeff Shaara. *Library Journal* 1 May 1996: 134.

Randal W. Allred

SHAARA, MICHAEL (1929–1988). Born in Jersey City, New Jersey, Shaara mixed his undergraduate education at Rutgers and graduate work at Columbia and the University of Vermont with varying careers as a merchant seaman, soldier, prizefighter, police officer, and freelance writer. In later years, he taught at Florida State University.

His 1975 Pulitzer Prize–winning novel *The Killer Angels* (1974) has been the most popular Civil War novel of the latter twentieth century. Praised for its authenticity and verisimilitude, the novel focuses on several historical characters who fought at Gettysburg; each is a recurring narrator, offering his own introspective view of the battle. These narrators include Joshua Lawrence Chamberlain and John Buford of the North and Robert E. Lee, James Longstreet, and Lewis Armistead of the South.

The novel characterizes the battle as a microcosm of the conflict between the old order and the coming modern age. Chamberlain is a modern man, liberal in his thinking and romantically committed to the cause of freedom. Educated and humane, this professor from Bowdoin College is surprised that he enjoys the exhilaration of battle. In spite of the slaughter, he relies on his reason and his heart to retain his optimistic perspective on the Civil War. Buford is somewhat of a maverick, exasperated by the restrictions of tradition and policy as well as the waste of good men in war. Thus, he eschews conventional cavalry tactics. Akin to him is Longstreet, who unlike the majority of Confederate officers is a modern thinker, a realist among romantics, willing to abandon military tradition in order to win. His innovative perspective opposes that of Lee the traditionalist, whose narrow loyalties to honor, God, and tradition cripple his genius. Lee feels honor-bound to attack the enemy on his chosen ground, as if the battle were a formal duel. Thus the debacle of Pickett's Charge and Southern defeat.

Civil War enthusiasts have commended the novel's authenticity in tactics and setting. Literary critics have appreciated its psychological realism and the focus on the "human dimension," as one early review put it: "The author makes little effort to analyze what brought the armies or any one man to this battlefield, and he doesn't attempt to glorify his soldier-hero or the causes." Another review observes this: "His achievement is combining these passages of apocalyptic immediacy with smaller scenes that dramatize the historian's cultural understandings." *The Killer Angels* owes much to **Hemingway** for its lean style and to **Crane** for its psychological realism and impressionistic narrative style.

Shaara's other works include *The Broken Place* (1968), the story of Tom McClain, who, scarred by the war in Korea, struggles to maintain belief in the face of tribulation and the grueling world of prizefighting. Shaara also wrote *The Herald* (1981), a science fiction story of intrigue, *Soldier Boy* (1982), a collection of short stories, and *For Love of the Game* (1991), a posthumously published novel about an aging baseball pitcher that has been made into a film by Kevin Costner.

Shaara was working with filmmaker Ronald F. Maxwell on a screenplay for *The Killer Angels* at the time of his death. In 1993 Maxwell made the novel into *Gettysburg*, a four-hour film that met mixed reviews. **Jeff Shaara** has written *Gods and Generals* and *The Last Full Measure* as companion novels to his father's *The Killer Angels*.

REFERENCES

Kauffmann, Stanley. "Life Struggles." Rev. of *Gettysburg*, by Michael Shaara and Ronald F. Maxwell. *New Republic* 8 November 1993: 32–33.
Le Clair, Thomas. Rev. of *The Killer Angels*, by Michael Shaara. *New York Times Book Review* 20 October 1974: 38–40.
Weeks, Edward. Rev. of *The Killer Angels*, by Michael Shaara. *The Atlantic Monthly* April 1975: 97–99.

Randal W. Allred

SHAPIRO, KARL (1913–2000). Karl Shapiro's celebrated work as a soldier–poet of World War II led him to a long, productive, and combative literary career. Born in Baltimore, Karl Shapiro grew up there and in Virginia, attending the University of Virginia and Johns Hopkins University without graduating. Shapiro was drafted into the army in March 1941. After training in Petersburg, Virginia (described in his poem "Conscription Camp"), he was sent to Australia on the *Queen Mary* and stationed in Melbourne and Sydney, where he wrote reports for a medical unit; he was then moved to New Guinea and the Trobriand Islands, where he came under Japanese bombardment, later receiving four bronze stars. In 1944 he returned to the United States on board a ship that also carried soldiers confined for mental illness. "Homecoming" (from *Trial of a Poet*, 1947) makes the return voyage stand for all of Shapiro's service: Its rough pentameters present a poet disturbed by the populous impersonality of army life, distressed that military lifestyles and colors seem to have covered the globe, and awed before the mysteries of the ocean.

Shapiro's first significant books, *Person, Place and Thing* (1942) and the Pulitzer Prize–winning *V-Letter and Other Poems* (1944), were published in the United States while he served overseas. Indebted to W. H. Auden, the poems garnered broad and immediate accolades from such disparate authorities as W. C. Williams and **Allen Tate**. Readers praised Shapiro's metrical fluency, his aggressively contemporary subjects—"Auto Wreck," "Drug Store," the cinema—and his raw, antisentimental observations of army life in poems like "Troop Train" (from *V-Letter*). The unhygienic soldiers of that poem seem to cross the whole world overland, reducing each country to the constricted dimensions of their own experience.

Shapiro called "Elegy on a Dead Soldier" (also from *V-Letter*) his "most anthologized poem." Opening with an improvised funeral in which a truck substitutes for a bier, Shapiro's twelve sonnetlike stanzas attempt to make this accidental fatality typify all the war dead: "We ask for no statistics of the killed."

Shapiro claimed in *V-Letter* that he had tried "to write freely, one day as a Christian, the next as a Jew, the next as a soldier who sees the gigantic slapstick of modern war." His subsequent changes in style and attitude have been unified by his antagonism toward whatever he viewed as current orthodoxy. He alternates high rhetorical seriousness with the consciously resentful, dyspeptic, or dysphemistic. He returned to his war experience in a few later poems, notably within the prose-poem sequence *The Bourgeois Poet* (1964), which includes his most vigorous, pugnacious, and individual writing. A rare description of combat is "Fox Hole," in which an anguished Shapiro watches his dying comrade.

The Younger Son (1988), Part 1 of Shapiro's projected three-part memoir *Poet*, describes Shapiro's childhood, adolescence, and wartime experience. (Part 2, *Reports of My Death*, appeared in 1990.) Shapiro's third-person narration, replacing all names by common nouns ("the poet," "the editor," "the Mother Sergeant"), produces a brusquely vivid chronicle, interrupted by Shapiro's appalled reactions to his own career: "He wouldn't like it later when critics called him a war poet. He was no such thing, only a poet who happened into a war, and how could you write poetry in the middle of a war and leave the war out?"

After World War II, Shapiro taught at Hopkins and at the Universities of Illinois, Nebraska, and California at Davis. He edited *Poetry* magazine from 1950 to 1956. His later work encompasses essays, compiled in *The Poetry Wreck* (1975); a novel, *Edsel* (1971); and other volumes of verse, including *Poems of a Jew* (1958), *Adult Bookstore* (1976), *Collected Poems 1940–1978* (which excludes much early work), and *The Wild Card: Selected Poems Early and Late* (1998), with a valuable introduction by M. L. Rosenthal.

REFERENCES

Reino, Joseph. *Karl Shapiro*. Boston: Twayne, 1981.

Shapiro, Karl. *The Wild Card: Selected Poems Early and Late*. Ed. Stanley Kunitz and David Ignatow. Urbana: University of Illinois Press, 1998.

———. *The Younger Son*. Chapel Hill: Algonquin Press, 1988.

Stephen Burt

SHAW, IRWIN (1913–1984). Irwin Gilbert Shamforoff grew up near Sheepshead Bay in New York City. By twelve he was writing stories, and at fifteen, as Irwin Shaw, he entered Brooklyn College, graduating in 1934. His alma mater would ultimately recognize with an honorary doctorate the man it had once expelled as a freshman. Student Shaw contributed theses for New York University students, articles for his school newspaper, plays for the dramatic group, and after graduation, two successful radio serials. His first major play, *Bury the Dead* (1936), was a pacifist fantasy dramatizing the futility of war. Echoing Gogol's *Dead Souls* and anticipating Kadare's *The General of the Dead Army*, in one short act it puts on stage six dead World War I privates who refuse to be buried and forgotten. Praised by Leslie Fiedler and others, it won the young playwright a strong following. A master teller of tales, Shaw then built a name for himself with some eighty-four stories published over the next fifty years. The title story in the twenty collected from *The New Yorker* and elsewhere for his *Sailor off the Bremen* (1939) prefigures America's entry into World War II. Shaw enlisted in 1942, covering the war in Africa, France, England, and Germany and rising in the ranks from private to warrant officer in the Signal Corps.

In the 1940s, Shaw produced other fiction, later reissued in his *Short Stories: Five Decades* (1978). Some treat obliquely the coming of war ("Free Conscience, Void of Offence," "Weep in Years to Come," "The City Was in Total Darkness," "Night, Birth and Opinion"). Others already suggest its dark consequences from behind the scenes or on the sidelines of battle ("Preach on the Dusty Roads," "Hamlets of the World," "Medal from Jerusalem," "Walking Wounded"). Three of the richest evoke aerial combat or Occupied Paris or the German front in order to underline American responsibility, German arrogance, and universal anti-Semitism ("Gunners' Passage," "Retreat," and especially "Act of Faith"). A last group point up enduring tensions through the ambiguities of denazification in Occupation Germany or the wartime legacies for a postwar Palestine ("The Man with One Arm" and "The Passion of Lance Corporal Hawkins").

Shaw's most influential work remains *The Young Lions* (1948). Taking his cue from lifelong Mussolini-sympathizer Marinetti's "Foundation of Futurism," Shaw in his first, prodigiously successful long novel shows how "like young lions we ran after Death." One of the best and most widely read novels of the war, it resembles a series of interrelated stories in linking the separate destinies of three soldiers: one Jew, one Gentile, and one Nazi, who kills the first but is killed by the second. Shaw painfully chronicles how the two American draftees achieve dignity and self-reliance despite individual failings and rank-and-file intolerance. The German remains an unredeemed fighting machine to the last. He becomes a sympathetic figure only in the film version when played by Marlon Brando, who was roundly chastised by Shaw for rewriting both history and fiction.

Shaw's eleven other novels earned him notoriety and riches but were criticized as lacking the moral engagement that characterized his youthful pacifism and mature wartime commitment. His greatest triumphs are certainly not the blockbusters, not even *The Young Lions*, but his sensitive and skillful portrayals of a gallery of figures caught up willy-nilly in World War II.

REFERENCES

Giles, James Richard. *Irwin Shaw*. Boston: Twayne, 1983.
———. *Irwin Shaw: A Study of the Short Fiction*. Boston: Twayne, 1991.
Shnayerson, Michael. *Irwin Shaw: A Biography*. New York: Putnam, 1989.

Roy Rosenstein

SHERWOOD, ROBERT (1896–1955). The chief subject of Robert Emmet Sherwood's plays is human warfare, and like his friend and fellow dramatist of war **Maxwell Anderson**, Sherwood's career is noteworthy for its radical shift from the post–World War I antiwar sensibility of his early plays to the fervidly militaristic dramas he wrote during the World War II era. His best-known screenplay, *The Best Years of Our Lives* (1946), is brutally frank in its portrayal of the traumatic effects of war on returning veterans and their families but is also firm in its fundamental avowal that their suffering and sacrifice were necessary in order to defeat the clearly defined evil of fascism.

The scion of a very prominent New York family, Sherwood was born in New Rochelle, New York, and attended prestigious boarding schools prior to his admission to Harvard in 1914. Almost immediately after his graduation in 1918, Sherwood attempted to enlist in the army and navy but was rejected because of his height. He then enlisted in the Canadian Expeditionary Force and served six months as an infantryman on the Western Front, where he was gassed twice and wounded in both leas. His experience as a soldier instilled in him an abhorrence for war that never would leave him, even when he became convinced of its necessity.

When he returned to New York, he began work as a journalist, and by the age of twenty-eight, he was editor of *Life* and a member of the famed Algonquin Round Table, a highly influential group of literati who included Dorothy Parker, Robert Benchley, and Alexander Woollcott. His first professional play, *The Road to Rome*, opened on Broadway in 1927 and was an almost immediate success. In this satirical antiwar comedy, a troubled Hannibal is visited by Amytis, the wife of a Roman senator, who is there not so much to convince him to spare Rome as to convince him that war is wrong. Hannibal finds her reasoning persuasive, but the issue is ultimately decided when Amytis seduces him so satisfactorily that he can no longer resist either her sexuality or her pacifist arguments. Having sufficiently "enlightened" Hannibal, Amytis then returns to her husband. The play's pacifism resonated well with already disillusioned veterans and placed Sherwood within the Lost Generation's generally antiwar perspective.

Sherwood returned to war-related themes in his fourth play, *Waterloo Bridge* (1930), the story of an American doughboy who falls for a London prostitute, a classic "whore with the heart of gold" who ultimately refuses to besmirch either his idealism or his innocence. Though the play never succeeded on Broadway, Hollywood liked it well enough to make three different versions: Universal in 1931 and MGM in 1940 and 1956.

When *Idiot's Delight*, perhaps Sherwood's most philosophical antiwar play, opened in 1936, it was becoming clear to many that the country might be headed into another war, and Sherwood's play explores the moral consequences of such a fate. He uses an international group of apparently peace-loving characters who are detained together in an Alpine hotel on the eve of war to demonstrate how vulnerable even the best of humanity are to the jingoistic patriotism spouted by nations in times of military crisis. When war does break out, a cancer researcher readily turns to designing chemical weapons, a young artist abandons his promising work and his new wife in his eagerness to enlist, and a munitions maker returns home to reap enormous profits. As the play closes, bombs are falling as two American entertainers launch into a raucous jazz version of "Onward Christian Soldiers."

But *Idiot's Delight* was his last pacifist play. In *Abe Lincoln in Illinois* (1939), Sherwood uses the pre–Civil War life of Abraham Lincoln as a vehicle for showing how necessary it is to stop appeasing one's enemies and stand up to them with military force. He continued his denunciation of isolationism in *There Shall Be No Night* (1940), in which a liberal pacifist ultimately takes up arms in defense of his freedom. Set in Finland during the time of its invasion by Russia, the play focuses on Dr. Kaarlo Valkonen, a neurologist and Nobel Prize winner, whose pacifist beliefs are steadily eroded by the reality of Russia's threat. After his son gives his life as a soldier in battle, Valkonen finally sees that war is a sometimes necessary evil and that freedom is worth dying for. Sherwood was accused of being a warmonger, but the play was a hit. It was to be his last popular success.

In 1940 Sherwood also became one of President Roosevelt's principal speechwriters, and during the war he served as director of the Overseas Branch of the Office of War Information. His interest in government continued after the war to the detriment of his playwriting. *The Rugged Path* (1945) is set during wartime, but it is a static piece of propaganda that preaches the importance of finding something one is willing to die for. In 1948 Sherwood published *Roosevelt and Hopkins, An Intimate History*, his monumental study of the relationship between the men that is generally considered one of the most important historical works about World War II.

REFERENCES

Brown, John Mason. *The Ordeal of a Playwright: Robert E. Sherwood and the Challenge of War*. New York: Harper and Row, 1970.
Meserve, Walter J. *Robert E. Sherwood: Reluctant Moralist*. New York: Pegasus, 1970.

Lucas Carpenter

SILKO, LESLIE MARMON (1948–   ). Silko, born in Albuquerque and raised on the Laguna Pueblo Reservation, is of mixed Laguna, Mexican, and white ancestry. She has taught at the Universities of New Mexico and Arizona, and she is married and has two sons.

Both a poet and fiction writer, Silko has won the Pushcart prize for poetry (1977) and other awards including a MacArthur foundation grant (1983). Her major work is *Ceremony* (1977), a novel. Other works include *Laguna Woman: Poems* (1974); *Storyteller* (1981); a collection of her correspondence with poet James Wright called *The Delicacy and Strength of Lace* (1986); a second novel, *Almanac of the Dead* (1991); and several volumes of memoirs and essays. Her works deal with the lives and stories of contemporary Native Americans.

In *Ceremony* Tayo, a mixed-blood veteran of World War II, has returned home to the Southwest but is unable to reconcile his wartime experience. He feels survivor's guilt over the death of his cousin, Rocky, on the Bataan Death March. Tayo has come home to a drought for which he feels responsible, because he cursed the rain on the Death March. Tayo goes through an unsuccessful healing ceremony carried out by Ku'oosh, a traditional, full-blood Navajo medicine man. He continues to weaken until he meets Ts'eh, who may be human or may be a supernatural figure, and Betonie, a mixed-blood healer who carries out a hybrid ceremony, a mix of traditional and modern elements, which finally heals Tayo of his guilt. Four other veterans, Harley, Emo, Leroy, and Pinky, corrupted by their war experiences, have been practicing witchery. A story told within the novel tells how indigenous witches created the witchery, of which the white people who invaded the Americas were a result. The ultimate form the witchery takes is the atomic bomb, made from uranium mined on the reservation. The novel is circular, ending where it began, with the witchery dead "for now." The novel is a powerfully told story of a veteran coming to terms with his war experience and reintegrating himself back into his home.

REFERENCES

Jahner, Elaine. "The Novel and Oral Tradition: An Interview with Leslie Marmon Silko." *Book Forum* 53 (1981): 383–388.

Jaskoski, Helen. "Thinking Woman's Children and the Bomb." *The Nightmare Considered: Critical Essays on Nuclear War Literature*. Ed. Nancy Anisfield. Bowling Green, OH: Bowling Green State University Popular Press, 1991.

Renny Christopher

SIMMS, WILLIAM GILMORE (1806–1870). Born in Charleston, South Carolina, Simms began writing verse as a child. He attended the College of Charleston, edited the Charleston *City Gazette*, and served in the state legislature. Although twentieth-century scholars consider Simms to be one of the most important antebellum writers, his contemporaries often criticized his writing as being sensationalized and melodramatic with flawed structures, plots, and characterizations while praising his imaginative and descriptive passages, especially of the Carolina low country.

Twentieth-century critics cite Simms's eight-volume American Revolution series as his best work. Most of these novels first appeared serialized in periodicals and were printed later as books. Fascinated by history and the conflicting loyalties among South Carolinians during the American Revolution, Simms created fictional stories based on real people and events; many characters such as the gallant soldier Porgy appear in different volumes. The series presents different aspects of the Revolution in South Carolina, often appearing out of historical sequence because of Simms's other writing commitments.

Simms's first Revolutionary romance, *The Partisan* (1835), was set at the 1780 Battle of Camden. Retaining historical integrity, Simms skillfully describes landscapes and stages battle scenes, although his plot and characters are often stereotypical and predictable. His second Revolutionary book, *Mellichampe* (1836), continues his narrative, featuring guerilla warfare on the Santee after the Battle of Camden. *The Kinsmen*—retitled *The Scout*—(1841), *Katharine Walton* (1851), and *The Sword and the Distaff*—reissued as *Woodcraft, or, Hawks about the Dovecote: A Story of the South at the Close of the Revolution*—(1852) discuss the British occupation of Charleston and postwar issues after the British left in 1782. *The Forayers* (1855) is set in Orangeburg before *Eutaw* (1856), which features the Battle of Eutaw Springs in September 1781 where the British were defeated. The final volume, *Joscelyn* (1867), is set in Augusta and the South Carolina back country in 1775.

Simms created powerful, energetic, intense stories that represent the folksy, oral tradition of the South. His protagonists are proud, patriotic, and idealistic colonists who persevere and use physical, spiritual, and intellectual strengths to become heroes securing freedom and defeating and expelling the British, who are depicted as immoral, brutish, and weak. Development of individual and national identity is a recurring theme. Characters are humorous and intelligent, talking in convincing Southern vernacular. Women are often unconventional and dress like male characters to symbolize their strength. Good versus evil is another frequent theme, with redemption for unsavory characters who are repentant. Because Simms was a prolific writer and his writing quickly serialized, much of his work lacks polish and cohesiveness. He overrelied on the plot device of a partisan and loyalist vying for the love of a woman and recycled scenes and characters. Some critics misinterpreted his acerbic anti-Northern comments as a propagandistic response to abolitionism. His novels are imaginative, with the common theme of culture replacing crudeness and showing Simms's optimism and vision for a better society both regionally and nationally.

War was a prevalent theme in Simms's writing, and he wrote about his personal experiences in the Civil War as well as essays and fiction about military subjects including the Mexican War, Indian conflicts, and the Alamo. Consulting primary sources, Simms wrote biographies of such military leaders as Francis Marion, John Laurens, and Nathanael Greene. Simms edited the anthology *War Poetry of the South* (1866) several years before his death. Simms's Revolutionary War novels were reprinted with scholarly notes for the Bicentennial.

REFERENCES

Guilds, John Caldwell. *Simms: Literary Life*. Fayetteville: University of Arkansas Press, 1992.

Oliphant, Mary C. Simms, Alfred Taylor Odell, and T. C. Duncan Eaves, eds. *The Letters of William Gilmore Simms*. 6 vols. Columbia: University of South Carolina Press, 1952–1982.

Watson, Charles S. *From Nationalism to Secessionism: The Changing Fiction of William Gilmore Simms*. Westport, CT: Greenwood Press, 1993.

Elizabeth D. Schafer

SIMPSON, LOUIS (1923–   ). Son of a Scottish colonial lawyer and an American mother, Louis Aston Marantz Simpson, born in Kingston, Jamaica, and educated at Munro College, emigrated to New York City in 1940 and was assigned three years later to the 101st Airborne Division. He saw extensive combat in France, Holland, Belgium, and Germany and fought in the murderous Battle of Bastogne. After being discharged in 1945, Simpson was hospitalized with posttraumatic stress and later claimed that writing poetry helped him recover. Combining poetry with an academic career, he gained his doctorate in 1959 from Columbia and took up a professorship of English at the State University of New York, Stony Brook. One of America's most distinguished postwar poets, Simpson's eminence was acknowledged by a Pulitzer Prize in 1963.

Explaining his objectives in writing war poems, Simpson stated that he firstly wished to remember, and then to portray, as exactly as possible what it was like to be an infantryman. *In the Arrivistes* (1949) several poems, including "The Men with Flame Throwers" and "Arm in Arm," which recreates a graveyard firefight in Verghel, Holland, fulfill these aims by achieving the formality and aesthetic distance of ballad. One of his finest war poems, "Carentan O Carentan," records his first experience of battle subconsciously transformed by a speaker whose guileless words ironically reveal his terror and helplessness. The tension between innocence and experience thus created lends "Carentan O Carentan" an archetypal resonance that is heightened by its menacing images.

Good News of Death (1955) includes one of Simpson's most restrained and coherent war poems, "The Battle." Whereas the three other war poems in the collection—"The Heroes," "The Ash and the Oak," and the poignant "Memories of a Lost War"—are marred to varying degrees by rhetorical strain, "The Battle" succinctly blends plain language with appropriate imagery. The Bastogne fighting is signified by an accumulation of precise, almost factual detail expressed syntactically in short sentences describing harsh wintry conditions and a punishing artillery barrage. Set against this evocation of unbearable pain are three striking images of redness that connote the human and spiritual dimensions of the conflict. The poem concludes with a metaphor suggestive of endurance and survival: The speaker's battlefield memories bring images of tired eyes as well as thin hands that hold a cigarette whose glowing ember "Would pulse with all the life there was within."

In contrast to the naturalistic mode of "The Battle," Simpson has written visionary war poems that are surreal in character. Found throughout his work such poems as "Old Soldiers," "The Heroes," "The Troika," and "The Laurel Tree" utilize dream imagery taken from the unconscious. One of the most impressive of such works is "I Dreamed That in a City Dark as Paris" from *A Dream of Governors* (1959), the key volume for understanding Simpson as a war poet. "I Dreamed That in a City Dark as Paris" describes how a dreaming war veteran finds himself abandoned in an empty city and takes on the identity of a French poilu from the World War I. The poem's conclusion affirms the legitimacy of visionary truth.

If the visionary mood is one way of communicating historical truth, then another route for Simpson is the narrative method employed in some of his most acclaimed poems such as "The Bird" and "A Story about Chicken Soup." Unlike his longest narrative poem, the conventionally realistic, semiautobiographical "The Runner," these poems have the immediacy and freshness of folk poetry. "The Bird" is a successful poetic representation of the Holocaust, which scales down massive historical events by focusing on the story of a concentration camp guard who sings plaintively each night before he gasses Jewish victims, and "A Story about Chicken Soup" acknowledges Allied guilt as well as Nazi atrocities. Written in flexible, rhymed quatrains and jaunty iambic meter, "The Bird" is one of America's greatest war poems: Largely adopting the callous point of view of a sentimental, patriotic German youth, the poem evokes the horror of mass extermination through sophisticated narrative variation and matter-of-fact language.

Although lacking the sense of mystery and narrative economy of these poems, Simpson's novel *Riverside Drive* (1962) provides insight into the author's imagination of war through the combat experience and subsequent amnesia of its hero, Duncan Bell.

REFERENCES

Moran, Ronald. *Louis Simpson*. New York: Troy Publishers, 1972.
Simpson, Louis. *Collected Poems*. New York: Paragon House, 1988.
————. *North of Jamaica*. New York: Harper and Row, 1972.

Jeff Walsh

SLOTKIN, RICHARD (1942–). Born in Brooklyn, New York, Richard Slotkin received his bachelor's degree from Brooklyn College in 1963 and his doctorate from Brown University in 1967. He joined the faculty of Wesleyan University in Middletown, Connecticut, in 1966 and is currently the director of the American Studies Program there. His analyses of the myth of the frontier provide theoretical underpinnings for his own provocative readings of American war literature and have influenced the readings of many other scholars.

Slotkin is best known for his trilogy of works exploring the Frontier Myth's influence on American identity. The first, *Regeneration through Violence: The*

Mythology of the American Frontier, 1600–1860 (1973), began as Slotkin's doctoral thesis and focuses on narratives by explorers, Puritans, and early American novelists to trace the development of a national literature as European colonists transform into Americans. The second book in the trilogy, *The Fatal Environment: The Myth of the Frontier in the Age of Industrialization, 1800–1890* (1985), further examines the influence of the frontier and demonstrates that, as the frontier recedes, the Frontier Myth intensifies and becomes more deeply embedded in our culture.

In *Gunfighter Nation: The Myth of the Frontier in Twentieth-Century America* (1992), the final volume in the trilogy, Slotkin analyzes the effects of the Frontier Myth on American perceptions of foreign relations and domestic issues. Brief summaries can't do justice to the complexities and subtleties of Slotkin's work; however, particularly influential to the study of American war literature is Slotkin's argument that the cultural metaphor of Cowboys and Indians has been invoked at various points in our nation's history to justify our participation in wars. *Gunfighter Nation* begins by discussing **Roosevelt**'s dramatization of the Spanish-American War battle of San Juan Hill in *The Rough Riders*. Roosevelt sets up his Rough Riders as an elite force who can act on behalf of the American masses who participate vicariously in the imperialism of the new frontier. Slotkin explains that Roosevelt links antiimperialists with "foolish sentimentalists" whose policies enraged Native Americans and caused them to kill white settlers. In this way the Frontier Myth is reconstituted in terms appropriate to the modern era.

Gunfighter Nation's discussion of the relationship between the movie western and the World War II combat film is exemplified by his analysis of links between 1943's *Bataan* and **Custer**'s Last Stand. Slotkin further argues that westerns create a history and a mythic landscape for Americans to colonize, and they influence understanding of the Cold War. In fact, he finds that the Golden Age of the Western (1948–1973) mirrors the development of the Cold War. Slotkin explains that the gunfighter version of the Frontier Hero reached its height during the Kennedy presidency and the Vietnam War. The book particularizes the connection between the American hero and Vietnam by describing the "John Wayne Syndrome," or the conflation of all Wayne's film characters that allows connections between the soldier and the frontier cowboy, between the American frontier and the contemporary quest of the American soldier.

Slotkin also coedited *So Dreadful a Judgment: Puritan Responses to King Philip's War* (1978), a collection of Puritan documents including sermons, poetry, and history. He wrote two novels, *The Crater: A Novel of the Civil War* (1980) and *The Return of Henry Starr* (1988). The first fictionalizes the Civil War Battle of the Crater during the summer of 1864. The second dramatizes the life of Henry Starr, Oklahoma Cherokee, nephew of outlaw heroine Belle Starr, bank robber, and silent screen actor. More recent articles by Slotkin focus on the movie western, **Mark Twain**'s frontier, and recent scholarship on the Civil War.

REFERENCES

Faragher, John Mack. "Gunslingers and Bureaucrats." *New Republic* 14 December 1992: 29–36.
Fredrickson, George M. "Redemption through Violence." *New York Review of Books* 21 November 1985: 38–42.
Perez, Gilberto. "The Frontier Dialect." *The Nation* 25 October 1993: 466–470.

Samantha J. Ward

SMITH, JOHN (1580–1631). Born in Lincolnshire, England, Captain John Smith nonetheless stands at the head of many traditional genres in American literature, among them geography, autobiography, and history. *A True Relation* (1608), his earliest account of his experiences in Virginia, is the first book in English written entirely in America. In it, Smith recounted the initial skirmishes of the Jamestown colonists and early fortifications against Indian attack. *A True Relation* also offered the first version of Smith's captivity by Powhatan. Smith, who had earned his captaincy fighting in eastern Europe and Asia Minor, ultimately became chiefly responsible for the defense of the colony, but a severe gunpowder burn forced him to return to England.

Although Smith billed himself as an expert colonizer and manipulator of native peoples, he made only one subsequent trip to the New World, which he described in *A Description of New England* in 1614. When the Pilgrims left for Massachusetts, they took not John Smith but his book as their guide. In 1624 Smith published his most ambitious work, *The Generall Historie of Virginia, New-England, and the Summer Isles*, a compilation of his own and other's writings in which Pocahontas, a minor figure in his earlier work, first emerges as the savior of John Smith.

Although frequently regarded as a knight-errant, Smith more accurately belongs to the class of pragmatic Indian fighters who have inhabited American literature since he consciously defined the type through his life and writings.

REFERENCES

Emerson, Everett. *Captain John Smith*. Rev. ed. New York: Twayne, 1993.
Smith, John. *The Complete Works of Captain John Smith (1580–1631)*. 3 vols. Ed. Philip Barbour. Chapel Hill: University of North Carolina Press, 1986.

Robert D. Madison

SMITH, THORNE (1892–1934). Born James Thorne Smith, Jr., at Annapolis, Maryland, the son of a naval commander, Smith received his education in private schools and attended Dartmouth for two years. Following family tradition, he enlisted in the navy from 1917 to 1919. After the war, he became a copywriter for several New York advertising agencies. He spent the late 1920s until his untimely death from a heart attack producing several novels.

Smith is well known for his humorous fantasy novel *Topper* (1926) in which a staid banker is transformed into a more fun-loving man by the ghosts of a wealthy and whimsical married couple. He also wrote several novels in this vein, such as *The Stray Lamb* (1929), *Turnabout* (1931), and *The Night Life of the Gods* (1931), which include supernatural or fantastic events.

While in the navy, Smith contributed a series of sketches of the misadventures of an inept navy recruit as he attempts to negotiate the navy's rules and regulations to the navy's magazine *The Broadside* in 1918. These episodic stories, later collected as *Biltmore Oswald: The Diary of a Hapless Recruit* (1919), are narrated by Oswald in diary form. The several illustrations by Richard "Dick" Dorgan within the book reinforce Oswald as a cartoonish and naive recruit.

Smith also published a sequel, *Out O'Luck: Biltmore Oswald Very Much at Sea* (1919), from sketches that appeared in *The Broadside* between 1918 and 1919 and illustrated by Dick Dorgan. They continue the saga of Oswald, this time on a ship at sea, as he tries to negotiate the war not very successfully. Both novels, pointing to the absurdities of naval life and including Smith's characteristic humor, are very much part of his early work.

Smith's only collection of poetry, *Haunts and By-Paths and Other Poems* (1919), contains several conventional and patriotic poems dealing with war. Most of them were originally published in *The Broadside* and celebrate the naval life of a sailor. In terms of style and content the poems are eminently forgettable. Smith's forte was in fiction.

REFERENCES

Jordon, Peter. "Wish Fulfillment: The Innocent Fantasies or Fantastic Innocence of Thorne Smith's Humor." *Studies in Popular Culture* 8.1 (1985): 53–62.
Scheetz, George H., and Rodney N. Henshaw. "Thorne Smith." *Bulletin of Bibliography* 41.1 (March 1984): 25–37.

Ymitri Jayasundera

SPANISH-AMERICAN WAR. America largely ignored Cuba's two-year-old guerilla war for independence against Spain until 1897, when American newspapers in competition for readership began reporting Spanish atrocities perpetrated against Cuban citizens, some of which were real and others manufactured. By 1898, the yellow press had created a public outcry for war, a call only heightened by the sinking of the U.S. battleship *Maine* in Havana harbor. Reluctant to engage in hostile military action, President McKinley relented after diplomatic efforts with Spain failed, asking Congress for a declaration of war. The four-month conflict that ensued from April to August of 1898 resulted in far more American fatalities from disease than combat, producing easy U.S. victories in Cuba and Puerto Rico and the destruction of the Spanish fleet in Manilla harbor.

Hostilities ceased with the signing of a treaty between the United States and Spain granting Cuba independence and ceding Puerto Rico, Guam, and the Philippines to the United States. With Senate ratification of the treaty in 1899, the United States had its overseas empire coveted by American expansionists.

Although relatively minimal in comparison to the volume emerging from other wars, the literature of the Spanish-American War reflects the debate over America's place in the global community at the turn of the twentieth century, a discussion that has continued ever since. Despite the yellow journalism of William Randolph Hearst's *New York Journal* and Joseph Pulitzer's *New York World*, even the most cynical commentator argued that America was morally obliged to defend Cuban independence due to its own successful struggle against European tyranny. **Mark Twain**, for example, in the essay "A Word of Encouragement for Our Blushing Exiles" (1899), decries the various crimes perpetrated throughout history by European nations, urging Americans to be proud of U.S. actions and motives in the region. Similarly, although his firsthand accounts of Spanish atrocities in Cuba questioned Hearst's "reportage," **Richard Harding Davis** in his *Cuba in Wartime* (1897) supported American involvement. This interventionist sentiment based on moral grounds, in combination with an economic downturn in the 1890s causing some to argue that America had to flex its muscle abroad to secure its own economic future, also fueled imperialists wishing to expand American world influence militarily. In fact, as early as 1895, Henry Cabot Lodge's call for a greater expansionist policy in "Our Blundering Foreign Policy" was first published in the popular journal *Forum*.

The most prolific and fervent expansionist thinkers were **Alfred Thayer Mahan**, in his widely read books *The Influence of America in Sea Power, Past and Present* (1897), *The Influence of Sea Power Upon History* (1899), and *Lessons of the War with Spain and Other Articles* (1899), and **Theodore Roosevelt**, in works like *The Rough Riders* (1899) and *The Strenuous Life: Essays and Addresses* (1910). Mahan argues for naval strength as the key to America's future world influence, providing U.S. justification for occupying the Philippines long after Spanish defeat. Moreover, Roosevelt's accounts of his daring combat experience made him the embodiment of a pure yet robust American masculinity and a spokesman for American interests and moral obligation at home and abroad. In a series of magazine articles and newspaper editorials, including "Expansion and Peace," published in *The Independent* in 1899, he argues for a strong U.S. military presence to keep the peace in newly liberated countries such as the Philippines. The collective expansionist imperative to abolish Old World tyranny would appear in other forms in the flagrantly patriotic poetry of **Clinton Scollard** (*A Man at Arms*, 1898) and **Elbert Hubbard**'s "A Message to Garcia" (1899), a sermonlike essay about a special envoy sent by President McKinley to Cuban insurrectionist leaders. Roosevelt's pro-Americanist influence would extend well into the twentieth century, as in **Henry Wilson Allen**'s *San Juan Hill* (1962) where Roosevelt appears as a character.

While expansionist sentiment offered moral and political justification for American intervention in Cuba, antiwar writers led by Mark Twain, **William Dean Howells, Peter Finley Dunne**, and others criticized America's wider imperial ambitions in essays, articles, and fiction. In "To a Person Sitting in Darkness" (1901), Twain exposes America's quest to liberate the Philippines as a ruse to take the country once the Spanish depart. Although a supporter of intervention in Cuba, he laments the greed and violence brought on by the new American imperialism in articles such as "The Great Dark" (1898), "A Salutation from the 19th Century to the 20th" (1901), and "The Battle Hymn of the Republic (Brought Down to Date)" (1901). Similarly, Twain's antiwar message is clear in "The War Prayer" (1905), where he portrays an angel who descends upon a congregation to expose them to the outcome of their prayers for victory in an unnamed conflict. The works of authors renowned for artistic achievements on other themes would offer similarly delayed reactions and influences, such as **Damon Runyon** in *The Tents of Trouble: Ballads of the Wanderbund and Other Verse* (1911) and *Rhymes of the Firing Line* (1912) and **Carl Sandburg** in selected works in *Chicago Poems* (1916).

Like his contemporary, William Dean Howells took up the call against war in "Editha" (1899), the tale of a soldier who reluctantly goes to war to appease his true love. When he dies in his first engagement, Editha visits his mother, a Civil War widow, who scolds the young woman for forcing her son to his death, a lesson Editha does not understand in the end. Although the Spanish-American War united North and South in a common cause, the story reflects the haunting Civil War battle memories Howells believes are lost in the fervor for war. The influence of the Civil War on conceptualizing the conflict with Spain can also be seen in **James A. Herne**'s failed Civil War drama *Griffith Davenport* (1899), a play critical of the South when the region was praised for its involvement in Cuban independence.

Besides fiction and literary nonfiction, journalism played an important part in defining the textual legacy of the Spanish-American War. In addition to the sensationalized "reporting" perpetrated by Hearst and Pulitzer and the eyewitness accounts of Davis, his aversion to the war moved Peter Finley Dunne to collect his Chicago newspaper columns into his first Mr. Dooley volume, *Mr. Dooley in Peace and War* (1898). Seasoned by his experiences covering the Greco-Turkish War and coming off the success of *The Red Badge of Courage* and numerous short stories, **Stephen Crane** wrote journalistic responses to the Spanish-American War, later collected in *Wounds in the Rain* (1899). Critical interest in Crane's "War Memoir" has been particularly active and laudatory.

As a clash between predominantly European or Anglo-American imperial ideologies, the Spanish-American War also raised serious questions about racial inequality and subjugation, a concern reflected in the literature of the era by non-Anglo authors. As early as 1895, in an essay called "Our America," revolutionary José Martí argued for the creation of a Cuba and western Caribbean free from Anglo-American and European domination. Moreover, Susie King Taylor's *Memoirs* reveals the conflicting loyalties of African Americans involving American imperialism. Debates over unflattering white portrayals of black Cubans and African American efforts to liberate Spanish possessions versus the American commitment to freeing Cuba and the Philippines divided the African

American community. In response, F. Grant Gilmore's *The Problem: A Military Novel* (1915) counters Roosevelt's conflicting impressions of the role of black troops during the charge up San Juan Hill with startlingly heroic depictions of the Ninth Calvary and its commander Sergeant William Henderson. First-person accounts, poetry, letters, and military records collected in Herschel Cashin's *Under Fire with the Tenth Calvary* (1899) testify to the real-life heroics of the black soldiers Gilmore fictionalizes.

As critic **Richard Slotkin** has asserted in *Gunfighter Nation* (1992), Roosevelt's conceptualization of the Rough Riders in the book of the same title perfectly carries over America's nineteenth-century Frontier Myth into twentieth-century American political and foreign policy arenas. For the commentators of the era, the Spanish-American War served as the ideological battlefield where American domestic and foreign policy was to be decided for the coming century. Justification for the stabilizing and purifying force of American imperialism on the territories liberated from Old World domination in the Western Hemisphere and around the world influenced, both thematically and technically, the comparatively naive chronicles of the First World War produced by Americans such as **Alan Seeger** in poems like "A Message to America," **Joyce Kilmer** in "The White Ships and the Red" and "The Peacemaker," and **Edith Wharton** in *The Marne*.

REFERENCES

Crisman, William. "Signaling Under Fire: Stephen Crane's Spanish-American War Writings at the American Literature Association Conference, 1991." *Stephen Crane Studies* 1.2 (Fall 1992): 9–11.

Payne, James Robert. "Afro-American Literature of the Spanish-American War." *Melus* 10.3 (Fall 1983): 19–32.

Venzon, Anne Cipriano. *The Spanish-American War: An Annotated Bibliography*. New York: Garland, 1990.

Michelle C. Morgan and Mark A. Graves

SPANISH CIVIL WAR. Many Americans became partisans of the anti-Fascist forces during the Spanish Civil War (1936–1939), and many American writers became spokespersons for the so-called Loyalist cause—though more than a few became disillusioned by the heavy hand of Soviet communism. Though the United States remained officially neutral, its citizens joined the Abraham Lincoln Battalion of the International Brigade—an unwieldy amalgamation of volunteers to the Loyalist (also called the Republican) cause.

The Spanish Civil War gave rise to major literary texts by British and Continental authors. However, most writings by Americans were pedestrian journalistic enterprises. And while some authors enjoyed the authority of writing from Spain, others made their stands without ever leaving the United States. Among those who protested the Franco regime were **William Faulkner, Archibald MacLeish, John Steinbeck, Lillian Hellman, John Dos Passos** (who fashioned a minor novel on the war), **Ernest Hemingway**, and **Martha Gellhorn**. Several of these writers worked with Hemingway on the documentary film *This Spanish Earth*. The most significant achievement is Hemingway's novel *For Whom the Bell Tolls*. This, along with a play and several short stories, constitute Hemingway's vital response to a war that engaged the imaginations, but not the creative energies, of many other writers.

American writers of lesser stature also fashioned important responses to this conflict. Among them are **Alvah Bessie**, whose memoir *Men in Battle* (1939) was praised by Hemingway, and **Edwin Rolfe**, a participant who wrote *The Lincoln Battalion* (1939)—a prose narrative—and several powerful poems collected in *First Love and Other Poems* (1951). **Genevieve Taggard** is another American poet whose work reflected strong feelings about the Spanish Civil War, while **Langston Hughes**, who also reported on the war, wrote several of the most penetrating poems to grow out of that experience. W. H. Auden, the great British poet who became an American citizen in 1946, contributed "Spain" (1937), perhaps the most frequently reprinted poem of that war.

REFERENCES

Benson, Frederick. *Writers in Arms: The Literary Impact of the Spanish Civil War.* London: London University Press, 1967.

Brown, Frieda S., et al., eds. *Rewriting the Good Fight: Critical Essays on the Literature of the Spanish Civil War.* East Lansing: Michigan State University Press, 1989.

Monteath, Peter. *Writing the Good Fight: Political Commitment in the International Literature of the Spanish Civil War.* Westport, CT: Greenwood Press, 1994.

Perez, Janet, and Wendell Aycock, eds. *The Spanish Civil War in Literature.* Lubbock: Texas Tech University Press, 1990.

Philip K. Jason

STALLINGS, LAURENCE (1894–1968). Few American writers who served in World War I wrote as much—or as well—about the subject as Laurence Stallings, whose war-related works include *What Price Glory?* (1924), *Plumes* (1924), *The First World War—A Pictorial History* (1933), and *The Doughboys* (1963), a still-definitive history of the American Expeditionary Force (AEF).

Born in Macon, Georgia, Stallings completed his B.A. in classical studies and biology at Wake Forest University in 1915. In 1918, he served in France as an officer in the Marine Corps and was seriously wounded at the battle of Belleau Wood; as a result, Stallings ultimately lost both of his legs. After the war, Stallings worked as a journalist in Washington, D.C., then as a reviewer for the *New York World*. In 1924, *What Price Glory?* (cowritten by Stallings and **Maxwell Anderson**, a fellow employee of the *World* and a pacifist) opened to critical acclaim at the Plymouth Theater and instantly established Stallings's reputation as a commentator on the war. Stallings spent the rest of his relatively long life working as a reviewer (for various newspapers), editor, screenwriter, and historian. During World War II, he reenlisted in the Marine Corps and served in the Pentagon.

What Price Glory? remains the most celebrated American drama of the Great War. Focused on the competition between two professional Marines, Captain Flagg and Sergeant Quirt, for the affections of a French girl, Charmain, the play offers an uneasy blend of service comedy and protest, alternating between scenes that stress the rowdy charm of the "old breed" and those that express horror over the Marines' appalling losses on the battlefield. By Act Two, the darker mood becomes dominant, as a shell-shocked soldier gives utterance to the emptiness at the heart of the war: "What price glory now? Why can't we all go home? . . . God damn every son of a bitch in the world who isn't here!" (56). Even the thoroughly professional Captain Flagg despairs: Weary of absurd orders (at one point, a general orders the men to plant propaganda posters in the enemy trenches) and teenage replacements, he refuses, at one point, to return his men to battle. Yet, in the end, both he and Quirt leave Charmain for the front, and the play stresses the hold that war has on its victims: "There's something rotten about this profession of arms," declares Flagg, "some kind of damned religion you can't shake. When they tell you to die, you have to do it" (74).

Stallings's novel *Plumes* offers a similarly skeptical commentary on the ability of human beings to escape the allure of warfare. The protagonist, Richard Plume, comes from a long line of Southern warriors and is a devotee of martial values—until his wounding in France and agonizing recovery. Unwilling to assume the role of "war hero," Richard becomes estranged from his family and dedicates himself to ending aggression. Ultimately, however, he concludes that the cultural forces aligned against pacifism are simply too powerful, and he ends his protest—though not before his young son Dickie learns, in the novel's chilling final scene, that a general is "a man . . . who makes little boys sleep in graves" (348).

REFERENCES

Brittain, Joan. *Laurence Stallings*. Boston: Twayne, 1975.
Cooperman, Stanley. *World War I and the American Novel*. Baltimore: Johns Hopkins University Press, 1967.

Steven Trout

STEIN, GERTRUDE (1874–1946). Born in Pennsylvania into a prosperous family of German-Jewish descent, Stein grew up in Oakland, California, and studied psychology at Harvard University and Johns Hopkins Medical School. Trafficking frequently between Europe and America in her formative years, in 1903 she moved to Paris permanently.

Stein lived in France the rest of her life, experiencing both world wars firsthand. Through World War I, she drove a truck for the American Fund for French Wounded. This and other wartime experiences are detailed in her critically acclaimed and best-selling *The Autobiography of Alice B. Toklas* (1933). A number of short World War I pieces also appear in *Geography and Plays* (1922) and *Useful Knowledge* (1928).

When Germany occupied France in 1939, Stein fled to the south, where she managed to elude Nazi officials. The experience of living through the Nazi occupation of France greatly affected her and provides the material for one of her best books, *Wars I Have Seen* (1945). In this her second best-selling auto-biographical work, Stein creates a rare portrait of civilian life in France during World War II. Against a backdrop of sensational postwar correspondent pieces just reaching the public at that time, Stein's text is extraordinary for its focus on the unexceptional and local, the "daily living" of herself and her community. In *Wars*, "daily living" is not only a matter of supply shortages and other inconveniences; it is also a matter of daily living within oneself, especially as to the psychology of civilians groping for a perspective on the war and the repressed terror of being a Jew in occupied France. *Paris, France* (1940) and her experimental novel *Mrs. Reynolds* (published posthumously) provide additional perspectives on World War II.

After the war, Stein moved back to Paris and opened her home to wandering American soldiers. Out of her appreciation for these men came *Brewsie and Willie*, a novel that tries to capture the rhythm of G.I. speech. This novel, in which Stein felt she had achieved a truly "American" mode of narration, is a montage of conversations between a group of enlisted men and army nurses. Having nothing left to think about but going home, these young American war veterans register their fears about reintegrating into a society of industrialism and waste, fears that implicitly raise the question, "We've always known what we have been fighting against, but what have we been fighting *for*?" Five days after it appeared in print in 1946, Stein died of cancer.

In her "Or More (or War)," collected in *Useful Knowledge*, Stein expresses a sentiment that can be taken as indicative of her perspective on war throughout her career:

> He goes, he goes when he is sent.
> When he comes, how many differences are there.
> Differences are differences between when he and when he does.
> Consider it as war.
> In the beginning consider it more.

As in all her war pieces, here Gertrude Stein is uninterested in the "differences" that propel wars; rather, she sees war through the eyes of ordinary people trying to navigate their way to survival and happiness. What interests her are those who "go when [they are] sent"—the soldiers driven into battle, the villagers driven from their homes. It is in the name of these anonymous people, these bystanders, that she implores all those who consider the alternative of war to "consider it more."

REFERENCES

Davis, Phoebe Stein. " 'Even Cake Gets to Have Another Meaning': History, Narrative, and 'Daily Living' in Gertrude Stein's World War II Writing." *Modern Fiction Studies* 44.3 (Fall 1998): 568–607.

Hobhouse, Janet. *Everybody Who Was Anybody: A Biography of Gertrude Stein.* New York: G. P. Putnam's Sons, 1975.

Hoffman, Michael J., ed. *Critical Essays on Gertrude Stein.* Boston: G. K. Hall, 1986.

Sutherland, Donald. *Gertrude Stein: A Biography of Her Work.* New Haven, CT: Yale University Press, 1951.

Eric Weitzel

STEINBECK, JOHN (1902–1968). John Steinbeck was born in California, which would be the setting of many of his novels. Although he never graduated, he attended Stanford University for several years. He died in New York City, having won the Nobel Prize in 1962. In novels such as *Of Mice and Men* (1937), *Cannery Row* (1945), and *East of Eden* (1952), Steinbeck demonstrates his sympathy with the plight of working-class Americans. The most widely acclaimed of these is *The Grapes of Wrath* (1939), an epic tale of one family's suffering the ravages of the American Dust Bowl era.

During World War II, Steinbeck worked as a European war correspondent, publishing articles in the *New York Herald Tribune* between June and December of 1943 that were later collected in *Once There Was a War* (1958). Divided into three sections—"England," "Africa," and "Italy"—the book contains dozens of Steinbeck's conversational accounts of the experiences of individual soldiers, bringing the war's events into more immediate focus for readers back home. His observations range from the conditions of anonymity imposed by the crowded conditions of the troopship to the often humorous exploits of individual soldiers such as the likable scammer Big Train Mulligan or the goat mascot of a regiment in the Royal Air Force. He remarks upon the odd juxtapositions to which war gives birth, such as the appearance in Algiers of modern machines of war alongside ancient transports of camels and wagons. The book ends with Steinbeck's account of the assault on Italy and its aftermath, in which Steinbeck observes, as his previous dispatches have already demonstrated, that the reality of battle is radically different from the image of orderly engagement that exists in the popular imagination.

Steinbeck also published a book about combat bombers, entitled *Bombs Away* (1942). A laudatory book, it follows squad members through precombat training and is a celebration of the skill and expertise of the American warrior in the air. As in his fiction, Steinbeck reveals his interest in the extraordinary nature of ordinary people, focusing here on the training of ordinary men not only to use machines of war but to become glorious war machines themselves.

REFERENCES

Benson, Jackson J. *Looking for Steinbeck's Ghost.* Norman: University of Oklahoma Press, 1988.

French, Warren. *John Steinbeck's Nonfiction Revisited*. New York: Twayne, 1994.
Parini, Jay. *John Steinbeck: A Biography*. New York: Henry Holt and Company, 1995.
Simmonds, Roy. *John Steinbeck: The War Years, 1939–1945*. Lewisburg: Bucknell University Press, 1996.
Steinbeck, John. *Bombs Away: The Story of a Bomber Team*. New York: Viking Press, 1942.
———. *Once There Was a War*. New York: Viking Press, 1958.

Thomas March

STEVENS, JAMES (1892–1971). Born and raised in Iowa, as a young man James Stevens found himself as a member of the working class in the Pacific Northwest. This setting became the backdrop for such books as *Paul Bunyan* (1925) and *The Saginaw Paul Bunyan* (1932), which retold the tall tales of lumbermen, and *Homer in the Sagebrush* (1928), a collection of short stories about the West. The time that James Stevens served in World War I, as part of the 152nd Infantry of the 41st Division, provided background for his semiautobiographical novel *Mattock* (1927).

In *Mattock*, Stevens satirizes the political, military, and religious aspects of World War I through the different moral struggles Private Parvin Mattock faces without ever having his protagonist reach the front lines. Mattock wants to be well liked in his company without becoming "duty-struck." Written in the first person, *Mattock* begins with the title character "down to the lowest place an infantry soldier could get," kitchen patrol (KP) duty. Mattock rises to become the hero of his unit, not through distinguished duty in the trenches but rather through defending his unit's honor against another unit during a fight in a whorehouse. Mattock eventually is promoted to corporal and becomes an assistant to the loyalty officer searching for Communists within his unit. By the end of the war, Mattock finds himself disliked by his fellow soldiers because of his actions. Despite his fundamentalist upbringing, Mattock turns to violence, drinking, and sex while in the military. He ends his service back where he started: demoted to private and on KP duty. After the war, Mattock returns home and has a "conversion," marrying a preacher's daughter and using his status as a veteran from the crusade for democracy to "fight the good fight against law-breakers, Reds, Romans, and foreigners."

However, Stevens has not created a character to be admired but to be satirized for being hypocritical. Mattock is not a hero but a moral vacuum who represents much of what is wrong with the Great War: the insistence on the virtues of patriotism, faith, and bravery through treachery, cynicism, and cowardice.

REFERENCE

Clare, Warren. "James Stevens: The Laborer and Literature." *Research Studies* 32 (1964): 355–367.

Sean C. F. McGurr

STOCKTON, ANNIS BOUDINOT (1736–1801). An often overlooked but quite significant dimension of the literature of the American Revolution is texts written by women. Throughout the colonies from Maine to the Carolinas, women writers such as **Mercy Otis Warren**, Abigail Adams, **Phillis Wheatley**, and Sarah Wister analyzed and celebrated the war for American independence in both prose and poetry. One such writer was Annis Boudinot Stockton, who, from her home in New Jersey, wrote numerous poems about the people and events involved in the war.

Born into a wealthy Pennsylvania family of Huguenot background, Annis Boudinot grew up in an atmosphere of wealth, learning, and privilege. Moving with her family in 1753 to Princeton, Boudinot later married Richard Stockton, whose family was one of the oldest and most distinguished in the region. Through her position as the wife of the college's first graduate trustee, Annis Stockton had the opportunity to know and befriend many of the important citizens of her day, including George and Martha Washington.

From an early age, Stockton prided herself on her literary achievements, many of which went unpublished during her lifetime but were nonetheless well known among the literati of the Middle Atlantic Colonies and gained her considerable reputation as a poet. As it did for several other women writers, the Revolutionary War provided a major catalyst for the development of Stockton's career. While popular sentiment generally prohibited early American women from pursuing a too-public career as a writer, wars frequently provided an exception to the prevailing rules of decorum regarding the writing and publication of texts by women. Throughout the seventeenth and eighteenth centuries, for example, the frontier wars between the English and the Indians had produced a flood of Indian captivity narratives written by women who would have otherwise gone unpublished and unnoticed, including **Mary Rowlandson**'s *Sovereignty and Goodness of God* (1682), now recognized as one of the most important martial texts of the seventeenth century.

Like most other poets of her day, Stockton espoused the neoclassical traditions popular during the late eighteenth century. In highly polished and sophisticated verse not unlike that of the great neoclassical poets of England, Annis Stockton commemorates important events and people associated with the war that was unfolding around her. Many of these poems were published in local newspapers and magazines, and several praised George Washington, whom she met during Princeton meetings of the Continental Congress and who considered her one of the leading literary talents of the war. Outliving her husband by many years, Annis Boudinot Stockton died in New Jersey in 1801.

REFERENCES

Butterfield, Lyman H. "Annis Stockton and the General: Mrs. Stockton's Poetic Eulogies of George Washington." *Princeton University Library Chronicle* 7 (1945): 19–30.

Cowell, Pattie. "Annis Stockton." *American Women Writers*. Ed. Lina Mainiero. New York: Frederick Ungar, 1982.

Mulford, Carla. "Annis Boudinot Stockton." *American National Biography*. New York: Oxford University Press, 1998.

————. *"Only for the Eve of a Friend"*: *The Poetry of Annis Boudinot Stockton*. Charlottesville: University Press of Virginia, 1995.

James A. Levernier

STONE, ROBERT (1937–   ). Born and raised in New York City, Stone enlisted in the navy in 1955. Discharged in 1958, he attended New York University for two years and later enrolled in Stanford University's creative writing program, where he met Ken Kesey, with whom he was briefly allied as part of the San Francisco psychedelic scene. From 1967 to 1971, Stone worked in Vietnam as a freelance writer and war correspondent. Stone has since held several academic positions while writing short stories and novels critical of a moral malaise he sees as endemic to contemporary American society.

Stone's contribution to the field of war literature rests principally on his second novel, *Dog Soldiers* (1974), which won the National Book Award in 1975. A metaphoric reworking of our Vietnam involvement, the novel opens in Vietnam with John Converse, a frustrated and feckless freelance war correspondent, reading a letter in which his wife Marge has agreed to join in a heroin-smuggling scheme. Unable to carry the heroin himself, Converse turns to a sometime marijuana smuggler and merchant seaman named Ray Hicks, whom he had met years before in the Marine Corps.

The title alludes to the nineteenth-century band of Plains Indians who fought with a fierce, fatalistic indifference to death. In their refusal to take any responsibility for their actions, Converse and Marge have essentially "taken leave of life." They qualify as "Dog Soldiers" in an ironic sense. The "converse" of this position is that occupied by Hicks, a "Dog Soldier" in the familiar sense of dogged persistence. A self-styled Samurai and modernist code hero who cultivates "the art of self-defense," Hicks almost gratuitously assumes complete responsibility for safeguarding both the heroin and Marge from a corrupt and ruthless federal agent named Antheil, who turns out to be the ringleader of the smuggling operation. The novel culminates in a gun battle in the Arizona mountains, with Hicks holding off Antheil's followers long enough for the Converses to escape. Hicks too escapes but is seriously wounded in the battle. He dies trying to carry the heroin to an agreed-upon rendezvous with the Converses. Unmoved by Hicks's sacrifice, John ties a white handkerchief to the heroin and leaves it behind as he and Marge drive off to resume their previously pointless lives together.

While it only starts out in Vietnam, *Dog Soldiers* has earned its high station in Vietnam War literature for bringing the war home in a symbolic and interpretive sense. A damning indictment of the culture that spawned the war, the novel explains Vietnam in terms of the tendency to push tolerance to insane heights and to tout moral disengagement as the new virtue during the 1960s. In our conduct as individuals, and as a nation, Stone suggests, we had grown solipsistic, recognizing no obligation beyond our own inchoate needs. But as Stone further suggests, these needs would never have coalesced into our Vietnam tragedy had it not been for a professional military that, in the manner of Ray Hicks, was all too willing to soldier bravely on in a bad cause. *Dog Soldiers* was made into the 1978 film *Who'll Stop the Rain.*

Three of Stone's later novels touch on war as a theme. *A Flag for Sunrise* (1981) is set against the backdrop of covert American efforts to counter a leftist insurgency in a Central American country, and the main character of *Outerbridge Reach* (1989) is a middle-aged Vietnam veteran whose unresolved feelings about the war lead to an ill-fated attempt to sail around the world alone. Stone's short story "Helping," reprinted in his 1997 collection *Bear and His Daughter,* likewise deals with the aftermath of the Vietnam experience.

In *Damascus Gate* (1998), Stone turns his attention from the violence inherent in the American experience to the violence endemic to religious fanaticism. In modern-day Jerusalem, against the backdrop of the Palestinian Intifada, a group of millenarian religious extremists form a coalition to fulfill biblical prophecy on their own terms. They enter into a plot to destroy the Temple Mount's Islamic mosques in order to clear the site for the rebuilding of the Second Temple. Their ultimate goal is to ignite a holy war that would rid Israel of its Arab presence and clear the political way for a theocratic Israeli government. In preparation for this outcome, the plotters employ a deluded messianic figure to arouse a general atmosphere of apocalyptic fervor and to cloak their ultimate objective under an appeal to religious syncretism. The plot is discovered by the novel's central character, Chris Lucas, a marginal freelance journalist whose own unresolved religious identity leads him to begin researching a book on religious extremism and to form a personal attachment to a well-meaning young woman on the periphery of the plot. Essentially a searcher after religious truth, she is herself unaware of the plotters' real intentions and has been manipulated toward their ends. Lucas finally proves to be a typically ineffectual Stone antihero. He plays no real role in thwarting the plot, and the reader, along with Lucas, is surprised to discover the actual genesis of what turns out to have been, from the outset, a political plot aimed at preserving the secular identity of the State of Israel.

REFERENCES

Beidler, Philip D. *Re-Writing America: Vietnam Authors in Their Generation.* Athens: University of Georgia Press, 1991. 237–264.

Melling, Philip H. *Vietnam in American Literature.* Boston: Twayne, 1990. 169–193.

Parks, John G. "Unfit Survivors: The Failed and Lost Pilgrims in the Fiction of Robert Stone." *CEA Critic* 53.1 (Fall 1990): 52–57.

Solartoff, Robert. *Robert Stone.* New York: Twayne, 1994.

Edward F. Palm

STOWE, HARRIET BEECHER (1811–1896). Renowned author, journalist, and educator Harriet Beecher Stowe lived amid a veritable God's Army— her father, six brothers, and husband were all ministers—whose impassioned

Calvinist evangelicalism profoundly influenced her writing, particularly her large body of abolitionist works. Her fiction and nonfiction alike breathed an ardently moral abolitionism that sparked the flames of controversy as slavery and states' rights severed the nation. No work, however, shook the world as did her *Uncle Tom's Cabin; or, Life among the Lowly*, the United States's best-selling book of the nineteenth century.

Serialized between June 5, 1851, and April 1, 1852, in the *National Era* and then published in book form in 1852, *Uncle Tom's Cabin* redefined both publishing and politics. Huge sales mirrored fiery public reactions to the tale that severely criticized the Fugitive Slave Law of 1850, the moral fiber of U.S. capitalism, and the justice of Southern slavery. Loved and despised, *Uncle Tom's Cabin* divided states and families, anticipating the national reaction to the Civil War, to which it has been intimately tied.

According to family legend, President Abraham Lincoln, upon meeting Stowe in 1862, claimed *Uncle Tom's Cabin* was responsible for the war. The book also spawned a huge cultural mania, from stage adaptations that played into the 1930s to reactionary novels, songs, and consumer goods that boasted an "anti-Tom" perspective. So tightly did "Uncle Tom" weave through the national fabric as a common phrase and racial stereotype that African American literature and culture still grapple with its ambivalent models of black manhood and personal dignity. The novel powerfully affected the Western Hemisphere as well, selling over a million copies in Britain in 1852 and spurring British and Irish women to send "An Affectionate and Christian Address" (1853) to U.S. women that begged them to save domesticity from slavery's evils.

Throughout the 1850s, Stowe's writings continued to address the building crises. Her 1854 "Appeal" to female solidarity to abolish slavery in the name of holy independence shortly preceded the Kansas-Nebraska Bill, which eradicated the Missouri Compromise of 1820, opened U.S. territories to slavery upon popular election, and precipitated a regional bloodbath between pro- and anti-slavery forces in Kansas. In 1856 she continued her novelistic attack with *Dred: A Tale of the Great Dismal Swamp*, which emphasizes the degrading effects of the institution upon white slaveholders.

When war came, Stowe personally felt its effects. Her son Frederick enlisted in the Northern army and took shrapnel in the ear at Gettysburg, an injury that plagued him throughout his life. Stowe's worry for him, coupled with many other woes, including ill health brought on by her many pregnancies, led her to write primarily on safe homey topics during the war years to escape the ravages on both national and personal domestic fronts.

Nevertheless, Stowe was far from mute about the Civil War. In the September 11, 1862, edition of *The Independent*, a religious, abolitionist New York weekly newspaper that first named the Civil War and for which Stowe wrote frequently, her column "Will You Take a Pilot?" challenged Lincoln's stand on preserving the Union over eliminating slavery. Confederate atrocities are the topic of her

May 1865 essay "The Noble Army of Martyrs," in which she tells the story of a Union soldier who dies in a Confederate prison.

REFERENCES

Hedrick, Joan D. *Harriet Beecher Stowe: A Life*. New York and Oxford: Oxford University Press, 1994.
Stowe, Harriet Beecher. *The Writings of Harriet Beecher Stowe*. 16 vols. Cambridge, MA: Riverside Press, 1896.
Sundquist, Eric J., ed. *New Essays on "Uncle Tom's Cabin."* Cambridge: Cambridge University Press, 1986.

Sandra Burr

STREETER, EDWARD (1891–1976). Streeter was born in Chestertown, New York. A Harvard graduate (1914) who edited the *Lampoon* his senior year, he worked briefly in business, then became a reporter for the *Buffalo Express*. A member of the New York National Guard, he was activated for duty, chasing Pancho Villa, in 1916, contributing newspaper pieces on his experiences. Reactivated in 1917, he served in France with the Field Artillery, then returned to a career in banking.

While serving in Texas, he wrote humorous imaginary letters for the post paper; training in South Carolina for the European war, he continued the letters, amassing a substantial number. With five days of New York leave before shipping overseas, he left an edited collection of the letters with a publisher, and the book *Dere Mable: Love Letters of a Rookie* (1918) became a best-seller. Three sequels followed: *That's Me All Over, Mable* (1919), *Same Old Bill, Eh, Mable* (1919), and *As You Were, Bill* (1920). Each volume is illustrated with pen-and-ink drawings by Corporal G. William (Bill) Breck. The letters are from a near-illiterate soldier, Bill Smith, to his sweetheart, Miss Mable Gimp, of Philopolis, New York. In them, Streeter employs every G.I. joke ever told, weaving them into the story of one simple doughboy caught up in the war to end all wars. Throughout, the humor centers on Bill's misunderstanding of military duties, his doubts about officers and noncoms, and his simple lack of sophistication socially and intellectually. Bill has a tendency toward malapropism, exaggeration, and mangled French, though his naive patriotism is perhaps what made him popular.

Streeter does not glorify war; instead, he uses black humor to show its reality. In a preface to *Same Old Bill*, the only volume that actually describes combat, Streeter defensively explains that such humor was the doughboy's choice: Barbs aimed at the army, about the French allies, and about battle are the release valve for troops in the midst of action (or of boredom while awaiting action). In one of the few letters dealing with actual combat, Streeter lets Bill express surprise that, in fact, wartime propaganda was false: The German soldiers were not chained to their weapons to fight, and there were no women conscripted to fill the battle line. With gruff humor, Bill describes the daily routine of doughboys soaked in water-filled trenches, befriending rats as closest acquaintances, and bearing seemingly meaningless reciprocal shelling. Slapstick lightly veils a usually boring, sometimes scary, and always lonely reality.

Streeter published no books between 1921 and 1938, concentrating instead on building his successful career in banking. He reprised the first two *Dere Mable* volumes for a collected edition in 1941. Once sufficiently established in banking, he resumed writing, publishing a number of humorous novels, including *Father of the Bride* (1949), *Mr. Hobbs' Vacation* (1954), and *Chairman of the Bored* (1961), as well as several travel books.

REFERENCES

Bell, Millicent. *Marquand: An American Life*. Boston: Atlantic–Little, Brown, 1979.
Cruse, Irma R. "Edward Streeter." *Encyclopedia of American Humorists*. Ed. Steven H. Gale. New York: Garland, 1988. 414–417.
Nichols, Lewis. "Edward Streeter, Humorist, Dies at 84." *New York Times* 2 April 1976: 34.
Swanson, Roy Arthur. "Edward Streeter." *Dictionary of Literary Biography*. Ed. Stanley Trachtenberg. Vol. 11. Detroit: Gale, 1982. 474–477.
Yates, Norris Wilson. *The American Humorist: Conscience of the Twentieth Century*. Ames: Iowa State University Press, 1964.

Mark D. Noe

STYRON, WILLIAM (1925–). William Styron was born in Newport News in Virginia's Tidewater region, a setting and a theme of much of his literary output. He attended Davidson College in North Carolina in 1942 and a year later joined the U.S. Marine Corps. He attended Duke University for a brief period while in the Marines, then returned to the service as a Marine lieutenant from 1944 to 1945. Styron was in Okinawa awaiting orders to take part in the expected invasion of Japan when the war ended in August 1945. He returned to Duke after the war and graduated in 1947. He then went to live in New York City and was briefly called to active duty in the Marine Corps during the Korean War.

Styron's first novel, *Lie Down in Darkness* (1951), which he began writing in 1947, is set in Tidewater Virginia and chronicles the fortunes of a young woman and her family. The book received high critical praise for its literary craftsmanship—including the Prix de Rome from the American Academy of Arts and Letters—and won Styron recognition as one of the leading authors of his generation.

The Long March, which Styron wrote in six weeks in Paris, was published in 1952 in *Discovery* magazine and in book form in 1956 by Modern Library. That novella is a psychological portrait of two U.S. Marine reserve officers called up to train for the Korean War. Both men are World War II veterans who are not exactly pleased to be under the command of a self-important colonel. The colonel forces the trainees to make a thirty-five-mile, full-pack march, which provides the book with its dramatic tension. *The Long March* later appeared in Charles Fenton's anthology *The Best Short Stories of World War II.*

Styron's play *In the Clap Shack* (1973) is a black comedy set in a U.S. Navy hospital's urology ward during World War II. Styron takes on the navy's medical system in this biting story of bureaucracy and ignorance run amok. The man who suffers is an eighteen-year-old Southern sailor who is wrongly believed to have syphilis. Styron's fourth novel, *The Confessions of Nat Turner* (1967), secured his reputation as one of the nation's top literary lights. The controversial book tells the story of an 1831 slave revolt in Virginia led by the title character who narrates the tale. Some critics accused Styron of racism, but he won the highest praise from others for his elegant prose and powerful psychological portraits. The book was awarded the Pulitzer Prize in 1968; two years later Styron received the Howells Medal from the American Academy of Arts and Letters.

His next novel, *Sophie's Choice*, won unstinting critical praise. The novel, which was adapted into a highly praised Hollywood film in 1982, is an autobiographical tale set in Brooklyn in 1947. Styron's alter ego, Stingo, is a struggling writer from Virginia who gets intricately involved with Sophie, a Polish Catholic who survived Auschwitz, and Nathan, her mad American lover. Filled with flashbacks to Sophie's days before and during the war, this coming of age novel chronicles Sophie's cataclysmic war experiences and Stingo's cathartic maturation. The elegantly written *Sophie's Choice* won the 1980 American Book Award.

By the mid-1980s, clinical depression slowed Styron's output, but he rallied to write about his illness in *Darkness Visible: A Memoir of Madness* (1990). *A Tidewater Morning*, three tales narrated by a boy who grew up in Tidewater Virginia, was published in 1993.

William Styron married Rose Burgunder in 1953. They have four children. He is a recipient of the Commandeur de l'Ordre des Arts et des Letters, the Commandeur Legion d'Honneur, and the Prix Mondial del Duca. Styron is a member of the American Academy of Arts and Sciences and the American Academy of Arts and Letters.

REFERENCES

Bryer, Jackson, R. *William Styron: A Reference Guide*. New York: G. K. Hall, 1978.
Ratner, Marc L. *William Styron*. New York: Twayne, 1972.
Ross, David W., ed. *The Critical Response to William Styron*. Westport, CT: Greenwood Press, 1995.
West, James L. W., III. *William Styron: A Life*. New York: Random House, 1998.

Marc Leepson

T

TAGGARD, GENEVIEVE (1894–1948). A poet, critic, editor, and social activist, Taggard was born in Waitsburg, Washington. Due to the missionary work of her parents, she lived in Hawaii for much of her childhood. Hawaii's multiracial culture had an enduring influence on Taggard and contributed to the liberal views that she had begun to form by the time she graduated from the University of California at Berkeley in 1920. The granddaughter of two Union soldiers, Taggard did her fighting as a poet of social protest and supporter of radical magazines. For example, she edited *May Days*, a 1925 anthology of verse published in *The Masses* and *The Liberator* that includes war poems by **Carl Sandburg**, Siegfried Sassoon, and **Edmund Wilson**. Taggard is best known for her trailblazing psychological study *The Life and Mind of Emily Dickinson* (1930); this work and her other efforts indicate the breadth of her literary endeavors.

Although she also wrote poems on love, nature, women's experiences, and social injustice, Taggard's poems on war are significant for their compelling descriptions and forthright appeals for change. "Silence in Mallorca" (1938) not only exemplifies these qualities but also rewrites Percy Bysshe Shelley's "Ode to the West Wind" as its collective speaker pleads for a just end to war. The poem calls on the wind to blow war away from the Spanish island and replace it with liberty, equality, a quiet land, and harmony within families and the government. "Silence in Mallorca," like "To Two Young Men Who Committed Suicide in Paris in 1932" (1937) and "Image" (1933)—later dedicated "to the heroic memory of Christopher Caudwell, author of *Illusion and Reality*, killed in action fighting with the government forces at Madrid, 1937"—shows the impact that the Spanish Civil War had on Taggard's imagination. Taggard's political involvement continued during World War II; she dedicated a 1942 pamphlet of her selected poems to war hero Liudmilla Pavlichenko in support of the Soviet Union against Germany.

REFERENCES

Taggard, Genevieve. *Collected Poems, 1918–1938*. New York and London: Harper, 1938.

————. *The Complete Works of Genevieve Taggard*. 3 reels. Ann Arbor, MI: University Microfilms International, 1974.

————, ed. *May Days: An Anthology of Masses–Liberator Verse, 1912–1924*. New York: Boni & Liveright, 1925.

Wilson, Martha A., and Gwendolyn Sell. "Lola Ridge and Genevieve Taggard: Voices of Resistance." *Arkansas Quarterly: A Journal of Criticism* 2.2 (Spring 1993): 124–133.

Catherine J. Tramontana

TATE, ALLEN (1899–1979). Born John Orley Allen Tate in Winchester, Kentucky, this writer, editor, critic, and university professor was one of the more important poets of the century, and his influence as a critic was widely felt as a leading figure among the New Critics. He was a member of the Fugitive group that grew out of Vanderbilt University, along with **Robert Penn Warren**, Donald Davidson, John Crowe Ransom, and others who changed the face of Southern literature and modern poetry. Tate also was something of a social reform theorist and wrote essays (including a piece in the 1930 Agrarian testament *I'll Take My Stand*) that condemn the debilitating effects of industrialism on the human community and evince a nostalgia for an agrarian lifestyle. He advocated a return to the perceived humanistic tradition of the Old South. In his earlier years Tate wrote biographies of Stonewall Jackson (1928) and Jefferson Davis (1929). But he is more noted for his critical essays, his several volumes of poems, and one novel, *The Fathers* (1938).

The Fathers, hailed by Arthur Mizener (in his introduction to the Swallow edition) as "the novel *Gone with the Wind* ought to have been," follows the coming of age of Lacy Buchan, the teenaged son of a high-minded Virginia gentleman in the years leading up to the Civil War. The narrator is Lacy as an old man, who reminisces about his young heart having been divided between the formal yet comforting tradition represented by his father, Major Buchan, and the lawless, destructive energy represented by his brother-in-law George Posey, whose romantic impulses leave the lives of his loved ones in shambles. As the war begins, the Old Order is overcome: The First Battle of Manassas is characterized as the beginning of the end of the traditional Southern lifestyle that the war was meant to preserve. Lacy and George, however, both choose that tradition and stability in the face of war's chaos.

Tate is perhaps best known for his poem "Ode to the Confederate Dead," a dense and introspective consideration of the sacrifices made by the title figures, written from the point of view of one who is trapped in the apparently meaningless void of modernity, where such heroic passion and selflessness seem scarcely feasible.

REFERENCES

Huff, Peter A. *Allen Tate and the Catholic Revival: Trace of the Fugitive Gods*. New York: Paulist Press, 1996.

Malvasi, Mark G. *The Unregenerate South: The Agrarian Thought of John Crowe Ransom, Allen Tate, and Donald Davidson.* Baton Rouge: Louisiana State University Press, 1997.
Meiners, Roger K. *The Last Alternatives: A Study of the Works of Allen Tate.* Denver, CO: Swallow, 1963.
Squires, Radcliffe. *Allen Tate: A Literary Biography.* New York: Pegasus, 1971.

Randal W. Allred

TERKEL, STUDS (1912–   ). Born Louis Terkel in New York City in 1912, he took the name "Studs" from James T. Farrell's colorful fictional character Studs Lonigan. Terkel earned a law degree from the University of Chicago in 1934. He then became a successful actor and later a broadcaster famous for his rapport with people of diverse backgrounds and occupations. When his liberal views led to cancellation of his television talk show, Terkel turned to writing oral histories based upon interviews with average people. As one correspondent stated, "Next to Richard Nixon, the person whose life has been most dramatically affected by the tape recorder is Studs Terkel." Although Terkel edits and occasionally guides his respondent's answers, he aims to capture "the essence of the man with nothing of me in it." Even critics who hold reservations about his methods readily acknowledge that his personal approach is a valuable tool in social research.

One of Terkel's most renown works is *"The Good War,"* for which he received a Pulitzer Prize in 1984. In this oral history, Terkel focuses on the responses of Americans to recreate an era of international crisis and domestic change. The interviewees' responses simultaneously express repulsion for the great misery and nostalgia for a time of national unity and moral certainty, a time that was both exhilarating and rehabilitating. Terkel demonstrates this dichotomy by placing the title in quotation marks. Terkel, adept at getting others to talk about their deepest thoughts and recollections, has turned oral history into a literary form. As with his other works, *"The Good War"* is an orchestrated jumble of voices, including the prominent and the unknown, the wealthy and the poor. Terkel drew critical praise for including interviews of black soldiers and their reminiscences of the segregationist policies of the era. Critics, however, note that Terkel carefully picks and chooses the viewpoints expressed, which largely mirror his own, thus undermining the work's claim to be inclusive. Most critics cite the shortcomings inherent in oral history, which relies upon memory. They also note that Terkel operates under a layman's false notion of history—that the facts speak for themselves and that the bits and pieces each person recollects of a specific major event will add up to a coherent whole. Terkel, however, presents no coherent theme and presents each story uncritically on its own terms. Terkel is best at presenting not the essence of the period but the odd, offbeat, and unique.

REFERENCES

Baker, James Thomas. *Studs Terkel.* New York: Twayne, 1992.
Parker, Tony. *Studs Terkel: A Life in Words.* New York: H. Holt, 1996.

Prescott, Peter S. Rev. of *The Good War*, by Studs Terkel. *Newsweek* 15 October 1984: 98.

Wainwright, Loudon. Rev. of *The Good War*, by Studs Terkel. *New York Times Book Review* 7 October 1984: 9.

William T. Hartley

TERRY, LUCY (ca. 1725–1821). Lucy Terry is the first known African American poet in colonial America. Part of the black diaspora, she was whirled from her native Africa to Rhode Island to Connecticut to Massachusetts by the time she was five years old. In Deerfield, Massachusetts, Lucy became one of two slaves of Ebenezer and Abigail Wells. Despite her social status she became renowned for having "a tenacious memory," being "a prodigy in conversation," and retaining a "knowledge of the holy scriptures [that] was uncommonly great"—aspects testifying to her skill in the arts of the European bard and the African griot. Indeed, her thirty-line poem "Bars Fight" (1746), the most vivid and complete extant account of the Indian raid on a party of haymakers in the Bars section of Deerfield on August 25, 1746, was a local favorite that Lucy was asked to recite throughout her life.

"Bars Fight" recounts a brief blitz in a barrage of hostilities in North America between the French, the British, and their Indian allies in the decade preceding the Seven Years' War (1756–1763). Deerfield residents, unaware that Pierre François Rigaud de Vaudreuil had captured Fort Massachusetts with a band of French and Indians on August 9, took no special precautions that August morning. Thus, the Indians' surprise ambush on the Allens and Amsdens as the families resumed haying quickly resulted in the deaths of three of the five adult men—Samuel Allen, his brother-in-law Eleazer Hawks, and one of two guards, Adonijah Gillett. As the second guard, John Saddler, escaped alive across the Deerfield River, the Indians slew the other man and his young brother—the Amsdens—severely wounded young Eunice Allen, and kidnapped Samuel Allen, the youngest. Nine-year-old Caleb Allen hid, undetected, in a nearby cornfield.

Lucy was intimately familiar with the themes of this poem precisely because she was a slave. Despair, horror, bloodshed, death, family separation, and the shock attendant upon forced and sometimes violent interaction with members of a different race and culture were part of her experience and, in a different but still painful way, those of the Allen and Amsden families.

REFERENCES

Foster, Frances Smith. " 'Sometimes by Simile, a Victory's Won': Lucy Terry Prince and Phillis Wheatley." *Written by Herself: Literary Production by African American Women, 1746–1892*. Bloomington and Indianapolis: Indiana University Press, 1993.

Proper, David R. *Lucy Terry Prince: Singer of History. A Biography*. Deerfield, MA: Pocumtuck Valley Memorial Association and Historic Deerfield, 1997.

Sandra Burr

TERRY, WALLACE (1938–   ). Wallace Houston Terry II was born in New York City, received his B.A. from Brown University in 1959, and was a Nieman Fellow at Harvard in 1970. He is an ordained minister (Disciples of Christ) and has worked as a journalist, covering the war in Vietnam as a correspondent for *Time* magazine from 1963 until 1971. He produced several oral histories concerning the role and experience of the African American soldier in the Vietnam War, including a record entitled *Guess Who's Coming Home: Black Fighting Men Recorded Live in Vietnam* (1972), with liner notes by Julian Bond.

Terry edited *Bloods: An Oral History of the Vietnam War by Black Veterans* (1984), which displays to a remarkable degree the vicissitudes black soldiers had to endure during their time in Vietnam, the effects of the war upon them, and the aftermath, as the soldiers tried to readjust to life in a still-racist United States. The title comes from the word black soldiers used to name themselves. The impetus for the collection came when Terry noticed that a special edition of *Life* magazine commemorating World War II had not a single picture of an African American soldier. He predicted that a similar and complete invisibility would occur to blacks in Vietnam by the year 2000. Made up of twenty narratives, the structure of *Bloods* is such that it demarcates the mythic sweep of the men in their full understanding of their situation and also describes in excruciatingly ironic detail the means of coping with prejudice and the racial hostility that the men must create in order to endure. In so doing, the work speaks to the efforts of these men as they come to terms with the promises of the Great Society and the hints of advancement embedded in the general tenor of the civil rights movement. The language of the black veterans preserves the difficulty, suspense, terror, and only some small moments of happiness during active duty and after. Speaking almost of a motif running throughout the work, one of Terry's subjects says: "I used to think that I wasn't affected by Vietnam, but I been livin' with Vietnam ever since I left."

REFERENCES

Karnow, Stanley. "Sharing the Ordeal of Vietnam." *New York Times Book Review* October 1984: 7–9.
Lomperis, Timothy J. *"Reading the Wind": The Literature of the Vietnam War*. Durham: Duke University Press, 1987.

Brian Adler

TIMROD, HENRY (1828–1867). Born in Charleston, South Carolina, Timrod attended the German Friendly Society School and the Classical School before entering the University of Georgia in 1845. After leaving the university in 1846, he returned to Charleston, tried a law apprenticeship, and then studied privately to become a college professor. Unsuccessful in attaining a university professorship, Timrod tutored on several plantations as he wrote and published his poetry. He collected this early work in *Poems* (1859).

Early in the Civil War period, Timrod wrote patriotic poetry praising the

South. His "Ethnogenesis," written during the meeting of the first Southern Congress in February 1861, heralds the birth of the Confederacy. Foreseeing the impending war with the North, Timrod asks God and Nature to protect the South. His poem concludes with a glorious vision of the South's future: "The rapturous sight would fill / Our eyes with happy tears!" "Cotton Boll" (1861) proclaims the power of Southern cotton; then, in closing, the poem becomes a war prayer: "Oh, help us, Lord! to roll the crimson flood / Back on its course." Timrod's prayer reveals his hostility towards the North: "strike with us! till the Goth shall cling / . . . and crave / Mercy." Another famous early war poem is "Carolina" (1862), which makes a desperate call to push back the Northern invaders who tread upon Carolina's "sacred sands."

In July 1861, Timrod volunteered in defense of the Beaufort coast, serving as quartermaster, secretary, and treasurer of the local company. Yet by September 1861, in accordance with a special clause, he left the company and returned to Charleston. Before March 1862, the tubercular Timrod once again enlisted, this time gaining appointment as a regimental clerk. Uninspired by his duties, Timrod left his clerkship to become a war correspondent for the *Mercury*. His new job brought him into contact with the Confederate army as it retreated after the battle of Shiloh. On account of his tuberculosis, his stay was short, and by late 1862, he returned to Charleston and his clerkship. Due to his continual health problems, the Confederate army discharged Timrod on December 15, 1862. He volunteered once more in July 1863 but was discharged after only a day.

Timrod was changed by what he saw. This change is evident in his poem "Christmas" (1862), in which Timrod struggles to reconcile holiday merriment with the wartime reality of widespread suffering and death. He explains that it is difficult to be merry "[w]hile some loved reveler of a year ago / Keeps his mute Christmas now beneath the snow." He struggles to find a way to sing of the holy day. Instead of a call for the death of his foes, Timrod asks for peace among the living and dead. By the end of the poem, there is a frantic insistence—"Peace, God of Peace! peace, peace, in all our / homes, / and peace in all our hearts!"—that expresses Timrod's weariness with the war. In "Spring" (1863), Timrod explores how the war has changed the meaning of spring from new life to more deaths. After a long winter Timrod looks forward to springtime as "[s]ome wondrous pageant," yet he also knows that this new season will also "rouse . . . A million men to arms." This poem concludes with an image of Spring kneeling on the ground, "Lifting her bloody daises up to God" and calling for the destruction of "the tyrants and the slaves / Who turn her meads to graves." In "Carmen Triumphale," which appeared in June 1863 prior to Vicksburg and Gettysburg, Timrod expresses renewed hope for victory. He experiences a "sober joy" with the North's defeat and exclaims, "Our foes are fallen! Flash, ye wires!" Again, he describes the Northerners as "tyrants" and asserts that "God gave the dastards to our hands." In July 1863, Timrod published "The

Unknown Dead," which praises the sacrifice of the common soldiers. He writes, "Beneath yon lonely mound . . . Lie the true martyrs of the fight."

After his final effort to join the Confederate army in 1863, Timrod did editorial work for the *Mercury* and *Daily South Carolinian*. In February 1864, he married Kate Godwin, and on Christmas Eve, she gave birth to their son Willie, whose death within a year completely devastated Timrod. From July 1863 to 1866, he published only one war-related poem. In June 1866 his "Ode," which commemorates the decoration of Confederate graves, was sung at the Magnolia Cemetery in Charleston. It poignantly captures the emotions of a proud but defeated South: "There is no holier spot of ground, / Than where defeated valor lies." Timrod's tuberculosis steadily intensified and eventually led to his death on October 7, 1867. For the verse that he created during the war, Timrod will be regarded as one of the most famous Southern poets of the nineteenth century.

REFERENCES

Parks, Edd Winfield. *Henry Timrod*. New York: Twayne, 1964.
Timrod, Henry. *The Collected Poems of Henry Timrod: A Variorum Edition*. Ed. Edd Winfield Parks and Aileen Wells Parks. Athens: University of Georgia Press, 1965.

Paul R. Cappucci

TOMPSON, BENJAMIN (1642–1714). Born in Braintree, Massachusetts, in 1642 to the zealous Reverend William Tompson and his wife, Benjamin Tompson was raised by two of his father's parishioners, Mr. and Mrs. Thomas Blanchard, after his mother's early death. His father, absent from home ministering to the local Indians, could not raise Benjamin alone. When Benjamin was quite young, the Blanchards moved to Cambridge, Massachusetts, and later sent him to Harvard College. He graduated in 1662 but followed a different path from most of his classmates, who became ministers. Benjamin became a schoolmaster and held several positions at prestigious schools, once even teaching Cotton Mather. After the death of his father in 1666, Benjamin married Susanna Kirtland in 1667. They had eight children before she died in 1693. Benjamin continued to teach at the Roxbury Latin School until his death in 1714.

Benjamin Tompson's contributions to American war literature take the form of poems about New England's deadly seventeenth-century conflict, King Philip's War. According to many scholars, Tompson's poem *New England's Crisis*, published in Boston in 1676, is America's first epic poem. Tompson's second poem about the war, *New England's Tears*, published in London in 1676, was originally designed as a continuation of *New England's Crisis*, but in reality both poems relate, for the most part, the same historical matter. Much of *New England's Tears* consists of reprinted text from the earlier poem, and accordingly they are here studied together as one poem.

Literary scholars have a hard time classifying Tompson's work. Most agree that he was writing "public verse" as a representative of the citizens of embattled

Massachusetts. However, the poems themselves are seen as a mixture of mock-epic, captivity narrative, journalism, and jeremiad. Other scholars classify the poems as verse histories filled with many tones, styles of writing, and fragmentary coverage of the war. Yet the "epic" label perseveres and with some justification. Tompson casts the forces of the war as epic characters, with the English colonists as Christian heroes or victims arrayed against the forces of evil and darkness, "pagan" Indians. Tompson, in an atypical turn for an epic, memorializes not individual heroes but entire Puritan communities that came under Indian attack. Scholars do agree, however, that Tompson's attempts at creating an American epic poem based on the war fail in the end as the poems degenerate into either jeremiad sermons or incomplete narratives of the war's progress.

REFERENCES

Eberwein, Jane Donahue. " 'Harvardine Quil': Benjamin Tompson's Poems on King Philip's War." *Early American Literature* 28.1 (1993): 1–20.
Slotkin, Richard, and James K. Folsom. "Benjamin Tompson: American Epic Poet." *So Dreadful a Judgment: Puritan Responses to King Philip's War, 1676–1677*. Middletown, CT: Wesleyan University Press, 1978.
Tompson, Benjamin, and Peter White. *Benjamin Tompson: Colonial Bard, a Critical Edition*. University Park and London: Pennsylvania University Press, 1980.
White, Peter. "Benjamin Tompson." *American Colonial Writers, 1606–1734*. Ed. Emory Elliott. Vol. 24 of *Dictionary of Literary Biography*. Detroit: Gale Research, 1984. 322–263.

Kyle F. Zelner

TOURGÉE, ALBION WINEGAR (1838–1905). Tourgée was born in Williamsfield, Ohio, and educated at the University of Rochester, New York. In April 1861 he enlisted in the Union army and was seriously wounded at the first Battle of Bull Run in July of that year. Following his recovery, Tourgée received a commission and served until 1864. While in the army Tourgée developed an abiding concern for the fate of black Americans, for their integration into American life, and for the reintegration of the South into the United States. This concern led him first to apply for a transfer to a regiment of United States Colored Troops, which was denied, and then, after the war, to a career in Reconstruction-era North Carolina, where he edited the Republican *Union Register*, served as a judge of the Superior Court, and held the post of United States Pension Agent.

Between 1874 and 1898 Tourgée authored more than fourteen books, all of which deal with the Civil War, its aftermath, and life in the Reconstruction South. *'Toinette: A Novel* (1874, reissued as *A Royal Gentleman* in 1881), is the story of the ante- and postbellum lives of Southern aristocrat Geoffrey Hunter and his slave mistress 'Toinette, through which Tourgée explores themes of racial and sexual equality and control, social limitations and opportunities, and miscegenation. Despite Hunter's love for 'Toinette and their child, he cannot marry her and break from the old order, thus illustrating the longevity of the slaveholding ethos and its metamorphosis into an emphasis on racial control in the postwar South.

Perhaps Tourgée's most important and most commercially successful work is the novel *A Fool's Errand* (1879), the story of an idealistic Northerner, Col. Comfort Servosse, who seeks to improve the plight of freedmen during Reconstruction. Servosse, a lawyer, is a carpetbagger but not the corrupt swindler of popular myth. He settles in North Carolina with his wife and daughter with hopes of improving his health and participating in the process of uplifting the defeated South by rebuilding it in the image of the more liberal North. Servosse's insistence upon a measure of equal rights for blacks enrages the local white populace, but he remains undeterred in his mission. Rising to leadership of the Union League, Servosse assumes responsibility for organizing freedmen and challenging unreconstructed Southerners for political power. Ultimately, however, Servosse fails in this fool's errand, for the Southerners will not be reformed or reconstructed.

Tourgée followed the success of *A Fool's Errand* with *Bricks without Straw* (1880), another novel about the difficulties of Reconstruction, and *The Invisible Empire* (1880), a factual account of the Ku Klux Klan. Although all of Tourgée's works are inspired by his own Civil War and Reconstruction experiences, the novel *Figs and Thistles* (1879) is the most closely autobiographical: The protagonist, Markham Churr, hails from Ohio and is wounded at First Bull Run. However, unlike Tourgée, Churr remains in the North after the war, where he confronts corruption and moral decision.

In 1878 Tourgée moved from North Carolina to New York, where he continued his literary career. In 1897, he was appointed U.S. consul at Bordeaux, where he died in 1905.

REFERENCES

Gross, Theodore L. *Albion W. Tourgée.* New York: Twayne, 1963.
Olsen, Otto H. *Carpetbagger's Crusade: The Life of Albion W. Tourgée.* Baltimore: Johns Hopkins University Press, 1965.
Tourgée, Albion Winegar. *A Fool's Errand.* Ed. John Hope Franklin. Cambridge, MA: Harvard University Press, 1961.

Ricardo A. Herrera

TRUMBO, DALTON (1905–1976). James Dalton Trumbo was born in Montrose, Colorado, and raised in Grand Junction, Colorado. He spent a year at the state university before his father's death forced him to leave school to support his mother and sisters. He began writing during the eight years (1925–1933) that he worked for a bakery. Trumbo wrote five successful novels but made his life as a screenwriter. He was one of the Hollywood Ten, blacklisted during the McCarthy era.

Johnny Got His Gun (1939) is based on the true story of a World War I soldier who survived a shell that cost him his arms, legs, mouth, eyes and nose. The novel takes place entirely in Joe Bonham's head. The novel's first section, "The Dead," shows Joe inching back to sanity; the second, "The Living," has Joe learn to calculate time, consider militarism, medical ethics, and religion. Using Morse code Joe contacts the army and begs to be put on display as a sign of war: They refuse. Trumbo's use of flashbacks and stream of consciousness blend powerfully with the novel's filmic techniques (Trumbo's film version was released in 1971).

The novel is a remarkable attack on war: The descriptions of Joe's sufferings are almost unbearable. He imagines himself as "a cut of meat" but a thinking one: "It was like a full grown man suddenly being stuffed back into his mother's body. . . . He was completely helpless." The novel is both claustrating and exhilarating; Joe's political purpose is to become a battlefield messiah: "Never before in the world had the dead spoken never since Lazarus and Lazarus didn't say anything. . . . He would speak from the dead. . . . He would tell all the secrets of the dead." The army responds: "WHAT YOU ASK IS AGAINST REGULATIONS."

If *Johnny* is the story of the ultimate victim, Trumbo's unfinished *Night of the Aurochs* (published posthumously in 1979) is about the ultimate tyrant, Ludwig Richard Johann Grieben, a fictional commander at Auschwitz-Birkenau. Grieben, a living expression of Germany's "unspoken folk-will," recounts the story of his boyhood systematic sexual torture of a young girl; his love for his friend Gunther Blobel (he will later assassinate him); his experience in the Freikorps, the Hitler youth, and the SS; and his obsession with a young Jewish ballet dancer whom he later enslaves. Grieben is delighted that the Confederate flag (and the racism it signifies) flies in contemporary America and notes that if the Auschwitz-Birkenau gas chambers are still, American prison gas chambers are busy.

Trumbo attacks cultural attitudes that have made war so popular: "the coarse decadent dreams of nineteenth-century romanticism energized and made real by the twentieth century's vision of pragmatic materialism." These are complex issues, Trumbo said eloquently when answering the chief investigator for the House Committee on Un-American Activities: "Very many questions can be answered 'Yes' or 'No' only by a moron or a slave."

REFERENCES

Cook, Bruce. *Dalton Trumbo*. New York: Charles Scribner's Sons, 1977.
Kriegel, Leonard. "Dalton Trumbo's 'Johnny Got His Gun.' " *Proletarian Writers of the Thirties*. Ed. David Madden. Carbondale; University of Southern Illinois Press, 1968. 106–114.

Tim Blackmore

TWAIN, MARK (1835–1910). A son of Missouri, Samuel Langhorne Clemens was at various times a printer, steamboat pilot, miner, and journalist before launching parallel careers as a lecturer and author that would make him, ultimately, one of the most celebrated public figures of his time.

When the war closed traffic on the Mississippi, ending his profession as a river pilot, Clemens joined a band of Confederate irregulars styled the "Marion Rangers." His two weeks of "service," which consisted entirely of avoiding combat, constitute his complete experience of military life. He then deserted and went to Nevada with his brother. While Clemens did not describe the Civil War directly in any of his best-known novels, some critics believe that the Grangerford-Shepardson feud presented in Chapter XVIII of *Huckleberry Finn* (1844) may be intended as a forecast in miniature of the great fraternal conflict.

The year after *Huckleberry Finn*, Clemens returned to his Marion Ranger memories in his essay "The Private History of a Campaign That Failed" (1885), which was published in a *Century Magazine* series on "Battles and Leaders of the Civil War." Through most of the essay he presents his fortnight of military hardship as a series of comic misadventures, recalling the make-believe of Tom Sawyer and his gang. He boasts that he learned "more about retreating than the man that invented retreating" (183). But near the end of the sketch there is an account—not otherwise verified—of the Rangers ambushing and killing an unarmed civilian. Whether this event was real or imagined, it represented for Clemens "the epitome of war . . . all war must be just that—the killing of strangers against whom you feel no personal animosity" (181). This view is maintained in "The War Prayer" (1905), probably written in slightly delayed response to the patriotic fever that had preceded the Spanish-American War. While a congregation prays for victory in the (unnamed) conflict, an angel appears to unmask what their prayer actually means in human pain: "help us to lay waste their humble homes with a hurricane of fire; help us wring the hearts of their unoffending widows with unavailing grief; help us to turn them out roofless with their little children to wander unfriended in the wastes of their desolated land."

Clemen's most graphic account of battle describes a war that never actually occurred. His satirical fantasy novel *A Connecticut Yankee in King Arthur's Court* (1889) concludes with a terrifying description of medieval knights annihilated by modern gatling guns, electric fences, and dynamite mines. While the description draws on the reality of colonial wars (which Clemens consistently opposed), readers today may find it a chilling prediction of the First World War.

REFERENCES

Emerson, Everett. *The Authentic Mark Twain: A Literary Biography of Samuel L. Clemens.* Philadelphia: University of Pennsylvania Press, 1985.

Robinson, Forrest, ed. *The Cambridge Companion to Mark Twain.* New York: Cambridge University Press, 1995.

Twain, Mark. *The Complete Essays of Mark Twain.* Ed. Charles Neider. Garden City, NY: Doubleday, 1963.

————. *The Complete Works of Mark Twain*. New York: Harper & Brothers, 1911.
————. *Tales, Speeches, Essays, and Sketches*. Ed. Tom Quirk. New York: Penguin, 1994.

Charles L. Crow

U

URIS, LEON (1924–). Born in Baltimore to Jewish parents of Russian Polish heritage, Leon Marcus Uris was educated in eastern seaboard public schools, abandoning high school in his last year to enlist in the Marine Corps. He served from 1942 to 1946, part of that time as a radio operator in the Pacific campaign. Determined at an early age to become a writer, Uris struggled for several years until his first novel, *Battle Cry* (1953), found publication. This transformation of Uris's World War II experiences was a critical and popular success, as was the screen version (1954) that he scripted. For the rest of his long career, Uris would continue to find subjects that kept him close to contemporary political conflicts. While he enchanted readers, millions of them, he did not continue to satisfy critics. Most find him an able storyteller but a mediocre stylist.

Battle Cry is one of the major novels of the Pacific campaign. Narrated by a hardboiled Marine sergeant and covering a wide range of sharply differentiated characters, most of them part of the sergeant's radio unit, the novel handles battles at Guadalcanal and Tarawa with intensity and convincing detail. Uris fashions a "melting pot" novel in which American character is delineated through its component ethnic ingredients. He gives half of the novel over to the preparations for combat: boot camp, specialty training, troop transport, and maintaining preparedness on foreign bases (particularly in New Zealand). *Battle Cry* is, first and foremost, a Marine novel of hard-drinking, hard-loving characters and the occasional sensitive soul who counterbalances the excesses of the others. It is also a novel that examines various leadership styles and their effectiveness. Uris handles the inevitable periods of anticipation and aftermath as keenly as he handles combat itself.

The Angry Hills (1955) is Uris's fictional adaptation of an uncle's diary. It is another World War II story, this time of a man who fought in Greece as part of the "Palestine Brigade" of the British Army. This novel, which was also turned into a film (released in 1959), initiated Uris's concern with contemporary Jewish history. *Exodus* (1958), an epic novel of the struggle for survival of

European Jewry culminating in the founding of contemporary Israel, is for many Uris's most important achievement. At once partisan and meticulously researched, *Exodus* is noteworthy for making an enormously complex stretch of history accessible and understandable. Like Uris's earlier works, it was the basis for an important motion picture (1960). Resistance in the Warsaw ghetto, treated in a segment of *Exodus*, becomes the main theme of *Mila 18* (1961). The war's aftermath, particularly the rebuilding of postwar Germany, is the subject of *Armageddon* (1964). The extension of Uris's concern with the history of the Mideast is found in *The Haj* (1984) and *Mitla Pass* (1988), the latter focusing on an Israeli soldier during the Sinai War.

Uris's other novels include *Topaz* (1967) and *QB VII* (1970), both of which can be called political thrillers. Better known, perhaps, are his enormous novels on contemporary Irish history: *Trinity* (1976) and *Redemption* (1995). In all of his works, Uris manages to achieve an orderly, manageable rendering of the complex social and political forces that lie behind the major conflicts of the twentieth century.

REFERENCE

Cain, Kathleen Shine. *Leon Uris: A Critical Companion*. Westport, CT: Greenwood Press, 1998.

Philip K. Jason

V

VIDAL, GORE (1925–   ). Born at the U.S. Military Academy, West Point, New York, where his father was an aviation instructor, Vidal spent his fourteenth year at Los Alamos Ranch School and later graduated from Phillips Exeter Academy. In 1943, he joined the army, studied engineering at Virginia Military Institute, then served as a deckhand on an army crash boat. In 1945, he became first mate aboard a freighter of the Army Transport Corps in the Aleutians.

Before, during, and after his time aboard the freighter, Vidal wrote *Williwaw* (1946), his only novel of men at war. Vidal saw no combat action, nor do the men in *Williwaw*, a lean, sullen drama, in the style of **Hemingway** and **Crane**, about the amorality of war and a military code that impels men to kill. The title is an Indian word for a wind that sweeps down from the mountains toward the sea, and such a wind rocks the supply boat on which the characters of *Williwaw* do their mundane duty. During the storm, the boat's surly second mate, Bervick, flings a hammer at the chief engineer, Duval, his rival for a woman, knocking Duval overboard. As the external storm rages, a beguiled Bervick, flush with repressed rage, watches Duval float away. He is neither caught nor punished, in part because no one really cares.

For Vidal, war has two meanings, one personal and one political. While a teenager at St. Albans School, Vidal began a passionate affair with a classmate, Jimmie Trimble, who later died at Iwo Jima. Vidal claims Jimmie is the only person he has ever loved, and he has replayed Jimmie's death in several novels. *The Season of Comfort* (1949), *Washington, D.C.* (1968), and *Two Sisters* (1970) each refers to or depicts, albeit briefly, the combat death of a Jimmie-like character. In *The Smithsonian Institution* (1998), Vidal's protagonist invents a time machine that transports him to the battle of Iwo Jima to alter Jimmie's fate.

Vidal claims that the United States wages war for one reason: to expand its international empire at the behest of money barons and the military. He develops this theme in his novels of American history: *Burr* (1973), *Lincoln* (1984), *1876* (1976), *Empire* (1987), *Hollywood* (1990), and *Washington, D.C.* In *Lincoln*, the president conducts the Civil War to turn America into a powerful modern industrial state. In the fin de siècle era of *Empire*, the American president discovers that entering World War I will transform America into an economic giant. In World War II–era *Washington, D.C.*, the Soviet menace is the perfect excuse for President Truman to create a national security state. And in *The Smithsonian Institution*, the time-traveling "T." attempts to prevent World War II by preventing World War I, but the government's genius for inventing war finds a way to make it happen anyway.

Finally, there's *Kalki* (1978), a science fiction novel about a Vietnam veteran who forms a religious cult and then kills everyone on earth with a lethal bacteria. This grim scenario explores Vidal's lifelong interest in how the media sells false prophets to a desperate, unsuspecting public—the very condition, Vidal argues, that allows the corporate-run American empire to wage war.

REFERENCES

Dick, Bernard F. *The Apostate Angel: A Critical Study of Gore Vidal.* New York: Random House, 1974.

Kiernan, Robert F. *Gore Vidal.* New York: Ungar, 1982.

Parini, Jay, ed. *Gore Vidal: Writer against the Grain.* New York: Columbia University Press, 1992.

Vidal, Gore. *The Essential Gore Vidal.* Ed. Fred Kaplan. New York: Random House, 1999.

Harry B. Kloman

VIETNAM WAR. American involvement in Indochina began toward the end of World War II, when it became clear that the Vietminh, a loose confederation of different Vietnamese nationalist factions increasingly dominated by Ho Chi Minh's Communists, would not willingly return to French rule after having helped liberate themselves from Japan and Vichy France. Following the stunning French defeat at Dien Bien Phu (despite a substantial infusion of American logistical support) and the subsequent partitioning of Indochina into the People's Republic of North Vietnam and the Republic of South Vietnam at the 14th Parallel by the Geneva Accords (1954), U.S. military aid shifted to the newly constituted, ostensibly democratic South Vietnam, gradually escalating from logistical support to the use of a steadily growing number of American military advisers to South Vietnamese military units. Having experienced firsthand the power of the Chinese Communist Army in the Korean War, the United States saw Vietnam as crucial in its Cold War strategy of "containing" the Communists, fearing that if South Vietnam fell, the rest of Southeast Asia would quickly follow suit in accordance with the controversial Domino Theory. As the South Vietnamese continued to lose ground, the United States used a murky incident in 1965 between two American destroyers and North Vietnamese patrol boats in the Tonkin Gulf to justify the bombing of North Vietnam and the introduction of U.S. ground troops along with air and naval forces.

After early success with its new airmobile tactics, the U.S. military soon became mired in the same kind of guerrilla war that had bedeviled the French. The siege of Khe Sanh, followed by the Communist Tet offensive of 1968, belied the favorable spin that General William Westmoreland and the Pentagon were trying to place on the war's progress and resulted in a serious erosion of public support of the war effort that ultimately led to President Lyndon Johnson's decision not to seek his party's nomination for a second term. Richard Nixon was subsequently elected president, largely on the basis of his promise to end the war, and he soon embarked on a program of "Vietnamization" of the war accompanied by a gradual withdrawal of the increasingly demoralized American troops. Direct negotiations were soon opened with the Communists in Paris, and by the time the Paris Accords were signed in 1973, the U.S. military presence in South Vietnam was reduced to practically nothing from an all-time high of more than a half-million troops of all branches of the armed forces in 1969. Nevertheless, neither the United States nor South Vietnam had ever won over the Vietnamese people, and even the best American efforts to train and equip the South Vietnamese armed forces had failed to make them adequate opposition to a disciplined, well-led, and well-equipped North Vietnamese army. Soon after the American withdrawal, the war entered its final phase when General Vo Nguyen Giap mounted a massive conventional armored offensive with heavy artillery support that eventually crushed South Vietnamese resistance. The ultimate fall of Saigon in 1975 included the bitterly ironic, well-publicized images of the chaotic helicopter evacuation of the American embassy.

The Vietnam War provoked an American literary expression almost from its inception, and one of the most frequently observed ironies of the war is that the one war the United States lost has also given rise to its most distinguished war literature. The first fictional treatment of America's involvement is Graham Greene's *The Quiet American* (1955), which features a thinly veiled version of Colonel Edward Lansdale, the legendary Central Intelligence Agency (CIA) operative who propagated disinformation programs designed to vilify the Communists in the eyes of the South Vietnamese. The first American book about the American involvement in Vietnam was **Eugene Burdick** and **William Lederer**'s *The Ugly American* (1958), which also includes a character based on Lansdale. The earliest American writing about the war was the work of journalists like Bernard B. Fall, **David Halberstam**, and Neil Sheehan, who sensed from the very outset that there was something seriously amiss with the United States's support of an autocratic regime simply because it was anti-Communist and pro-American. As the war progressed, reporters like **Gloria Emerson**, Seymore Hersh, Joseph Kraft, and Jonathan Schell added their contributions to exceptional journalism of the Vietnam War, an impressive body of writing best represented in *Reporting Vietnam*, a two-volume collection by The Library of America (1998). The war also proved to be instrumental in the development of the self-reflexive, highly subjective New Journalism practiced most notably by **Norman Mailer** in *Armies of the Night* (1968), his rendering of the 1967 antiwar march on the Pentagon, and **Michael Herr** in *Dispatches* (1974), a series of hallucinogenic meditations on the nature of the Vietnam War and its place in the American psyche.

The first American poetry, drama, and fiction of the Vietnam War began to appear soon after the United States entered in force in 1965. The earliest poetry was a product of the burgeoning antiwar sentiment in the mid-1960s and included work by Robert Bly, Daniel Berrigan, Denise Levertov, and Allen Ginsberg (see *A Poetry Reading against the Vietnam War*, 1967). Soon, however, poetry by returning veterans began to appear, beginning with **John Balaban**'s chapbook *Vietnam Poems* (London, 1970) and the influential early anthology *Winning Hearts and Minds* (1972). Balaban's first full-length collection, *After Our War* (1974), won the Lamont Prize. (Balaban, who did alternative service in Vietnam, is not, strictly speaking, a veteran.) Other significant volumes of poetry include D. C. Berry's *saigon cemetery* (1972); Michael Casey's *Obscenities* (1972); **Walter McDonald**'s *Caliban in Blue* (1976), *After the Noise of Saigon* (1988), and *Night Landings* (1989); **Bruce Weigl**'s *A Romance* (1979), *The Monkey Wars* (1985), and *Song of Napalm* (1988); and **Yusef Komunyakaa**'s *Dien Cai Dau* (1988). Of more recent vintage are Doug Anderson's *The Moon Reflected Fire* and Kevin Bowen's *Playing Basketball with the Viet Cong* (both 1994). **W. D. Ehrhart** has published several volumes of Vietnam War poetry, of which *To Those Who Have Gone Home Tired* (1984) is most notable; he is also the editor of two trailblazing anthologies: *Carrying the Darkness* (1985) and *Unaccustomed Mercy* (1989).

Likewise, plays about the Vietnam War appeared early on, and some of the earliest efforts came from the civilian antiwar perspective, commencing with Gerome Ragney and James Rado's wildly popular *Hair* (1966) and including with Megan Terry's *Viet Rock* (1966), Tuli Kupferberg's *Fuck Nam* (1967), Terrence McNally's *Botticelli* (1968), **Arthur Kopit**'s allegorical *Indians* (1969), and Michael Wells's *Moonchildren* (1971). These were soon followed by *Still Life* (1979), Emily Mann's drama of a Vietnam veteran's postwar family; Amlin Gray's *How I Got That Story* (1981), a drama of the New Journalism in Vietnam; Lanford Wilson's *The Fifth of July* (1982), the story of an inner-city veteran; and *Tracers* (1986), a collective composition by eight Vietnam veterans. The central achievement in Vietnam War drama is **David Rabe**'s Vietnam cycle consisting of *The Basic Training of Pavlo Hummel* (1969), *Sticks and Bones* (1972), *The Orphan* (1975), and *Streamers* (1977). Rabe, a combat veteran and experimental playwright, was the first to blend theater of the absurd and theater of cruelty with the American experience in Vietnam and to link Vietnam with dark primal forces of the national collective unconscious.

Certainly the dominant genre of Vietnam War literature is the novel. John Newman's *Vietnam War Literature: Annotated Bibliography* (1982; 3rd ed., 1995) lists an ominous 666 Vietnam War novels, and the number continues to grow. From the outset, the evolution of Vietnam War fiction has followed a twofold path. Novels like David Halberstam's *One Very Hot Day* (1967) and Ronald J. Glasser's *365 Days* (1971) continued the realistic-naturalistic, "war is hell" mode of the American war novel, a tradition extending from **Stephen Crane** through **Ernest Hemingway** and **John Dos Passos** to Norman Mailer and **James Jones**. Many other "traditional" war novels followed, including Josiah Bunting's *The Lionheads* (1972), Winston Groom's *Better Times Than These* (1978), **James Webb**'s *Fields of Fire* (1978), and **John Del Vecchio**'s epic *The 13th Valley* (1982).

On the other hand, *Catch-22* (1961), **Joseph Heller**'s darkly humorous, surrealist satire of World War II, revealed an abundance of new possibilities for the novelists of the Vietnam War, many of whom were strongly influenced by Heller's novel, and the publication of Norman Mailer's *Why Are We In Vietnam?* (1967), a story about a hunting trip in Alaska that never mentions Vietnam, made it clear that the Vietnam War would also be chronicled in strikingly nontraditional ways. For example, **William Eastlake** in *The Bamboo Bed* (1969), Asa Baber in *The Land of a Million Elephants* (1970), and Loyd Little in *Parthian Shot* (1975) incorporated the absurd and surreal into their narratives, as did **Robert Stone** in *Dog Soldiers* (1973), **Ward Just** in *Stringer* (1974), and John Clark Pratt in *The Laotian Fragments* (1994), while **Larry Heinemann**'s *Close Quarters* (1974) and **Gustav Hasford**'s *The Short-Timers* (1979) added a lyrical, hallucinatory rendering of the ultraviolence of war. Perhaps the best examples of the resulting "new" Vietnam novel are Stephen Wright's profoundly absurd *Meditations in Green* (1983), Gustav Hasford's intricate *The Phantom Blooper* (1990), and **Tim O'Brien**'s surreal fantasy *Going After Cacciato* (1978) and his metafictional *The Things They Carried* (1990). Many of these novels are important not only as war literature but also as key documents in the charting of American literary postmodernism.

Particularly noteworthy is **Robert Olen Butler**'s Vietnam trilogy: *The Alleys of Eden* (1981), *Sun Dogs* (1982) and *On Distant Ground* (1985). Butler's contribution also includes his prize-winning *A Good Scent from a Strange Mountain* (1992) and *The Deep Green Sea* (1997).

The effects of the war on the returning Vietnam veteran have been explored not only by Larry Heinemann in *Paco's Story* (1986), **Philip Caputo** in *Indian Country* (1987), and Tim O'Brien in *In the Lake of the Woods* (1994) but also by women writers like Susan Fromberg Schaeffer in *Buffalo Afternoon* (1989) and **Bobbie Ann Mason** in *In Country* (1985). Of the hundreds of personal memoirs spawned by the war, the most frequently noted are Tim O'Brien's *If I Die in a Combat Zone* (1973), Ron Kovic's *Born on the Fourth of July* (1976), and Philip Caputo's *A Rumor of War* (1977), all of which are strongly influenced by the New Journalism. W. D. Ehrhart's *Vietnam-Perkasie* (1983), Lynda Van Devanter's *Home before Morning: The Story of an Army Nurse in Vietnam* (1983), John Balaban's *Remembering Heaven's Face* (1991), and **Tobias Wolff**'s *In Pharaoh's Army* (1994) provide additional first-person perspectives on the war. Also of significance are Frances Fitzgerald's meditative history *Fire in the Lake* (1972) and Myra MacPherson's *Long Time Passing: Vietnam and the Haunted Generation* (1984). The diversity of ethnic and cultural perspectives on America's Vietnam experience is presented in such oral histories as Al Santoli's *Everything We Had* (1981) and **Wallace Terry**'s *Bloods: An Oral History of the Vietnam War by Black Veterans* (1984), as well as in anthologies like George Mariscal's *Aztlan and Vietnam: Chicano and Chicana Experiences of the War* (1999). Also of interest is Eric James Schroeder's *Vietnam, We've All Been There: Interviews with American Writers* (1992).

The growing body of scholarship devoted to literature of the Vietnam War is best represented by Philip Beidler's *American Literature and the Experience of Vietnam* (1982) and *Re-Writing America: Vietnam Authors in Their Generation* (1991), James C. Wilson's *Vietnam in Prose and Film* (1982), John Hellmann's *American Myth and the Legacy of Vietnam* (1986), Timothy J. Lomperis's *"Reading the Wind": The Literature of the Vietnam War* (1987), Thomas Myers's *Walking Point: American Narratives of Vietnam* (1988), Susan Jeffords's *The Remasculinization of America: Gender and the Vietnam War* (1989), Philip H. Melling's *Vietnam in American Literature* (1990), Tobey C. Herzog's *Vietnam War Stories: Innocence Lost* (1992), Owen Gilman's *Vietnam and the Southern Imagination* (1992), Andrew Martin's *Receptions of War: Vietnam in American Culture* (1993), Vince Gotera's *Radical Visions: Poetry by Vietnam Veterans* (1994), Donald Ringnalda's *Fighting and Writing the Vietnam War* (1994), John Newman et al.'s *Vietnam War Literature: An Annotated Bibliography* (1982; 3rd ed., 1995), and Milton J. Bates's *The Wars We Took to Vietnam: Cultural Conflict and Storytelling* (1996). *America Rediscovered* (1990), edited by Owen Gilman and Lorrie Smith, and *Fourteen Landing Zones* (1991), edited by Philip K. Jason, are noteworthy collections of cultural and critical essays.

Lucas Carpenter

VIGILANTES. This now largely forgotten group, described in its literature as "a patriotic, anti-pacifist, non-partisan organization of authors, artists and others," was founded in New York City in 1916 by writers Julian Street, Porter Emerson Browne, and Hermann Hagedom, with the assistance of Charles Hanson Towne, then editor of the social reform–slanted magazine *McClure's*. In the months preceding America's entry into the war, the group announced that its aims were:

To arouse the country to a realization of the importance of the problems confronting the American people. To awaken and cultivate in the youth of the country a sense of public service and an intelligent interest in citizenship and national problems. To work vigorously for preparedness, mental, moral, and physical. To work with especial vigor for Universal Military Training and Service under exclusive Federal control, as a basic principle of American democracy.

Among the Vigilantes' 146 charter members were such luminaries as **Theodore Roosevelt**, George Ade, Kate Douglas Wiggin, Booth Tarkington, Don Marquis, Charles Dana Gibson, Rupert Hughes, Edwin Arlington Robinson, Irvin S.

Cobb, Bliss Carman, **George Washington Cable**, Ida Tarbell, Thornton Burgess, George Randolph Chester, Faith Baldwin, and James Montgomery Flagg. In March 1917, the group realized where its true power lay and shifted its focus to pro-American propaganda, which members disseminated in narrative advertisements (via a managing editor) and through mainstream poems, short stories, and novels.

The majority of Vigilantes worked quietly, without drawing attention to their membership or the group's aims. One exception was humorist Ellis Parker Butler, best remembered as the author of the 1905 tall tale "Pigs Is Pigs." A banker by profession, he composed—among hundreds of other war writings—the instructional booklet *Robinson Crusoe and Thrift Stamps* (National War Savings Committee for New Jersey, 1919), which bears the byline "Ellis Parker Butler of the Vigilantes"; it explains in lighthearted fashion how spending one's pennies on Uncle Sam instead of on luxuries assists the war effort and economic recovery. This writer also made a less-than-subtle plea to his peers in the short story "An American Britling" (*Green Book Magazine*, December 1917), by making its main character, Mr. Bartlett, a physical double for himself, with the same dual job and an identical home life. When America enters the war, Mr. Bartlett joins the Vigilantes and works with them tirelessly to promote the virtues of financial responsibility and thrift. Any of the hundreds of nonmember writers who knew Butler personally would have recognized this as a strong hint that they stop thinking solely of themselves and do likewise.

The organization was sapped of its literary strength in August 1917, with the formation of the Division of Syndicate Features (and a similar group for artists) by the War Department's Committee on Public Information (CPI). Given the chance to continue their propaganda work on an official basis, many Vigilantes switched over. Still more left to contribute to the Foreign Mail Service, a governmental press agency that provided weekly or monthly essays by famous writers to overseas newspapers. Hermann Hagedorn made a case for the earlier group in "What Is the Vigilantes? What Is It Doing for This Country?" published in the art magazine *The Touchstone* (October 1917: 91–98), but by the time the article appeared, the Vigilantes had all but dissolved. A few stalwarts remained with the group or—like Butler—did double duty with the CPI through the end of the war; *McClure's* continued its pro-American campaign until long after the Armistice.

REFERENCES

"Authors Map War Work: Vigilantes Will Write to Forward Patriotism." *New York Times* 30 March 1917: 11.

Browne, Porter Emerson. "Vigilantes: Why and What They Are." *Outlook* May 1918: 67–69.

"Society of Prominent Authors and Illustrators." *Bookman* June 1917: 420.

"Writers for Army Bill: 'Vigilantes' to Appeal to Nation for Universal Service." *New York Times* 18 March 1917: 11.

Katherine Harper

VONNEGUT, KURT (1922–   ). "That's the attractive thing about war," says
Eliot Rosewater in *Slaughterhouse Five*. "Absolutely everybody gets a little
something." What Kurt Vonnegut, Jr., born in Indianapolis, got from his three
years of experience as a World War II infantry scout was material for at least
four novels (as a prisoner of war [POW], Vonnegut survived the Allied firebombing of Dresden). Vonnegut studied but completed no degrees at the University of Tennessee, the University of Chicago, Cornell, and Carnegie Tech.
He worked for General Electric, and he taught at the Iowa Writer's Workshop
(1965–1966).

Mother Night (1961) is a metanarrative about Howard W. Campbell, Jr., a
fluent bilingual American German playwright recruited as a spy in 1938; Campbell's anti-Semitic radio broadcasts send coded messages to the Allies. After his
wife Helga disappears, Campbell leaves Germany for postwar New York, where
he is watched by Soviet and American spies. A string of betrayals draws Campbell to Israel for punishment: When it becomes evident he will be released,
Campbell commits suicide.

Campbell's world is apolitical: His love for Helga is strong enough to create
a "nation of two" that shuts out Nazism. Helga's death robs Campbell of his
created "nation of two" as well as his sense of purpose. Vonnegut warns: "We
are what we pretend to be, so we must be careful about what we pretend to be."
Another character is less certain: "A moral? It's a big enough job just to burying
the dead, without trying to draw a moral from each death."

Cat's Cradle (1963) is a satirical tale of a literal cold war. Writing about
Felix Hoenikker, one of the "fathers of the atomic bomb," Jonah discovers that
each of the three Hoenikker children possesses "ice-nine" invented by their
father (all water freezes on contact with ice-nine). The Hoenikkers make deals
in exchange for their ice-nine. On an island where one of the children has given
ice-nine to an insane dictator, Jonah is introduced to the antireligion of Boko-
nonism just before ice-nine renders the planet a sterile blue-white ball. The
natives commit suicide, and Bokonon urges Jonah to join them. *Cat's Cradle*,
like Jonah's own book, is "a history of human stupidity" and a satire on scientific
positivism: "Science is magic that works," says one character. Science is an
unknowing, amoral force that makes killing superbly easy, argues Vonnegut.

God Bless You, Mr. Rosewater (1965) follows the shell-shocked Eliot Rosewater as he becomes an American saint of lost causes. Rosewater's experiences
in the infantry have given him eccentrically sane views about America's war
culture. Rosewater's vision looks to Vonnegut's next novel, *Slaughterhouse Five*
(1969), the story of Billy Pilgrim's progress through life after he has come
"unstuck in time." Trapped behind German lines in World War II, Billy jitters
through future and past, fated to relive his life (and death) as a series of nonlinear
moments, moving between his experiences as a POW, his survival of the Dresden firebombing, his dreary suburban life as an optometrist, and his position as
a star exhibit in a zoo on the planet Tralfamadore.

"There are almost no characters in this story," writes Vonnegut about (and in) *Slaughterhouse Five*, "and almost no dramatic confrontations, because most of the people in it are so sick and so much the listless playthings of enormous forces." Whereas *Mother Night* is a story about evil arising out of good intentions, Vonnegut's later narratives suggest humans are largely helpless in the face of chaos. Vonnegut's assessment that people love evil, "that large part of every man that wants to hate without limit" (*Mother Night*), is answered by his plea for common decency.

REFERENCES

Broer, Lawrence R. *Sanity Plea: Schizophrenia and the Novels of Kurt Vonnegut*. Ann Arbor: UMI Research Press, 1989.

Goldsmith, David H. *Kurt Vonnegut: Fantasist of Fire and Ice*. Bowling Green, OH: Bowling Green State University Popular Press, 1972.

Klinkowitz, Jerome, and John Somer, eds. *The Vonnegut Statement*. New York: Dell, 1973.

Morse, Donald E. *Kurt Vonnegut*. Starmont Reader's Guide No. 61. San Bernardino, CA: Starmont House, 1992.

Reed, Peter J. *Kurt Vonnegut, Jr*. New York: Warner, 1972.

Tim Blackmore

W

WARREN, MERCY OTIS (1728–1814). Born in Barnstable, Massachusetts, Warren was a member of a prosperous and politically influential family. While not formally educated, she was tutored in history and literature. As tensions increased in the early 1770s over the exercise of royal authority, she joined her husband, James Warren, and brother, James Otis (a leader among the Sons of Liberty), in organizing committees of correspondence. Warren also wrote dramatic satires aimed at Governor Thomas Hutchinson and the prominent Loyalists who participated in his administration. While never performed, these plays were widely circulated in newspapers and pamphlets.

Her work included *The Adulateur* (1773), a satire in which Rapatio (Hutchinson), the governor of the fictional Upper Servia, is pitted against Brutus (Otis) and Cassius (Sam Adams). Warren provocatively implied that Hutchinson was responsible for encouraging the Boston Massacre. An incomplete play, "The Defeat," appeared in newspapers shortly thereafter, and two years later Warren published *The Group* (1775), her most widely circulated satire. In these plays she continued her sharp attacks on royal officials and castigated Boston's leading Tories as "court sycophants, hungry harpies and unprincipled danglers." Two additional patriotic dramas, *The Blockheads* (1776) and *The Motley Assembly* (1779), have been attributed to her, but the case for Warren's authorship is inconclusive.

In the postwar period Warren wrote in opposition to the adoption of the Constitution, which cost her the friendship of John Adams. She also published a collection of poems in 1790 that included "The Squabble of the Sea Nymphs," a mock epic based on the Boston Tea Party. However, her most impressive work was not fictional but rather her three-volume *History of the Rise, Progress and Termination of the American Revolution* (1805). It stands with David Ramsay's 1789 account as one of the most important contemporary histories of the war. Given her background, Warren was able to provide precise details concerning local acts of resistance in Massachusetts during the early stages of the struggle. In broader terms, Warren's chronological narrative of the major events of the war led to incisive reflections on the character of those who fought, as well as the pressing issue of the viability of the Republic.

REFERENCES

Anthony, Katherine. *First Lady of the Revolution*. Garden City, NY: Doubleday, 1958.

Cohen, Lester. "Explaining the Revolution: Ideology and Ethics in Mercy Otis Warren's Historical Theory." *William and Mary Quarterly* 37 (1980): 200–218.

Richards, Jeffrey H. *Mercy Otis Warren*. New York: Twayne, 1995.

Warren, Mercy Otis. *History of the Rise, Progress, and Termination of the American Revolution*. Ed. Lester H. Cohen. 2 vols. Indianapolis: Liberty Classics, 1988.

———. *The Plays and Poems of Mercy Otis Warren*. Ed. Benjamin Franklin V. Delmar. New York: Scholars Facsimiles, 1980.

Robert D. Sturr

WARREN, ROBERT PENN (1905–1989). One of the most versatile figures in twentieth-century American letters, Warren left his mark as a novelist, essayist, literary critic, and perhaps most important, poet. Warren was born in Guthrie, Kentucky, educated mostly in the South, and worked as a professor at his alma mater Vanderbilt and later at Louisiana State University. Even when he took up residency in New England, he maintained a distinct Southern regionalism.

Like his fellow Southern Agrarians, a large portion of Warren's work is based in an attempt to reinterpret Southern history, especially that revolving around the Civil War. Yet Warren was from the beginning less regional in his work than the other Agrarians. His first book, *John Brown, the Making of a Martyr* (1929), is an unromantic demythologizing of Brown, the "ungodly godlike man." Warren contributed to the Agrarian *I'll Take My Stand* (1930), a "spiritual secessionist" anthology of essays that sought to ennoble the values of the old agrarian South within the context of a prevailing Northern industrialism. Thirty-five years later, Warren published *Who Speaks for the Negro?*—which, in effect, repudiates his earlier views on "anachronistic and inhuman" slavery.

Warren's most enduring extended work on the Civil War is *The Legacy of the Civil War* (1961), which attempts to explain some of the war's ambivalences. The war, he posits, gave both sides distinct "psychological heritages"—the North, "the Treasury of Virtue," and the South, "the Great Alibi." While neither inherited view is wholly fallacious, they fail to acknowledge man's basic corrupted nature (a major theme in virtually all of Warren's work).

Best known for *All the King's Men* (for which he received the first of his three Pulitzer Prizes in 1947), some of Warren's other historical-fictional works are set in the Civil War. *Band of Angels* (1955) is the story of Amantha Starr, who, light-skinned and unaware that her mother was a slave, is sold to collect her late father's debts. In *Wilderness: A Tale of the Civil War* (1961), an idealistic Bavarian Jew becomes a Union soldier only to discover that his fellow soldiers care nothing for emancipation. The cruelty of warfare is a theme in several of Warren's poems, including "Terror," "Shoes in Rain Jungle," "Two Studies in Idealism: Short Survey of American, and Human, History," and the book-length *Chief Joseph of the Nez Perce* (1983).

REFERENCES

Aaron, Daniel. *The Unwritten War: American Writers and the Civil War.* Madison: University of Wisconsin Press, 1987.
Blotner, Joseph. *Robert Penn Warren: A Biography.* New York: Random House, 1997.

Bryan L. Moore

WATKINS, SAMUEL R. (1839–1901). Samuel Watkins wrote only one book, but it is a memorable one—*Co. Aytch: A Side Show of the Big Show*, an accurate and gripping account of the Confederate soldier's experience in the Civil War. Born June 26, 1839, near Columbia, Maury County, Tennessee, Watkins attended Jackson College in Columbia before enlisting in the First Tennessee Regiment at the outbreak of the war. As a member of this unit, known as the "Maury Grays," Watkins participated in all of its major battles, from Shiloh and Chickamauga to Nashville and its final surrender on April 26, 1865, to General Sherman in Greensboro, North Carolina. Of the original 1,250 men who enlisted in the regiment in 1861, only 65 officers and men were left in Greensboro. Of these, Watkins was 1 of 7 of the original 120 men in Company H.

Watkins serialized his memoir in his hometown paper, the Columbia *Herald*, in 1881–1882 and shortly thereafter published it as a book. Throughout the volume, Watkins balances humorous descriptions and stories with graphic details of battle and episodes of heroism that ultimately prove meaningless. "Our cause was lost from the beginning," Watkins asserts; in his view "the private soldier fought and starved for naught" because of disagreements among the populace about secession and generals' and politicians' greater concern with self-advancement than the effective prosecution of the war.

Throughout, Watkins repeatedly emphasizes that this is *his* story, told from *his*—a *private's*—point of view. He makes it clear that he does not expect historians to remember his memoir, thinking they will favor those of the famous generals like Sherman, Grant, and Lee. Watkins was mistaken here, as subsequent printings attest to the fact that he is not forgotten, due largely to his remarkable detail and his considerable gifts as a storyteller.

REFERENCES

Hall, Dennis R. "Sam R. Watkins' 'Co. Aytch': A Literary Nonfiction." *Kentucky Philological Review* 8 (1993): 15–20.
Inge, M. Thomas. "Sam Watkins: Another Source for Crane's *The Red Badge of Courage.*" *Stephen Crane Studies* 3.1 (Spring 1994): 11–16.
Watkins, Samuel R. *Co. Aytch: A Side Show of the Big Show.* Ed. Roy P. Basler. New York: Macmillan, 1962.

Sandra Alagona

WEBB, JAMES (1946–). James H. Webb, Jr., has had three successful careers: military, governmental, and literary. After graduating from the U.S. Naval Academy in 1968, Webb served with distinction as a Marine in Vietnam; received the Navy Cross, Silver Star, two Bronze Stars, two Purple Hearts, and a National Achievement Medal; and rose to the rank of captain.

After retiring from the Marines because of his war wounds, Webb attended Georgetown University Law School, earning his J.D. in 1975. Webb then entered government service, holding such positions as minority counsel to the Committee on Veterans Affairs of the U.S. House of Representatives and assistant secretary of defense for Reserve Affairs. In 1987, he was nominated by President Ronald Reagan to be secretary of the navy. Webb found the political aspects of being navy secretary sufficiently frustrating that he left the position after less than one year.

James Webb's first novel, *Fields of Fire*, published in 1978, reflects the author's own combat experience as well as his belief that the role of combat soldier is an honorable profession. The main character, Robert E. Lee Hodges, Jr., patterned after the author's own background (Southern families steeped in military tradition), states, "Man's noblest moment is the one spent on the fields of fire."

Fields of Fire was a major financial and critical success. It also proved generally popular with Vietnam veterans, although some critics and other readers have objected to its defense of war as ennobling. The book offers a dramatic and realistic view of combat as it affects the average soldier. Although the Vietnam War is presented as seriously flawed, the failure of the war effort is blamed on misguided policy made by civilian leaders and high-ranking military officers—not because the war was fought for unjust reasons or incorrect geopolitical motives, or that war itself is inherently immoral. The novel also argues that leaders of the war effort and civilians insufficiently understood and honored those who did the fighting and dying (such as Lieutenant Hodges and Snake, the latter a street-smart kid from a northern slum who, although in many ways the antithesis of the main character, becomes Hodges's close friend and comrade in arms).

The novel is unusually ambitious, especially for a first novel, as it also argues for the nobility and courage of the South Vietnamese soldier, explores race relations in the military, and attacks the antiwar movement (through Will Goodrich, a failed soldier and dupe of the antiwar movement who only at the end of the book begins to realize the value of the men he had betrayed).

Although James Webb's subsequent novels—*A Sense of Honor* (1981), *A Country Such as This* (1983), and *Something to Die For* (1991)—did not enjoy the same degree of popularity as *Fields of Fire*, they are vivid and readable narratives that explore such important issues as how to prepare courageous and honorable warriors, how to resolve conflicts between principled (and sometimes unprincipled) governmental leaders, and whether political machinations endanger the very survival of a still-honorable military tradition.

REFERENCES

Gilman, Owen W., Jr. *Vietnam and the Southern Imagination.* Jackson: University Press
of Mississippi, 1992. 29–44.
Herzog, Tobey C. *Vietnam War Stories: Innocence Lost.* New York and London: Rout-
ledge, 1992. 110–125.
Lomperis, Timothy J. *"Reading the Wind": The Literature of the Vietnam War.* Durham,
NC: Duke University Press, 1987. 13–24.

Edward J. Rielly

WEIGL, BRUCE (1949–   ). Bruce Weigl was born in Lorain, Ohio, an
industrial town that, next to the Vietnam War, would prove to be the most
common setting for his poetry. Weigl served in the U.S. Army from 1967 until
1970, including a stretch from 1967 to 1968 with the First Air Cavalry in Vietnam, and received the Bronze Star.

After the war, Weigl attended Oberlin College and later earned a master's
degree from the University of New Hampshire (1975) and a doctorate from the
University of Utah (1979). He taught at several institutions before joining the
faculty of Pennsylvania State University.

In his first collections of poetry, *Executioner* (1976) and *Like a Sack Full of
Old Quarrels* (1977), Weigl found his primary subject, the Vietnam War. Although he would write about other matters, the war would continue to be his
primary focus throughout such books as *A Romance* (1979); *The Monkey Wars*
(1984); *Song of Napalm* (1988), which includes new as well as previously published poems and is even more consistently and explicitly about the Vietnam
War than the earlier books; *What Saves Us* (1992); and *Sweet Lorain* (1996).
Weigl's Vietnam War–related books also include *Poems from Captured Documents*, edited and translated by Weigl and Thanh T. Nguyen (1994), a collection
of poems written by North Vietnamese and Viet Cong soldiers; and *Writing
Between the Lines: An Anthology on War and Its Social Consequences* (1997),
which Weigl edited with Kevin Bowen.

Among U.S. poets writing about the Vietnam War, Weigl may give the most
attention to the aesthetics of poetry. His poetry demonstrates an ability to step
back from the subject in order to fashion through words a work of art, as in the
Pushcart Prize poem "Temple Near Quang Tri, Not on the Map." The poem
depicts U.S. soldiers entering a temple to find a Vietnamese man crouched and
mumbling in a corner. As he is lifted upright, the charge, wired so that the man
himself is a booby trap, goes off. The poem concludes with sparrows bursting
"off the walls into the jungle," as the poet opts artfully for suggesting to convey
the effect. Another of Weigl's most famous poems is "Song of Napalm," in
which the narrator stands at his door back home looking out into the night. The
night sky, horses, and fences give way to images of war, especially a girl trying
to outrun the napalm that is burning her. The union of Vietnam and U.S. experiences is common in his poetry, to the extent that even poems such as "Snowy

Egret," without ever mentioning the war, take on an additional resonance because of the Vietnam context surrounding Weigl's life and poetry.

In later poetry, Weigl looks more often at postwar Vietnam. "Her Life Runs Like a Red Silk Flag" and "Why Nothing Changes for Miss Ngo Tri Thanh" in *What Saves Us* and "Fever Dream in Hanoi" in *Sweet Lorain* are just a few examples of poems that transport the reader, as Weigl himself has journeyed, to contemporary Vietnam.

Bruce Weigl's many poetry awards include a fellowship from the National Endowment for the Arts, the Academy of American Poets Prize, Breadloaf and Yaddo Foundation fellowships, and an award from Vietnam Veterans of America for "Contributions to American Culture."

REFERENCES

Gotera, Vince. *Radical Visions: Poetry by Vietnam Veterans*. Athens. University of Georgia Press, 1994. 283–301.

Rielly, Edward J. "Bruce Weigl: Out of the Landscape of His Past." *Journal of American Culture* 16.3 (1993): 47–52.

Schroeder, Eric James, ed. "Bruce Weigl: 'Poetry Grabbed Me by the Throat.' " *Vietnam, We've All Been There: Interviews with American Writers*. Westport, CT: Praeger, 1992.

Smith, Lorrie. "Resistance and Revision in Poetry by Vietnam War Veterans." *Fourteen Landing Zones: Approaches to Vietnam War Literature*. Ed. Philip K. Jason. Iowa City: Iowa University Press, 1991.

Edward J. Rielly

WELCH, JAMES (1940–   ). The Blackfeet Reservation town of Browning, Montana, was Welch's birthplace. Of Blackfeet and Gros Ventre Indian descent, like many Native Americans he is a mixed blood with European bloodlines as well. He attended reservation schools for much of his public education, Montana state schools for college and graduate work.

Of his two books detailing warfare, Welch's third novel, *Fools Crow* (1986), is perhaps the finest novel by or about Native Americans. Among its incidents of war, the work includes nicely drawn, highly accurate descriptions of intertribal warfare just before the advent of Anglo domination in the western United States. Perhaps the most important of these events is the one early in the novel when Fools Crow earns his name. As a member of Blackfeet horse-stealing party, he kills an even younger Crow Indian, producing a wide range of thoughts and emotions within him. Moreover, these accounts of intertribal warfare make for intriguing comparisons to later incidents of Anglo-Indian martial conflicts. One of these latter "battles" includes an incident common in Native American literature: the U.S. military's slaughter of an Indian group mainly composed of women and children. The intertribal conflicts thus simultaneously underscore actual differences between the warfare practiced by colliding Native American and white cultures and prevent Welch's Indians from becoming caricatured as

Noble Savages. Welch also individualizes smaller-scale hostilities between the two races. One such instance details a frightened father and son's murder of an aged Blackfeet man; another involves a tribally disowned group of Indian renegades and their own less-than-honorable "guerrilla warfare" slaughter of whites.

Equally well balanced is Welch's foray into nonfiction, *Killing Custer: The Battle of the Little Bighorn and the Fate of the Plains Indians* (1994). The book is an outgrowth of his scriptwriting research conducted along with director Paul Stekler, whose Afterword discusses their working together to make the documentary film *Last Stand at Little Bighorn*. It chronicles perhaps the most legendary and defining battle in U.S. history as well as numerous interconnected historical and cultural events preceding and following it. Though few, if any, of the volume's details or photographs are themselves new, the book provides the best published Native American examination of what might be termed "The Plains Indians' Last Stand." Welch's novelistic gifts serve him well in numerous descriptions of battles, evoking at times a sense of actual presence amid the dust and clamor and confusion.

REFERENCES

Bevis, William W. "James Welch." *Western American Literature* 32.1 (1997): 33–53.
Owens, Louis. "Earthboy's Return: James Welch's Acts of Recovery." *Other Destinies: Understanding the American Indian Novel.* Norman: University of Oklahoma Press, 1992.

David N. Cremean

WHARTON, EDITH (1862–1937). Among the most talented of the American writers who supported the Allies' cause in World War I, Edith Wharton had a ringside view on the fracas from her home in Paris. In addition to devoting her energies to organizing and aiding a variety of war relief charities, for which she was awarded the French Legion of Honor in March 1916, she also contributed several books, both of fiction and nonfiction, to the literature of the Great War. At times hilariously satirical, at other times as propagandistic as a recruiting poster, Wharton's war writings have been largely overlooked by scholars.

Born to a distinguished New York family, Wharton spent much of her childhood abroad and was privately educated. As a child she tried her hand at fiction and poetry. Later, as an adult bored with her social milieu and unhappy in her marriage, she found an escape in writing. In 1907 she moved to France, and by the time that war broke out in Europe, her reputation as a writer already was well established; she had published a half-dozen short story collections, novels, and novellas.

During the early years of the war, Wharton's charity work sapped much of her energy, but she still found time for some war writing. In the first half of 1915, under the auspices of the French Red Cross, Wharton made several visits to the French front. Her impressions of these visits, and of wartime Paris, were collected in a series of essays that appeared in monthly installments in *Scribner's*

Magazine and then were collected as *Fighting France: From Dunkerque to Belfort* (1915). In these essays, written in the first person, Wharton has nothing but praise for the courage of the men and women of France. Of French troops on the march, she records, "Close as the men were, they seemed allegorically splendid." They seemed ready to "ride straight into glory." But Wharton was not blind to war's horrors. In another of the essays, she muses, "War is the greatest of paradoxes: the most senseless and disheartening of human retrogressions, and yet the stimulant of qualities of soul which, in every race, can seemingly find no other means of renewal."

Wharton's next full-length work about the war, *The Marne* (1918), is clearly the work of a war-backer. Throughout its 158 pages of large type, Wharton's novel follows the travails and records the angst of young Troy Belknap, the scion of a wealthy and well-traveled New York family. Troy's one regret in life is that he is too young to partake in the war as a soldier. During the early days of the war, he must sit idly in the marble-lobbied hotels of Paris and watch as the Germans overrun his much-loved France. Eventually, Troy contrives to join an American ambulance unit in France, and during the Second Battle of the Marne, he seizes an unexpected opportunity to join in the fighting. He volunteers for a dangerous scouting mission, proves his bravery, and is fatally wounded while carrying an injured soldier to safety.

Although it is a work of fiction, *The Marne* is unambiguous in its message. The proper place for every worthy American young man is at the front. With arch wit, Wharton ridicules wealthy Americans who are not duly attuned to Europe's suffering, and she has nothing but contempt for pacifists. Describing the United States's belated entrance into the war, Wharton writes in *The Marne*, "America tore the gag of neutrality from her lips, and with all the strength of her liberated lungs claimed her right to a place in the struggle. The pacifists crept into their holes."

A second work of war fiction titled *A Son at the Front*, on which Wharton had worked intermittently since the spring of 1918, was published in installments in *Scribner's* (from December 1922 to September 1923) and then published as a full-length novel in late 1923. At the center of this work is John Campton, a divorced American painter living in Paris. The book explores Campton's reaction when his son (who was born in France but raised in America) is called up for military duty in the French army. Campton wants his boy to be safe, but he also wants his son to be a hero. At story's end, the boy dies, and Campton designs the statue that will be placed over his grave.

Much lengthier than *The Marne, A Son at the Front* enjoyed neither good sales nor good reviews. A critic for the *Bookman* called it "a belated essay in propaganda." In a decade in which postwar disillusionment already had begun to set in, *A Son at the Front* struck many readers as being maudlin and outdated.

In addition to writing the above-mentioned works, Wharton also edited *The Book of the Homeless* (1916), an anthology of works by prominent writers and artists published to raise funds for Belgian refugees. She also set her novel *The*

Mother's Recompense (1925) against the backdrop of the war. Finally, in her autobiography, *A Backward Glance* (1934), Wharton recorded her memories of the war years and offered insight into her creative process.

REFERENCES

Benstock, Shari. *No Gifts from Chance: A Biography of Edith Wharton.* New York: Charles Scribner's Sons, 1994.

Lewis, R.W.B. *Edith Wharton: A Biography.* New York: Harper & Row, 1975.

Price, Alan. *The End of the Age of Innocence: Edith Wharton and the First World War.* New York: St. Martin's Press, 1996.

Cynthia Wachtell

WHEATLEY, PHILLIS (ca. 1753–1784). Since the publication in England in 1772 of *Poems on Various Subjects, Religious and Moral*, Phillis Wheatley has been celebrated primarily for her contribution to American literature as the first African American woman to publish a volume of poems. Captured in her homeland of Senegal and brought to Boston via the Middle Passage in 1761, Wheatley spent her adolescent and early adult years in the very hub of New England revolutionary activity. As a member of the Old South Church, she both heard and was befriended by the leading patriot preachers and politicians of Boston, including Andrew Elliot, Samuel Cooper, John Lathrop, and John Hancock, among many others. From the Wheatley residence on Queen Street, she witnessed the Boston Massacre, and during George Washington's stay in Cambridge, Wheatley met Washington.

Like other enslaved black Americans of her day, Wheatley took a keen interest in the revolution unfolding around her. The humanitarian rhetoric of the Revolution offered her and others in her situation the hope that the events of the war would awaken in her Euro-American contemporaries an awareness that the very rights for which they struggled were the same rights that they withheld from hundreds of thousands of African American slaves. As she wrote in a 1774 letter to the Native American evangelist Samson Occom, "How well the Cry for Liberty, and the reverse Disposition for the Exercise of oppressive Power over others agree,—I humbly think it does not require the Penetration of a Philosopher to determine."

Unable for fear of reprisals to write more openly about her abolitionist concerns, Wheatley encoded these concerns throughout her poetry, particularly in those poems about the Revolution. In arguing for the liberties and rights of the American colonists in such poems as "To the Right Honourable William, Earl of Dartmouth," "To His Excellency General Washington," "On the Capture of General Lee," "Liberty and Peace," and "America," Wheatley subtly draws attention to the disparity between what the Euro-American patriots of the Revolution were claiming for themselves and what they were denying to others. Like the dying Revolutionary War general she eulogizes in her poem "On the Death of General Wooster," Wheatley translates the war into a greater and ultimately more important struggle to free "Afric's blameless race."

Had she not died in poverty in 1781, Wheatley would have been deeply disappointed that the so-called patriots of the Revolution did not extend their newly won liberties to their African American sisters and brothers. Nonetheless, the militancy and urgency that lie beneath the surface of her eighteenth-century poetic diction indicate her absolute confidence that slavery would one day end, and she can be viewed as both an important African American poet of the American Revolution and a prophetic poet of the Civil War to come.

REFERENCES

Akers, Charles W. " 'Our Modern Egyptians': Phillis Wheatley and the Whig Campaign against Slavery in Revolutionary Boston." *Journal of Negro History* 60 (1975): 397–410.

Levernier, James A. "Phillis Wheatley and the New England Clergy." *Early American Literature* 26 (1991): 21–38.

———. "Style as Protest in the Poetry of Phillis Wheatley." *Style* 27 (1993): 172–193.

Wheatley, Phillis. *The Collected Works of Phillis Wheatley*. Ed. John Shields. New York: Oxford University Press, 1988.

James A. Levernier

WHITMAN, WALT (1819–1892). Walter Whitman was born on Long Island on May 31, 1819. Prior to the Civil War, Whitman worked, among other jobs, as a printer, a schoolteacher, and an editor of various newspapers. Whitman published poems, tracts, articles, and even a temperance novel, *Franklin Evans* (1842), during the 1840s and early 1850s; nevertheless, the appearance of the first edition of *Leaves of Grass* in 1855 would eventually secure his reputation as one of America's greatest poets.

In 1862, upon hearing that his younger brother George had been wounded in the battle of Fredericksburg (December 13, 1862), Whitman relocated to Washington, D.C., where he stayed until 1873. During the war, Whitman tended the war wounded, playing the role of wound dresser, comforter, and volunteer nurse to the soldiers in the army hospitals. Out of these experiences grew some of his best poetry and some of the best poetry of the Civil War. *Drum-Taps*, Whitman's collection of Civil War poems, was first published in 1865. After Lincoln's assassination that same year, Whitman released *Sequel to Drum-Taps*, which contained several poems in honor of the late president, including the powerful elegy "When Lilacs Last in the Dooryard Bloom'd" as well as the more popular "O Captain! My Captain!" *Drum-Taps* was incorporated into the fourth edition of *Leaves of Grass* in 1867, but only as a hasty addendum at the end of the volume. When the fifth edition was published in 1871–1872, *Drum-Taps* was more carefully integrated into the volume.

Taken as a whole, *Drum-Taps* is a masterful collection of war poetry. Read sequentially, the poems take the reader from the first summons to enlistment in

1861 to the end of the conflict in 1865. The collection begins with Whitman recalling the energetic call to arms of Manhattan citizens in "First O Songs for a Prelude." Soon, however, initial energy dissipates into harsh reality as the conflict ensues, and poems such as "Eighteen Sixty-One" and "Beat! Beat! Drums!" both celebrate the rush to battle and lament the foreboding violence of that "hurrying, crashing, sad, distracted year." One of the more interesting early poems is "The Centenarian's Story," in which an elderly veteran of the Revolutionary War recounts his experiences as Civil War recruits practice drills on a nearby field—a field still harboring the "phantoms" of Washington's army.

The poems that comprise the middle of the collection are notable for their imagistic representation of army maneuvers—for instance, "Cavalry Crossing a Ford" and "An Army Corps on the March"—and for their graphic presentation of the horrific outcome of battle. Of this latter group, poems such as "Vigil Strange I Kept on the Field One Night" and "A Sight in Camp in the Daybreak Gray and Dim" are remarkable in their depiction of the casualties of war. In "Vigil," for instance, the narrator sits through the night next to a boy fallen in battle; then, at daybreak, wrapping him in a blanket, the narrator "buried him where he fell." One of the climactic middle poems is "The Wound-Dresser," in which Whitman vividly details his duties as a volunteer nurse. In this poem the carnage of war is depicted as Whitman recounts changing the bandages of amputees and other wounded.

The mood begins to change toward the end of the collection, however, as poems such as "Over the Carnage Rose Prophetic a Voice" hint at the end of the conflict and at a reunified United States. This prophetic vision is carried over into "The Artilleryman's Vision," in which a veteran, at home after the end of the war, is tormented with visions of battle. Finally, in "Spirit Whose Work Is Done," "Turn O Libertad," and "To the Leaven'd Soil They Trod," Whitman concludes *Drum-Taps* with poems celebrating the end of the war.

Whitman's other major war document was his prose work *Memoranda of the War*, which was based on journal entries made during the war but not published until Whitman issued it in a small edition in 1875. Later, *Memoranda of the War* was incorporated into the larger *Specimen Days and Collect* (1882). Composed mainly of brief autobiographical sketches, the text recounts snapshots of the war, from crowds standing on Broadway in the evening reading in stunned silence the news of the firing upon Fort Sumter, through the aftermath of the battles of Fredericksburg, Chancellorsville, and Gettysburg, the death of Lincoln, the return of Northern prisoners of war from camps such as Andersonville, and finally, to the closing of the army hospitals in the late fall of 1865. The strength of Whitman's vignettes lies in their stark and graphic descriptions of the casualties of war, made all the more vivid because most of them recount Whitman's firsthand experiences treating such casualties.

REFERENCES

Greenspan, Ezra, ed. *The Cambridge Companion to Walt Whitman*. Cambridge: Cambridge University Press, 1995.

Kaplan, Justin. *Walt Whitman: A Life*. New York: Simon and Schuster, 1980.

Miller, James E., Jr. *Walt Whitman*. New York: Twayne, 1962.

Whitman, Walt. *The Collected Writings of Walt Whitman*. Gay Wilson Allen and Sculley Bradley, General eds. New York: New York University Press, 1961– .

———. *Complete Poetry and Collected Prose*. Ed. Justin Kaplan. New York: Library of America, 1982.

Eric Carl Link

WHITTIER, JOHN GREENLEAF (1807–1892). One of America's best-loved "Fireside Poets," Whittier's New England roots ran deep. Born and raised on land that five generations of his family had farmed in Essex County, Massachusetts, the young Whittier grew up surrounded by a simple Quaker piety. Poor, yet with his religion's belief in the equality of all mankind, Whittier was attracted to writing when his ill health impaired his ability to work the family farm.

Through his friend William Lloyd Garrison, the aspiring writer obtained an editorial position at the *American Manufacturer* in Boston. There, in 1829, but especially in Hartford, Connecticut, at the *New England Weekly Review* for several years thereafter, Whittier wrote on a variety of topics, especially historical and political ones. Early explorations into the theme of war appeared in essays such as "The Stormed Fort: A Tale of 1756" and "A Soldier's Story." Although several essays in these newspapers are of uncertain authorship, what is clearly Whittier's work both affirms the bravery of the individuals involved and disapproves of the violence of war. In these early years Whittier was also developing strong political ties with the antislavery movement in metropolitan centers as far south as Philadelphia, where he wrote for the *Pennsylvania Freeman*.

Although in 1840 Whittier broke with the radical elements of the abolitionist movement, he remained staunchly committed to the principles of emancipation in his early public poems. One of the clearest examples occurs in "Massachusetts to Virginia" (1843), where he says, as a pacifist, "we wage no war, we lift no arm" in active militarism. Yet even here the warlike images predominate, with the narrator speaking of "blasts," "marching files," and "the shaft of Bunker." Like the later "Ichabod" (1850), a satiric attack on Daniel Webster's reversion from emancipation's principles, and his troubled "Brown at Ossawatomie" (1859), a poem telling of John Brown's Raid, Whittier's attitude is troubled, torn between a love of country and a moral indignation against slavery, on the one hand, and on the other hand, a fear of the consequences of violent militarism.

Whittier's twenty-eight poems written during the tumultuous Civil War years are collected in *In War Time and Other Poems* (1864). Interspersed with occasional verse, a number of powerful poems appear here that attempt to chronicle historical events of the war. In "To John C. Fremont," Whittier lauds the general for announcing the freedom of Missouri-based slaves; although premature, Whittier's persona praises the act by saying, "Still take thy courage! God has spoken through thee, / Irrevocable, the mighty words, Be Free!" A more timely poem is "Astrea at the Capitol," written to praise the abolition of slavery in the District of Columbia in 1862. Here, in highly allusive lines, Whittier rejoices the freedom of these slaves.

Collected in the same volume, poems such as "At Port Royal," with its interpolated "Song of the Negro Boatmen," and "The Battle Autumn of 1862" capture, in microcosm, the importance of specific Civil War events. Whittier's most important poem in this collection, however, is the symbolic "Barbara Frietchie," set in Frederick, Maryland. The protagonist of the ballad, one of Whittier's favorite poetic forms, saves, through almost superhuman effort, the Union flag from the attacking rebel soldiers. The final couplets end in lines typical of Whittier's intention:

> Peace and order and beauty draw
> Round the symbol of light and law;
>
> And ever the stars above look down
> On thy stars below in Frederick town!

Her act of bravery, important in itself, is thus for a higher purpose, saving, symbolically at least, the "light and law" of the nation.

When, three years later, the war ends, Whittier turns his attention to other matters: In the nostalgic and extraordinary popular *Snow-Bound: A Winter Idyll* (1866), he creates what he calls a "Yankee pastoral"; in other works, published nearly until his death in 1892, his concerns with emancipation are replaced by religious themes. His early poetry and prose had made him well known, his Civil War poems and *Snow-Bound* had brought him great popularity, and his later poems, attuned to the times, had solidified his reputation. Whittier was, with his clear and direct poetry and his firm moral purpose, a writer who spoke to, and for, the people of our country.

REFERENCES

Kribbs, Jayne K., ed. *Critical Essays on John Greenleaf Whittier*. Boston: Hall, 1980.
Whittier, John Greenleaf. *The Writings of John Greenleaf Whittier*. 7 vols. New York: Riverside, 1888–1889. Rev. ed. 1894.
Woodwell, Roland H. *John Greenleaf Whittier: A Biography*. Haverhill, MA: Trustees of the John Greenleaf Whittier Papers, 1985.

Charles J. Gaspar

WILBUR, RICHARD (1921–). Former Poet Laureate of the United States, Richard Wilbur was born in New York City and raised in North Caldwell, New Jersey. From Amherst College, he enlisted in the U.S. Army and served in World War II from 1943 to 1945, reaching the rank of staff sergeant. Upon his return, he attended Harvard on the G.I. Bill, published his first book of poetry, *The Beautiful Changes and Other Poems* (1947), and embarked on a career of writing and teaching. Wilbur's graceful craftsmanship and his rage for order within the lines of his work and in his vision of the world are, in part, a legacy of his World War II experience. He commented to Stanley Kunitz that "it was not until World War II took me to Cassino, Anzio, and the Siegfried Line that I began to versify in earnest." *The Beautiful Changes* includes eight poems that deal specifically with the war.

"Tywater" describes the death of a simple, knife-throwing, lariat-roping Texan and expresses Wilbur's shock at the randomness of death on the battlefield. His vision of the modern battlefield depicted in "Mined Country" is especially prophetic given the contemporary international concern over the proliferation of land mines. Wilbur speculates that the consequence of war is a natural world of lost trust; yet he is able to embrace a wary faith that love can be resurrected. Wilbur's sense of paradox is present in the "Comical-delicate" poem "Potato," where Wilbur playfully puns on "savor" and "savior" and connects the unpretentious spud of the G.I.'s kitchen police to Christ's tomb. War, for Wilbur, helped him see what Clara Claiborne Park termed the "brilliant positive" in something even so lowly and absurd as the potato. In "Place Pigalle," Wilbur mimics the language of courtly love in a contemplation of a whore with "eyes as pale as air" and a "priestgoat" faced soldier, but even in this obvious parody, Wilbur conveys a deeper intellectual appreciation of paradoxical affinities between love and war. The poem "On the Eyes of an SS Officer" succeeds in capturing Wilbur's strongest emotions against those responsible for much of the suffering he observed on the line. Wilbur's unambiguous curse is an uncharacteristic emotional response to war not central to the purpose of his poetry.

Wilbur's aesthetic responses to war are most fully expressed in "First Snow at Alsace," where the newly fallen snow changes things by embracing and smoothing the roofs of homes, disguising the fact that they are "Fear gutted, trustless and estranged." Wilbur, even in the wreckage that is war, can celebrate a sense of the regenerative goodness of the natural things of this world—the first snow promises some relationship between material and spiritual realms. There is a shock of recognition and an assurance of order revealed in and through the natural act of creation—opposed to man's act of destruction. His poem does not dwell on abstract despair but attempts to find in the desolate landscape transformed by first snow a hint of the "I-Thou" relationship of man to nature and natural things. In the process of reconciling the paradoxes of war, Wilbur discovered the sacramental in even things as simple as potatoes and first snow.

REFERENCES

Kunitz, Stanley, ed. *Twentieth Century Authors*. First Supplement. New York: Wilson, 1980.

Park, Clara Claiborne. "Called to Praise: Richard Wilbur's Brilliant Positive." *Christianity and Literature* 42.4 (Summer 1993): 551–567.

Salinger, Wendy, ed. *Richard Wilbur's Creation*. Ann Arbor: University of Michigan Press, 1981.

Wilbur, Richard. *New and Collected Poems*. New York: Harcourt Brace Jovanovich, 1988.

Joseph T. Cox

WILLIAMS, BEN AMES (1899–1953). Born in Macon, Mississippi, Williams was reared in Jackson, Ohio, where he worked for his father, who was editor and publisher of the local newspaper, the *Standard Journal*. After graduating from Dartmouth in 1910, Williams worked as reporter for the *Boston American* and also began submitting stories to pulp magazines. From 1915 to 1917 Williams published his short stories exclusively in the pulps, but in 1917 the *Saturday Evening Post* accepted his story "The Mate of Suzie Oakes." Williams was to publish a total of 135 short stories, thirty-five serials, and seven articles in that magazine over the next twenty-four years. His best-known work of this period is "All the Brothers Were Valiant." "Great Oaks" marks Williams's first attempt at writing about war; the story of life on an island off the coast of Georgia focuses on seven major historical events, concluding with the Civil War. Another serial, "Thread of Scarlet," is Williams's first full-fledged war story. It takes place in Nantucket during the War of 1812. The protagonist is a young American who cannot decide whether or not to fight in the war but finally decides to do so.

Because most of his serials were also published in book form (*Great Oaks* was so published in 1930), Williams had had thirty books published before he wrote his first novel. *Come Spring* (1940) is the story of a Maine Village during the Revolutionary War. Inspired by actual events, the book focuses more on the conflicts between the settlers and the Native Americans than on the war itself. Maine is also the setting for Williams's next novel, *The Strange Woman* (1941). Spanning the years from the War of 1812 to the Civil War, the novel depicts the life of one woman as told by seven different men, including her father and several lovers.

With *In Time of Peace: September 26, 1930–December 7, 1941* (1942), Williams examines the decade leading up to America's entry into World War II. Many of the novel's characters are uncertain as to what American policy should be regarding the conflict in Europe; *In Time of Peace* shows in detail the anti-Roosevelt sentiment that was commonplace in America at the time and also attempts to present the German point of view.

House Divided (1947) is Williams's magnum opus, a Civil War novel that took twelve years to research and over four years to write. Spanning the years 1859 to 1865, it focuses on the Currain family, owner of plantations in North Carolina and Virginia. Williams's great-uncle General James Longstreet is also a character in the novel. In *House Divided*, Williams examines the politics that lead to war and the political machinations that occur during wartime. The Currains are pro-secession though not pro-slavery and are rabid opponents of Abraham Lincoln, whom they learn ironically is their father's illegitimate grandson. *House Divided* does not present a lengthy depiction of the Civil War itself, nor does it detail the events leading to and following the war. It is, like many of Williams's novels, primarily a romantic adventure story that emphasizes its characters' personal lives more than the war. *The Unconquered* (1953), which depicts Reconstruction in Louisiana, is its sequel.

In addition to his fiction, Williams edited two noteworthy books about war. *A Diary from Dixie* (1949), by **Mary Boykin Chesnut**, is the journal of a Southern woman written during the Civil War: It was one of Williams's primary resources when writing *House Divided. Amateurs at War: The American Soldier in Action* (1943) consists of profiles of American servicemen.

REFERENCES

Geismar, Maxwell. Rev. of *House Divided*, by Ben Ames Williams. *Saturday Review of Literature* 13 September 1947: 10.

Rev. of *House Divided*, by Ben Ames Williams. *The New Yorker* 13 September 1947: 119.

Van Gelder, Robert. *Writers and Writing*. New York: Scribner's, 1946.

Warfel, Harry Redcay. *American Novelists of Today*. New York: American Book Company, 1951.

Randall Clark

WILLIAMS, JOHN A. (1925–   ) Born in Jackson, Mississippi, novelist John A. Williams was raised in Syracuse, New York. Upon hearing of the Japanese bombing of Pearl Harbor, the writer dropped out of high school to enlist in the navy, receiving an honorable discharge in 1946. Williams later attended Syracuse University, majoring in journalism. While distinguishing himself in broadcast and print media, Williams also committed himself to fiction writing, publishing his first novel, *The Angry Ones*, in 1960, followed by eight more works of fiction and several books of nonfiction. His most celebrated publications include the novel *The Man Who Cried I Am* (1967) and *The King God Didn't Save* (1970), a groundbreaking study of the life of Martin Luther King, Jr.

Originally conceived as a nonfictional analysis of African American military service, *Captain Blackman* (1972) may very well be Williams's most ambitious, artistically satisfying novel. A sprawling postmortem historical novel blurring the lines between fact and fiction, Williams merges his journalistic sensibility with his talents as a fiction writer to create a work that incorporates every major American military conflict from the American Revolution to the Vietnam War. The novel begins in 1971 as Captain Abraham Blackman, an exemplary, seasoned soldier, is pinned under machine gun fire from the Viet Cong. Knowing that his loyal squad will attempt to rescue him, Blackman is faced with a choice: to let them risk their lives or to divert enemy fire, saving the men he has sworn to protect. Choosing the latter, the captain throws himself into the open. Critically injured, Blackman falls into a long, hallucinatory dream in which he appears as a soldier, fighting alongside the black Revolutionary War hero Peter Salem.

The narrative continues to alternate between Blackman's historical reveries and his fight to stay alive on the operating table. The main tension in the novel stems from Blackman's relationship to Major Ishmael Whittman, a white officer and Blackman's superior in rank only. Over the span of their careers, Blackman has forced Whittman to understand that he is only half the soldier Blackman is; race, not ability, has determined their differing statuses in the military. In the dream sequences, Whittman appears as an ineffectual leader, lauding his unearned power over his black troops. Each episode ends with a factual document—letters from General Pershing, Andrew Jackson's statements after the War of 1812, for example—testifying to the military's conflicting, wavering attitudes toward black military service. The novel ends as the still-unconscious captain imagines a futuristic war in which African Americans take over the military. It is unfortunate Blackman's only true victory lies within a bittersweet dream of vengeance.

In his 1999 *Clifford's Blues*, Williams returns to World War II with the story of a jazz musician imprisoned in Dachau. Clifford leads a band of prisoner musicians who entertain their captors and thus keep themselves alive.

REFERENCE

Muller, Gilbert. *John A. Williams*. Boston: Twayne, 1984.

Jennifer C. James

WILSON, EDMUND (1895–1972). Wilson was born in Red Bank, New Jersey, and graduated from Princeton University in 1916. He was a reporter in New York (1916–1917) and served unhappily in the army in France, first as a base-hospital orderly, then as an Intelligence Corps sergeant (1917–1919). He resumed his journalistic career, became a distinguished literary editor, and established himself as a versatile writer and a superb literary critic. *I Thought of Daisy* (1929), his first novel, includes descriptions of his handling of gruesome war casualties in France. After much professional success, he disputed with the Internal Revenue Service, which in 1958 charged him for failing to file tax returns and not paying taxes from 1946 to 1957. In 1960 it froze his sources of income. In the wrong and facing ruin, Wilson paid but turned the episode into a political-protest diatribe, *The Cold War and the Income Tax: A Protest* (1963). It is full of vitriolic, leftist comments against bureaucratic inefficiency and waste, paranoid fear of communism, the arms and space races, and the entire military-industrial establishment.

Wilson was the author of forty-six other books but only one exclusively concerned with war, *Patriotic Gore: Studies in the Literature of the American Civil War* (1962). He offers a mainly sociopolitical treatment of thirty-odd authors living in the 1860s and often active thereafter and in the process analyzes their cultural and professional backgrounds and publications. He contrasts Northern mercantile crusaders, often treacherous, and gallant, aristocratic Southerners, often mushy, during their quasi-Calvinistic conflict supposedly of good versus evil; but then he shows that during Reconstruction the North became so pseudovirtuous, the South so unforgiving, that many gifted writers in both regions seemed tongue-tied—some by what they had suffered, others by trying unsuccessfully to write in ways acceptable to their mainly female readers. Especially perceptive are Wilson's discussions of generals Ulysses Grant and William Sherman; Southern diarist **Mary Chesnut**, guerrilla Colonel John Mosby, and politician Alexander Stephens; writers **Ambrose Bierce**, **John De Forest**, and **Albion Tourgée**; and Justice Oliver Wendell Holmes. Several minor writers are resurrected, vivified, or redeemed.

REFERENCES

Aaron, Daniel. *The Unwritten War: American Writers and the Civil War*. New York: Knopf, 1973.
Bewley, Marius. "Northern Saints and Southern Knights." *Hudson Review* 15 (Autumn 1962): 431–439.
Meyers, Jeffrey. *Edmund Wilson: A Biography*. Boston: Houghton Mifflin, 1995.
Warren, Robert Penn. "Edmund Wilson's Civil War." *Commentary* 34 (August 1962): 151–158.

Robert L. Gale

WILSON, KEITH (1927–). Born in Clovis, New Mexico, Wilson aspired to a career as a naval officer. Graduating from Annapolis, he served three tours in Korean waters between 1950 and 1953. At first proud to be part of the United Nations effort, he came to believe that it was in reality only a fig leaf covering far less altruistic American policy aims. Disillusioned, he left the navy and embarked on a career as a university professor and poet.

Wilson's Korean War experiences provide the foundation for perhaps his most important book. First published in 1969 as *Graves Registry & Other Poems*, it contained poems about the war along with poems about his native American Southwest. Says Wilson, "I started writing *Graves Registry* in the winter of 1966 in anger that my government was again fighting an undeclared war in a situation that I, from my experiences in Korea, knew we could never win." In 1992, Wilson published an updated edition of the book called simply *Graves Registry* and containing the original Korean War poems, additional poems from his 1972 *Midwatch* (including a number that deal explicitly with the Vietnam War), and fifty newer poems. Taken together, they weave the literary and the political into a single tableau that moves skillfully across time and geography.

Wilson's Korean War poems are not about the big battalions and the pitched battles but about coastal operations and guerrilla raids, shattered villages and shattered ideals. They are peopled by Americans but also by Koreans and Japanese, by refugees and cripples, by warriors, but also and more so by the defenseless and the innocent who always become the wreckage of war. "O, do not dream of peace," he scolds in "Commentary," while "such bodies / line the beaches & dead men float / the seas, waving[.]" As he writes in "December 1952," Wilson's poems force us to confront "the cost of lies, tricks / that blind the eyes of the young. *Freedom. / Death. A Life Safe for.* The Dead." They are his explanation of how he began his life expecting to kill people and ended up dedicating it to teaching people instead.

REFERENCE

Ehrhart, W. D. "Soldier-Poets of the Korean War." *War, Literature & the Arts* 9.2 (Fall–Winter 1997): 33–38.

W. D. Ehrhart

WOLFF, TOBIAS (1945–). Wolff was born in Birmingham, Alabama, and holds degrees from both Oxford and Stanford. He has worked as a reporter for the *Washington Post* and has held academic positions at Stanford, Goddard College, Arizona State University, and most recently at Syracuse University. With the rank of lieutenant in the U.S. Army he served as an adviser to an Army of the Republic of Vietnam (ARVN) battalion during the Vietnam War.

Both Wolff's early (disowned) war novel *Ugly Rumors* (1975) and his war memoir *In Pharaoh's Army: Memories of the Lost War* (1994) portray men isolated from the army and believing themselves to be unfit for much of what is required of them. They are not stereotypical soldier-heroes, just as much of Wolff's war fiction questions the stereotypes associated with military service. For example, in "Wingfield" (*In the Garden of North American Martyrs*, 1981), the title character is pegged as having no chance to survive his tour in Vietnam due to his lazy, unmilitary bearing, yet he does come back alive somehow. In "Soldier's Joy" (*Back in the World*, 1985), camaraderie is established not in battle but when two soldiers fabricate a story to cover up the senseless murder of a third soldier during guard duty. With "The Other Miller" (*The Night in Question*, 1996) the main character happily allows himself to be taken away from his company during a war game rather than admit he is not the man being sought. And in "Casualty" (*The Night in Question*), B. D. experiences relief instead of grief over the mortal wounding of his friend Ryan because he no longer has to face the moral dilemma of whether or not to intervene on Ryan's behalf. But Wolff's most complete questioning of soldierly stereotypes comes with his novella *The Barracks Thief* (1984).

While pulling guard duty at an ammo dump, Phil, Lewis, and Hubbard refuse to leave their posts despite the approach of a forest fire. This loyalty in the face of danger creates a sense of camaraderie among the three—but it is short-lived. Both Phil and Hubbard become absorbed by personal problems, and Lewis begins stealing from the men in the barracks. By the end of the novella, Lewis is caught and dishonorably discharged, Hubbard deserts before being shipped to Vietnam, and years later Phil reflects on how he has become "addicted to comfort"—so unlike the man he was that night at the ammo dump. None of these characters achieves a satisfactory masculine identity or a lasting sense of comradeship, making *The Barracks Thief*, along with Wolff's short stories, a serious argument against the myth of manly fellowship under arms.

REFERENCES

Bates, Milton J. *The Wars We Took to Vietnam: Cultural Conflict and Storytelling.* Berkeley: University of California Press, 1996. 207–210.

Hannah, James. *Tobias Wolff: A Study of the Short Fiction.* New York: Twayne, 1996.

Lyons, Bonnie, and Bill Oliver. "An Interview with Tobias Wolff." *Contemporary Literature* 31.1 (Spring 1990):1–16.

Joe Sarnowski

WOOD, CHARLES ERSKINE SCOTT (1852–1944). Charles Erskine Scott Wood was born in Erie, Pennsylvania, but the family moved near Baltimore after the American Civil War. Wood's navy father pushed his unwilling son through West Point, but Wood's performance was lackluster, and he was sent to the Pacific Northwest after graduation. He resigned his commission in 1884 and entered law in Portland, Oregon, beginning his writing career soon after. Wood wrote novels, poetry, and sociopolitical commentary but always considered himself a poet. He is perhaps most famous for "transcribing" Chief Joseph's surrender speech in 1877. *A Book of Tales* (1901) is his collection of Native American legends. *The Poet in the Desert* (1915), his long poetic work, is divided into fifty-two cantos, many of which address his love of the Oregon landscape and describe his "philosophical anarchism." Wood's *Heavenly Discourse* (1927), written during and primarily about World War I, was his most popular work, consisting of forty-one dialogues by various historical figures and ranging in topics from censorship to war. *The Masses*, in which many of the discourses appeared, was pulled from newsstands when it printed a dialogue in which Jesus asks God, "Father, were you and mother ever married?"

One discourse, "Satan Brings the United States into the War," discusses the way the United States and other countries have propagandized war. "You ought to see the patriots club their fellow-citizens in the name of freedom and the good old flag of liberty," Satan says. "I nearly die laughing." Eventually, God decides that as long as people are "stupid sheep," Satan can rule earth as he sees fit. Another discourse, "A Pacifist Enters Heaven—in Bits," displays the hypocrisy patriotism breeds. A soul reaches heaven, battered for not rising during the "Star-Spangled Banner" by "the patriots—the one hundred percenters; those who encourage other people to die for freedom, democracy, etc., while they stay home to beat up."

While Wood wrote many essays and poems on the western landscape and his experiences with the army as it tried to settle conflicts with the Native American population, he also wrote antiimperialist literature. His short story "The Juniper Post" is about a ranchwoman's son who returns alive from fighting in the Philippines after having been reported dead, a theme also developed in his *Heavenly Discourse*.

REFERENCES

Bingham, Edwin R. *Charles Erskine Scott Wood*. Boise: Boise State University Printing and Graphics Services, 1990.
Barnes, Tim. "Beyond the Bear Paw Mountains: Charles Erskine Scott Wood's Literary Campaign for Freedom." *Sweet Reason* (Fall 1986): 12–22.

Cristie L. March

WORLD WAR I. *See* **First World War**.

WORLD WAR II. *See* **Second World War**.

WOUK, HERMAN (1915–). The eldest child of Russian Jewish immigrants, Herman Wouk was born in New York City where his father ran a laundry business. Educated at the prestigious Townsend Harris High and Columbia College, he spent nearly a decade working as a gag writer for vaudeville and radio comics while struggling to write plays for Broadway. After the United States entered World War II, Wouk volunteered for service in the navy, attending officer candidate school at Columbia. Assigned to the Pacific Theater, he served aboard the USS *Zane*, a destroyer-minesweeper, rising to the position of executive officer. After the war, he married Betty Brown and returned to New York to take up a career as a full-time writer. The Wouk family moved several times over the next four decades—to the Virgin Islands, Washington, D.C., and finally Palm Springs, California.

Wouk's novels can be classified into three major groups: accounts of Jewish life in America, stories about the founding and history of the modern State of Israel, and chronicles of America's involvement in World War II. Although not always well received by critics, Wouk's novels have always had a large readership.

By far the most well known of Wouk's war novels is his Pulitzer Prize–winning *The Caine Mutiny* (1951). Informed by Wouk's personal experiences at sea aboard a destroyer-minesweeper, *The Caine Mutiny* examines a young officer's passage from pampered civilian dilettante to seasoned war veteran. Willie Keith, Columbia graduate and reluctant warrior, finds himself aboard a ship that sees virtually no combat. Instead, the USS *Caine* trudges back and forth across the Pacific in an inglorious support role to the major naval combatants. Life aboard the *Caine* is anything but dull, however, after new captain Philip Queeg takes command. An incompetent martinet, Queeg alienates both officers and crew. His loyal executive officer Steve Maryk tries to defend him, but gradually Maryk is convinced by another officer, Tom Keefer, that Queeg is insane. Maryk eventually relieves Queeg of command while the ship founders in a storm, involving Willie in the process. Both are court-martialed for mutiny, but their attorney casts doubt on Queeg's sanity and convinces the judges to issue reprimands rather than stiffer punishment. The euphoria the mutineers feel in besting Queeg is short-lived, however, when their attorney accuses them of leading an easy life in America while Queeg and his fellow professional officers were making great sacrifices to keep America free.

Considered by many a novel in the tradition of the bildungsroman, *The Caine Mutiny* traces the story of its hero, and by extension, his country, in their progress from rash egocentrism to a more reasoned appreciation for community values. Nevertheless, many academic critics have faulted Wouk for presenting a story that first vilifies the professional naval officer and then exonerates him.

A conservative viewpoint also permeates Wouk's two novels about World War II. In *The Winds of War*, Wouk introduces the Henrys, a fictional navy family. Victor "Pug" Henry, a career naval officer, is all that Philip Queeg is not: highly professional, imaginative, loyal to both his country and his family, concerned about the common good rather than personal advancement. Befriended by President Franklin Roosevelt, Henry receives assignments that bring him into contact with all of the major world leaders. Not surprisingly, the Henrys find their family relationships disrupted as America moves toward war: Both sons marry in haste, only to leave their brides for naval service, while Pug and his wife, Rhoda, find their own marriage under strain. The novel ends with Pug surveying the damage done by the Japanese at Pearl Harbor.

War and Remembrance picks up the Henrys' story as America goes to war. Pug and his sons exhibit gallantry under fire, with one son losing his life at the Battle of Midway. Meanwhile, on the home front Pug's wife drifts away from him, leaving him free at last to marry a young British correspondent with whom he has a chaste relationship throughout the war.

Both novels paint a convincing portrait of the sacrifices Americans made to bring about victory for the Allies. Additionally, much of both novels is devoted to an examination of the plight of the Jews under Hitler.

All of Wouk's major war novels became subjects for screen treatment: *The Caine Mutiny* was an Academy Award–winning film in 1953, and *The Winds of War* and *War and Remembrance* each formed the basis for major television miniseries. The dramatic court-martial scene from *The Caine Mutiny* was revised by Wouk himself into a Broadway play that received highly favorable reviews and numerous revivals. As a consequence, millions of Americans for over four generations have come under the spell of this popular writer who has used his fiction to promote a decidedly conservative, patriotic vision of a country about which he feels passionately.

REFERENCES

Beichman, Arnold. *Herman Wouk: The Novelist as Social Historian.* New Brunswick, NJ: Transaction Books, 1984.
Mazzeno, Laurence W. *Herman Wouk.* New York: Twayne, 1994.

Laurence W. Mazzeno

Y

YAMADA, MITSUYE (1923–). With her Japanese American cultural heritage, Mitsuye Yamada has explored her multicultural experience with her poetry, short fiction, and essays. Born in Kyushu, Japan, and raised in Seattle, Washington, Yamada and her family were interred in a U.S. concentration camp in Idaho during World War II. Her first collection of poems, *Camp Notes and Other Poems* (1976), examines her experience growing up with Issei parents, the family's incarceration in Idaho, and her eventual repatriation into American culture.

Divided into three parts, *Camp Notes* begins with "My Issei Parents / Twice Pioneers / Now I Hear Them," a section that explores Yamada's familial connections and her family's arrival in the United States. Through the voices of her great-grandmother, her mother, her father, and her childhood self, Yamada examines the paradoxical messages she received as a Nisei child. In "Enryo" Yamada relates the confusing translations of values and styles that confront her hybrid self, wondering how ingrained habits of deference and courtesy can support or project the pride she is told is her inheritance. These poems lead into Section Two, "Camp Notes," which explores Yamada's experience in Camp Harmony, Idaho.

The paradox of a prison named Harmony and the experience of Japanese American children is explored in these poems. In "Evacuation," Yamada notes the irony of her obedient smile, used as propaganda, as she boards the bus for her internment, which she sarcastically likens to a lifelong vacation. Her father, imprisoned on charges of "possible espionage," remains incarcerated. Yamada's use of ironic tone is most powerful in "Desert Storm." As the inhabitants take cover from an Idaho dust storm, she observes how the cover phrase of "relocation" masks their imprisonment. Nonetheless, Yamada insists, those held in detention camps lived their lives "just like people," emphasizing the dehumanizing effect of her experiences with the humanizing images of her poetry. The third section, "Other Poems," further examines issues of cultural assimilation and difference. These poems are powerful in their simplicity and provide a stunning vision of the Japanese American experience. Yamada returns to these themes in her second collection of poems, *Desert Run* (1988).

REFERENCES

Schwiek, Susan. "A Needle with Mama's Voice: Mitsuye Yamada's *Camp Notes* and the American Canon of War Poetry." *Arms and the Woman: War, Gender, and Literary Representation*. Ed. Helen M. Cooper, Adrienne Auslander Munich, and Susan Merrill Squier. Chapel Hill: University of North Carolina Press, 1989.

Yamada, Mitsuye. *Camp Notes and Other Writings*. New Brunswick, NJ: Rutgers University Press, 1998.

Amy L. Wink

YOUNG, STARK (1881–1963). Born in Como, Mississippi, Young was educated at the University of Mississippi (B.A., 1901) and at Columbia (M.A., 1902). After teaching English at Mississippi, the University of Texas, and Amherst, he became drama critic for the *New Republic* and then for the *New York Times* and served as editor of *Theatre Arts Magazine*. After several volumes of poems and plays, Young turned to fiction with *Heaven Trees* (1926), *The Torches Flare* (1928), and *River House* (1929). All three novels explore the relationship between the modern South and its past, Young's ideas about which take explicit form in his essay "Not in Memoriam, but in Defense" in the Agrarian manifesto *I'll Take My Stand* (1930).

Making trips to Mississippi to research the historical background, Young used both published and unpublished materials to give *So Red the Rose* (1934) historical authenticity. Told from the perspective of members of the Bedford and McGehee families living in Natchez, the novel records the Southern debate over secession, involves characters in military action at the battle of Shiloh, and dramatizes the experience of Federal occupation. Hugh McGehee and his son Edward are slave owners who cannot see a fair way to bring the institution to an end. They believe in maintaining the Federal Union, but Edward finds a hero in Jefferson Davis and enlists in the Southern army. One of the most moving sections of the novel is Young's account of Agnes McGehee's trip to the Shiloh battlefield to locate her son's body and bring it home for burial.

By contrast, Edward's cousin Duncan Bedford sees Davis as the unheroic architect of the South's defeat. He respects Robert E. Lee, who after the war accepts the presidency of Washington College, for demonstrating the way the South can retain traditional values but move into the changed postwar world. In addition to Davis and Lee, Young uses William Tecumseh Sherman to clarify his ideas about the relationship of the South to its past. When Hugh and Agnes McGehee encounter Sherman, who before the war had taught Edward at the Louisiana Military Academy, they recognize his ability to separate his human feelings from his military objective of destroying the South. His mind is the industrialized impulse at odds with their agricultural culture, and clearly Young uses *So Red the Rose* to make an argument more about the South of the early 1930s than of the 1860s.

A film version of *So Red the Rose*, directed by King Vidor, was released in 1935; an edition of the novel, with an introduction by fellow Agrarian Donald Davidson, was issued in 1953. Young followed up the novel with a collection of stories entitled *Feliciana* (1935). In 1951 he published an account of his early life entitled *The Pavilion*. Young was buried in Como, Mississippi.

REFERENCES

Pilkington, John. *Stark Young*. Boston: Twayne, 1985.

Young, Stark. *The Pavilion: Of People and Times Remembered, of Stories and Places*. New York: Charles Scribner's Sons, 1951.

————. *Stark Young: A Life in the Arts: Letters, 1900–1962*. Ed. John Pilkington. 2 vols. Baton Rouge: Louisiana State University Press, 1975.

Robert C. Petersen

SELECTED BIBLIOGRAPHY

Aichinger, Peter. *The American Soldier in Fiction, 1880–1963: A History of Attitudes toward Warfare and the Military Establishment.* Ames: Iowa State University Press, 1975.

Aldridge, John W. *After the Lost Generation: A Critical Study of the Writers of Two Wars.* New York: McGraw-Hill, 1951.

Alter, Nora M. *Vietnam Protest Theatre: The Television War on Stage.* Bloomington: Indiana University Press, 1996.

Axelsson, Arne. *Restrained Response: American Novels of the Cold War and Korea, 1945–1962.* New York: Greenwood Press, 1990.

Bates, Milton J. *The Wars We Took to Vietnam: Cultural Conflict and Storytelling.* Berkeley: University of California Press, 1996.

Beidler, Philip D. *American Literature and the Experience of Vietnam.* Athens: University of Georgia Press, 1982.

———. *The Good War's Greatest Hits: World War II and American Remembering.* Athens: University of Georgia Press, 1998.

———. *Re-Writing America: Vietnam Authors in Their Generation.* Athens: University of Georgia Press, 1991.

Bergonzi, Bernard. *Heroes' Twilight.* New York: Coward-McCann, 1966.

Bevan, David, ed. *Literature and War.* Amsterdam: Rodopi, 1990.

Bippy, Michael. *Hearts and Minds: Bodies, Poetry, and Resistance in the Vietnam Era.* New Brunswick: Rutgers University Press, 1996.

Buitenhuis, Peter. "American Literature of the Great War." *American Studies International* 23.2 (October 1985): 79–86.

———. *The Great War of Words: British, American, and Canadian Propaganda and Fiction, 1914–1933.* Vancouver: University of British Columbia Press, 1987.

Burnham, Michelle. *Captivity and Sentiment: Cultural Exchange in American Literature, 1882–1861.* Hanover, NH: University Press of New England, 1997.

Christopher, Renny. *The Viet Nam War/The American War: Images and Representations in Euro-American and Vietnamese Exile Narratives.* Amherst: University of Massachusetts Press, 1995.

Cobley, Evelyn. *Representing War: Form and Ideology in First World War Narratives.* Toronto: University of Toronto Press, 1993.

Cooper, Helen M., Adrienne Auslander Munich, and Susan Merrill Squier, eds. *Arms and the Woman: War, Gender, and Literary Representation*. Chapel Hill: University of North Carolina Press, 1989.

Cooperman, Stanley. *World War I and the American Novel*. Baltimore: Johns Hopkins University Press, 1967.

Cowley, Malcolm. *Exile's Return: A Literary Odyssey of the 1920s*. New York: Norton, 1934.

Cullen, Jim. *The Civil War in Popular Culture: A Reusable Past*. Washington, DC: Smithsonian Institution Press, 1995.

Derounian-Stodola, Kathryn Zabelle, and James A. Levernier. *The Indian Captivity Narrative. 1500–1900*. New York: Twayne, 1992.

Doherty, Thomas. *Projections of War: Hollywood, American Culture, and World War II*. New York: Columbia University Press, 1993.

Doyle, Robert C. *Voices from Captivity: Interpreting the American POW Narrative*. Lawrence: University of Kansas Press, 1994.

Drinnon, Richard. *Facing West: The Metaphysics of Indian-Hating and Empire-Building*. Norman: University of Oklahoma Press, 1997.

Ebersole, Gary L. *Captured by Texts: Puritan to Postmodern Images of Indian Captivity*. Charlottesville: University Press of Virginia, 1995.

Edwards, Paul M. *A Guide to Films on the Korean War*. Westport, CT: Greenwood Press, 1997.

Ehrhart, W. D., and Philip K. Jason, eds. *Retrieving Bones: Stories and Poems of the Korean War*. New Brunswick, NJ: Rutgers University Press, 1999.

Eisinger, Chester E. "The American War Novel: An Affirming Flame." *Pacific Spectator* (Summer 1955): 272–287.

Eksteins, Modris. *Rites of Spring: The Great War and the Birth of the Modern Age*. New York: Anchor-Doubleday, 1990.

Erenberg, Lewis A., and Susan E. Hirsch, eds. *The War in American Culture: Society and Consciousness during World War II*. Chicago: University of Chicago Press, 1996.

Fenton, Charles. "A Literary Fracture of World War I." *American Quarterly* 12 (Summer 1960): 119–132.

Fussell, Paul. *The Great War and Modern Memory*. New York: Oxford University Press, 1975.

———. *Wartime: Understanding and Behavior in the Second World War*. New York: Oxford University Press, 1989.

———, ed. *The Norton Book of Modern War*. New York: Norton, 1991.

Gatlin, Jesse C., Jr. *The U.S. Air Force in Fiction: The First Twenty-five Years*. Research Report 73–3. [Colorado Springs,] CO: U.S. Air Force Academy, 1973.

Genthe, Charles. *American War Narratives 1917–1918: A Study and Bibliography*. New York: David Lewis, 1969.

Gilman, Owen W., Jr. *Vietnam and the Southern Imagination*. Jackson: University Press of Mississippi, 1992.

Gilman, Owen W., Jr., and Lorrie Smith, eds. *America Rediscovered: Critical Essays on Literature and Film of the Vietnam War*. New York: Garland, 1990.

Goldman, Dorothy. *Women Writers and the Great War*. New York: Twayne, 1995.

Gotera, Vince. *Radical Visions: Poetry by Vietnam Veterans*. Athens: University of Georgia Press, 1994.

Hager, Philip E., and Desmond Taylor. *The Novels of World War I: An Annotated Bibliography*. New York: Garland, 1981.

Hanley, Lynne. *Writing War: Fiction, Gender & Memory*. Amherst: University of Massachusetts Press, 1991.

Hellmann, John. *American Myth and the Legacy of Vietnam*. New York: Columbia University Press, 1986.

Herzog, Tobey C. *Vietnam War Stories: Innocence Lost*. New York and London: Routledge, 1992.

Hillstrom, Kevin, and Laurie Collier Hillstrom, eds. *The Vietnam Experience: A Concise Encyclopedia of American Literature, Songs, and Films*. Westport, CT: Greenwood Press, 1998.

Hinz, Evelyn J., ed. *Troops versus Tropes: War and Literature*. Winnipeg: University of Manitoba Press, 1990. A special issue of *Mosaic* 23.3 (Summer 1990).

Hoelbling, Walter. *Fiktionen vom Krieg im neueren amerikanischen Roman*. Tübingen: Gunther Narr, 1987.

Holsinger, M. Paul, and Mary Anne Schofield. *Visions of War: World War II in Popular Literature and Culture*. Bowling Green, OH: Bowling Green State University Popular Press, 1992.

Hynes, Samuel. *The Soldiers' Tale: Bearing Witness to Modern War*. New York: Allen Lane/Penguin, 1997.

Jason, Philip K. *Acts and Shadows: The Vietnam War in American Literary Culture*. Lanham, MD: Rowman & Littlefield, 2000.

———. *The Vietnam War in Literature: An Annotated Bibliography of Criticism*. Pasadena, CA: Salem Press, 1992.

———, ed. *Fourteen Landing Zones: Approaches to Vietnam War Literature*. Iowa City: Iowa University Press, 1991.

Jeffords, Susan. *The Remasculinization of America: Gender and the Vietnam War*. Bloomington: Indiana University Press, 1989.

Jones, Peter G. *War and the Novelist: Appraising the American War Novel*. Columbia: University of Missouri Press, 1976.

Kirschke, James J. *Willa Cather and Six Writers from the Great War*. Lanham, MD: University Press of America, 1991.

Klein, Holger, ed. *The First World War in Fiction: A Collection of Critical Essays*. New York: Barnes & Noble, 1977.

Kolko, Gabriel. *Century of War: Politics, Conflict and Society since 1914*. New York: New Press, 1994.

Lepore, Jill. *The Name of War: King Philip's War and the Origins of American Identity*. New York: Knopf, 1998.

Lewis, Lloyd B. *The Tainted War: Culture and Identity in Vietnam War Narratives*. Westport, CT: Greenwood Press, 1985.

Limon, John. *Writing After War: American War Fiction from Realism to Postmodernism*. New York: Oxford University Press, 1994.

Lomperis, Timothy J. *"Reading the Wind": The Literature of the Vietnam War*. With a "Bibliographic Commentary" by John Clark Pratt. Durham, NC: Duke University Press, 1987.

Louvre, Alf, and Jeffrey Walsh, eds. *Tell Me Lies about Vietnam: Cultural Battles for the Meaning of the War*. Philadelphia: Open University Press, 1988.

Malo, Jean-Jacques, and Tony Williams. *Vietnam War Films*. Jefferson, NC: McFarland, 1994.

Mariani, Giorgio. *Spectacular Narratives: Representatives of Class and War in Stephen Crane and the American 1890s*. New York: Peter Lang, 1992.

Martin, Andrew. *Receptions of War: Vietnam in American Culture*. Norman: Oklahoma University Press, 1993.

Matsen, William E. *The Great War and the American Novel*. New York: Peter Lang, 1993.

Melling, Philip H. *Vietnam in American Literature*. Boston: Twayne, 1990.

Meredith, James H., ed. *Understanding the Literature of World War II: A Student Casebook to Issues, Sources, and Historical Documents*. Westport, CT: Greenwood Press, 1999.

Miller, Wayne Charles. *An Armed America: Its Face in Fiction—A History of the American Military Novel*. New York: New York University Press, 1970.

Myers, Thomas. *Walking Point: American Narratives of Vietnam*. New York: Oxford University Press, 1988.

Neilson, Jim. *Warring Fictions: American Literary Culture and the Vietnam War Narrative*. Jackson: University Press of Mississippi, 1998.

Newman, John, David A. Willson, David J. DeRose, Stephen P. Hidalgo, and Nancy J. Kendall. *Vietnam War Literature: An Annotated Bibliography*. 3rd ed. Lanham, MD: Scarecrow, 1995.

Perez, Janet, and Wendell Aycock, eds. *The Spanish Civil War in Literature*. Lubbock: Texas Tech University Press, 1990.

Pisapia, Bianca Maria, Ugo Ribeo, and Anna Scacchi, eds. *Red Badges of Courage: Wars and Conflicts in American Culture*. Rome: Bulzoni Editore, 1998.

Quinn, Patrick, and Steven Trout, eds. *New Perspectives on the Literature of the Great War*. New York: St. Martin's Press, 1999.

Ringnalda, Donald. *Fighting and Writing the Vietnam War*. Jackson: University Press of Mississippi, 1994.

Rowe, John Carlos, and Rick Berg, eds. *The Vietnam War and American Culture*. New York: Columbia University Press, 1991.

Schaefer, Michael W. *Just What War Is: The Civil War Writings of De Forest and Bierce*. Knoxville: University of Tennessee Press, 1997.

Schweik, Susan. *A Gulf So Deeply Cut: American Women Poets and the Second World War*. Madison: University of Wisconsin Press, 1991.

Searle, William J., ed. *Search and Clear: Critical Responses to Selected Literature and Films of the Vietnam War*. Bowling Green, OH: Bowling Green State University Popular Press, 1988.

Sheldon, Sayre P., ed. *Her War Story: Twentieth-Century Women Write about War*. Carbondale: Southern Illinois University Press, 1999.

Slotkin, Richard. *The Fatal Environment: The Myth of the Frontier in the Age of Industrialization, 1800–1890*. New York: Atheneum, 1985.

———. *Gunfighter Nation: The Myth of the Frontier in Twentieth-Century America*. New York: HarperCollins, 1992.

———. *Regeneration through Violence: The Mythology of the American Frontier, 1600–1860*. Middletown, CT: Wesleyan University Press, 1973.

Stokesbury, Leon, ed. *Articles of War. A Collection of American Poetry about World*

War II. Introduction by Paul Fussell. Fayetteville: University of Arkansas Press, 1990.

Tal, Kali. *Worlds of Hurt: Reading the Literatures of Trauma*. New York: Cambridge University Press, 1996.

Tylee, Claire M. *The Great War and Women's Consciousness: Images of Militarism and Womanhood in Women's Writings, 1914–1964*. London: Macmillan, 1990.

Tyler, Moses Coit. *The Literary History of the American Revolution, 1763–1783*. 2 vols. 1897. New York: Ungar, 1963.

Waldmeir, Joseph. *American Novels of the Second World War*. The Hague: Mouton, 1971.

Walsh, Jeffrey. *American War Literature 1914 to Vietnam*. New York: St. Martin's Press, 1982.

Walsh, Jeffrey, and James Aulich, eds. *Vietnam Images: War and Representation*. New York: St. Martin's Press, 1989.

Wilson, Edmund. *Patriotic Gore: Studies in the Literature of the Civil War*. New York: Oxford University Press, 1962.

Wilson, James C. *Vietnam in Prose and Film*. Jefferson, NC: McFarland, 1982.

Winkler, Allan M. *The Politics of Propaganda. The Office of War Information 1942–1945*. New Haven, CT: Yale University Press, 1978.

Woodward, David R., and Robert Franklin Maddox. *America and World War I: A Selected Annotated Bibliography of English Language Sources*. New York: Garland, 1985.

INDEX

Boldface page numbers indicate the location of main entries.

ABOUT THE EDITORS AND CONTRIBUTORS

PHILIP K. JASON is Professor of English at the United States Naval Academy. His fifteen previous books include *Retrieving Bones: Stories and Poems of the Korean War* (coedited with W. D. Ehrhart) and *Acts and Shadows: The Vietnam War in American Literary Culture*. He has edited several volumes of poetry and literary criticism, including *The Critical Response to Anais Nin* for Greenwood Press (1996). A widely published poet, he is coauthor (with Allan B. Lefcowitz) of the *Creative Writer's Handbook*.

MARK A. GRAVES is an Instructor in the Department of English, Foreign Languages, and Philosophy at Morehead State University (Kentucky). He has formerly taught at Bowling Green State University and at Michigan State University. Graves's publications on Wilfred Owen, Ellen Glasgow, John Dos Passos, and American playwright George Kelly have appeared in journals such as *English Language Notes, Ellen Glasgow Newsletter, CLAJ*, and *Theatre Annual*. He is the author of *George Kelly: A Research and Production Sourcebook* from Greenwood Press (1999).

ROBERT D. MADISON is Professor of English at the United States Naval Academy. A specialist in nineteenth-century American literature as well as earlier periods, he has published widely on sea literature, James Fenimore Cooper, and Herman Melville. Professor Madison is the editor of the Penguin edition of Charles Wentworth Higginson's *Army Life in a Black Regiment*.

MICHAEL W. SCHAEFER is Associate Professor of English at the University of Central Arkansas. A specialist on the literature of the Civil War, he is the author of *A Reader's Guide to the Short Stories of Stephen Crane* and *Just What War Is: The Civil War Writings of De Forest and Bierce*.

BRIAN ADLER is a Professor in the English Department at Valdosta State University (Georgia).

SANDRA ALAGONA is an Adjunct Professor in the English Department at Mt. San Antonio College (Walnut, California).

RANDAL W. ALLRED is an Associate Professor in the English and Communications Studies Department at Brigham Young University (Hawaii).

STEVE ANDERSON is a Professor in the English Department at the University of Arkansas at Little Rock.

DEBRA A. BENKO is a Ph.D. candidate in English and Creative Writing at Bowling Green State University.

TIM BLACKMORE is an Assistant Professor in the Faculty of Information and Media Studies at the University of Western Ontario.

DAVID A. BOXWELL is an Associate Professor in the English Department at the United States Air Force Academy.

SANDRA BURR is a Ph.D. candidate in the American Studies Department at the College of William and Mary.

STEPHEN BURT is a Ph.D. candidate in the English Department at Yale University.

CATHERINE CALLOWAY is a Professor in the English Department at Arkansas State University.

PAUL R. CAPPUCCI is a graduate student in the English Department at Drew University (Madison, New Jersey).

LUCAS CARPENTER is a Professor in the English Department at Oxford College of Emory University.

CHIH-PING CHEN is an Instructor and Ph.D. candidate in the English Department at the University of Massachusetts at Amherst.

LAURA M. CHMIELEWSKI is a Ph.D. candidate in the History Department at the City University of New York.

RENNY CHRISTOPHER is an Associate Professor in the English Department at California State University at Stanislaus.

RANDALL CLARK is an Assistant Professor in the Language and Literature Department at Pfeiffer University (Misenheimer, North Carolina).

MARY S. COMFORT is a member of the Adjunct Faculty in the English Department at Moravian College (Bethlehem, Pennsylvania).

JOSEPH T. COX is Headmaster of The Haverford School (Haverford, Pennsylvania).

DAVID N. CREMEAN is an Instructor in the English Department at Black Hills State University (South Dakota).

CHARLES L. CROW is Professor Emeritus in the English Department at Bowling Green State University.

DEAN DeFINO is an Assistant Professor in the English/Film Studies Department at Sweet Briar College.

JAMES I. DEUTSCH is an Adjunct Professor in the School of Media and Public Affairs at George Washington University.

JAMES M. DUBINKSY is an Assistant Professor in the English Department at Virginia Polytechnic Institute and State University.

W. D. EHRHART is a Research Fellow in the American Studies Department at the University of Wales.

JONATHAN R. ELLER is a Professor in the English Department at Indiana University–Purdue University at Indianapolis.

ROBERT L. GALE is Professor Emeritus in the English Department at the University of Pittsburgh.

CHARLES J. GASPAR is a Professor in the English Department at Brenau University (Georgia).

PRISCILLA GLANVILLE is an Instructor in the English Department at the University of South Florida at Tampa.

KATHERINE HARPER is a Ph.D. candidate in the English Department at Bowling Green State University.

JENNIFER HARRISON is associated with the Learning Resource Center at Virginia Wesleyan College (Norfolk).

WILLIAM T. HARTLEY is a Ph.D. candidate in the History Department at the University of Tennessee at Knoxville.

JENNIFER A. HAYTOCK is a Visiting Assistant Professor in the English Department at John Carroll University (Ohio).

RICARDO A. HERRERA is an Assistant Professor and Chair of the History and Geography Department at Texas Lutheran University.

WALTER W. HOELBLING is an Associate Professor in the American Studies Department at Karl-Franzens-University (Graz, Austria).

SHAWN HOLLIDAY is an Assistant Professor in the English and Foreign Languages Department at Alice Lloyd College (Kentucky).

MARY HRICKO is an Assistant Professor in Library and Media Services at Kent State University at Geauga.

JENNIFER C. JAMES is an Associate Professor in the English Department at Montgomery College (Rockville, Maryland).

YMITRI JAYASUNDERA is a Ph.D. candidate and Instructor in the English Department at the University of Massachusetts at Amherst.

PATRICK JULIAN is on the dance faculty of the Department of Theater and Dance at Eastern New Mexico University.

PETER KATOPES is Dean of University College at Adelphi University.

JAMES KELLEY is a Ph.D. candidate in the English Department at the University of Tulsa.

JAMES R. KERIN, JR. is an Associate Professor in the English Department at the United States Military Academy.

DAVID KILPATRICK is an Instructor in the Literature Department at Mercy College (Dobbs Ferry, New York).

HARRY B. KLOMAN is a Journalism Instructor in the English Department at the University of Pittsburgh.

MARC LEEPSON is Arts Editor of *The VVA Veteran*, a publication of the Vietnam Veterans of America.

JAMES A. LEVERNIER is a Professor in the English Department at the University of Arkansas at Little Rock.

ERIC CARL LINK is Hugh Shott Professor of English in the Department of Language and Literature at North Georgia College and State University.

BRAD E. LUCAS is a Ph.D. candidate in the English Department at the University of Nevada at Reno.

CRISTIE L. MARCH is an Assistant Adjunct Professor in the English Department at La Salle University.

THOMAS MARCH is a Ph.D. candidate in the English Department at New York University.

LAURENCE W. MAZZENO is President of Alvernia College in Reading, Pennsylvania.

SEAN C. F. McGURR is an Independent Scholar from Columbus, Ohio.

BRYAN L. MOORE is an Assistant Professor in the English Department at Arkansas State University.

PAMELA MONACO is an Assistant Professor in the English Department at Thomas Nelson Community College (Hampton, Virginia).

MICHELLE C. MORGAN is a Ph.D. candidate in the History Department at Columbia University.

MARK D. NOE is an Associate Professor in the English Department at Penn College of Technology (Williamsport, Pennsylvania).

TED OLSON is an Assistant Professor in the English Department at East Tennessee State University.

EDWARD F. PALM is a Professor and Chair of the Division of Language and Literature at Glenville State College (West Virginia).

DONNA L. PASTERNAK is an Assistant Professor in the English Department at Marshall University.

ROBERT C. PETERSEN is an Associate Professor in the English Department at Middle Tennessee State University.

RENATE W. PRESCOTT is an Assistant Professor in the English Department at Kent State University at Geauga.

DEAN REHBERGER is a Professor in the Department of American Thought and Language at Michigan State University.

EDWARD J. RIELLY is a Professor in the English Department at Saint Joseph's College (Maine).

ROY ROSENSTEIN is a Professor in the Comparative Literature Department at The American University of Paris.

JOE SARNOWSKI is a Ph.D. candidate in the English Department at the University of Toledo.

ELIZABETH D. SCHAFER is an Independent Scholar from Loàchàpokà, Alabama.

ROBERT M. SLABEY is Professor Emeritus in the English Department of the University of Notre Dame.

ROBERT D. STURR is an Assistant Professor in the English Department at Kent State University at Stark.

CATHERINE J. TRAMONTANA is a Ph.D. candidate in the Literatures in English Department at Rutgers University.

STEVEN TROUT is an Associate Professor in the English Department at Fort Hays State University (Kansas).

CYNTHIA WACHTELL is an Instructor in the Humanities Division at New School University.

JEFF WALSH is a Professor in the English Department at Manchester Metropolitan University (England).

SAMANTHA J. WARD is a Visiting Lecturer in the English Department at the University of Oklahoma.

ERIC WEITZEL is a Ph.D. candidate in English at the University of California at Santa Barbara.

JULIANNE WHITE is a Ph.D. candidate in the English Department at the University of New Mexico.

AMY L. WINK is a Visiting Assistant Professor in the Division of English at Emporia State University (Kansas).

KYLE F. ZELNER is a Ph.D. candidate and Teaching Fellow in the History Department at the College of William and Mary.